WHEN EVEN
ANGELS WEPT

The Senator Joseph McCarthy Affair—
A Story Without a Hero

ALSO BY LATELY THOMAS

A Pride of Lions
Storming Heaven
The Mayor Who Mastered New York
The First President Johnson
The Vanishing Evangelist
A Debonair Scoundrel
Sam Ward: King of the Lobby
Delmonico's: A Century of Splendor
Between Two Empires

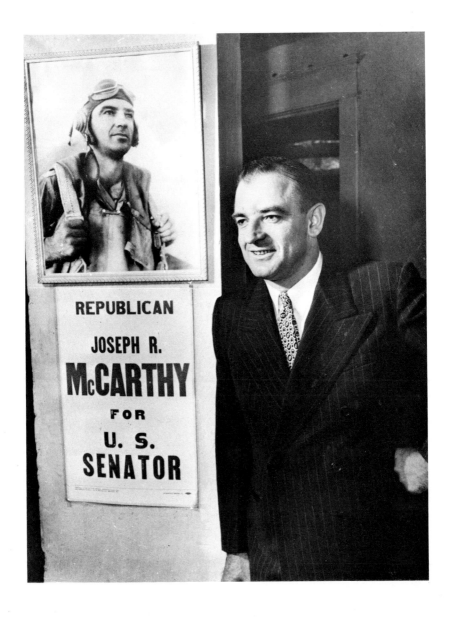

ENTRANCES AND EXITS. November, 1946. Judge Joseph McCarthy, having defeated veteran Senator Robert LaFollette for the GOP Senatorial nomination in the Wisconsin primary, pauses beside one of his campaign posters depicting him in his Marine Air Corps uniform. *Credit: Wide World Photos.* Overleaf: December 2, 1954. His right arm in a sling, Senator McCarthy enters the U.S. Senate chamber on the day of censure. *Photo courtesy of U.S. News & World Report.*

WHEN EVEN ANGELS WEPT

The Senator Joseph McCarthy Affair—
A Story Without a Hero

Lately Thomas

Steele, Robert V P

William Morrow & Company, Inc.
NEW YORK 1973

Library of Congress Catalog Card Number: 75-170233

ISBN 0-688-00148-3

To
Those Who Were Not There
and to
Some Who Were

Contents

PART THREE
Pirate with a Cause

PART FOUR
The Power and the Glory

PART FIVE
Fugue on an Army Theme

PART SIX
Buccaneer at Bay

PART SEVEN
A Daniel Come to Judgment

"But man, proud man,
Dress'd in a little brief authority . . .
Plays such fantastic tricks before high heaven
As make the angels weep."

—Measure for Measure

The Argument of the Play

During his lifetime and since his death, Joseph Raymond Mc-Carthy, the late senator from Wisconsin, was and has been the subject of interminable controversy; analyzed, exculpated, and condemned. What he was, what he did, what effect he had or did not have on his generation has been debated in millions of impassioned words. And this massive commentary has rested, and still rests, upon a common premise, namely, a moral appreciation of the man. It has been impossible to discuss the late senator without passing moral judgment upon him.

This approach, it seems to this author, misses the point of the episode, for in all essential respects, basically, Joseph McCarthy was a pirate, and one does not, one cannot, pass valid moral judgments upon pirates.

This is meant in no facetious or superficial sense. The close similarity between McCarthy's character, mentality, and motives and the basic patterns of piracy is clear. The distinction which sets the freebooter apart from the violent revolutionary, for example, or from the man who wages a war for some purpose other than plunder, appears in McCarthy, the essence of this distinction being that the pirate is not amenable to moral laws because he recognizes none. By the very act of becoming a pirate he has forced the moral code, which is binding on other men, to walk the plank. A man cannot be held morally answerable to laws of which he is incognizant; hence the pirate, entertaining no scruples whatsoever, is freed of their encumbrance.

Joseph McCarthy was true to the prototype of a roving corsair as few exemplars of freebooting have ever been. In his own category he had few flaws. And when viewed in that light, his career and impact, which are otherwise incomprehensible, become understandable.

1

Whether we are aware of the fact or not, we do not pass moral judgments upon pirates, either the worst or the best of them—Blackbeard, Captain Kidd, or Long John Silver—because intuitively we grasp that their ways and standards of conduct lie outside the confines of conventional morality. Ways deplorable, doubtless, antisocial and even horrible, yet, when regarded impersonally and from behind a buffer of distance, often fascinating. Moral conformity is not the pirate's concern. For him, rapine is no more reprehensible than is preaching to a parson or lending money at interest to a banker. We may, if we are strong enough, hold the pirate sternly accountable under statute law; we may even stretch his neck; but morally he will not be answerable to us. Admonish Captain Teach that he is flouting the law of ownership, and he whips out his pistol and shoots you dead; nor will his action, from his point of view, be morally indefensible. No, in the long run, while we may fear and execrate the pirate, especially if he injures us personally, we do not sucessfully pass moral judgment upon him.

And one reason why he is impervious to our moral sanctions is because in him we dimly sense certain latent atavisms deeply buried in our own natures. In us all lurks a vestigial bent toward buccaneering, if we dared and the times were propitious. We do not scruple to thrill vicariously to the gory exploits of Morgan, the scourge of the Spanish Main, or shrink from deliciously shuddering over the horrors of his sack of Panama. How many of us are moral because of the presence of the policeman? The pirate has no inhibitions. Is he opposed? Out flashes the cutlass and the opponent is struck down. Does the pirate then suffer remorse? On the contrary, he would be remorseful if he did not summarily eliminate the obstacle to his will.

Fortunately for those of us who live by the morality of our conventionalities, true pirates are rare. Unfortunately for us, they are usually able; they are not petty thieves or brawling hoodlums. When one of the authentic breed does appear among us, we are at a loss for a while to cope with him; for there can be no coming to grips with him until we realize that we are facing a being who is exempt from moral restraints, a man without moral perceptions turned loose in a moral world—one who will break all the rules because for him there are none.

A pirate story is entertaining, but it can be instructive, too; from the career of a freebooter on a grand scale there is much to be learned. And if the pirate be of sufficient stature to overshadow events, personages, and policies greater than himself, then his success and his inevitable downfall (for he lives by chance as well as audacity; luck and daring are his twin fickle supports) will comprise a tale not less sweeping in scope and grandeur than those of some moral heroes.

The McCarthy affair was, next to war, the most prolonged and profound political upheaval to shake the United States during the first half of this century. As a drama the episode was unsurpassable; it was played on the world stage before a rapt audience of millions. The object of this narrative is to recount that drama as it unfolded from day to day, not as it may be viewed through the superciliously lifted lorgnette of retrospect, and without the slightest attempt to convert or condemn.

The drama centers on a freebooter who outtopped all his rivals in singularity, in the brilliance and swiftness of his ascent, and in the totality of his decline. He dazzled like a meteor, and was snuffed out as abruptly. He lived by words, and for a while his word was a lever to move nations. This was no mean feat. Let us see him as he was—not prejudged or travestied, but in action—corsair and raider, living for the moment only, yet perversely achieving an immemorial notoriety. Let us see the other actors in the play as *they* were, without partisanship—fallible and egregious at times, not always praiseworthy; for as the title page has announced, this is a story without a hero. As for the attitude of the author, to echo the disabused candor of Talleyrand, who never found a hero:

"Pray consider, sirs, that I neither blame nor approve; I relate."

PART ONE

The Making of a Buccaneer

"Some sins do bear their
privilege on earth."
　　　　—*King John*

Say "Cheese"

The state of Wisconsin has long been noted for its dairy products and maverick statesmen, several of the latter having been quite as renowned as the state's famous cheese. Milwaukee's Socialist mayor, Daniel Hoan, in his heyday was a national wonder, and Robert Marion LaFollette ("Fighting Bob"), whose "Wisconsin Idea" of social legislation anticipated the New Deal by thirty years, was one of the United States Senate's foremost figures. But no more egregious maverick was ever engendered by the political and hereditary crosscurrents of Wisconsin than the son who was born to Timothy and Bridget McCarthy on their farm in Grand Chute Township, on November 14, 1908. This, their fifth son, the couple named Joseph Raymond, and they destined him routinely to a life of unremitting toil, frugality, and Catholic virtue. In one respect—his having been born to work—Joseph McCarthy never outgrew his vocation.

Grand Chute, in the center of the state just north of Lake Winnebago, was a district of farmlands of indifferent productivity. Most of the farmers were Irish, although Timothy McCarthy had a streak of German, too; but Bridget came from Ireland. Their farm produced the usual crops of oats, corn, barley, potatoes, and cabbages, and to make it turn a profit the children were expected to pitch in with the chores almost before they were out of diapers. Little Joe did his share, even attracting attention by the air of grim determination with which he went about his tasks. Among people he was shy, sometimes running off and hiding rather than face strangers.

In due course he was sent to the one-room county schoolhouse, where all eight grades of pupils studied and recited together. He seemed to learn easily, but classwork did not interest him, and upon

7

graduation he went to work for his father. Stubbornly independent, he often fought with his older brothers, who teased him by laughing at his resemblance to a bear cub—stocky, with thick chest, short arms, and pawlike hands. Joe would sail into all four of them with fists flying. Occasionally, if the tormenting became unbearable, he would run for protection to his mother, who encouraged him not to be afraid of hard knocks, but to stand up for his own in spite of everybody.

Timothy McCarthy had a rough tongue and demanded implicit obedience from his family. Joe stood his father's surliness as long as he could, then hired out to a neighboring farmer. There he scrimped until he had saved $65. With this, he told his father, he proposed to raise chickens, and Timothy rented him one acre of land at the going rate, warning, however, that he could count on no help from the family.

In two years Joe parlayed his $65 and acre of ground into a large chicken house, 2,000 laying hens, 10,000 broilers, a truck to carry his products to markets as far away as Chicago, and a bank account.

Then came reverses. Rounding a curve, his truck overturned, scattering hens, eggs, crates, and feathers. This meant a serious loss. Next, coming out of the heated chicken house into the bitter winter air, he caught a chill that developed into influenza and sent him to bed. Because he had no reserve cash, he was unable to hire a competent substitute to look after his flock, and the two school-boys whom he asked to take over neglected the job. By the time Joe was on his feet again, most of his flock was dead.

That finished his hankering for farm life. Driving to Manawa, a town of about five thousand population twenty miles away, he talked himself into a job managing a new branch of a grocery chain. He was eighteen, and from that time on his personality changed: no longer shy, he became loud and assertive, a pronounced extrovert, eager for friendship and praise, and burning with ambition. His breezy, backslapping manner pleased the customers, and soon his store was making a bigger profit than any other in the chain.

He went about the accepted forms of recreation with the same energy with which he ran the store. One day a group of young fellows heading for a swim invited him to come along, and he trotted away with them, although he could not swim and was afraid of the water. His companions were not given any hint of this, and at the swimming hole they shucked off their clothes and one by one leaped from a diving board into the pool. When his turn came, Joe clutched an inner tube around his waist, ran out, and jumped. He came up floundering, but fought off his friends' offers to pull him out and made it to shore himself. Then, to the others' surprise, he immediately ran out on the board and jumped again, repeating this over and over until all were ready to leave. By then the inner tube had slapped his sides black and blue, but he had learned to swim and had lost his fear of the water.

Joe was observant, and it became clear to him that his ambition wouldn't carry him very far without more education. He was twenty years old, but he enrolled as a freshman in Little Wolf High School. He felt foolish at first in the midst of schoolmates of thirteen and fourteen; but encouraged by the motherly woman who ran his boardinghouse, and tutored by admiring teachers, he hurled himself at his textbooks, developing an ability to cram that would stand him in good stead in later life. As a result, he completed four years of studies in one year. His work at the store suffered, of course, sales fell off, and reluctantly the management fired him. But he got a job as usher in a movie house, persevered, and was graduated at the end of the year with honors, having passed all tests brilliantly. Thereafter for years he would boast that he could make himself an expert on any subject in twenty-four hours by resorting to his system of cramming.

[II]

Joe McCarthy took the next step in his hop-skip-and-jump education by matriculating at Marquette University, a Jesuit-conducted college in Milwaukee. In filling out the entrance form, he displayed a jaunty attitude toward the rules. In answer to the question, "Did you attend four years of high school?" he put down, "Yes," intending, his high school principal later said, to tell the Marquette people the truth "when they got to know him better." There appeared to be no need, for about McCarthy's qualification to handle academic work at the university there arose no question.

He had enrolled in the engineering school, but soon realized that he lacked a proper foundation of mathematics to excel at that pursuit; and besides, the engineering students he found dull, unimaginative, literal. The cocky, argumentative law students were more to his taste, so he transferred to law.

His story as a student at Marquette was that of innumerable others: odd jobs to pay the way—driving a truck, short-order cooking, washing dishes, selling tires—combined with a little help from his father. He developed a flair for cooking and liked to show off before friends. Academically he had no difficulty, although his teachers sometimes wondered how much of what he stored in his tenacious memory he understood. Thanks to his skill in cramming, he always did well in examinations; his lowest mark was in Legal Ethics.

He showed no aptitude for sports, and little real interest. In high school he had gone out for basketball, but was too big and rough for the rest of the team, and besides, he seemed unable to learn the rules. Also, he seemed to derive no fun from the game; he just played to win. At Marquette he took up boxing, but never learned to protect himself. It didn't seem to bother him; he would bound out of his corner in a wide-open, slashing attack, throwing punches wildly with no thought of defense. Inevitably he took many a beating, but he would absorb punishment as if he enjoyed it, and keep lunging in even when bloodied and groggy. Such disregard for self-preservation earned him a name on campus, and in his senior year, when the boxing coach resigned, Joe fell heir to the job and hung up his gloves.

Another accomplishment that gained him respect was his demonic poker playing. The game was no pastime to him, but every hand a life-and-death struggle. He bluffed so outrageously it was impossible to outguess him, and consequently, when he won, he frequently won big.

His first attempt at public speaking failed ignominiously, but with the same grim determination with which he had tackled his high school studies, Joe set out to overcome this handicap. He joined a debating society and (still in a hurry) defied precedent by at once running for president of the club. He lost by a landslide, but got himself talked about, and later ran for class president against the same student who had trounced him in the club election. By this time Joe was better known, he campaigned tirelessly, and the vote was a tie. Joe's opponent proposed that they cut cards to decide who had won, but McCarthy demanded that they vote again a week later. He won the argument and a week later won

the runoff election by two votes. His rival was infuriated. He reminded Joe that each had agreed to vote for the other, and accused
McCarthy of having switched and voted for himself. McCarthy
admitted this. "You wanted the best man to win, didn't you?" He
grinned.

The incident rankled, but Joe's innate and almost irresistible
friendliness healed the breach shortly afterward when the classmate's father died. On the day of the funeral, who should come
rolling up to the bereaved home in a battered Ford but Joe Mc-
Carthy? He had cut classes, turned down a job that he needed,
borrowed the car, and driven out to be with his friend. That was
typical of Joe. Win or lose, he never bore a grudge against an
opponent, and he could not believe that anybody could bear a
grudge against him. People liked Joe, brassy as he was, and it
wasn't his fault if he saw everything—boxing, poker, politics, life
itself—in terms of a game to be won at all costs, using whatever
means were handy. That was his frame of mind when he left
Marquette with his law degree, and it would remain his frame of
mind throughout life.

[III]

It is said that McCarthy hung out his shingle six hours after
being handed his law diploma, thereby winning a bet from a fellow
graduate. Brash though he was, he had no intention of entering
into competition with big-city lawyers; rather, he went back to
the rural district where he had been brought up, whose manners
and prejudices he understood, and opened an office in the county
seat of Waupaca. His stay there lasted nine precarious months.
County records show that only four cases were handled by Counsel-
lor McCarthy during that time, and two of those suits were dismissed perfunctorily. His prowess at poker managed to keep him
going. In a roadhouse outside town there was nearly always a
game in progress, and Joe became a fixture there. His audacity
baffled other players; he asked no quarter and he gave none; consequently there was no fun in playing against him. But his winnings
paid the board bill.

One day a popular attorney from Shawano, named Mike Eberlein, dropped into McCarthy's cubbyhole office and asked, "Joe,
why don't you close up this dump and come to work for me?"

"Why don't you close that dump of yours and come to work for me?" Joe shot back, and Eberlein laughed; he liked the young man's spunk.

The upshot was that a deal was struck; and at nine o'clock the next morning the door of Eberlein's office burst open and an aggressive young man announced to a startled typist:

"Hello. I'm your new boy. You just watch; I'll be at the top of the heap in a few years."

McCarthy was twenty-eight. (Actually, with his habitual carelessness about dates and figures, he represented himself as twenty-seven, stating that he had been born in 1909 instead of 1908. It is quite likely that he believed it, never having verified the record.)

His Marquette experiences had steered McCarthy toward a career in politics, a natural step for a lawyer. He had amused his classmates by insisting on stopping, whenever they happened to drive through a county seat, and introducing himself to the local judges. "It makes you known," he would explain seriously. "Might help later on." Already he understood that making oneself known to voters was the first step toward political success. Eberlein was a Republican and Joe was a Democrat, but having both parties represented in the firm was good for business. So were the partners' religious associations, McCarthy's Catholic background counterbalancing Eberlein's Lutheranism.

Joe became a whirlwind joiner, signing up with the Lions, Junior Chamber of Commerce, County Bar Association, social and church groups, just about everything. And he made himself useful, volunteering to get up a bazaar or picnic, sell tickets, or make a speech. So it was not surprising that he should be elected president of the Young Democratic clubs of the Seventh Congressional District, embracing ten counties. Although the Democrats amounted to little in the state, this position gave McCarthy official standing, and he announced his intention to run for district attorney of Shawano County. In view of his downy age and his political affiliation, the news caused not a ruffle in the opposition camps. In the state as in Shawano County, the Progressive party of the reigning La-Follettes was the dominant force, with the Republicans next in line; the Democrats just weren't there.

Young and inexperienced as he was, McCarthy already sensed the political verity that voters are not interested in ideas, but in personalities. Since it was inconceivable to him that anybody should not wish to vote for him, once they got to know him, he offered the voters not a platform, but himself, as the answer to all their needs and questions. Elect him, the unspoken premise ran, and everything needful would follow. He became the greatest hand-shaker that Shawano had ever seen, even shaking close friends' hands when he met them on the street. For campaign purposes he identified himself with the Democrats nationally and with President Franklin D. Roosevelt, who was bidding for a second term that year. County newspapers tagged the youthful campaigner "a dedicated F. D. R. man and militant New Dealer," although they had little in the way of professed doctrine to go on.

The primary election came off in September. Each of the three parties, in order to comply with the mechanics of Wisconsin's election laws, had entered a single candidate, unopposed; the result, therefore, was a rough indicator of the relative strength of the three parties in the county. The Progressive candidate got 3,014 votes; the Republican got 692; and unlucky Joe got 577. Plainly the Democratic cause in Shawano was a forlorn hope. McCarthy, however, announced that although he hadn't the slightest chance of winning, he would stay in the race for the November election as a public service, explaining and clarifying the issues to the voters, and incidentally continuing and expanding the process of making his face and name familiar to the public.

Such selfless activity bore fruit. In November, when the ballots were counted, the Progressive candidate was found to have won handily, as expected, polling 6,175 votes; but Joe, the lowly Democrat, had pulled himself up into second place with 3,422 votes, against the trailing Republican's mere 2,842. It was quite a feat, considering that in all contests for state and county offices throughout Wisconsin, only four Democratic candidates had succeeded in reaching even second place. A friend who knew McCarthy at that time described his frame of mind:

"Joe was so ambitious it was terrifying."

"Good Morning, Judge"

Mike Eberlein had drudged for the Republicans for years, and the time had come, he thought, when he would be justified in claiming his reward. A judgeship would nicely round out his legal career, and there was an election coming up in 1939 for circuit judge of the Tenth Judicial District, which took in Shawano, Outagamie, and Langdale counties. Eberlein thought he had a good chance of winning, and in the spring of that year he confided his hopes to his partner. Joe gave him a hearty handshake and told him he was sure he'd make it.

Eberlein's indignation, therefore, may be imagined when, shortly after receiving that loyal blessing, he heard that McCarthy had jumped into the same judicial race.

Joe stated his reasons in an open letter to the voters of the district. Actually they boiled down to one, namely, that the incumbent, Judge Edgar V. Werner, was too old. Worn out by twenty-four years on the bench, the honored old man had earned retirement, Joe intimated. He himself, just three years out of law school, was thirty.

The business relationship between Eberlein and McCarthy terminated abruptly. Outwardly they preserved the amenities, Mike saying that Joe "preferred to go his own way," and McCarthy pointing out that since he would have to campaign night and day, it would not be fair for him to remain on the firm's payroll.

Joe's campaign strategy was simple and direct: in an ancient automobile with a loudspeaker mounted on top, he set out to visit every farm in the three counties at least once. Not a politician in the district gave him a ghost of a chance of beating Judge Werner. His approach to each prospective source of a vote was systematic. While gassing up at a filling station, or swapping chaff with a

14

country storekeeper, he would pick up the name of a nearby farm family, together with details about their ages, peculiarities, crops, cattle, and religious preferences. Then when visiting that farm he would glean similar information about families farther along the road, and these names and facts he would enter in a permanent file. He never discussed his qualifications for the judgeship, but simply exhibited himself as a clean-cut, likable, energetic young man who had a down-to-earth understanding of the problems of ordinary folks.

One farmer described a typical visit:

"He didn't know me from Adam, but somehow he had learned my name, and my wife's name, and our kids' names, and even the name of our dog. By the time I first noticed him, he was outside petting the dog, and before I could get to the door he was handing my little girl a lollipop and Indian-wrestling with my boy. At first I pegged him for a salesman, but when he grabbed my hand and introduced himself I remembered him from a letter he sent me, saying he wanted to beat old man Werner because the judge was too old for the job."

Joe didn't mention the election, the farmer said; what he was interested in was the farm, how it was doing, its layout, livestock, crops, and poultry.

"He wanted to know if I'd let him milk a cow. Said he liked to keep his hand in. He milked good." But what really floored the man was Joe's suddenly asking, "Say, how's that sick mare of yours? Any better?" Touched by such solicitude, the farmer took his visitor out to the barn, and McCarthy "treated that mare like it was his own flesh and blood. He acted like it was the saddest thing in the world that my mare was sick. And he promised he'd do all he could to help."

The clincher came a week later, when the farmer got a letter from McCarthy listing all the ways to cure a sick mare that he had been able to find out, and wishing the farmer good luck, with kind regards to his wife, his children, and his dog.

The personal letter was a basic element in McCarthy's strategy. After he left a house, he would pull over to the side of the road, plug a recording machine into the car's generator, and dictate a letter to the person just interviewed while his memory was fresh. These recordings he would send to a typist to transcribe and mail out over Joe's signature.

Week after week, Joe covered the Tenth District in a blackslap-
ping, handshaking blitz of jollification. He kissed babies, praised
housewives' pies and cakes, and agreed with oldtimers that the
country was just falling apart. With the help of relatives and well-
wishers (mostly middle-aged women who yearned to mother big,
boyish Joe), he sent out thousands of postcards supposedly signed
by himself, bearing down on the issue of Judge Werner's age. He
stated Werner's date of birth as 1866, making him seventy-three
years old, although in fact Werner had been born in 1873 and was
sixty-six years old. This was a mentally confusing trick, like juggling
1492 and 1942, and often it got by. Joe was never disrespectful
of the older man, but spoke deferentially of "my worthy opponent,"
"my distinguished opponent," "that fine jurist," and then artfully
alluded to the judge's supposed decrepitude.

The tactic was effective because the idea of "old judges" who
couldn't keep up with the times was in the public mind as a result
of President Roosevelt's recent attack on the "nine old men" of
the United States Supreme Court. In the congressional elections
of the year before, the President had lost his attempt to get rid of
men like Senator Millard Tydings of Maryland, who had opposed
his "court-packing" plan, and the issue was still alive. McCarthy
benefited from it.

For a while Judge Werner ignored the attacks, but under such
constant misrepresentation he lost his temper and took to denying
that he was ready for the chimney corner. This played into Mc-
Carthy's hands, and in a newspaper advertisement headed, "What
About This Age Question?" he expressed regret at causing Judge
Werner distress, and explained that he had raised the issue only as
an intended tribute to "my seventy-three-year-old opponent's faith-
ful service," in one capacity or another over a period of thirty-
five years, "at a total income of $170,000 to $200,000."

A little mental arithmetic would have showed that this grand
total of Judge Werner's emoluments as a public official worked out
at a very modest annual income; but that was not the impression
Joe conveyed.

On election eve every voter in the district received a postcard
in the mail, signed with McCarthy's name and "hoping for your
vote on election day." The card carried a snapshot of a winsome,
freckle-faced boy clutching a baseball bat. In default of any identification, the recipients could hardly be blamed if they assumed

(not knowing that McCarthy was a bachelor) that the cute kid was his own—a serious miscalculation; for in this election, the one "cute kid" was Joe. When the tally was in, McCarthy had won by 15,160 votes against Judge Werner's 11,154, a third candidate trailing with 9,071.

Joe, who had never been out of debt since his chicken farm collapsed, made instant use of his $8,000 judicial salary to buy a house in Appleton. Then he took square aim on his next target—the United States Senate.

[II]

One day a Marquette acquaintance dropped into Judge McCarthy's chambers and during the conversation said with a trace of envy:

"Joe, you've got everything. You hold a position that most lawyers expect to reach only after years of effort. You can stay a judge for the rest of your life. If you play your cards right, you might even become governor."

Joe swiveled back and forth restlessly. "I'm not interested in small jobs," he replied, and he meant it. Not that he disliked being "Wisconsin's youngest judge"; but he had set his sights on something much more alluring. Meanwhile, the function of a court of law being to render speedy justice, he set about doing that in his own headlong fashion. The process made headlines for Judge Joseph R. McCarthy in a most gratifying way.

When McCarthy took over, his court had a backlog of two hundred and fifty cases. In a few months he not only cleared the docket, but thereafter he never fell behind. This he accomplished only by strenuous work, but work McCarthy seemed to dote upon. He abolished the regular terms of court, which had a way of fostering postponements, and held himself available to go to any part of his circuit where lawyers were ready to go to trial. During one stretch of forty-four days, he held his court in session until after midnight twelve times. The pace he set was exhausting; but the prosy, the dull, and the dilatory were forced to keep up. One evening, after adjourning court in one town, the judge drove three hundred miles through a blizzard in order to hold court in another town in the morning.

Wisconsin judges were permitted to exchange positions occasionally and hear cases in each other's courts, and McCarthy availed himself of this privilege extensively; it was another means of widening the circle of people who knew him and of him. Newspapermen especially came to look forward to the periodic appearances of Judge McCarthy because of his insistence on picking up every bar tab in sight.

Judgeships in Wisconsin are at least nominally nonpartisan offices, and McCarthy had not been required to indicate any party affiliation in his own campaign. He never repudiated the Democrats. But the evidence was overwhelming that the state's voters, when they did not elect Progressives, normally elected Republicans; and this fact of political life Joe stored away in memory as he breezed through his judicial duties.

In the courtroom his manner was informal and lively. He did not disdain to play to the gallery, and there was always a sense of drama and excitement when he was presiding. He might interrupt testimony to tell a joke, or enforce decorum in a way that brought a chuckle. Once, halting a witness, he stood up and pointing his gavel at a lawyer in the back of the room barked:

"Bill, if you want to win a case in this court, put out that cigar!"

McCarthy himself had given up smoking at Marquette; it distracted him from work, and work was his obsession. Although he could be a two-fisted drinker on occasion, he was never incapacitated by a few bourbons; his backslapping just became a little more boisterous, that was all. His free-and-easy courtroom ways did not escape criticism, of course, but that didn't bother Joe. He laid no claim to scholarship, yet his record on reversals stacked up favorably with those of far more learned judges. One of his first actions on being elected had been to acquire a three-volume work on the rules of evidence and stuff it into his brain by his high-school cramming method. And he resorted shrewdly to other means to make up for his deficiencies. For example, when he had to make an important ruling, he might appeal to counsel for one side, saying, "Now, Jim, what would you say on this point?" The lawyer would give a rundown on the law and precedents in his favor. Then McCarthy would turn to opposing counsel and say, "Well, Tom, how would you answer Jim here?" And that lawyer would expound until he was talked out. Then McCarthy, fortified by this well-posted analysis of the salient points, would hand down a decision that stood a good chance of being upheld if the case should go to appeal.

Also, Joe was always prepared to serve as peacemaker, and often he summoned opposing counsel to his chambers and talked them into settling out of court. Anything that would expedite the business of the law he was game to try, regardless of immediate praise or blame. As for criticism, he ignored it, even though, in one case, it was of the most formidable kind, culminating in a stern rebuke by the state supreme court. Because in the course of time some of the records unaccountably went astray, certain aspects of this case were never disclosed, but the essential facts were these:

At the urging of the state Department of Agriculture, McCarthy had slapped an injunction on the Quaker Dairy Company, a milk processor and distributor, prohibiting them from continuing pricing practices which discriminated against small farmers. Violation of state law was claimed. Quaker Dairy obtained a six-month postponement, pending which Judge McCarthy suspended his temporary injunction.

When finally the suit came to a hearing, McCarthy ruled that although violations had indeed occurred, the law that had been broken was due to expire in six months and was practically a dead letter already; therefore he voided his own injunction, and when the state's attorney moved for trial of the company on the ground of the past violations, he ruled that a trial would work undue hardship on the company and be a "waste of time," and dismissed the action.

The indignant state's attorney appealed to the state supreme court for an order directing McCarthy to try the suit. The supreme court sent for a transcript of the evidence and McCarthy's decision, and was informed that the reporter's notes had been destroyed. McCarthy took full responsibility, saying he had ordered the notes destroyed because they were not material.

This high-handed procedure shocked the justices and they delivered a stinging reprimand, stigmatizing McCarthy's action as "highly improper . . . an abuse of judicial power." Chief Justice Marvin S. Rosenberry wrote that "the destruction of evidence under these circumstances could only be open to the inference that the evidence destroyed contained statements of fact contrary to the position taken by the person destroying the evidence." This strong

hint of malfeasance was backed up by an order to restore the
original injunction and try the case.

McCarthy complied with the order, reinstated the restraining
order, and then, after a curt trial session, tongue-lashed the state's
attorney as a "troublemaker." The incensed lawyer tried to get a
transcript of the judge's remarks in order to seek redress, but was
put off repeatedly. Finally the Agriculture Department, embarrassed by the dispute, dropped its complaint and discharged the
abused attorney. (Years later, when application was made to the
supreme court library for access to the briefs in the Quaker Dairy
appeal, those briefs had disappeared, nobody could say how.)
Characteristically, McCarthy never bothered to excuse or explain
his conduct; with the true aggressor's instinct he met an attack by
counterattack, and very often by sheer audacity he would make
it stick.

[III]

One way and another, all this while Joe was broadening his
political base. His objective was the United States Senate, nothing
less; but from a county judgeship to the Capitol in Washington was
a giant leap; it would take time. Outside his judicial circuit Mc-
Carthy was still little known, and a problem that constantly engaged
his restless mind was how to introduce himself to voters elsewhere.
The situation seemed critical, too, because he discerned a possible
rival to his ambition in the virile young mayor of Milwaukee, Carl
F. Zeidler, whose recent defeat of the veteran Daniel Hoan had been
a sensation.

Zeidler was tall, blond, and magnetic. He spoke for the state's
large German element, and the crowds loved him. Pearl Harbor
came, and in the first wave of patriotic enthusiasm he enlisted in
the Navy. Thereupon photographs of him in his ensign's uniform appeared in newspapers throughout the state, to McCarthy's
chagrin. The publicity buildup, he realized, would provide a spring-
board for higher political office after the war (it couldn't last
forever), and Zeidler might snatch the prize Joe had set his sights
upon. The dilemma was acute, and McCarthy met it in his customary style, by a vigorous counterattack.

Consulting friends, he asked what uniform carried more public
appeal than Navy gold braid? The uniform of a United States

Marine, came the reply. That suited McCarthy's natural pugnacity, and on June 2, 1942, he wrote on court stationery to Major Saxon Holt, Marine Corps recruiting officer in Milwaukee, setting forth his qualifications and applying for a commission. Always in a hurry, two days later he drove to Milwaukee and spoke with Major Holt personally. At the same time he informed the press that he was determined to get into combat "as a private or in any other way the Marines can use me." The *Milwaukee Journal* reported approvingly that "Judge McCarthy, who has been earning $8,000 a year, applied to Marine Headquarters here Wednesday, offering to enlist 'as a private, an officer, or anything else you want me to be. I want to join up for the duration.'" Coming from the state's leading newspaper, this was a heady mention.

The *Appleton Post-Crescent* said more definitely:

"Judge McCarthy is entering the Marines with no promise of a commission or special favors, but is hopeful that he will be able to earn his way into officers training school. He said that right now he is 'more interested in a gun than a commission.' . . . Although he is automatically deferred because he is a judge, McCarthy said that he had reached the conclusion that 'we can't win the war by letting our neighbors do the fighting,' so he will take a hand in it himself."

All this brought Joe heaps of praise. There was no question about his patriotism, and although he was thirty-three and rated deferment, he was enlisting voluntarily in the toughest branch of the nation's armed forces. Photographs of the belligerent judge, resplendent in a hastily procured Marine uniform, blossomed in newspapers throughout the state. Little attention was paid to the fact that the uniform was not that of a private; on Joe's shoulders gleamed the silver bars of a first lieutenant. On June 4, two days after he had applied to join the service, he had been handed his commission.

As a sentimental gesture, Judge McCarthy permitted himself to be photographed presiding in court in uniform, and the press covered the event royally. Said the *Milwaukee Journal:*

"The judge's bench of Branch 2 of Milwaukee's municipal court was occupied briefly Wednesday by a lieutenant of the Marines in uniform. He heard one case as a farewell gesture to judicial robes until the war is over. The Marine officer is Judge Joseph McCarthy, 34 [sic], of Appleton, Wis., the youngest circuit judge in this state.

Judge McCarthy obtained his commission in the Marine Corps June 4 and left at 11:30 A.M. Wednesday for the Marine base at Quantico, Va. Circuit Judge Gerald Boileau of Wausau, who had been presiding in Branch 2, invited Judge McCarthy to sit in for one case when the latter called on friends in the building."

It was an effective curtain scene.

Then Lieutenant Joe headed off to the war with a boyish grin and the good wishes of a host of people who would be wishing him every ill a few years hence.

"To the Shores of Tripoli"

Joe's departure had not been accomplished without some grumbling on the part of the man who was responsible for running Wisconsin's judicial circuits, Judge Arnold F. Murphy. Joe had obtained a preliminary leave to clear up personal affairs, and on July 6 Judge Murphy, acting as chairman of the board of circuit judges, had written urging McCarthy to reconsider; in Murphy's opinion, his value to the community as a judge would exceed that of his service as a Marine. Murphy was especially concerned over McCarthy's failure to resign from the bench; he was merely waiving the salary for the duration of his service. This precluded the appointment or election of a replacement who could help to carry the circuit's heavy load of litigation. McCarthy had persuaded two colleagues to take over his share of the work, and about their ability to meet these fresh demands Judge Murphy had serious misgivings.

But McCarthy dissented, and on August 4 he was sworn into the service, reporting for duty at Quantico on August 12, 1942. There he sweated through the rigorous Marine training with zeal and zest, although matching himself against enlistees of eighteen and nineteen he admitted was rough. "I thought I was in good shape," he would recall, "but in that first week's training at Quantico I thought I'd die—and was afraid I wouldn't." In one respect—that of aggressiveness—he left nothing to be desired.

His training completed, he was assigned to various duties until April, 1943, when he was promoted to captain and shipped to the Pacific war zone aboard the seaplane tender *Chandeleur*. There was a stopover in Hawaii and on June 12 the voyage was resumed from Pearl Harbor, headed for Espiritu Santo, in the New Hebrides.

On June 22, the *Chandeleur* crossed the equator, and in keeping with sea tradition, the crew was allowed to haze the "polliwogs" who were crossing the line for the first time. Before "King Neptune," throned on the boat deck, the neophytes were subjected to dousing with hoses, paddling, the forced reciting of gibberish, prodding with an electric trident, and head shaving. Rank meant nothing; there were no exemptions.

McCarthy joined in the horseplay with good spirit. Dressed in pajamas, barefoot, with a bucket tied to one ankle, he was thumping down a bulkhead ladder to the jeers of the "shellbacks" when he slipped and fell backward. His foot caught between the bottom rung and the bulkhead and three bones were broken. The foot was put in a cast; but the patient refused to remain in sick bay, and went hobbling about the deck on crutches. His fellow officers joked about his "war wound," and he joked about it himself, but begged the others never to divulge how it had been sustained, for the circumstances were too humiliating. By the time the *Chandeleur* reached Espiritu Santo the injury was healed, leaving a scar but no other ill effects, and McCarthy entered directly upon his duties as an intelligence officer attached to the Fourth Marine Air Base Wing.

His job was to interrogate pilots returning from reconnaisance and bombing missions to determine their success—whether they had got through to the targets, what air and ground resistance they had encountered, and whether they had knocked out strategic facilities. These data McCarthy would digest and evaluate for use in plotting future strikes. The work was important and he did it well; but, after all, it was ground work, and Joe itched to be in the air with his finger on the trigger of a machine gun. He took to practicing target shooting and became so addicted (he once fired 4,700 rounds in an afternoon) that a wag hung up a sign:

SAVE OUR COCONUT TREES—SEND MC CARTHY BACK
TO WISCONSIN.

Intelligence officers sometimes volunteered to go on bombing missions in order to check the accuracy of their reports and familiarize themselves with actual flight conditions. At his own request, Captain McCarthy flew a number of missions, and one of his pilots subsequently reported that "the judge sure loved to shoot those guns; he was really eager in that rear seat."

During the next two years, Captain McCarthy was shuttled to various posts—Guadalcanal (with the First Marine Air Wing temporarily) and Munda—and he flew on convoy cover duty in the

Empress Augusta Bay landings, spotting Japanese batteries for artillery and dive-bomber strafing. He raked enemy airfields with his twin .30-caliber guns, and out of it all acquired, or coined for himself, a nickname—"Tail-Gunner Joe." Splashed under photographs of the modestly smiling judge, looking rakish in a Devil Dog helmet and flying gear, it proved irresistible to Wisconsin newspapers, avid for war stories with a local tie-in. Shawano and Appleton were proud of their fighting Marine.

Joe's jaunty self-confidence and his resourcefulness as a scrounger on behalf of his messmates made him popular. Somehow he could talk the Army or the Seabees into loosening up on beer, and wangle meat and fresh vegetables out of tough supply officers on transports. He was always ready to get up some entertainment for off-duty hours, and his poker playing became famous. The fliers called him "Judge" and listened indulgently when he talked about cracking the U.S. Senate when the war was over. They thought it was a joke when he draped a banner across his tent:

HEADQUARTERS—MC CARTHY FOR U. S. SENATE

They laughed when he painted "McCarthy for U. S. Senate" on the sides of two trucks, and Joe laughed with them. But he meant it.

[II]

Back in Wisconsin, friends kept the newspapers posted on the doings of Tail-Gunner Joe. He himself varied the monotony by taking a whirl in the stock market. Just how he did it McCarthy never explained—perhaps through a fortunate tip and certainly with the help of luck—but operating from a beachhead thousands of miles away, he turned a profit of $42,353.92 in 1943 by speculating in securities. He ran into income tax difficulties on this when he claimed the entire sum was exempt from the Wisconsin state tax because it had been earned while he was "not a resident of the state." The state auditors disallowed this claim, and after a struggle McCarthy paid both state and federal income taxes on the windfall. Anyway, he had often said, and would repeat, that for him money was "the easiest thing to get."

Meanwhile this remote-control financier was the proud recipient of a citation for meritorious service signed by Fleet Admiral Chester Nimitz. Only the most outstanding citations were signed by Nimitz, those of less importance being issued through lower channels. The citation had been recommended by Joe's first commanding officer in the Pacific, Colonel E. E. Munn, commanding Marine Scout Bombing Squadron 235. The recommendation, dated February 11, 1944, praised Captain McCarthy's devotion to duty in the words:

"On 22 June 1943 Captain McCarthy suffered a broken and burned foot and leg. He, however, refused to be hospitalized and continued doing an excellent job as intelligence officer, working on crutches."

Admiral Nimitz echoed Colonel Munn's praise, and also paid tribute to McCarthy's voluntary participation in many combat missions. The citation read:

"For meritorious and efficient performance of duty as an observer and rear gunner of a dive bomber attached to a Marine scout bombing squadron operating in the Solomon Islands area from September 1 to December 31, 1943. He participated in a large number of combat missions, and in addition to his regular duties, acted as aerial photographer. He obtained excellent photographs of enemy gun positions, despite intense anti-aircraft fire, thereby gaining valuable information which contributed materially to the success of subsequent strikes in the area. Although suffering from a severe leg injury he refused to be hospitalized and continued to carry out his duties as an intelligence officer in a highly efficient manner. His courageous devotion to duty was in keeping with the highest traditions of the naval service."

In Wisconsin, there was widespread speculation about how Captain McCarthy had sustained his injury. Modestly Joe declined to discuss it, and the impression spread that he had been hit by shrapnel, although it was also said that he had been injured when his bomber, returning from a mission, groundlooped on landing and burst into flames. Either way, the judge was a hero.

News of Joe's citation was received by his war buddies with mixed feelings. Nobody questioned his courage, and he certainly had been injured on June 22, 1943, but not on any combat mission; it was by falling off a ladder on the *Chandeleur*. There was no doubt, also, that Joe was liked by the top brass. Major General H. R. Harmon, Army commander in the Solomons, wrote that Captain McCarthy was "well liked and respected by his associates," and mentioned his "unfailing good nature and ready wit." Another of McCarthy's commanders, Major General Field Harris, of the Marines, added his personal congratulations to Nimitz's action, and assured the proud judge that "the Marine Corps will not forget the fine contribution you have made."

A combat flier who knew Joe well put it differently. With a whistle of admiration he exclaimed:

"That guy could promote anything—up to and including the Medal of Honor!"

[III]

With money to spend, a glamorous war record, and an accumulated head of steam that threatened to blow out all safety valves, in the spring of 1944 McCarthy made an opening move toward attaining his goal, the United States Senate. Wisconsin was to elect a senator in the fall, and influential Republican leaders had endorsed the incumbent, Alexander Wiley, as their choice for the party's nomination in the primary election. Under Wisconsin's "open primary" law, anybody could declare himself a candidate for the nomination of any party, and anyone could vote in the primary of his choice, without previous party registration. Brashly, Captain McCarthy entered his name in the Republican primary contest. This did not require repudiation of his Democratic affiliation, and Joe offered no apology or explanation of the switchover. Senator Wiley, he realized, would be hard to beat, but Joe was as eager as an excited terrier to try. At least he would not have to buck a rival war hero, for Carl Zeidler, whose example had helped to put McCarthy into uniform, had been lost at sea in a night submarine attack.

The spectacle of a Marine on Bougainville entering the political lists half a world away was sufficiently novel to attract attention, and McCarthy's comrades in the Corps shed their last reservations about the extent of his nerve. He announced his decision in a letter to friends, replying to a question which they had never asked, namely, whether he would be "willing to serve if elected to the Senate." The answer to that was easy: after revolving the matter earnestly, he said, he must truthfully reply, "Yes." But he added a caution:

"You understand, of course, that I shall take no part in the campaign. In fact, I do not expect to be in the United States before the election, and I cannot, because of military regulations, discuss political issues. I must of necessity leave this campaign to my friends and the voters of Wisconsin."

His friends gave this letter to the press, and the campaign was launched by a sketchy Committee to Elect Joseph R. McCarthy U. S. Senator, composed mainly of Joe's relatives.

McCarthy was indeed prohibited by military regulations from electioneering; according to some critics, he was also disqualified from running for an office like that of senator as long as he remained a judge, and Joe had not resigned from the bench. The Wisconsin state constitution provided that judges could "hold no office of public trust, except a judicial one, during the term for which they are respectively elected, and all votes for either of them for any public office, except a judicial office, shall be void."

In the excitement of sending up trial balloons, Joe's backers seemingly failed to recollect this provision, and the favorable reaction of the press to McCarthy's novel daring did nothing to jog their memory. The absentee candidate was widely praised. The *Wisconsin State Journal,* published in Madison, the capital city, saw in McCarthy's candidacy an indication of a public awakening to "the need of vigorous intellects in high office." The *Shawano Evening Leader* was sure that Joe, who had "put everything he had" into his job as a Marine, would devote himself as unstintingly to the public weal in a higher capacity. The *Appleton Post-Crescent* propounded the question: "If a combination of the McCarthy qualities cannot make a statesman, then what can?" It was the question that Joe had asked himself many times, and another one to which the answer was easy.

A few sour notes were not wholly smothered in the chorus of praise for a self-sacrificing war hero. Wisconsin's Secretary of State Fred R. Zimmerman read the state's constitution and refused to certify McCarthy's name on the ballot; but he was overruled by the state's attorney general, who cited a 1922 precedent. Joe's backers contended, and they found lawyers to agree, that the state could not set the qualifications for a United States senator, that field having been preempted by the United States Constitution. And the U. S. Constitution stipulated only that a senator must be at least thirty years of age, at least nine years a citizen, and a resident of the state from which elected. Reluctantly Zimmerman complied with the attorney general's decision.

Again eyebrows were raised when it was remarked that Mc-

Carthy, long identified with the Democrats, had barged into the Republican primary without a by-your-leave or declaration of a change in his political loyalties. When had he switched? No date could be found, for he had never openly broken with the Democrats and had never joined the Republicans. To the conservative Republicans of Wisconsin, this nebulous situation was distasteful, but Joe couldn't have shown less concern. Always willing and eager to be friendly, he knew that any party can use a winner.

The Committee for Joe threw the direct-mail machinery into gear again and praise of McCarthy flowed out to press and electorate. It painted a beguiling picture of Tail-Gunner Joe, stressing his patriotic relinquishing of a safe berth on the bench and a substantial salary in order to serve in the front lines. And if every statement in this campaign literature was not literally true, well, political broadsides are not supposed to be sworn testimony. Captain McCarthy, blazing away at Japanese Zeroes, was not to be held accountable for everything his friends might say about him. True, a couple of years might be knocked off his age, to make his meteoric rise appear more dazzling; but about the rise there could be no question, and he *was* young for his position and achievements. Maybe it wasn't true that he had enlisted as a private; but he had offered to, hadn't he, and he *had* distinguished himself in combat, unless Admiral Nimitz was strangely mistaken. And there were always those photographs of Tail-Gunner Joe in flying togs, which couldn't be brushed aside.

In July, McCarthy sprang a surprise by wangling a thirty-day leave and showing up in time to steamroller the drive through the final weeks. Wearing his combat decorations, he stumped the state at a pace that had his campaign manager reeling.

"I set up a meeting in Milwaukee and he turns up speaking in Fond du Lac, on Lake Winnebago!" moaned that harassed individual.

Gunner Joe blazed away, and rules and schedules that got in the way joined the casualties of war. He edged around military regulations forbidding political speeches by stating frankly that he was gagged, then going on to say what he would say if he were free to say it. He told the Milwaukee League of Women Voters:

"I wish I could discuss the importance of oil and of maintaining a strong Army and Navy to be used in the event that any international organization breaks down. But I may not do so."

In Appleton, he told an audience of civic-minded women, "If I were able to speak, here is what I would say," and went on to say it.

He was modest about his service record. "Mind you," he would say, "I don't take any special credit for doing my job." He spoke feelingly about "our boys" and praised their bravery in all sincerity. Only once was he taken aback, and then only momentarily. A rumor was circulating that the mighty Marine was wearing elevator shoes, and it was a fact: in a passing spasm of vanity, Joe was adding an inch to his stature in uniform. During an appearance in Badger Village, a heckler yelled, "Why do you wear built-up shoes?"

For a second, Joe was stumped. Then, pulling off one shoe, he held it up and pointed to the platform built into the heel.

"I'll tell you why I wear this shoe," he replied evenly. "It's because I carry ten pounds of shrapnel in this leg."

Whereupon the crowd turned upon the abashed heckler, and Joe finished his nonspeaking speech. Nobody reflected that it was impossible for a man to carry ten pounds of shrapnel in his leg, or any other portion of his body, and stay alive.

With his captain's bars and his irrepressible friendliness, his energy and disclaimers of special merit, and his cheerful willingness to serve, McCarthy proved attractive to the voters, although the portents all pointed to Wiley's winning the nomination. And so he did, polling 153,570 votes. But McCarthy got 79,380, completely snowing under two minor candidates. Joe had every reason to be elated by the result: he had made himself known throughout the state, and without party backing or any but an amateur organization he had rolled up an impressive total at the polls.

On August 20, McCarthy reported back for duty at the Marine Corps station at El Centro, California; but observing that the war was progressing favorably without his help, on October 19 he applied for another leave—of sixty days this time—pleading the need to catch up on his long-neglected judicial duties. His application was turned down, and when he persisted, he was offered an opportunity to resign. Although he had enlisted "for the duration," he accepted this offer; on February 20, 1945, he was relieved of active duty, and his resignation became effective on March 29.

Back to Wisconsin McCarthy went, well in advance of the tide of homecoming veterans. His recent buddies in the Pacific faced months more of bitter fighting before they could join him in civilian life.

[IV]

Just before McCarthy's severance from the Marines, he was re-elected without opposition as judge of Wisconsin's Tenth Judicial District. But after the excitements of war and a taste of big-time campaigning, the bench palled, and he devoted more and more time to furthering his Senate ambition. There seemed to be no call for his services from any party organization, a situation that Joe found intolerable; so he set out to correct it. Crisscrossing the state, shaking hands and making speeches wherever two or more voters came together (it seemed), he injected himself into the affairs of the Young Republicans, and pumping some of his own vitality into that lackadaisical body, he succeeded in steering its direction into the hands of a small band of believers in his future. He then turned his attention to making himself felt by the real rulers of the state's Republican party, the Republican Voluntary Committee.

Wisconsin's peculiar election laws so hemmed in the regular party organizations as to render them ineffectual. The Voluntary Committee was one answer to this situation; composed of conservative Republican leaders, it functioned as a shadow party, really controlling nominations and setting party policy. The committee could function unofficially in ways that the official party organization could not. For example, it could spend as much money as it liked to elect its candidates, so long as there was a public accounting, although the party was limited in this regard. Whereas the party convention was forbidden to endorse any candidate in advance of the primary elections, the committee's convention could endorse at will. Under the leadership of Thomas J. Coleman, a wealthy industrialist, the Voluntary Committee had become an undisputed power in Wisconsin politics. McCarthy set out to woo the committee.

On December 1, 1945, he addressed a letter to the committee's several hundred members, offering himself as the party's nominee for the Senate in the 1946 election. The letter was ignored.

Shortly after this rebuff, the Young Republicans convened in Milwaukee and lined up in McCarthy's support. Staying in the same hotel was Coleman, and McCarthy introduced himself to the dignified, white-haired boss in the hotel dining room. Coleman doubted the sincerity of Joe's conversion to Republicanism, and he listened to the young man coolly. He was not wholly unimpressed.

"Joe," he finally said, "you're a nice guy and I like you. But you have no background in the Republican party. You just don't fit into the senatorial picture for next year. If you keep on working the way you have been and gain some support, you may have a chance some time in the future."

Looking Coleman in the eye, McCarthy retorted with cheerful cockiness:

"Tom, you're a nice guy and I like you. But I've got news for you. When the committee's convention is over next spring, Joe McCarthy will be the Republican-endorsed candidate for the United States Senate."

Coleman stiffened. Rising, he snapped, "What you need is some self-confidence," and strode away. But the cheek of the young upstart, his very impudence, left an impression which Coleman did not quickly shake off. As for Joe, he was confident that he could cram himself down Coleman's throat.

[V]

Changes had been taking place in the Wisconsin political lineup. The great name in the state still was LaFollette. "Fighting Bob" LaFollette's two sons had carried on the tradition, Philip as three-term governor, and Robert M., Jr., as United States senator since his father's death in 1925.

Until 1934, the brothers had remained in the Republican fold, but in that year they broke away and formed their own party, the Progressive. Through it since then they had held Wisconsin virtually in fief. But recently the New Deal had given the Democrats a boost, and at the same time some Progressives who did not like certain aspects of the New Deal had been trending toward a renewal of Republican ties. Both these trends had drained the Progressive party, and by 1945 the double drift had become so pronounced that "Young Bob" proposed that the Progressive party disband and its members move back into the Republican ranks, with the avowed intention of capturing control of that party and liberalizing it. Despite heated opposition, LaFollette's view prevailed and the Progressive party disappeared, while LaFollette entered the Republican primary for nomination to another term in the Senate.

This move met resistance on two fronts: Coleman and his conservatives hated the LaFollettes and resented their apostasy, while the more liberal Progressives were angered by the failure to merge with the Democrats. However, the political realities seemed to indicate that Young Bob's reelection was inevitable: in Wisconsin the name "LaFollette" had long been invincible. Few political hopefuls were willing to run against the senator, in view of almost certain humiliating defeat; but no such trepidation hampered Joe McCarthy. The Voluntary Committee was due to meet in the spring and endorse its choice for the Republican nomination, and McCarthy opened a frontal attack on this hitherto hostile group. He addressed a letter—another letter—to the committee's members scattered over the state, announcing his readiness to play Jack the Giant Killer against the dreaded LaFollette. Again the response was nil.

In no way deterred, McCarthy set out to buttonhole the members personally. In seventy-one towns and villages he elbowed his way into meetings of the local branches, shook hands, and endlessly repeated the glad tidings he had handed to Coleman. His reception was lukewarm to frigid.

At the same time he tackled potential rivals who might be tempted to try their luck by calling on them privately and exposing in all candor the risks they would run, because, first of all, no matter whom the committee's convention endorsed, Joe was in the race to stay; and second, why try to beat a combat veteran so soon after the war? Every possible competitor felt the force of the argument with one exception: Governor Julius P. Heil, a rich manufacturer who took pride in being referred to as "Julius the Just."

As a confirmed check-grabber, Heil was a match for McCarthy, and he had had long experience in cultivating good will by means of lavish parties. On the evening before the Voluntary Committee opened its convention in Oshkosh, "Julius the Just" was host to a throng of politicians in his hotel suite. But as the evening wore on, a strange thing happened: delegate after delegate sidled up to the host and, after assuring him of his vote, added with an air of melancholy regret that it was a shame, but the "Coleman crowd" had secretly decided to ditch Heil and endorse Joe McCarthy. After hearing this disconcerting bit of news half a dozen times, Heil began to worry. He worried all night, and in the morning, convinced that he had been double-crossed, he angrily withdrew from the contest. What he did not learn until later was that those bearers of bad tidings had been prompted to it by Judge McCarthy.

Although now the field seemed wide open, McCarthy did not relax his generalship. Noticing that the Milwaukee delegation was short several members, he telephoned a friend in Milwaukee and told him to "get ten men up to Oshkosh immediately."

"How can I get that many guys on such short notice?" the friend demanded. "How do I know they'll be for you?"

"Go down to the Marine Corps League and get the names of ten Marines in Milwaukee," McCarthy rapped out. "They all know me. Say Joe wants them and they'll come."

"But some of them may be Democrats."

"Listen. If you ask them, they'll come. And they'll vote for me."

The result was foreseeable. On the first ballot McCarthy won the convention's endorsement by 2,328 votes to 298 for his closest opponent.

Still Joe was not out of the woods. Coleman and his aides balked at entrusting the party's hopes of retiring LaFollette to an inexperienced country judge, and an inner committee beat the bushes for a more impressive candidate. Their choice fell on Walter J. Kohler, Jr., son of a former governor, wealthy, personable, and popular.

McCarthy met this challenge in his usual head-on fashion. Calling on Kohler, he discussed the political outlook, and in the course of the chat mentioned that any candidate who had a divorce in his background would have to expect some pretty distasteful attacks. Also, it was only fair to let Kohler know that no matter who else ran, Joe was in the race to stay, with or without organization backing.

Kohler had been divorced recently. He was a gentleman and shrank from "nastiness." After pondering the situation, he announced that rather than split the anti-LaFollette vote, he would not run.

That left Joe, the political outsider armed principally with colossal nerve, to face the Goliath of vote-getters in Wisconsin, Young Bob LaFollette. Like it or not, Coleman's committee were forced to support their convention's nominee; Joe had crammed himself down their reluctant throats.

How to Win an Election, McCarthy Style

[I]

That campaign went down in the annals as a cyclone of activity. McCarthy opened in Milwaukee on March 18, promising a "very rough but clean fight." It proved to be rough; whether it was clean depended on one's understanding of the word.

Joe dropped all other interests, even poker, as he dashed up and down and around and across the state, leaving a trail like a spider's web. On one four-day stretch he canvassed twenty-seven towns, making speeches, shaking hands, barging into bars, barber shops, restaurants, hotel lobbies—any place that might contain a voter.* He stopped strangers on the street, snatched their hands with a brisk, "Hello, I'm Judge McCarthy, running for the Senate, you know," and, before the person accosted could reply, darted along to buttonhole another prospect. He cultivated farmers and ex-servicemen especially, but also businessmen, factory workers, clergymen, students, housewives. He whipped through Rock County, in the western part of the state, in a day of activity that started at ten in the morning and continued long after midnight. Entering a town, he would jump out of his car and charge along the main street, darting into the stores, speaking briefly before special groups—in Edgerton before the town's lawyers; at Beloit donning overalls and chatting with workers in the machine shops—telling how he had worked as a foundry helper while earning his way through college. He talked with veterans about war days. Usually there was a luncheon address, and at night a dinner speech, and midnight would find him hobnobbing over drinks at the Young Republican head-

---

* The towns were: Alma Center, Arcadia, Augusta, Barron, Black River Falls, Blair, Bloomer, Cameron, Chetek, Chippewa Falls, Cumberland, Durand, Eau Claire, Ellsworth, Fairchild, Hudson, Independence, Menominee, Mondovi, Niellsville, New Richmond, Osseo, Owen, Rice Lake, River Falls, Thorp, and Whitehall.

35

quarters, the American Legion club rooms, or some other convivial gathering place.

Such energy attracted helpers by the dozens. One enthusiastic booster was a young lawyer named Urban P. Van Susteren. They met at a charity bazaar, and Van Susteren remarked during their conversation that he might be able to introduce McCarthy to some friends who could help. At 7:30 the next morning Joe was on Van Susteren's doorstep, demanding that they get started on those introductions. Van Susteren was so impressed he became McCarthy's campaign manager and remained one of his most devoted lieutenants.

Coleman's organization, meanwhile, having been left with no choice but to accept the astonishing judge as their candidate, poured money and system into the campaign, printing and distributing 750,000 copies of a twelve-page brochure depicting McCarthy in the rear seat of a bomber and carrying the slogan, *"Washington Needs a Tail-Gunner."* Newspaper advertisements capitalized on McCarthy's service with the Marines. An appeal published in the *Milwaukee Journal,* a paper unfriendly to Joe, read:

"JOE McCARTHY was a TAIL-GUNNER in World War II. When the war began Joe had a soft job as a Judge at EIGHT GRAND a year. He was EXEMPT from military duty. He resigned to enlist as a PRIVATE in the MARINES. He fought on LAND and in the AIR all through the Pacific. He and millions of other guys kept YOU from talking Japanese. TODAY JOE McCARTHY IS HOME. He wants to SERVE America in the SENATE. Yes, folks. CONGRESS NEEDS A TAIL GUNNER . . . AMERICA NEEDS FIGHTING MEN . . ."

By way of contrast, the McCarthy literature listed LaFollette's record—"sat out the war in Washington, lived on his Virginia plantation," while drawing his Senate salary and "fat rations" although "15,000,000 Americans were fighting the war and 130,000,000 more were building the sinews of war."

"Did the newspaper publishers who suggest that Joseph R. McCarthy resign his judgeship while being a candidate for office give up their $30,000 and $50,000 incomes per year?" the broadside challenged. "Did the Progressive senator who returns to the state only intermittently from his estate in Virginia, chiefly for campaign purposes, make any sacrifice at all?"

[II]

LaFollette, busy in Washington with his massive program for reorganizing the government, disdained to answer such attacks. The polls indicated that he would win by three to one, and he saw no reason to demean himself; Young Bob was not like his aggressive father: he lacked Fighting Bob's magnetic appeal and he disliked crowds and campaigning. In Washington he had turned his abilities to matters of national scope, relying on the prestige of his name and the tradition of progressivism that he symbolized to sustain him at home, and in consequence had come to appear neglectful of the regional interests of his constituents. In the international field he had broken sharply with Franklin Roosevelt's interventionist policy, reverting in large measure to his father's isolationism. In particular, LaFollette had become a bitter critic of Soviet Russia and communism. In May, 1945, he had attacked the Soviets in the Senate, charging that they intended to enslave the free peoples, if they could. This speech had alienated many supporters who favored the Roosevelt administration, including many members of the Progressive party.

McCarthy kept up his stinging allusions to the "absentee senator" and upbraided LaFollette for refusing to engage in a public debate. He hammered on the charge that while he was sweating out the war in the Marines, LaFollette and his wife had collected $47,339.78 in "war profits" from their part ownership of a Milwaukee radio station. The LaFollettes had invested in the station when it was started, and the profits were dividends; but McCarthy charged a conflict of interest because the station was licensed by the government (all radio stations were), and LaFollette voted funds for the licensing agency. "HOW DID LaFOLLETTE GET THAT MONEY?" the newspaper advertisements demanded; and when LaFollette said nothing, Joe stepped up the attack.

The tempo of his barnstorming became frenetic. One day he started at 5 A.M. from Marinette, a town on Green Bay in the rugged north country, to drive to Superior, 250 miles away, where he was due to speak over the radio at 5 P.M. and make a public appearance at 8:30. Pushing along over rutted roads, he frequently hit seventy miles an hour and in the first hundred miles had four blowouts. In every town and hamlet he stopped for a street corner talk. At Rhinelander he abandoned the automobile and took passage in a small commercial plane plying to Superior, but over Butternut the craft developed an oil leak and was forced down in a field of oats. Joe had learned to fly during the war, so he borrowed a light plane belonging to a lawyer in Ashland and flew himself the rest of the way. He reached Superior too late for the radio broadcast, but was on hand, full of pluck and vim, at the public meeting.

No chance for him to present himself and harass his opponent was overlooked. In a night club at Eagle River, he collected each person's share of the dinner check and, having walked over to the cashier, slapped down the money with a loud, "I'm Judge McCarthy, running for the Senate. This is on me."

Philip LaFollette was scheduled to speak on behalf of his brother at a dinner meeting of accountants in Milwaukee, and McCarthy showed up. When Philip started his speech, Joe started table-hopping, introducing himself in a stage whisper as "'the man who is running against Bob, you know." Phil's speech was ruined, and several days later, when he ran into McCarthy on the street, he demanded angrily how a country judge ever hoped to beat Bob LaFollette in Wisconsin.

Replied Joe cheerily: "I'll tell you how. We've got thirty-five guys who are built like Bob and who have rubber masks that look exactly like him. They are going to travel the state, bumping into people and asking who do they think they are, bumping into a United States senator."

And away he scooted, leaving the nonplussed Philip wondering whether he really meant it.

Joe could snub an embarrassing friend, too. One day an associate of the Shawano days who had worked with McCarthy as a fellow Democrat back in 1935 and 1938, spotted the judge in a hotel bar, conferring with several Republican politicians. Approaching Joe's table, the friend held out his hand with a hearty, "Hi, Joe," and wished him luck in the primary.

McCarthy looked the intruder up and down. "I don't believe I've met you," he said coldly, and turned away.

The indignant Democrat later had to admire Joe's quick-wittedness: as the candidate of the Republicans, the judge could hardly be expected to show cordiality to or even recognition of a figure from his Democratic past.

Although McCarthy had support in the county press of the state, the larger newspapers, including both the *Milwaukee Journal* and the *Madison Capital Times,* were antagonistic. One front on which they attacked the judge was his judicial shortcuts; among other questionable practices, it was averred, he was running a "quickie divorce mill." Although the charge was general, only two instances were cited. In each case, both parties concerned wanted the divorce, and agreement had been reached on the terms; but the actions had been stalled in the clogged Milwaukee courts for months, and relief was being denied to the litigants. State law permitted the transfer of a cause from one jurisdiction to another, and in these two instances the transfer was made to McCarthy's circuit. There, everything being in order, Joe snipped the marital knot in a jiffy.

McCarthy's opposition found that in each of the two cases, one of the lawyers concerned had contributed to Joe's campaign chest in his 1944 primary race; one lawyer had donated $50, and the other had parted with $46.95. On this slender evidence, the cry was raised that the state's corrupt-practices act might have been infringed, although no formal charge was preferred by anyone. The allegation was investigated independently by the *Capital Times,* which yielded to nobody in its antipathy to McCarthy, and was dismissed as farfetched, inasmuch as the transferring of suits to another circuit, particularly from Milwaukee, was common practice, and there were numerous other cases of out-of-circuit divorces with no hint of any irregularity. McCarthy didn't bother to refute the accusation, nor would he ever, although it would outlive himself.

[III]

Two weeks before the election, LaFollette finally put in an appearance. Since not a political writer in the state gave McCarthy a chance, Young Bob was blandly confident. The contest was primarily one of personalities: the forty-year tradition that clung to his family name was massively in LaFollette's favor; but McCarthy crackled with youth and vitality. LaFollette was able, honest, earnest, and dull; Joe put on a show. When the senator attempted to offer a dignified, reasoned rejoinder to Joe's wild punches, the latter bore in with the warning that information had come that "this smear campaign will hit a new high, or rather I should say a new low, in the last few days of this election."

Then, on the eve of the voting, half a million postcards were dumped into the mails, carrying a picture of Tail-Gunner Joe and a handwritten message:

> Dear Jim (or Harry or Tom or August): Your vote
> Tuesday will be greatly appreciated by
> *Joe McCarthy.*

Volunteers had been signing the candidate's name to these cards for weeks.

On August 20, the voters trooped to the polls, and the early returns looked bad for McCarthy. In rural areas where he had been expected to take a commanding lead, he and LaFollette were running neck-and-neck, the figures shifting back and forth inconclusively. Since LaFollette's strength always had lain in the industrial districts of Milwaukee, Kenosha, and Racine, Joe's hopes sank when the returns from these points began to come in. Then surprisingly he assumed the lead, and held it tenaciously. He carried Milwaukee county by 10,000, although six years before LaFollette had swept it by a margin of 50,000. The political experts were dumfounded. Then Kenosha fell to McCarthy, and Sheboygan, and the final figures showed that he had accomplished the impossible: he had ended the era of LaFollette by 5,396 votes. It was a narrow triumph, but it was enough; LaFollette never recovered from the blow.

Groggy after the all-night vigil, McCarthy hastened back to Appleton, led a victory snake dance along College Avenue, then tumbled into bed and slept for twenty-four hours. Awakened by a reporter who greeted him as "Senator," Joe muttered, "Not yet; we've got a tough fight ahead," rolled over and slept some more. But soon he was up and running in the direction of the general election in November.

A Crisscross of Colors

A new political picture of the state had emerged from the primary election. With the Progressive party eliminated, the Republicans had swept up sufficient strength to become the dominant faction. McCarthy's election in November, therefore, seemed fairly certain, although he did not relax his high-powered electioneering in the least.

Lamentations over LaFollette's downfall were loud. The senator's mouthpiece, the weekly *Progressive,* bitterly assailed the ingratitude of organized labor especially, charging that large segments of the labor vote had "buried their knife in the back of one of the best friends they ever had."

Less partisan observers viewed the situation differently. The *Milwaukee Journal* believed LaFollette had brought about his own defeat by "losing touch with the home folks." His organization had been eroded by neglect, and to crown a long series of mistakes, he had made an "unimpressive campaign . . . avoiding the issues." By contrast, the *Journal* noted, McCarthy had offered youth and vigor persuasively, and he was close to the people.

The operation of the peculiar Wisconsin primary law also had helped McCarthy, because many Democrats had voted in the Republican primary. Two motives had impelled these voters. First, they thought that McCarthy would be a weaker candidate than LaFollette, thereby improving the Democrats' chances of success in November; and second, many former Progressives who had swung into the Democratic fold upon the disbanding of their own party had borne a grudge against LaFollette for "defecting" to the Republicans, and had voted against him in revenge.

Still another complication that was apparent in the primary vote led to a charge that would follow McCarthy to the grave, namely,

41

that he owed his victory to Communist support. Such an accusation could be made plausibly only in Wisconsin in 1946, for only in that state did there exist a Communist vote large enough and well enough organized to decide an election.

Joe probably brought the charge on himself by attacking his Democratic opponent, Howard McMurray, a political science professor at the University of Wisconsin, on a vulnerable point at the very outset of their campaign. McMurray, earnest, informed, and well-intentioned, was decidedly leftish in his political views; he was also, unfortunately, inept, easily flustered, and unimpressive as a speaker. Early in the campaign McCarthy had told a Milwaukee audience that his opponent was "Communistically inclined." White-faced and trembling with anger, McMurray had denied the imputation, calling the statement "a little below the belt." Joe thereupon flashed clippings from two Wisconsin newspapers quoting the *Daily Worker,* the Communist party organ, as speaking well of McMurray, even calling him a "fellow traveler." Did he or did he not accept this endorsement? Joe inquired. McMurray repudiated the *Worker's* support, denied ever having been aware of it, and termed the papers carrying the quotation the "most reactionary" in the state.

McCarthy stuck to his question.

"The *Daily Worker* called you a fellow traveler, meaning a Communist," he said. "I regret bringing this up, but you forced me to do it."

Since the *Daily Worker* was not known to speak favorably of persons whom they deemed inimical to their cause, despite all McMurray's denials, the suspicion remained. Even Norman Thomas, the usually equable spokesman of the Socialists, wanted to know whether McMurray "accepted the 'fellow traveler' label the *Daily Worker* has pinned on you," and the peculiarities of Wisconsin's current political setup made the issue important.

The Communist strength in the state was centered in the state's CIO (Congress of Industrial Organizations), particularly in the huge Allis-Chalmers local of the Auto Workers Union in Milwaukee. That local was dominated by Harold Cristoffel, who eventually would be convicted of perjury for denying his Communist party membership. The state secretary of the CIO belonged to the party, and the Milwaukee garbage collectors' union was bossed by Communists. The Communists thus had a powerful grip on the state's 750,000 CIO members, and the party's leadership had been infuriated by LaFollette's attacks on the Soviet Union. But Joe McCarthy they considered the candidate of the most reactionary elements in the state.

As told later by Communist party leaders, their headquarters in Milwaukee was visited, several weeks before the August primary, by a Republican campaign worker named Harlan Kelley, who suggested that in view of the Reds' known hatred of LaFollette, they cooperate with the Republicans to insure his defeat. Another target of both factions was included in the proposal—Representative Andrew J. Biemiller, Democratic congressman from the state's Fifth District. Biemiller had been even more aggressively outspoken against Soviet Russia and communism than LaFollette; he even disdained the liberals in his own party, charging that the Democratic state ticket was so loaded with fellow travelers that it looked "like a Communist picnic."

"See here," Kelley was quoted as telling the Communist party chiefs, "you fellows have been highly critical of Biemiller and La-Follette. You must have in your possession a lot of damaging material on both of them. I am here to suggest that you make that material available to us so that we can use it in our campaign. Despite our opposition to each other, we are both opposed to Biemiller and LaFollette, so why can't we get together to beat them?"

The Communists declined to cooperate because, they said, they found McCarthy, and the candidate opposing Biemiller, Charles J. Kerstan, too reactionary altogether for their stomachs. This opinion was made official by the party's chairman directly after the primary election, when he reported by wire to the *Daily Worker* his view of the Republican winner, McCarthy. Calling the judge "an open imperialist Red-baiter," he warned that "he is a good campaigner and will be heavily financed."

After the primary, the party chairman told William T. Evjue, publisher of the anti-McCarthy *Capital Times,* that the Reds would support McMurray (not McCarthy) in November, not because they liked the Democratic nominee, but because he offered the only alternative to the "reactionary" Republican slate. And during the autumn campaign, the Communists' own candidate for governor, Sigmund G. Eisenacher, urged "progressive Democrats, Socialists, Progressives, and Republican liberals" to unite with the Communists to defeat "reactionary Republicans like McCarthy."

It was when McCarthy raised the issue of Communist support against McMurray that the Democratic chairman of Shawano County, Kenneth Traeger, made the public charge that McCarthy owed his primary victory to Communist votes. Traeger prefaced his accusation by saying that at the start of the primary campaign he had tended to favor McCarthy, but had changed his mind when his brother, Bernard Traeger, an FBI agent, told him that McCarthy had "the support of the Cristoffel-Communist group in the Allis-Chalmers union."

Kenneth Traeger said he had confronted McCarthy with this statement and urged him to issue a public disclaimer, but Joe had refused, allegedly quipping: "I guess Communists have as much right to vote as anybody else, haven't they?" *

Although there was no substantiation of Kenneth Traeger's assertion, the story was picked up and circulated as undoubted truth, LaFollette's own *Progressive* stating flatly that McCarthy's primary success was due to "the Communists, who own the Milwaukee county CIO lock, stock, and barrel." And that statement would continue to be repeated throughout McCarthy's career and long after his death.

[II]

McCarthy himself did not lay stress on the Communist issue during the fall campaign. He opposed farm price controls, played up his war record, and excoriated New Deal "bureaucrats" and the Truman administraiton generally. He did taunt his opponent with being "a megaphone for the Communist-controlled PAC" (Political Action Committee, the political arm of the CIO); and he took up the Communist theme in the last few days when he sensed a responsiveness to that line of attack in his audiences. But in this regard he was only following the example of his party nationwide. In state after state, Republican orators were accusing the Demo-

---

* Long afterward, Bernard Traeger would state in writing that Kenneth's story was false; that he had never dissuaded his brother from supporting McCarthy, and had never given any information that there was a Communist plan to back McCarthy's campaign. The Reds indeed had opposed LaFollette, Bernard Traeger confirmed, but they had voted in the Democratic primary, not the Republican, and later they had voted for McMurray against McCarthy. That many Communists had invaded the Democratic primary was admitted later by Harold Cristoffel. For sources and documentation on this point, see, among others, *The Rise of McCarthyism,* by John Steinke, unpublished master's thesis, University of Wisconsin, 1960.

crats of being "soft on Reds." In Tennessee, Congressman B. Carroll Reese, the Republican national chairman, was saying that the choice was "between Communism and Americanism," and this was a keynote of the whole Republican campaign. Senator Wiley reflected this in Wisconsin when he predicted McCarthy's election for the reason that "the people want the government to stand for Americanism and not Communism." Joe was merely following his party's line.

He was forced, however, to weather another squall in the form of a legal challenge of his right to run for senator while clinging to the judge's robe, in apparent violation of the state's constitution.

This attack grew out of the refusal of the state treasurer, John Smith, acting in his capacity as a member of the state board of canvassers, to certify Joe's primary victory. Pressure was brought to bear, and reluctantly he yielded. But an eccentric insurance man in Appleton, Fred Felix Wettengel, took up the fight independently. Helping himself to a liberal dose of outrage, after denouncing Wisconsin lawyers as "a bunch of weak sisters," he petitioned the state supreme court as a concerned citizen to erase Joe's name from the ballot in the November election. The court deliberated and issued a decision that embraced several interesting points: (1) that McCarthy's name already was on the ballot, and "wrongs already perpetrated cannot be corrected by an injunction"; (2) that the secretary of state had merely performed a duty in putting the name on the ballot, having no discretionary power to exclude it; (3) that the court felt it should not intrude in a field that had been preempted by the United States Constitution; and (4) that many things might happen that would dispose of the issue—Joe might withdraw, he might be defeated, he might even die. Holding out this triplicity of possibilities, the court denied Wettengel's plea. McCarthy interpreted the ruling as a vindication, and there the matter rested. What one not unfriendly critic called "cutting ethical corners" had become standard practice with hurry-up McCarthy.

Rocketing down to the wire in November, he was vindicated by the voters, who handed him a thumping majority—620,430 to McMurray's 378,772.

The *Milwaukee Journal* construed the landslide as "chiefly an extension of the national revolt against the New Deal," a revolt so emphatic it gave the Republicans control of both houses of

Congress. Beyond a doubt, 1946 was a Republican year, and Joe
had benefited from the national trend. But there was another factor
which he pinpointed for the press when he was quizzed on what
he thought were the reasons for his success. Pondering a moment,
he came up with a simple answer to the riddle: "I don't claim to
be any smarter than the next fellow, but I do claim that I work
twice as hard."

Deeming it unfair to deprive the national capital of an immediate
glimpse of the Peck's bad boy of the Wisconsin woods, early in
December, a full month before he could take his seat in the Senate,
McCarthy grabbed a fistful of calamitous neckties, stuffed them
and some equally loud shirts into a bag, and took off for Washington. Already he was thrilling to his first taste of national publicity:
Time magazine had carried a flattering report on his stunning defeat of the veteran LaFollette, including a photograph of Joe flashing his boyish grin.

By coincidence (or was it fate?) on the same page appeared a
report on another Republican primary victory, with a photograph
of the winner—an elderly man with a whimsical expression, smoking a pipe. He came from Vermont, and his name was Ralph E.
Flanders.

A Badger in the House

When Joseph R. McCarthy, senator-elect, stepped off the train in Washington, he glanced around and uttered the famous first words: "Hell, it's raining!"

It seemed disloyal of the weather not to welcome him with a salvo of sunshine.

The inconspicuousness of his arrival he rectified promptly by calling a press conference. Curious to learn what a senator-to-be might have to communicate in the midst of coal strike that threatened to paralyze the national economy, a handful of correspondents showed up. Joe gave them his solution of the crisis: let President Truman draft John L. Lewis and his coal miners into the Army and order them back to work. The newsmen were impressed, but not by the feasibility of the proposal. What if the miners refused to obey the President, they asked. Why, martial law took care of insubordination, said Joe. Did he mean—shoot John L. Lewis? Or jail the entire membership of the United Mine Workers?

"Nonsense," said McCarthy. "All this talk about you can't put 400,000 men in jail is stuff. They won't go to jail. They'll mine coal first."

"You're new around here, aren't you?" the reporters grunted as they straggled out.

This first discouraging encounter with the press McCarthy soon overcame by arranging to keep the National Press Club bar permanently supplied with wheels of Wisconsin cheese. For a group of women correspondents he turned on the Irish charm and served them a dinner cooked by himself. They considered him quite the jolliest thing that had hit Capitol Hill in years.

Joe adapted quickly to Washington. He got rid of his sunset-hued neckties and acquired a tuxedo. As an unattached "extra man" he was in demand by hostesses, and accepted invitations so profusely he found himself dining out every night in the week. But it dawned on him that this treadmill would take him nowhere, and he became selective in his socializing. Actually, social activities bored him unless they could be made to serve his political ambition.

In the Senate he attracted no more attention than is customarily bestowed upon freshmen members, which is little. His committee assignments were from the bottom of the barrel with one exception —a place on the Banking and Currency Committee. Personally he was well-liked, there being no pose in his affability, and there was always a bottle in his desk when a visitor came by. He eagerly wanted to be liked by others; he craved friendship.

He lived with Spartan simplicity, not because of asceticism, but because of indifference to creature comforts. He rented a room in the Anacostia apartment of his administrative assistant, Ray Kiermas, and set himself to master the rules of the new world he was entering. Applying his cramming method, he pored over reports and books of reference, boning up on economic issues, foreign relations, and parliamentary procedure.

On the Senate floor he spoke seldom, and when he did he pleased by his brevity; his modesty in refraining from pushing himself was approved. He realized that he was at a disadvantage because of his youth; in this body of men ruled by precedence and seniority, he was ten years younger than the average senator, and twenty-five years younger than most chairmen of important committees. This was a challenge to his temperament, because he disliked to wait, but he met it.

His voting record was undistinguished, leaning rather toward the liberal side than toward the conservative. He interested himself in veterans' welfare and joined his colleague, Senator Wiley, in pushing a measure to assist Wisconsin's fur farmers. Passage of this bill evoked so grateful a mail response that Joe bragged to reporters, "Now the fur people think I'm God!"

In the field of foreign relations, he generally supported the administration. He voted for military aid to Greece and Turkey, implementing the Truman policy of halting Soviet expansion, and he would vote for both the Marshall Plan and the North Atlantic Treaty Organization. The only hand he took in regard to Communist infiltration was to offer an amendment to the Taft-Hartley bill authorizing employers to dismiss Communist employes. Taft brushed the amendment aside as superfluous. Altogether, during his early months as a senator, Joe steered a middle course between the extremes of his colleagues, and cultivated popularity outside the chamber by his personality and his unquenchable friendliness.

Openhanded in spending, he got rid of every cent he received. He liked nothing better than to show up at a friend's home with a sack of hamburgers and a bottle of champagne. He insisted on informality, required his staff to call him "Joe" and not "Senator," and franked his mail "Joe McCarthy." And he kept up his addiction to roughhouse poker. From time to time, apparently without system, he plunged into the stock market, and he amazed friends by his reckless betting on any kind of a racetrack tip. His prowess at the poker table caused comment, one Wisconsin opponent grimly advising anyone playing against Joe either to play for table stakes or "get some big bank to back you. He raises on the poor hands and always comes out the winner."

But in spite of all activity, the new senator, after those long strides in Wisconsin, seemed to have lost momentum. He seemed boxed in.

A Time of Turmoil

Much the same was true of the nation during the years of Mc-
Carthy's Senate apprenticeship. It was a period of great confusion
and national frustration. After the giant accomplishment of winning World War II, the United States was struggling to readjust to
a peacetime basis, and finding it increasingly difficult to do. At
home there were shortages of housing and of foodstuffs, threats of
unemployment, and problems created by tremendous shifts in the
population. The prolonging of privations that had been borne
patiently during the fighting bred protest and discontent. This had
been clearly reflected in the 1946 elections, and was so openly
acknowledged on Capitol Hill that the Republicans who rode into
Congress on the backwash of that discontent were jocularly known
as the "meat shortage boys."

Abroad the United States was headed into uncharted waters. A
new world had opened up, filled with unanswered questions. In
the postwar redistribution of world power America found itself the
dominant force—not by choice, and even against the fervent wishes
of many of its citizens, but by the simple exhaustion and abdication
of its partners. The wartime alliance with Soviet Russia had dis-
solved; more and more plainly it was seen that our erstwhile ally
had embarked upon a program of aggrandizement, employing the
two-pronged technique of coercion and hidden guile—infiltration
and betrayal.

To Americans the situation was unnerving. They had no tradition
that fit the new realities. In the government, expertise was lacking,
and the public was even less well equipped to understand the radical
changes in shifting world policy. Absorbed in the irritations of their
domestic readjustments, Americans only gradually, after much
blundering and reluctance, came to understand that there could be

no return to world conditions of an earlier date. All that had been wiped out by the technological and social upheavals produced by the war. The process of learning to cope with the new world equation was fitful and painful—a stumbling forward rather than a smooth, steady, coordinated advance.

In March, 1946, Winston Churchill, in his "Iron Curtain" speech at Fulton, Missouri, had defined the nature and implacability of the current struggle, calling it a "cold war." A month previously, Secretary of State James F. Byrnes had indicated a first stiffening of American resistance to Soviet aggressions. A year later, in March, 1947, enunciation of the Truman Doctrine made clear the intention of the United States to resist the Soviet threat to the free world. Senator McCarthy voted to implement this policy by force of arms. Yet still the Red tide spread. Czechoslovakia was taken over by means of subversion and treachery. In the United Nations, the United States almost daily was subjected to insults as a "warmonger." Then came the Communist blockade of Berlin and the United States airlift which fed and warmed Berliners for a year.

All the while, for the first time in their national experience, Americans faced an organized, sustained, and sinister external threat—not alone to their material interests, but to their very existence as a nation. The threat also was internal, and in that sphere so terrible in its potentialities for great harm that the subject was avoided in day-to-day conversation.

Domestically the threat lay in the use of espionage and penetration of social organizations by the Communists, for the furtherance of Soviet Russia's aims. These activities, the world outside Russia gradually learned, were being carried on constantly, mainly by stealth, on a scale of magnitude and effrontery transcending all previous experience. Diplomacy had been debased to a game of spy and counterspy, embassies reduced to nests of secret agents, while apologists for Russia spun their exculpations on all sides.

Some of Russia's sympathizers were sincere; some were hoodwinked by the Russians' trumpeting of their devotion to praiseworthy ends. Important labor unions had been infiltrated, and so had been segments of the news and entertainment worlds—channels of communication invaluable for disseminating covert propaganda.

This web of infiltration had been exposed to the public bit by bit, always against intense resistance. As early as 1930 a congressional inquiry had been ordered into Communist subversion, and the disclosures had been hooted down by Russia's apologists as ridiculously alarmist. The term "fellow traveler" had come into use to describe those abettors of Communist activity who accepted at face value the Reds' professed altruism, but fastidiously held aloof from open alignment with the party.

Despite the storms of protest raised by these early investigations, the facts they managed to bring to light did kindle suspicion in the minds of many people, and, as the disclosures continued, that suspicion would not down. As gradually defined, it became a conscious suspicion that something was amiss—and at the very top. Otherwise, why was the peril not being combatted with greater success? Why, at times, was the very existence of the danger denied? Spokesmen for the nation's intellectual, political, and academic worlds from time to time insisted that everything needful was being done, but concrete events pointed to a different conclusion. Public mistrust built up steadily, not always clearcut and seldom logically reasoned, but confused and deep-rooted.

Revelations produced by the House Committee on Un-American Activities had shocked and angered millions of Americans, while others denounced the committee and its findings as a "witch hunt," a betrayal of American ideals, and called its members "smear-mongers" and "Fascists." Yet in spite of these outcries, month after month the public witnessed a parade of contumacious witnesses who reviled their questioners and retreated into defiant silence when asked about possible involvement in Soviet espionage. As this sordid pantomime was performed over and over again, the minds of Americans struggling with their own postwar readjustments stirred uneasily. Reaching into official circles, this sense of danger in 1947 impelled President Truman to authorize procedures for screening all federal employes in reference to their loyalty, and a comprehensive check of personnel got under way in August of that year.

A prime target of this screening program was the State Department, which was laboring under special disabilities because of the indiscriminate blanketing into its payroll of some 13,000 employes of disbanded wartime agencies. From the discontinued Office of War Information alone 7,482 employes had been transferred to the State Department; and although thousands of these soon left the government service voluntarily, 4,000 remained. Thousands of these employes, it was discovered, had never had their backgrounds checked at all. Thus a situation of almost hopeless complexity had been created with which the department's loyalty board had to cope.

The regaining of control of Congress by the Republicans in the 1946 election had set off several inquiries into the working of the screening program, which from the moment of its inauguration had been harshly attacked and bitterly defended. Some facts emerging from these investigations had tended to strengthen the feeling among a wide segment of the public that something was radically wrong in the government itself—something that at the best might be muddleheadedness, and at the worst might be treachery.

There was, for example, the *Amerasia* case, with its trails that led into, but never out of, a baffling Communist maze. The case was and would remain one of the most inscrutable mysteries of the cold war.

[II]

Amerasia was the name of a magazine of limited circulation (never more than 2,000) read mainly by professional diplomats. It dealt with questions of foreign policy, specifically in Asia. In February, 1945, a Far East analyst in the Office of Strategic Services (the wartime cloak-and-dagger agency of espionage and intrigue) read an article in *Amerasia* on British-American relations in Siam. It startled him because it paralleled almost identically a highly secret report he had once prepared on the subject, not only paraphrasing the OSS report, but lifting entire paragraphs verbatim. Obviously the writer had had access to this report, which was classified, and it seemed likely that he had had a copy in front of him while he wrote.

This was a serious leak, pointing toward espionage. The facts were referred at once to the OSS director in New York, Frank Bielaski, who placed the *Amerasia* office at 225 Fifth Avenue under surveillance. Inquiries quickly established that the editor, Philip Jaffe, was known as a generous contributor to Communist causes; that he was in regular touch with known Communists; and that he had written for a Communist publication, *China Today*, under a different name. Jaffe seemed to be prosperous, deriving an income from a nonunion printing plant which manufactured greeting cards.

A check of the files showed that *Amerasia* had published articles on the Far East by such experts as Frederick Vanderbilt Field, Anna Louise Strong, Owen Lattimore, and Benjamin Kizer, all of whom were identified more or less openly with the interests of the Chinese Communists in their stuggle with the Nationalists under Chiang Kai-shek.

One thing that seemed odd to Bielaski was that night after night the *Amerasia* offices were brightly lighted. Why should so modest a publication require so much overtime work? Finally on March 11, 1945, a Sunday night, when the building was dark, Bielaski led a squad of agents there. Flashing badges, they induced the janitor to let them into the *Amerasia* suite. In the outer office they found nothing unusual, although in an adjoining room was elaborate photocopying equipment capable of turning out a quantity of work much greater than anything *Amerasia* would require.

Jaffe's private office then was entered, and there the raiders found piled on the desk photocopies of ultra-secret classified government documents. There were personal reports to the Secretary of State, reports from military attachés in China and elsewhere, and data gathered by Naval Intelligence. All were plainly stamped "confidential" or otherwise classified as secret. Both originals and freshly made copies were on the desk, in profusion. The raiders doubted their eyesight.

Then behind a door they found a heavy suitcase and two briefcases literally stuffed with classified documents, all of them originals except for the OSS report that had been used for the article and had led to the search; both the original and four copies of this document were found.* And there were other OSS documents, which had not yet been missed, all secret, one stamped boldly, "Top Secret." As Bielaski later would testify:

"I took this stuff and spread it around. It covered almost every department in the government except the FBI. . . . There were documents from the British intelligence, naval intelligence, G-2 [Army Intelligence], Office of Censorship, Office of Strategic Supply. . . . There were so many we could not list them. These documents were from three or four to 150 pages. There were 300 documents. Every one of them bore the stamp that possession of

---

* The unanswered question: Why should a publication of such modest editorial needs require *several* copies of a classified document in its unauthorized possession, unless the material was to be passed along, or shared with, other unauthorized persons?

these documents is a violation of the espionage act. It was stamped all over them.

"About that time one of my men who had gone into the library came in and said he had found something. He had an envelope which was not sealed. It was a large manila envelope. In that envelope were, I should say, fifteen or twenty documents. . . . In between these documents, every other one, we found six top secret documents of the Navy Department. . . . One of them was entitled, 'The Bombing Program for Japan.' It was top secret. I read it. It showed how Japan was to be bombed progressively in the industrial cities, and it named cities.

"The second one that I read gave the location of all the ships of the Japanese fleet, subsequent to the Battle of Leyte; I guess it was October 1944. It gave the ships by name, and where they were located."

Other documents that he saw, Bielaski testified, included information on the disposition of Nationalist Chinese troops (information of priceless value to the Chinese Communists), and one document, contained in an envelope lying open on a table, that was marked " 'A' Bomb." Bielaski assumed it was a code abbreviation for some new type of ordnance, for he had never heard of an atomic bomb at the time.

Convinced that if he went to his superiors and told them what he had seen, "they just wouldn't believe me," he selected a dozen or so of the documents, including all the copies of the OSS report he was after, and put them in his pocket to use as proof. Then arranging everything as they had found it, the raiders departed.

A few hours later, Bielaski was in the office of Archbold Van Buren, OSS security chief, in Washington, reporting on his find. One by one he placed the documents he had carried away on Van Buren's desk. One dealt with the German order of battle. Another was marked, "For the Attention of the Director of Naval Intelligence Only." Still another (FBI records would confirm this) contained one of the most tightly guarded secrets of the war, namely, that the Navy had broken the Japanese code.

Van Buren also could hardly believe his senses; but there were the tangible proofs, documents that could not be brushed aside as imaginary, and every one of them, in his stated opinion, "of benefit to an enemy of the United States." And the United States was still at war.

Van Buren called General William Donovan, the head of the

OSS, and then took the evidence to him. Donovan noticed that each of the documents bore the seal of the Department of State, and he at once called Secretary of State Edward Stettinius, Jr., at the latter's Wardman Park apartment, requesting an immediate interview. Assistant Secretary of State Julius Holmes was with Stettinius when Donovan arrived. The documents were handed to the Secretary, who read them, exclaiming at one point to his assistant, "Good God, Julius, if we can get to the bottom of this we will stop a lot of things that have been plaguing us!"

He offered no explanation. Later it would be recalled that President Roosevelt had complained about the way State Department secrets were leaking to the press.

Six days after the talk with Stettinius, the FBI was put on the case. Jaffe and *Amerasia* were placed under intensive surveillance. This brought to light a curiously persistent relationship between Jaffe, his associates, and the Institute of Pacific Relations, a Far East study group sponsored by some of the most eminent names in American industry and scholarship.

On June 6, 1945, six persons were arrested, charged with violations of the espionage act, and the public got its first word of the devious affair. Those arrested were Jaffe; Kate Louise Mitchell, coeditor of *Amerasia;* Emmanuel S. Larsen, who had spent years in China and during the war had been employed by both Naval Intelligence and the State Department in positions involving the handling of secret documents; Andrew Roth, until the day previous to his arrest a lieutenant in Naval Intelligence (the reason for his abrupt severance was never disclosed); Mark Gayn, born in Manchuria of Russian parents and long resident in China, and since his naturalization in 1944 a free-lance newspaper and magazine writer specializing in Far Eastern topics; and John Stewart Service, State Department career diplomat recently returned from China, where he had been assigned to positions close to Chiang Kai-shek and at one time had been an observer at the headquarters of Mao Tsetung, the Communist commander. In the magazine's office and in the possession of those arrested were found some 1,700 classified documents from government files, most of them dealing with Far Eastern affairs.

After some delay, the cases of the six arrested were brought before two grand juries, and the second panel indicted Jaffe, Larsen, and Roth on the minor charge of illegal possession of government property. Espionage could not be proved, the government attorneys contended, because no evidence had been found indicating that the purloined material had been transmitted to a foreign power. Miss Mitchell, Gayn, and Service were not indicted, and Service, who had been suspended by the State Department pending disposition of the case, was reinstated, with a letter of congratulations from the Secretary of State.

It was noted at the time that a bitter feud between two factions in the State Department holding opposite views of the way to deal with conquered Japan, Russia, and the Red Chinese, was resolved precisely at this juncture with victory for the faction headed by Assistant Secretary Dean Acheson. Undersecretary Joseph Grew and Assistant Secretary Holmes, who had advocated a "tough" policy against Soviet expansion and had vigorously backed the FBI's presentation of the *Amerasia* affair, were retired, and Acheson moved into Grew's spot as Undersecretary—next in rank to the Secretary.

The apparent reluctance of the Justice Department to proceed to trial of the three indicted persons drew adverse comment in the press; the public had been shocked by the disclosures so far made, guarded as these were. Then suddenly, on the morning of Saturday, September 29, without advance notice being given to the press, Jaffe was taken before a judge in New York. The judge asked the government prosecutor how much time he would require to develop his case, and the attorney replied, "Less than five minutes." And in five minutes he did make clear to the court that there was no evidence of disloyalty on Jaffe's part, simply lack of discretion and overzeal as a journalist bent on getting his facts straight. The defendant was fined $2,500 and released. Then Larsen pleaded nolo contendere and was let off with a $500 fine. On the government's motion, the indictment against Roth was dismissed.*

[III]

There this curious case had rested, but the unanswered questions it had raised would not stay down. In a vague way, many Americans saw sinister influences at work, culminating in what seemed to be an insolent disregard for the national safety, if nothing worse —and worse was suspected. The Justice Department's suave ex-

* Both Roth and Gayn later became contributors to *The Nation*.

planation that the evidence against the accused persons was legally tainted because it had been gathered in the first instance without a search warrant and in part by wiretapping, would not wash, and the FBI contended that it had presented an "ironclad" case. And strangely, an influential section of the conservative press insisted upon viewing the arrests as altogether outrageous. The *New York Herald Tribune* called them "Red-baiting," and said they were "a serious omen if they mean that anyone in the government [must] maintain a mouselike quiet if he is to the political left of the State Department." Calling in the FBI and "bringing about arrests which resulted in headlines concerning 'spies' and 'espionage' " the same paper reprobated as a grievous mistake: "It might have been better . . . to have dismissed the men concerned."

Curiously, the Communists' own mouthpiece, the *Daily Worker,* echoed this demurrer, calling the affair a "witch-hunt" traceable to the malign influence of Grew and J. Edgar Hoover, director of the FBI, and "aimed essentially at freedom of the press."

Other newspapers, however, expressed strong resentment of the cavalier disposal of the mass of evidence, and the case provided the Republicans with a political issue. The Democrats defensively pooh-poohed the episode as "teacup gossip," and Grew's homely explanation ("We heard somebody in the chicken coop and went to see who was there") was ignored by the Acheson faction in the department. Jaffe made a remark to Larsen, after their slap-on-the-wrist fines, that may have been illuminating: "Well, we've suffered a lot—but anyhow, we got Grew out."

The outcry threatened to do so much damage to the Truman administration that in the spring of 1946 a House Judiciary sub-committee, under the chairmanship of Samuel F. Hobbs, an astute Alabama Democrat, undertook an investigation. The subcommittee held one public hearing, then listened to a parade of witnesses in executive secrecy. Bielaski told his story, the Justice Department defended its action, Larsen was heard, and after several months the subcommittee issued two reports, majority and minority, diametrically opposed. The Democratic majority found that a prosecution could not have succeeded for technical reasons; the Republican minority maintained that convictions could have been obtained. The minority found that the government had bungled, but said there seemed to be no evidence of a deliberate "fix." The transcript of the testimony taken was not published.

And so an uneasy ghost was laid—permanently, the administration hoped. But a case which could inspire cartoons like the one that appeared in the *Detroit Free Press*—showing a trail of footprints labeled *"Amerasia Fix"* leading straight into the White House —was not likely to stay buried long.

[IV]

In this excitement and in the various investigations of Communist influence in the government, real or alleged—particularly in the State Department—occurring at this period Senator McCarthy took no visible interest. Nor did he protest the action of President Truman when, midway through one inquiry conducted by the Senate Judiciary Committee and just when investigators began turning up significant evidence, the President forbade the disclosure of any personnel data to congressional committees. The directive, issued on March 13, 1948, instructed the heads of all departments to pay no heed to any subpoena, request, or demand for such data emanating from Capitol Hill.

This abrupt shutting off of the only source of authoritative information regarding personnel put an end to the Judiciary investigation. The shutoff occurred, it was noted—whether or not by coincidence was a matter of opinion—simultaneously with a burst of criticism of the Presidential screening program as an affront to freeborn citizens, an oppressive denial of constitutionally guaranteed rights, a "terrorist" tactic aimed at the suppression of free speech, and other things equally heinous, illicit, and reprehensible.

This conflict of views was one expression of the irreconcilability of two basically opposite ideological credos that had solidified during the postwar turmoil. On the one side, the rights of the individual were held to be supreme; on the other, the rights of the nation, of the people as a whole, were deemed paramount. Proponents of the latter view argued that conditions unforeseen by the framers of the Constitution had arisen, involving a new type of warfare—the cold war—which was every bit as desperate and as fateful for the nation as a war fought with tanks and bayonets; and that in prosecuting this newstyle warfare, every available resource not only could be, but as a matter of patriotic self-preservation ought to be employed, since the life of the nation was at stake. One available resource was exposure of the subterranean workings of the nation's enemies and of those who either deliberately or ignorantly abetted the enemy's cause.

From the liberal viewpoint, this reasoning was fallacious and inadmissible. In their opinion the threat to the United States was external, not internal, and the Communist party in the United States was a lawfully constituted political organization, openly advocating principles which might be abhorrent to most Americans, but which could be legitimately advanced for all that. Communists had as much right to combine and function as a political party, ran this argument, as had Republicans, Democrats, Socialists, or Prohibitionists. The Communist party did so function, nominating candidates for public office and propounding their program in the approved ways; and no citizen, the liberals contended, should be harassed or embarrassed or penalized because he believed in Communist theories.

Opposed to this was the conviction on the part of many Americans, informed and uninformed, that the Communist party in the United States, aligned with a bewildering array of "fronts" and other more or less concealed adjuncts, was not a political party acting in good faith, by constitutional means, but was an arm of an international conspiracy directed against the government of the United States and in effect against the entire free world. This conspiracy, it was believed, was intent upon supplanting free government with an atheistic toltalitarian tyranny, not by open and lawful means, through the ballot box, but by stealth, deceit, and treachery, and by the use of force and violence.

This conflict of views was irreconcilable because obviously one viewpoint or the other must be false; both could not be true. And because the opposing attitudes were irreconcilable, they led inevitably to extreme asseverations by partisans on both sides. Year after year the clamor had persisted, rising and falling in direct ratio to the degree of cordiality or hostility governing our relations with the Russians at the time. Thus by the late 1940's Americans were troubled; but Wisconsin's junior senator gave no indication whatever of being concerned with the Communist issue.

Diversions of a Senator

If some shrewd observer had watched the junior senator from Wisconsin expecting to detect in his actions a fixed line of policy, the expectation would have been dashed, for Joe's legislative style was the same as that of his boxing—furious bouts of wild punching, conforming to no consistent pattern, and plunges from topic to topic without any bridging logic. At one moment he was swinging at the inequity of sugar rationing, and at another impugning the honesty of the United States Army. His motives often puzzled his colleagues, which was scarcely to be wondered at, since the emotional and mental stresses that underlay his drive were not comprehended by the man himself. Joe McCarthy was almost devoid of the introspective faculty, and many members of the Senate, as well as the majority of both his adherents and his opponents, never would understand him. It was plain from his legislative actions that he responded readily to the claims of friendship and good-fellowship, and any cause he espoused he promoted and defended with reckless tenacity; he was a bulldog for holding on.

McCarthy introduced or seconded bills dealing with veterans' welfare, a politically profitable field for legislative record-making directly after the war, but he enjoyed no monopoly there. While he supported the entire military establishment in a general way, his real favor went to the Marine Corps. This was only natural; but since McCarthy dealt habitually in exaggeration, he seemed over-endowed with suspicion of the rival military branches.

One talent that had served him well in Wisconsin he brought into the Senate. This was his skill in transforming an orderly debate into a general scuffle. He did this both as a tactic and instinctively, without personal animus and sometimes without particular point. The only way of fighting he knew was attack; defense he did not

61

understand, and consequently he scorned it. His aim in debate was to fluster his opponent at the outset by a hail of unexpected blows and open the way to a knockout later. Once a bout was over, Joe became his hearty, friendly self again, grinning with good humor.

The first major controversy to which the senator contributed his specialized style of attack was that over the lifting of wartime controls on sugar. The beet sugar producers of Wisconsin were agitating to end rationing, and the Wisconsin legislature had memorialized Congress in support of such action. Responding to this pressure, McCarthy introduced a bill "to prevent sugar hoarding and to continue export controls, as a gradual way out of rationing." Senators Charles W. Tobey of New Hampshire and Ralph Flanders of Vermont, two states where housewives did much home canning, protested that decontrol would benefit only large industrial users and commodity speculators. The debate became acrid.

Senator Tobey, a senior member of the Senate, was hot-tempered and jealous of his privileges; Flanders was the practical Yankee philosopher, skeptical, shrewd, wryly humorous, with a personality like the tang of a winter apple. Self-educated, he had married the daughter of a machine tools manufacturer and had inherited the business, which he ran efficiently. Unlike Senator Tobey, he was not easily baited, but Joe managed to plunge him into incredulous bewilderment with one easy speech.

In making out a case for his bill, McCarthy united imagination with audacity. Beginning, in his flat, unemotional, commonplace tone (he was always a poor speaker, stumbling and halting over his words), the junior representative of the Badger State preluded: "Either we have sufficient sugar to do away with rationing, or we do not. It is a matter of tons."

Proceeding from this incontrovertible fact, Joe read off an array of statistics, threaded on a commentary that traced a trail of sugar around the world. Included were figures on imports and exports, estimates of the Cuban crop, price fluctuations, international agreements, and surpluses of sugar conjured up in Brazil, Argentina, and Peru; all leading to the comforting conclusion that there were lying about "791,000 tons of sugar upon which we had not counted."

Flanders protested that his Wisconsin colleague was violating an elementary rule of arithmetic, namely, that apples and oranges cannot be added in the same column. "The senator from Wisconsin has raised questions so fast that I am having difficulty in keeping up with him. We cannot deal cavalierly with the question of sugar stocks, figures regarding the Cuban crop, the receipts, the amounts——"

McCarthy broke in: "Mr. President, I sat here for four hours yesterday while the senator held the floor on this subject. I do not object to being asked questions, but I do not think the senator should make a speech."

Flanders protested he was merely trying to unscramble a mess, but Joe would not allow it, hitting his critic with unexpected objections from all sides. Tobey took a hand when he heard McCarthy say he was acting in the interest of the nation's housewives and add with an air of finality: "Within the past ten minutes I have received word from the Department of Agriculture that they . . . wish to discuss with us the possibility of agreeing to make available to the housewife during the third quarter—that is, during the canning season—a total allotment of twenty pounds of sugar."

Tobey had received directly contrary information from the same source. Leaving the chamber, he telephoned to the Secretary of Agriculture, Clinton P. Anderson. Returning to the floor, he challenged McCarthy's statement, saying:

"Here is the answer which came from Secretary Anderson just three minutes ago, over the telephone, to me: 'I authorize you to state that I have not at any time made a statement that we can give more sugar for home consumption now. . . . There is no more sugar available for home consumption. But if any more does come across the horizon, we will allocate it to the housewives.' That is exactly Secretary Anderson's statement, and it refutes the statement which has been made by the senator from Wisconsin."

"Then, Mr. President," McCarthy retorted with the brusquerie of a man dealing with a stupid objection, "I don't give a tinker's dam what Secretary Anderson says about the matter. The sugar is there!"

Tobey flushed. "On the question of veracity," he shot back, "I would not choose between the two gentlemen, but on a question of fact I take the Secretary of Agriculture every time!"

Whereupon McCarthy, in effect, raised the ante, and with an air of pained reluctance informed the senators that, only a few days before, Tobey had confided that he intended to introduce "some type of fictitious amendment" to Joe's bill, which would "do nothing more or less than deceive the housewife."

Infuriated by this personal attack, Tobey demanded the floor and got into the record his defiant response that "the senator's statement, I submit, far contravenes the truth, to put it plainly!" McCarthy interrupted, but Tobey shouted on: "I am not quite through yet, sir! I point out that the senator is confusing the Senate of the United States by a heterogeneous mass of figures which will not stand the test of accuracy!"

The decorum of the Senate was shattered, and in the end sugar controls were extended, although McCarthy did squeeze in a provision lifting them five months earlier than had been proposed by the administration. Tobey, who frequently mixed his metaphors, exclaimed, when Joe's amendment was adopted: "The speculators are singing a Te Deum in their hearts tonight! They are singing 'Hail, hail, the gang's all here! We are ready for the kill!' "

At the end McCarthy ironically voted against the bill, even though it contained his amendment; he was annoyed because another amendment of his had been rejected, which would have allowed industrial users to share equally with home consumers in any extra supplies of sugar that might turn up.

McCarthy's actions in this controversy gave rise to some cynical reflections. It was true that he had acted in accordance with the expressed views of his constituency, and there was nothing objectionable in that. What was questionable was McCarthy's noticeable intimacy at this time with a lobbyist for the Pepsi-Cola Company, Russell M. Arundel. The parties thrown by this big spender were the talk of Washington; he once was host to some three hundred prominent Democrats, President Truman among them, for two days on Jefferson Island in Chesapeake Bay, and the *Boston Herald* had described the stag affair as comparing favorably with Belshazzar's celebrated feast. Arundel had an interest in Pepsi-Cola bottling plants, and the company had been having difficulty in obtaining sugar. During the debate over lifting controls, McCarthy was often seen with Arundel, and in fact he appeared so openly to be carrying the ball for the company that he was nicknamed around the Capitol "The Pepsi-Cola Kid." He grinned and didn't mind.

Shortly after the showdown on sugar, McCarthy took a beating in the stock market, and his bank in Appleton called for more collateral to cover his loans. After repeated appeals from the bank's president, Matthew Shuh, an old friend, McCarthy sent a note for $20,000, payable in six months, endorsed by Russell M. Arundel, whose credit, he told Shuh, "I assume you have looked up . . . and find that he is good for an amount far in excess of this."

Four months later Shuh began to worry, because, he wrote to McCarthy, "Mr. Arundel hasn't any liquid assets shown on his statement," and the bank examiners had placed his note on the "objectionable list." The note would have to be paid within ten days, Shuh pleaded, or it would "surely put both you and me in the doghouse."

Joe met that crisis one way or another, and in the process did not cease to be known in Capitol corridors as "The Pepsi-Cola Kid."

[II]

It was not the position that McCarthy took on sugar rationing that was significant; it was the way he carried out his role of spokesman for the interests, legitimate or otherwise, whom he chose to represent. Flanders had been pelted with a jumble of unrelated data until he was dizzy, with bland disregard for statistical gaps so gross that an auditor for the Commodity Credit Corporation needed six single-spaced typewritten pages to expose thirteen major errors. The excitable Tobey had been trapped into sputtering incoherency by a "tinker's dam" and an imputation of political fakery, flung out on the floor of the Senate in violation of all rules of courtesy and mutual respect. Yet in spite of these breaches of custom, Joe continued to be not unpopular with many of his colleagues off the floor. He resembled a romping, awkward dog, upsetting the furniture in furious demonstrations of friendliness, hardly to be held accountable. In some ways Joe was still countrified and naive.

A friend had been struck by an incident that occurred shortly after McCarthy's arrival in Washington. He was lunching with Joe in the Senate dining room when Senator Claude Pepper of Florida entered. At that time Pepper was a headline figure, much in the news, and Joe often had read about him and his prominence in Washington's inner circles. Forgetting lunch and companion, McCarthy had stared in open awe at the celebrated senator.

The consciousness of not quite belonging stuck with McCarthy, senator though he was. A year after arriving in Washington, he stood nursing a martini during a reception; the room was crowded with men and women bearing famous names—people in positions of power. As he took in the throng, McCarthy murmured to the guest beside him, "I wonder what these people would think if they knew I once raised chickens."

[III]

But no flutter of insufficiency distinguished his next legislative foray. This concerned the long, impassioned debate over public versus privately financed housing to meet the desperate postwar shortage. Millions of Americans had a direct interest in this controversy and feeling ran high. The trail of Joe's participation in the complex affair is long and at times serpentine, and again it was not his stand on the main issue, which was open to sincere conviction either way, but the way he played his hand that was significant.

In August, 1947, Congress had set up a joint Senate-House committee, composed of members of the Banking and Currency committees of both houses, to study the problem and recommend legislation. Under the accepted rules of seniority, Senator Tobey was slated to head the joint committee. McCarthy, who had asked for and had been assigned membership, had different ideas.

On August 19, the committee met to organize. The rules of the Senate permitted proxy voting; those of the House did not. Tobey held the proxies of four members. McCarthy moved that the rule of the House prevail and proxies be disallowed.

Tobey begged that the wishes of members unable to be on hand for the preliminaries be respected. McCarthy retorted that members who didn't bother to attend meetings shouldn't have any say in the proceedings; he had counted noses and knew he had a majority on his side. So the motion was put and carried, knocking Tobey out of the controlling chairmanship.

Then McCarthy nominated as chairman Representative Ralph A. Gamble of New York, a fervent advocate of private housing. Gamble was elected, with McCarthy his substitute in case of absence. Later, to reporters, McCarthy explained why he had blocked Tobey: "I frankly didn't want him to be chairman. He thinks the sole answer to the problem is public housing. . . . However, it doesn't make much difference who the chairman is. We shouldn't be sidetracked by personal animosity between two senators." Gamble's leaning toward private housing was not mentioned in this interview.

Senator Tobey was outraged. "This child is born of malpractice," he exclaimed. "I hope the forceps didn't hurt it! But behold, I am a soldier in the ranks, with malice toward none, but I do like straight-shooting!"

Hearings were held by the joint committee all over the country during that summer and fall. Meanwhile, an omnibus housing bill containing a public-housing provision was offered in the Senate by the Republican leader, Robert A. Taft of Ohio, cosponsored by two Democratic senators, Robert F. Wagner of New York and Allen J. Ellender of Louisiana.

With this bill pending, the joint committee issued a report over the signature of Chairman Gamble, deploring the use of federal funds to finance housing and predicting that, if persisted in, it would lead to "further and more extensive reluctance of private capital to enter the field." The correct solution, Gamble and McCarthy contended, lay in the stimulation of mass-produced prefabricated houses.

But by that time Senator Tobey had wrested back committee control, and a contrary report was issued over his signature, rejecting the Gamble-McCarthy conclusions and calling for passage of the Taft-Wagner-Ellender bill. McCarthy countered with a substitute measure. Then the omnibus bill was stymied in the House by the Gamble faction, and Taft gave up the struggle and allowed McCarthy's substitute to be enacted over Tobey's protest.

In the debate McCarthy again demonstrated his aggressiveness and his instinct for attacking an opponent at his weak point. Explaining these "terrier tactics" of Joe's the *New York Post* wrote:

"With a senator like Flanders, who spoke in broad philosophical terms, McCarthy would interrupt repeatedly to ask his impression of the meaning of some words on the fifth line of page twenty-seven, offering revisions, modifications, and corrections of his own until Flanders was dizzy. Then he would purringly sympathize with Flanders for not knowing what the measure was all about. With a senator like Sparkman [Alabama Democrat], who understood the technicalities of the bill as well as he did or better, McCarthy would resort to rhetorical broadsides about 'socialism.' "

It was quite a show, and some senators who were not under the gun rather enjoyed watching Joe's gymnastics; overlooking, in the fascination of the spectacle, that their turn might come next.

Nor did anyone except McCarthy's most devoted critics and the embittered proponents of public housing object that during this period the senator's relations with representatives of real-estate interests and makers of prefab housing were particularly cozy. McCarthy was a member of the Senate Banking and Currency Committee, which among other things acted as watchdog over the Reconstruction Finance Corporation, the agency that extended government financing to home builders. A manufacturer of prefabricated houses using porcelain and aluminum as novel materials, the Lustron Corporation, was granted loans totaling $37,500,000 and these loans, with other RFC transactions, were under constant review by the Banking Committee.

Several months after the housing bill was passed, McCarthy called reporters to his office and handed them copies of his first literary work—a 7,000-word manual titled "A Dollar's Worth of Housing for Every Dollar Spent." It was issued by the Lustron Corporation. Addressed primarily to veterans, it explained the ins and outs of buying a home, methods of financing, pitfalls to avoid, and other practical details. Obviously it contained much valuable information. McCarthy said he had written the pamphlet for Lustron under a royalty agreement, and when pressed to say how much he had received replied that the amount was "embarrassingly small," and he had had to "split it with ten people who helped me."

Joe was proud of his bantling, and he had reason to preen himself on the payment he had received from Lustron—$10,000. According to one calculation, this worked out at $1.43 a word, a figure that topped all known records for remuneration paid to authors. Such generosity on the part of Lustron was to create embarrassment for Joe, directly and indirectly, when the company finally went bankrupt, still owing the RFC $37,500,000. It was brought out that Lustron's president, Carl Stranlund, on several occasions had obliged Senator McCarthy by cashing the latter's checks at racetracks around Washington, where Joe was seen regularly. There was a rumor that Stranlund had subsequently torn up those checks, but he denied it.

[IV]

The view of the senator taken in Wisconsin remained favorable. To many, Joe's political monkeyshines had been amusing, and the saving grace had been that he usually won. By perhaps the majority of Wisconsiners, his crudities were tolerated, although conceded to be in poor taste. To a tenacious minority, McCarthy had been objectionable from the beginning, and his record in Washington was not making him any less so. In 1948 this minority launched a fresh attempt to discredit him and just possibly get him out of the Senate.

The attempt centered on a revival of the contention that McCarthy had been elected to the Senate in contravention of Wisconsin law, and hence held his seat illegally. Miles McMillen, an editorial writer and sometime Washington correspondent of the *Madison Capital Times,* in July, 1948, filed a complaint with the state board of bar commissioners, setting forth that in running for the Senate while a judge McCarthy had violated the canon of judicial ethics. This started the action. The commissioners mulled over the matter for six months, and in December found that McCarthy indeed had chosen to "defy the rules of ethical conduct prescribed by the constitution, the laws of the state of Wisconsin, and the members of the profession, in order to gain a selfish personal advantage. It is difficult to conceive," the judgment went on, "of any conduct on the part of a presiding judge which would bring judges into greater disrepute and contempt," and the Wisconsin Supreme Court was requested to disbar him.

This indictment, stern though tardy, the supreme court pondered for another six months, then found that in accepting election as a United States senator, McCarthy had indeed violated "the terms of the constitution and laws of Wisconsin" and had broken "his oath as a circuit judge and as an attorney-at-law." But the court declined to take punitive action for several reasons. First, the barn door theory: the voters had had a chance to pass on the issue and they had seen fit to send McCarthy to the Senate and he was there, so why an empty gesture of locking the barn door now? Second, McCarthy had practiced law for years and had never been found "derelict in the discharge of his duties and obligations as a lawyer." Third and finally, the violation stood "in a class by itself, which is not likely to be repeated."

In taking refuge behind this last conclusion the justices ran no risk of contradiction whatever, for it certainly was inconceivable that Joseph McCarthy would ever again run for the United States Senate while a circuit judge of Wisconsin.

Joe hailed the outcome as a complete vindication, and paid his disrespects to the bar commissioners by saying that either they had known their case had no merit, and were playing politics, or else they were completely incompetent. Either way, he called their action "a disgrace to every honest, decent lawyer in the state of Wisconsin and they ought to resign."

This was his reaction in public. Privately he explained with a grin that what the verdict really meant was, "Yes, it was illegal—Joe was a naughty boy—but we don't think he'll do it again."

[V]

Coincident with this rebuff, the *Capital Times* and other unindulgent observers of McCarthy's two-step through the rules that hedge ordinary mortals found fresh grounds for their antagonism in Joe's puzzling role as apologist, or at least public advocate, for a group of convicted Nazi war criminals. The case was extraordinary in many ways. The men had been found guilty in Germany of the massacre of American prisoners during the Battle of the Bulge, in 1944. At the crossroads village of Malmédy, in Belgium, some 150 American prisoners had been herded into a field and mowed down by machine gunners of the First SS Panzer Division. After the war, 73 of the executioners were tried and 43 were sentenced to death. Subsequently the trials were reviewed by the Judge Advocate General's office and some of the sentences were set aside or reduced.

Meanwhile, the convicted men had petitioned the United States Supreme Court to intervene, alleging that they had been convicted on the basis of confessions extracted by physical torture and psychological intimidation, through resort to such devices as staging mock trials and simulated hangings to terrify the accused under interrogation. The Supreme Court ruled it had no jurisdiction; but the attendant publicity led to separate inquiries, one by the Judge Advocate General, the other by an independent panel of state judges. These investigations reported finding no proof of physical violence, but they did find irregularities in the prosecution, and commutation of the remaining death sentences to life imprisonment was recommended.

Throughout this period, the "Malmédy massacre" was widely publicized, both in Germany and in the United States. In Germany the accusations of brutality on the part of the United States Army prosecutors fed anti-American sentiment, while at home sufficient doubt was generated to prod the Senate into undertaking its own investigation, early in 1949. Pursuant to a resolution introduced by Senator Raymond E. Baldwin of Connecticut, the inquiry was assigned to the Armed Services Committee, of which Baldwin was a member, and he was named chairman of the subcommittee to carry out the task.

Baldwin was serving in the Senate as a matter of civic duty and party loyalty. He had not wished to be elected at all. Having served ably as his state's governor, in 1946 he had announced his retirement from politics to devote himself to law practice. The Republicans of Connecticut, facing a sharp contest for the Senate seat, already had decided on Mrs. Clare Boothe Luce as their best hope of turning back the Democratic challenge; but Mrs. Luce, who was completing a term in Congress, also wished to abandon political life for the time being and pursue other interests. Upon her withdrawal, the party turned to Baldwin, and he was elected. Dignified, reserved, with a strong sense of public responsibility, Baldwin disliked clamor and strife.

As a first step Baldwin proposed to call the prosecutors in the Malmédy trials and allow them to tell their story; up to now they had not been permitted to testify. It happened that one of the prosecutors was a member of Baldwin's law firm in Connecticut. Senator McCarthy, although not a member of the investigating subcommittee, had asked the senatorial courtesy of permission to sit in on the hearings. This was granted, and next, by sheer overbearing, he obtained permission to cross-examine witnesses. From that moment he assumed command and swiftly turned what had been intended as a temperate fact-finding into a Donnybrook of acrimony and confusion.

Citing the law partner prosecutor, he bore down on Baldwin's supposed conflict of interest and demanded that the chairman resign. This Baldwin heatedly refused to do, whereupon McCarthy made himself the defender of the convicted Nazis and the unsparing accuser of the Army for its supposed misconduct of the trials. There was nothing temperate about his attack; he was scornful, bitter, venomous, and contemptuous. Baldwin, convinced of his own rectitude but handicapped by his ambiguous position, vainly tried to curb his fellow senator.

McCarthy's motives in all this remained enigmatic. He never explained, but that was his way. He attacked, and left the explaining to others. Certainly in this instance he baffled his closest associates.

As a former Marine, aggressively patriotic, he seemed an unlikely person to intervene on behalf of storm troopers who had been convicted of barbarities against American prisoners of war. Yet intervene he did, and subsequent developments indicated that there had been some merit to his case. But his methods were in contempt of every standard of Senate procedure. He bullied the chair and harried witnesses. He confused the transcript with irrelevancies, and imputed the basest motives to spokesmen for the Army. He gave Baldwin such a miserable time that the other members of the Armed Services Committee felt obliged to come to their colleague's rescue, and they unanimously adopted a resolution expressing their confidence in his conduct of the hearings, a most unusual step.

The Democratic members of the subcommittees, Senators Estes Kefauver of Tennessee and Lester C. Hunt of Wyoming, lent little support to the chairman, Kefauver seldom appearing at the hearings and the mild-manered Hunt proving incapable of standing up to McCarthy's assaults. McCarthy called the American military judges "morons." He would snap at a witness, "I think you are lying," or, in his insistent, cutting voice, "It makes me rather sick down inside to hear you testify what you think is proper or improper." Statements made by the Secretary of the Army or the Judge Advocate General he dismissed as "fantastic" or "the most phenomenal I ever heard." He misquoted the transcript or garbled it so that other senators became lost in a maze trying to follow him; and after weeks of confusing the issues, he peremptorily demanded that the entire American interrogation team submit to a lie-detector test. This was refused, of course, whereupon McCarthy stalked out of the hearing and branded the investigation a "whitewash" and "shameful episode," for which he held Baldwin personally accountable. On the Senate floor he charged Baldwin with being "criminally responsible" for a miscarriage of justice; and when Senator Tobey and others protested this violation of the rule forbidding personal attacks, McCarthy flew at them. Baldwin hit back, and the committee's course was angrily defended by Hunt and Kefauver. McCarthy did not retreat an inch, but taunted the distressed Baldwin that he would live to "bitterly regret this deliberate and very clever attempt to whitewash" the American officials involved.

The subcommittee's report, approved by the full committee, found that there indeed had been some malpractice on the part of over-zealous prosecutors, but no evidence of "beatings and physical vi-

olence in such forms as could only be devised by warped minds"—
which was what McCarthy had charged. On the whole, the report
concluded, the men had received fair trials. But despite this rallying-
round-the-flag, it was conceded generally that McCarthy's insistence
upon the impropriety of Baldwin's directing the inquiry had not
been without some shadow of justification; and after the storm had
blown itself out, the Army canceled the remaining death sentences.

But Baldwin was not finished. Sickened by the abuse to which he
had been subjected, when an offer was made of a seat on the Connecticut supreme bench, he accepted it gratefully and resigned
from the Senate. McCarthy's behavior, he made plain, had been
the last straw, ending his association with politics.

The question of McCarthy's motives would always remain
clouded. Doubtless they were mixed, as are the motives of most
human beings. It is likely that he was reacting in part to pressure
from Wisconsin's large and influential German element. During
World War I, Wisconsin's German population had been cruelly
harassed by self-appointed vigilante groups, and their lasting resentment had provided the elder LaFollette with his most solid
support after the war. Then during the 1930's Wisconsin had been
at the very center of the isolationist movement, largely pro-German
in its origins, and the younger LaFollette had benefited from this.
McCarthy was bound to be politically sensitive to this influence.
Some of his financial backers were German, notably the wealthy
Milwaukee industrialist Walter Harnischfeger. During the Malmédy
hearings, a school chum of McCarthy's, a lawyer named Tom Korb,
came to Washington to help in threading through the legal intricacies of the complicated affair, and Korb was a lawyer for
Harnischfeger's company.

But McCarthy's actions cannot be accounted for by the superficial appearances. At no time was he ever consistently and avowedly
pro-German. Later it came to light that at least some of McCarthy's
"documentary evidence" of the Army's asserted brutality had originated with a man named Rudolph Aschenauer, living in Frankfurt,
whom Army Intelligence identified as a Communist agent engaged
in stirring up anti-American feeling in West Germany. McCarthy
would deny having any contact with Aschenauer, and the evidence
is not clear. But McCarthy's uncritical acceptance of data which
had been channeled to him surreptitiously, or under surface plausi-
bility, would have been consistent with his practice in other cases;

he would become notorious for his carelessness regarding sources.

The tangled knot of motivation, however, will not yield to any easy unraveling. Perhaps in the senator's subconscious a contributory factor was the latent suspicion, if not active hostility, that every true Marine feels for the Army. McCarthy had been a Marine, and had been imbued with the attitudes and traditions of the Corps. The Marines' opinion of their sister services is unflattering at best (to call a Marine a soldier is a gross insult), and he may have felt unconsciously that the Army's word should not be accepted without skepticism, prudence dictating that a sharp, even when friendly, eye be kept on all Army claims and activities. In a case of political infighting, the Army thus might seem fair game to a Marine of McCarthy's pugnacity; and this, however vaguely, might have given direction and color to the conglomerate of his motives.*

Still another contributing motive, perhaps the most impelling of all, might have come from the response of the press to the Malmédy incident. Day after day the hearings were headlined, with McCarthy's name displayed prominently. *The New York Times,* for instance, carried headlines such as "McCarthy Challenges Testimony," "McCarthy Scores Brutality," "McCarthy Charges 'Whitewash' "—all directing to the public's notice a certain minor senator from the Midwest. While the hearings went on he was "somebody." When he entered the Senate dining room, now and then a stranger's gaze would fasten on him with a look of recognition. He had become a person who counted; and while Joe McCarthy wanted to be liked, before all else he wanted to be known. So, if any stick will serve to beat a dog, why might he not belabor the Army? After all, politics was a game, and those who played it rough were most apt to win. Harry Truman (who would have scorned to share even this opinion knowingly with Joe McCarthy) had stated the first rule of politics: "If you can't stand the heat, get out of the kitchen."

McCarthy could stand the heat. And he loved to make a clatter at the range.

---

* Witness the concluding lines of "The Marine Hymn," invariably sung with rousing defiance:
> "If the Army and the Navy ever gaze on heaven's scenes,
> They will find the streets are guarded by United States Marines."

A Time of Ripening

At the start of 1950 it was plain to newsmen in Washington, whose job it is to keep tabs on the personalities in government, that Senator Joseph McCarthy was not in favor with the leaders of the Senate. Socially popular he might be among the less fastidious members, but the leadership on both sides of the aisle mistrusted him. His manners in debate were execrable, and the resolution of confidence in the badgered Baldwin voted by the Armed Services Committee was a studied rebuke to the upstart from Wisconsin carrying the names of such respected and influential party chiefs as Senators Lyndon Baines Johnson of Texas, Richard Russell of Georgia, and Millard Tydings of Maryland, on the Democratic side, and Republicans Leverett Saltonstall of Massachusetts, Styles Bridges of New Hampshire, and William Knowland of California. By 1950, therefore, McCarthy was a congressional outsider—a lightweight tolerated rather than accepted—a maverick, in the bad graces of the political establishment in Washington and left largely to make his own way.

The basic cause of this isolation was, of course, Joe himself. His driving energy had been unable so far to focus on any sustained, rewarding political goal. So long as his ambition had been centered on attaining the United States Senate, he had forged ahead swiftly and steadily, cutting corners and quite gracelessly thumbing his nose at conventions and scruples. But since achieving his goal, he had been without direction, flitting restlessly from the frivolous to the dubious—from sugar to housing to Malmédy—and finding the most congenial outlet for his fiercely competitive energy in marathon sessions of cutthroat poker. The causes he embraced from moment to moment never claimed him irrevocably; he was not locked into them; he participated but did not dominate. Erratically he came

75

and went, in ways that puzzled onlookers because they seemed to have no settled purpose, no logical bent.

The continued lack of an adequate means for burning off his surging energy was bad for his health. When Congress was in session he frequently flew to Wisconsin for weekends of roughing it in the woods, hunting and fishing, trying to discharge his tensions by strenuous physical exertion. After attending the 1948 Republican National Convention in Philadelphia, he took off for the Montana wheatfields and worked twelve hours a day as a harvest hand, incognito. If he was detained in Washington for a protracted period his temper, always hot and unruly, would fray, and he would be victimized by sinus headaches that sent him to the hospital for relief.

Reports from home indicated that his political popularity was waning, although he was confident of his ability to arrest the decline. His danger really was slight, for he retained the backing of the party machine, and personally he was hail-fellow with the voters. His enemies had sedulously publicized, with sinister overtones, his annual disputes with the tax collectors. Like thousands of other taxpayers, Joe tried to cut corners in that game, too, and when the revenue authorities disallowed his claims, he paid up. Sometimes the disputes grew rancorous, but no violation of the tax laws was demonstrated; still, his antagonists found these altercations useful as examples of the senator's propensity to make unfounded claims and to overreach himself.

In 1948, Wisconsin had moved into the Democratic column, and nationally that party won back control of both houses of Congress. This pushed McCarthy into minority status and further lessened his standing in the Senate. When the 81st Congress organized in January of 1949, he was dropped from his one major committee assignment, Banking and Currency; the incoming chairman, Senator Burnet R. Maybank of South Carolina, had flatly declined to serve if "that troublemaker," as he termed McCarthy, remained. Obligingly, the Republicans demoted Joe to the Committee on the District of Columbia, just about the foot of the ladder. He was not abashed; but with his term due to expire in 1952, he realized that it behooved him to start thinking about winning reelection. Shadowboxing with issues really not his own had led nowhere; he needed something special to give direction to his free-swinging. And destiny had been building up just the issue that would enable him to focus all his peculiar abilities with maximum effectiveness. Joe would not discover this issue; it would be handed to him.

[II]

A man of genius must be born into the right time if he is to make a mark on history; despite his gifts, if he is born out of his time, the world probably will hear little or nothing of him. The conjunction of time, place, and conditions is requisite for the unique personality to precipitate a crisis; unless the time is propitious, genius cannot flower.

Imagine Napoleone Buonaparte born fifty years sooner, in 1719 instead of 1769. In 1719, Corsica was a dependency of Genoa, as it had been for centuries, and this Napoleone, assuming that he would have gone into his country's army, would have been thirty-five years old, with twenty years of soldiering behind him, when Paoli struck the first major blow at Genoese rule, the event that eventually led to the absorption of Corsica by France. As an alien career officer in the French service, enjoying neither wealth nor influence nor even French antecedents, Buonaparte would have encountered great difficulty in rising above the rank of colonel, and there would have been little likelihood of his getting a chance to show the amazing stuff that was in him. Continuing our supposition and assuming that he would have lived the same number of years that he did, this Buonaparte would have been dead four years before the outbreak of the American Revolution, with the French Revolution still a distant prospect. History then would contain no record of Napoleon Bonaparte, of epic marches across a continent, of the overthrowing of dynasties and the seating of Bonapartes on the thrones of Europe. The pages inscribed with the legend that even today stirs wishful emulation would be blank.

Napoleon's fulfillment was dependent upon his point in time, and upon the chance of place as well. Again stretch the imagination to conceive of Bonaparte's being born in the Russia of Catherine the Great, or in the backwoods of colonial Pennsylvania. Where would the Napoleonic legend be then?

And so, in this one respect, it was with McCarthy: had he arrived on the national scene sooner or later, or had he not been endowed with special qualities of recklessness and audacity that responded

to the psychosis of the time, it is probable that while his name would
be recoverable by archeologists burrowing in the Senate archives,
the word "McCarthyism" would not be in the dictionaries. Joseph
Raymond McCarthy was not the inventor of his era, he was its
apotheosis. Make no mistake, this man of loud noises, of checkered
career, of violent, destructive impulses, possessed in abundant degree that super-quality which in the theater distinguishes a star from
a merely accomplished performer. From the moment of his first
bounding onto center stage, he dominated the drama. And it was
a drama of no mean proportions. In time it would swell to terrifying
dimensions.

The Stage Is Set

As 1950 dawned, there was a malaise abroad in the land. Despite periodic assurances from Washington that all was well in the best of all possible Democratic worlds, the mass of people were uneasy. Treachery or the potentiality of treachery seemed to many to be endemic in official circles. Public confidence in both the effectiveness and the sincerity of the measures being taken to win the cold war had been undermined by a long series of shocks. That since the 1930's Communists had successfully infiltrated numerous departments of the government was no longer denied; the questions now were how deeply had they dug in, and had they really been dug out? The various angry, irreconcilable answers given to these anxious questions left the issue suspended, unresolved.

Already the published list of infiltrators and those accused as such was long. It included Lauchlin Currie, an executive assistant to the President; Harry Dexter White, an Assistant Secretary of the Treasury; John J. Abt, chief counsel of the Senate subcommittee on civil liberties; Victor Perlo, chief of the statistical branch of the War Production Board; Edwin A. Smith, member of the National Labor Relations Board; David Weintraub, national research director of the Works Progress Administration. These were not men holding insignificant clerkships, and all of them, with others, had been linked to Communist spy rings by the Federal Bureau of Investigation in the early 1940's. Then in 1945, the *Amerasia* case had raised a suspicion of a protective cover-up of treasonous Communist activities reaching even into the White House. In 1946, Carlo Aldo Marzani, who had been transferred to the State Department from the wartime Office of Strategic Services, was indicted and the next year was convicted of perjury in denying his Communist party affiliation. In 1946, too, the Igor Gouzenko spy ring disclosures in Canada shocked the free world into realization of the extent to which Soviet Russia had converted its diplomatic service into a worldwide spy apparatus.

There followed, in 1947, the case of George Shaw Wheeler, who was dropped from government employment after being denounced as a Soviet spy, and who later fled behind the Iron Curtain. In 1948, H. Julian Wadleigh was accused of espionage, and later admitted the fact. The crowning shock came in August, 1948 (in the midst of the Berlin airlift crisis), when Whittaker Chambers, former Soviet spy-ring courier, named Alger Hiss before the House Committee on Un-American Activities as a wartime Soviet spy who had stolen State Department secrets for transmittal to Moscow. In rapid succession there followed Chambers' turning over of copies of the documents stolen, and then the microfilmed so-called pumpkin papers; the glimpsing through a veil of attempted secrecy of the frantic efforts made to bury the scandal; the indictment of Hiss for perjury (the statute of limitations having run out on espionage); his two sensational trials; and finally, in January, 1950, his conviction and sentence to prison.

Millions of Americans watched the unfolding of this drama with rising alarm and indignation. Sentiment ran high, both for and against Hiss or Chambers, and a question heard with growing frequency was: with so much that has been hidden coming to light, how much more treasonable activity is there which has not been disclosed? Presumably Hiss had not acted alone; who had been his collaborators? Were they still in positions of influence? What was being done to identify and expose them? When no satisfactory answers came from Washington, but only self-serving assurances that everything was being taken care of, not a few Americans jumped to the conclusion that the situation was worse than they had feared.

Such suspicions were fed by the events. Had not President Truman, when faced with documentary proof of Hiss's treason, stubbornly repeated his sneer that the uproar was a Republican trick—a "red herring"? Had he not used that phrase contemptuously three times in public, even authorizing the press to quote him directly—a permission that was seldom given for Presidential press conference asides?

What was to be thought when the Secretary of State, Dean Acheson, stated unctuously, after Hiss's conviction, "I will not turn my back on Alger Hiss"?

In the face of such apparent lofty contempt or blind disregard for the safety of the nation, whom could the man in the street *not* suspect? The ordinary voter was no splitter of hairs, nor did he feel that the guardians of the nation were entitled to treat a convicted traitor with saintlike forebearance. And again the question arose: with one Alger Hiss routed out and defanged, how many others might still be nesting in the government? Sooner or later someone would give voice to that unresolved question in a tone that would compel a responsive answer.

The Hiss sensation was not the sole alarm occurring in the months of late 1949 and early 1950. While the cold war threatened to grow hot, with the Communists besieging Berlin, in New York eleven top officers of the Communist party in the United States had gone on trial for conspiracy to advocate the overthrow of the government by force and violence. After months of uproarious obstructionism before Judge Harold Medina, the eleven were convicted and sent to prison.

Then, on September 23, 1949, President Truman had announced that the Soviets had detonated an atmoic bomb, and the monopoly held by the United States on the "doomsday weapon" was ended. The speed with which the Russians had caught up to the United States in the arms race stunned Americans; but the mystery was explained in part when, on February 3, 1950, the British authorities arrested a German-born, British-naturalized atomic scientist named Klaus Fuchs, accusing him of passing atomic secrets to the Russians. During the war Fuchs had worked at Los Alamos, where the first atomic bomb was constructed.

In the same period the specter of infiltration of the government by Communists surfaced again when Judith Coplon, an analyst in the Justice Department, was picked up on the street in the act of passing secret FBI data to Valentin Gubitchev, attached to the Soviet delegation to the United Nations. Early in 1950 both were on trial in New York City for espionage.

In the midst of all this, word came out of Washington of a fierce controversy among America's atomic scientists over both the utility and the morality of constructing the theoretically possible hydrogen, or "hell-bomb," with intimations that some of the physicists were motivated less by love of humanity than by an urge to help the Communist cause. In eight-column headlines, newspapers across the country carried warnings from such respected authorities as Dr.

Vannevar Bush that no defense was possible against the H-bomb. Albert Einstein declared that all life on earth could be obliterated by the bomb, and in India Prime Minister Nehru put the equation neatly:

"It is the hydrogen bomb or the world. If we have come to the conclusion that the world is a bad show, let the hydrogen bomb put an end to it. Otherwise put an end to the hydrogen bomb."

Almost nobody took seriously the possibility that the Russians might refrain from constructing an H-bomb of their own. They had proved they could build one, and every action and statement of their leaders breathed belligerence. A tremendous buildup of Soviet air power was known to be under way, and in the United States the fear of sudden attack grew so acute that the wartime air raid warning system was reactivated on the Pacific coast. This fear was strengthened by the news from Formosa, to which island the remnants of Chiang Kai-shek's defeated Nationalist Chinese were fleeing from the mainland, leaving all China to the victorious Communists under Mao Tse-tung. With the rout of Chiang, all Asia, with its enormous human and material resources, was threatened with absorption into the Communist sphere.

Under these successive shocks, Americans were bewildered, anxious, and suspicious as 1950 rolled in. Responsible spokesmen saw the nation drifting toward disaster, through ineptitude if not through deliberate betrayal. In the Far East we were reaping the bitter harvest of our failure or inability to settle on any steady, coherent policy. Venerable Bernard Baruch pictured the government as "staggering from crisis to crisis" in that area.

During the agony of China, neither the opposition raised to Chiang nor the support given to Mao had been clearcut; the opposition in American quarters had been devious and concealed, the support clandestine and tricked out in specious disguises. The whole China question was riddled with irony, subtlety, and stealth. And despite the placebos spooned out by the government's apologists, Americans sensed dimly, or they feared, that something was radically amiss. Members of the voiceless majority—the grocer, the farmer, the banker, the housewife, the factory hand—as well as many thoughtful, well-informed, articulate watchers of world trends, were jittery. They had doubts, and no one was answering them in a positive, satisfying way. In a time of crisis, the instinct of the ordinary mortal is to *act,* to *do something,* and there was an unspoken dread that those in control were insufficient to the task—that they were proving themselves *talkers* while the Communists *acted*.

Into this picture stepped Senator McCarthy, not as its cause but as its culmination. The crisis was one of fear, of foreboding, of frustration, suspicion, and disillusion, and he mirrored all these, at the same time uttering a rallying-cry of resistance against them.

[II]

Sometimes in history the resolving of an intolerable condition has come about by chance or sheer inadvertence. When Napoleon gave the command to rake the mob in the rue St. Roche with grape-shot, he was responding to a mere military impulse; yet it was that unpremeditated impulse which ended the Revolution and earned Bonaparte an empire.

Many stories have been told about how McCarthy became interested in the issue of Communists in government. Roy Cohn, who knew the senator intimately, believed that McCarthy "bought" the Communist issue as he might have bought an automobile—listening to the sales talk, looking under the hood, kicking the tires, trying the seats, taking a test drive, thinking over the price, and deciding that the car would do. "It was just as cold as that," Cohn has insisted. But this view excludes much.

Cohn says that McCarthy told him that up to 1949 he had no particular interest in communism, and in fact knew little about it.* That was possible, considering his furious concentration on reaching the Senate, and his fumbling about since getting there. But it happened, at the start of 1950, that he was looking for a strong basic issue on which he could pitch his bid for a second term; the election was coming up in 1952, and the Coleman machine seemed to have been rather cool recently; there was no disputing that the senator's war-hero glamor had rubbed thin.

Late in 1949, according to Cohn, McCarthy was approached by a young Army officer in G-2 (Intelligence) who had a copy of a memorandum compiled in 1947 for a House Appropriations sub-committee during its abortive investigation of Communist influences

* Frederick Woltman, a leading anti-Communist writer for the Scripps-Howard newspapers and a close friend of McCarthy, is reported to have disclosed that in the spring of 1950, the senator admitted to Woltman's wife that he had been aware of the Communist issue for only the last two and one-half months.

in the State Department. The officer felt strongly that the information contained in the memorandum should be given to the public, and he hoped to induce McCarthy to undertake the job.

What was in this memorandum? First, it was addressed to the then Secretary of State, General George C. Marshall, and it conveyed the subcommittee's alarm over what it termed "a deliberate, calculated program being carried out not only to protect Communist personnel in high places [read here *Amerasia* case], but to reduce security and intelligence protection to a nullity. . . .

"On file in the [State] Department [the memorandum continued] is a copy of a preliminary report of the FBI on Soviet espionage activities in the United States, which involves a large number of State Department employes, some in high official positions. This report has been challenged and ignored by those charged with the apparent tacit approval of Mr. Acheson [then Undersecretary of State]. Should this case break before the State Department acts, it will be a national disgrace."

This explicit warning was dated June 10, 1947. Alger Hiss had left the State Department a few months previously to head the Carnegie Endowment for International Peace.

The State Department, under heavy pressure, had opened its loyalty files to the subcommittee's investigators, headed by Robert E. Lee, who had taken notes on the files of 108 past, present, and prospective State Department employes. Then President Truman had clamped his secrecy ban on security files, forbidding their being shown to congressional investigators, and the subcommittee's work had come to an abrupt halt. The Lee Report, so-called, containing the data taken from the files before they were closed by White House directive, had been filed away in the subcommittee's records without action. At least two copies had been passed along to other congressional committees, one of them the Senate Committee on Expenditures in the Executive Department, of which McCarthy was a member; there is no indication that he became aware of the report at that time, although he certainly would have had access to it.

The young G-2 officer, according to Cohn's version, came upon the Lee Report and the memorandum in 1949. He was shocked by its contents, which, if verified through a congressional inquiry, would seem to prove that the government's whole security program was being sabotaged, either by laxity or by conscious design. Believing the facts should be made known, the G-2 officer had approached three Republican senators before speaking to McCarthy, but these had shied away from touching what looked like political dynamite. The officer then came to McCarthy as his fourth choice, and Joe promised to look over the young man's papers. He stuffed the bulky file into his briefcase and went home, and after dinner he settled down to examine it. He did not stop reading until he had finished the last page, and his reaction, as he described it to Cohn, was: "Fantastic! Unbelievable! Take any spy story you ever read, any movie about international intrigue, and this is more startling!"

The next morning he telephoned his G-2 informant and said he would "buy the package."

This is the story told by Cohn, and it is probable that it contains elements of the facts in a garbled form; McCarthy was notoriously careless about dates, details, and recollections.

What is certain is that one evening late in January, 1950, Mc-Carthy had dinner with three friends in Washington's Colony restaurant. The three were the Reverend Edmund A. Walsh, dean of the School of Foreign Service at Georgetown University; Charles A. Kraus, a political science instructor at Georgetown; and William A. Roberts, a liberal-oriented lawyer. Over the meal the senator said he was looking for a strong issue to take to the voters in Wisconsin in 1952. The friends suggested several possibilities. The St. Lawrence Seaway, for instance. Joe turned thumbs down on that: no sex appeal. He broached an idea for an all-inclusive pension plan that would pay every person sixty-five years old or older $100 a month, but his companions called it economically ridiculous. Father Walsh, a scholar long dedicated to combatting communism and Soviet expansion, proposed Communist subversion. That would make a strong issue, all agreed, but it would call for a fighter. Well, Joe was a fighter; he said he might give it a whirl. There was no insincerity in his coolness; in political matters McCarthy often showed a keen sense of timing, and his political judgment, when not warped by his personal interests, was usually shrewd.

Deciding to test the political weather, he instructed his staff to whip together a suitable speech. It was a patchwork affair, assembled from numerous sources, including the *Chicago Tribune,* a speech made recently by Richard M. Nixon in the House of Representatives, and the *Congressional Record.* From the *Record* was retrieved a letter that Secretary of State Byrnes had written to Representative Adolph J. Sabath of Illinois on January 26, 1946, giving a report on the progress of the State Department's loyalty screening program. Out of some 3,000 persons screened, Byrnes reported, adverse recommendations had been returned against 285 employes and applicants for jobs, and of the employes included, 79 had been dismissed. The inference was that no action had been taken as of that date against the remaining 206 (or 205, the figure would vary) who had been rated unsuitable for government employment.

Pieced together though it was, the speech bristled with McCarthy touches. There was the blunt simplicity of phrasing (no wearisome hairsplitting or philosophical equivocation); there was the positive accusation (names named, no beating about the bush, a spade called a spade, a traitor called a traitor); and sides taken frankly (no apology for one's stand). Most important, there was a sense of drama. A fighter by instinct, thriving on battle, McCarthy was inherently dramatic; every scene, every idea, every event he became identified with was thereby infused with the excitement of conflict.

The speech had to be thrown together in a hurry because the senator was about to do his stint of party tub-thumping in a series of Lincoln Day appearances. On Thursday, February 9, he was booked to address the Republican Women's Club of Ohio County in Wheeling, West Virginia. Next he would speak in Reno, Nevada, traveling by way of Salt Lake City, where he would be interviewed on the radio with Senator George W. Malone of Nevada, a fellow Republican. Finally he would fly to Huron, North Dakota, for a speech, then back to Washington. Joe did not expect to garner any great acclaim by anything he might say on such an itinerary; he was trying out an idea.

[III]

On the afternoon of February 9, McCarthy flew to Wheeling. He was met at the airport by Tom Sweeney, who was to be his host; Congressman Francis J. Love; and Frank Desmond, a reporter for the *Wheeling Intelligencer*. The local radio station, WWVA, wanted to broadcast the senator's speech later in the evening and had sent word by Sweeney that they would like an advance copy. Joe explained that he had only a rough draft, from which he was bound to depart, but Sweeney thought that would serve and he took a copy to deliver to the studio. Desmond took another copy. McCarthy kept the third, to do some last-minute work on it, he said.

That evening he spoke in the McClure Hotel, and his restlessness on the platform attracted quite as much attention as what he said. He spoke in a clipped, unemotional tone, incisive but often halting over words. Frequently he referred to his notes, lying on the speaker's stand, and read passages from them. Other portions of his speech seemed to be extemporaneous. An engineer from WWVA was on hand, making a recording for the station's use later.

The burden of McCarthy's address was a bitter indictment of America's five-year retreat in the cold war—the disasters in Asia; the loss of China to the Reds; the culpability of the State Department policy planners who had masterminded the nation's cave-in to the Communists at home and abroad. Such men, McCarthy said, were still engaged in their work of blundering and betrayal, and either they were Communist-inclined, or they were Communist-controlled. The fastidious Secretary of State, Dean Acheson, Joe pilloried as "this pompous diplomat in striped pants with a phony British accent," who, by refusing to "turn his back" on the convicted traitor Alger Hiss, had "endorsed communism, high treason, and betrayal of a sacred trust."

If McCarthy had expected to set Wheeling on fire, he failed signally. Actually he had no such expectations. The newspapers didn't see much in the speech, the big city dailies, with one exception, ignoring it. The exception was the *Chicago Tribune,* which was feuding with Acheson on its own account and gave Joe's disparaging description of the Secretary a few lines on an inside page. The *Denver Post* lived up to its reputation for eccentricity by according McCarthy page-one honors; but the *Post* was hardly one of the nation's first-rank newspapers.

In Wheeling, the *Intelligencer* dealt with the speech more extensively, giving numerous direct quotations from the senator's text. McCarthy was reported as saying, as he brandished a document picked from the pile before him:

"While I cannot take the time to name all of the men in the State Department who have been named as members of the Communist party and members of a spy ring, I have here in my hand a list of two hundred and five that were known to the Secretary of State as being members of the Communist party, and who, nevertheless, are still working and shaping the policy in the State Department."

In the radio broadcast that followed, station WWVA played its recording of McCarthy's spoken words. No unusual listener reaction was manifested, and the next morning, in keeping with standard practice, the tape was "scrubbed," the recording erased.

On Friday, February 10, Senator McCarthy hustled aboard a plane for Denver, Salt Lake City, and Reno. And because his recorded words had been "scrubbed," nobody would ever be able to say with certainty exactly what Senator McCarthy did tell the Republican ladies of Wheeling on the 9th of February, 1950. Yet that date might justly be labeled Founder's Day in the chronology of the McCarthy Episode.

McCarthy did not speak in a vacuum. The day after the senator unburdened himself in Wheeling, Klaus Fuchs, a lodger in Wandsworth prison, unburdened himself in London of a full confession of his atomic spying for the Soviet Union. He named confederates—names that would haunt the American public in the months ahead—David Greenglass, Morton Sobel, Harry Gold, Julius and Ethel Rosenberg. Fuchs's telling it all was the tug on the trigger that would explode McCarthy's delayed blockbuster.

"What Did You Say, Senator?"

At Denver McCarthy was obliged to change planes, and he was surprised to find newspaper reporters at the airport, waiting to question him about those 205 Communists nestling in the crannies of the State Department. Did he really have such a list? Certainly he had, the senator replied, and he would show it, but for the moment the plane for Salt Lake City was loading and he must get aboard.

That evening, Friday, February 10, Joe appeared in the radio interview with Senator Malone in Salt Lake City, and was questioned about his Wheeling speech. Said he, "Last night I discussed the Communists in the State Department. I stated that I had the names of fifty-seven card-carrying members of the Communist party." Furthermore, Secretary of State Acheson could have those names at any time if he would promise to take action on them, although McCarthy intimated his strong belief that no action would be taken.

"In other words, senator," the interviewer pressed, "if Secretary of State Dean Acheson would call you at the Hotel Utah tonight in Salt Lake City, you would tell him fifty-seven names of actual card-carrying Communists in the State Department—actual card-carrying Communists?"

"Not only can I, Dan, but I will, as I say, on condition," McCarthy replied.

This rubbed a sensitive nerve in Washington, and that same Friday Lincoln White, State Department press officer, issued a hasty denial that the department harbored any Communists, promising that "if we find any, they will be summarily dismissed. We did not furnish Senator McCarthy with any such list," he added for the benefit of those who were curious about the senator's source of information, "and we would be interested in seeing his."

Immediately McCarthy blanketed White's denial by jumping the dispute to a higher level—the White House. This was a maneuver in which Joe would excel. In a telegram to President Truman, he alluded to White's curiosity and told the President that he could establish the truth of McCarthy's statements by simply picking up the telephone, calling Dean Acheson, and asking the Secretary how many of some 300 employes who had been certified for dismissal by the President's own loyalty board had actually been fired. According to his own source (this was the Byrnes letter, although he did not name it), only about 80 of the 300 or so had been got rid of, McCarthy said, and "this was done after a lengthy consultation with Alger Hiss." He pointed to the fact (implying a sinister conjunction of dates) that President Truman's directive shutting off all loyalty files from inspection by any congressional body had been issued *after* the House Un-American Activities Committee had linked Hiss with a Communist spy ring.

"Despite this State Department blackout," the senator wired, "we have been able to compile a list of fifty-seven Communists in the State Department. This list is available to you, but you can get a much longer list by ordering Secretary Acheson to give you a list of those whom your board listed as being disloyal and who are still working in the State Department."

Then he offered the President two "suggestions":

"1. That you demand that Acheson give you and the proper Congressional committee the names and complete report on all those who were placed in the department by Alger Hiss and all of those who are still working in the State Department who are listed by your security board as bad security risks because of their Communist connections.

"2. That you promptly revoke the order in which you provided that under no circumstances could a Congressional committee get any information or help from the executive department in exposing Communists."

Then McCarthy struck home with a charge that would cause infinite bitterness and embarrassment to the Democrats:

"Failure on your part will label the Democratic party as being the bedfellow of international communism. Certainly this label is not deserved by hundreds of thousands of loyal Democrats throughout the nation and by the sizable number of able and loyal Democrats in both the Senate and the House."

[II]

The fat was in the fire, and in his speech in Reno on Saturday Joe fanned the flames. He repeated his Salt Lake City charge, altering the phrasing somewhat to: "I have in my hand fifty-seven cases of individuals who would appear to be either card-carrying members or certainly loyal to the Communist party, but who nevertheless are still helping to shape our foreign policy."

Thereafter the figures might vary, but the basic allegation remained unchanged, namely, that actual Communists or their tools were in the State Department, in policy-making positions, even though the department's own loyalty board had spotted them as loyalty or security risks. If this were true, the long sequence of our defeats in the cold war became understandable: not blundering, but treason, had carried us from disaster to disaster.

McCarthy's startling accusations, made with all the confidence of a man who was sure, came at a moment of almost unbearably accumulated tensions. Scarcely three weeks before, Hiss had been convicted, with the accompanying shocks of "red herring" and Acheson's refusal to turn his back on the perjurer. Our rout in China—our loss of the atomic bomb monopoly—the appalling warnings of an H-bomb holocaust—the frightening confessions of Klaus Fuchs—these were all fresh in people's minds, creating an atmosphere of foreboding in which the "truth-telling" of one bold, unmannered but positive Irishman found an explosive response.

The administration, recognizing that the blaze McCarthy was lighting might spread destructively, acted swiftly to stamp it out. A higher authority than Lincoln White—John E. Peurifoy, Deputy Undersecretary of State in charge of the department's entire security program—moved into the picture and assured Washington newsmen that McCarthy's charges were false. He said that he had telegraphed to the senator a demand that the latter, "as a loyal American," turn over the names of his "fifty-seven card-carrying Communists," and "if I can find a single one, he will be fired by sundown." This of course was nonsensical, in view of the long, intricate process prescribed, under both loyalty and civil service rules, for dismissing government workers. One dubious reporter asked whether the department's procedures could, for example, "screen out a Klaus Fuchs?"

"All I can say is that our system is a continuing process," Peurifoy responded. "It is a difficult job and we keep at it."

Since 1947, he said, 16,075 employes had been investigated, and not one case of disloyalty had been found—not one. Two employes had been dropped as security risks, not necessarily disloyal (they might have been heavy drinkers, or just blabbermouths), he said, and "security questions had been raised about two hundred and two others who had left the department since January 1, 1947, either through resignation or by reduction in force."

The public, meanwhile, remained jittery. There had been much dissatisfaction with the administration's screening program, some condemning it as harsh and arbitrary, others faulting it as too lenient to be effective. There was instant interest, therefore, in what facts McCarthy had to back up his accusations. It was hard to tell what to believe, going by the mere record. For instance, McCarthy's use of the term "card-carrying members of the Communist party" meant nothing because for several years membership cards had been abolished, and all those outstanding called in, as an aid to secrecy. On the other hand, Peurifoy's proud claim that out of 16,075 State Department workers screened, not one had been found disloyal, seemed shocking on its face: either far too many individuals were being subjected to harassment, or undesirables were slipping through the net. In either case, the procedures being used must be at fault.

There was also the debate over whether McCarthy had said 205, or 207, or 208, or 57 Communists at Wheeling, since no actual recording had been preserved. Persons who had heard the speech disagreed entirely. McCarthy inserted in the *Record* the text of the speech he had given in both Wheeling and Reno—the same speech in both places, he told the Senate—and in this he used the figure 57.

Since these are the words by which McCarthy consented to be judged, and since it is the only complete purported text surviving, a glance at it is needful if one wishes to understand the man and the impact that his words produced with such startling rapidity. Picture one's self at Wheeling, or at Reno, and listen while the senator fires his own shot that was destined to be heard around the world:

> Ladies and gentlemen, tonight as we celebrate the one hundred and forty-first birthday of one of the greatest men in American history, I would like to be able to talk about what a glorious day today is in the history of the world. As we cele-

brate the birth of this man who with his whole heart and soul hated war, I would like to be able to speak of peace in our time, of war being outlawed, and of worldwide disarmament. These would be truly appropriate things to be able to mention as we celebrate the birthday of Abraham Lincoln.

Five years after a world war has been won, men's hearts should anticipate a long peace, and men's minds should be free from the heavy weight that comes with war. But this is not such a period—for this is not a period of peace. This is a time of the "cold war." This is a time when all the world is split into two vast, increasingly hostile camps—a time of a great armaments race. Today we can almost physically hear the mutterings and rumblings of an invigorated god of war. You can see it, feel it, and hear it all the way from the hills of Indo-China, from the shores of Formosa, right over into the very heart of Europe itself.

The one encouraging thing is that the "mad moment" has not yet arrived for the firing of guns or the exploding of the bomb which will set our civilization about the final task of destroying itself. There is still a hope for peace if we finally decide that no longer can we safely blind our eyes and close our ears to those facts which are shaping up more and more clearly. And that is that we are now engaged in a showdown fight—not the usual war between nations for land areas or other material gains, but a war between two diametrically opposed ideologies.

The great difference between our Western Christian world and the atheistic Communist world is not political, ladies and gentlemen, it is moral. There are other differences, of course, but these could be reconciled. . . . The real, basic difference . . . lies in the religion of immoralism—invented by Marx, preached feverishly by Lenin, and carried to unimaginable extremes by Stalin. This religion of immoralism, if the Red half of the world wins—and well it may—this religion of immoralism will more deeply wound and damage mankind than any conceivable economic or political system. . . .

While Lincoln was a relatively young man in his late thirties, Karl Marx boasted that the Communist specter was haunting Europe. Since that time, hundreds of millions of people and vast areas of the world have fallen under Communist domination. Today, less than one hundred years after Lincoln's death, Stalin brags that this Communist specter is not only haunting the world, but is about to completely subjugate it.

Today we are engaged in a final, all-out battle between Communistic atheism and Christianity. The modern champions of communism have selected this as the time. And, ladies and gentlemen, the chips are down—they are truly down.

Lest there be any doubt that the time has been chosen, let us go directly to the leader of communism today—Joseph Stalin. Here is what he said—not back in 1928, not before the war, not during the war—but two years after the last war was ended: "To think that the Communist revolution can be carried out peacefully, within the framework of a Christian democracy, means one has either gone out of one's mind and lost all normal understanding, or has grossly and openly repudiated the Communist revolution." . . .

Ladies and gentlemen, can there be anyone here tonight who is so blind as to say that the war is not on? Can there be anyone who fails to realize that the Communist world has said, "The time is now"—that this is the time for the showdown between the democratic Christian world and the Communist atheistic world? . . .

At war's end we were physically the strongest nation on earth, and, at least potentially, the most powerful intellectually and morally. Ours could have been the honor of being a beacon in the desert of destruction. . . . Unfortunately, we have failed miserably and tragically. . . . The reason why we find ourselves in a position of impotency is not because our only powerful potential enemy has sent men to invade our shores, but rather because of the traitorous actions of those who have been treated so well by this nation. It has not been the less fortunate or members of minority groups who have been selling this nation out, but rather those who have had all the benefits that the wealthiest nation on earth has had to offer—the finest homes, the finest college education, and the finest jobs in government we can give.

This is glaringly true in the State Department. There the bright young men who are born with silver spoons in their mouths are the ones who have been the worst.

Now I know it is very easy for anyone to condemn a particular bureau or department in general terms. Therefore, I would like to cite one rather unusual case—the case of a man who has done much to shape our foreign policy.

When Chiang Kai-shek was fighting our war, the State Department had in China a young man named John S. Service. His task, obviously, was not to work for the communization of China. Strangely enough, he sent official reports back to the State Department urging that we torpedo our ally Chiang Kai-shek and stating, in effect, that communism was the best hope of China.

Later, this man—John Service—was picked up by the Federal Bureau of Investigation for turning over to the Communists secret State Department information. Strangely, however, he was never prosecuted. However, Joseph Grew, the Undersecretary of State, who insisted on his prosecution, was forced to resign. Two days after Grew's successor, Dean Acheson, took over as Undersecretary of State, this man—John Service—who had been picked up by the FBI and who had previously urged that communism was the best hope of China, was not only reinstated in the State Department but promoted, and finally, under Acheson, placed in charge of all placements and promotions.

Today, ladies and gentlemen, this man Service is on his way to represent the State Department and Acheson in Calcutta— by far and away the most important listening post in the Far East.

Now, let's see what happens when individuals with Communist connections are forced out of the State Department. Gustave Duran, who was labeled (I quote) "a notorious international Communist," was made assistant to the Assistant Secretary of State in charge of Latin American affairs. He was taken into the State Department from his job as a lieutenant colonel in the Communist International Brigade. Finally, after intense Congressional pressure and criticism, he resigned in 1946 from the State Department—and, ladies and gentlemen, where do you think he is now? He took a high-salaried job as chief of the cultural activities section in the office of the Assistant Secretary General of the United Nations.

Then there was a Mrs. Mary Jane Kenny, from the Board of Economic Warfare in the State Department, who was named in an FBI report and in a House committee report as a courier for the Communist party while working for the government. And where do you think Mrs. Kenny is—she is now an editor in the United Nations document bureau.

Another interesting case is that of H. Julian Wadleigh, economist in the trade agreements section of the State Department for eleven years, who was sent to Turkey and Italy and other countries as United States representative. After the statute of limitations had run so he could not be prosecuted for treason, he openly and brazenly not only admitted but proclaimed that he had been a member of the Communist party . . . that while working for the State Department he stole a vast number of secret documents . . . and furnished these documents to the Russian spy ring of which he was a part.

You will recall last spring there was held in New York what was known as the World Peace Conference—a conference which was labeled by the State Department and Mr. Truman as the sounding board for Communist propaganda and a front for Russia. Dr. Harlow Shapley was the chairman of that conference. Interesting enough, according to the news release put out by the State Department in July, the Secretary of State appointed Shapley on a commission which acts as liaison between UNESCO and the State Department.

This, ladies and gentlemen, gives you somewhat of a picture of the type of individuals who have been helping to shape our foreign policy. In my opinion the State Department, which is one of the most important government departments, is thoroughly infested with Communists.

I have in my hand fifty-seven cases of individuals who would appear to be either card-carrying members or certainly loyal to the Communist party, but who nevertheless are still helping to shape our foreign policy.

One thing to remember in discussing the Communists in our government is that we are not dealing with spies who get thirty pieces of silver to steal the blueprints of a new weapon. We are dealing with a far more sinister type of activity because it permits the enemy to guide and shape our policy. . . .*

This brings us down to the case of one Alger Hiss, who is important not as an individual any more, but rather because he is so representative of a group in the State Department. It is unnecessary to go over the sordid events showing how he sold out the nation which had given him so much. Those are rather fresh in all our minds. However, it should be remembered that the facts in regard to his connection with this international Communist spy ring were made known to the then Undersecretary of State Berle three days after Hitler and Stalin signed the Russo-German alliance pact. At that time one Whittaker Chambers—who was also part of the spy ring—apparently decided that with Russia on Hitler's side, he could no longer betray our nation to Russia. He gave Undersecretary of State Berle—and this is all a matter of record—practically all, if not more, of the facts upon which Hiss' conviction was based.

Undersecretary Berle promptly contacted Dean Acheson and

---

* A passage lifted almost verbatim from a speech made by Richard M. Nixon in the House of Representatives on January 26, 1950.

received word that Acheson (and I quote) "could vouch for Hiss absolutely"—at which time the matter was dropped. And this, you understand, was at a time when Russia was an ally of Germany. This condition existed while Russia and Germany were invading and dismembering Poland, and while the Communist groups here were screaming "warmonger" at the Untied States for their support of the Allied nations.

Again, in 1943, the FBI had occasion to investigate the facts surrounding Hiss' contacts with the Russian spy ring. But even after the FBI report was submitted, nothing was done.

Then late in 1948—on August 5—when the Un-American Activities Committee called Alger Hiss to give an accounting, President Truman at once issued a presidential directive ordering all government agencies to refuse to turn over any information whatsoever in regard to the Communist activities of any government employe to a Congressional committee.

Incidentally, even after Hiss was convicted—it is interesting to note that the President still labeled the exposé of Hiss as a "red herring." *

If time permitted, it might be well to go into detail about the fact that Hiss was Roosevelt's chief adviser at Yalta when Roosevelt was admittedly in ill health and tired physically and mentally . . . and when, according to the Secretary of State [Stettinius], Hiss and Gromyko drafted the report on the conference. . . . Of the results of this conference, Arthur Bliss Lane of the State Department had this to say: "As I glanced over the document, I could not believe my eyes. To me, almost every line spoke of a surrender to Stalin."

As you hear this story of high treason, I know that you are saying to yourself, "Well, why doesn't the Congress do something about it?" Actually, ladies and gentlemen, one of the important reasons for the graft, the corruption, the dishonesty, the disloyalty, the treason in high government positions—one of the most important reasons why this continues—is a lack of moral uprising on the part of the one hundred and forty million American people. . . . However, the morals of our people have not been destroyed. They still exist. This cloak of numbness and apathy has needed only a spark to rekindle them. Happily, this spark has finally been supplied.

As you know, very recently the Secretary of State proclaimed

* When inserting the speech in the *Record,* McCarthy noted that this wording was not accurate, that the passage should have read "even after Hiss was indicted," instead of "convicted."

his loyalty to a man guilty of what has always been considered as the most abominable of all crimes—of being a traitor to the people who gave him a position of great trust. The Secretary of State, in attempting to justify his continued devotion to the man who sold out the Christian world to the atheistic world, referred to Christ's Sermon on the Mount as a justification and reason therefor, and the reaction of the American people to this would have made the heart of Lincoln happy.

When this pompous diplomat in striped pants, with a phony British accent, proclaimed to the American people that Christ on the Mount endorsed communism, high treason, and betrayal of a sacred trust, the blasphemy was so great that it awakened the dormant indignation of the American people.

He has lighted the spark which is resulting in a moral uprising and will end only when the whole sorry mess of twisted, warped thinkers are swept from the national scene so that we have a new birth of national honesty and decency in government.

These are not the words that would be attributed to McCarthy by some; they are the words he vouched for, and except for the one paragraph above set in italics they have never been seriously questioned.

Here are all the ingredients of the man: his simplistic creed; his savage directness; his scorn of compromise; the unqualified accusation; exaggeration habitual and deliberate, knowing its effect; dramatic intensity; discourtesy and rudeness thinly veneered with senatorial gloss; the cocksureness of a man who thinks in terms of black and white, blind to intermediate hues; the skilled 'jabbing at an opponent's tender spot; the rank appeal to an audience's emotions; the poorly educated man's repugnance for intellectuals and "pansy-pants" effetes; the stubbornness and truculence; and through it all immense self-assurance. There was nothing *mesquin* or affected about the performance; no rant, no bluster; but a sort of earnest clumsiness and cheerful pugnacity.

PART TWO

Letters of Marque
and Reprisal

"What cracker is this same that deafs our ears
With this abundance of superfluous breath?"
—*King John*

The Senate Resolves

When McCarthy got back to Washington, the reaction to his Western speeches surprised him. Reporters were waiting at the airport to question him about that list of "fifty-seven card-carrying Communists" who he maintained were in the State Department. Certainly he had such a list, he said, and he would show it to them; but rummaging in his briefcase failed to locate it, and he guessed it must be in his checked luggage. Cameramen snapped him peering into the briefcase in search of the document.

The Democrats were seething, while Joe's fellow Republicans spoke warily: in view of the temper of the voters, this issue packed dynamite. Just how much evidence did McCarthy have to back up his charges? What if they should boomerang? Politicians are seldom remarkable for boldness, and until there was more information available the Republican senators held gingerly aloof.

The President was scornful: not a word of truth in anything that fellow said, was his contemptuous dismissal of reporters' questions. Senator Scott Lucas of Illinois, the Senate's majority leader, as an administration spokesman deplored McCarthy's "shameful" slur on the State Department. Lucas had not been aware of the Wheeling speech until reporters called it to his attention and the mail began pouring into his office, indicating an unexpected response throughout the country; then he realized that Joe's charges must be met squarely and turned back on the accuser.

Rallying to the defense of the four individuals named by McCarthy at Wheeling, the State Department's Peurifoy put out a statement emphasizing that John Stewart Service had been cleared in the *Amerasia* affair and had come through two subsequent loyalty checks successfully, and that not one of the other three was still connected with the department; Shapley, the Harvard astronomer,

never had been employed. But raising on a poor hand was Mc-
Carthy's way of playing the game, and he announced his intention
of carrying his attack to the Senate floor. Not only did he have a
live issue, but his love of battle was aroused, and he told insistent
newsmen that he would document his case to the hilt in the Senate.

[II]

True to his promise, on February 20 McCarthy met the challenge
of the opposition party in a hectic, eight-hour session. From somewhere—the source is not clear—he had obtained a copy of the so-
called Lee Report, summarizing adverse data contained in the State
Department's security files on 108 persons. He had made no reference to this report on his Western tour, but it furnished the basis
for his unprecedented attack on the State Department in the Senate
on February 20.

The business being discussed by the Senate that afternoon was a
measure to set up a permanent subcommittee on the problems of
small business, when McCarthy arose for the purpose of making an
announcement. At 4 P.M., he said—which would be as early as he
could get the floor—he intended to discuss "a subject and give facts
which I think will be of great interest to the Senate and the press";
and in consequence he hoped that as many senators as possible
would be on hand. "My remarks will deal with the extent to which
Communists have infiltrated into the State Department and are
shaping State Department policy. I intend to cover that subject in
detail."

Senator Lucas immediately passed the word quietly that no vote
of importance would be taken that day, in effect notifying the members that they might absent themselves. This was an unwise move.
Many senators did depart, so that when McCarthy began his speech
at four o'clock he faced an almost empty chamber. But true to his
fighting technique, Joe came out swinging, and within two minutes
he had landed a stinging blow on the unwary Lucas.

"Mr. President," he began, "I wish to discuss a subject tonight
which concerns me more than any other subject I have ever discussed before this body, and perhaps more than any other subject
I shall ever have the good fortune to discuss in the future. It not
only concerns me, but it disturbs and frightens me."

Recalling his speech at Wheeling, he read the telegram he had

sent to President Truman and said that he had received no acknowledgment or answer except that Truman had said at a press conference that there was "not a word of truth" in it.

"Subsequently, the Democratic leader of the Senate—at least, the
alleged leader," Joe went on, glancing toward Lucas, "made a
speech in Chicago in which he repeated substantially what the
President said, except that he went one step further and stated:
'If I had said the nasty things that McCarthy has said about the
State Department, I would be ashamed all the rest of my life.' He
also said there was not a word of truth in my charge. I think it is
unfortunate, not because I am concerned with what the senior
senator from Illinois happens to think, but because he occupies such
an important position. . . ."

This brought Lucas to his feet with a challenge: "Mr. President,
will the senator yield?"

McCarthy: "Wait till I finish. If the senator will stay with me for
the next few hours he will learn a great many facts. . . . I think a
group of twisted-minded intellectuals has taken over both the Democratic and Republican parties, to try to wrest control from them."

The indignant Lucas protested that he was as much against communism as McCarthy was, and "what I am asking the senator to do
is to follow through with the speech that he made at Wheeling. . . .
I want him to name those Communists. The senator is privileged to
name them all in the Senate, and if these people are not Communists
he will be protected. . . ."

This brought the instant retort from McCarthy: "I wish to thank
the distinguished senator from Illinois for his views, but I should
like to assure him that I will not say anything on the Senate floor
which I will not say off the floor. On the day when I take advantage
of the security we have on the Senate floor, on that day I will resign
from the Senate."

From this point on the encounter grew steadily more bitter. Lucas
interrupted some eighty times, and other senators joined in a continuous heckling of the speaker. When McCarthy attempted to read
Secretary of State Byrnes's letter of 1948, Lucas objected, demanding to know what was the point. The point, McCarthy explained,
was that this letter was the basis for some of the things he had said
in Wheeling, but "the President said, 'It's just a lie. There is nothing
to it.' "

Lucas bore in: "Did the senator say at Wheeling last Thursday night that two hundred and five persons working for the State Department were known by the Secretary of State to be members of the Communist party, or words to that effect? Did he call the attention of the country to the fact that two hundred and five men in the State Department were card-carrying Communists? Did the senator say that? That's what I'd like to know."

Thereupon McCarthy asked unanimous consent to insert in the *Record* "a copy of the speech I made at Wheeling, West Virginia."

Lucas: "Can't the senator answer yes or no?"

McCarthy: "I ask the senator please not to interrupt me. I will yield to him later. I will give him all the chance in the world."

But Lucas was insistent, repeating, "I asked the senator a very simple question," although, like many another allegedly simple question, his was not simple at all, nor susceptible to a yes or no answer.

McCarthy renewed his request for unanimous consent to insert his speech unread, but Lucas objected, so the request failed. McCarthy then read aloud, word for word, the speech "which I made at Wheeling, West Virginia, and at Reno, Nevada. It was the same speech." This achieved his purpose—to place in the *Record* the only authenticated text of the speech which he said he had delivered in both places.

But the reading consumed time, and in an ostentatious display of boredom Lucas strolled toward the door.

"I hope the senator from Illinois will stay for this," McCarthy called after him, and Lucas instantly halted.

"I shall be right here," he flung back. "I am coming over to the Republican side of the aisle so that I will not miss anything."

At this point Senator Henry Cabot Lodge, Jr., Massachusetts Republican, broke in to say that he was vitally interested in what McCarthy had to say, although he did not know whether his colleague was right or wrong; but questions of grave importance were involved, and as a member of the Foreign Affairs Committee he intended to ask for a thorough investigation of the charges. He regretted that he must leave the chamber to keep an appointment, but promised to read the entire speech with great care the next day.

McCarthy welcomed the suggestion of a thorough investigation. Indeed, he made that a keynote of his discourse. Again and again he was interrupted by Democratic senators demanding to know why he had not turned over the information he claimed to have to "proper authorities," such as the FBI, the State Department, or "some appropriate committee." Patiently he explained why he had chosen his present course. He had, he said, summaries of the files on eighty-one persons who were, or had been, employed by the State Department; these summaries had been compiled from the State Department's own records, and they had long been available to the Secretary of State. The information was not new, he stressed; any other senator might have dug it out. But precisely because the data had been available for so long, without anybody taking any action on it, he had cast about for a way that would insure its being thoroughly looked into.

"I originally thought possibly we could hope for some cooperation from the State Department and the President," he explained. "However, in going over the material and finding that all of it, of course, has been available to the State Department, for it is all from their files, it seemed that nothing could be gained by calling it to their attention again. The President, I felt, had demonstrated his lack of interest quite thoroughly during the Hiss investigation. Then, when I sent him a telegram and said, 'Mr. President, I have the fifty-seven names; they are yours if you want them,' and when he answered by calling me a liar, I felt I could get no cooperation from the President."

Senator Brien McMahon of Connecticut wanted to know why McCarthy had not turned over his data to the Senate Foreign Relations Committee. McCarthy replied that he had considered that course, also; but "keeping in mind that the members of the . . . committee and all the senators have had substantially the same knowledge and opportunity that I have had, I questioned whether anything would be gained unless the President changed his mind and said, 'I will give you the information.' "

Then coming to the crux of his choice of procedure, which he said he would adhere to undeviatingly, he announced: "I thought the only thing to do was what I have done, namely, to let the people of the country know what is going on, and then hope that the presure of public opinion would be great enough to force the President to clean house.*

"Frankly, I think he will not clean house until he determines

---

* By way of historical curiosity, if nothing more, compare this with the legal defense advanced on almost identical grounds by *The New York Times, Washington Post,* and other newspapers for their unauthorized publication of the secret Pentagon Papers in 1971.

it is politcially inexpedient for him to do otherwise. I think the
President is one of the cleverest politicians this nation has ever
had. I think when he discovers that the people of the country do
not want a continuation of what is going on, there will be a housecleaning."

Alone, he stressed, he could do little to establish the truth. "I
do not have any tremendous investigative agency to get the facts.
I do not have a counter-espionage group of my own. . . . I do
not have [even] the complete State Department files in these
matters. I very greatly wish I did. That is one of the things I
hope one of our committees will succeed in getting."

[III]

By now the attendance had fallen off further, and the few
senators remaining stood about talking in low tones. Senator
Kenneth S. Wherry, the minority leader, directed the chair's attention to the lack of a quorum, but Senator Lucas objected to
a roll call. Sticking to his insistence that McCarthy say what he
had said at Wheeling (although the entire speech, as vouched for
by McCarthy, had been read aloud), Lucas produced clippings
from three newspapers—the *Washington Post, New York Times,*
and *Chicago Tribune*—all reporting that McCarthy had said "two
hundred and five Communists" at Wheeling, and challenged the
senator to repudiate them.

"If the senator is going to make a farce of this," McCarthy interjected, and Lucas hastily protested that he was in earnest. But
the studied lack of attention was irking Joe, and he demanded a
roll call. Twenty-four senators answered to their names, and five
more were pried out of various rooms; forty-nine were required
for a quorum. Under the rules, therefore, Lucas was compelled
to move to adjourn, and the motion was voted down, 18 to 16,
with sixty-two senators listed as absent. Thereupon the sergeant-
at-arms was instructed to round up a quorum—the first time in
five years that this has been necessary.

After a thirty-five-minute lull, enough senators were prodded
into making their appearance, some of them grumpy and resentful, and then McCarthy proceeded with his report on the cases
in his file. He said he would give the facts on all eighty-one, and
he actually did cover seventy-six. McCarthy identified the cases

by numbers, not by names, saying he would give the names only if the Senate ordered him to do so. He stressed that he was not evaluating the data he presented. "Everything I have is from the State Department's own files," he said again and again. "I shall not attempt to present a detailed case on each one, a case which would convince a jury. All I am going to do is to develop sufficient evidence so that anyone who reads the *Record* will have a good idea of the number of Communists in the State Department."

When pressed to disclose the names, he warned that to do so at that time might work gross injustice. "I am not indicting the eighty-one," he made clear. "It is possible that some of these persons will get a clean bill of health. I know that some of them will not." And he disclaimed knowing whether all of the persons in the list were still with the State Department, although some he did know were still there. "I know they have all been there at some time. A sizable number is still there."

The Democrats kept demanding that he produce names. Said Senator Tydings of Maryland: "I want to remain here until he names them."

Senator Withers of Kentucky prodded: "I should like to ask the senator what reason he has for not calling names. Does not the senator think it would be a fine thing to let the public know who the guilty are? Is not the senator privileged?"

But McCarthy stuck to his refusal to involve perhaps innocent people. Investigate first, he counterdemanded; then name the accused.

[IV]

The crowded gallery, alerted in advance that the senator would make startling revelations, leaned forward expectantly as McCarthy began to read off his numbered cases. The source of his information he indicated only as "from State Department files," where it had been "a long time. . . . The records are completely secret, except what I could get from loyal State Department employes." Indeed, he added, "if it were not for some good, loyal Americans in the State Department—and there are many of them—I should not have been able to present this picture tonight."

He led off with what he called the "big three"—Cases 1, 2, and 81. These "three big Communists," he said, "are tremendously important and of great value to Russia. . . . I cannot possibly conceive of any Secretary of State allowing [them] . . . to remain in the State Department. I do not believe President Truman knows about them. I cannot help but feel that he is merely the prisoner of a bunch of twisted intellectuals who tell him what they want him to know."

Case No. 1 he described as "employed in the office of an Assistant Secretary of State." Intelligence agents had shadowed him and "found him contacting members of an espionage group." He also had succeeded in obtaining "important positions" for two other Communists by hoodwinking "a well known general" into recommending them, a tactic which the senator described as "the usual modus operandi: if there is one Communist in the department, he will get some other individual to recommend another Communist so that the breed can be increased."

Lucas was on his feet with the by now repetitious demand: "Will the senator tell us the name of the man for the record? We are entitled to know who he is."

Once more McCarthy declined, emphasizing that he did not have all the information in the cases, including possibly extenuating data, "but I have enough to convince me that either they are members of the Communist party, or they have given great aid to the Communists. That is why I said that unless the Senate demanded that I do so, I would not submit this publicly, but I would submit it to any committee, and would let the committee go over these [cases] in executive session."

Senator Neely of West Virginia was disgusted. Let the presiding officer enforce the rule against irrelevant interruptions and let McCarthy finish, he demanded, so "we will not be required to sit up all night like wild cats and . . . sleep all day tomorrow like hoot owls!"

McCarthy plodded through his dossiers, case by case. No. 9 he thought the Senate might even enjoy, since "this individual, after investigation, was *not* given clearance by the State Department. After failing to obtain clearance by the State Department he secured a job in the office of the Secretary of Defense! And where do senators think that man is today? He is now a speech writer in the White House! . . . I think I am doing Mr. Truman a favor by telling him this. I don't think he knows it. I don't think he would have this individual there writing speeches for him if he knew it.

But the individual referred to, and his wife—this is in the file of the investigative agency—are members of Communist-front organizations. He has a relative who has a financial interest in the *Daily Worker.* . . . The State Department used good judgment not to clear this individual."

Another case was described as that of a former analyst in the OSS who had joined the intelligence service of the State Department's military assistance program—highly sensitive employment —although he was reported to be the close friend of a Communist and a regular reader of the *Worker,* and was "known to have stated that the Communists should take over in this country."

Then there was a man whom the senator identified as "a foreign service officer" in the Information and Cultural Division of the State Department, who had visited Soviet Russia in 1947 as a delegate of a trade union later disavowed by the American Federation of Labor. This man was listed in the Chicago police files as having been a Communist since 1930.

Another man, McCarthy said, had transferred from the OSS to the Office of Research and Intelligence in the State Department in 1945, although the department's own reports identified him as a member of Red fronts and an associate of known Communists. Subsequently his department superiors had complained of his being oversympathetic to Russia and his blaming "the capitalists" for all the difficulties incident to the postwar readjustment.

Still another individual on McCarthy's list was identified as "one of our foreign ministers," who allegedly had passed secret information to a known Soviet agent, in spite of which he was now serving in an important listening post in Europe.

Case No. 53 McCarthy termed "rather important—in fact, they are all important." He said it involved a person "who has been named by a confessed Communist spy as part of his spy ring. . . . This individual is, in my opinion, Mr. President, one of the most dangerous Communists in the State Department.

"Next, I come to Case No. 81. I think this individual has been doing this nation untold damage because of the high position she holds in the Voice of America. . . . The file in this case contains a wealth of information indicating that this individual is an extremely dangerous and active Communist, completely disloyal to the United States, and loyal to Russia. . . . It is perhaps sufficient to point out that the witnesses without exception have stated in essence that this individual has collected in her office a mixture of fellow travelers and pseudo-liberals and outright Communists. These witnesses indicate that the group is close-knit and attempts a vicious character assassination of anyone who disagrees with them, and apparently rather successfully so. . . . Immediate steps should be taken, in my opinion, to obtain not only the discharge but the prosecution of this individual."

Vainly the Democrats tried to force McCarthy to stop. At times the exchanges descended to bathos. When McCarthy exclaimed that a thing that "walks like a duck, talks like a duck, and acts like a duck" it is pretty safe to identify as a duck, Senator Herbert Lehman, New York's elderly Liberal-Democrat, took exception and demanded whether that meant that McCarthy could tell a Communist by his gait, or that all Communists walked like ducks. Joe replied that his questioner was not stupid, and "I am afraid if it is not clear to the senator now, I shall never be able to make it clear to him, no matter how much further explanation I make." The old man, whose walk indulgent friends sometimes likened to a duck's waddle, padded back to his seat, and in this way the time of the Senate was consumed.

Senator McMahon, whom the sergeant-at-arms had called away from a dinner party, breezed in in evening dress while McCarthy was dwelling on Case No. 34, and on being told what number it was devoutly hoped he would be home in bed before they reached the bottom of the list. McMahon, a handsome Irishman, was quite as pugnacious as McCarthy but more polished. For a while he spelled off the weary Lucas in hammering at Joe to name the persons he was accusing under a thin camouflage of numbers.

"If the senator from Connecticut had been here a little earlier," McCarthy shot back, "he would have heard the majority leader demanding we do exactly that. He demanded that I present the names and indict these people before the country without giving them a chance to be heard. I said, 'No, I will not do that unless the Senate demands it.' "

No senator moved to make such a demand, although individual members on the Democratic side kept calling on McCarthy to disclose the names on his own authority, on the basis of the admittedly incomplete data he held. McMahon asked McCarthy whether he did not think "it is the American system, that when a man is accused, he shall be given a hearing, that all witnesses for him and against him shall be heard and adjudged? Star chambers are not for the United States of America, nor are trials *ex parte,* on the basis of the files of the persons concerned, on the floor of the United States Senate."

That was exactly what he did want, McCarthy repeated—full hearings on the full information, so that the country might know what the situation in the State Department was, in regard to the security of the nation. On the surface, from the limited facts in his possession, the situation looked black.

McMahon would not have it so; he wanted the names now, although he refrained from urging the Senate formally to demand them. And he bore down on the charge that McCarthy was presenting only derogatory material taken from the files, ignoring or withholding any counterbalancing favorable information. In the rest of the cases he proposed to submit, McMahon wanted to know, would he present both derogatory and favorable information? McCarthy tried to answer, but McMahon wanted a straight yes-or-no: "That is a yes-or-no question."

McCarthy: "The answer is that I obviously do not have photostats of all the files."

McMahon: "Has the senator got——"

McCarthy: "Let me finish. . . . The senator understands that I do not have complete State Department files in these matters. . . . The senator flatters me when he says it is my duty to present the entire file to the Senate and to give all the information. The President has said we shall not get that file, and, as of the present moment, since we are not on a 'Dear Joe, Dear Harry' basis, I cannot go to the White House and say, 'Harry, give me this file because Senator McMahon insists that you give me this information.' All I can do is to give senators what I can dig up. I have given the senators the fullest, most complete, fairest resumé of the files that I possibly could."

Doubtless, he conceded, there would be found favorable information in the complete files; even a Communist might be a kind husband and a loving father.

Senator Brewster of Maine broke in to wonder what difference it would make how many good points might be in a file if the person were a Communist sympathizer or fellow traveler. "Our jails are filled with persons who were perfectly honest up to the time they performed the deeds or acts that got them convicted," he added.

But Lucas protested that McCarthy was accusing people wholesale; where was his proof? In reply Joe read him the political facts of life: "Since when has it been the job of a senator who is a member of the minority . . . to clean house for an executive department? That is the task of the majority, and I hope they take the task on their shoulders. . . . Does the senator feel it is my job to probe behind the [Truman] iron curtain and get the information?"

"The senator from Wisconsin has already been behind the iron curtain," Lucas retorted bitterly; nevertheless, he promised that "we will ferret this out, from top to bottom."

"Isn't it a fact, to boil all this down," Senator Wherry interposed, that McCarthy was simply asking an investigation to determine whether there were disloyal persons in the State Department?

Absolutely, Joe agreed, adding: "I think the condition today is so fraught with danger, I think that we are in a period today so close to war, that even if we do damage some of the honest employes, I must take the only method I know of whereby I think we can secure a housecleaning." The repsonsibility lay squarely on the Democratic majority, he repeated, for "the only way to clean out the State Department is not by laws, but by the cooperation of the President."

Lucas pledged all assistance in getting McCarthy "a hearing under oath," whereupon Joe rejoined that "the senator thinks this should be a trial of the man digging out the Communists, and not of the Communists themselves."

That exclamation and another made by McCarthy midway through the long battle Lucas would have occasion to remember ruefully during the coming months. At one point the exasperated Joe had snapped at his tormentors: "I do not fancy at all this condemnation of an attempt to bring this matter before the Senate! I intend to give all the facts!"

At 11:43 P.M. the exhausted and bedraggled Senate adjourned, leaving McCarthy in effect master of the field; he was ready to go several rounds more.

[V]

Whatever might have been the thoughts of the denizens of the Senate press gallery as their ears rang with the din on the floor, they were aware that they were witnessing a virtuoso performance on the part of Wisconsin's junior senator, and perhaps the emergence of a new force in the Senate. The irrepressible McCarthy had a tremendous issue, and in his fashion he was making the most of it. He had held out against a massive assault, even though clumsily; in the words of one correspondent, he had exhibited "all the deftness of a bulldozer." And the question was wide open whether McCarthy really had some fresh information. If only a fraction of what he said was true, the nation might well be uneasy.

For the most part the press reports of McCarthy's action were factual and straightforward. *The New York Times* headlined (on Page 13):

M'CARTHY CHARGES SPY FOR RUSSIA HAS A HIGH STATE DEPARTMENT POST

But if the newspapers were hesitant to take sides, the Democrats were not. A Senate understrapper had managed to put the party's leadership on the defensive for eight furious hours. He had been challenged, derided, ridiculed, and he had not retreated one inch. Again and again by parliamentary devices Senator Lucas had tried to wrest the floor from him, but McCarthy had succeeded in "stating the facts" so that the whole country heard them. It was all very well for the Democrats to decry his charges, but the Hiss scandal was too recent, the shock of Klaus Fuchs too profound for such accusations to be shrugged off. And the Democratic leadership did not treat the attack on its integrity lightly. The day after McCarthy spoke Senator Lucas spent in consultation with the party's membership of the Senate and with the Democratic policy committee. The result was a decision to meet the peril head-on and in a full-dress investigation force McCarthy to make his words good, or expose his own falsity. Senator Lucas thereupon introduced Senate Resolution 231, calling for such an inquiry.

The debate on the resolution brought out eighty-six senators, so worked up were partisan feelings. The Republicans certainly wanted the investigation, McCarthy favored it, and the Democrats sensed that any attempt to hush the matter would bring down the wrath of a host of voters.

At Republican urging, amendments were offered, broadening the scope of the inquiry. Senator Morse of Oregon fought hard to have the hearings open to the public. Lucas, also, favored the widest publicity for the inquiry.

"So far as I am concerned," he said, "it will be in the open, where every individual in America, every newspaperman can attend, so that they will know definitely, as soon as possible, just who is being charged and who is not being charged with being Communists. That is only fair . . . every individual in the State Department tonight is under a cloud."

McCarthy took part in the debate only once. That was when Lucas asked whether he was willing to disclose the sources of his information. Where documentary evidence was concerned, McCarthy replied, he would never tell; otherwise the jobs of any informants he had in the State Department would not "be worth a tinker's dam."

"I hope that the investigating committee will insist that he name the sources of his information," Lucas commented sternly. "He is responsible for this investigation. He cannot hide behind anonymous informants. His duty, as a senator and as an American, is to tell the committee exactly where he got his information and to name names."

McCarthy sat through it stoically; he seemed capable of absorbing any amount of punishment. Then he assured Lucas that the latter "knew perfectly well" that he would cooperate with the investigation.

The amended resolution was adopted unanimously. Its mandate was explicit. Since what the Senate ordered the investigating committee to do, and what was subsequently done, were to lead to endless wrangling, inflaming the controversy rather than quenching it, the exact wording of Senate Resolution 231, as presented below, is important:

> RESOLVED, that the Senate Committee on Foreign Relations, or any duly authorized subcommittee thereof, is authorized and directed to conduct a full and complete study and investigation as to whether persons who are disloyal to the United States or have been employed by the Department of State. The committee shall report to the Senate at the earliest practicable date the results of its investigation, together with such recommendations as it may deem desirable, and if said recommendations are to include formal charges of disloyalty against any individual, then the committee, before making such recommendations, shall give said individual open hearings for the purpose of taking evidence or testimony on said charges. In the conduct of this study and investigation, the committee is directed to procure, by subpena, and examine the complete loyalty and employment files and records of all government employees in the Department of State and such other agencies against whom charges have been made.

Ready on the Right,
Ready on the Left...

[I]

Senator Millard E. Tydings of Maryland was named chairman of the subcommittee of three Democrats and two Republicans entrusted with the duty of carrying out the mandate of the Senate.

The Tydings Committee, as it became popularly known, is generally credited with having "made" Senator Joe McCarthy, and it "unmade" Tydings. In the words of one commentary, the investigation carried on under the direction of Tydings "established McCarthy, in the eyes of a few articulate, and millions of inarticulate, anti-Communists, as the standard-bearer in the fight to expose Communist infiltration of the federal government. In the minds of many other Americans, especially of almost all members of our intelligensia, it established McCarthy as the arch-villain of mid-twentieth century politics." *

There were, of course, deep-seated reasons for this development, reasons which lay within McCarthy and within his antagonists mutually. Conformable to Newton's third law of motion, action produces reaction of equal intensity, and violence produces counterviolence equally extreme, and Joe McCarthy was the embodiment of the most audacious violence. Never profound and completely unoriginal (from start to finish of his career he would use the same hackneyed phrases lifted from others, and the same dog-eared appeals), he was constantly effective in dramatizing the lurking thoughts and tumultuous emotions of his listeners, pro and con; and this by none of the usual artifices of the rabble-rouser, for he had no oratorical power, but by his gift for infusing the commonplace words with a sense of drama—the drama of hyper-

---

* *McCarthy and His Enemies,* William F. Buckley, Jr., and L. Brent Bozell, Regnery, Chicago, 1954.

bole, boldness, conflict. Other men, in and out of government, as he himself would point out, had been saying much that he said, and had "landed back among the want ads." He knew the "open sesame," the key, to the front pages. Where others generalized, he was specific. *Treason* is hard to visualize, it is diffuse, intangible, shadowy, but a *traitor* is a person who can be identified and satisfactorily hated.

An example of McCarthy's ability to energize the utterances of others was his incessant arraignment of the State Department for "coddling Communists." The phrase was not his. In 1948, for instance, Earl Warren, governor of California, while campaigning as the Republican vice-presidential candidate, accused the Democratic administration of "coddling Communists," and there was no public hysteria. No shrieks of outrage resounded from coast to coast. But when McCarthy spoke the words, they became surcharged with the energy of his own nature, dark, dynamic, and dramatic. And the reaction induced was correspondingly energetic.*

The antagonism to McCarthy displayed instantaneously and automatically by America's academic and intellectual communities was predicated upon the ideological divisions of the previous twenty years. Gradually, with many hesitations and internal struggles, the bellwethers of liberalism had been drifting away from their flirtatious association with Marxism and Soviet totalitarianism. During the Depression years, to be pro-Communist had been not only fashionable, it had been a hallmark of right-thinking, of mental clarity and moral decency. The traditional ideals of the nation were at a discount, and expressions of vestigial faith in these supposedly outmoded concepts was written off as either naive or nefarious.

The unnatural Hitler-Stalin alliance had disabused many liberals of their roseate illusions; but to abjure publicly a faith held so positively for so long was an act of contrition of which few were capable: no one likes to look foolish, no one likes to don the dunce cap before the crowd and admit that one has been taken in. For those too thin-skinned to bear the odium of an abrupt apostasy, the false dawn of Soviet-American amity during World War II had provided a means of "tapering off" from the heavy involvements of

---

* Napoleon, the supreme embodiment of energy, believed that "energy is the inspirer, or source, of intelligence"; which it need not be, although sufficient energy can produce the appearance of intelligence.

the previous decade without total loss of dignity: the virtues of the Russian people could still be extolled without subscribing to the Communist postulates. In this way self-esteem was preserved, and self-esteem is the most prized of human possessions.

By 1950, the shocking revelations of the Communists' real aims had shaken most of the liberal left loose from their infatuation with Stalinism; but this disillusioned element preferred to manifest their tardy conversion in ways they believed seemly, at their own pace, without panic or presenting the ludicrous spectacle of scrambling to an opposite extreme. The jarring irruption of a Johnny-come-lately from Wisconsin, with his crass cry of "Forward charge!" struck the liberal left on their most exposed nerve, and the groans of anguish that it provoked were visceral in their instinctiveness and intensity. The penitents who shuffle with reluctant steps toward the confessional do not relish being hustled along by a boorish beadle: no one likes to have his thunder stolen. And Joe McCarthy on a rampage was as heedless of ideological sensitivities as any other pirate on a raid.

Hardly had he fired his shot in Wheeling when the political seismologists detected the concussion. The articulate *Nation* promptly mocked the senator as a hunter on the prowl with a blunderbuss. "He started out by saying there were 57 card-carrying Communists" in the State Department. "If he fails to bag any game at all . . . [he] will have suffered no serious loss, his reputation as a statesman being negligible to begin with."

The *New Republic* castigated Joe for having held up a settlement of the current potato crop crisis by his midnight filibuster —"for which many senators were routed out of their homes and dinner parties." The whole affair, while reprehensible, was obviously small-bore.

[II]

Senator Tydings organized his committee, promising in a radio broadcast that the investigation would be thorough, but "neither a witch-hunt nor a whitewash." Senator McCarthy, said Tydings, would be allowed to present his facts "in any manner he chooses," and it would be up to him to prove everything he had said. The majority members of the committee, besides Tydings, were Senators McMahon of Connecticut and Theodore F. Green of Rhode Island.

The Republicans were Senators Bourke B. Hickenlooper of Iowa and Henry Cabot Lodge, Jr., of Massachusetts.

Senator Tydings was an excellent choice to conduct such an inquiry. A veteran of the Senate, wealthy, patrician in bearing, he was a skillful controversialist, able, in the words of one admirer, to "decapitate with a phrase." Although a stout party man, he did not hesitate to speak out independently on occasion. His prestige in the Senate was enormous because of the way he had turned back the attempt of President Franklin D. Roosevelt to purge him in the 1938 election. Tydings' popularity in Maryland was solidly established and his political defenses were considered impregnable. He would be coming up for reelection in November of this year, and the McCarthy inquiry should enable him to chalk up credits for use in that campaign.

Senator McMahon, one of the younger members of the Senate, was an adroit fighter, charged with grave responsibilities as chairman of the Joint Committee on Atomic Energy. With some aspects of the administration's policy toward Soviet Russia he disagreed, and said so; he was haunted by the dread that the H-bomb might mean the doom of civilization, unless the arms race were halted.

Octogenarian Senator Green, who had been an ardent New Dealer in the stirring days of Roosevelt's first administration, was still one. A party wheelhorse, he could be counted upon to support the chairman wholeheartedly.

Senator Hickenlooper, a heavy-set, deliberate Iowan, strongly conservative in his views, offered a sharp contrast to his colleague, Lodge. The latter, fastidiously educated, energetic, and independent, was politically liberal-with-reservations. As it turned out, Lodge would be unavoidably distracted by personal matters throughout the investigation.

There was another factor that would play an important, though unacknowledged, part in the coming battle, and that was the antagonism, inherent and mutual, that separated McCarthy from the men arrayed against him—an antagonism based on geographical and cultural differences. Coming from the Midwest, McCarthy typified certain aspects of the people of that region, including a profound belief in the superiority of Midwesterners. He considered them more "American," truer to the nation's traditional values, less susceptible to "foreign" influences and ideas than their contemporaries on either coast. "There is something about the men from the Midwest," he would say, striving to put his meaning into words, clasping and unclasping his hands and cracking his knuckles in the intensity of the effort.

On the Tydings Committee, only Senator Hickenlooper would share this regional prejudice. The other four senators, including Lodge, who would be at least nominally on McCarthy's side in a party division, were members—influential, affluent members—of the Eastern establishment, shaped and guided by the cultural environment of the North Atlantic seaboard. The intellectual center of the nation lay in that area roughly; most of the prestigious universities were there, and politically that region looked toward Europe. At the outbreak of World War II the Northeast had been strongly interventionist in sentiment, while the Midwest had been isolationist. The populist movements of the last century had originated and flourished in the West, not in the East. The East—Wall Street—signified financial interests which the rural Midwest had long considered inimical. Put all these factors together, add the effects of a rudimentary education and a sense of social inferiority, and Joe McCarthy, their embodiment, plainly came from the wrong side of the tracks; he was and always would remain an outsider in the eyes of the East, offensive by reason of his very background. And his own bias against Eastern influences and Eastern mannerisms would stand out as plainly. Even his wartime experience, having been in the Pacific theater of action, had focused his attention on the Orient and away from Europe, about which he knew nothing at first hand.

[III]

With the formation of the Tydings Committee, McCarthy realized that the time had come to put up or shut up. He welcomed the prospect, although he would be fighting virtually alone. The Democrats were insistent that he make good on the numbered but unnamed "cases" he had presented in the Senate; the Republicans hoped he could, but they doubted it (Senator Taft thought the man was out of his mind); and the press was stumbling in confusion. McCarthy had showered down "cases" so profusely, and then had crosshatched the original accusations with so many qualifications, that no one could say with confidence where the truth might lie. It seemed unlikely that he would deliberately bamboozle the Senate; so a reasonable assumption seemed to be that he had stumbled upon something tremendous. On the other hand, this trigger-happy swashbuckler might be about to fall flat on his face. McCarthy-on-a-tear was a phenomenon not yet plumbed by the members of the National Press Club, and these waited impatiently for the opening of the hearings on Wednesday, March 8.

McCarthy reserved a room in the Library of Congress and started to cram. He had some assistance, not much. A few members of Congress who had been fighting communism long before Joe passed along data and advice; Richard Nixon, who had been instrumental in developing the case against Hiss, opened his files; several newspapermen provided leads and editorial help. The work went on around the clock, Joe practically giving up sleep, even giving up poker. In the early hours he would fling himself on a couch in his office and sleep for an hour or two, then plunge into work again.

The Republican Policy Committee of the Senate had canvassed whether to make the fight a matter of official party concern and had voted against it; Joe was on his own.

During the interval of preparation, two events further excited the public's uneasiness about the Communist threat.

On March 1, Klaus Fuchs was sentenced to fourteen years in prison, and the headlines recapitulated the extent of the help he had given to the Russians. For Americans it was frightening reading.

The day before, Secretary of State Acheson had appeared before the Senate Appropriations Committee on behalf of funds for the department, and had offered a public "clarification" of his statement that he would "not turn his back" on Alger Hiss. He confessed he felt humiliated that any explanation should be necessary. His words had been misconstrued and misrepresented, he stated to the coolly listening senators, and the questioning turned to what criteria the State Department's loyalty board used to screen out disloyalty or security risks. By way of reply, Acheson read from the department's own manual of instructions this definition of what in its view constituted a presumptive risk:

"Participation . . . in organizations which are fronts for, or controlled by, [the Communist] party . . . whether by membership therein, taking part in its executive direction or control, contribution of funds thereto, attendance at meetings . . . or by written evidence or oral expressions, by speeches or otherwise, of political, economic, or social views, will be taken into account, together with such mitigating circumstances as may exist." *

Senator Styles Bridges of New Hampshire asked icily whether "a friend of a person convicted of perjury in connection with a treasonable act" would be considered a security risk. With matching frostiness Acheson replied, "I think it would be a matter to be looked into."

To troubled Americans, such exchanges, reported in the press, fanned their fears that the direction of the country's foreign policy, in this time of urgent crisis, was in dubious, or at least inept, hands. This heightened the interest in the Tydings-McCarthy inquiry, and when the hearings opened on March 8, every seat in the ornate marble-and-gilt Senate caucus room was occupied.

* To many persons having an average grasp of English this read suspiciously like a comprehensive definition of "guilt by association," a deviltry that would become identified as a positive element of "McCarthyism."

Then Ho! For the Spanish Main!

The committee had decided upon giving their proceedings the widest possible publicity, including television coverage, and the caucus room was cluttered with cameras, lights, and trailing cables.

McCarthy showed up promptly, and at 10:30 A.M. the session was called to order. Joe was sworn as the first witness.

McCarthy had prepared an opening statement outlining his case, and he requested permission to read it. Permission was granted; but he had barely started when he was interrupted by the chair, and further interruptions followed so rapidly that within fifteen minutes the hearing had been transformed into a public brawl.

Senator McMahon broke in with the point-blank question, "Senator, is it your intention to name individuals against whom you are making charges?" But to this question McMahon tacked on the observation that naming names publicly might work "a grave injustice" on "decent American citizens" who might be accused and later exonerated. Didn't McCarthy understand this?

So well had McCarthy understood this that he had urged Tydings to hold the first sessions in private, so that any persons named on the basis of the admittedly incomplete information he held, and later cleared as the committee developed further information, should not be subjected to a public "smear." Tydings had turned down the request, and when the entire committee voted on the question, the three Democrats had held out for conducting all hearings in public, the two Republicans voting against it. Now McMahon, who had already refused the protection of closed sessions to any persons who might be accused wrongly, was demanding that McCarthy name those he accused over television, before a national audience, before any investigation was made into the validity of the charges.

McCarthy fought back. He had been assured by the chairman, he said, that he might present his case in any way he chose, and he was merely following the customary procedure by first out-lining his contentions in a connected statement, after which he would submit to cross-examination.

Tydings was unmoved. He demanded the name of the "high State Department official" whom McCarthy had accused in the Senate of exerting pressure to reinstate a discharged employe described as a notorious homosexual and security risk. The employe had been fired on February 16, 1946, and had been rehired on April 1, McCarthy said; the name was in the State Department files and could be obtained by the committee very easily—simply by sub-poenaing the records, as the Senate had instructed and authorized the committee to do.

Jabbing a finger at the witness, Tydings retorted: "You are in the position of being the man who occasioned this hearing, and so far as I am concerned in this committee you are going to get one of the most complete investigations ever given in the history of the republic, so far as my abilities permit." *

The wrangling grew heated, and Hickenlooper shouted protests against heckling the witness. McCarthy stuck doggedly to the read-ing of his statement. "I intend," he said, "to submit to the com-mittee information bearing upon the disloyalty, the bad security risks, in the State Department. Then it is up to the committee to investigate those particular cases."

"Give us the names," Tydings demanded repeatedly, but Mc-Carthy would not.

"The committee has been allowed, I believe, $25,000 or $50,000 to do that," he said. "I do not have the investigative staff, I do not have access to the files, to make any complete investigation and make any formal charges. All I intend to do . . . is to submit the evidence I have gathered."

Senator Lodge insisted that McCarthy be allowed to develop his case in his own way. "I think to interrupt the witness every time and break up his continuity and destroy the flow of his argument, the way we are doing, is not the right procedure," he protested. "For some reason that has not been made clear to me, whether it

---

* McCarthy had had relayed to him Tydings' reported boast: "Let me have McCarthy for three days in public hearings and he will never show his face in the Senate again!"

is to rattle or whether it is to confuse, I don't know, we have an entirely different procedure here today. . . . I am objecting to the constant interruption of the witness so that he never gets a fair shake."

But the Democrats had determined that McCarthy was not to get a fair shake. In his first 250 minutes on the stand, he was allowed to read his statement only 17 minutes, and was interrupted 85 times. As Christopher Emmet would comment in the liberal Catholic weekly *Commonweal,* the investigation already had taken on the appearance of "an unequal contest between an enraged hick and an accomplished city slicker, with the latter, in the person of Tydings, getting the applause and the laughs."

Senator Green prodded: "Senator, there are two words in the English language—'yes' and 'no.' If you would use just one of them we could get along here. Do you have the names?" Tydings insisted that it was of the "highest importance" that the name of the "high State Department official" be divulged at once, so the department could deny him further access to classified information. To which Lodge retorted that since McCarthy's charge was already three weeks old, the department had had plenty of time to take action if it really cared to.

Slugging his way through his preliminary statement, at the critical point McCarthy stressed again that he thought it fairer to offer his evidence in closed sessions—and was answered sharply by Tydings that "if it is your desire to give [the names] in open session, that is your responsibility." McCarthy read on, and the names began to fall:

"Let us take the case of Dorothy Kenyon. This lady has been affiliated with at least twenty-eight Communist front organizations, all of which have been declared subversive by an official government agency."

Nine of the organizations had been cited by the Attorney General, he said, the rest by various state and national authorities. From his bulging briefcase he pulled a sheaf of photostated letterheads, reports, and newspaper clippings to support his charge; the file made an impressive display. He ticked off the organizations with which he said Miss Kenyon had been affiliated. One was the American Russian Institute, which was on the Attorney General's subversive list, and at this point McCarthy negligently brought in a celebrated name, doing it so casually that some reporters failed to catch it, and others thought they had misheard. He said, in his flat voice:

"Although I shall discuss the unusual affinity of Mr. Philip C. Jessup, of the State Department, for Communist causes, I think it pertinent to note that this gentleman, now formulating top-flight policy in the Far East affecting half the civilized world, was also a sponsor of the American Russian Institute."

At noon the hearing recessed until the next day, with McCarthy scarcely halfway through his statement. But the newspapers had their headlines; and so great was the ability of this terrierlike attacker to galvanize and excite the press, those headlines played up McCarthy. The *Washington Times-Herald* reported the whole hectic session under the screaming headline:

JESSUP PAL OF REDS—M'CARTHY

[II]

Miss Kenyon's name had drawn a blank in the packed caucus room. Although she was a former municipal judge of New York City, and had been an inveterate joiner of liberal and feminist causes, she was virtually unknown outside her own city. Her only association with the State Department had been as a delegate since 1947 to the United Nations Commission on the Status of Women. She immediately telegraphed to Senator Tydings, denouncing McCarthy as an "unmitigated liar" and a coward hiding behind senatorial immunity. She also demanded an opportunity to appear before the committee and "attack Senator McCarthy's outrageous and maliciously false charges against me." Tydings read her telegram into the record and announced that she would testify as soon as McCarthy finished his statement.* Whereupon the latter amplified his charges against Miss Kenyon. Particularly alarming, he said, was the fact that although she had belonged to or aided twenty-eight Communist fronts over the years, the State Department's security officers had never questioned her about them. He said that President Truman should call in the loyalty board

---

* Reporters in New York who hastened to interview Miss Kenyon were met with the blank response, "Who is McCarthy?" Television cameras were brought in to record her reaction; and in later years of her long and active career she would recall with amusement that at her first words the equipment blew out every fuse in the building.

members and find out why she had been given clearance sight unseen.

Snapped Tydings, "That is a speech, and not testimony." McCarthy struck back that the chair was constantly trying to throw him off his pace, and Senators Green and McMahon joined in, demanding the names of those "loyal Americans" in the State Department who, McCarthy said, were feeding him information.

"You are not fooling me!" Joe flashed defiantly, leaning across the table. "You want the information so that heads will fall in the State Department! I am surprised that this committee would become the tools of the State Department—not seeking the names of bad security risks, but seeking rather to find out the names of my informants so they can be kicked out of the State Department tomorrow!"

Senator McMahon, his face flushed and his knuckles white, thrust his bulk forward belligerently and rapped out, pounding the tabletop: "I am profoundly shocked by the irresponsible speech just made by the senator from Wisconsin! His imputation of any such motive is something I repudiate and denounce! It is unworthy of any senator of the United States! When you start making charges of that sort about me, you had better reflect on it, and more than once!"

"I have reflected!" McCarthy retorted, returning glare for glare. The crowd was tense, but the moment passed without blows being exchanged though the bitterness remained.

The battle went on for an hour, with McCarthy placing more names in the record, pulling their dossiers from his overflowing briefcase. To illustrate how Red fronts roped in fine, patriotic people to conceal their designs, he held up the letterhead of an organization of housewives which long since had been exposed as a Communist setup, on which appeared, listed as a "sponsor," the name of the wife of the Secretary of State, Dean Acheson.*

At the weekend the hearing was recessed with honors even: the Democrats were still convinced that McCarthy was bluffing, and the senator had not given way under fire.

On Monday the battle was resumed, with only slightly less acri-

---

* Swiftly interviewed at the State Department, Acheson acknowledged with a smile that several years before his wife had given $10 to a group of women shoppers interested in getting more for their money in the food markets, and that subsequently her name had been used without authorization as a "sponsor." He doubted that even Senator McCarthy would call his wife subversive.

mony. McCarthy produced four more names—Haldore Hanson, an administrator of the Point Four program of assistance to undeveloped nations; Stephen Brunauer, a scientist in Navy ordnance; his wife, Esther Calkin Brunauer, a longtime State Department employe; and Owen Lattimore, a professor and writer on Far Eastern topics. Lattimore, McCarthy called a "policy-making State Department attaché collaborating with those who have sworn to destroy this nation by force or violence." Hanson, he termed a man "with a mission to Communize the world," and in naming Brunauer, he called on the committee to subpoena the files of Navy Intelligence, the State Department, and the FBI, to determine whether or not Brunauer had been "a close friend of Noel Field, a known Communist, who recently and mysteriously disappeared behind the Iron Curtain."

At the noon recess McCarthy still had not finished; but he served notice that he would not appear at afternoon sessions. This was allowable under Senate practice. But the next morning he was back with more names, explaining that he was forced to go into details because over the weekend the State Department had been "screaming that I didn't present details." This day he ticked off the names of Gustavo Duran, whom he had already named in Wheeling; Dr. Harlow Shapley, Harvard astronomer; and Dr. Frederick Schuman, of Williams College; and the much investigated John Stewart Service.

The "Communist affiliations" of Service, a career diplomat for seventeen years, McCarthy said were "crystal clear. . . . I earnestly request that this committee ascertain immediately if Service was not considered a bad security risk by the loyalty [review] board* . . . in a post-audit decision handed down on March 3 of this year [a date only a little more than a week before]. I understand that the board returned the file of Mr. Service with the report that they did not feel they could give him clearance and requested that a new board be appointed for the consideration of his case."

Service, McCarthy contended, was "one of the small, potent group of 'untouchables' who year after year formulate and carry out plans for the State Department and its dealing with foreign nations, particularly in the Far East." He adverted to Service's ambiguous role in the *Amerasia* case, and indicated his own belief that Service should have been indicted and tried.

---

* A sort of higher court, which could overrule decisions of the departmental loyalty boards.

Immediately after McCarthy's statement, the State Department denied having any knowledge of the loyalty review board's supposed action on Service. Then at 3:30 P.M., three hours after Joe had left the stand, the department announced that the communication from the loyalty review board had just been received, and that it was dated March 14, that very day. The Service file, it was explained, had been sent to the review board in January of the previous year, and in compliance with the board's recommendation, Service had been ordered home at once to undergo further questioning. John Peurifoy angrily defended the accused man, saying:

"In the person of Jack Service we have an able, conscientious, and a demonstrably loyal foreign service officer . . . one of our outstanding experts on Far Eastern affairs. . . . As a result of Senator McCarthy's resuscitation of dead, discredited, disproven charges . . . Mr. Service finds his character once more called into question . . . and his brilliant career as a diplomat once more interrupted so that he can be defended, and can defend himself, against such baseless allegations all over again. . . . It's a shame and a disgrace. . . . The sympathy and good wishes of the entire department go out to them [Service and his family]."

McCarthy pounced on this as a virtual command to the department's loyalty board to clear Service before any evidence had been presented. "Can there be any doubt what action will be taken by the . . . board after this mandate from their boss that they give Service a complete and thorough whitewash?" he demanded bitterly. "This is the sort of thing that we know goes on behind closed doors, but this is the first time the department has had the effrontery to publicly tell the loyalty board how to prejudge the case before hearing the facts."

And he fired off a letter to Seth W. Richardson, the chairman of the review board, asking "how it could have taken eleven days for the [Service recommendation] to go the few blocks from your board to the State Department? Why did the executive secretary of your board attempt to mislead the public by publicly stating, 'I have never heard of the Service case'? What caused the thirteen-month delay in the audit [review] by your board in this case?"

These were embarrassing questions, and they indicated that McCarthy had inside sources of information. And many observers suspected that in Service the senator had found a vulnerable target, for the odor of *Amerasia* lingered.

[III]

But a stunning setback awaited McCarthy. Dorothy Kenyon appeared before the committee at an afternoon session, and in keeping with his announced intention, the senator was not present. Miss Kenyon proved to be a handsome, graying woman of sixty-two, dressed in black silk, and was only too happy to demonstrate that Joe McCarthy was a liar. She gave her background calmly, then submitted documentary evidence that, among other anti-Communist activities, in 1939 she had criticized Soviet Russia and the Stalin-Hitler pact, and as late as 1949 she had been denounced in Soviet propaganda for "irresponsible drivel" and "slandering the Soviet people." She described herself politically as "an independent, liberal, Rooseveltian Democrat," and conceded that her name might have been used, "even at times with my consent," in connection with organizations that later proved to be subversive, but which at the time seemed to her to be engaged in activities or dedicated to objectives that she "could and did approve." Questioned specifically about the groups named by McCarthy (he had named only twenty-four of the alleged twenty-eight), she said she had been affiliated with twelve, had withdrawn from four of these upon learning of their Communist complexion; two she denied ever having belonged to; and regarding the remainder she had no recollection. At present, she said, she was affiliated with none of them, and in fact many of them had been disbanded years ago.

The spectators plainly were moved by the witness's candor and sincerity. She confessed she was prone to error, but denied that she had ever thought or acted disloyally.

"With all the mistakes and errors of judgment which the best of us can and do commit only too frequently," she concluded, "I submit that the record proves without a question that I am a lover of democracy, of individual freedom, and of human rights for everybody; a battler, perhaps a little too much of a battler sometimes, for the rights of the little fellow who gets forgotten or frightened or shunned because of unpopular views. . . . The converse of these things—dictatorship, cruelty, oppression, and slavery—are to me intolerable. I cannot live in their air, I must fight back. This is perhaps not a very wise or prudent way to live, but it is my way. . . . There is not a Communist bone in my body!"

The audience burst into applause at the end of this emotional declaration of faith. Then Senator Hickenlooper put a few fumbling questions in cross-examination, winding up by asking her whether anybody at the State Department had ever questioned her about her association with so many dubious causes. "Never," was her answer. She did concede that in a recent speech she had said that the perjury trial of Alger Hiss was "a product of hysteria created by the House Committee on Un-American Activities," and she still held that opinion. She also had said, she testified, that "in the present temper of the country," she doubted that Hiss could get a fair trial.

Miss Kenyon was dismissed with a gallant avowal from Hickenlooper: so far as he was concerned, he said, there was not the slightest reason to believe that she was or had been "in any way subversive or disloyal."

The Democrats gloated over this "surrender" by their Republican colleague, but they had not fully gauged McCarthy's tenacity or resourcefulness. In the newspapers he was already a winner, as day after day his name appeared on the front pages. He had become big news; tourists recognized him as he hurried along the Capitol corridors. Paradoxically, elements of the press that liked him the least gave him the most telling display. The very vehemence of their revulsion played into his hands. When John Peurifoy issued almost daily bulletins repudiating McCarthy's charges, and the senator retorted in terms so crass as to make a diplomat shudder, publications disliking Joe could not forbear printing his "gutter talk." They thought that the very vulgarity of his language would discredit him with the public; unfortunately for them, Joe's "straight talk," as his supporters construed his stinging phrases, served to build him up.

An example of this was McCarthy's commiseration with Peurifoy over having to act, Joe said, as Acheson's "front and shield." He wondered when the Secretary of State would have "the guts to stand up and say, 'This is my baby,' take the blame for this sorry situation, and quit making a goat of young Peurifoy, who has to do as he is told or lose his job."

Papers hostile to Joe printed every word of this abrasively coarse defiance; but for every reader who was genuinely distressed, many more were attracted to this man who dared to speak up in everyday language and refused to be overawed by the "cookie pushers."

[IV]

Before the Tydings Committee, things were not going well for Joe. Not yet an experienced controversialist, he fell into traps set by his opponents. Pursuant to the policy announced by Tydings at the outset, all persons named by McCarthy were invited to appear in their own defense if they cared to, and six did, entering positive denials; others filed rebuttal statements that were placed in the record. Every consideration was shown for those who testified. They were allowed to consult counsel without limitation, and could call supporting witnesses. The committee offered to bring in by subpoena any witnesses reluctant to appear, and no step was omitted that might help McCarthy's targets to vindicate themselves.

The senator on his side could only refer the investigation to the State Department's files for substantiating evidence. It was all there, he maintained—the full facts on every case he had brought forward; subpoena these and it would all be found. But to subpoena the files would invite open conflict with the executive branch, for those files had been sealed from congressional inspection by Presidential directive, and the Democratic majority on the Tydings Committee wanted no tug of war with the White House—especially while they were engaged, in effect, in vindicating the honor of the administration.

Haldore Hanson appeared and swore that he was no Communist, never had been a Communist, and resented this attack on his loyalty. "Senator McCarthy," he said, "produced no new facts before this committee which were not available to [FBI] interrogators. In fact, he produced nothing that I hadn't put in a public library."

Although McCarthy had said nothing about Philip Jessup except that he seemed to have an "unusual affinity" for Communist causes, the roving ambassador had flown back from Pakistan to face the committee. The public was familiar with Jessup's name, for as United States representative in the United Nations he had been a trial to the Russians, and he had been one of the prominent Americans who testified as character witness for Alger Hiss. Most of these witnesses had testified only in Hiss's first trial; Jessup had repeated his testimony in the second trial.

Before the committee he denied with quiet dignity that he was a Communist or Communist sympathizer. He offered letters from Generals Marshall and Eisenhower praising him in terms of the utmost esteem. The letters were read into the record by Tydings and were picked up by the press. Jessup pointed out that while he was in the Far East he had been attacked simultaneously by *Izvestia* and Senator McCarthy, and commented that "anyone who believes in the concept of guilt by association might draw some startling conclusions from this fact."

Under tactful questioning he maintained that "McCarthy's innuendoes" were doing the nation a disservice by shaking the faith of foreign governments in our representatives abroad. Doubts had been raised that Americans were "really united in combatting Communism," he said, and the senator's reckless actions were "smirching" the good name of the United States.

McCarthy, who was present during this testimony, requested permission to cross-examine the witness, but was refused, Tydings ruling that it would not be fair because Jessup had not been present to cross-examine McCarthy when he first introduced the ambassador's name. Protesting against this ruling, McCarthy fed a few questions to Senator Hickenlooper, who put them to the witness; but Jessup fielded these to the contentment of the majority. Hickenlooper was not equipped to press the issue, and the examination soon ended.

With a cordial handclasp, Senator McMahon assured Jessup that he added his personal endorsement to those of the two generals. "You are entitled to the thanks of all our people for the magnificent job you have done," he told Jessup warmly.

So far in the parade of witnesses McCarthy had shown up poorly; but though groggy from the punishment, he kept punching. He certainly had not flushed out one provable, identifiable, or self-confessed "card-carrying Communist," and if the press was to be believed, the outlook was dark for Joe. Yet, oddly, across the nation interest in the fracas appeared to be mounting instead of diminishing. *Time* magazine assured its million and a half subscribers that "loud-mouthed Joe McCarthy" was making "a wretched burlesque of the serious and necessary business of loyalty checking," although he had "probably damaged no reputations permanently except his own."

But there appeared to be some readers of *Time* who did not agree with this conclusion. Among them was Joe McCarthy.

"Stand or Fall"

To censure, to condemn, to disapprove is the birthright of every freeborn American, and Joe's critics were availing themselves of this prerogative to the fullest extent. During the first month of the protracted Tydings hearings, Senator McCarthy and his charges preempted the front pages of the nation's daily newspapers more than twenty times, and nearly always invidiously. The periodical press was just as liberal in allotting space to the "bull-shouldered" disrupter of Senate decorum and his obstreperous tactics. Joe was not spared. The *New Republic* deplored his "reckless disregard for truth" as a measure of the "decline in our common sense and respect for human dignity," and termed his failure to sit through Miss Kenyon's "brilliant reply" one of the "most contemptible acts in a long time." The voters of Wisconsin the *New Republic* reprobated for "the shame they have brought on their state and their government."

The Nation, determined to extract some consolation from the lamentable spectacle, took comfort in reflecting that Joe's charges were "so flimsy" and his conduct "so shabby" that he had weakened the political value of "the smear technique," and was actually debasing the currency of blackguardism.

The politicians were more guarded in their pronouncements. The Democrats in Congress generally avoided crying out too loudly against McCarthy, although they damned him heartily in private, fearing that another "red herring" blunder might finish their chances in the coming election. The Republicans were ready to encourage Joe from the sidelines, but preferred not to get involved in the fight directly. (Senator Taft was rumored to have counseled McCarthy unofficially to keep pitching, to "try one case after another, because if one doesn't stick the next one may," but Taft denied this.) Not a few Republican senators were convinced that McCarthy was right about the State Department, but they doubted that he could prove it. Should he be discredited, they wished to steer clear of the wreckage. On the other hand, if he could make his charges stick, the party would gladly claim him for its own.

At least one congressman, Representative Eugene Cox, a Georgia Democrat, was revolted by such pusillanimous pussyfooting and said so. In the House he expressed his "supremest contempt for the timidity or cowardice, or both, which are now operating to restrain the people from coming to Senator McCarthy's aid." The senator, Cox declared, was merely trying to "put out of the State Department the friends of Stalin, and every informed person in Washington" believed such were there. "God help our country if public opinion permits the appeasers of Russia to crucify a man who has manifested the loyalty and decency to speak up for America!"

Representative Clarence J. Brown, an Ohio Republican, had qualms. Although the State Department now admitted that some of its officials might have "played footsie with fellow travelers" in the past, he pointed out, it still was accepting their unsupported word that they had changed their ways. He asked reasonably, "Would you trust your money to a bank whose directors were reformed embezzlers?"

One answer to that question appeared in the flood of mail that daily inundated McCarthy's office. The very newspapers that carried Representative Cox's speech published a photograph of Joe looking over letters piled high on his desk. Most contained fervent pleas to keep up the fight. Although at first there had been the customary influx of "crackpots and neurotics," his staff reported, the quality of the mail had improved very quickly, and now the favorable reaction was from solid citizens—teachers, farmers, businessmen, and especially war veterans. Often a donation to "help the cause" was enclosed, a dollar bill, perhaps, or a small check.

Backed by this evidence that he did not lack popular support, McCarthy defiantly doubled his bets, informing the Tydings Committee that he would give them the name of the "top Russian espionage agent" in the United States—a man who, he said, was currently connected with the State Department.

"The man I am talking about was Hiss' onetime boss in the espionage ring," he said earnestly. "He has a desk in the State Department and has access to the files—or at least he did until four or five weeks ago. I am perfectly willing to stand or fall on this one. If I am shown to be wrong on this, I think the subcommittee will be justified in not taking my other cases too seriously. If they find I am one hundred percent right—as they will—it should convince them of the seriousness of the situation."

This set off repercussions all over Washington. Was Joe bluffing, or did he hold the winning ace? In a closed session he gave the committee the name of the man and said that proof of his accusation could be found in the confidential files of the FBI and the State Department. And he challenged President Truman to "put up or shut up" on releasing those files.

Tydings declined to reveal the identity of McCarthy's target, but in Washington "secret" information leaks as readily as water through a sieve, and within two days it became known that the man was Owen Lattimore, head of the Walter Hines Page School of International Relations at Johns Hopkins University in Baltimore. Drew Pearson, a Washington news columnist, divulged the name over the radio.

The situation was critical for the administration. If McCarthy really had incriminating evidence, another "Hiss—red herring" sensation might be in the making, the scandal of which would probably cost the Democrats control of the government. Truman tried to skirt around the danger by secretly permitting the Tydings group to examine an FBI summary of its file on Lattimore, although stipulating that the action should not be construed as setting a precedent. Elaborate precautions were imposed, and only the summary or digest of the "raw" file was shown, not the complete dossier. The President also authorized FBI chief J. Edgar Hoover to testify on the subject publicly. This was an extraordinary step, which indicated the seriousness the administration attached to this attack.

The examination of the summary was carried out by Senators Tydings, McMahon, Green, and Lodge in the office of Attorney General Howard McGrath. One member of the committee, Senator Hickenlooper, was absent, on a visit to his home state. Then Hoover, in an almost unprecedented appearance as a witness, testified before the committee. He said that opening the bureau's "raw" files would destroy the agency's effectiveness completely; but he stated that the complete file on Lattimore did not contain proof of McCarthy's assertion.

Over the radio, then, Senator Tydings urged anyone who knew where Lattimore had a desk in the State Department to speak up, because the department knew nothing about it.

At the same time, the most powerful broadside yet aimed at the rampaging "Wisconsinner" was fired by the elder statesman and former cabinet member, Henry L. Stimson. In a letter to *The New York Times,* Stimson asserted that McCarthy's real motive was not "to get rid of Communists in the State Department; he is hoping against hope he will find some. . . . No matter what else may occur, the present charges have already spattered mud upon individuals of the highest integrity, and in the present state of the world the denial cannot always overtake the accusation. . . . Indiscriminate accusations of this sort . . . damage the innocent, and they help protect the guilty. For if the accuser is so stupid as to connect a man like Ambassador Jessup with Communists, are not all such accusations made suspect? . . . This is no time to let the noisy antics of a few affect the steady purpose of our country or distract our leaders from their proper course. This is rather a time for stern rebuke of such antics."

This honestly indignant but still somewhat *ex parte* protest by a man who himself had once headed the Department of State reminded some people unpleasantly of those floods of letters from prominent Americans that had been rained on Alger Hiss, expressing unbounded confidence in his innocence, before the evidence was in, and McCarthy's mail reflected this suspicion. Nevertheless, Stimson's letter was a severe blow, jubilantly hailed by the senator's opponents.

Printed in the *Times* side by side with Stimson's rebuke was a report by Anne O'Hare McCormick, the paper's chief writer on international affairs, on the decline of American prestige abroad during recent weeks, thanks to the McCarthy sideshow.

"Not since the war has American leadership been so widely questioned by our friends," this writer found. "Reports and press comments from every country in Western Europe show that we are losing influence. The current attacks upon our Secretary of State and the Department of State shock and bewilder our allies. The charges of disloyalty batted around pell-mell in Congress, and the time and attention they receive from Congress and the public, throw doubt upon the seriousness and reliability of our foreign policy." And so the jeremiad continued to the foot of the page.

McCarthy was not impressed. "I am going to prove everything I said, right down the line," he insisted with that air of cheerful stubbornness that had once led a friend to observe that the surest way to get Joe McCarthy to tackle a hopeless job was to tell him he would be crazy to try it.

Retiring to a hotel with several members of his staff, two stenographers, Charles Kersten, a former Milwaukee congressman, and Freda Utley, a New York schoolteacher and former Communist, he flung off his coat, yanked open his collar, rolled up his sleeves, and flanked by stacks of documents and plates of sandwiches, plunged into a super-super-cram session.

[II]

Meanwhile, the man who a few days before had been totally unknown to the general public, but whose name now had been scrawled indelibly on a page of history—Owen Lattimore *—was on his way back from Afghanistan, where he had gone on a United Nations mission. As jaunty and cocksure as his accuser, he had cabled at first word of his involvement: MC CARTHY'S OFF RECORD RANTINGS PURE MOONSHINE. DELIGHTED HIS WHOLE CASE RESTS ON ME AS THIS MEANS HE WILL FALL FLAT ON HIS FACE. . . . WILL BE HOME IN A FEW DAYS.

And at each halt during his progress home he contributed another scathing comment. In London, after calling McCarthy an obvious lunatic and his charges "unmitigated lies," he added that "nevertheless one does not like to be splattered with mud even by a madman." And on landing at New York he termed McCarthy a "base and miserable creature," a "hit-and-run politician," who hurled accusations "falsely, irresponsibly, and libelously." He suggested that the senator merited being decorated by Stalin for "telling the kind of lies about the United States that Russian propagandists couldn't invent."

That was Harry Truman's feeling, too. Vacationing in Key West, the President kept in daily consultation by telephone with the Attorney General and Senator Tydings about "this man McCarthy"; but despite Tydings' pleas, the President refused to open State Department or FBI files generally to the committee. And when

---

* Often called, in print and orally, Owen J. Lattimore, although he protested he had no middle name or initial.

Tydings finally did subpoena the department's files, Secretary Acheson ignored the summons.

Adding to the tension was the testimony offered by two witnesses before the Tydings group, who were called to throw light on the operations of the loyalty boards. One witness was the chairman of the State Department's own loyalty screening board, General Conrad Snow; the second was the chairman of the loyalty review board, Seth Richardson. Richardson testified that his board had conducted 10,000 full-field investigations over a period of three years, without turning up one instance of spying. Reminded of the Judith Coplon case, Richardson said the Justice Department had handled that one. General Snow testified to the same effect.

Which led President Truman to pooh-pooh that all the ruckus was part of a Republican plot to "get" Dean Acheson, led by Senators McCarthy, Wherry, and Bridges. Those three, he said, were "the Kremlin's biggest assets" in the cold war.

Retorted Senator Taft, "The greatest Kremlin asset in our history has been the pro-Communist group in the State Department who surrendered to every demand of Russia at Yalta and Potsdam, and promoted at every opportunity the Communist cause in China, until today communism threatens to take over all of Asia." Senator Wherry snapped that President Truman was "mighty bold in accusing us after placing the loyalty files under lock and key." And Senator Homer Ferguson of Michigan commented on the secrecy order as saying in effect that "five senators . . . are not as competent to look at the files as twenty-three appointive members of a loyalty board."

Joining in the tumult, in the House of Representatives Franklin D. Roosevelt, Jr., stigmatized McCarthy's slur on Jessup as "unfair, unjust, and un-American," while in a letter to Senator Tydings, Haldore Hanson angrily informed the committee that since he had been singled out by McCarthy, he and his family had been bedeviled by their neighbors and threatened by telephone. He dared McCarthy to repeat his charges off the Senate floor and promised to sue for libel if he did. Tydings made the letter public and announced that Hanson had been cleared by the State Department three times after a "complete loyalty and security check."

At the same time Mrs. Brunauer reported that she had been threatened by telephone callers at all hours of the night and day. And the bitter commotion was carried into the Senate when Senator

Malone accused Tydings of according "kid-glove treatment" to witnesses adverse to McCarthy, and ignoring the Senate's mandate to "investigate Communist infiltration of the State Department." Instead, he charged, they seemed to be interested in nothing but "coddling and protecting" persons whose connections gave rise to "serious doubts" about their loyalty. Capitol attendants wondered what had happened to the tradition of mutual courtesy that had prevailed among senators for so long.

[III]

Armed with fresh documentation, McCarthy alerted the press that he was going to take the Senate floor, and at the same time requested J. Edgar Hoover to have an FBI agent on hand to whom he might hand some documents on the spot.

On the appointed day, when the signal was flashed that McCarthy was about to speak, the Senate galleries filled with a rush. Members of the House came over from their wing to witness the performance. The air was tense with expectancy.

Right on time, McCarthy bustled in, followed by attendants carrying piles of papers. These they stacked on two desks and chairs; conspicuous among them was the senator's open briefcase, crammed with photostats.

At 2:06 P.M., McCarthy started to speak, and he continued without a break until 6:18. Now and then he paused to sip cough medicine sent over from the Navy hospital, or to gulp a glass of milk. And the burden of his speech was that Owen Lattimore had influenced United States foreign policy disastrously in the past, and was influencing it still—always in favor of Soviet Russia. From Lattimore's prolific writings he quoted passages which proved, he contended, that the professor had consistently followed the Communist party line. He said he could produce a witness, a person formerly high up in the Communist ranks, who would testify that Lattimore was known to him to be a member of the party. Harking back to the *Amerasia* scandal, the senator flourished an affidavit (which he said he was giving to the FBI) stating that "the night before John S. Service, Lieutenant Andrew Roth, and four co-defendants in the *Amerasia* case were arrested, this man was at the home of Lattimore. . . . He states that Roth, Lattimore, and Service spent a great deal of time by themselves, discussing certain papers or manuscripts." (McCarthy did not read the affidavit, but explained later that his informant had sworn that the papers being examined were classified government documents.)

Next McCarthy read from a letter written by Lattimore, when he was with the Office of War Information during the war, to Joseph Barnes, an OWI official, which the senator said amounted to instructing Barnes to employ only Chinese with Communist sympathies.

He presented another affidavit, by a former general in Red Army Intelligence, stating that the affiant had been told in Moscow that Lattimore was helping the Soviets.

He cited a trip Lattimore had made to farthest-north Point Barrow, Alaska, on which he had carried two cameras and had taken photographs; also that Lattimore's home contained a darkroom. And he went into the tangled background and affiliations of the Institute of Pacific Relations during the period when Lattimore was editing the institute's periodical, *Pacific Affairs.*

On one point McCarthy did backtrack. "I may have perhaps placed too much stress on the question of whether or not he [Lattimore] has been an espionage agent," he confessed; what really mattered was the fact that Lattimore had served as a "chief architect of our Far Eastern policy." For the time being, he added, any question of "membership in the Communist party or participation in espionage" was immaterial, for on his general charge he stood firm. And he would not, despite challenges from the Democratic side, reveal the sources of his information. On the contrary, he served notice that "regardless of whether any senator may disagree with me, that is the procedure which I intend to follow."

At one point McCarthy offered to let any interested senator read his documents, but when Senator Lehman stepped across the aisle to take the paper McCarthy was waving, Joe snatched it back. For a moment the two men stood eyeing each other; then McCarthy, with his odd, high-pitched titter (a "strange, rather terrifying giggle," one critic described it), said, "Go back to your seat, old man." * As Lehman waddled back to his seat, Stewart Alsop, sitting in the press gallery, whispered to his wife, "There goes the end of the republic!"

---

* Although the words do not appear in the *Congressional Record,* newsmen stated that they heard them spoken.

Throughout McCarthy's tirade, the Democratic leaders of the Senate sat mute. Not once was any rebuttal attempted. The public galleries noisily applauded McCarthy time and again, and his Republican colleagues let him run on. Plainly he was making an impression, and at the close even so conservative and unexcitable a senator as Saltonstall of Massachusetts told Joe, "This is terrible! I really am worried!"

The *New Republic*'s Washington reporter was impressed, also, but drew different conclusions. McCarthy, this observer felt, was a new phenomenon, "the most formidable figure to hit the Senate since Huey Long. . . . Coolly calculating, fully aware of what he is doing, gambling for the highest stakes, bold and daring and elusive and slippery . . . McCarthy is as hard to catch as a mist— a mist that carries lethal contagion."

So the stage was set for a confrontation between the senator and the professor, McCarthy and Lattimore.

A Paladin! A Paladin!

To McCarthy's enemies, and they were many, the unnerving aspect of this novel phenomenon was that, although batted down again and again, Joe refused to stay flattened. So far the consensus was that his attack had fizzled badly, although there was some suspicion that in Lattimore he might have hit upon a valid case. His announced willingness to "stand or fall on this one" was not taken lightly, and the high-ceilinged caucus room was filled with a select audience on April 6, when the confrontation was to take place.

The setting bespoke the importance attached to this meeting between the embattled senator and the peppery professor. The cream of the political and academic worlds was present, admission being by card only, and the customary throng of students and tourists being turned away. The crowd was well-dressed, generally middle-aged, and conscious of the searching eyes of the television cameras. The ladies wore their best hats and brightest smiles, and the men assumed appropriate expressions of dignified detachment. The press table overflowed. In a row facing the witness chair were seated all five members of the subcommittee. This in itself was unusual, for Lodge had attended few sessions, and Senator Hickenlooper had missed several while campaigning in Iowa. The three Democrats, on the contrary, had been assiduous in attendance.

McCarthy entered and took a seat directly behind the committee, facing the witness chair. His thinning hair glistened under the lights, and his swarthy jowls justified the quip of one wit that they always looked "several hours beyond the five o'clock shadow." His lips were set tightly, but his manner radiated confidence as he wisecracked with the reporters.

Opposite him sat his adversary, Owen Lattimore, slight, schoolmasterish, with sandy hair and mustache and receding brow, a little owl-like behind his spectacles. His manner was self-assured, a little supercilious; apparently he felt quite capable of knocking down an opponent of McCarthy's mental attainments.

Both fighters were entering the ring with several strikes against them. McCarthy's disadvantages were his failure thus far to make good on a single charge, his shifting and weaving under fire, and the astonishing sloppiness of his "homework," his research. Accuracy was not in him, and he constantly drifted off into inflated generalizations and flights of hyperbole. One critic (Arthur Krock, in *The New York Times*) had commented that "Mr. McCarthy would have many more defenders if he had not discredited whatever case he may have by trying to stretch his indictments to dimensions they emphatically have failed to reach."

Not that McCarthy was devoid of defenders. In the Senate, Senator H. Alexander Smith of New Jersey had declared that McCarthy was simply doing his "obvious duty" and had begged him not to be deflected from it. Senator Taft also had approved McCarthy's pertinacity in hammering home his accusations, and Taft's reputation made ridiculous any suggestion that he would employ or condone character assassination. In McCarthy's favor, also, were the letters and telegrams that continued to pour into the Capitol, mirroring the deep concern of a wide section of the voters, and their feeling that all was not well in the State Department especially.

The strikes against Lattimore were more tenuous and intangible. They grew out of his record of activities, about which the public at this time knew little. His had been a long career as a political journalist of some ambiguity. He was forty-nine, the son of a schoolteacher. He had grown up in China, a land he had come to know intimately, having fraternized with Uzbek traders and Mongolian camel drivers. He had written eleven books and hundreds of articles on Far Eastern topics. His books, while unofficial, had been considered almost "must" reading in the State Department; consequently Lattimore's influence in that quarter was understood to have been extensive. He had played a part in the downfall of Chiang Kai-shek, having served as a political adviser to Chiang during World War II. Becoming disillusioned with the Kuomintang (Chiang's Nationalists), he had taken to calling the Nationalists the "war party" and the Communists the "peace party" and had argued for an accommodation with the Reds. He had inveighed against the inefficiency and corruption of Chiang's regime and in subtle ways apparently had helped to smooth the way for the Communists' eventual triumph. All this, however, even when viewed in the least creditable light, added up to far less than "espionage agent" or even "bad security risk." Also, Lattimore was not employed by the State Department at all, but by Johns Hopkins University.

Upon reaching Washington, he had told reporters at the airport:

"I am not and never have been a Communist, a member of the party or a Communist sympathizer, or affiliated or associated with the Communist party. I have never advocated or supported the cause of communism, either within the United States, in China, in the Far East, or anywhere in the world. The fact of the matter is that I and my writings have been denounced by Soviet, Mongol, Japanese, and Chinese writers, as well as [here his voice grew acidulous] some intemperate Americans. A Soviet publication recently called me a 'learned lackey of imperialism.' I am advised that at least one of my books has been banned in the Soviet Union. Others have been honored by typical Communist denunciations. If anybody has sworn that I have been or am a member of the Communist party he is a perjurer."

That was categorical enough. Now, as he stepped to the witness chair in the suddenly hushed caucus room, he was to repeat his protestations under oath—with the possibility of a perjury prosecution hanging on his words.

[II]

At a nod from the chairman, the witness began to read a preliminary statement. It ran to forty-two pages. Now and then he glanced up from the text, which he knew almost by heart, and later would state that he had noticed one thing quickly—that Senator McCarthy could not look a man in the eye.*

Lattimore's statement was prolix, but closely reasoned; it had been put together largely with the help of his attorney, Abe Fortas. McCarthy listened impassively, allowing himself an occasional in-

* This would conflict strikingly with the impression of others who faced Senator McCarthy under similar circumstances, and who spoke of the senator's baleful glare as a he ground down a witness. The truth may be that McCarthy did have a habit, acquired on the bench and common to not a few judges, of letting his glance stray toward the ceiling or a far corner of the room while listening to a prolix witness or a prosy counsel.

dulgent smile as the professor tore into him with sarcasm, defiance, and righteous wrath, plentifully studded with invective. He apologized for not knowing just what he was accused of, since McCarthy had demoted him successively from "master spy" to "chief architect" to "bad security risk"; this was distressing to a man who liked to be precise. The senator's accusations were repelled *in toto* as "base and contemptuous lies," the net effect of which had been to impair the government's effectiveness in dealing with its friends and allies, and to render the United States "an object of suspicion in the eyes of the anti-Communist world, and undoubtedly the laughing-stock of the Communist governments."

"Gentlemen," Lattimore lectured his auditors (the classroom manner often peeked through), "I speak to you as a private citizen. I owe no obligation to anyone except my country and my conscience. I have spent my life in the study of the problems of the Far East and . . . in writing about those problems as I saw them."

That did not imply disloyalty, and errors of judgment, if such were made, did not constitute treason. The witness poured scorn on the apparent source of McCarthy's allegations—the so-called "China lobby." This loose aggregation of apologists for the Chiang regime had drawn the special hatred of American liberals and the morbid detestation of the Communists. Depicting McCarthy as the "willing tool" of the "China lobby," Lattimore traced the senator's information to mixed Chinese and Russian sources—"or perhaps I should say that some of his exotic material on Mongolia appears to trace back to some Russian sources of distinctly low caliber."

The tone of sarcasm and irony was pronounced. It was "the learned senator," from whose lips issued "sound and fury"; "absurd cloak-and-dagger yarns"; and "these preposterous and villainous names that have been uttered by Senator McCarthy." The reader's voice took on stridency in the repeated allusions to the "China lobby," described by Lattimore as a "bitter and implacable group of people" whose methods were "to intimidate persons like me and even officials of the United States government from expressing views that are contrary to their own. Their weapon of intimidation is McCarthy's machinegun."

He confessed that he had derived "a certain amount of wry amusement" from the fact that some of these "China lobby fanatics" were ex-Communists. "Perhaps that status gives them a special right to criticize those of us who happen not to be Communists, ex or otherwise. Certainly it provides them with ideal training and unique skill for the kind of campaign vilification and distortion that the so-called 'China lobby' is conducting through the instrumentality of the senator from Wisconsin.

"I am not and never have been a member of the Communist party," the witness read on, finally coming to the crux of the statement. "I have never been affiliated or associated with the Communist party. I have never believed in the principles of communism nor subscribed to nor advocated the Communist or Soviet form of government either within the United States, in China, in the Far East, or anywhere in the world. I have never consciously or deliberately advocated or participated in promoting the cause of communism anywhere in the world."

Other explicit refutations of allegations by McCarthy were heaped up. The charge that the Institute of Pacific Relations was an instrument of Soviet intelligence was called absurd, considering that its current chairman was Gerard Swope, former head of General Electric, and trustees or distinguished members included General Marshall, Sumner Welles, Ray Lyman Wilbur, Robert Gordon Sproul—the illustrious names rolled out in a stream, and for good measure the witness threw in letters commending him, written by Nelson T. Johnson, former ambassador to China; Demaree Bess, associate editor of *The Saturday Evening Post;* and Generalissimo Chiang Kai-shek.

It was a brilliant exercise in the tactic of "innocence by association."

Turning then to McCarthy's innuendo of "guilt by association" in linking Lattimore to two of the men arrested in the *Amerasia* case—Service and Roth—the witness said that, yes, those men had been at his home three days before their arrest; but the purpose of their being there had not been to look over classified documents, but to join in a barbecue picnic in the Lattimores' backyard. There had been other guests, two Johns Hopkins professors and their wives and children, and the time had been passed in cooking hamburgers over an open fire. As for the "classified papers" so suspiciously mentioned by McCarthy's informer, they were the galley proofs of a forthcoming book by Roth, entitled *Dilemma in Japan,* the material for which had all been cleared by Navy security officers.

Having hacked his way through the "jungle of McCarthy's

charges, allegations, and threats," Lattimore went on to analyze "the meaning of these vicious charges." In the foreground he saw "the unscrupulous ambitions of a shady politician willing to machinegun his way to the front pages of the newspapers, reckless of any damage to the reputations of innocent persons. . . . Senator McCarthy's characterization of my writings, his summaries and quotations, are sufficiently perverse and twisted to make any Communist critics green with envy."

A factor contributing to the current "hysteria" Lattimore described as the "spreading sense of uneasiness and fear" regarding unknown and mysterious Asia, an uneasiness for which he realized there was some justification. This vague apprehension (a feeling that "something must be terribly wrong there") had led, Lattimore contended, to "a growing, hysterical willingness" to find a scapegoat.

In what increasingly resembled a seminar lecture, the witness then reviewed recent events in China and gave his opinion that "we have failed" there. But he disclaimed responsibility for that failure; others must bear that blame: "Senator McCarthy does me the honor of saying that I am the architect of this policy which has failed. Let me point out that even if this were true, it would not be disloyalty. It would mean that I am a poor architect. The fact of the matter, however, is quite the contrary. The fact is I have never held a position in the United States government in which I could make policy. The fact is that I have been very little consulted by those who do make policy—before Pearl Harbor, during the war, or since the war. I think I can fairly claim—with great regret— that I am the least consulted man of all those who have a public reputation in this country as specialists on the Far East."

The classroom manner peeped out once more in the witness's peroration. With all solemnity he advised the attentive senators:

"I say to you, gentlemen, that the sure way to destroy freedom of speech and the free expression of ideas and views is to attach to that freedom the penalty of abuse and vilification. If the people of this country can differ with the so-called 'China lobby' or with Senator McCarthy only at the risk of the abuse to which I have been subjected, freedom will not long survive. . . . It is only from a diversity of views freely expressed and strongly advocated that sound policy is distilled. He who contributes to the destruction of this process is either a fool or an enemy of his country."

Then demonstrating that he was not afraid to look an opponent in the eye, Lattimore turned squarely toward the taut-lipped
McCarthy and said, "Let Senator McCarthy take note of this."

The audience burst into applause. And on that note the smiling
chairman rapped for a recess.

[III]

During the recess Lattimore was all but smothered with com-
pliments. Senator Tom Connally of Texas, chairman of the Foreign
Relations Committee, of which the Tydings group was a sub-
branch, wrung the gratified professor's hand, dilating bitterly upon
McCarthy's "conscienceless extremes." Other spectators poured out
expressions of admiration and relief that the revulsion against Joe
had found so able and fearless a voice. And their admiration was
increased at the afternoon session (attended by neither Senator
McCarthy nor Senator Lodge) when, under some perfunctory questioning by Senators Green and McMahon, and an inept cross-
examination conducted by Senator Hickenlooper (no match for
Lattimore's agility and expertise), the witness went over the entire
China policy controversy and pungently defended the State Department's course in Asia.

The hearing closed with an unexpected climax. For several days
Senator Tydings had been noticeably cheerful, without telling why.
When all the questions had been asked, he arose and with a trium-
phant smile addressed the witness:

"Dr. Lattimore, your case has been designated as the number
one case, finally, in the charges made by Senator McCarthy. You
have been called, substantially, I think, if not accurately quoting,
the top Red spy in America. We have been told that if we had
access to certain files that this will be shown. I think as chairman
of this committee that I owe it to you and to the country to tell
you that four of the five members of this committee, in the presence
of Mr. J. Edgar Hoover, the head of the FBI, had a complete summary of your file made available to them. Mr. Hoover himself
prepared those data. . . . And at the conclusion of the reading
of that summary, in great detail, it was the universal opinion of
all of the members of the committee present, and all others in the
room . . . that there was nothing in that file to show that you
were a Communist or had ever been a Communist, or that you

were in any way connected with any espionage information or charges; so that the FBI file puts you completely, up to this moment, at least, in the clear."

Excitement swept the room, and as Tydings declared the hearing adjourned his smile grew broader and broader.

When word of Tydings' statement reached McCarthy he shot back a reply:

"If Tydings said that, then he is not telling the truth. Period."

Then he took off for Passaic, New Jersey, to receive the national Americanism award of the Marine Corps League. And the *New Republic* jubilantly nominated the McCarthy show "The Greatest Flopperoo of All Time."

The Crisis Deepens

Instead of settling matters, Owen Lattimore's testimony stoked the fires of mutual crimination. William S. White, reporting from Washington to *The New York Times,* wrote that not since the war, "in this city of easy partisan angers and easy forgetfulness," had the actions of a single member of Congress—"in any way or on any subject"—created such profound bitterness. The paradox was that the cause of all the rancor was a "heavy-shouldered, black-browed man of forty," so eager to be liked that White pictured him as endowed with a smile which "even among politicians is extraordinarily ready"—a junior senator, who never had been and still was not admitted to his party's inner councils. The reason for his power over the emotions of others was an enigma. His own manner was not emotional at all; at hearings he appeared alone, earnest but cool, aided by no assistants except those in a clerical capacity. He ran a one-man show. Yet the mere mention of his name seemed to touch off headlines. And his fame was an overnight sensation. Six months, even a few weeks, before he might have said whatever he chose and the press would have overlooked him. Now his words and his very silences were the subject of heated debate. What had caused this change? The man's nature had not changed. The difference, of course, lay in the issue he had suddenly espoused. That issue had been building in the public mind, waiting for someone to present it with dramatic belligerence. This McCarthy had done, and the response, both for and against him personally, had been as violent as his own choice of words.

A storm had blown up over his selection by the Marine Corps League to receive its Americanism award. The judge advocate of the New York City branch of the league had denounced the action as "disgraceful and unauthorized," and had been in his turn disavowed and reprimanded by higher authority. At the convention in Passaic McCarthy was thunderously applauded when he repeated his attack on Jessup and Lattimore, charging that they had followed policies identical with those of the Communists; but he refrained from calling the two men Communists outright. Reverting to the taunts of Peurifoy and Lattimore that he was "weaseling," Joe said that he had done what he had promised to do, namely, repeated his attack outside the Senate, without benefit of immunity, and his words were libelous if they were not true; so let anybody who felt himself libeled sue. Nobody did.

One feature of Lattimore's excoriation had been the coining, or at least the "uttering" (the legal term for putting into circulation), of the word "McCarthyism" to describe everything about the Wisconsin senator that his critics abhorred.* "McCarthyism" covered a multitude of meanings. To anti-McCarthyites it connoted reckless accusation, "smearing," disregard for truth, lying, equivocation, "guilt by association," character assassination. To McCarthy the word was a badge of honor: "McCarthyism," he said, "is Americanism." His definition at least had the merit of being more concise.

[II]

During the weekend of McCarthy's Passaic triumph the air waves were rank with the controversy over the senator. Radios crackled and television sets glowed as verbal blows were traded in a round table of talk, which, like all round tables, had no start or middle or end. Tydings, Peurifoy, Lattimore, Hickenlooper, McCarthy himself—Republicans and Democrats—all were heard. Hickenlooper got in a swipe at Senator Tydings for the latter's sensational "clearance" of Lattimore. Hickenlooper had not been present when the other senators looked over the summary of Lattimore's FBI file; but the day after Tydings made his statement that the examination had cleared Lattimore ("up to this moment, at least") the Iowan read the summary and "entirely disagreed" with Tydings. He could find no warrant, he said, for a sweeping exoneration, and until the complete file was made available, he was withholding judgment.

* Who first used the word has been disputed. McCarthy said it was invented by the *Daily Worker*. However, Lattimore's appears to have been the first authenticated instance of its use, and it received immediate acceptance.

Then Senator Lodge, who had inspected the summary but had not been present when Tydings spoke, also made clear that there was no unanimity on the subject. Stressing that he had not been consulted about Tydings' statement, Lodge said he had reached "no final conclusions whatever on any phases of this investigation, and I certainly will not reach any until I have questioned a number of witnesses in executive session. When I do I shall announce them myself. No one is authorized to speak for me. I still believe the present procedure is very defective, and the sooner these proceedings are brought behind closed doors the better."

This reflected a growing feeling among many onlookers that the political overtones of the investigation were becoming more and more distinct and any impartial judgment less and less likely to be reached. Representative Richard Nixon called for turning over the inquiry to a nonpartisan commission to be appointed by the President; but Truman felt that such a move would be a tacit repudiation of the Democrats who were conducting the investigation. McCarthy said the President was "afraid" to open the State Department's confidential files even to members of his own party, and to reporters pictured his own position as analogous to that of a prosecutor confronted with a corpse (the China policy) and a man standing over it with a smoking gun. "The defendant says it was accidental, and the corpse can't be questioned. The issue is whether it was an accidental killing, or murder." That was all he was trying to find out, he said.

At the same time he gave Tydings the name of a witness whom he wished to have called to testify in regard to Lattimore's Communist connections. It speedily became known that this witness was Louis F. Budenz, former editor of the Communist party's newspaper, the *Daily Worker,* and a longtime informant and consultant to the FBI. Trusted and vouched for by that bureau, Budenz was corrosively detested by many liberals, as well as, naturally, by all true-blue (or true-red?) Communists.

The subpoena was issued, and at the same time the committee's counsel, Edward P. Morgan, demanded in writing that McCarthy submit within seven days "the names of any witnesses or any and all information you intend to present."

The Senator refused to be hurried. In a manner which some deemed gracious and others denounced as insolent, he replied that he would "continue to supply the committee with such information and the names of such witnesses as come to my attention." And when Tydings announced that the committee was going to look into matters beyond McCarthy's specific charges, Joe applauded the intention, although stressing that "I won't believe it until I see it. It's the first sign we've had that Tydings and McMahon are not dedicated to the proposition that the truth about Communists and perverts must not come out."

The fires of anticipation thus were kept blazing brightly during the few intervening days before Budenz was scheduled to appear. *Times* correspondent White reported that the coming session had aroused more feverish interest than any other event of recent years, and Senate attendants reported the demand for seats exceeded even the record set by the Pearl Harbor hearings in 1945.

In response to the identification of Budenz as McCarthy's "mystery witness," Lattimore, through his counsel, Fortas, had denied knowing Budenz or, "to the best of my knowledge," ever having met or been associated in any way with him.

Republican support seemed to be swinging behind McCarthy. Senator Taft again accused President Truman of libeling McCarthy by calling him a "Kremlin asset" and revived the President's unlucky use of "red herring" in the Hiss case. The Democrats, Taft charged, were simply trying McCarthy rather than carrying out the real purpose of the investigation. "Whether Senator McCarthy has legal evidence, whether he has overstated or understated his case, is of lesser importance," said Taft. "The question is whether the Communist influence in the State Department still exists."

Truman's scornful retort was that he didn't think it was possible to libel McCarthy. Senator Connally repelled as "base slander" the insinuation that the Democrats had caused China to fall to the Reds. And on another front Edward Barrett, Assistant Secretary of State, told a UNESCO group that Senator McCarthy had been guilty of "the most shockingly irresponsible performance," while the executive committee of another UNESCO commission voted a resolution commending Mrs. Brunauer for her "distinguished services" and calling the charges against her (none of which, so far as anybody knew, had been investigated yet) "wholly without foundation."

While this was going on, in a speech in New York, Methodist Bishop G. Bromley Oxnam joined in the clamor by denouncing "self-appointed vigilantes masquerading in patriotic robes" and "hysterical men whose political ambition causes them to label distinguished public servants as subversive." And Democrats and Republicans continued to argue the issues in radio forums, the Democrats sneering that McCarthy's charges were "old stuff," purely political, and the Republicans retorting that their opponents were trying to avoid looking into the facts by shouting "smear." Senator Hickenlooper was reported to be ready to resign from the investigating committee in disgust over its palpably partisan bias. Lodge brought out adroitly that Tydings, McMahon, and Hickenlooper all were up for reelection this year, and might be hunting campaign material.

The news magazines, meanwhile, added to the hubbub by a drum-fire of commentary, almost all derogatory to McCarthy. *The Nation* spoke of "the panting little demagogue from Wisconsin," and of Hickenlooper as "his slow-footed stooge." Lattimore's self-defense was lauded as "a magnificent performance," a fitting offset to the virtuoso feats of McCarthy himself on the Senate floor. But *The Nation* warned that it would not do "to let McCarthy squirm free"; his "shrill defiance" must be silenced permanently. Had he not proved himself to be "as crafty as a coyote, as dangerous as a trapped bear," and "an albatross around the neck of the Republican party?" It was all "a miserable and repulsive business"—but somehow the fascination remained.

The *New Republic* was slightly more hopeful; it had a hunch that the public was "getting sick of McCarthy." Of course, "McCarthyism" might outlive its originator, because its roots ran deep in the national fabric.

That McCarthy was exciting opposition even among his coreligionists was made plain by the *Catholic Review,* a publication sponsored by the Washington-Baltimore archdiocese, which called on the senator to "put up or shut up." This set off a whole new line of speculation over the sources and extent of McCarthy's support, as this was being manifested more and more abundantly by the mail reaching senatorial desks. So widely did the waves of rumor spread that in London *The Economist,* a publication enjoying a worldwide reputation for reliability, stated boldly that Senator McCarthy had thrown the United States into an uproar with his charges, "in quest of his consuming ambition—to be the first Catholic President of the United States." This pronouncement simply caused the political pots to boil more furiously, Senator Lucas pleading with Illinois audiences that "this is a time for all true Americans to put an end to partisan tactics," and Democratic National Chairman William M. Boyle, Jr., cautioning party leaders to refrain from making "intemperate replies" to attacks on the administration's foreign policy, that issue being much too touchy to be treated recklessly. Contrariwise, Senator Taft reminded his own constituents in Ohio that McCarthy had accused nobody publicly until he was forced to by the opposition's demands.

[III]

In the midst of this tumult, on the eve of Budenz's tensely awaited appearance, an event occurred that, while not directly connected with McCarthy or the current furor, revived at an inopportune moment old animosities and old bitterness: the United States Supreme Court denied a rehearing to Dalton Trumbo and John Howard Lawson, members of the "Hollywood Ten" convicted of contempt of Congress for refusing to answer questions regarding communism before the House Un-American Activities Committee. Since the other eight persons cited at the same time—Ring Lardner, Jr., Albert Maltz, Herbert Biberman, Alvah Bessie, Samuel Ornitz, Edward Dmytryk, Adrian Scott, and Lester Cole—had entered into a stipulation that their cases should be tried without a jury if Trumbo and Lawson lost their appeal, their conviction seemed assured.

In a blast of vituperation aimed at the Supreme Court the ten stated publicly:

"By this decision it has been announced that only those Americans will be safe from inquisition and intimidation who will crawl before men like J. Parnell Thomas, John Rankin, and Senator McCarthy." *

In a not dissimilar strain, the *New Republic* was speaking of McCarthy's "diabolism" and a "paranoia of fear" that was gripping the country, while Lattimore sounded a leitmotif that would recur again and again—a "reign of terror" was being imposed upon Americans by simple (but not simpleminded) Joe.

Lattimore had been warned by his counsel of the possible peril in which he stood the moment Tydings announced that Budenz

---

* Rankin and Thomas were former chairmen of the Un-American Activities Committee, the first a bigoted anti-Semite, and the second convicted of accepting kickbacks from his staff. Bracketing McCarthy with them was lowering him to the bottommost pit of damnation, from a Communist point of view.

would testify. The extent of the danger could not possibly be exaggerated, Fortas said bluntly, because McCarthy had gone "a long way out on a limb" and terrific political pressures were building up. "The report that Budenz will testify against you has shaken everyone in Washington," Lattimore quoted Fortas as saying; so what course should they adopt? Should they fall back on a carefully guarded statement which would reduce the chance of "entrapment by fake evidence"? Or should they meet the threat directly and fight it? By his own account, Lattimore replied that there must be no pussyfooting—"meet the thing head on and slug it out."

Well, that was McCarthy's way of fighting; he was satisfied. He realized that Budenz's testimony would be fateful for himself, and he had been careful to state publicly that he had never met Budenz, and did not know him, but did know substantially what he was expected to say. On his side, Budenz had disclaimed ever having seen or talked with McCarthy.

Counterattack

Thursday, April 10, was the day of the big encounter. Lattimore was the first of the principals to arrive. The caucus room was jammed, seven hundred people being crammed into space designed to hold three hundred. As he entered, Lattimore was greeted by a smattering of applause, noticeably not unanimous. He paused, smiling, and raised his clasped hands above his head, like a boxer entering the ring. Then he and his wife took seats in the front row. Directly before them was the witness chair. McCarthy came in and took a seat behind the committee table, facing the witness chair, and at 10:29 A.M., one minute before the scheduled opening time, Chairman Tydings slapped the table with a roll of papers to still the chittering audience, and Budenz entered. He strode at once to the witness chair, brushing Lattimore's sleeve as he passed. A hush fell over the room as the witness was sworn.

Who was this stocky, stolid-featured man in a rumpled double-breasted blue suit who began to speak rapidly in a high-pitched, emotionless voice with a nasal twang? His public reputation was immense. Born in Indianapolis fifty-eight years before, he had grown up in the Roman Catholic faith, but soon after graduation from law school he had married a divorcee and been excommunicated. Plunging into socialist and labor activities, he became a union organizer, well-known to the police of street-fighting details. In 1935, he had joined the Communist party. Rising through the ranks, he had achieved membership in the party's national committee, or "politburo," and finally had become managing editor of the *Daily Worker*. In that capacity he was necessarily privy to the party's secrets and thoroughly acquainted with its personnel. His job had required him to identify the party's friends and its foes, and to know the roles that each played. In 1945, he had broken

157

with communism, and now was an economics instructor in Fordham University, operated by the Jesuits in New York City.

Budenz had been prominently associated with several notorious anti-Communist cases. He had been one of those identifying Alger Hiss as a Communist. He had exposed Gerhart Eisler (who fled to East Germany) as the top Soviet espionage agent in the United States. He had been the government's chief witness in the trial and conviction of eleven Communist party leaders the year previous. In addition, he had testified for the FBI in numerous instances and had given the bureau a vast amount of data on Communist activities in the United States. The FBI vouched for his dependability, having established that on every point on which corroboration was possible, his word stood up. Obviously he was a witness well equipped to testify in such a case as the one before the Tydings committee; whatever his testimony, it would be hard to brush it aside.

[II]

First Budenz sketched his background and stated his qualifications as a onetime Communist functionary. He mentioned the Institute of Pacific Relations and described it as originally an independent study group, later infiltrated by Communists. There had been a Communist cell in the IPR, he said: "I knew of this in 1936 and from then on." The leaders of this cell, he said, were Philip Jaffe, the *Amerasia* editor, and Frederick Vanderbilt Field, millionaire great-great-grandson of Cornelius Vanderbilt, the founder of the fortune. Jaffe and Field, Budenz said positively, "to my knowledge are solely espionage agents. In this cell there was also Owen Lattimore."

At this statement a gasp swept the audience. The three wire-service correspondents leaped up and shoved and jostled their way to the door, and in seven hundred minds the headlines took shape:

LATTIMORE NAMED BY BUDENZ AS RED

Lattimore had been taking notes furiously, grimacing and pretending to whistle at some of Budenz's statements. Later he would say that at that instant he heard "the baying of the bloodhounds on the trail." He had noticed on entering the chamber a feeling of reserve and even hostility; with few exceptions, this crowd was cold, contrasting with the warmth and friendliness in the same room on the day he had testified. He thought he saw a clue in the presence of numerous priests, conspicuous by their black garments; also, the fact that the Daughters of the American Revolution were meeting that week in Washington explained to him the preponderance of middle-aged and elderly women of severe aspect.

Budenz had hardly begun. He went on to tell why he knew Lattimore was a Communist, although they had never met. As editor of the *Worker,* the witness explained, his duty had required him to "keep in his head" the names of perhaps a thousand persons, disclosure of whose connection with communism would destroy their usefulness to the party. These were not "small fry," but "large-sized individuals," whom the *Worker* was expected to treat with respect. Politburo instructions were transmitted in the form of "onionskin documents," sent to a mail drop, which the recipients were ordered to read, then tear into small pieces and flush down the toilet. In these instructions, Budenz went on evenly, "L or XL in Far Eastern affairs referred to Mr. Lattimore. I was so advised by Jack Stachel," the party's disciplinarian.

There definitely had been a Communist conspiracy to influnce United States policy toward China, the witness continued, and "Mr. Lattimore can be placed in that conspiracy." At a 1937 meeting of the politburo that he attended, Budenz said, Earl Browder, then head of the party but later expelled, had "commended Mr. Lattimore's zeal in seeing that Communists were placed as writers in *Pacific Affairs.* It was agreed that Mr. Lattimore should be given general direction of organizing the writers and influencing the writers in representing the Chinese Communists as 'agrarian reformers.' "

At a meeting of the politburo in 1943, Budenz went on, Field had reported that Lattimore had been advised by the party to change his line on China—to start representing Chiang as the head of "feudal China" and the Chinese Reds as the leaders of "democratic China." One result of this had been the planting in *Pacific Affairs* of a pro-Communist article by T. A. Bisson, who at one time had accompanied Lattimore on a trip to Yenan, in Red Chinese territory.

In 1944, when Lattimore, as chief of the Pacific division of the Office of War Information, was with Henry Wallace on a presidential mission to China, Stachel had come to the *Worker* office,

Budenz said, and "advised me to consider Owen Lattimore as a Communist. To me, that meant to treat as authoritative anything he said."

Under severe questioning by Tydings, and less vigorous grilling by the Republican senators, the witness admitted that he had never seen Lattimore, but had only been told that he was a Communist. But to Senator Green he added, "I had never seen Mr. Alger Hiss, either, but I knew he was a Communist and so testified." The lights seemed to glare angrily as he answered the questions in a carefully phrased monotone. No, he had no personal knowledge that Lattimore was a Communist, outside of what he had been told officially by party leaders; but he assured the senators that corroboration could be obtained if they would dig for it.

He could not, of his own knowledge, state that Lattimore's books peddled a pro-Communist line because he had read only one, and that one cursorily; but he had no doubt about what a careful analysis would reveal.

How about the fact that Lattimore had contributed money to the Finns during the Russo-Finnish war, and had supported the Marshall Plan, which was aimed at halting the advance of communism in Europe? Budenz explained that "concealed Communists" were given leeway in such matters, in order the better to disguise their real purposes. Similarly, the statement contained in a *Daily Worker* review of one of Lattimore's books that the author went "completely off the beam" in discussing social and economic evolution in China, Budenz said, was in line with the party's policy of promoting the works of their hidden friends by means of "faint damns." The *Worker,* he added, "knows very well that Lattimore in his position has to be with the capitalists."

The witness had alleged elsewhere that there were some four hundred "concealed Communists" active in the United States whom he could name but would not, because of their policy of "bleeding their betrayers white" with libel suits that they never hoped to win but used to destroy their accusers. For this reason, he said, he had recently taken Lattimore's name out of an interview that appeared in *Collier's* magazine. Also, although he had been feeding the FBI information on Communists for five years, he had mentioned Lattimore's name to the bureau for the first time a couple of days after the committee had been shown the summary of Lattimore's file. Why had he never mentioned him sooner? Because, he replied, he simply had not got around to him.

In regard to one of McCarthy's charges—that Lattimore was "the top Russian espionage agent in the United States"—Budenz stated: "To my knowledge, that statement is not technically accurate."

[III]

It was late afternoon when the witness concluded. His voice was husky from fatigue, and he leaned back in his chair wearily for a moment as the merciless TV lights flicked off. But soon they came on again for the testimony of a witness called on behalf of Lattimore, retired Brigadier General Elliott R. Thorpe, during World War II General Douglas MacArthur's chief of counterintelligence.

Thorpe told the committee that three times—in the 1930's, in 1944, and in 1947—he had investigated Owen Lattimore, and "never in my experience as an intelligence officer have I heard a man so frequently referred to as a Communist, with so little basis in fact." Lattimore's ability to spy for a foreign government—unless he had access to secret information, of which there was no evidence—General Thorpe rated as "so small as to be of no value." Finally, he went on record as believing that the professor was entirely loyal and "would always act as a loyal American citizen."

When Thorpe stepped down, Abe Fortas tried hard to introduce an affidavit by Bella V. Dodd, an ex-Communist then practicing law in New York City, which he said "struck materially" at Budenz's testimony, but the chair declined to receive the document at that time. Thereupon Fortas gave it to the press. Its most pertinent portion stated that although Mrs. Dodd and Budenz had served on the party's national committee at the same time, she had "never met Owen Lattimore" and had never heard of him until the present controversy arose. "In all my association with the Communist party I never heard his name mentioned by party leaders or friends of the party as a party member or a friend of the party," read this declaration.

So ended a long day of heat, glare, and tension. As Lattimore slowly worked his way toward the exit there was no applause, and among those around him smiles were few.

McCarthy had remained on hand throughout. He was bubbling with confidence as he bounded off to address the convention of the American Society of Newspaper Editors.

There he appeared in fine form. Taking a fresh swing at his detractors, he castigated the State Department's repeated clearances of John Service as "almost a deliberate mischievous playing with American security." He bore down on former Secretary of State General Marshall as "a pathetic thing . . . totally unfitted for a cabinet position," whom it had been "almost a crime" to place in charge of "persons like Service and Lattimore" when the fate of China was in the balance. He told the assembled editors, representing the elite of the nation's press, that he had been vilified as a "revolving son-of-a-bitch," * but "knew it would be thus"— that anyone attacking Communists in government had to expect "vilification, smears, and falsehoods, peddled by the Reds, their minions, and the egg-sucking phony liberals who litter Washington with their persons and clutter American thinking with their simpleminded arguments."

The editors had greeted the senator with perfunctory handclapping. At the close they applauded him resoundingly.

* An old joke: "a son-of-a-bitch any way you look at him."

Jumping on Joe

[I]

Macaulay, in his essay on Lord Bacon, comments upon a trait in human nature which makes us reluctant to "admit the truth of any disgraceful story about a person whose society we like; . . ." He notes "how long we struggle against evidence, how fondly, when the facts cannot be disputed, we cling to the hope that there may be some explanation or some extenuating circumstance." And also with what difficulty we bring ourselves to think well of "those by whom we are thwarted or depressed," while we are receptive to "every excuse for the vices of those who are useful or agreeable to us." This trait Macaulay ascribed to all human beings, believing it cannot be effaced or eradicated either by experience or by reflection.

Here lies one of the keys to the career of Senator Joe McCarthy. Had not a situation—a climate of dread and distrust—been created over a long period of time, McCarthy's words would have lighted no fires of resentment; they would have been pointless. And the fact, constantly denied by those whom his manner, quite as much as his matter, mortally offended, was that the situation which made him possible had been created by the collective behavior of precisely those who formed his most inveterate critics. Human vanity rebels against being detected in a foolish action. No one likes to be told that he has been something of a chump, especially no one who, however modestly, considers himself endowed with the superior insights of the intellectual elite; yet this was the net effect upon many of Senator McCarthy's bludgeon blows.*

* In December, 1951, *Freeman* magazine, commenting on the "cataclysmic eruptions that, for almost a year now, have emanated from all the better-appointed editorial offices of Manhattan and Washington, D. C.," suspected that the cause must be "something in Mr. McCarthy's makeup . . . a sort of animal, negative-

Even before the senator's appearance, the validity of Macaulay's observation had been demonstrated by the reaction of the articulate, liberal community to the Hiss affair. At first, seemingly, every right-thinking liberal, and many persons of plain goodwill, had rushed to condole with Alger Hiss and express revulsion for his accuser. The first was a creditable reaction; but the second, before the evidence was in and before any investigation of the very grave accusations raised against Hiss had been undertaken, was less ingenuous. Hiss's defenders tumbled over each other to vindicate him, albeit on the basis of nothing more substantial than their predilection; and during the long attrition of their expressed confidence thereafter they had retreated only step by step from their emotional, unreasoning, and basically illiberal initial endorsement. Many merely withdrew into silence and never recanted; others, more contentious, took up positions behind breastworks of semantics, sedulously refusing to admit that any question of spying was involved and primly pointing out that Hiss had been convicted of nothing but perjury, which of course was legally exact.* The Hiss case had caused the liberal press and some liberal spokesmen great embarrassment; therefore the reaction to Budenz and his testimony was more circumspect and wary. The fact was inescapable that his statements and those of Lattimore could not be reconciled. Both men had been under oath. Obviously one or the other was grossly mistaken, or deliberately lying.

The liberal left was convinced that Lattimore was being traduced, but Budenz's positive identification could not be brushed aside as of no weight whatever. His effectiveness as a witness and his unquestionable sincerity were conceded even by such pronounced exponents of liberalism as the *New Republic*, although with a trace of wryness. ("From the Bible down, Prodigal Sons have had a certain glamor.") True, the testimony offered regarding Lattimore's Communist links had been hearsay, but "strong hear-

---

pole magnetism, which repels alumni of Harvard, Princeton, and Yale. We think we know what it is: this young man is constitutionally incapable of deference to social status." This is a trait, of course, which irrevocably condemns its possessor to perpetual exclusion as an "outsider," and nothing can overcome the repugnance which it inspires.

* Hiss could not be prosecuted for espionage because the statute of limitations had run on that charge.

say . . . it went further than we expected." Nevertheless, the magazine concluded, if the tests of loyalty and patriotism propounded by Senator McCarthy were to prevail, we should wind up with "half the American people suspecting the other half" and that "is exactly what Stalin wants, we assume."

The moderation of this editorial opinion was somewhat offset by the same magazine's recruiting of an expert in McCarthy-hating and a past master of vituperation, Harold Ickes. For years the self-styled "Old Curmudgeon" (who had provided mirth for Washington ribalds by tumbling out of bed on his autumnal honeymoon) had been displaying his virtuosity as a male fishwife, assailing persons and things, high and low, of which he disapproved. At a loose end since resigning from President Truman's cabinet (parting with a gratuitous insult for his chief), from now on Ickes would level his venomous (and frequently funny) darts at the junior senator from Wisconsin, rechristened in the Ickes lexicon "Joseph Rank Muck-Carthy."

Ickes, of course, was not alone in tossing verbal brickbats at Joe. A culling of the terms of opprobrium applied to McCarthy during the first few weeks of his anti-Communist activity attests the degree of hatred he aroused; how bitter, deep-seated, and at times irrational it was. A sampling of the choice billingsgate, taken at random from the writings of some of Joe's more articulate opponents, yields the following phrases, among others equally odious:

"Political profiteer"; "briefcase demagogue"; "dangerous adventurer"; "misleader of the people"; "our No. 1 Fascist"; "imposter"; "political thuggery"; "Piltdown politician"; "a primitive form of political obscenity"; "evil unmatched in malice";* "political hoodlum"; "whirling dervish"; "revolving Ananias"; "moral leprosy"; "madman"; "nauseating character assassin"; "poolroom politician"; "political gangster"; "gutter brawler"; "malodorous Marine"; "roustabout"; "powerful pettifogger"; "loud-mouthed rowdy"; "medicine man from Appleton"; "irresponsible bounder"; "town tough"; "Wisconsin fly-by-night"; "jackal McCarthy"; "preposterous, egregious, ineffable, discredited bombast"; "bullyboy"; "spiteful and delinquent mental patient." †

* Later a theologian would label McCarthy "one of the disguises of the Devil."
† These epithets are all taken from a press that was constantly talking about censorship, the threat of suppression, and the risk of expressing their views.

Ickes outbayed the pack. "A fig-leaf for McCarthy!" he cried, accusing the senator of "indecent intellectual exposure." Let the Senate provide smelling salts for the occupants of the visitors gallery when McCarthy was "befouling the chamber," was another Ickes suggestion; senators might grow accustomed to the noxious stench of "MuckCarthy," but no visitor could unless he chanced to work in the stockyards or a glue factory. This "political charlatan from Wisconsin," with his "cheap claptrap . . . his numerous progeny of lies . . . his monstrous prevarications . . . his obscenities against the institutions of his country . . . this congenital liar . . . shameless liar . . . notorious Jack Ketch of character . . ."—with such shrill eloquence Ickes maintained the high intellectual level of the debate. It required no effort for him to spit out that the "repellent McCarthy . . . our own pocket-size demagogue" need never go into court to prove to himself and others that "once a political guttersnipe, always a political guttersnipe."

Against such ingenious abuse, McCarthy, for all his aptitude, found himself at a loss; he had the will, but lacked the vocabulary.

[II]

After a month and a half of hearings, Senator Tydings was feeling the strain. Word had sifted down from the highest levels that Joe McCarthy must be squelched; yet so far few of his original charges had been absolutely disproved. The denials entered by those accused were to some extent necessarily self-serving, and they had been clinched by no hard evidence independently obtained. Although the Tydings Committee had been created to investigate the entire subject of State Department loyalty, no real investigation had been made; the committee had simply called the officials responsible for the department's loyalty screening program, asked them whether their work was effective, and accepted their word that all was well. The unpalatable truth was that McCarthy's charges, instead of having been booted into oblivion, as anticipated, had blown up a storm that daily grew wilder, and with an election coming up, Capitol Hill was feeling the draft. The Democrats were apprehensive: How it had come about they did not understand, but in a ridiculously brief time a lone senator—one possessing no impressive background and commanding no party influence—had become the active symbol of the frustrations of an aroused electorate. The mystery was frightening. One senator, of many years' service, confided to *Times* correspondent White that "the answers [to McCarthy] so far have plainly not caught up with the charges. We had thought earlier that they were catching up. We still hope and think the public ultimately will come over to the administration's side. But not yet, not yet."

To illustrate, the senator pushed across the desk a typed postcard, heavily underlined in red, reading: "Why don't you get the Red rats out of the State Dept.?" Thousands of similar messages were coming daily, and senators experienced in estimating the spontaneity of such barrages were convinced that this one was a genuine expression of popular feeling; they were frankly alarmed by its vigor and apparent depth in the country. The Democratic leaders, therefore, decided that McCarthy, the visible source and instigator of this revolt, must be "totally and eternally destroyed." *

The strategy was worked out at a conference in Senator Tydings' Washington apartment. Present were Edward P. Morgan, chief counsel for the Tydings Committee; the senator; John Peurifoy; and other State Department officials.

The first move, it was agreed, should be a concerted attack in Congress, based on the contention that McCarthy had lied to the Senate when he denied having said "two hundred and five Com-

---

* The excited condition of a large portion of the nation was illustrated by a May Day stunt that received coast-to-coast attention. On May 1, a mock takeover by Reds was staged in the town of Mosinee, Wisconsin, in McCarthy territory. Masked American Legionnaires, posing as Communists, Russian-style, routed the mayor and police chief out of their beds before dawn, set up roadblocks with barbed-wire defenses, halted persons for identity and ration cards, and herded objectors into hastily erected "concentration camps" near "Red Square." At 10:15 A.M., the mayor, still in slippers and bathrobe, standing with a pistol in his back, announced the town's complete surrender to the "United Soviet States of America," and urged everyone to "submit to the accomplished fact" and avoid bloodshed; "God must have willed it this way, and maybe it's for the best." At the same hour, the Lutheran minister was seized in the midst of an opposition sermon and his church was "confiscated" as an "institution against the working class." All business activities (except those of the post office) were "nationalized," the public library was "purged" of anti-Communist books, and a film about Cardinal Mindszenty playing at the local theater was banned. In the stores, men's suits that had been selling for $42 were marked up to $242, and coffee to $4.14 a pound. Lunch rooms by command served nothing but black bread and potato soup. At the end of the day everybody unmasked at a grand patriotic rally in the town square; but such was the shock of this freakish demonstration enacted with spine-chilling realism that the mayor suffered a real heart attack that evening.

munists, known to the Secretary of State," in his Wheeling speech. Affidavits had been obtained from employes of radio station WWVA affirming that they had checked the broadcast at the time against McCarthy's advance text, and the words "two hundred and five" occurred in both. These affidavits, it was decided, should be read on the Senate floor. (*Newsweek* magazine stated that a tape recording also would be played.)

Next would come the disclosure of the source of the "eighty-one cases" that McCarthy had listed in his February 20 speech—the so-called Lee Report—all "old stuff, long discredited," which McCarthy had dusted off and presented as new, it would be charged. West Virginia's two senators, Harley Kilgore and Matthew Neely, would be entrusted with this attack.

In the interim, Secretary Acheson fought back on another front. Two days after McCarthy was applauded by the American Society of Newspaper Editors, Acheson addressed the same assemblage and delivered a forty-minute blast at McCarthy and his method of combatting subversion. The senator, sitting at a side table, heard it all. McCarthy's clamor, Acheson said, was like saying the best way to fight fires was to ring every alarm in town—"not because you know of any fire, but if you get all the apparatus out and have it wheeling through the streets, you might find one." Alluding to McCarthy's accusations as "this filthy business," the Secretary challenged the editors to live up to their responsibility to the public and stop being participants ("unwilling participants, disgusted participants, yet nevertheless participants") in keeping the farce alive.

The three hundred delegates, who two days before had applauded McCarthy, stood up and cheered Acheson. Hands dug into pockets, McCarthy kept his seat. Krock of the *Times* took a sampling of delegate reaction and found it about evenly divided for and against the senator; although many expressed their belief that if the personnel files would prove Joe a liar, Truman would order them "opened tomorrow."

[III]

Budenz had been called back by Tydings for further questioning, this time in secret session, after Lattimore branded his testimony "a plain, unvarnished lie." A furious row erupted when Tydings barred McCarthy from this closed hearing, although he was willing to let Lattimore and his counsel, Fortas, sit in. Also excluded was Robert Morris, counsel for the committee's minority members, whom Tydings had engaged reluctantly on the Republicans' insistence. When McCarthy objected strenuously, Tydings changed his mind about letting Lattimore and his attorney attend.

Repairing to the Senate, McCarthy denounced his exclusion and proceeded to give a rundown on the testimony he said Budenz even then was giving. Senator Jenner, accusing Tydings and his Democratic colleagues of trying to protect the administration at any cost, labeled the whole inquiry "Whitewash, Inc." * Whereupon Tydings stormed into the Senate and demanded an end to "this wild charging in the newspapers, this baloney! Let's get on, stop this heckling and bitterness and pettiness and find the Reds, if there are any!"

Senator Wherry (Ickes had a name for him, too—"the merry mortician") hotly reminded Tydings that President Truman had called senators "Kremlin assets" with no rebuke from any Democrat. "Let him prove it!" Wherry shouted. Tydings, he charged, was putting on a "pantomime show," having no intention of uncovering anything.

The acrimony was in no way allayed by the committee's performance when it called as witnesses Frederick Vanderbilt Field and two former Communists who had been expelled from the party, Earl Browder and Bella V. Dodd.

From Browder and Field the committee wheedled statements that "to the best of their personal knowledge," neither Lattimore nor other individuals named by McCarthy were Communists. Browder said that he had never met, spoken to, or even seen Lattimore, although the latter himself had stated that in 1936 he had talked with Browder about China. Browder, former chairman of the Communist party in the United States, was openly contemptuous of the committee, and so was Field, and the deferential manner of Senators McMahon and Tydings toward these witnesses did not pass unnoticed. The transcript was replete with such courtly expressions as "thank you very much for cooperating," "in the interest of fairness and truth," "I see your point of view, but," "I should be very grateful to you," and (Tydings to Browder) "I want to thank you for your cooperation, and hope, after the conference with your attorney, you can go into other areas," and (to Field), "thank you."

* The phrase had sinister topical connotations just then because of the recent exposure of a killer-for-hire organization known as "Murder, Inc."

This despite Browder's unconcealed scorn and Field's belligerent reluctance to answer even such questions as whether he owned a farm in Connecticut.

Mrs. Dodd, a short, plump, middle-aged woman in a blue polka-dot dress, thumped the arms of the witness chair as she repeated that she had never met Lattimore, had never seen him in party circles, and had never even heard of him until recently. As for his books, she maintained that the party considered them "anathema." *

Tydings next introduced letters from three former Secretaries of State repudiating the suggestion that their policies had been in any way "masterminded" by Lattimore. General Marshall repelled the insinuation as "completely without basis in fact. So far as I and my associates can recall I never even met Mr. Lattimore." † Cordell Hull: "I am not aware that . . . he had any appreciable influence." James F. Byrnes: "I do not know Mr. Lattimore. If he ever wrote me about the Far Eastern policy the letter was not brought to my attention." To which Dean Acheson added: "Mr. Lattimore, so far as I am concerned, or am aware, has had no influence."

A question was raised in the newspapers at this point as to what Senator Tydings was trying to prove. Nobody, least of all the Communists, attached the slightest credibility to the word of Earl Browder, and the other recent witnesses had been about as suspect. *Newsweek* was for dismissing the investigation outright as "an exercise in futility."

[IV]

McCarthy, having flown to Arizona for a brief vacation, returned to Washington as Dr. John King Fairbank, professor of history at

---

* It was commented at the time that these ex-Communists, forcibly expelled from the society of their comrades, displayed an evident nostalgia for the old faith, despite their professed recantations. Also, in their search for a new discipline, they relied almost hypnotically on the virtue of key words and shibboleths. Mentally they dwelt in the world of slogans and hair-splitting, the never-never land of dialectic. Few seemed liberated from these tendencies.

† This was perhaps an oversight. In October, 1949, General Marshall and Lattimore sat together at a round table conference at the State Department convened by Philip Jessup, during which Lattimore, in Marshall's presence, advocated a policy favorable to withdrawing United States support from Chiang Kai-shek and placing no obstacle in the way of a Communist takeover of China. Presumably those attending this supersecret discussion were at least introduced to each other. This conference was to figure in later investigations that would result in serious consequences for both Lattimore and Jessup.

Harvard, was denouncing him at a rally in New York, calling him indeed an asset to the Kremlin—worth ten divisions to the Chinese Reds, and many more to Russia. The senator fired back that "regardless of professors," he would continue the fight to expose Reds, using "bare knuckles" whenever necessary. In reply to Acheson, he said that "the simple fact remains that the State Department has adopted the official Communist program [on China] right down to the last comma. And if Mr. Lattimore was not the salesman for the Communist party, then I ask Mr. Acheson, who did the selling job?"

In the same broadcast speech the senator accused Tydings of "putting obstacles in my way," and asserted that he himself was doing the work the committee was supposed to do. "I've almost gone bankrupt hiring former FBI men to develop the facts," he stated. At present he had four investigators on his payroll, he said, and had been forced to let one go "because I'm getting too close to the bottom of the barrel." He said his investigators were excellent but expensive, costing him from $23 to $35 a day, plus expenses. However, he was getting some financial help from a "sizable number" of good Americans who were mailing in their "crumpled dollar bills" and urging him to keep up the fight.

For a second time before the Tydings investigators, Lattimore went to bat. This time his manner was less restrained. Shouting and pounding the table, he called Budenz's testimony "a tissue of falsehoods," uttered for the sole purpose of "personal profit." He characterized Budenz as a "professional informer," "a twisted and malignant personality," "man of sinister melodrama," living in his "own lurid world of Conspiracy," "a smear artist," and other terms equally scathing. He let fly at McCarthy in a manner that might have aroused envy in the atrabilious Ickes, denouncing the senator as "a despoiler of the character of good American citizens," surrounded by a "motley crew of crackpots, professional informers, hysterics, and ex-Communists," whose "unprincipled attacks" and "spurious sensationalism . . . unjustly slandering" people had "debased the processes of the Senate and disgraced his party and the people of his state and nation." The witness said he had received 170 letters praising him for resisting the "bullying of any man who stands up for an independent opinion." He quoted Harvard's Professor Zechariah Chafee, Jr., who likened McCarthy's actions to a "barbarian invasion."

Finally, less with anger than with the waspish asperity of an injured schoolmarm, Lattimore lectured the senators on their proper course, admonishing them that "a tide of fear has swept Washington and is undermining the freedom of the nation," and that "professional character assassins" like their colleague "must not be permitted to run riot or to spread publicly their venom. . . . Put an end to this nonsense."

Although again Lattimore was applauded, he had noted—with a sense of relief—that during this session the television lights had been turned on only intermittently, not continuously, as before, which seemed to point toward a subsidence of public interest. McCarthy was not on hand to hear this testimony, having flown back to Arizona, where he had many friends. Nor was he present when a witness whose name he had given to the committee, insisting that she be called, did appear and testify. She was Freda Utley, a former Communist who had seen the party from the inside, having been married to a Russian who disappeared during the purges of the 1930's. Having escaped to Western Europe, she had since then written extensively on Communist doctrine, and in a preliminary statement read to the committee she analyzed Lattimore's writings insofar as they touched on Communist theory, and stated her findings, namely that:

"Soviet Russia, in all of Lattimore's writings, is always sinned against and is always represented by Lattimore as standing like a beacon of hope for the peoples of Asia, even when she is collaborating with the Nazis or aggressing on her own account. Russia is never in the wrong, and if he is forced to take cognizance of a few slight misdemeanors on her part, he excuses them only as a reaction to American imperialism or some other country's misdeeds."

With McCarthy's charges she found only one fault—they did not go far enough. The senator underestimated Lattimore, she explained:

"To suggest that Mr. Lattimore's great talents have been utilized in espionage seems to me to be as absurd as to suggest that Mr. Gromyko or Mr. Molotov employ their leisure hours at Lake Success [United Nations headquarters], or at international conferences, in snitching documents."

She had no personal knowledge that Lattimore was in literal fact a Communist, she replied to questioning, but he was something far more dangerous—he was like the "Judas cow" in a stockyard that leads the other animals to slaughter.

There was no courtliness in Tydings' manner as he tartly admonished this witness: "We don't take opinion evidence here. We want facts, f-a-c-t-s. We are getting very few of them. We are getting mostly opinion."

Mrs. Utley replied that her "opinions" were "expert knowledge," but the chairman found his patience exhausted and called the next witness—Demaree Bess, of *The Saturday Evening Post*, who expressed his firm opinion that Lattimore was no Communist. No demand for "f-a-c-t-s" was pressed upon him.

Lattimore had his own sneering opinion of Freda Utley as a "disillusioned intellectual" regurgitating "bits of old, turgid, but still bitter sectarian dispute. It has nothing to do with me." He took a passing swipe at Senator McCarthy as "that profound political scientist" and pointed out with a touch of unction that "unlike Budenz and Utley, I have never been a member of the Communist party or subscribed to a conspiracy to overthrow and subvert established governments. Unlike Budenz, I have never engaged in a conspiracy to commit murder or espionage."

[V]

But McCarthy was on hand when the Democrats opened their carefully planned major attack in the Senate, leading to a scene more vitriolic than anything the oldest senators could recollect. As *Newsweek* observed, this assault was intended to be lethal, because plainly McCarthy's charges were making an impression on the country—not so much by their substance, as because of the frantic efforts that so obviously were being made to discredit their author.

The Senate attack had been preceded by a speech in the House of Representatives by Frank Karsten, who disclosed publicly for the first time that the list of eighty-one "suspicious characters" which McCarthy had presented to the Senate on February 20 was the so-called Lee Report, examined and rejected as worthless, he contended, long before. "I have complete contempt for anyone who, through deceit or fraud, would seek to inflame and hoodwink the American people," was his righteous condemnation of the senator from Wisconsin.

Scott Lucas, the majority leader, led off in the Senate by reading a statement by Peurifoy reviewing the Wheeling speech, McCarthy's "shopworn" list of cases, and the Lattimore charges.

"There is no shred of truth to the senator's statement——"
Lucas cried, but Wherry cut him short for violating Senate Rule
19, which forbids a senator to call another senator a liar. Vice-
President Alben Barkley ordered Lucas to sit down; but a motion
to override the chair was immediately offered and carried, and
Lucas resumed.

Then Senator Kilgore read the affidavits of the Wheeling radio
men who had monitored McCarthy's speech and swore that the
words "two hundred and five" had been used. Lucas stormed that
"the entire United States press" had reported McCarthy's use of
that figure, and facing McCarthy, he cried: "The time has come
to call a spade a spade. I am willing to take what the press of the
country said, and not what Senator McCarthy says he said on that
occasion." Did he or did he not use that figure? That was the sole
question, and Senator Tydings insisted that "any honest man" could
give a yes-or-no answer to that. Senator Neely offered copies of the
Wheeling Intelligencer quoting McCarthy as saying "two hundred
and five" and demanded, "I want to know whether the senator did
say, or did not say, that he had the names of two hundred and five
Communists in the State Department."

McCarthy replied that the speech he made in Wheeling was in
the *Record*. Neely shouted that if the charges against the State
Department should be proved false, "those responsible should be
scourged from the company of decent men." Accusing his opponents of playing "a silly numbers game," McCarthy went on:
"There is no doubt in the mind of Senator Tydings at all as to what
was said. The President of the United States himself received a
wire from me as to exactly what I said."

Neely: "That is not the question. Did the senator write in the
Wheeling speech that he had the names of two hundred and five?
Will the senator say yes or no?"

McCarthy: "I call for the regular order."

"It is perfectly evident——" Senator Lehman interjected, but Mc-
Carthy cut him off, repeating, "I call for the regular order." But
Lehman went on doggedly, "——that he has not denied."

McCarthy: "Point of order, Mr. President!"

Tydings: "I should like to put the question again, yes or no. It
is the kind of question that can be answered yes or no by any honest
man."

McCarthy: "You have had twenty hours to cross-examine me in
committee; you are not going to question me here on this floor.

Does the senator not know that the only money he has spent in investigating so far has been to send men to West Virginia to investigate me? Is not the important question here to try to get rid of Communist individuals, whether there are ten, fifty, or a hundred?"

Neely retorted that the Tydings Committee ought to investigate "where the truth lies in the Wheeling speech, because somebody is lying at a rate Ananias never lied!" Ominously he added that if McCarthy's charge of "two hundred and five Communists in the State Department" proved to be groundless, "I think the senator will have destroyed himself in the Senate and will have destroyed his usefulness in the country."

The words sounded like a knell, but to McCarthy the sound was mere tintinnabulation. Having sat through Neely's outburst, he gathered up his papers and stalked out.

And the next day the White House added its strength to the campaign to "destroy McCarthy" by announcing that the President had consented to open to inspection by the Tydings committee the State Department's confidential files on all eighty-one of McCarthy's "cases." So now there could be no dispute over what the files contained.

In the meantime, the committee had started a new inquiry into the *Amerasia* affair. Frank Bielaski, the man who had led the original raid on the *Amerasia* offices, was called to testify in a closed session from which McCarthy was excluded. The senator thereupon gave to the press what he said was the gist of the testimony Bielaski was even then giving. Releasing the report in the form of an open letter to Senator Tydings, McCarthy reminded the committee chairman that every witness whose testimony might damage Joe had been heard in public, but that witnesses who might help him and others who were "trying to expose Communists in government" were heard in secret. Therefore he felt duty bound to let the American people know what was going on.

McCarthy also announcd that the State Department was giving John S. Service access to material for use in his forthcoming loyalty review that was being denied to the Senate. In response to which, General Snow, chairman of the department's loyalty board, stated that the board felt an obligation to give Service "fullest opportunity to prepare and present his case."

No wonder Senator Lodge was pleading, "Let's get this show off the road." Senator Flanders of Vermont thought that would be a good idea, too.

A Matter of Consciences

The conditions under which President Truman had opened the loyalty files to the subcommittee were stringent. The senators would be allowed to examine them at the White House, in the presence of representatives of the State and Justice Departments, but they could make no written notes or take anything out of the room. They would have to rely on memory alone as to the contents of the files.

The three Democrats showed up promptly to begin their task. Brimming with confidence, they posed laughingly for a group photograph, appearing in the merriest of moods, serenely sure that now they had access to the wherewithal to nail McCarthy and his outrageous allegations to the barn door.

The files were in the cabinet room. Each senator was at liberty to take one or more at random and study its contents. The work was slow and tedious, the information in each dossier comprising a loose mass of data, much of it trivial, unarranged and undigested. In two days of steady application, Tydings managed to struggle through thirteen "cases."

Senator Hickenlooper got a belated start on the work because of his temporary absence on a campaigning visit to Iowa. He brought back the news that public interest in the investigation had taken a sharp turn upward in his state during the last month; whereas previously it had drawn little attention, now it was being "talked about a lot," he said.

Another indication of spreading interest was seen in the steady flow of invitations to speak coming into McCarthy's office, far more than he could possibly accept, although he did accept many, carrying his message directly to audiences particularly in the Midwest.

In Chicago he ridiculed Truman's "phony generosity" in opening the security files, saying they had been "stripped" of inconvenient data. Moving along to Janesville, Wisconsin, he told a cheering crowd of Young Republicans that the file on his "Case No. 2"— involving a United States minister to a foreign nation—had been "thoroughly raped," and said that if the complete file were opened, "even the President's puppets would rise above politics and have this minister fired immediately." And again he pledged that "no matter how McCarthy bleeds in the process, the job will continue until we have a thorough housecleaning."

"Rape" being a headline word, the senator's accusation was published all over the country, with all its sensational connotations. Senator Tydings was furious. "We've got everything that the government has got—FBI, QXY, the whole damn thing!" he sputtered. "There will be no excuses this time!" But Senator Hickenlooper retorted that they did not have "the whole damn thing" because the FBI files were not included. Tydings countered that Peyton Ford, an Assistant Attorney General, had given assurance in a letter that a special inquiry by the FBI had found that "the files are intact, that they have not been 'raped' or tampered with in any way, and that the material turned over to the State Department by the FBI is still in the files. Thus," Tydings concluded triumphantly, "the McCarthy charges are not sustained by the facts."

But a weakness in this exculpation, as some reporters saw it, was the extreme secrecy surrounding Peyton Ford's letter. When reporters asked to see the letter, or to have its exact text given out, Tydings put them off, saying that the names of accused persons would be disclosed. The result was to raise a fresh set of doubts, and the matter of the files was further muddled when Senator Lodge, after looking over what he identified as "a representative cross-section," figuratively threw up his hands and declared that to try to make sense out of the undigested hodgepodge would be "a waste of time."

[II]

Meanwhile, in the Senate the campaign to thwart McCarthy took a surprise turn when Senator Dennis Chavez of New Mexico, sixty-two and ailing, introduced the religious issue. This was toying with fire indeed. Rising to speak on the dispute, Chavez preluded his attack by saying that for the first time in his nineteen years in Congress he was making "a deliberate point of referring to my religion. I am a Roman Catholic." And because of his faith, he felt it was a matter of conscience to protest, "not only as a Catholic but as an American," when he saw his church, which had so staunchly opposed communism, being used as "a shield and a cloak" by an individual—Senator McCarthy's key witness, Louis Francis Budenz—"now elevated to the unique position of America's No. 1 professional witness in all matters concerning loyalty, patriotism, and political reliability."

Actually, Chavez went on, Budenz had led a life of "bawdy personal excesses," had had three children by his wife before marrying her in 1945, and had been arrested twenty-one times (as a labor agitator) "before he joined the Communists in 1935 at the tender age of forty-four. . . . I believe in clemency to sinners, but with repentance should go humility, not hypocrisy. . . . My ancestors brought the Cross to this hemisphere. Louis Budenz has been using the Cross as a club. . . . It has become the fashion to lionize and extol the ex-Communist in America today. Ex-Communists are treated as heroes of the republic. They are rushed to forums from which to denounce good citizens who always opposed communism, but refused to make merchandise of their patriotism."

This attack was a dangerous expedient, the purpose of which was to discredit McCarthy by discrediting his witness. Subsequently it became known that the material for the attack traced back through Owen Lattimore. Chavez had not acted independently. The damaging information against Budenz came from secret testimony given in a deportation hearing against a Communist, in which Budenz had been a witness. The only copy of this secret testimony had been in the possession of an attorney appearing for Communists, and from him it was leaked to receptive quarters. Although Senators Tydings and Lucas, the Democratic leader, did officially associate themselves with Chavez's attack, Senators Lodge and Hickenlooper, minority members of the Tydings Committee, had no inkling of the charges before they were aired in the Senate.

This raising of the religious issue was generally considered below the belt, for at no time had Senator McCarthy exploited his Catholic connection. Also, it was common knowledge that some elements of Catholicism fervently opposed him. The three Catholic friends who reportedly had originally instigated Joe to take up the issue of Reds in government, including Father Walsh of George-town, were understood to have repudiated him. McCarthy was not present when Chavez spoke, but he contented himself with replying that the likable New Mexican was a "dupe," that somebody else was pulling the strings. A pointed rebuke to Chavez was adminis-tered by the Reverend Laurence J. McGinley, S. J., president of Fordham University, and McCarthy was invited to address the Catholic Press Association at its convention in Rochester, New York. The senator told reporters he was getting "quite a bit" of financial help by donations mailed in, and that he now had four investigators working full time and a fifth part time. "We're getting along all right," he said, adding that he positively was not receiving one penny of Republican party funds.

The Catholic press convention gave the senator a standing ova-tion, a fact that *Commonweal* reported with sorrow. Although there appeared to be some delegates who were critical, no voice was raised against the speaker. At the outset McCarthy made it clear that he was not speaking for the Church or for anybody except Joe McCarthy, and he answered questions put by the dele-gates at great length. He said he was receiving money donations and pledges of support from Democrats and Republicans alike—good Americans, who believed in their country and in his aims. One reminder to stand fast that he kept on his desk, he said, was thirty-seven cents mailed to him by a nine-year-old boy who wanted his birthday money used "to fight communism."

Patrick Scanlan, editor of the *Brooklyn Tablet,* in introducing the senator, described him as a man of courage, the victim of slan-der and a nationwide smear campaign. After hearing McCarthy's speech, Scanlan resorted to baseball slang to confess that previously he had harbored some doubts about the senator's "control," but he now was convinced that it was as good as his "speed."

At Johns Hopkins University, Owen Lattimore was tendered a testimonial dinner and reception by his faculty associates, in token of their continued faith in his "integrity as a scholar and loyalty as a citizen."

And intermixed with these happenings came an announcement from Philadelphia of the arrest there of one Harry Gold, who had helped Klaus Fuchs pass atomic bomb secrets to the Russians—while the revived *Amerasia* inquiry spread from the Tydings Com-mittee to a "runaway" grand jury which had undertaken to look into the evidence on its own initiative, without being instructed to do so. Justice Department spokesmen were shuttling between the two investigations, earnestly repeating their previous assertions that the evidence was so tainted no convictions could have been obtained. Tydings released his own summary of testimony given in secret session by the original prosecutor in the case, but failed to release any supporting transcript. and McCarthy promptly branded the action "an almost unbelievable development in 'Operation Whitewash.' This new practice of hearing a witness in secret, and carefully selecting the parts of his testimony which will be made public and the parts which will be kept secret, is fantastic beyond belief!" *

Senator Hickenlooper said the country would be "appalled when the whole truth becomes known"; but the Justice Department scouted the notion that there was anything in the evidence "remotely resembling" what Hickenlooper suggested. McCarthy demanded that the six persons arrested in the *Amerasia* case be questioned, and Tydings made preparations to call Jaffe, Larsen, and Service. And almost daily the State Department fulminated against the accusations that were thickening the air, and against McCarthy personally.

[III]

Amid this "hysteria and confusion" (the lamentation of one segment of the press) a voice of recall to simple sanity was suddenly heard. "This McCarthy business" had kept the Senate tied in knots for nearly four months when on June 1, Senator Margaret Chase Smith, Republican of Maine, introduced a note of reason. Sparing neither Democrats nor Republicans, she warned that there had been aroused in the land a "feeling of fear and frustration that could result in national suicide and the end of everything we Americans hold dear." In recent weeks, she said, the Senate of the United States had been "too often debased to the level of a forum of hate and character assassination sheltered by the shield of Congressional immunity. I am not proud of the reckless abandon in which unproved charges have been hurled from this side of the aisle. I am not proud of the

---

* Interestingly Senator McCarthy would be harshly criticized for allegedly adopting this practice brought so forcefully to his attention during the Tydings inquiry.

obviously staged, undignified countercharges that have been attempted in retaliation. The American people are sick and tired of being afraid to speak their minds lest they be politically smeared as 'Communists' or 'Fascists.' Freedom of speech is not what it used to be in America. It has been so abused by some that it is not exercised by others. . . . The American people are sick and tired of seeing innocent people smeared and guilty people whitewashed. But there have been enough proved cases to cause nationwide distrust and strong suspicion that there may be something to unproved, sensational accusations. There are enough proved cases to make this point without diluting our criticism with unproved charges. . . . I don't want to see the Republican party ride to political victory on the four horsemen of calumny—Fear, Ignorance, Bigotry, and Smear."

Then she presented to the Senate a Declaration of Conscience, which she had drawn up and which had been signed by herself and six other Republican senators. McCarthy sat white-faced and grim only three feet behind her as she read the manifesto:

"We are Republicans, but we are Americans first. It is as Americans that we express our concern with the growing confusion that threatens the security and stability of our country. Democrats and Republicans alike have contributed to that confusion." The Democrats were blamed for "complacency to the threat of Communism here at home and the leak of vital secrets to Russia through key officials of the administration." They were castigated for "lack of effective leadership," for "oversensitiveness to rightful criticism" and "petty bitterness against their critics." The Republicans were held accountable no less for uttering "irresponsible words of bitterness" and for "selfish political opportunism" in hope of political gain.

The senators who signed this declaration, besides Mrs. Smith, were Irving M. Ives of New York, Charles W. Tobey of New Hampshire, George D. Aiken of Vermont, Robert C. Hendrickson of New Jersey, Edward J. Thye of Minnesota, and Wayne L. Morse of Oregon.

The Senate listened in startled silence to the plucky voice of one of its most respected members, and at the end McCarthy walked out. Hugging to their lacerated bosoms this sign of a rift in Republican ranks over "McCarthyism," the Democrats glided over the strictures against their party and praised its overall wisdom and moderation. Senator Tydings called it "fair," "temperate," and an act of "stateswomanship." The *New Republic,* battered by recent events, even ventured to express hope that "the nation is catching up with McCarthy."

The next day McCarthy, undeterred, attacked President Truman anew for defending "the vested interests of Communists by keeping their agents in the State Department." Without mentioning Mrs. Smith or her Declaration, he replied obliquely—in obedience to the promptings of his own conscience, he said:

"Let me make clear to the administration, to the Senate, and to the country that this fight against communism, this attempt to expose and neutralize the efforts of those who are attempting to betray this country, shall not stop, regardless of what any group in this Senate or in the administration might do. I hold myself accountable not to them, but first to the people of my state, and secondly to the people of the nation, and thirdly to civilization as a whole."

[IV]

The Tydings Committee did summon Jaffe, Larsen, and Service. But the former *Amerasia* editor, with his counsel, John Rogge, sitting beside him, refused more than one hundred times to answer questions, taking refuge each time in the Fifth Amendment, pleading possible self-incrimination. After trying to get a response for three and a half hours, Senator Green admitted that "we are right where we started."

Then Larsen testified in a closed hearing, and McCarthy, speaking before the National Editorial Association, charged that this witness had discussed his testimony with John Peurifoy in advance and had been offered free counsel in the *Amerasia* inquiry, and loyalty clearance later, in return for testimony favorable to the government and a promise not to testify against Service. According to McCarthy, Larsen had assured Peurifoy, "Don't worry, I won't testify against John." Although Larsen's testimony was secret, McCarthy described it as mainly an attempt to repudiate all his earlier statements and unload the *Amerasia* blame on everybody else—"smearing anyone and everyone within reach who has been exposing Communists."

Peurifoy denied McCarthy's charge and said that on the contrary the senator had tried to subvert Larsen. Larsen himself called Mc-

Carthy a liar; but Larsen's credibility had been about destroyed by now.

Then the "runaway" grand jury in New York, under intense pressure from Washington, closed its *Amerasia* inquiry and disbanded after issuing a statement that the Justice Department hailed as completely vindicating its course of action, although the foreman of the grand jury denied that it had been meant to do any such thing.

That week Senator McCarthy was a topic of active speculation at the National Governors Conference. Governors Earl Warren of California and James Duff of Pennsylvania expressed disapproval of the senator's methods, but they also scored the administration for the obvious bias of the Tydings Committee. Governor Thomas E. Dewey of New York had mixed feelings about McCarthy.

The Wisconsin Republican convention, however, entertained no reservations in regard to Senator McCarthy's "courage, patriotism, and loyalty" and his "unswerving fidelity" in the face of "merciless and unceasing vilification and abuse." A resolution was passed endorsing his "untiring efforts to root out and destroy treasonable, Communistic, disloyal elements" infecting the Truman administration.

Then David Greenglass was arrested as another atomic spy, while the secret testimony given by J. Edgar Hoover before a Senate committee two months earlier was released, in which the FBI chief for the first time gave an official estimate of the strength of communism in the United States—"a potential fifth column of 540,000 people." This, he said, included roughly 40,000 known Reds and 500,000 sympathizers. Communists at that moment, he said, were more active than Nazi or Fascist operatives ever had been in World War II, although so shaken by defections and information leaks that they had instituted their own purge program. Even the party's thirteen-member central committee was being made subject to check, Hoover reported; in fact, the Communists had set up forty-nine separate "loyalty boards" of their own to combat defections.

A Gallup Poll survey indicated that the nation, if not "catching up" with McCarthy, certainly was "waking up" to him. Of the people questioned, 84 percent knew about McCarthy's allegations, and 46.4 percent thought they were "a good thing for the country." Only 34.5 percent thought they had done harm; 19.1 percent held no opinion.

Then another New York grand jury indicted William W. Remington, an economist employed by the Commerce Department, for perjury in denying membership in the Communist party. He had been identified as a Communist by several former Reds. Another Hiss sensation seemed to be in the making, and McCarthy, although he had nothing to do directly with the indictment, was credited with it; Remington had been "Case No. 19" on the list McCarthy had read to the Senate on February 20. The Tydings Committee had declined to look into the matter because Remington was not a State Department employe.

At the same time, the executive committee of the American Veterans Committee called for the impeachment of Senator McCarthy for "high crimes and misdemeanors." The committee also called him a liar. But over the radio Senator Wherry maintained that McCarthy had done the American people "a great service" in alerting them to the danger of subversion, whether or not his approach was right.

And in *The New York Times,* Hanson W. Baldwin, military affairs writer, while deploring McCarthy's net effect on the nation's defenses, admitted that the senator's "Quixotic anxiety about loyalty and righteousness in the State Department" was "only one manifestation of Congressional and public concern with security in the atomic age." And Baldwin noted other indications of "grass roots interest in security, and awareness that we must guard against the termites that attack from within as well as the enemies that assault from without." The trouble about McCarthy, in Baldwin's view, was that he was impelling the government toward greater and greater secrecy, "which breeds not security but fear."

In the Senate, Senator William Benton of Connecticut, dapper, aggressive former advertising tycoon, took a harsher line toward McCarthy, saying, "He doesn't argue. He doesn't answer. He doesn't reason. He hits and runs."

The phrase proved popular, and soon Lattimore was alluding to "the disreputable McCarthy and his hit-run campaign of libelous charges under senatorial immunity."

Then John Stewart Service faced the Tydings group in a public hearing and conceded that he had given Jaffe confidential military information which might be "technically considered secret"; but if he did, he contended, it was only because no discussion of China at that time could have been kept separate from the war then in progress. Service testified calmly, scarcely glancing at McCarthy sitting a few feet away, as he accused the senator of giving false testimony against him. All his efforts regarding China, Service insisted, had been aimed at keeping that nation out of the hands of the Reds. He had an apt explanation for everything; but so had McCarthy.

In the midst of this, reporters digging through the debris of the bankrupt Lustron Corporation came across the check for $10,000 made out to Joseph R. McCarthy, and asked him about it. That was payment for authoring the booklet, "A Dollar's Worth of Housing," Joe explained, and there was nothing new about the incident except the disclosure of the amount of the payment. There was no illegality involved, McCarthy said easily; it was just as ethical for him to accept $10,000 for writing a pamphlet as for Vice-President Barkley, for example, to accept $5,000 for making a speech, or for Senator Morse to accept $500. "I just sold to the highest bidder."

Joe was correct in his contention of no illegality, but variously slanted headlines, ranging from the sardonic to the morally outraged, reflected the raised eyebrows of many a citizen. *Time* magazine's headline read, "Author! Author!" while *Newsweek,* having in mind both McCarthy and Service, headlined its report, "Ready Explanation Week," and compared Joe to "a small boy caught with his fist in the cookie jar and jam smeared over his face."

Then, on June 25, when everyone concerned was looking for some way to "get this incredible show off the road," the North Korean Communists, backed by Soviet Russia, launched their blitz against the Republic of Korea, President Truman ordered United States land, sea, and air forces to the defense of South Korea, the United Nations condemned North Korea's aggression—and Joe McCarthy was off the front pages. It had taken a shooting war to do it.

Whose Fraud? Whose Hoax?

Politically apprehensive Democrats in Washington and elsewhere were hopeful that the national emergency, by depriving McCarthy of the front pages, would put an end to his attacks, and McCarthy was said to be resigned to temporary eclipse. "My forum is the front page," he was said to have told a reporter. "I don't have that now, so I'll keep quiet." But "quiet" with McCarthy was a relative word, and he did make page two of *The New York Times* with a television interview in which he charged that "American boys are dying in Korea" because the military aid voted by Congress for South Korea had been "sabotaged" by a group of "untouchables" in the State Department. All the Koreans got, he said, was "about $52,000 worth of baling wire."

Then in close succession the State Department gave John S. Service his sixth security and loyalty clearance, one day after he had testified before the Tydings Committee, and a howl went up in Congress that his testimony there had not been considered by the loyalty board. Backtracking hastily, the department explained that the clearance would not become final until the loyalty review board had looked into the case once more. And four days after the Communist armies swarmed into South Korea, Tydings announced that his committee would hold no further hearings, but would set about preparing an "interim" report.

The decision had been taken over the strenuous objections of the two minority members. Senator Hickenlooper protested that the investigation had "barely scratched the surface," and he served notice that he would sign no report, because no basis for making a report existed. He offered to submit a list of twenty or thirty witnesses who he felt should be called, "and you can have it tomorrow

186

afternoon." Said Tydings: "I think our work is pretty well concluded."

Lodge's protest also was disregarded. To point up the superficiality of the investigation, he read into the record nineteen questions relating to State Department security which he believed needed answering. The questions were not his own, he stressed, but had been raised by others, in some instances publicly and loudly. All had been brushed aside by the chairman. And when Robert Morris, the minority counsel, begged permission to call up "just one case," he was rebuffed huffily. Snapped Tydings: "Mr. Morris, we can mention cases from now until doomsday." Morris urged, "It is all in the record, senator; may I just finish?" "You are not a member of the committee," was the cutting reply. "When we want counsel to speak we will ask them."

Senator Lodge interposed that he should like to hear what Morris had to say, and with that the counsel was allowed to go on:

"There is a case of a man who has been an employe of the State Department. He is now one of Paul Hoffman's top assistants . . . doing work that is quasi-State Department in character. I have gotten some witnesses together who will testify that he was a member of the same Communist party unit as they were, and I think we would be delinquent if in the face of the evidence that is now in the record——"

Tydings cut him short: "Why didn't you tell us this? Why did you wait until this hour to tell me?"

"I am not waiting," Morris protested. "One day Senator Green made me a witness and I put it all in the record."

"You haven't told me about it," Tydings insisted obstinately. "This is the first time I have heard about it."

"Senator, I assume that you are aware of everything that is in the record."

"No, there are some things in the record I haven't been able to read. Turn it over to the FBI or do something with it. I'd like to get a decision here; we don't want to waste this afternoon." Brusquely Tydings put the motion to suspend the inquiry and it was carried by three to two. Hickenlooper stated that he would have some comments to make in the Senate, and Lodge announced that he would file his own "individual views."

McCarthy agreed that the investigation should be wound up— "the most fantastic exhibition I have ever seen," he called it—and said the ending of such a "whitewash operation" would be good news for the country. "Tydings and McMahon have succeeded in making the subcommittee a disgrace to the Senate and an insult to the intelligence of the country. My investigation will continue; I've now got five investigators working round the clock, and unless some other committee is formed to do an honest job, I will be forced to take the evidence to the Senate floor."

So the issue was still very much alive—kept alive largely by Tydings and the Democrats.

McCarthy also denied, at this time, that he was in trouble with the Wisconsin income tax authorities, who had requested more detailed explanation of his returns. He also breezily defended the $10,000 Lustron payment.

This enabled Secretary of Agriculture Brannan to blister Joe before a Democratic rally, identifying him only as "a certain high-priced author on housing," whose "shouting from the housetops has exposed no Communists, brought no traitors to justice," but only "created fear, confusion." The rally displayed neither fear nor confusion nor disunity nor discord as it whistled and cheered the speaker.

And McCarthy came back with an open letter to President Truman saying that he had evidence that in 1946 the State Department had destroyed files bearing on the loyalty of its staff. To the letter he attached photostatic copies of statements made by four individuals to the effect that they, as department clerks, had helped to carry out the rifling job.

The department countered that the asserted "weeding out" of the files had been merely a re-sorting under a new filing system, in anticipation of a new loyalty program; nothing, it said, had been destroyed.

Then Tydings released to the press advance copies of the report he intended to submit on the long-drawn-out struggle.

[II]

One glance at this document and the hackles of the Republican senators rose: In effect, they protested, the report found the defendants in the case innocent, and the prosecutor guilty! The report asserted that Senator McCarthy had hatched a "nefarious plot" to practice fraud and deceit upon the Senate, meanwhile living in "mortal fear" that he would be exposed. His charges against the

State Department, it was maintained, were not only baseless and false, but an example of the technique of the "big lie" used by Adolf Hitler. Name by name the report ticked off the persons whom Mc-Carthy had placed under suspicion, and all were cleared. Against Mrs. Esther C. Brunauer there had been found "no evidence of disloyalty." Gustavo Duran had resigned "before the loyalty program was instituted," and therefore rated no attention.* Haldore Hanson was held not accountable for having published articles in Communist magazines. Philip Jessup had definitely belonged to two Red fronts (not five as McCarthy charged), but whether or not his name had been used without his permission in the others had not been shown. Certainly Dorothy Kenyon had been "less than judicious" and "gullible" in letting herself be linked with "twenty cited organizations," but in this she had had "a great deal of distinguished company." † And while Service had been "extremely indiscreet" in his dealings with Jaffe, he was neither disloyal nor a security risk, and had been "framed" by the "China lobby." John Carter Vincent was completely exonerated as to disloyalty, and Owen Lattimore was neither a Communist nor a spy nor an employe of the State Department; and while he had "not exercised discretion" in his contacts, he had "never knowingly associated with Communists," and he was rated loyal. To cap the verdict, in the *Amerasia* case the committee had found "not one shred of evidence to support the unwarranted charge that the case was 'fixed' in any manner," all the government agencies involved having acted in good faith and properly.

The report was signed by Senators Tydings, McMahon, and Green. It had not been seen by Senator Hickenlooper until the day after it was handed to the press (a reporter gave the senator his first glimpse of it); and Senator Lodge, in a 20,000-word dissenting opinion, ripped into the committee's procedure, saying that "the investigation must be set down as superficial and inconclusive. The proceedings often lacked impartiality. . . . The subcommittee's record is a tangle of loose threads, of witnesses who were not subpoenaed, of leads which were not followed up." In the *Amerasia* case, he said, "no satisfactory answer was obtained to the question

* This although the Senate had "authorized and directed" the subcommittee "to conduct a full and complete study and investigation as to whether persons who are disloyal to the United States *are or have been* employed by the Department of State."
† Innocence by association? again asked the committee's critics.

as to why . . . the Justice Department failed to prosecute Jaffe, Larsen, and Roth with vigor . . . resourcefulness, and enthusiasm." McCarthy's charges Lodge put down as "not proved" (a Scotch verdict), but he declined to give blanket exoneration to anyone named, not even Jessup. "We simply did not investigate him," he pointed out, so no conclusion was possible, although personally he was quite ready to accept the word of Generals Marshall and Eisenhower that the ambassador was perfectly loyal.

The language of the majority report was so vitriolic—all aimed at Senator McCarthy—that the Republicans felt compelled to make the matter a party issue and attempt at least to tone down the wording. If that should fail, the party as a unit would fight to prevent acceptance of the report by the Senate.

This decision altered McCarthy's position in the Senate profoundly. Up to now he had been alone, cheered on by some of his party colleagues, but not backed or endorsed by the leadership. Now his defense became Republican doctrine, and the initiative for asserting it passed from his hands to those of the party strategists. It was a sweeping change, and the Democratic leadership took note of it by swiftly calling a caucus of their members, at which Tydings put the issue to them squarely. For months, he contended, he, McMahon, and Green had been subjected to every kind of abuse, and they had kept silent. He personally had "stuck his chin out" to get a fair investigation, he declared, and his fellow Democrats now "have got to back me up." Despite some misgivings that perhaps they were committing a blunder, the caucus voted to support the committee absolutely.

[III]

While this behind-the-scenes debate was going on, McCarthy expressed his hope that the report would be filed as written, and he told Senator Taft, the policy leader, that any attempt to prevent its being presented would be a mistake. The report, he said, would "perform a valuable function in that a reading of it by any fair-minded person will indicate the extent to which the subcommittee has gone to protect Communists. I can stand up to the smear. I have expected it."

Taft agreed with Senator Lodge that the subcommittee had failed to carry out its mission, but had concocted a political report that was insulting to McCarthy and inferentially to every Republican who agreed with him.

The Foreign Relations Committee received its subcommittee's report, as written, and voted, 9 to 2, to "transmit" it to the Senate without recommendations. Lodge and Hickenlooper cast the two negative votes. Some of the members did not bother to read the report before voting. Two paragraphs, criticizing Lodge and Hickenlooper for absenteeism and for issuing misleading statements, were deleted, but otherwise nothing was changed. And on July 20—five months to the day since McCarthy's Senate speech had set off the long turbulence—the storm broke in the Senate, with a violence unwitnessed there since Civil War-Reconstruction days. The *New Republic*'s correspondent, looking back on a quarter of a century of reporting the Senate, could recall nothing to equal it for bitterness.

Tydings opened the battle, and the galleries tensed as he unreeled a long electric cord attached to a phonograph beside his desk. The Democrats crouched in their seats, "positively growling for revenge," the *New Republic* reported. "You could actually hear a hoarse, angry mutter."

At the beginning Tydings stumbled, but was deftly helped to recover by Vice-President Barkley.

"Mr. President," Tydings addressed the chair, "I send to the desk a report of the Subcommittee of the Committee on Foreign Relations, pursuant to Senate Resolution 231——"

Barkley interrupted with a parliamentary reminder that a report from a subcommittee was not acceptable; the Senate receives reports only from its committees, not their branches. Said Barkley loudly, "The chair would say that a report from the subcommittee is not in order."

Tydings was hurrying on, and managed to get out "which I have been instructed," when Barkley again broke in, more sharply. "If it is a report from the full committee it is in order."

This time Tydings caught the cue and urbanely continued: "I referred to it as I did only for identification. I am instructed by the full committee to submit the report to the Senate, and that I now do."

Barkley: "The report is filed."

This was the critical moment. Senator Wherry, minority leader, was on his feet immediately to inquire whose this report was, the subcommittee's or the committee's. Senators Lodge and Alexander Smith of New Jersey, both members of the Foreign Relations Committee, explained that it was a report from the subcommittee which the full committee had voted to "transmit" to the Senate—mechanically, that is, the way one hands a letter to another person—without expressing approval or disapproval, and in fact without making any recommendation or comment on it whatever. Therefore it was a subcommittee report, not one from the full committee. But the chair overruled this interpretation; whereupon Wherry appealed to the Senate to overrule the chair. The vote was 45 to 37 to uphold the chair. The depth of feeling on both sides, in this conflict, was laid bare by this division, for the Democrats had voted as a unit, and the Republicans the same, something almost unknown in the Senate. This dispelled the last doubt that the struggle would be grim.

Twice more the Republicans tried to have the report refused on technical grounds, and each time they were beaten back by a straight party vote. There was no pretense of conducting a debate: whenever a Republican arose to speak, the buzz of conversation on the Democratic side became so loud that finally the chair was impelled to request all senators who did not care to listen to leave the floor. None did, and few listened to the Republican objections. Protesting this studied inattention, Senator Jenner of Indiana exclaimed in disgust, "How can we get the Reds out of Korea if we cannot get them out of Washington?"

At length Tydings was able to launch into his speech, a two-hour display of showmanship in which he hammered McCarthy from every side, in voice and manner expressing denunciation, ridicule, outrage, disgust. With humor, sarcasm, and appeals to patriotism, he charged that McCarthy had "stooped to a new low" of irresponsibility, and pictured the ordeal of the investigation he had just concluded. For three months, he said, he had "taken punishment by a colleague of mine, who used every epithet and every form of opprobrium and calumny to blackguard me, the senator from Connecticut [McMahon], and others. But I have not returned the favor because I did not want to sink to that kind of level, even off the Senate floor." Looking directly at McCarthy, he added scornfully, "And anything I say or do on the Senate floor I shall say outside the Senate floor, and I shall not retract it afterward!"

Applause came from the galleries, and the Vice-President admonished against interruptions.

Next Tydings tore into McCarthy's tangle of figures on the number of Communists supposed to be in the State Department, coming to the conclusion that "in making his speech at Wheeling, on February 9, Senator McCarthy was talking of a subject and circumstances about which he knew nothing," and thereby he had put his party on a spot so that it had to come to his rescue:

"When a senator says there are five hundred and sixteen, two hundred and five, fifty-seven, one hundred and eight or twenty-five spies, or one spy even, in the State Department, it is not the statement of a man on the corner of 9th and G Streets who is carrying on a casual conversation with people who are going home from work. It is the voice of the republic. It is the voice of the government. People think it is so." For this reason, Tydings went on, it had been necessary to nail this use of the Hitler technique of the "big lie," and he had reluctantly taken on the task, realizing that it would "bring no plaudits for me, but only scars and wounds for myself from men of little character."

What had McCarthy really said at Wheeling? That, Tydings continued, had been the first thing the investigators had tried to establish, and they had established it. He called attention to the first of eight huge charts, blowups of newspaper reports of McCarthy's speeches in the West. The first was from the *Wheeling Intelligencer.* Tydings had the chart placed on an easel in plain view, and using a five-foot pointer, he indicated the headline:

McCARTHY CHARGES REDS HOLD JOBS; TRUMAN
BLASTED FOR RELUCTANCE TO PRESS PROBE

Then he pointed to the words said to have been spoken by the senator: "I have in my hand a list of two hundred and five members of the Communist party . . ."

Tydings whacked the chart with the pointer and the crack sounded like a gunshot. Think of it, he cried, "here is a Secretary of State with two hundred and five known Communists in his department . . . and he is so low and vile and unpatriotic that he permits them to stay there and whittle away the vitals of our government!"

But the next day, he went on, referring to accounts of Joe's subsequent speeches as reported in the press, the figure had changed to fifty-seven, and it kept on changing, with McCarthy finally denying under oath that he ever said "two hundred and five" at Wheeling. Well, Tydings had affidavits by the reporter for the *Intelligencer* and two officials of radio station WWVA who had monitored the broadcast, and here was the advance copy of the speech given to them by McCarthy, and the figure 205 was confirmed by them all.

Then Tydings held up a phonograph record and asked unanimous consent to play it. Such a thing had never been done in the Senate chamber, but Tydings explained that "I am not asking the senators to take my word, but to hear the senator's voice."

Excited murmurs ran through the press gallery—the lost recording of the Wheeling speech must have been found!

Senator Wherry arose and said dubiously that he wished to "reserve my right to object" to unanimous consent, because there were "certain rules——"

Before he could finish Tydings cut in with, "I withdraw the request."

"Just a moment, please," Wherry remonstrated.

"I withdraw the request," Tydings repeated.

"I should like to state my reasons," Wherry insisted; but distinctly and stubbornly Tydings twice repeated that he withdrew the request, adding, "I will play the record off the Senate floor in due time— but admission will be *by card* only."

This jibe at McCarthy's "card-carrying Communists" drew a laugh from the galleries and Democrats on the floor. Tydings proceeded to announce that he had a recording of the senator's radio interview in Salt Lake City *also* and would be happy to play it outside the chamber. "And if this gets broken," he said, holding up the record in his hand, "I have duplicates."

Then he diverted the Senate with travesty and burlesque. "This is what the record would say if I could play it," he chuckled, "but my hearers will never get the full beauty they would through hearing the golden voice itself telling it. Here it is; I will try to imitate it a little. Listen to this. This is Dan Valentine, the radio announcer." And mimicking McCarthy's voice, he read from the script of the Salt Lake City colloquy containing the words "fifty-seven card-carrying members of the Communist party."

"This is what the senator said in Salt Lake City, not what he said to the Senate he said either in Wheeling or at Salt Lake City, but his own voice shows what he said," Tydings concluded. Then his voice grew vibrant with anger as he exclaimed: "Mr. President, there is too much evidence to doubt what was actually said, particularly when we have a voice here [he gestured toward the record] which can speak louder than the silent exhibits I have already shown to the Senate. That is why I said a hoax and a fraud was practiced on the people of the United States, and by the eternal gods, that is true!"

The galleries applauded as the speaker rampaged on. "That is not the half of it! There was next detailed in this sordid episode the cases of eighty-one individuals . . . Oh, my, how the newspapers did lap up those things! 'Eighty-one spies in the State Department!' 'Eighty-one Communists known to Acheson!' 'He'll not do anything about it!' Day after day, 'Tydings and his gang are whitewashing!' "

By means of charts he showed the parallels between McCarthy's numbered list and the Lee Report, which, he said, had been thoroughly looked into by four separate committees of a Republican-controlled Congress and "nobody asking that a single [person] be fired or a report made to Congress. So when some shout about 'whitewash,' I am going to show the senator that we Democrats are in some very 'extinguished' company!" Advancing toward Senator Jenner [the senator who had spoken of "Whitewash, Inc."] Tydings berated him with a contemptuous bitterness so personal that the chair ordered him to desist and sit down. But a Democratic motion to override the chair was carried instantly, by another straight party vote, and Tydings resumed his tongue-lashing. The Marylander recalled his own service as a machine gunner in World War I and his citation by General Pershing for the Distinguished Service Cross—something the senator from Indiana perhaps wouldn't know about, he sneered. "When it is suggested that I would protect Communist spies in the country that I love, I find—no, I cannot say here what I would wish to say!" And taunting Jenner with having voted against the Marshall Plan and the Atlantic Pact, he accused him of "always, always, following the same thing that Stalin is saying, that the *Daily Worker* is saying."

As for McCarthy, Tydings said he was making no attack on him; "I have simply dealt with the facts." The Republicans' position he sympathized with, he said, and drew more laughter by quoting Emmanuel S. Larsen, of *Amerasia* notoriety, as having testified that Senator Wherry had told him, after McCarthy's Wheeling speech, "Oh, Mac's gone out on a limb and kind of made a fool of himself, and we have to back him up now."

This brought Wherry to his feet again with an angry denial that he had ever made the statement, and he even doubted that Larsen had ever said such a thing, although Senator Lodge confirmed that he had heard Larsen so testify. Wherry in turn was contemptuous as he retorted that if the rest of Tydings' report were no more authentic than that, the public could "throw it in the ashcan." Taking umbrage at the presence on the floor of Edward Morgan, the Tydings Committee counsel—who had been sitting beside Tydings, acting as prompter—Wherry tried in vain to have him expelled from the chamber. He suspected Morgan of having inserted this particular "garbage" into the report, and during an intermission he moved across and threw a punch at the attorney. Senator Connally of Texas rushed to separate the combatants.

In concluding, Tydings demanded dramatically: "What is there here other than a fraud and a hoax? They represent perhaps the most nefarious campaign of half-truths and untruths in the history of this republic! It ought to make Americans' blood boil that they have been told these foul charges! Here is the record [picking up the phonograph record] to prove what I say! At a time of great national peril, if this body has any idea of maintaining its integrity, it might well ponder these matters. If you are still in doubt, come to my office and hear this record. You will find out who has been 'whitewashing—'whitewashing' with mud, with slime, with filth, with the dregs of publicity at the expense of the people's love for their own country! I ask the Senate: 'What are you going to do about it?' I leave it up to the Senate's conscience."

Again the galleries applauded, and there was even a spatter of handclapping on the floor. Tydings had spoken for two hours and five minutes, and at the close his shirt was drenched with perspiration. Twenty or more Democrats crowded to shake his hand. McCarthy, who had sat throughout without flinching, left the chamber quietly, but had a word for the reporters outside.

"Today," he said, "Tydings tried to notify the Communists in government that they are safe in their positions. However, I want to assure them that they are not safe. We started out with eighty-one. Two have been gotten rid of already. Case No. 19, William Remington, has been indicted by a grand jury for perjury in connection with his membership in the Communist party, although the Tydings group gave the entire eighty-one a clean bill of health. That means two down and seventy-nine to go. The others will be dug out, one by one."

[IV]

The next day the Republicans counterattacked, centering their fire on the failure of the Tydings Committee to do the job it had been ordered to do. Senator Ives of New York, who only a few weeks before had signed the Declaration of Conscience with Margaret Chase Smith, led off. Charges of "a fraud and a hoax," he said, "should not be allowed to serve as camouflage for dereliction in duty or failure in performance on the part of those preferring the charges. Errors in commission by some should not blind us to errors in omission by others." Tydings' stinging phrase Ives bounced back, saying that if any fraud or hoax had been perpetrated, it was the deliberate action of the subcommittee in "disregarding the will of the Senate." This support for McCarthy seemed somewhat backhanded, but the speech underlined the unanimous disassociation of the Republican side from the Democratic attack on the Wisconsin senator.

Senator Lodge, who had filed his "individual views" dismissing the investigation as "superficial and inconclusive," said the majority's conclusions amounted to "God's in His heaven, all's right with the world." Again he pleaded for a system of nonpartisan, nonpolitical commissions to handle such investigations in the future. When Senator Lehman found it "incomprehensible" that Lodge should refuse to clear a man like Philip Jessup of suspicion of disloyalty, Lodge explained again that while he personally had confidence in Jessup's integrity, "why try to say we investigated him when we did not investigate at all—except to be clever or put somebody on the spot?" And he declined to be a party to something labeled a report on an investigation that had never taken place.

Senator Hickenlooper termed the report "a mysterious document mysteriously conceived," and was revolted by the thought of being associated with it. Tydings' brag about the transcript of the hearings running to 3,000,000 words, filling 4,000 pages, with testimony by 35 witnesses, he ridiculed. Lodge observed that if "a group of smart young lawyers were to go through the majority report and take out everything in it . . . that savors of personal vituperation, there would be very little left."

Senator Jenner answered Tydings' philippic by one even more vitriolic, winding up with "All trained seals have to stoop to pick up the ball when they drop it, and the attack of the senator from Maryland on me is only an indication of how low he is willing to stoop to pick up the administration's ball, no matter how rotten the filth it has rolled through." The "pro-Communist" smear he flung back, averring that Tydings deserved another citation—one from Stalin—reading, "Thanks for a job well done!"

An unexpected sensation was provided when Senator Flanders called attention to the new title page that had been clipped to the report overnight, identifying it as a report by the Foreign Relations Committee. The Republicans tried to prevent its circulation under this misleading cover, and again were voted down on straight party lines.

Several days later Senator Lodge discovered that forty-five pages of matter he had inserted in the record, including all the "unanswered questions" he had listed, had been cut out. To his indignant protest Senator McMahon replied that it was a mistake, some clerk's error, committed unintentionally; but Lodge showed by the clumsy way in which the portion preceding the excised passage had been joined to the portion following it that the deletion had been deliberate. McMahon offered to have the omitted matter added as an appendix, but Lodge insisted that it be restored to its proper place, although he could not halt distribution of the copies already prepared.

Never had Capitol reporters witnessed such bitterness in the Senate. The McCarthy issue, which many had believed buried by the Korean fighting, was back again, in the words of *Newsweek,* "bigger and dirtier than ever." More importantly, the situation had been changed. Until now Joe McCarthy had been the lone freebooter, sustained by nothing but his audacity and his skill in maneuver. Now he had come under the party's wing, he had acquired party backing, and his support among the people, thanks to the eminence conferred upon him by the long Tydings imbroglio, was many times widened. From the inquiry's rancorous infighting he had emerged, not unscathed, but paradoxically strengthened by the wounds he had suffered. No longer was he a corsair: the Republican high command had unwittingly issued him letters of marque and reprisal, authorizing him to prey on anything he might suspect of flying the Red flag. And for the next four years he would ravage all the coasts of Bohemia with impunity, secure in his new status as a jolly privateer.

PART THREE

Pirate with a Cause

"Either be hot or cold; God doth despise,
Abhor, and spew out all neutralities."
—Herrick

Dead Men Tell No Tales

[I]

In February, 1950, Joseph R. McCarthy, senator from Wisconsin, was virtually unknown to the American public at large, and even little known to the group of newspapermen whose occupation it was to keep posted on the powers and personalities of Washington. By the end of July, 1950, Senator Joe McCarthy was as widely known as the President, his features were familiar to millions, and his words and actions—even his supposed thoughts—were being chronicled by gossip columnists and pondered by political pundits. Between those two dates he had been the target of political and personal attacks of an intensity, scope, and vigor such as seldom have been directed against any public figure. The swiftness of his transformation from an indistinguishable senator to an object of nationwide adulation or detestation was as unprecedented as it was breathtaking. Like a rocket he had shot upward, and there seemed to be no end to his ascent. How had this come about?

The times and world and national developments had set the stage for him, true; but the activating factor still had been McCarthy. He was, or certainly he seemed to be, unprecedented. He conformed to no conventional pattern. And it was his unique qualities that had lifted him into prominence and would continue to propel him higher and higher. He had found a cause that would absorb him completely, one that it was already plain promised immense if vague political benefits. It is a truism that sooner or later the prophet becomes his own disciple, the salesman sells himself; and although before 1950 McCarthy had given little thought to communism, once he began to delve into it, enthusiasm kindled simultaneously with his patriotism. No man can read another's mind absolutely, but on balance it seems fair to say that at this point McCarthy was reasonably sincere in his objective, even though his tactics were cal-

culating and shifty. An instinctive guerilla fighter, he was brilliant
in that role; even his opponents grudgingly admired his rapidity of
movement and skillful escapes. The *New Republic* had commented
on the fascination of "watching lumberjack McCarthy agilely leap
from log to log . . . and leave each stump just before it throws
him. How long can he do it?" But he kept on doing it, to the baffle-
ment of ill-wishers. And regarding the depth and sincerity of his
patriotism, as he comprehended that sentiment, there could be no
question. The playing of "The Marine Hymn" would bring tears
to Joe McCarthy's eyes, and they were not tears shed on cue.

McCarthy also was capable of surprising, "out-of-character" behavior. A future colleague, Charles E. Potter, a combat veteran
who had lost both legs in the Battle of the Bulge and who would
become a senator from Michigan, had a veteran's keen eye for
patriotic humbug, and he would attest to McCarthy's striking ability
to pass from one role to another with convincing sincerity. One
minute he would be Joe the rough diamond, a Prince Charming in
the raw; the next, the glowering district attorney beating down a
witness; one moment the rabble-rouser spouting inflammatory inani-
ties, and in a twinkling "good old Joe," the drinking man's companion. He might be the hearty outdoorsman, tramping the Wisconsin
woods, fishing, hunting, carousing, sitting out exhausting poker sessions; and then the steadfast friend, compassionate, generous, understanding; only suddenly to transform himself into a ruthless grand
inquisitor. As Macaulay wrote of Horace Walpole, of McCarthy,
too, it might have been said that "his features were covered by mask
within mask . . . he played innumerable parts, and overacted them
all." And like Walpole, "he loved mischief"—mischief that might
be malicious, or simply mischief for mischief-making's sake.

A mischief-maker who acts on impulse is difficult to cope with,
because he deals in illogic and the unexpected. Born combative,
stimulated rather than deterred by hard knocks, McCarthy, with a
privateer's bravado, would lay aboard an adversary of superior
weight against all prudence and reason, and the very impetuosity
and recklessness of his onslaught often enabled him to beat down
opposition and make off with the prize. Because he acts from different motives than the majority of mankind, the freebooter can cut
through conventional courses, and attack or scuttle away as the
exigency of the moment may require.

By the time the Tydings Report was filed in the Senate, McCarthy had passed through his first major battle, had learned his craft and felt his strength; henceforward he need fear nothing but himself— which in itself is an attitude hard for the conventional-minded to grasp.

[II]

McCarthy's opposition betrayed their inability to come to grips effectively with the unusual phenomenon they faced by their muddled and contradictory reaction to the Tydings affair. *The New York Times* said roundly that "McCarthy and 'McCarthyism' have been exposed for what they are—and the sight is not a pretty one"; but it also conceded that the "net effect of the report is uncertain." The *Times* suspected that the Tydings Report, rather than extinguishing, may have added "new fuel to the political fires that have surrounded the case from the beginning." The only thing the *Times* was sure about was that as long as the Democrats ruled Congress, there would be no more investigations of McCarthy; tangling with him had proved too risky. If he had accomplished nothing else, he at least had united the Democrats on this issue, which was itself a feat hardly paralleled.

To *The Nation,* the notion that the Senate might let the matter drop was anathema. "If McCarthy is guilty as charged (and the evidence against him is black as pitch), it is monstrous to assume that we must endure him as a maker of our laws until the people of Wisconsin have a chance to vote on him two and a half years from now," was *The Nation*'s feeling. In plain words, McCarthy should be expelled from the Senate, even though Senator Wherry would "set up the howl expected," and though Senator Taft had found the Tydings Report "derogatory and insulting to the Senate." (To *The Nation,* this conclusion indicated merely that Taft's "highly touted intellect" had become "curiously perverted.")

The *New Republic* rejoiced over the outcome of the wrangle, believing that Tydings had written an end to a "chapter of hysteria such as America has rarely known." Premature jubilation over the elimination of Senator McCarthy would become a recurrent theme among his enemies.

The undenominational Protestant weekly *Christian Century* felt that the Tydings investigation had done nothing to clear the atmosphere, nor had it "convinced many who were not convinced before. Partisan votes can confirm partisans in their partisanship, but they do little more." The only report that *Christian Century* deemed worthy of "serious attention by fair-minded citizens" was Senator Lodge's, denouncing the inquiry's procedure as tending to "besmirch the reputations of innocent persons, hamper the work of government investigative agencies, impair the position of the United States before the world, reflect unjustly on many excellent persons in the State Department . . . and, after all these misfortunes, end up with only a most superficial and inconclusive finding." With this summation *Christian Century* heartily agreed, although it expressed relief that "while the Korean war goes on there will be no more hullabaloo in Washington about Communists in the State Department."

These editorial reactions, typical of the generality of published comment, merely underscored the political gains that McCarthy had made. *Newsweek* brought this into focus by a single item of news: with congressional elections close at hand, Senator McCarthy was receiving more bids to speak from all over the country than all other senators combined, and the Republican National Committee had requested him to funnel these invitations through party headquarters. GOP strategy, it was plain to see, set great store on Joe's effectiveness as a stump speaker, especially in the states where the Senate races were the hottest.

McCarthy was happy to oblige. Nearly every weekend he flew out of Washington to keep a speaking engagement, and his theme was always the same: " 'McCarthyism' means 'Americanism.' " In most places he was received with noisy enthusiasm, acclaimed as the hero of his cause. And each of these forays lifted him higher in the respectful esteem of his party mates. For those who could see it, Joe was consolidating his victory with a view toward more audacious exploits.

[III]

The commotion at the Capitol, after Tydings' tear in the Senate, did not abate. While Republican assaults on the subcommittee report continued, McCarthy brought a fresh accusation in the Senate, charging that a "Mr. X," an economist in the Eastern European division of the State Department, was a hidden Communist, born in Moscow and active in numerous Red fronts. He declined to name the man, but waved a photostat copy of an FBI report highly derogatory of the man. From clues in the document Senator McMahon identified "Mr X" as Edward G. Posniak and warmly defended his loyalty, offering to put twenty-five affidavits into the record attesting Posniak's patriotism. One of the affidavits was by Republican Senator Wayne Morse, McMahon said; whereupon Morse insisted that his entire statement be read. This revealed that Morse had indeed endorsed the man, but with the reservation that he had had no contact with Posniak since 1930 and could not vouch for anything after that date. Posniak himself termed false everything that McCarthy said except that he had been born in Moscow; his parents had fled the Bolsheviks in 1917, he said, and as "an early victim" of the Reds he had been a lifelong antagonist of Communists.

The effect of it all was to throw the Senate into renewed turmoil, especially when McCarthy asserted that the State Department's clearance of Posniak, in the face of the FBI information, was only to be expected, inasmuch as members of Secretary Acheson's law firm made a practice of appearing before the department's loyalty board as attorneys for persons accused.

"Think of it!" he exclaimed; "Acheson's law partners appearing before the loyalty board of which Acheson is boss!"

McCarthy also charged that President Truman was out to "get" him, by fair means or foul, and had assigned two income tax agents to "collect all the bad information about McCarthy they could. They ought to come to me. I know more about McCarthy than anybody else does. McCarthy doesn't claim to be a great saint or a great sinner—just a normal man."

This was said at a time when widespread publicity was being given to the senator's dispute with the Wisconsin tax authorities over his 1949 return. The state tax department revealed that Joe had listed his income for that year as $17,120, but interest payments of $15,172 and stock losses of $2,290 had left him with a net deficit of $342, so he had paid no tax at all. The state was seeking a more detailed explanation, it was said, and McCarthy supplied one, listing payments to six relatives, six banks, and a finance company. Auditing of the return proceeded slowly, with Joe's critics releasing figures and rumors at intervals. But this was small shot that rattled harmlessly off McCarthy's armor, and really it was intended only to annoy.

A matter on which he did return a point-blank fire was the phonograph record which Tydings had waved so triumphantly in the Senate. Although nowhere in his long tirade had Tydings unequivocally identified the recording as one of McCarthy's Wheeling speech, the implication had been inescapable, and the press generally had so identified the disc in their accounts.*

As the days went by, some Capitol reporters did feel that it was odd that neither McCarthy nor anybody else had challenged the identification of the recording at the time. When reporters asked Tydings to play it in his office, as he had promised he would, they were put off with excuses.

What the press did not know was that McCarthy himself was endeavoring to track down a recording of his words in Wheeling. On June 28, three weeks before Tydings submitted his report, McCarthy had written confidentially to Herman Gieske, editor of the *Wheeling Intelligencer,* suggesting that since there were many radio hams who made a hobby of transcribing broadcast programs perhaps one of these amateurs might have taken the speech off the air. A recording, he told Gieske, would "effectively discredit . . . the false claim" that he had used the figure 205 on the air, and he asked Gieske to keep the matter confidential, because otherwise "I would have the press services on my neck looking for a statement." This search was still going on when Tydings reported to the Senate on July 20. Some time after that, Gieske informed McCarthy that no recording had been found, and that positively none was known to exist.

On August 4, in the Senate, McCarthy called Tydings' bluff. Tydings was not present, although McCarthy had sent word of what he was going to say. Recalling that the crux of the dispute was whether he had said "fifty-seven" or "two hundred and five" in Wheeling, McCarthy read Tydings' words, and also Tydings' subsequent complaint about the scant newspaper coverage that his speech was apt to get.

"Well, this statement of Senator Tydings got coverage," Joe said.

---

* *The New York Times,* for example, adhering to the strictest accuracy, had reported that while Tydings "was never heard to state directly and precisely where and when the recording had been made," he had explicitly asserted that it "would show that Mr. McCarthy had falsified in disclaiming a use of the 205." Since nobody ever accused McCarthy of using the "205" figure anywhere except in the Wheeling speech, no attribution except to Wheeling could thus logically be made.

"The press apparently understood the senator from Maryland. I have before me a copy of the Washington edition of the *Daily Worker*, the *Washington Post* [this had become McCarthy's habitual salute to his arch-foe], from which I quote:

" 'All the apparatus was in place. Tydings was about to let the senators hear the Wisconsin Republican's own voice charging that there were 205 card-carrying Communists in the State Department. McCarthy had made the claim over station WWVA in Wheeling, West Virginia, last February.'

"I have before me a copy of the *Milwaukee Journal* of July 21, 1950," McCarthy continued, "in which it is said:

" 'Tydings said he had a phonograph recording of the West Virginia speech to prove McCarthy lied, but was not permitted to play it on the Senate floor.'

"Mr. President, it is very important, I think, to determine whether the senator from Wisconsin or the senator from Maryland lied. That one of them lied is obvious. . . . I think it is important to have a decision on the matter, once and for all, so that the Senate and the country can better evaluate the report of the majority members of the subcommittee, and other statements made by the Senator from Maryland."

McCarthy then challenged the integrity of the press, saying:

"I do not know how the Senate can force the senator from Maryland to play that recording. I do not know how it can call his bluff. This is one time when the press can perform a service to the country and to the Senate. Members of the press can go to the office of the senator from Maryland and say, 'Millard, let us hear that recording. Let us hear the voice of McCarthy using the figure two hundred and five.' . . . As I have said, whether it is two hundred and five or fifty-seven may not be important in itself, but it becomes important when the senator from Maryland says McCarthy has perpetrated a fraud on the Senate in saying he used the figure fifty-seven when he actually used the figure two hundred and five. It is now important to know whether the senator from Maryland may not have been practicing a fraud when he stated he had a recording of my speech which would prove that the senator from Wisconsin had lied. . . . It is a very simple matter to find out who spoke falsely."

Anyone who looked in the newspapers the next day for any conspicuous display given to this challenge would have been disappointed. Some reporters did approach Tydings again with requests to hear the record, and again they were put off.*

[IV]

At the time McCarthy spoke, Tydings was conducting his primary campaign for the nomination to a fifth term in the Senate. About the outcome no one expressed any doubt; the senator was popular and entrenched in the state's Democratic organization. And when, as expected, in early September he crushed his primary opponent by a 3 to 1 vote, his reelection in November over the colorless, little-known candidate picked by the Republicans was taken for granted. President Truman, although no fervent admirer of Tydings, thought the primary result a highly satisfactory answer to McCarthy's "smears."

Joe himself had been feverishly busy during the summer and autumn. In constant demand to speak, he appeared in fifteen states. He spoke several times in Illinois, where Scott Lucas, the man who had first tangled with McCarthy over the Wheeling speech, was seeking another term with every prospect of success. Lucas' opponent was Everett M. Dirksen, a member of the House of Representatives and a firm ally of McCarthy, and "McCarthyism" was a leading issue in the campaign.

In Connecticut, both Senators McMahon and Benton were up for reelection, and McCarthy made several appearances against them. He also campaigned energetically in the West, always on the same issue—clean out the State Department—flush out the infiltrators. His name was invoked by the Democrats generally as a symbol of loathing. In California, a bitter contest for the Senate was being carried on between Richard M. Nixon and Helen Gahagan Douglas. Nixon, without naming McCarthy, echoed the demand for a clean sweep of the State Department, while Mrs. Douglas claimed that McCarthy was stumping the state for Nixon, although "the Republican press is so ashamed of McCarthy that it doesn't publish a word about it." Actually McCarthy made one speech in California, and it was reported in the press.

All over the nation Democrats were under fire for the twin evils

---

* It may be noted that years later, in a deposition hearing, Tydings, when questioned about this matter, replied only that he had "never said" the recording was of the Wheeling speech.

of corruption and "being soft on communism." McCarthy needed only mention Alger Hiss to arouse an audience's anger; the issue was everywhere, and, thanks mainly to the efforts of Tydings and the opposition press, McCarthy had come to symbolize that issue. The besieged Democrats could only contend that they had been even rougher on the comrades than had been their opponents, but only Democrats—and by no means all Democrats—believed this; the Republicans certainly had the richer ammunition. What was most noticeable about the campaign, however, was not the issues, but the new spirit that seemed to infuse the long-dispirited Republicans—a spirit of "git up and git," as *Time* put it—a foresense of victory. And this invigoration, Republican strategists frankly admitted, was due in substantial part to the emergence of McCarthy.

Maryland was where McCarthy concentrated his electioneering activity. He sent members of his staff into the state, raised money, and laid out plans. Tydings' opponent was John Marshall Butler, a Baltimore attorney making his first bid for public office. The Republican organization in Maryland was weak (Democrats formed 70 percent of the voter registration) and money was needed to introduce their candidate to the electorate properly. Large contributions came in from wealthy friends of McCarthy in Chicago, Texas, and elsewhere outside the state. A Chicago public relations expert, Jon M. Jonkel, was brought east to supervise Butler's campaign, and since Maryland law forbade out-of-state political managers, Jonkel was officially engaged as an adviser, although actually he bossed the entire campaign and handled most of the money. Tydings' voting record—against fair employment, antilynching, and racial-integration legislation—was raised against him; but chief emphasis was on his "whitewash" of the State Department. Day after day he was assailed for "giving the green light to Stalin's agents to gnaw at the foundations of our national security." McCarthy himself made three speeches, hammering on the "whitewash" theme. "Lucas provided the whitewash when I charged there were Communists in high places," Joe declared; "McMahon brought the bucket; Tydings the brush." And Tydings, by "protecting Communists for political reasons," was shielding traitors "at a time when the survival of Western non-atheistic civilization hangs in the balance."

The disheartening setbacks being suffered by the United Nations forces in Korea, where the Chinese had swarmed across the border

and were pressing irresistibly southward, lent dramatic urgency to
these appeals. General MacArthur was pleading for authority to
strike at the Chinese in their "privileged sanctuary" just beyond
the Yalu River, while in Washington, especially from the State Department, a cry went up that any such aggressive action would
bring Soviet Russia into the war.

The postcard-barrage technique that had worked so well for Joe
in Wisconsin was put into service again, and half a million cards
"personally signed" by Butler (but actually by crews of women
paid at so much per thousand signatures) flooded the state, begging
for votes to "keep Communists out of the government." The master
stroke, however, was the publication of a four-page tabloid, titled
"From the Record," in which were restated all McCarthy's charges
against Tydings. And as proof that Tydings indeed had been "soft
on Reds," there was a photograph showing Tydings and Earl
Browder apparently engaged in earnest conversation. The caption
under it read:

> Communist Earl Browder, shown at left in this composite pic-
> ture, was a star witness at the Tydings committee hearings, and
> was cajoled into saying Owen Lattimore and others accused of
> disloyalty were not Communists. Tydings (right) answered,
> "Oh, thank you, sir." Browder testified in the best interests of
> those accused, naturally.

The catch lay in the word "composite," slipped in so unob-
trusively that it registered with few readers. The photograph was
a fake, produced by taking separate photographs of the two men,
pasting them together in the desired pose, and then photographing
the whole as a single picture. It produced the effect intended, and
hundreds of thousands of copies were distributed in the last days
of the campaign. Butler's official campaign manager repudiated the
device as "stupid, puerile, and in bad taste," and a volunteer worker
for Butler who called it "an insult to people's intelligence" later
claimed to have burned or sold for scrap 150,000 copies.

The result of the vote in November stunned Tydings, the Democrats, the Congress, and the nation, for Tydings was defeated by
more than 40,000 votes. What Franklin Delano Roosevelt, with
all the power and prestige of the Presidency at his beck, had been
unable to do, McCarthy, it appeared, had accomplished. Nor was
that all. In Illinois, Lucas, apparently invincible, went down to

defeat before Dirksen. In California, Nixon was elected to the Senate. In Connecticut, while both McMahon and Benton were reelected, the former handily, Benton's margin of votes was cut to 1,200 and a recount was being called for.

Elsewhere, candidates in whose behalf McCarthy had spoken were elected, and others, on whom he had pinned the "soft on Reds" label, were trounced. He was credited with contributing materially to the defeat of two noted liberals, Senators Frank Graham of North Carolina and Claude Pepper of Florida—the same mighty Pepper at whom Joe McCarthy had gawked in awe four years before. Even in areas where the determining factors had been largely local, the issue which the press and the public alike held to have been decisive had been "McCarthyism." * And although the Democrats retained control of Congress, they had suffered severe losses for which Senator McCarthy was given the credit or the blame.

He was satisfied: his pirate revenge was complete. Dead men tell no tales.

* The power of McCarthy's name in Wisconsin already had been startlingly demonstrated in the primary elections there. A Lakeville working man, night sacker in a soybean mill, fifty-five years old, living with his wife and six children in a tar-paper shack, entered his name in the Democratic-Farmer Labor primary contest for nomination as state railroad and warehouse commissioner. During the campaign he made no speeches, sent out no literature, never asked for a vote, just kept on sacking beans. When the ballots were counted he was the winner by 50,000 votes, swamping four rivals. His only vote-getting asset was his name— Joe McCarthy.

Maryland and Marshall—Oh, My!

As 1950 closed, the atmosphere in Washington was heavy with gloom. In November the nation had been shocked by the attempt of two Puerto Ricans to assassinate President Truman. One of the assassins had been shot dead outside Blair House, and the other, after being tried and convicted, would have his death sentence commuted to life imprisonment by the President. Here was evidence of continued danger from internal subversion.

In Korea the situation was grave, with the forces of General MacArthur being overrun by hordes of Chinese. In Europe, one heard threats and warnings of war. The Russians were truculent, and the debacle of United States policy in the Far East seemed complete. In its Christmas issue, *Newsweek* magazine started a review of the diplomatic outlook with the lugubrious question:

"Will this be the last Christmas of peace on earth?"

In Moscow the Soviet press greeted the new year with a boast that in the second half of the twentieth century "all roads will lead to communism," with Marxism triumphant everywhere.

It was not a time of national confidence; things had gone wrong, and Americans were trying to understand why. Secretary of State Acheson, who just one year before had been ridiculing the Chinese Nationalists, exhorting the Dutch and French to recognize that "a revolution has taken place in Asia," and stating that the first rule of American policy in the Far East must be to do nothing that would weld the Chinese and Russians together in common enmity to the United States, now, a year later, appeared to have executed a pirouette in the opposite direction. As James Reston of *The New York Times* saw it, the Secretary now was all for giving more help to Chiang, insisting that military conditions must determine United States policy toward the future of Formosa, conducting a policy of

212

economic sanctions against the Peiping government, and urging the
United Nations to get together on a policy of collective action
against that regime. Other observers stated plainly that the Secretary seemed to have accepted a World War III as inevitable and
imminent.

Amid these alarms, the 82nd Congress of the United States, with
its Republican accretions, met and organized, and correspondents
noted a marked change in the Senate's attitude toward the junior
senator from Wisconsin. Only a few months previously, not a few
Republican senators had taken care not to pass McCarthy's desk
and had avoided any public display of friendliness. These snubs
had made no impression on smiling Joe. But as a result of the election, the atmosphere had changed, and now Joe McCarthy, in
William S. White's view, was "the most politically powerful first-
term senator in this Congress. The desk of Senator McCarthy is
not, these days, avoided very often by his Republican colleagues.
. . . The man who pursued Acheson now finds the GOP membership of Congress officially demanding Acheson's head. The man
who pursued across the country the two most formidable Democratic fighters—Lucas and Tydings—now surveys a scene where
both are returned to private life. The lessons of these facts have
not been lost. Nor have the Democrats ignored McCarthy as so
long they have tried to do. . . . 'McCarthyism' is simply today a
very considerable force in the Congress of the United States. And
it seems here to stay."

Christian Century, a periodical not prone to forming hasty conclusions, held the same opinion. "Whether we like it or not—and
we do not like it," ran their commentary, "the Wisconsin senator
has become an influential factor in American life."

To unreflective tourists Senator McCarthy had become a sought-
after celebrity, a "must" sight in the Capitol. Now visitors to the
Senate dining room stared in awe at the dark jowls and thinning
hair of the great McCarthy, and he took it as his due, without
losing any of his bucolic bonhomie.

An indication of the political spell cast by McCarthy was the
action of the Democratic caucus in seating Tydings' conqueror,
Butler. Although Tydings had filed a complaint of gross irregularities in the election, Butler was seated "without prejudice," meaning the action was final and might not be reversed except for grave
cause. Off the record the Democrats admitted that they had adopted

this course because "what happened to Tydings could happen to any of us."

McCarthy breezily announced that he intended to look into the Commerce and Agriculture departments during the new session, as well as State. His appointment to the Appropriations Committee, which had jurisdiction over the operating funds of these three departments, drew a howl of protest, Senator Benton expressing outrage at giving to the State Department's "implacable and irresponsible enemy" power of life and death over its fund. It could lead only to "chaos and unspeakable danger," he protested. "Now State Department officials must suffer not only in silence, but in another way. They will find their budgets manipulated by their tormentor, activity by activity, division by division, behind closed doors, and for no reason they can fathom or refute. The junior senator from Wisconsin is to be the judge, jury, and prosecutor of the State Department. By this appointment he becomes his own kangaroo court. . . ."

"We can each of us have his own opinion of the sneak attacks against the State Department on the floor last year," Benton continued, "and there is no doubt what the private consensus is, though few have chosen to state it publicly. That performance can be summed up in the slogan: 'If you can't make one libel stick—try, try another.'" Having once served in the State Department, Benton was watchful for its welfare.

Senator Kenneth McKellar of Tennessee, chairman of the Appropriations Committee, said he had appointed McCarthy at the request of the Republican leadership, and the latter said that Joe was entitled to the place by seniority. Senator Wherry defended McCarthy from Benton's attack, saying: "He has done more than anybody I know to establish the confidence of the public. When the record is written, when his service is done, it's going down in glory."

McCarthy, who was absent during Benton's outburst, shrugged off his critic as a "mental midget" and flung out the taunt: "Connecticut has many mothers and wives of brave men who have been killed in Korea. Many more from Connecticut will die because of the traitorous acts of the dupes and stooges of the Kremlin in our State Department. Benton was elected by those wives and mothers to fight for America, not against it. Yet he squeals and beats his breast because the day of judgment is at hand for the crimson clique in the State Department and because the State Department may be called upon to render an accounting of its stewardship."

Shortly afterward, Senator McKellar bumped McCarthy off the important subcommittee, and McCarthy paid off an old score by bumping Margaret Chase Smith from the Expenditures subcommittee that he headed. No question of revenge involved, he said, as he replaced Senator Smith with newcomer Richard Nixon. And to the hinterlands Joe flashed word that the job of "cleaning out the skunks" would go on—"a dirty, foul, unpleasant, smelly job, but it has to be done, and it will be done—in spite of the high-pitched squealing of those left-wing bleeding hearts of the press and radio."

[II]

Inspiring excitement in headlines was Joe's way of conducting business, and his offstage activities sometimes commanded more newspaper space than did his Senate speeches. Just before Christmas he had a set-to with one of his most persistent detractors, Drew Pearson, the columnist and radio commentator. Pearson had been attacking Joe steadily, for various derelictions, when one evening they met as guests at a dinner party in Washington's Sulgrave Club. With Joe was Nixon, and the two were seated at a table with Pearson and Representative Charles E. Bennett of Florida. What subsequently happened was recounted in several versions later on, but substantially this appears to have been the sequence:

After coffee, most of the guests got up to dance, leaving the four mentioned at the table. Leaning across Bennett, who was seated between them, McCarthy told Pearson that he intended to speak about him in the Senate the next day, "to say some things the country should know." To which Pearson answered that he had some things to say about Joe, and "I've never gone after a man yet that I haven't gotten in the end." McCarthy retorted that Pearson could say anything he pleased; "I've been called everything in the world." Then Pearson: "Why don't you give a speech about your income tax? Tell them how you keep out of jail."

At this McCarthy lunged and grabbed Pearson by the scruff of the neck. Bennett, who was lame from childhood polio, attempted to separate the two and fell, and while McCarthy was helping him up, Pearson walked away.

Later the antagonists met in the cloakroom. Slapping Pearson on the back, Joe exclaimed, "Well, Drew, a pleasant evening, wasn't it?"

Flushing with anger, Pearson plunged his hand into his coat pocket, groping for the check; but McCarthy barked, "Don't you reach into your pocket like that," and seizing Pearson's arms, he kneed him. Sputtered Pearson, "When are they going to put you in the booby hatch?" Whereupon McCarthy slapped him twice, movie-villain fashion, right and left. Nixon came in at that moment, but McCarthy wasn't finished: Swinging far back, he let fly with his open palm, slapping Pearson so hard he fell down.

Nixon moved in. "Let's go, Joe," he urged, but McCarthy stood firm. "I won't turn my back on that son of a bitch," he growled. "He's got to go first!"

Hastily Pearson departed. Nixon would say later that he had never seen a man slapped as hard as Joe walloped the capital's best known, and beyond all doubt most hated and least trusted news commentator.

The next day Fulton Lewis, Jr., a close friend of McCarthy, told of the affair over the radio, and twenty-four senators telephoned Joe congratulations. Austere Senator Arthur Watkins of Utah, a former judge, encountering McCarthy in the Capitol elevator, remarked dryly: "Joe, I've read conflicting accounts of where you hit Pearson. I hope both are true."

McCarthy delivered the promised speech, putting into the *Record* quotations from more than forty prominent Americans, including Franklin D. Roosevelt, Harry Truman, Admiral Halsey, Cordell Hull, Jesse Jones, and Walter Reuther, in which "liar" was the least of the epithets of loathing they had applied to the columnist. McCarthy added his own, calling Pearson the "voice of international communism," serving as a stooge for one David Karr, a man once employed by Pearson and a contributor to the *Daily Worker.*

"It appears that Pearson never actually signed up as a member of the Communist party and never paid dues," McCarthy said; but he served notice on all "loyal newspaper editors and publishers and radio station owners" that if they refused to buy Pearson's syndicated column, "this disguised, sugar-coated voice of Russia, the mockingbirds who have followed the Pearson line would disappear." The American people, too, could do their part, he said, by telling their newspapers that they "do not want this Moscow-directed character assassin being brought into their homes to poison the well of information at which their children drink." And they could let the Adam Hat Company, Pearson's $5,000-a-week radio sponsor, know "what they think of their sponsoring this man" by boycotting Adam hats. "Anyone who buys an Adam hat, any store that stocks an Adam hat, is unknowingly and innocently contributing at least something to the cause of international communism by keeping this Communist spokesman on the air."

Pearson replied wrathfully that his record of fighting communism was longer and better than Joe's, and dared him to repeat his remarks without immunity. McCarthy offered to if Pearson would waive "his own special kind of immunity," created by signing over his property to his wife, frustrating any attempt to collect damages. Eventually Pearson did sue for libel and $5,100,000.*

After much shadow-boxing, this suit, like others of the kind, resulted in nothing more concrete than the very startled reaction of the highly paid, eminent attorney retained by Pearson when McCarthy called him a "shyster."

But the line of defense adopted by Pearson pointed up a weakness shared among Joe's opponents: too many of them answered his attacks by contending that they had been even rougher on Reds than he had himself. Granting that McCarthy was as unscrupulous as his critics said, the implication this carried seemed to be that they had been even less scrupulous, which was hardly a defensible position; it was like fighting vice with more flagrant vice, or sin with superior sin. For all his achievements, Joe's enemies were still underestimating him, mainly because they misunderstood the sort of fighter they were pitted against, or the extent of his popular influence. One source that did not underestimate him was the Adam Hat Company; rather than face a boycott of their products, they canceled their contract with Drew Pearson.

[III]

Another brush with the "enemy" (as McCarthy had come to be) failed to aid the cause of the downcast Tydings, when Earl Browder, cited for contempt of the Tydings Committee, pleaded in defense (1) that the chairman had never admonished him; (2) that he had

---

* Commented Ickes, "McCarthy will doubtless plead immunity, as another would intoxication."

indeed answered some 150 questions, while refusing to answer others; (3) that at the close he had been publicly thanked by the chair. And as a corroborating witness Browder called Senator McCarthy. Joe testified: "In all my experience, I don't think I have seen more perfect cooperation of a chairman and a witness." Browder, he said, "obviously was doing what the chairman wanted him to do—that was, to conduct Operation Whitewash." The judge ordered a verdict of acquittal.

Tydings got in his licks in hearings before the Senate subcommittee on privileges and elections, investigating his charges of illegality in the Maryland election. Testifying in a jam-packed room, with sixty reporters on hand and half a dozen senators listening attentively, he said that he was appearing as a private citizen, without political ambition, to "disclose certain scandalous, scurrilous, libellous, and unlawful practices" in the campaign. His defeat, he contended, had been brought about by a "tissue of lies" in a campaign of "moral squalor." He did not ask that Butler be unseated. Nor did he demand direct action against McCarthy. His main fire was concentrated on the "From the Record" tabloid, and on the broadcasts of Fulton Lewis, Jr. The tabloid, it was brought out, had been printed on the presses of the *Washington Times-Herald,* at McCarthy's suggestion. The *Times-Herald* was published by Mrs. Ruth ("Bazy") McCormick Miller, niece of Colonel Robert R. McCormick, publisher of the *Chicago Tribune,* and 500,000 copies of the tabloid had been run off at the ridiculously low price of $1,440. The editorial content had been prepared by a member of the newspaper's staff.

McCarthy had given his research assistant, Miss Jean Kerr, leave of absence to work in the campaign, and she had helped to raise money outside Maryland. Before the subcommittee she defended the use of the tabloid, saying it contained the sort of information that should go out in campaigns, and her only criticism was that it didn't go far enough; its original wording had been toned down, she grieved to say. Whereupon Senator Hennings wondered aloud, "Who was the sissy in the crowd?"

Irregularities in financing the campaign were brought out; some $27,000 in donations had been funneled directly to Jonkel and never reported, an oversight which he corrected by filing an amended report, thus mitigating the penalty. Eventually he would be tried for this and other violations of the Maryland election laws and be fined $5,000, which he paid without a quiver, his ears still ringing from the dressing-down administered by the bench.

Tydings asked that Mrs. Miller, Frank Smith, of the *Times-Herald* editorial staff, and Fulton Lewis, Jr., be prosecuted for criminal libel. McCarthy did not appear before the subcommittee, although he indicated his willingness to do so.

After weeks of delay, the subcommittee pieced together a report from the separate conclusions submitted by each member. It was caustic in tone. In effect, it said, there had been two campaigns in Maryland—the "front street" campaign conducted by Butler and "responsible" supporters, and a "despicable 'back street' type of campaign, which usually, if exposed in time, backfires. Such campaign methods and tactics," the subcommittee warned, "are destroying the very foundations of our government." The question of McCarthy's participation was dealt with severely, the report stating that "any sitting senator, regardless of whether he is a candidate in the election himself, should be subject to expulsion by action of the Senate, if it finds such senator engaging in practices and behavior that make him, in the opinion of the Senate, unfit to hold the position of United States senator." But the subcommittee refrained from recommending McCarthy's expulsion.

McCarthy's reply was prompt. His first reaction to the report, he said, was one of surprise that "small-minded politicians" should "continue to underestimate the intelligence of the American public." He defended Butler's campaign as "intelligent and courageous," maintained that Communists in government had been the issue, and laid down the rule that "no loyal American is an outsider when it comes to getting rid of Communists. As long as puny politicians try to encourage other puny politicians to ignore or whitewash Communist influences in our government, America will remain in grave danger." Taking a swipe at the two Republicans who signed the report—Margaret Chase Smith of Maine and Robert Hendrickson of New Jersey—he said he was not surprised, for "after all, they went on record last year approving Tydings' whitewash and condemning me for getting rough with Communists." Later he told *U.S. News & World Report* that he thought the Maryland campaign had been "one of the cleanest campaigns in the country."

As a member of the parent Rules Committee, McCarthy served notice that he would file a minority report if the subcommittee's should be adopted, which it was, by a 9 to 3 vote, Wherry, Jenner, and McCarthy being the three dissenters. One change McCarthy did secure: at his request, it was made clear that Miss Kerr had not endorsed the use of the Browder-Tydings composite photograph.

Comment on the subcommittee's report was mainly adverse to Joe, one of the sharpest blows coming from the moderate *Commonweal*. Already *Christian Century,* the Protestant counterpart of Catholic *Commonweal,* had bemoaned that "step by step the power of Senator Joseph R. McCarthy is growing, and that fact portends no good for American democracy." Now *Commonweal,* alluding in an editorial to the current scandal of West Point cadets who had admitted that they had cheated in examinations, asked: "If the cadets are to be tried for cheating, why not McCarthy? Has he done less than these cadets to debase the integrity and honesty of our national life? The issue here is not whether or not communism must be fought at home: it must. The issue is whether or not we . . . will leave the job—and our liberties—to a man who runs along the back streets to do his cheating when he hasn't the stuff to do things the straight and open way."

Such strictures left no mark on the senator. He was constantly on the go, always in a hurry, speaking out of town often and always on the same theme: get the "crimson clique" out of the government. Having dubbed the meticulously garbed Secretary of State the "Red Dean of Fashion," he belabored Acheson with the phrase ceaselessly. And ascending even higher in the hierarchy of public figures, he drew a bead on no less a man than General George Catlett Marshall, who had been drafted by President Truman to serve as Secretary of Defense during the Korean emergency.

[IV]

With McCarthy's flair for utilizing the press, the attack was well-heralded. Richard Rovere, *The New Yorker*'s Washington correspondent, amusingly attributed to Senator McCarthy that ingenious invention, "the press conference to announce a press conference." The senator would summon newsmen to his office in the morning to inform them that he would have something important to say in the afternoon, perhaps hinting slightly at the nature of his forthcoming disclosure. The afternoon newspapers would carry this news under the headline McCARTHY TO NAME NAMES; then the next day's morning editions would carry the second news conference under the headline McCARTHY NAMES NAMES. This gave the senator double mileage from the one item of news. McCarthy was expert in using this transparent device, and the Capitol reporters, never sure what he would say, were forced to play his game.

McCarthy had attacked General Marshall before, terming him unfit to be Secretary of State and a pawn in Acheson's "sellout" of China. During the debates over General MacArthur's plea that the Korean fighting be carried into the Chinese "sanctuaries," the senator had urged that Marshall be sent back to his farm in Leesburg, and that MacArthur be ordered to give the Chinese "the roughest and toughest treatment of which we are capable."

The Senate galleries were crowded when McCarthy arose on June 14 and started to read a 60,000-word indictment of a man who was as close to being a revered national hero as any American alive. Few senators were on the floor, and most of these straggled out before Joe had gone very far. The burden of the speech was that there existed a conspiracy aimed at paving the way for the conquest of the United States by Soviet Russia—"a conspiracy so immense and an infamy so black as to dwarf any such previous venture in the history of man." Both Marshall and Acheson were linked to this unimaginable plot.

The indictment was elaborately detailed. It covered Marshall's war record and his actions as Secretary of State. He was described as "steeped in blood" (an accusation that can be brought against any commander in war, who must march to victory across slain men), and was said to have sponsored policies identical with those of the Kremlin ever since 1942. President Truman was exonerated of blame. "I do not believe that Mr. Truman is a conscious party to the great conspiracy," McCarthy said. On the contrary, he thought the President was "only dimly aware" of what was going on. With supporting documentation from the writings of Winston Churchill, Cordell Hull, Admiral Leahy, Henry L. Stimson, Hanson W. Baldwin, and others, McCarthy deduced that Marshall had:

1. opposed the invasion of Italy in World War II and the conquest of the Balkans before the Russians could get there;

2. advocated the "enticement" of Russia into the war with Japan, by means of the concessions made at Yalta and Teheran;

3. refused to demand a corridor of access to Berlin, resulting in the blockade that the airlift had, with great difficulty, broken;

4. created the China policy that turned that country over to the Reds;

5. excluded West Germany, Spain, Turkey, and Greece from military participation in the North Atlantic alliance.

"We have declined so precipitously in relation to the Soviet Union in the last six years, how much swifter may be our fall into disaster with Marshall at the helm?" McCarthy demanded. "If Marshall is innocent of guilty intent, how can he be trusted to guide the defense of the nation," with a record like that?

The conspiracy in which Marshall was a prime agent, the speaker went on, was intended to "diminish the United States in world affairs, to weaken us militarily, to confuse our spirit with talk of surrender in the Far East, and to impair our will to resist evil. To what end? To the end that we shall be contained, frustrated, and finally fall victim to Soviet intrigue from within and Russian military might from without."

The speech sounded little like McCarthy's usual flamboyant style except in the occasional bursts of familiar expletives—"crimson clique," "high-pitched screaming and squealing," and Marshall's alleged "affinity for Chinese Reds." By and large the language was scholarly, the tone academic, the wording that of a historian and dialectician. The senator stumbled over words as he read on, in his flat, droning voice, for nearly three hours, to a diminishing audience. Then he gave up and inserted the rest of the document in the *Record* unread.

Neither McCarthy nor his staff had the capacity to compile such a treatise; that was plain at the merest glance. So obviously he was reading the work of a ghost-writer or writers better versed in scholarship and better informed in regard to foreign policy than he would ever show himself to be. Even though he subsequently put the speech between covers and published it over his own signature as *America's Retreat From Victory,* no competent critic ever seriously credited McCarthy with such a nugget of erudition as this:

"I am reminded of a wise and axiomatic utterance . . . by the great Swedish chancellor Oxenstiern, to his son departing on the tour of Europe. He said: 'Go forth, my son, and see with what folly the affairs of mankind are governed.' "

Imagination boggles at the notion of this sage admonition issuing from the compendium of Joe's learning; to borrow McCarthy's own phrase, that would indeed be "the most fantastic thing ever heard of."

[V]

Once this broadside had been fired against the man whom McCarthy characterized as having been, by some malign "alchemy of propaganda," enshrined as the "greatest living American," Joe paid it little further heed. General Marshall, accustomed to a more sophisticated weaponry, disdained to notice the blunderbuss thunderclap; yet the shock value of Joe's reckless action was immeasurable, and he reaped benefit from it.

Engaged in incessant and generally enjoyable combat on several fronts, McCarthy was, to the sometimes despair of his reeling opponents, making headway. Besides lambasting Acheson ("Red Dean of Fashion") at every opportunity, and the Secretary's coterie of diplomatic "cookie-pushers," he stepped up his attack on Philip Jessup, whose nomination by the President to be a delegate to the United Nations already was meeting with disfavor in Senate circles. Richard Nixon had called Jessup "the architect of our Far Eastern policy" before McCarthy lifted the phrase to pin it on Owen Lattimore, and crusty Tom Connally of Texas, chairman of the Foreign Relations Committee, had grumbled, "I do not like Mr. Jessup." But Truman insisted on the appointment, and the result was a tendentious hearing before a subcommittee. McCarthy testified for two days, repeating all his former charges against Jessup. Then the attack widened when Harold Stassen, former governor of Minnesota, precipitated a hot argument by blaming Jessup directly for the United States' ruinous policy in China. Senator John J. Sparkman of Alabama, who headed the subcommittee, accused Stassen of piling "inference onto inference onto inference onto inference" to arrive at the wrong conclusion, and Senator J. William Fulbright of Arkansas evaluated McCarthy's testimony in a sentence: "You can put together a number of zeros and still not arrive at the figure one." The clashes became so heated that the subcommittee finally voted, 3 to 2, *not* to approve the nomination, and action was held over until Congress adjourned, when the President was able to make an interim appointment. And McCarthy pointed to another victory.

Owen Lattimore was back in the news defending himself copiously against involvement with the dubious activities of the Institute of Pacific Relations. In a raid on a barn in Massachusetts, the stored files of the institute were seized and correspondence was discovered indicating that Lattimore had been less than candid in his testimony before the Tydings Committee. He was due for further grilling, this time before Senator Pat McCarran's Internal Security Committee, with McCarthy sitting in as assistant inquisitor.

William Remington went on trial for perjury, one of the prosecutors being a "whiz kid" prodigy attached to the United States attorney's office in New York City, named Roy M. Cohn. Remington was convicted and sentenced to prison, only to win a reversal on appeal and undergo a second trial.

Julius and Ethel Rosenberg were put on trial for wartime espionage, which carried the death penalty, and Harry Gold and David Greenglass, their confessed accomplices, testified to the multiple treacheries of that spy ring on behalf of the Russians. Julius Rosenberg swore that he was a loyal American, but he would not tell the jury whether he was a Communist.

Again and again the name Hiss appeared in the news until the climactic headline, HISS STARTS PRISON TERM. He was represented as embittered but confident of ultimate vindication.

In April, General Douglas MacArthur had been relieved of command in Korea, and the shocked nation had followed intently the resulting Senate inquiry. In that the whole controversy over our failure in Asia was gone over once more; but the investigation was conducted by Senator Russell of Georgia with such discretion and impartiality that the heat was dissipated and a potential national crisis averted.

During these months the press continued to serve McCarthy's ends, unwillingly but not unwittingly. He had positive support in a few quarters, principally the *Chicago Tribune* and its affiliates, and the Hearst newspaper chain. Otherwise most of the nation's leading journals opposed him, many strongly, and he struck back at them freely; to maintain their claims to impartiality in reporting the news, they were obliged to print what he said, and to carry the subsequent inevitable echoing exchanges. At one time or another he accused these newspapers and magazines (none notably left wing) of aping the Communist line: *The New York Times, St. Louis Post-Dispatch, Milwaukee Journal, Denver Post, Syracuse Post-Standard, Christian Science Monitor, Time, Life, The Saturday Evening Post.*

For the *Washington Post, Madison Capital Times,* and *New York Post* he reserved special scorn, terming them local editions of the *Daily Worker.* They on their side hated him so obsessively that they could scarcely keep him off a page, and his really hard-core antagonists went even further. An assiduous reader of the *New Republic* counted the number of times *McCarthy* or *McCarthyism* appeared in a single issue and came up with a total of forty, in four separate articles. Harold Ickes alone accounted for seventeen mentions in his routine abuse of "Joseph Rank MuckCarthy."

McCarthy gloried in the vituperation; he said it raised him in the esteem of all true Americans, and also, he considered it purely professional, in no way personal; politics was a rough game, and he could take punishment. His discomfited enemies, however, often found themselves left more dazed than determined after some fresh attempt to end his rampage had failed, with the senator simply growing bolder. Once looked upon as a man who would stop at nothing, he seemed to have become a man whom nothing could stop. Only an assault by the heaviest artillery could flatten this whirling dervish of improbability, it had become apparent, and at last the heaviest gun of all—the President—was trundled out to finish the fight that so many were fumbling.

But before Truman could deliver his barrage, Senator William Benton made his bid to be known as "Bill the Bogey-Killer" by getting McCarthy kicked out of the Senate, if he should refuse to resign. Rashly, Benton introduced a resolution to that effect.

"Moral Leprosy?"
Or "McCarthy for President?"

[I]

Before taking this step, the junior senator from Connecticut had been warned that he would be toying with political extinction. He was invited to view the grisly remains of Lucas and Tydings, and was reminded that Joe had almost beaten Benton in the recent election, and next time it might be different. But Benton often behaved in an unsenatorial fashion.

The Senate was made up principally of lawyers, and Benton was a businessman, direct, aggressive, and accustomed to succeed. His credentials were impressive, although not political. In 1929, with Chester Bowles, he had founded the advertising agency of Benton & Bowles. Radio was coming in, and the firm was quick to grasp its commercial possibilities. During the Depression they had been innovators in exploiting that medium, to their own prosperity. Retiring from business, both partners had turned to public service (in atonement, some wags held, for having invented the singing commercial). Bowles would become governor of Connecticut, ambassador to India, and Undersecretary of State, while Benton, after serving as vice-president of the University of Chicago and chairman of the board of *Encyclopaedia Britannica,* became an Assistant Secretary of State in charge of information programs under President Truman. In 1949, he had been appointed to the Senate to succeed the resigned Baldwin, an early McCarthy casualty. Recently he had been elected to fill out the remainder of Baldwin's term, and two years hence he would be up for election to a full term. Thus he had everything to lose by taking on Joe, and the professional politicians told him so.

It was the report on the Maryland campaign that stirred Benton to action. Suspecting that the report would be pigeonholed and forgotten, he introduced a resolution calling on McCarthy to resign

226

or face investigation to determine whether he should be expelled from the Senate. Not only McCarthy's part in the Maryland campaign, but his other activities should be looked into with a view to expulsion, Benton said; meanwhile, pending disposition of his resolution, he invited McCarthy to refrain from taking part in the business of the Senate.

"In my opinion," Benton told his colleagues, "Senator McCarthy has weakened the respect of decent people for representative government by his attacks upon the character of respectable citizens from the sanctuary of the Senate floor."

Only Senator Lehman arose to thank Benton for taking a stand against a "character assassin," and Benton's resolution was referred to the Rules Committee's subcommittee on privileges and elections, where presumably it would gather dust.

McCarthy was not present when Benton acted, but he promptly issued a statement in reply, coupled with a threat. The statement read:

"Tonight Senator Benton has established himself as the hero of every Communist and crook in and out of government. I am sure that Owen Lattimore and all the Alger Hisses and William Remingtons still in government will agree with the resolution. I call the attention of all honest Democrats to how men of little minds are destroying a once great party."

The threat was even more pointed:

"Lucky for this country that Connecticut's mental midget does not run the Senate! Benton will learn that the people of Connecticut do not like Communists and crooks in government any more than the people of Maryland like them."

Two days later Joe called in reporters and offered to give them the names of twenty-six past or present employes of the State Department whose loyalty had been questioned. There was one condition: the reporters must print the names. Since statements made off the floor of the Senate are not exempt from the libel laws, the reporters demurred, although Joe told them there were some "very high officials" on the list. He said he had suggested to Acheson that these persons be suspended, and had sought assurances that they at least were not having access to classified papers; but back had come a letter saying in effect, "Go to hell." Now, Joe pointed out logically, "if a bank employe is charged with embezzling, you don't let him still have access to the till."

The next day he read this list of names in the Senate. It included "the prize of them all," Jessup, and also John Carter Vincent, who had been "Case No. 2" on McCarthy's original list, given to the Tydings Committee. He linked both men to Communist fronts or to "known Soviet espionage activities," and some others on the list he termed Soviet agents outright.*

The new Democratic majority leader, Ernest McFarland of Arizona, successor to the purged Lucas, bitterly condemned McCarthy's action as "character assassination," and Senator Lehman again called such charges a "smear" and "dastardly." Senator Wherry, on the Republican side, invoked Rule 19, the rule of senatorial courtesy, and McCarthy in retort to McFarland repeated that he and other Democrats were turning their party into one of "Communists and crooks." No one but the two Democratic senators spoke against McCarthy, although their side of the chamber glowered collectively, and the reaction in the press to this "name-calling" was violent. *Newsweek* headlined its report of the fracas, "Democrats Fume at McCarthy, But He Has Them Terrorized." In New York the *Times,* noting that Joe was "at it again," groaned that the Kremlin must rejoice every time the senator opened his mouth, for he was doing his utmost to "destroy the confidence of the American people in the honor, the integrity, and the loyalty of some of their most highly placed public servants, from Secretary of State and on down."

Next President Truman took up the cudgels against the onetime Marine and circuit judge of Wisconsin. Speaking at the dedication of the American Legion's new headquarters in Washington, the President lit into "character assassins" and "scandalmongers" who were "trying to divide us and confuse us and tear up the Bill of Rights." He called on the Legion to "rise up and put a stop to this terrible business . . . take the lead against the hysteria that threatens the government from within."

These "scandalmongers and hatemongers," the President went

---

* One named was Mrs. Esther Brunauer. McCarthy said he understood that she had been suspended by the State Department, although he had been unable to get confirmation. Actually, Mrs. Brunauer had been suspended on April 10, four months previously, just after her husband, Stephen Brunauer, had been suspended by the Navy for security reasons. He had then resigned, on June 18, before his case had been looked into by the Navy's loyalty board. A year later, on June 16, 1952—two years after McCarthy had first raised the question of Mrs. Brunauer's reliability, with typical overstatement calling hers "one of the most fantastic cases I know of"—Mrs. Brunauer would be dismissed from the State Department, as a security risk.

on, warming to his subject, were "chipping away at our basic free-
doms" more effectively than Communists could. They were creating
"such a wave of fear and uncertainty that their attacks upon our
liberties go almost unchallenged. They are filling the air with the
most irresponsible accusations against other people. They are trying
to get us to believe that our government is riddled with Communists
and corruption, when the fact is that we have the finest and most
loyal body of civil servants in the world. The scandalmongers are
trying to get us so hysterical that no one will stand up to them for
fear of being called a Communist. Character assassination is their
stock in trade. Guilt by association is their motto. Many people are
frightened—and frightened people don't protest."

The speech was mildly applauded, and Earle Cocke, Jr., national
commander, admitted that he was not enthusiastic about it; certainly
he was not going to lead the Legion in any campaign against Mc-
Carthy.

Although Truman had never spoken McCarthy's name, everybody understood that the attack was aimed squarely at Joe. And
that suited Joe fine. The very editions that carried the President's
blast also carried McCarthy's challenge to the President to stop
"trying to protect the dupes and stooges of the Kremlin by using
his high office to attack—not the facts—but whoever attempts to
bring the facts to the attention of the American people. If only Mr.
Truman realized that the disgrace and shame is not to find Communists high in government, but that the disgrace and shame comes
when politicians of little minds and less morals try to protect them.
The American people are getting extremely tired and sick of the
administration's clever method of defense by smearing whoever
exposes Communists and corruption in government."

Then he demanded free radio time to answer the President—and
got it without a quibble. All four networks—NBC, CBS, ABC, and
Mutual—granted him time to reply, and his rebuttal was duly
broadcast. It included another attack on Philip Jessup, McCarthy
saying that he held in his hand a copy of a petition signed by Jessup
favoring destruction of all material capable of making an atomic
bomb, by dumping it in the ocean. He also said that Jessup, when
chairman of the Pacific Council of the Institute of Pacific Relations,
had a staff of twenty-three, of whom "ten have been named under
oath" as Reds, three as spy agents, and three as "probably Reds."
And he assailed Truman again for the directive barring release of
any loyalty data to Congress. He appealed to his millions of listen-

ers: "Can you think of one reason on God's earth why Mr. Truman has issued this order making it an offense against the government to give Congress the truth about Communists who are in our government? Is not this order an admission that they know about and are trying to protect the Communists in government?"

The charges against Jessup the State Department derisively called "quarter-truths, half-truths, and untruths." At the same time the department's security chief issued a warning that any employe caught giving information to Senator McCarthy would be fired forthwith.

[II]

If McCarthy was on the run, few could see signs of it. Capitol newsmen reported him as active as ever. He spoke seldom in the Senate, and then almost always on the one topic, but he was constantly dashing off to make a speech elsewhere. He paid little attention to routine Senate business, but his cockiness on and off the floor of the Senate was unmistakable. Nobody on Capitol Hill expected that Benton would get even a hearing on his resolution, and the expulsion of Joe seemed too unlikely to be seriously considered.

But Benton kept pushing, promising that if he were given a public hearing he would present a bill of particulars against McCarthy so damaging that a full investigation would be unavoidable. And finally he won consent.

Although newsreel, radio, and television crews were shut out of the hearing room, a full press contingent and an overflow audience were on hand when Benton offered his 30,000-word, 59-page indictment of McCarthy on ten specific counts, each buttressed by a mass of documentary evidence. The charges were not new; rather, they summarized what had been brought out piecemeal before.

The first charge accused McCarthy of perjury in denying that he had said he had a list of 205 Communists in his speech at Wheeling. On this count Benton urged that the senator be prosecuted. But the entire field of McCarthy's activities was covered—the $10,000 Lustron check; the tax squabbles; his "deceitful" promise to repeat outside the Senate anything he said there under immunity; his contumacy before the Tydings Committee. He called McCarthy an "amoral man," who "used the lie as an instrument of policy"—a man of "corruptibility and mendacity" and of "gross irresponsibility," who followed "a pattern of dictatorship and deceit. . . . He has borne false witness and deliberately and repeatedly corrupted and subverted facts."

The weighty document ended with bitter humor. The next step after investigation of the charges, Benton said, should be to refer the evidence to the Justice Department for prosecution. "If that is done," he concluded, "I concede cheerfully that my resolution asking for Senator McCarthy's expulsion from this body becomes somewhat academic. After all, a senator in jail, for all practical purposes, has been expelled. Freedom to lie is not a freedom which membership in the United States Senate confers upon any man."

McCarthy had been invited to appear in answer to Benton, but he declined. In a letter addressed to the subcommittee chairman, Senator Guy M. Gillette of Iowa, and beginning chummily "Dear Guy," Joe explained: "I am not in the least concerned with what this subcommittee does insofar as my fight to expose communism and corruption in Washington is concerned. This subcommittee cannot in the slightest influence my activities. . . . The Benton type of material can be found in the *Daily Worker* almost any day of the week and will continue to flow from the mouths and pens of the camp followers as long as I continue to fight against Communists in government. Frankly, Guy, I have not and do not intend to read, much less answer, Benton's smear attack. I have said before that I will not waste my time on this mental midget."

Then he accused the two Republicans on the subcommittee— Margaret Smith of Maine and Robert C. Hendrickson of New Jersey—of being biased against him because they had signed the Maryland election report, prepared by the same subcommittee. And in a letter to Senator Tom Hennings of Missouri, a Democratic member of the subcommittee, McCarthy accused him in effect of stacking the cards in advance, because a law partner of Hennings was currently acting as counsel for John Gates, editor of the *Daily Worker*, in the latter's appeal from conviction under the Smith Act; * and also because Hennings' law firm was counsel for the *St. Louis Post-Dispatch*, which McCarthy said "has editorialized against my anti-Communist fight along the same lines followed by the *Daily Worker*."

The dignified Hennings replied in the Senate. He termed McCarthy's "Dear Tom" letter "an affront to the entire Senate" which required an answer. His law partner, he said, not only was serving

---

* Passed in 1940, making it a felony to advocate, or belong to an organization advocating, the overthrow of the government by force and violence.

as Gates's counsel without fee, but had undertaken the task because of his belief that every man, even a Communist, was entitled to the basic rights guaranteed by the Constitution. Furthermore, the partner's action had been praised by the *Journal* of the American Bar Association as "an example of advocacy at its purest and noblest."

Hennings was incensed that McCarthy's letter had been released to the press before he received it; and in sympathetic revulsion the subcommittee voted to go ahead with a thorough investigation of Benton's charges.

Hennings' sturdy repulse of an imputed slur, following Benton's detailed impeachment of the rollicking senator, raised a flicker of hope, here and there, that the tide might be turning against Mc-Carthy. *Commonweal* reported that "many men are rejoicing that McCarthy is being, at last, stood up to, that he is being attacked, that responsible men are beginning to fight back." And *The Nation* commented, with what degree of confidence only its editors knew: "A reaction to McCarthyism is in the making; it is not much larger than a man's fist today, but it could become quite a cloud by November, 1952." In an editorial headed "Joe Stubs His Toe," *The Nation* argued that his hasty charges of bias and his "sudden effusions of friendship" for "Dear Margaret," "Dear Tom," and "Dear Guy" had alienated senators who might otherwise have held aloof. But the magazine at the same time warned that "today McCarthy is not too impossible a candidate for the Republican Vice-Presidential nomination as a running mate for that model of sterling integrity, Robert A. Taft."

That prospect was frightening others, too, and *Life* magazine pleaded with Senator Taft to "renounce and repudiate all political connections" with McCarthy. "Thousands, maybe millions, of Americans would willingly and tearfully vote for Taft and integrity in corrupt times like these. But how will they vote if his name is also associated with 'McCarthyism'? The cumulative debasement of United States politics has gone far enough. Somebody must forgo the pleasure of further groin-and-eyeball fighting. . . . The nation owes no debt to Joe McCarthy."

[III]

But the feeble flame fanned by Joe's critics soon died out. Let "intellectuals" denounce and obstruct as they might, the "mass of common Americans," so often and so often erroneously invoked, seemed bent on heeding McCarthy rather than Benton. At the annual encampment of the Veterans of Foreign Wars in the Hotel Astor in New York City, Maurice J. Tobin, Truman's personable Secretary of Labor, delivered a slashing attack on "men who spread "irresponsible slander from the privileged sanctuary of the United States Senate. . . . It is my view that the men who founded this nation did not intend the Senate to be a citadel for slanderers to hide in from libel suits." Tobin named no names, but only one was thought of.

Hardly had the speaker ended before James J. Davis, Jr., commander of the Pennsylvania department of the VFW, grabbed the microphone to protest against "the inference here against one of our comrades. I demand that we invite Comrade Joe McCarthy to give us the other side of this story!" And amid cheers and a few boos, Commander-in-Chief Charles C. Ralls, of Seattle, appointed Davis a committee of one to extend the invitation.

Davis got on the telephone. McCarthy was in Idaho on a speaking tour. Reached in Boise, he agreed to fly east immediately. And the next day McCarthy burst into the convention amid scenes of absolute tumult.

Coming straight from LaGuardia Airport, he strode into the grand ballroom and almost ran down the aisle, gripping his inseparable briefcase and grinning at the thunderous welcome. As he sprang onto the platform, the delegates arose and whistled, cheered, and applauded for five minutes. "Give 'em hell, Joe!" came shouts from the floor, and "McCarthy for President!"

For an hour and a quarter he spoke, to constant applause. He ripped again into Jessup and "Red Dean of Fashion" Acheson. Without mentioning Tobin by name, he spoke of "a fine young gentleman who was ordered to do the job he did," and quoting Tobin's remark that every accused person is entitled to "a fair trial in a courtroom," suggested a trial before a jury of his charges against the two State Department leaders. "No immunity exists on the podium," he pointed out, and if his charges were false, those slandered could sue; he personally would act as prosecutor, and the others could have "as many lawyers as they want to defend them." Hammering home this offer, he declared that if his evidence was untrue, "then they have been grossly libeled, and they can start their lawsuits tomorrow." And if the verdict went against him, he pledged that he would resign from the Senate; but if he won, then "the whole motley crew" must agree to get out.

Halfway through his speech he peeled off his coat and rolled up his sleeves. He pulled papers and pamphlets from his briefcase, holding them up to view and inviting the delegates to write to him in Washington for photostatic copies. From transcripts of congressional hearings he read excerpts which indicated, he said, that Jessup had been affiliated with "not one, not two, not three, not four, but five organizations officially named as fronts and doing the work of the Communist party." A pandemonium of applause greeted this statement.

Stop McCarthy? This demonstration seemed to put a quietus on any such hope. And Joe's dramatic appearance before the convention was not the sole indication. Two hours before he spoke, the delegates had voted a resolution of "no confidence" in Acheson and other State Department "policy-making officials," calling for the Secretary's dismissal. The resolution had been passed, the *Times* said, by a "roaring" voice vote, with almost no dissent. This had expressed the mood of the delegates before Joe spoke; his appearance had intensified that mood of anger and focused it on himself.

By the autumn of 1951, *Newsweek* reported that McCarthy's opponents were in the depths of gloom. *Time* already had noted that after three unsuccessful attempts to squelch the senator, administration strategists were beginning to despair. Neither "anguished denials of communism in the State Department nor vitriolic attacks on McCarthy and his witnesses" had been able to calm the uproar he caused; if anything, it had grown louder and rowdier. Even Truman's assault, with all the force of the White House behind it, had fallen flat, and, like the President, some people were anxiously asking, "Where is this leading us?" Were the editors of *The Nation,* for example, justified in speaking of the "moral leprosy of 'McCarthyism' "?* Was *Commonweal* right in deploring with a shudder "the malignant thing called 'McCarthyism' [that] spreads itself still like a miasmic cloud sail across the honor of our sky"? Was it really to be—"McCarthy for President"?

---

* McCarthyites also had their phrase to express their feelings toward the policies of Dean Acheson, as being "a little to the left of leprosy."

A Concert of Discords

In the fall of 1951, having once more plunged the Senate into snarling confusion, McCarthy flew to Arizona for a vacation. His health was not good. He had been increasingly bothered by a tremor of the hands and head, and his sinuses, always troublesome, were acting up.

No man worked harder or more continuously. His outer office was crowded daily with visitors—furtive characters and solid citizens, crackpots, flag-wavers, and concerned voters alarmed by what they saw as a disastrous trend in national affairs. A reporter quipped that a Hollywood spy thriller might be cast any day in McCarthy's waiting room. The senator's own mannerisms were dramatic, attention-getting. While telephoning he would let the tap water run noisily, or keep rapping the mouthpiece with a pencil; this was supposed to foil any recording device.

His desk was strewn with letters, documents, photostats, clippings, which he would shift from pile to pile, arrange and rearrange nervously, while conversing. Now and then he would pull out a paper in support of what he was saying, and if the guest failed to grasp the cogency of the document, would say that, of course, taken by itself, it meant nothing; but match it against *this* (extracting another paper from the litter), or *this* (a third paper, same business), together with a fourth or fifth (ditto), and the pieces of the jigsaw puzzle would fall into place and give one "the full picture." Many a caller departed with his brain in a whirl, understanding nothing, but more than half convinced that so much documentation *must* mean something.

In public McCarthy seemed to be always hurried, running against time. He gave interviews while trotting along a corridor. He ate at odd hours, paid little attention to what he devoured, and when his

235

digestive system rebelled, as it often did, subdued it by gulping quantities of bicarbonate of soda. With sure instinct, he deliberately cultivated the role in which he realized he had been cast—uncouth hero or villain of villains. He burped and patted his belly in public. He encouraged a dark stubble of beard, rolled up his shirt sleeves to show his hairy arms, and allowed photographers to snap him bleary-eyed and disheveled. His crudity fascinated even those who were most repelled. He winked and leered at pretty girls, airing himself as a lady-killer, although anybody who watched him could see that he had no time for dalliance, even if he were inclined that way. His one interest in life had become the role into which he had been thrust by circumstances, and he played it to the hilt.

Offstage he was still the country boy, eager to be liked, and aware of his newly acquired power. Addicted to bourbon in copious quantities, he would pour a drink for the most casual visitor, and could shift into informality over a glass amazingly. How he did this was a mystery to associates, and strangers were astonished by his character transformations. Privately there seemed to be no malice in the man, and the accusatory manner he assumed in public was like the pathos of a clever trial lawyer playing on the heartstrings of a jury—laid aside the moment court adjourns.

To Joe's antagonists this faculty was frustrating. Senator Lehman credited him with total insensitivity. "He was the most insensitive man I ever knew," Lehman would describe him long afterward. "You couldn't insult him. I would assail him in the most scathing terms, and after the debate he would come up grinning, throw his arm around my shoulders, and inquire, 'How are you, Herb?' He seemed to have no sense of the fact that principles of right or wrong were involved. His activities were all part of a political game. If anyone got hurt, it was too bad; but it was part of the game."

"Explaining Joe" had become a Washington pastime, and all the explanations differed. Benton even hinted at insanity, but nobody really believed this. The *Christian Science Monitor* theorized that the reason for Joe's recklessness in attack was his understanding of himself and his opponents—that "he really does not care what others say about him, although others do care what he says about them." This of course would give him an enormous advantage in encounter, for it would render him invulnerable while his adversary was smarting under his ferocious blows.

Dean Acheson was subjected to Joe's ambivalence in a famous

episode. The Secretary was in a Capitol elevator one day when Mc-Carthy stepped in. Putting out his hand, Joe said pleasantly, "How are you, Dean?" Acheson flushed and stared straight ahead, and at the next stop marched out. McCarthy was baffled by such behavior. "What's the matter with the man?" he asked friends sincerely. That a man could take umbrage over a political roughhouse, to the extent of refusing a civil greeting, was beyond Joe's comprehension.

If one's taste ran to lodge-night humor, the senator was hard to resist. Richard Rovere has put into print a story that went the rounds in Washington, and which, while probably apochryphal, portrays McCarthy's infectious friendliness in social contacts. An eminent British journalist, the story went, read about the terrible senator and determined to expose and crush him in a series of articles. Coming to Washington to study his subject, he telephoned McCarthy's office for an appointment and was jolted when the senator told him to come right on over. Joe never high-hatted a reporter needlessly. The eminent journalist found the senator in shirt sleeves. He started to explain his mission candidly, disdaining to do anything behind his victim's back. Joe waved the explanation aside and suggested they have a drink. No thank you, the guest replied, and again started to make clear that his purpose was to destroy the senator utterly, without pity. Joe nodded and stuck to the idea of a drink. "Straight or with water?" he asked. "We can talk later."

"Senator McCarthy," the Britisher stated, "I will talk now, and I warn you that you can expect no——"

"For chrissake," snapped Joe, "are you going to have a drink or not? Let's settle that first."

With a restatement that hospitality would earn McCarthy no favors, the journalist harrumphed that he might perhaps accept a little something, with perhaps just a dash of soda.

"Good," grunted Joe. "Want ice?"

Then, Rovere recounts, the interview started, and it went on for an hour or so. "The Londoner could not put a question without telling McCarthy what a foul and poisonous creature he was. McCarthy could not answer without offering some more whiskey —with perhaps just a dash of soda. Both were loaded almost to the muzzle when McCarthy was reminded that he had a dentist's appointment. He invited St. George to come along, and the interview went on insofar as was possible with McCarthy's great jaw clamped open, and a dentist with trembling hands working over

McCarthy's cavities and trying to keep his head in an atmosphere blue with talk and quavering with the fumes of the bourbon he had consented to allow the patient to use as a rinse. Back in McCarthy's apartment, the interview still continued, in a much degenerated form. It carried over to the next morning. Finally it ended. The Englishman wrote his articles; they burned with moral outrage; but they weren't quite so powerful an assault on McCarthy as they were planned to be. He was not destroyed."

In line with this presumably fictitious example of McCarthy's ability to handle an avowed critic, when the comradely mood was upon him, was the belief of one of the senator's Wisconsin lieutenants, Urban P. Van Susteren, that Joe could meet any situation and master it by just "plain, honest-to-God straight talk." If Joe were President of the United States, Urban P. would say, he would end the cold war by simply picking up the telephone and calling Joe Stalin. "This is Joe McCarthy," he would say. "I'm coming over tomorrow to talk about things. Meet me at the Moscow airport at one o'clock."

In Moscow, Joe would "sit down with Stalin in a closed room. First thing he'd tell a coupla dirty jokes. Then he'd look Stalin right in the eye and say, 'Joe, what do you want?' And Stalin would tell him. The two would talk man to man, not like a lot of pansy diplomats. They'd find out what each of them wanted and settle their differences. But when Joe left, he'd tell Stalin, 'The first time I catch you breaking this agreement, I'll blow you and your whole goddam country off the map.' " *

It was indubitable that McCarthy's personality did have an ameliorating effect on some individuals who were outraged by his actions. Most newspapermen could not help liking him as a person. One cause of their sometimes reluctant admiration was the way he dared to take on anybody and anything in sight—the entire establishment—without a moment's hesitation. His audacity at times was dumfounding; again and again he had outfought, outwitted, or outrun antagonists stronger than himself, and he had never cried uncle.

Even for his friends, he was a hard man to backstop; he positively preferred to fight alone. Senator Wherry had discovered

* We shall see how so astute an intellectual as Bertrand Russell would indulge in the same fantasy.

this at the time of the Maryland election report, when he congratulated the two Republican subcommittee members, Smith and Hendrickson, on having done "a whale of a job" under great difficulties. McCarthy took exception to this and corrected Wherry sharply, saying, "I personally think they did the foulest conceivable political job." And later, during a meeting of the Rules Committee, when Wherry ventured to intervene on McCarthy's behalf, Joe snapped: "I don't need your protection and I don't want it. I can take care of myself."

It was said that this defiant attitude had cost McCarthy a place on the potent Republican Policy Committee. But he wanted no share in a divided command; he demanded freedom to tack and reach, dash in or scuttle out, as chance offered and the spirit impelled. And on returning to Washington at the start of 1952 he resumed his forays on several fronts.

[II]

McCarthy had put in the latter part of December, 1951, in the naval hospital at San Diego, California, having his sinuses treated. The pain of the ordeal had been assuaged to some extent by the news that on December 13, John Stewart Service, six times cleared by the State Department's loyalty board and once exonerated by the Tydings Committee, had finally been dismissed on the recommendation of the loyalty review board. A principal consideration in arriving at the decision had been the transcript of a 1945 conversation between Service and Philip Jaffe, editor of *Amerasia,* which the FBI had obtained by wire-tapping and therefore had been inadmissable as evidence in court. The conversation revealed that Service had in fact given Jaffe military secrets, despite his denial before the Tydings Committee, and that he knew of Jaffe's Communist reputation at the time. The review board had written to Dean Acheson, "To say that his course of conduct does not raise a reasonable doubt as to Service's own loyalty, would, we are forced to think, stretch the mantle of charity much too far." Thereupon the Secretary, using his discretionary power to overrule his own department's loyalty board, ordered Service's dismissal. Collecting some $10,000 in accumulated pay and pension money, Service said good-bye to government employment.

Soon after returning to Washington for the second session of the 82nd Congress, McCarthy began leaking to a Senate committee the secret minutes of a meeting of the loyalty review board, held nearly one year before, on February 13–14, 1951. Hiram Bingham, a former Republican senator from Connecticut, had succeeded Seth Richardson as chairman of the review board one month previously, and the minutes revealed the board's intense dissatisfaction with the State Department. Bingham was quoted as saying:

"I think it fair to say that the State Department, as you know, has the worst record of any department in the action of its loyalty board. The loyalty board, in all the cases that have been considered in the State Department, has not found one—shall I say 'guilty' under our rules. It is the only board which has acted in that way. . . . I called Acheson's attention to the fact that his board was out of step with all other agency boards. In the Post Office Department, 10 percent of all persons examined were found to be worthy of separation from the government. In the Commerce Department, 6.5 percent. The average was about 6 percent. The State Department, zero. . . . I told him, 'You've got to tell the loyalty board members to behave themselves.' "

As evidence of this astonishing laxity, Bingham cited an instance in which only one member of the State Department board had heard all the witnesses. "After the first hearing or two, one board member . . . was sent abroad on a mission to Gibraltar, or some other place, and then after the next hearing, another member of the board was given some other duty." In addition, the chairman of the State Department board, General Snow, had permitted the wife of the man under investigation—although she herself had been denounced as a Communist—to sit beside him during the hearings and coach him on his answers.

Another member of the review board, the minutes of this meeting showed, had spoken of the State Department practice of calling in an employe against whom derogatory information had been filed, explaining the situation to him, and allowing him to resign, without making any entry on his personnel record showing why he had resigned, thus enabling him to take a position in another government department.

Still another member of the board had joined in with the question: "What are you going to do when the attorney who is presenting the charges acts as though he were the attorney for the incumbent? I read one hundred pages of a record where the three members of the board were acting as attorneys for the employe."

To which the executive secretary had rejoined: "Oh, they've taken the attitude that they're there to clear the employe and not to protect the government. We've been arguing with them since the program started."

"That brings up a question that has been on my mind a little," still another member had volunteered. "I've been disturbed about the State Department—their remarkable record of never having fired anybody for loyalty—and yet we do nothing about it . . . I have been troubled about whether or not we owe the duty of having somebody call the attention of the President, for example, to the fact that the program simply does not work in that department and let him worry about it. It seems to me that we assume more responsibility when we sit back (as we have done for three years) and know that the country rests in a false sense of security that we are looking after their interests here, when we know darn well that it is completely ineffective in one of the most important departments of the government . . ."

This frank talk among members of the Truman-appointed review board had taken place a full year after Senator McCarthy first called the nation's attention to a loyalty situation in the State Department, and had asked for a searching look into that department's record. Obviously no changes had been made in the meantime; nor had any of consequence occurred by the time McCarthy made public the review board's concern—a whole year after the quoted meeting. The conclusion the public drew from these startling disclosures boosted the senator's stock; he had cried "Danger!" when he stood alone, and facts belatedly coming to light seemed to bear him out. Why, then, his supporters asked, the bitter outcry against him as a conscienceless liar and traducer?

[III]

When the death of Senator Wherry created a vacancy on the Appropriations subcommittee handling State Department funds, McCarthy won back his place there, and with the help of the subcommittee chairman, Senator McCarran, the State Department's

loyalty deficiencies were at length searchingly explored. General
Snow was reduced to stammering humiliation as he laid bare his
ignorance of facts that had been common knowledge for years.
He did not know whether Dean Acheson had been in the State
Department at all at a time when Acheson was Undersecretary of
State. Questioned about speeches he had made in denunciation of
McCarthy at George Washington University and the Harvard
Club the previous autumn, Snow confessed that although he had
assured his audiences at the start that he spoke only as an individual, he had referred to himself later as representing the State
Department. He admitted that department personnel had helped
to write the speeches; that the department had cleared them in
advance; and had printed and circulated them. In these speeches
Snow had defined *McCarthyism* as "the making of baseless accusations regarding the loyalty and integrity of public officers and
employes," but when McCarthy asked him to name one person
against whom "baseless accusations" had been made, Snow retreated behind the plea that he could not "discuss cases." He had
not read various records that were available to the public; he
had not been aware of disclosures that had appeared in the newspapers; and when he was asked by Senator Ferguson whether he
would make the same speeches over again, he abjectly sighed,
"Oh, no, certainly not!"

Thereupon, McCarthy, revealing a side of his nature that had
been overlooked by most of the press (certainly it was never
mentioned in *The Nation* or *New Republic*), summed up his impression of General Snow in a far from vindictive manner, calling
him a man too kind-hearted for the country's good:

"I may say, in fairness to Mr. Snow, I think I understand his
reasoning better than some of his friends do. He is the son of a
judge, his grandfather was a judge. I understand they were kindly
men. I think that he is in effect trying criminal cases; that he must
give everyone the benefit of the doubt, and if there are any doubts
which can be resolved in favor of the employe, he resolves them
in favor of the employe. It is the kindly thing to do, but makes
him completely incompetent to act as head of that board. I do
not accuse you of being an evil man, Mr. Snow, but watching the
results that come from your board, I am trying to find out what
prompts you. And I have talked with some of your friends. The

general report is that you are a kindly individual who just dislikes seeing a man lose his job." *

For millions of Americans, McCarthy had pinpointed the issue neatly: leniency toward an employe against whom there existed strongly suspicious evidence must not be allowed to override the requirements of national security. The public had learned the extent of the review board's apprehension and the State Department's apparent extreme laxity through McCarthy's disclosures, and he reaped the benefit. He had given copies of the secret minutes to the Appropriations Committee, and also to the wire services. The latter had sent out brief digests of some of the remarks. Where this material was published at all, it was inconspicuously. Official Washington, meanwhile, had been thrown into a dither, and a frantic search was launched to track down his source of information. He declined to reveal how he had come into possession of the minutes, although their authenticity was not denied.

The wire services promptly locked up or "mislaid" their copies of the document, while the reaction of the liberal left was condensed by the *New Republic* into a curt warning to the members of the loyalty board to "watch out how they vote and speak, lest the omnipotent and all-hearing Joe McCarthy become aroused enough to accuse *them* of Communist sympathies."

* A similar tendency to leniency had been expressed by the former head of the loyalty review board, Seth Richardson. Writing to Mrs. Eleanor Roosevelt on December 6, 1949, Richardson had stated that "the penalty of a disloyalty discharge is so disastrous that the loyalty review board has inclined toward resolving all doubts in favor of an involved employe." And in February, 1952, Richardson explained to an editor of the *New Republic:* "I regret the destruction of any government employe. It's a terrible penalty to be called disloyal. That's why the board has leaned back in the way it has." Yet during exactly the above period, the loyalty boards were under constant fire from liberal spokesmen for their asserted severity, harshness, and injustice.

A Lesson in Tactics

McCarthy was able to make hay, at about this time, out of the State Department's handling of the security investigation of Oliver Edmund Clubb, a Far Eastern expert who had been with the department for twenty-four years. Clubb's name had been given to the Tydings Committee by McCarthy, although not prominently, and the committee had cleared him. Then on June 27, 1951 (a year after the Tydings Report), the department suspended Clubb pending investigation. This was an unusual step; the department did not customarily suspend an accused employe pending disposition of his case. Then on February 11, 1952, the department told the press that Clubb had been cleared of all charges on both loyalty and security grounds, and had been restored to duty. Then Clubb resigned.

Senators Ferguson and McCarthy set to work, and two weeks later came up with the information that after the department's loyalty board (under General Snow) had unanimously recommended Clubb's dismissal as a security risk, Secretary Acheson had overruled the recommendation and allowed Clubb to resign. In that way Clubb salvaged his $5,800-a-year pension, which he would have forfeited if he had been fired. McCarthy said the deal had been arranged between Acheson and Clubb ahead of time.

The State Department was mum until Acheson confirmed that he had overruled his own board, as all department heads had the authority to do. He said he had not studied the record in the case —didn't have time for that—but had turned it over to a friend in whose judgment he had confidence, and had acted on the friend's advice. Why a friend should be better qualified to return an equitable verdict than his own loyalty board the Secretary did not say.

244

Clubb he described as "one of our most experienced and trusted officers."

McCarthy did not fail to chalk up another credit on this admission by the "Red Dean of Fashion." And during the same period he grappled with a major press critic—*Time* magazine. The previous autumn *Time* had done a cover story on Joe, taxing him with failure to make good on his charges, and concluding: "After nearly two years of tramping the nation, shouting that he was 'rooting out the skunks,' just how many Communists has Joe rooted out? The answer is none. . . . No regard for fair play, no scruple for exact truth hampers Joe's political course. If his accusations destroy reputations, if they subvert the principle that a man is innocent until proved guilty, he is oblivious. Joe, immersed in the joy of battle, does not even seem to realize the gravity of his charges."

With its circulation of more than a million and a half readers (backed by the five million circulation of *Life,* its sister publication), *Time* was a formidable adversary, but Joe was not daunted. In a letter to Henry Luce, the publisher, he served notice that inasmuch as the magazine had not "corrected a single one of the false statements" contained in the article, he was preparing to lay the facts before *Time*'s advertisers. The letter read in part:

"I send you copies of your own files to show that your staff, who prepared this story, deliberately and with full knowledge of the true facts misrepresented the case. . . . [The files] will give you some idea of the viciousness of the lying smear attack which *Time* magazine made in its attempt to hamper my efforts to get rid of Communists in high positions in our government. As you of course know, I am preparing material on *Time* magazine to furnish all of your advertisers, so they may be fully aware of the type of publication which they are supporting."

This was immediately and widely interpreted as an attempt to intimidate the press—nobody bothering to ask the obvious question, namely, whether a large section of the press had not been doing its best to intimidate Joe. The unequal odds—one senator against the resources of the Luce empire—were not commented upon, although, if one were to accept at face value the anguished cries of the "intimidated" press, Joe seemed to enjoy a decided edge.

The same observation applied to a fresh confrontation between

McCarthy and President Truman. The senator had drawn a bead on a member of the White House staff, Philleo Nash, an adviser on minority groups, saying that FBI reports had named Nash as a Communist and a close associate of a member of a Canadian spy ring. He added that although the White House had cleared Nash, the loyalty review board had not been able to act on his case because one of Truman's assistants refused to yield the files. Nash instantly replied that the charge was a "contemptible lie," and the President used sulphurous language in denouncing McCarthy as a pathological liar and character assassin who had never told the truth, to Truman's knowledge. The FBI denied it had given any information on Nash to McCarthy, and the round ended with McCarthy still defiant.

"Instead of name calling," he retorted, "the President should answer several questions:

"Did I properly quote from the White House loyalty board records?

"If not, where did I misquote?

"If he admits I quoted properly . . . why is he willing to keep Nash on as an adviser?"

To the average American—the plain citizen who did not command any public forum—the very incessancy and acerbity of the attacks made against Joe were redounding in his favor. The sentiment of a wide segment of ordinary voters had been expressed a long while before by a Milwaukeean in a radio interview: "I don't care if Joe doesn't uncover a single Commie in the State Department. He'll scare the rats out!"

But the senator's cut-and-thrust continued to inspire a resentment among his antagonists that sometimes betrayed them into injudicious outbursts of temper. Such a lapse was fatal to Newbold Morris, an eminent New York lawyer who had been brought in by President Truman to clean up the corruption in the government, the money scandals particularly having become too flagrant to ignore any longer. Morris had barely begun his work when he was called before the Senate's subcommittee on investigations to explain a sale of war-surplus tankers reported to be running oil into Communist China. The tankers had been sold to United Tanker Corporation, which in turn was owned by China International Foundation, of which Morris was president. The subcommittee wanted to know whether Morris had profited by the deal—and how about those hot cargoes, if any?

Morris, a man with a tindery temper, arrived with a large piece of cardboard on which was scrawled, "Keep your shirt on!!!" His wife had given it to him, and he placed it on the table in front of him, face up, as the questioning started. First he took back a previous denial that he had profited by the tanker sale; he had checked, he said, and through his law firm, which handled the deal, he had made $30,000. But he denied knowledge of any cargoes to China.

Snapped Senator McCarthy: "Since your foundation owned all the stock in United, and you helped to sign the death warrant of American boys in Korea, you were either the biggest dupe or the biggest dope of all history, because you made enormous profits out of those shipments."

Morris' face turned scarlet. Flipping the warning card over, face down, he shouted at Joe: "You've knocked off a lot of characters before, but you're not going to knock mine off! My patriotism's at stake!"

The whole train of the inquiry was derailed, and when Senators Nixon and Mundt tried to get it back on the rails, Morris flew at them, and talked about "diseased minds" and "mental brutality" of the same sort that the Communists were using on Cardinal Mindszenty in Hungary. Pounding the table, the witness fumed at McCarthy's "frightful distortion," and shouted: "Down here in Washington in the last three years you've created an atmosphere so vile the people have lost confidence in their government!"

Later he carried the attack into a press conference, and then offered to explain the tanker deal to Mundt over a luncheon; but the latter declined, saying, "I'd probably get stuck with the check." Nixon remarked that of twenty witnesses called, Morris had been the only uncooperative one. The upshot was sympathetic headlines for McCarthy (oil shipments to the enemy in Korea touched a sensitive nerve) and the speedy termination of Morris' usefulness in Washington. Drawled Senator Underwood of Kentucky, "I'm afraid he ain't gonna be around much longer," and he wasn't.

[II]

Meanwhile the Rules Committee had instructed its subcommittee on privileges and elections to include in its examination of Senator Benton's accusations McCarthy's alleged attempts to intimidate the press and radio. His relations with his press critics in Wisconsin, also, the subcommittee was advised to look into, mainly at the instance of the *Madison Capital Times* and the *Milwaukee Journal*. Both these major dailies had been carrying on a vendetta against "the abominable Joe-man," although among the country and weekly newspapers of the state McCarthy had widespread support.

The subcommittee, under Senator Gillette, had been experiencing rough going. Directly on the reassembling of Congress, Margaret Chase Smith requested to be relieved of the assignment, and she had been replaced by Senator Welker of Idaho, a staunch McCarthy supporter. Senator Hendrickson, the other Republican member, also had signified a desire to withdraw, but had been persuaded to remain.

Then the committee suffered embarrassment by the defection of one of its investigators, Daniel G. Buckley, a young New York lawyer. Sent to Wheeling to check again on what McCarthy had said there, Buckley soon realized, he told the press, that although he had understood his obligation had been "to seek the truth relating to the charges against Senator McCarthy," he really was expected to "substantiate Senator Benton's charges . . . at the expense of the truth."

"My job in Wheeling," he said, "I thought was to find the facts, to find whether, as Senator Benton charged, McCarthy had said that he had a list of two hundred and five Communists in the State Department, or whether, as Senator McCarthy maintained, he had said he had a list of fifty-seven individuals, either members of [the party] or loyal to communism. I thoroughly interviewed a large number of witnesses who were in a position to know what Senator McCarthy had said. Every one of those witnesses save one supplied information which cast grave doubt and suspicion on Senator Benton's story and substantially corroborated Senator McCarthy's account."

This was a startling development, but Buckley detailed his report, saying he had interviewed the two WWVA radio men who had made affidavits for the Tydings Committee claiming that they had heard McCarthy use the "205" figure, and that both now admitted that they could not recall actually hearing it. The one who had checked the broadcast against McCarthy's advance text confessed that he had "spot-checked" the speech only, and was not even aware, until it was pointed out to him, that the text contained a number of factual errors so gross as to be ludicrous, which certainly would have attracted attention if they had been broadcast as written. The radio men and the *Intelligencer* reporter all said that their original statements had been given to insistent investigators for the State Department, not aides of the Tydings Committee. Other witnesses who had heard McCarthy speak, Buckley said, almost unanimously doubted that McCarthy had said "two hundred and five"; several recalled that he had used some figure "like fifty-seven."

Buckley said that when he reported his findings he was taken off the McCarthy investigation and assigned to an inquiry into an election in Ohio, and shortly afterward was dropped.

McCarthy's opponents scoffed at Buckley's statement, terming it a blatant attempt to "subvert" the subcommittee, although no detailed refutation was offered, merely the general charge. Because telephone records showed that Buckley had been in touch with Miss Jean Kerr, a McCarthy assistant, the senator was said to have "plotted" Buckley's action in a campaign to torpedo the Gillette investigation. Then it turned out that one of the reasons why Senator Margaret Chase Smith had asked to be relieved was the "extreme partisanship" (against McCarthy) which she felt was animating the subcommittee.

Months had passed, and the investigation had seemed headed for a pigeonhole when Buckley's disclosures fanned it into life again. In a letter to Gillette, McCarthy flatly accused the committee of spending "tens of thousands" of dollars without authorization for the sole purpose of digging up material "for the Democratic party for the coming campaign against McCarthy." The subcommittee, he said, was "guilty of stealing just as clearly as though the members engaged in picking the pockets of the taxpayers and turning the loot over to the Democratic National Committee. . . . While the actions of Benton and some of the committee members do not surprise me, I cannot understand your willingness to label Guy Gillette as a man who will head a committee which is stealing from the pockets of the American taxpayer and then using this money to protect the Democratic party from the political effects of the exposure of Communists in government." He thought the Gillette committee was proving itself "even more dishonest than the Tydings committee."

[III]

Being called a thief and a pickpocket was too much for Senator Mike Monroney of Oklahoma, a Democratic member of the subcommittee, and he appealed to the parent Rules Committee for protection. Let the full committee, Monroney urged, challenge McCarthy to ask that the Senate discharge the subcommittee; the result, Monroney said, would be either a vote of confidence in the investigators or a vote of confidence for McCarthy.

Stung by the charge of dishonesty, the Rules Committee did introduce in the Senate a resolution to discharge their subcommittee, and an entire afternoon was consumed in vitriolic debate. During the uproar McCarthy again demonstrated his mastery of the maneuver of working his opponents into incoherent fury, and then, when the turmoil was at its height, creating a diversion by opening a second front—attacking suddenly from a different direction, catching his enemies in a cross fire, and while they milled in wrangling confusion, flitting out of sight. It was the tactic of a raider, the surprise blow dealt with utter audacity, of which McCarthy was a master.

First McCarthy said he would vote to discharge the subcommittee, because "after the fantastic activities of the [same] subcommittee in the Maryland elections case, I can have no confidence in it." Then he reversed himself and said he would vote to sustain the subcommittee, because he wanted them to investigate Senator Benton, too. And he presented a list of charges covering Benton's official, business, and personal activities almost as long as Benton's indictment against him.

Senator Monroney, whose boiling temper had about reached the pitch of calling for hanging Joe on the spot, fought against this attempt to distract the senators' attention from accusations of "picking pockets" and "spending vast sums of money" without warrant. The subcommittee, he said, had laid out $3,200 for forty-five days' work by three investigators, working on cases involving three of the largest states—and that was all.

Senator Hickenlooper professed to be mystified by the commotion, and Margaret Chase Smith flew at him, demanding: "Will the senator from Iowa tell me whether he was ever accused of being a thief? . . . Would the senator ever become callous enough not to mind being called a thief by a fellow senator?"

Hickenlooper allowed as not, but thought his fellow members were being "hypersensitive" to McCarthy's letter, "highly critical" and "caustic" though it was. "Members are constantly charged with things of which they are not guilty."

Did his Iowa colleague think that "even one charge, repeated nine times, that we are stealing the taxpayers' money, is a matter of casual criticism which one should lightly brush off?" Monroney demanded, and went on: "I get worried about democracy sometimes. I get worried when some forces in this nation try to shake the very foundation stones of our government and try to stir up suspicion, distrust, and religious hatred, and do other things that are completely inimical to free and democratic government. We have seen the same pattern overseas, where we saw many governments fail because of these very attacks on the foundations of government by people who created doubt."

Similar allusions to McCarthy as an incipient Hitler, a Mussolini, or other authoritarian conspirator had been growing daily bolder, although they had not been made so directly in the Senate before.

Senator Benton joined the debate and linked McCarthy to the methods used by Communists to undermine and confuse. Here was a brilliant display, he said, of "the tactics of hitting and running, of never standing still, of never answering charges, of hitting, of hitting again, of running again." Terming McCarthy "the skillful propagandist which all of us know him to be," Benton predicted that "it is what he said [against Benton] that will appear in the newspaper headlines," not the bitter exchanges on the floor.

Benton was right. McCarthy's demand that his rival be investigated captured the headlines, and little appeared about the unseemly and futile wrangle, although it had terminated with a still more brilliant use by infighter Joe of exactly the tactics that Benton deplored. Pressed hard by Monroney, McCarthy suddenly introduced the name of Darrell St. Claire, chief clerk of the Rules Committee. St. Claire had once been a member of the State Department's loyalty board, and Joe flew at him, accusing him of having cast the vote that cleared Edward G. Posniak, a department economist, "although there had been twelve separate FBI reports opposing it." St. Claire, McCarthy charged, had helped the Gillette subcommittee write the Maryland election report (which had nothing to do with the present debate) and had also drafted the subcommittee's current "scurrilous" attack on him.

Senators all but fell over each other springing up to defend St. Claire. Margaret Chase Smith swore that he had "never sat with the subcommittee, never had anything to do with the typing of the report or anything to do with the Maryland or the Benton resolution that I know of." Monroney called McCarthy's charge "completely misinformed," and hotly resented "the effort to connect a member of a Senate committee staff with pro-Communist tendencies." Senator Gillette added his denial that St. Claire had had "anything whatsoever to do with the writing of any report of the subcommittee," and Carl Hayden of Arizona, chairman of the Rules Committee, protested that St. Claire's name had been dragged into the debate "without any basis in fact whatsoever."

Adding his own few words, Senator Hubert Humphrey of Minnesota defended St. Claire, crying: "What are we going to do—let another man be thrown to the wolves? I submit that in this country a man is innocent until he is proved guilty. Something terrible has happened to us. We go around accusing people day after day and demanding that they prove their innocence. That is totalitarian law, not democratic law. It is Anglo-Saxon jurisprudence upside down. . . . It is like the days of Nero when innocent people are thrown into the arena to be destroyed. I think it is time we stated that we are not going to let people be ruined, their reputations destroyed, and their names defiled because we happen to be in the great American game of politics. If that is what politics is coming to, I am getting out." *

Saying he was "shocked" by the "policy of indicting by smear," Senator Lehman called on the Senate not to "pussyfoot on a matter of as tremendous importance as that which we are discussing."

Having thrown the Senate into utter turmoil, Nero-Joe walked out. He had to catch a plane, he told reporters, to make a speech on "Ethics and Honor in Government."

Frustrated and disgusted, as much with themselves as with their tormentor, the crestfallen senators voted, 60-0, to sustain their subcommittee and let the investigation go on.

---

* The date of this threat, not immediately carried out, was April 10, 1952.

Lattimore, Ever Lattimore

[I]

Repeatedly Senator Benton had challenged McCarthy to sue him for slander, offering to waive immunity for anything he had said in the Senate, and finally Joe accepted the dare. Filing suit in federal district court in Washington, he asked $2,000,000 damages.

The action overjoyed McCarthy's adversaries. Senator Lehman thanked Benton publicly for rendering "a great service to our country," and *Commonweal* said that "all Americans, touched with dignity and honor and self-respect, owe endless gratitude" to Benton. Between the principals no amenities were wasted: McCarthy called Benton's waiver of immunity a "cheap, phony bluff," while Benton labeled Joe's suit "a grandstand gesture."

"If I never attacked Communists in government, Bill Benton would never be attacking McCarthy," was the latter's retort. "I want to get people like Benton on the stand under oath and make them either tell the truth or perjure themselves. When I get through, the American people will have a better idea of who and what are behind Benton in his attack on McCarthy for exposing Communists."

The phrases seemed to have become obsessive, but they were McCarthy's; like a shrewd advocate, he stuck to his one issue, and never skipped an opportunity to hammer it home.

With the court docket running two years behind, there was little chance that the action would come to trial before the November elections, when both men would be bidding for another term. At the same time, Senator Gillette, speaking for his subcommittee, intimated that their inquiry would proceed slowly, in order to avoid prejudicing either senator in the coming campaign.

McCarthy's stock was receiving a further boost, meanwhile, from disclosures before the Senate Internal Security subcommittee presided over by tough, seventy-five-year-old Pat McCarran of Nevada. He ran his committee autocratically, and his influence in the Senate was legendary; he had been known to silence an objector in the middle of a speech by merely stepping in front of him and looking the man in the eye. McCarran hated Communists and fellow travelers as bitterly as did McCarthy, and he was more thorough in "rooting them out."

Since the Tydings Committee investigation, much evidence had come to light regarding the role played by the Institute of Pacific Relations in shaping the Asian policy of the United States. Much of this evidence had been acquired through the seizure of some 150,000 items of IPR correspondence stored in a Massachusetts barn owned by Edward C. Carter, director of the IPR, and in Frederick Vanderbilt Field's cellar. Through this correspondence, a clearer picture emerged of the influence that Field, John Carter Vincent, and especially Owen Lattimore had exerted on State Department policy during the critical years in the Far East.

Vincent had been active in the diplomatic maneuvering that had brought the Communists into power in China, and the seized IPR files revealed the close association that had existed between Vincent and Lattimore when the latter was editor of *Pacific Affairs*.

Under questioning, Vincent could offer no helpful comment on such statements as that in a letter written by Carter to Lattimore in 1947, regarding a book, *The Unfinished Revolution in China*, just published. Carter had written that it was of the "utmost importance" that Lattimore "devise some means of getting it read at an early date, among others by Secretary of State George Marshall, Senators Vandenberg, Morse, and Ives, John Foster Dulles, and John Carter Vincent of the State Department." The book, Carter explained, was "so full of profound understanding and admiration of the Chinese people . . . it might become a military and political handbook for Vietnam and in other Asiatic areas. . . ." So strongly had Carter felt that, in a postscript after a postscript, he suggested: "I assume that John Carter Vincent . . . might persuade General Marshall to read it from cover to cover."

The political tone of the book was indicated by the reviews it received: In *The New York Times*, Owen Lattimore had reviewed it glowingly, declaring that the author had placed himself in distinguished company by his "outspoken support of the Chinese

Communists"; while the *Daily Worker* placed the book "at the top of the list."

Confronted with a pamphlet which he had endorsed during the war, and which drew parallels between the Communist movement in China and the "grass roots" populist movements of the last century in the United States, Vincent acknowledged that the booklet might be viewed as Communist propaganda, although it had not been so judged at the time, when Russia was our ally.

He was unable to recall, despite persistent questioning, whether, at the time of the *Amerasia* arrests, he had spoken to Lattimore and Lattimore's wife of his fear that the IPR might be attacked as subversive, and he differed with his questioners over the significance of that incident, if indeed it had occurred. Again and again the committee accused him of evasiveness.

All this, however, was relatively small-time. Interest picked up when Lattimore was called, for McCarthy's foes had never ceased to remind the public that the senator had said he was willing to "stand or fall" on the case of Lattimore.

The professor came into the arena swinging belligerently, as was his style. Again, as in 1950, he had a preliminary statement to place in the record; it ran to 17,500 words and 50 typewritten pages, and contained terms of vituperation such as had seldom been given voice in a congressional hearing. But this time he had no respectfully listening audience; after the opening sentence, in which he boldly accused the committee of suppression and distortion of evidence, and of welcoming "stacked" testimony, which was destroying innocent men and jeopardizing the nation, he ran into a barrage of interruptions from the senators. So abundant were the challenges that by the end of the day he had been able to read only eight pages of the statement, although he had given it to the press for release in full at the start of the hearing.

The witness's allegation of a McCarthy-induced "reign of terror" in the State Department drew Senator McCarran's comment that such a charge was "not at all out of line with the general procedure of the Communist party." McCarran reminded Lattimore that for months Judge Harold Medina, when trying the party's leaders in New York under the Smith Act, had been forced to put up with "all kinds of condemnatory remarks and insulting expressions," and pointed out that although the committee might refuse to admit the statement, they were refraining from such "suppression."

"Notwithstanding the insulting and offensive remarks that appear in the statement by the witness, he may proceed," said McCarran, "with the understanding that from time to time as he goes along, counsel for the committee will interrogate him."

Counsel for the committee was Robert Morris, who had been so reluctantly assigned as minority counsel in the Tydings probe, and throughout that inquiry had been snubbed, shut out, and barely tolerated by the Democratic members. Now Morris dug into Lattimore's connections with the Institute of Pacific Relations, among other matters, relentlessly.

In his statement Lattimore bestowed upon Senator McCarthy such epithets as "the Wisconsin whimperer" and "graduate witch-burner." Harold Stassen was called a "roadshow McCarthy" and "the perpetual presidential candidate." Seconded and advised from time to time by his counsel, Abe Fortas, the witness denounced the "reign of terror" which he said was being conducted against foreign-service personnel and against the "inquiring mind" in general, as well as against anyone who opposed the "China lobby." Almost line by line he was interrupted by challenges from the committee members and counsel, and at length he blurted that he had no expectation of getting a fair hearing, and by five o'clock complained that his mind was "in a maze." Fortas protested against the "inhuman treatment" of the witness, but McCarran coolly ordered Lattimore to return the next day.

At that time, still cocky, Lattimore picked up the reading of his statement, and wept as he spoke again of a "reign of terror" in the State Department that already had victimized three old friends—Service, Clubb, and Vincent. He accused the committee of fomenting "a nightmare of outrageous lies, shaky hearsay, and undisguised personal spite" out of the IPR files. "Concerning my reputation and character, you have now for many months been publishing to the world an incredible mass of unsubstantiated accusations, allegations, and insinuations. For months a long line of witnesses has set me in the midst of a murky atmosphere of pretended plots and conspiracies so that it is now practically impossible for my fellow citizens to follow in detail the specific refutation of each lie and smear."

The witness was never at a loss for terms of abuse. Louis Budenz he scorched as "a glib liar," and Senator Knowland he alluded to sneeringly as "the senator from Formosa." When Senator Ferguson interposed, "That is the Communist line, isn't it?" Lattimore replied with apparent satisfaction, "They may have picked it up." Commented McCarran, "Everybody is in bad faith except Lattimore," and ordered the witness back the next day.

On the third day the statement was finally struggled through, and cross-examination began. The atmosphere was so tense that extra policemen were stationed about the room, and the spectators were warned that any demonstration whatever would lead to arrests. From 10 A.M. until dusk, Lattimore fought off questions. Members of the committee repeatedly accused him of arrogance and making countercharges that he could not substantiate. Pressed on that point, he said that what he had just stated was opinion, yes; but so many witnesses against him had only given their opinions, was he not to be permitted to do the same? No, said the chair, and Lattimore complained that he could no longer think under "this kind of hammering."

But "this kind of hammering" went on the next day, and for days afterward, with the witness making admission after admission that contradicted his testimony of 1950. Confronted with documentary proof, including his own letters in the IPR files, he conceded that although he had said in 1950 that never during his editorship of *Pacific Affairs* had he considered Field a Communist, he must have been aware as early as 1939 that Field was "a close fellow traveler of the Russians."

He conceded that in 1950 he had sworn that he had never had the privilege of answering Lauchlin Currie's mail, whereas his own letters, now produced, stated that he had.

He conceded that his testimony to the Tydings Committee that he never had a desk in the State Department was false, because for a while he had had a desk in Currie's office in the State Department building. And whereas he had previously said that his use of Currie's office had been "irregular and infrequent," he acknowledged as his own a letter dated 1942 in which he had said, "I am in Washington about four days a week and when there can always be reached at Currie's office."

Counsel Morris asked: "Did you know that there has been testimony here that Lauchlin Currie aided an espionage ring during the war?" Lattimore answered that it was news to him, and at the close of the fourth day he begged a "two-day respite" because he was tired. Rejoined Senator McCarran, "We are all tired," and ordered him back.

[II]

All this made headlines on the nation's front pages and was highly embarrassing to the liberals who had flocked to Lattimore's defense at the time of the Tydings inquiry. A "quickie" book, *Ordeal by Slander,* which Lattimore had rushed into print in 1950, had been rapturously reviewed at the time in many leading journals and had sold profitably. Its whiplash literacy had given heart then to those among McCarthy's opponents who were repelled both by the tenor of his charges and by his deplorable syntax; here was one scholar who could pay back Joe in his own coin. The professor who refused to be pushed around by the bully-boy from Wisconsin had been something of a hero to the anti-McCarthy forces; but now, under the astute "hammering" of Senator McCarran, the rallying cry of "Lattimore" was beginning to sound hollow. And McCarthy's stock rose correspondingly.

Through a sixth, a seventh, and finally a twelfth day, the questioning kept on, and each day it became clearer that the nimble professor who had been so capable of answering for himself, had more things to answer for than most people had imagined. The most destructive evidence came when documents were produced showing that during the war Lattimore had met with Constantine Oumansky, the Soviet ambassador, and had confided to him the yet secret information that he, Lattimore, had been assigned as political adviser to Chiang Kai-shek—a piece of news of great value to the Communists. The facts were contained in IPR correspondence regarding a luncheon at the Mayflower Hotel in Washington on June 18, 1941, attended by Oumansky, Vladimir Rogoff, a Russian newsman, Lattimore, Field, and Carter, director of the Institute of Pacific Relations. The correspondence stated that Alger Hiss had been requested to set up the luncheon, but had declined; whereupon Carter had arranged it. In a letter written subsequently by Carter to Philip Jessup appeared these lines:

"It so happened that last week I had lunch with Oumansky on Wednesday [June 18]. We talked for a couple of hours. I was fortunate in getting Lattimore over from Baltimore, as I thought it was pretty important to have a long talk with Oumansky, in view of his job and the evolving world situation. It was a most illuminating two hours."

So it went, day after day, with Lattimore making concession after concession while accusing the committee of placing him in "multiple jeopardy" by reviving charges on which the Tydings Committee had already cleared him. He admitted that he had passed off his call at the White House on the eve of the Potsdam conference by saying it had lasted "about three minutes," without mentioning that he had left with President Truman a memorandum outlining his views on foreign policy. Asked why he had not disclosed this memorandum to the Tydings Committee, he replied that he had not been asked about it, and he felt no obligation to volunteer any information. And finally, after persistently evading the question, he admitted that as editor of *Pacific Affairs* he had leaned backwards to favor the Soviet Union by such actions as deleting from a contributor's article passages objectionable to the Russians. He kept complaining of fatigue, denied again and again that he was a Communist or Communist sympathizer, and became entangled in such a web of contradictions that he himself indicated that a perjury prosecution seemed unavoidable.

Finally, after one of the longest cross-examinations in congressional history, he was dismissed, but not before receiving a 2,500-word tongue-lashing from Senator McCarran, speaking on behalf of all seven members of the subcommittee. The witness was accused of evading and trying to obscure the truth, and of many outright falsifications. His conduct before the committee was reprobated as "flagrantly defiant . . . consistently evasive, contentious, and belligerent." He was called "insolent, overbearing, arrogant, and disdainful," and was reproached for "willful unresponsiveness, hair-splitting, and intemperate, provocative, and abusive language." Finally, five "patent untruths" that had been uttered by him were set forth specifically.

In reply Lattimore defended his conduct as "vigorous" but not "contemptuous," and said he had only stood up to a savage cross-examination persisted in for many days: "I refused to defend myself by cringing."

In its report, filed on June 27, 1952, the McCarran group found that the Institute of Pacific Relations had "possessed close organic relations with the State Department . . . Owen Lattimore and

John Carter Vincent were influential in bringing about a change in United States policy in 1945 favorable to the Chinese Communists . . . Owen Lattimore was, from some time beginning in the 1930s, a conscious articulate instrument of the Soviet conspiracy . . . Owen Lattimore testified falsely before the subcommittee with reference to at least five separate matters that were relevant to the inquiry and substantial in import."

The committee thereupon transmitted the record to the Justice Department, and before the year was out, Owen Lattimore would be indicted for perjury on seven counts.

The daily press had covered Lattimore's debacle in detail and for the most part with exemplary impartiality, although some of the more extremely liberal periodicals, after initially eulogizing "Lattimore's counterattack," had lapsed into silence as his retreat became painfully clear. McCarthy had staked his credibility on the case, and even *The New York Times,* which was steadily growing more decidedly hostile to Joe, conceded that the McCarran findings came close to bearing out McCarthy's description of Lattimore as "chief architect" of the disastrous policy followed by the United States in regard to China.

Americans who were less fastidious than the *Times,* although no less logical in their deductions, chalked up the names of Service, Clubb, Vincent, Jessup, Brunauer, Lattimore—all on McCarthy's lists—and refused to believe that Joe could be "all wrong." Rather they credited him with rendering a patriotic service, in the face of the most determined opposition, by exposing to public view a rank growth in the body politic that had been condoned and denied too long. His methods might be crude, brassy, scattergun, but they were getting results. At least, so ran a wide consensus.

Five Aces Are Hard to Beat

Well before Owen Lattimore would be indicted, the nation's attention would be absorbed by an event of greater interest—the election of a President. And a question already being hotly debated was whether "McCarthyism" would be a major issue in the campaign. The Republicans said yes, the Democrats groaned no.

The Democrats were running scared, and the Republicans were running confidently. To the Republicans the overriding issue was the "mess in Washington"—the Korea "mess," the influence-peddler "mess," the sale of post office jobs "mess," the tax scandals "mess," the communism "mess." This last brought in McCarthy, long since established in the national consciousness as the most vocal and insistent expression of the people's revulsion from the encroachments of Soviet Russia abroad, and the toleration of Russia's allies, apologists, and infiltrating agents at home. This eminence he had achieved single-handed, by daring and by sticking to one definite objective. It was a cause in which he could believe utterly (although he did not find it necessary to believe every word he said). Sweeping generalizations and exaggeration for effect were the weapons he fought with; and his most abhorring enemies were matching him, violence for violence, hyperbole for hyperbole.

Professional politicians did not really regard McCarthy as a second Hitler; like themselves, he was playing what Senator Humphrey had frankly called "the great American game of politics," although with fewer inhibitions about the rules and, it was ruefully admitted, often with greater success. That Joe was a political power in 1952 no politician denied; the only difference in their expressed estimates of his strength was in regard to its magnitude and its intensity.

261

About the place that McCarthy would occupy in the coming campaign there were many guesses. Months before, *Life* magazine had reported that "half the Democrats and most of the Republicans in Congress are paralyzed with fear of Joe," and his stock had not fallen since that time; his presence, therefore, whether in the foreground or in the background of the campaign, was expected to bode ill for some who had crossed his path, and to be of good augury for some with whom he agreed. Senators, especially, trod warily around Joe these days: they were haunted by the wraiths of Lucas, Tydings, Pepper, and others, wailing disconsolately through Capitol corridors and gibbering in dim corners, banished from the fondly familiar chamber. Yet paradoxically, in this election apparently so propitious for his party, Joe's opponents believed they discerned their best hope yet for whisking him out of the Senate and delivering the nation from his detestable deviltries.

The hope was based on the struggle within the party to capture the nomination for President. The conservative wing was doggedly supporting Senator Robert A. Taft of Ohio; the moderate or liberal wing was pinning its hopes on General Dwight D. Eisenhower.

McCarthy had been inclining generally toward Taft, but he had kept his lines of communication with other avowed candidates open, and his opponents feared that he might opportunistically switch to Eisenhower—and that Eisenhower might accept his endorsement. *The Nation* had contemplated the possibility of a Taft-McCarthy ticket ("given the degree of paranoia that exists") with an appropriate shudder; and as Eisenhower scored victories in the state primaries, the apprehension became feverish. Would the supposedly politically naive General reject the spurious nostrums hawked by "the medicine man from Wisconsin" and repudiate McCarthy? Or would he bow to political expediency and "walk with the devil"? Those were the questions which *The Nation* and like-minded anti-McCarthyites propounded agonizingly, week after anxious week.

Eisenhower faced the dilemma publicly for the first time a month before the convention. In a television hookup from Abilene, Kansas, the General said, in reply to questions, that he would support any Republican candidate who subscribed to the party's principles, although to his mind the thing to concentrate on was the need to get rid of the "umbrella of fear" that overshadowed the entire world. Reporters were not satisfied: would he support Senator McCarthy for reelection? he was asked point-blank. Ike (whom everyone liked) replied that he did not intend to "indulge in personalities." Nobody was more determined than himself, he went on, that "any kind of Communistic, subversive, or pinkish influences be uprooted from responsible places in our government," and he believed the job could be done without "besmirching the reputation of any innocent man, or condemning by loose association."

To both the friends and the foes of McCarthy this was pretty thin gruel; but it set the pattern for a series of evasive and obfuscating statements on the subject by Eisenhower. While "I Like Ike" buttons bloomed, whom Ike would like in Wisconsin remained the unanswered question.

[II]

Intense pressures were being brought to bear on the General by the rival factions among his advisers. To the liberals the situation was crystal-clear: honesty required that a stand be taken, and how could Eisenhower justify the slightest contact, personal or political, with the man who had sullied the name of Ike's commander, sponsor, and intimate friend, General George C. Marshall? The possibility was unthinkable, although many thought it, even though Ike was known to have been furious at McCarthy's "slanderous" attack.

The practical politicians, on the other hand, advised realistically that without McCarthy's help it was doubtful that Eisenhower could carry Wisconsin, and he would need that state to win.

As the argument raged, the liberals alternately hoped and despaired. Over the last two years they had suffered a succession of traumatic shocks in their efforts to muzzle McCarthy. As far back as November of the previous year, *Christian Century* had announced that the "effort to clear the Republican party of the 'McCarthyism' taint" had started. Even before that *The New York Times* had ventured its belief that the tide was turning against Joe, that more Democrats, and even a few Republicans, seemed to be willing to face up to the Wisconsin terror. And *The Nation,* after virtually dedicating its pages to a "stamp out Joe" crusade, had rejoiced when McCarthy sued Benton for slander, interpreting the move as an indication that Joe was on the ropes—calling the suit an act "not so much of brashness as of desperation."

Back early in 1951, William T. Evjue, editor of the *Madison Capital Times,* on a visit to Washington had been astonished by "the terror a poolroom politician from my home state could instil in men holding responsible positions in the government"; but now, with Eisenhower surely unable to stomach Joe, Evjue was confidently reporting "the hysteria responsible for 'McCarthyism' " was "clearly on the wane in Wisconsin." And the ever hopeful *Nation,* just one week before the Republican convention, foresaw "stormy weather" ahead for Joe. To this extent had McCarthy's opposition rallied from their previous defeats and were looking with confidence to the coming test.

The New York Times, chastened by experience, was less sanguine; in mid-May it interpreted the omens for McCarthy's own reelection as favorable. Against formidable opposition, within his own and the Democratic party," ran the *Times'* conclusion, "he seems a shoo-in." True, there remained the possibility, in case he should be reelected and in the event of a damaging report by the Gillette subcommittee, that the Senate might deny him his seat— a tenuous possibility, but one offering at least hope.

McCarthy himself displayed no anxiety. Having announced his entrance in the primary election to be held on September 9, he went about his affairs without change, circulating in the Senate with his ever-ready smile, cheerfully gregarious, betraying no lack of confidence that he would be with "Dear Guy" and "Bill" and "Herb" for a long while to come.

Making good his threat to Henry Luce, he had sent letters to prominent advertisers in *Time,* suggesting that they withdraw their accounts. Many persons, he wrote, were "not aware of the facts, and because of that are unknowingly helping to pollute and poison the waterholes of information"; and since he felt it was "more important to expose a liar, a crook, or a traitor who is able to poison the streams of information flowing into a vast number of American homes, than it is to expose an equally vicious crook, liar, or traitor who has no magazine outlet for his poison," he was bringing the facts to his correspondents' attention. *Time* reported no cancellations and Joe went on to other things.

In addition to his suit against Senator Benton, he was suing the *Syracuse Post-Standard* for $500,000, charging libel in an editorial against him; and this suit he would win, with payment of a nominal sum and a public retraction and apology by the paper.

[III]

The Republican national convention met in Chicago in July. A special interest attached to it because it would be the first political convention to be televised nationally, and millions of voters would see the party's headliners in action for the first time.

One headline speaker was Senator Joe McCarthy. The invitation to address the delegates had been issued only after a bruising struggle behind the scenes. The liberal element was in agony: allowing McCarthy to appear before television viewers as an accredited spokesman for the party they believed would kill all chances of victory in November. The professionals arranging the program urged just as truculently that McCarthy could not be ignored without offending a host of voters who favored him, and that far from being a detriment to the party, he would prove one of its chief assets. Joe had his party in as big a snarl as he sometimes had the Senate.

About the reaction of the delegates when McCarthy appeared there was no doubt. He was rousingly introduced by the temporary chairman, who told the crowd: "When they tell you Joe McCarthy has smeared the names of innocent men, ask them to name just one. Every man exposed has been publicly fired or quietly allowed to leave the government service. We will not 'turn our backs' at any time on that fighting Marine, the Honorable Joe McCarthy!"

The hall erupted with applause and a demonstration. While the band played "On Wisconsin" and "The Marine Hymn," delegates carrying fish-shaped placards labeled "Acheson," "Hiss," "Lattimore," and "Red Herring" paraded in front of the platform. *The New York Times,* bravely reporting what actually happened, certainly without bias in favor of Joe, said the demonstration lasted four minutes, the longest of the convention up to that point. The applause, the *Times* carefully added, was not unanimous and "many delegates sat or stood unmoved."

But there was no question about the response to Joe's fighting speech. Between salvos of cheers he told the convention that he would not soften his blows, because "a rough fight is the only fight that Communists understand. We can't fight Communists in the Acheson-Lattimore fashion of hitting them with a perfumed silk handkerchief at the front door, while they batter our friends with brass knuckles at the back door!"

He called on "the millions of loyal Democrats" to look at the record and see that their party had "deserted" them. Even one Red in the State Department was too many, he cried; and as regarded the stalemate in Korea, he pledged that if the Republicans won, "we won't be in any war which we are afraid to win." The real issue of the election, he contended, was whether the United States should "continue to squander her blood, waste her resources, and sacrifice her position of world leadership—just that and nothing more."

The next morning, *The New York Times,* in an editorial headed "Low Point," mourned:

"At precisely 3:21 P.M. yesterday, Eastern daylight saving time, the Republican convention in Chicago reached rock bottom. This was when Senator Joseph R. McCarthy of Wisconsin, the traducer of reputations and mudslinger extraordinary, sponsor (under the libel-proof privileges of the Senate) of the incredible charge that General George C. Marshall has been part of a 'conspiracy so immense and an infamy so black as to dwarf any previous such venture in the history of man,' mounted the rostrum to address the assembled delegates. He did so at the explicit invitation of the Republican National Committee, tendered by it for reasons best known to itself. This is the low point. From now on the course must certainly be upward."

What the convention went on to was the nomination of Dwight D. Eisenhower for President and Richard M. Nixon for Vice President.

McCarthy returned to Washington and went on to Bethesda Naval Hospital, suffering, it was said, from a sinus infection. But the medical bulletin was quickly amended to state that the senator had undergone major surgery, and would be out of action indefinitely.

[IV]

This surprise development threw his opposition in Wisconsin off balance. They had been prepared for a hard-hitting campaign, but not for lack of a visible target to lash at. Belaboring Joe when he was too sick to fight back would only win sympathy for him; so a whole new strategy of campaign had to be devised.

McCarthy's operation had been to mend a ruptured diaphragm. Postsurgery bulletins reported the patient recovering satisfactorily, although he probably would be unable to do any public speaking for at least two months—beyond the date of the primary.

On July 28 he was reported "past the danger point." *

On August 2 McCarthy left the hospital and was flown to Wisconsin to recuperate at a north woods resort; his staff reported him "coming along nicely." The primary election was five weeks off.

Not all of McCarthy's enemies accepted the medical bulletins at face value. *The Nation* insinuated that Joe had deliberately timed the operation ("which may or may not have had to do with a diaphragm distended by screaming 'big lies' in the Senate") to upset the primary's normal schedule and rattle his opponents. "Medical sources," said *The Nation,* "report that the operation was not necessary at this time, that he might safely have waited until mid-November." As matters stood, Joe, "either as an invalid or as a martyr," would be able to "pace his campaign in an unexpected way," and it seemed very unfair. The "medical sources" quoted were not identified.†

During August every weapon that could be raised against Joseph R. McCarthy was brought into play.

In Washington, the result of a nationwide poll of political scientists was published, rating the members of the Senate in order of their relative effectiveness, and McCarthy stood at the bottom of the list.

In Wisconsin, a group calling themselves the Wisconsin Citizens Committee on McCarthy's Record, issued a 136-page booklet titled *The McCarthy Record,* which *Christian Century* welcomed as "at last an intelligent effort to protect the voters of Wisconsin against [the senator's] cuttlefish technique. . . . It's all there, factual, calm, documented, damning. The whole story of the junior senator from

---

* That same day another headline reported the death of Senator McMahon, an implacable McCarthy foe. McMahon had succumbed to a spinal ailment; he was forty-eight.

† In the interest of fairness, it ought to be noted that *The Nation's* failure to identify these anonymous "medical sources," invoked as a screen behind which to accuse the senator of a gross deception, was the very thing for which McCarthy was excoriated so bitterly by *The Nation* and others, namely, spreading unsubstantiated insinuations and making accusations, based on anonymous sources. This was held to be the essence of "McCarthyism." See *Random House Dictionary:* "McCARTHYISM: public accusation of disloyalty . . . in many instances unsupported by proof or based on slight, doubtful, or irrelevant evidence. . . ." Also *American Heritage Dictionary:* "McCARTHYISM: political practice of publicizing accusations . . . with insufficient regard to evidence. . . ."

Wisconsin, from the day when he launched his ambitions as a Democratic candidate for county district attorney to his present notorious eminence, is told. There's the story of the way in which the Wisconsin supreme court and bar association rebuked him for his actions as a state circuit judge. There's the very queer story of his state income tax troubles. There's the Lustron check. There's the shifting of figures in his accusations against the State Department. There are the promises to make his charges without benefit of senatorial immunity and the welshing on those promises. And much more; it's all there. If the citizens of Wisconsin read this booklet, we are confident they will take care of McCarthy's bid for reelection."

McCarthy was facing a field of seven in the primary contest, since his incapacitation had prompted several dark horses to jump into the scramble. The only serious contender, however, was Leonard F. Schmitt, a personable young lawyer from Merrill. He had been induced to make the fight by backers of Eisenhower, and although at the start he had gone easy on the recuperating "invalid or martyr," he soon shifted to a no-holds-barred attack.* Working against his chances were two powerful factors: the state's party organization, led by Coleman's Voluntary Committee, had endorsed McCarthy; and Eisenhower had taken the course of refusing to endorse any candidate whatever in a primary contest. Wisconsin's Governor Walter J. Kohler, Jr., who was extremely popular in the state, also had endorsed McCarthy, although he disliked the senator intensely.

Schmitt based his chief hope on Wisconsin's peculiar election law, which permitted anyone to vote in a primary regardless of party affiliation. Schmitt believed that many Democrats, to whom McCarthy was anathema, would cross over and vote in the Republican column, just to unseat the senator. Some political experts concurred with Schmitt in this prognostication, and to stimulate this trend, the anti-McCarthy forces applied pressure at Republican national headquarters to get Eisenhower to say at least whether he would or would not support the senator in November, should he be renominated. The hope was that Ike would indicate such lack

---

* Schmitt was the first political candidate, apparently, to make extensive use of the "talkathon," staying for hours in front of a television camera talking and answering questions telephoned by listeners. In one session he remained on the air for twenty-five hours consecutively, a feat which attracted national notice.

of enthusiasm for Joe that Schmitt's campaign would benefit; and an encouraging sign was seen in the report coming from Washington, toward the end of August, that in his forthcoming tour of Wisconsin, Senator Nixon, the Vice-Presidential candidate, would attack McCarthy at least inferentially.

This was front-page news, and William S. White informed *The New York Times* that "adequate authority" confirmed that Nixon would support a continuing drive to get Communists out of the government, wherever they might have imbedded themselves under the benign neglect of the Truman administration; but he would stress that no charges should be brought against individuals without the facts to back them up. This would be tantamount to taking the Communist issue away from Joe—or trying to.

A furious hassle followed in the Republican high command, and the next day the front pages carried columns of type denying the Nixon report. From his campaign train in Colorado, Eisenhower said flatly that while he would not give a blanket endorsement to Senator McCarthy, or campaign for him, he would support any Republican running against any Democrat this year. Expressing sharp disagreement with methods which he implied McCarthy used, Ike made a spirited defense of General Marshall. Asked whether he would appear on the platform with McCarthy, he replied that he did not think it "a heinous thing" to be seen with the senator; and he reminded the press that if he were elected he would need a Republican Congress to make an effective administration.

In Washington, Nixon averred that both Eisenhower and he would support McCarthy in the general election, if the senator won the nomination, but added: "In supporting any particular candidate, neither I nor General Eisenhower will endorse the methods of Republican candidates which happen to be different from our own."

The Democrats professed to be scandalized by this flirting with the "moral leprosy" of "McCarthyism." *The Nation* appealed to Eisenhower's conscience, pleading that since he "must repudiate McCarthy sooner or later . . . it is much better that he do so now. . . . Independent voters want to be assured of more than the general's personal attitude; they want McCarthy to be defeated. If the general fails them now, they will remember in November."

Before the national convention of the American Legion, Governor Adlai Stevenson of Illinois, the Democrats' nominee for the

Presidency, advised Eisenhower, who was describing himself as a "middle-of-the-road" man, to get rid of his "middle-of-the-gutter" advisers. Although he did not name McCarthy, Stevenson's target was obvious, and the applause which he received for his remark was described as "polite."

At the end of August, McCarthy let it be known that he was flying to Washington to consult doctors on his condition and, if they approved, he would make one speech, in Milwaukee, on September 3, six days before the primary voting.

[V]

Just then an interesting sidelight came from Baltimore, where in a pretrial hearing in McCarthy's suit against Senator Benton, former Senator Tydings was questioned about that purported recording of McCarthy's Wheeling speech which he had attempted to play in the Senate. "I have four records showing McCarthy was a liar," Tydings testified, but he admitted explicitly that he had no recording of McCarthy's words at Wheeling.

An anti-McCarthy group immediately invited Tydings to come to Wisconsin and debate McCarthy, and he responded that he would do so "with pleasure." But McCarthy, passing through Milwaukee on his way east, merely shrugged. "I'm not going to waste time debating with the dead," said he.

In a final flurry, *The Nation,* speaking in what its editors saw as a desperate hour for American liberties, appealed again to Eisenhower to disembarrass himself of the "albatross" of McCarthy. "Speak up, general," *The Nation* exhorted; there was still time to redeem himself. "Let his supporters . . . explain to him that McCarthyism is not a partisan issue. . . . McCarthy is bad medicine for the Republicans."

Another article in the same issue, brightened by a gorilla-like caricature of the junior senator, concluded hopefully that "McCarthy's performance has found no echo in Wisconsin and is looked upon as a fundamentally dishonest performance, 'all malarky.' " The author's prayer was that the voters would "expunge this 'ism' from our politics and the word from our language."

Subjoined were statements by thirteen "representative men"— professors, labor leaders, churchmen, officeholders, journalists, attorneys—telling why they opposed the senator. The mildest testimonial was by a minister in Sheboygan, who granted that "Joe McCarthy is a pleasant person. He can be ingratiating and as friendly as a puppy. He has the gift of disarming his critics. But attractive as this personal quality is . . . on the basis of his record, he does not qualify to be a United States senator."

McCarthy returned from Washington with medical permission to speak, and in Milwaukee, on September 3, before 1,700 cheering supporters, he described his hours of despondency during his enforced silence. Schmitt's campaign had worried him, he admitted, and he wondered, too, why he had been singled out for attack by Stevenson. Since becoming the Democratic standard-bearer, McCarthy said, Stevenson had gone out of his way to berate him three times. "Why?" he asked. "Why the bitterness? Could you be disturbed, Mr. Stevenson, because I am checking your record since the day you entered government service at about the same time and in the same department as the Hiss, Abt, Witt, and Pressman group?" Saying that Stevenson had given "all-out support to Alger Hiss," McCarthy declared that he was checking the nominee's record "not only for proof of guilt by association, but of guilt by collaboration."

Reporting the speech in the staunchly Republican *New York Herald Tribune,* Joseph Alsop would write that the senator had worked his audience up to "paroxysms of hatred," and so far as his words might affect the primary, certainly they were not designed to entice Democrats.

The voter turnout on September 9 was so heavy that many polling places kept open after the announced closing time. And down to the wire McCarthy romped, winning in a veritable landslide of 538,000 votes to 211,000 for Schmitt. Of the nearly million votes cast, the senator took 55 percent; he not only routed Schmitt by better than 2½ to 1, but rolled up 100,000 more votes than all the other senatorial candidates in both parties combined—five Republicans and two Democrats.

The crushing fact to McCarthy's opponents was that Schmitt's appeals to Democrats to vote in the Republican column had been overwhelmingly successful. Democrats *had* crossed over in droves; but instead of voting against McCarthy they had handed him the nomination. Joe had held all the winning cards in his own deck, plus an ace from his opponents' hand. Five aces are hard to beat.

To the Conqueror,
Medals of Valor

"Shell-shocked" described McCarthy's opposition the day after Wisconsin voted, and the most shocking aspect of his triumph was that it was a purely personal achievement: Joe, not party drum-beating, had caused the record turnout and the size of his vote. On this point everyone agreed.

Schmitt was "appalled" by the people's refusal to repudiate "the man with the most corrupt record ever made by a Wisconsin senator." The only ready answer to the enigma Schmitt could offer was that the election had become a contest between two Joes—Joe McCarthy and Joe Stalin. If you weren't for McCarthy you had to be for Stalin, and vice versa.

McCarthy took the result in stride. "I don't see any real need for a victory statement," he said, proceeding to make one. "The people of Wisconsin have voted for me. The people of Wisconsin have made their statement about the issues of corruption, communism, and the suicidal foreign policy that has been so good for Russia and so bad for America. They have given full endorsement to my campaign to rid the government of subversive forces that would destroy it." His grin was sufficient testimonial to his elation.

Party leaders were swift to congratulate the winner. In Cincinnati, Senator Taft said he was "delighted. . . . I didn't endorse him because I stay out of primaries, but I did and do approve of his accomplishments in rooting out Communists and subversion in government." Senator Wiley, McCarthy's Wisconsin colleague, who also had held aloof from the primary fight, pledged his support and urged all Republicans to work for McCarthy's election in November.

Democratic spokesmen wept tears of sympathy for poor Eisenhower, saddled with an incubus by the Wisconsin electorate. Senator Benton deduced that the voters "didn't have the facts," although they had been pelted with them for weeks. Senator Sparkman thought "this must be one of Eisenhower's darkest days." The odor of crocodile was rank.

The Nation tried to take a broader view. McCarthy's "thumping victory," in its estimation, had been due to no last-minute pressure or trickery; McCarthy had conducted a remarkably quiet campaign, it conceded. The vote, *The Nation* concluded, was not so much a positive ratification of McCarthy and his methods, as an expression of "a strong groundswell of fear, irrational hatred, and a compulsive drive to subordinate every issue, foreign and domestic, to the negative purpose of 'fighting communism.'" Unfortunately for the Republicans, *The Nation* deduced, a maneuver which the moderates had expected to "outflank the right wing" had ended in "Eisenhower's encirclement."

The *New Republic* glumly admitted that the chance of reversing the primary victory in November appeared slight.

Perhaps a poll conducted among Milwaukee clergymen on the eve of the primary came as close as any analysis to digging down to the bedrock basis of McCarthy's voter appeal. All but five of those polled had responded, and 134 had said they favored McCarthy's return to the Senate, against 57 who wished to retire him. The most striking feature, however, was the stamp of approval placed on McCarthy as a fighter, engaged in a good cause. People "need someone to stir them up," wrote one minister. Other typical comments were: "We need more such fearless men." "Admire him for his courage." So it was as "Fighting Joe" that he had rallied the state to his support.

Commonweal, in an even-tempered review of the election, recognized the plain fact that McCarthy was a hero to thousands, endowed with "the kind of emotional appeal which is impervious to arguments"; nor was the fact that his record showed him to be "something less than a knight in shining armor" likely to shatter the loyalty of his admirers. Rejecting the position that Catholics should support McCarthy because their church also was anti-Communist, *Commonweal* announced its intention to fight the senator, without bitterness but relentlessly, to the last gasp. In words as doughty as Joe's own it served notice:

"We have opposed McCarthy in the past and we will continue to oppose him in the future. We can hear the measured voices . . .

saying, 'Of course, one cannot possibly approve of his methods, but he *is* anti-Communist.' Not for us. We have heard that song before, and we can't buy it."

[II]

Agreement seemed to be general that McCarthy would prove an embarrassment to his party's national ticket. He merely said that he intended to speak for Republican candidates wherever he might be invited, and of course he would work for the election of Eisenhower and Nixon, regardless of whether they came out for him.

He started carrying out this pledge by invading Connecticut, where Senator Benton was waging an uphill battle. "You ain't seen nothing yet in the fight on communism," he assured his audience. "It's going to get rougher and rougher and rougher. Some people claim they don't like McCarthy's methods, but, my friends, you can't fight communism in the State Department manner. If skunks are killing your chickens, the more successful your skunk hunt is, the worse smell you have when you come back."

Then he caught a plane for home, and in driving away from the airfield in Madison narrowly escaped injury when his car was rammed by another. Shrugging off the accident, he joined Governor Kohler and Republican National Committeeman Henry Ringling in a flight to Peoria, Illinois, to pick up Eisenhower's campaign train.

On his swing from South Carolina to North Dakota, the General was about to enter Wisconsin, and a frantic struggle was going on backstage over what Ike should say in McCarthy's bailiwick. It had been given out that in a major speech in Milwaukee, Eisenhower would couple an attack on the Truman administration's lethargy in combatting the Communist menace at home with a vigorous defense of General Marshall.

The anti-McCarthy crowd was on tenterhooks. Old-line advisers on the campaign train were telling Eisenhower that he could not afford to snub the best vote-getter the party had. Eisenhower needed Wisconsin to win, and McCarthy's domination of that state had just been demonstrated. But Ike was stubborn: Loyalty to a devoted comrade required that he speak out at a time and place that would give his words weight. The draft of the speech already prepared for his use in Milwaukee contained this passage:

"The right to question a man's judgment carries with it no automatic right to question his honor. Let me be specific. I know that charges of disloyalty have, in the past, been leveled against General George C. Marshall personally. I know him, as a man and as a soldier, to be dedicated with singular selflessness and the profoundest patriotism to the service of America."

Then Kohler, Ringling, and McCarthy flew into Peoria. After a huddle with campaign managers, word was conveyed to Ike that the passage would cause offense and might even split the party, and without party solidarity the election would be lost. Eisenhower himself talked with McCarthy for half an hour, and afterward the senator admitted that the speech had been discussed. He had told the General, McCarthy said, that he didn't have the slightest objection to Eisenhower's saying anything he wanted to, but he thought Milwaukee was the wrong place to say it. The tribute to Marshall thereupon was deleted; and the next day at Green Bay, the first stop in Joe's state, Eisenhower called for the election of all Republican candidates.

McCarthy stood with the party bigwigs on the rear platform of the special train as Eisenhower went on to explain that his and McCarthy's aims were identical when it came to "ridding this government of the incompetents, the subversive, and disloyal," though they differed over method. And at every stop thereafter, the senator appeared on the platform and was photographed in a somewhat long-range handclasp with the candidate, ostensibly sealing their alliance.

At Appleton Joe introduced the General, and in Milwaukee that evening, before an audience that only three-quarters filled the arena, Eisenhower coupled an appeal for McCarthy's reelection with a scathing attack on the Democratic administration for "tolerating the penetration of the government by Communists and treason itself." The future of the nation, he said, "belongs to courageous men, and not to those who have sneered at the warnings of men trying to drive Communists from high places, but who themselves have never had the sense or stamina to take after the Communists themselves."

After that speech Wisconsin was considered safe for Eisenhower; but the senator's critics were aghast. Arthur Hays Sulzberger, strongly pro-Eisenhower publisher of *The New York Times,* wired Sherman Adams on the Eisenhower train, "I am sick at heart."

276   When Even Angels Wept

Editorially the *Times* grieved over "an unhappy day" in the General's "strange journey" through Wisconsin. "We have deeply regretted that General Eisenhower's understandable dread of the splinter-party system has led him to the length of endorsing McCarthy," was the mournful plaint.

Eisenhower kept on vowing to rout the "pinks" out of Washington, and deploring the errors of policy that had led the United States into "two world wars in the last seven years." And McCarthy shuttled about the country, his own campaign neglected, speaking wherever he was invited. He spoke in Arizona at the invitation of Barry Goldwater, who was opposing Senate Majority Leader McFarland. In Ohio he spoke at the invitation of Taft.

Tremendous advance publicity was given to a speech he was to make in Chicago on election eve against Adlai Stevenson. The event was a $50-a-plate dinner in the Palmer House, and the senator's appearance was to be nationally televised. The speech was delivered, and to viewers across the nation McCarthy presented what he termed "the facts . . . the coldly documented history of this man who says 'I want to be your President.'" He alluded to Stevenson as running on "the Truman-Acheson ticket; I don't want to call it the Democratic ticket because it would be a great insult to all the good Democrats in this nation. . . . Unfortunately, the millions of loyal Democrats no longer have a party in Washington."

Much of the speech dealt with Stevenson's political advisers and speech writers, specifically Arthur Schlesinger, Jr., and Archibald MacLeish. Turning back on Stevenson the latter's recent advice to Eisenhower to get rid of his "middle-of-the-gutter" advisers, Joe said laughingly that if they would let him aboard the Stevenson train with "a slippery elm stick," he would guarantee to make "good Americans" out of Adlai's idea men.

But the jibe that drove Joe's opponents to fury was a slip of the tongue, real or calculated, that confused Stevenson with Alger Hiss. Tracing Stevenson's alleged devious record on the Communist menace, the words slipped out: "Strangely Alger—I mean Adlai . . ."

The diners laughed, but listening Democrats sent up a roar of anger; obviously McCarthy had touched a sensitive nerve. *The New York Times* reported receiving more than 200 telephone calls within thirty minutes protesting Joe's "foul blow" and berating the *Times* for its continued support of Eisenhower since the General's "surrender" to the ogre from Wisconsin. Well, the *Times* concluded editorially the next day, McCarthy had delivered his widely heralded speech, and the republic still stood. But to sound out election sentiment in the senator's state after this blast, the *Times* sent its own reporter to Wisconsin. The report, as of election eve, was that the state stood solidly for Joe.

Said a country editor: "Sure, I'm for McCarthy. I'm against communism. He's the only one doing anything about the Communists. I think there's more good than evil in Joe and that's why I'm going to vote for him."

A farmer in a field: "Yes, I guess about everybody in this part of the country is for McCarthy. If he wasn't telling the truth they'd a hung him long ago. He's one of the greatest Americans we ever had."

A Milwaukee bartender: "Well, he's got some pretty good enemies and I like him for that. Perhaps he isn't much of a senator, but he's a real fighter. He may be a stinker—but he's a Wisconsin stinker."

The reporter found that the very quantity and virulence of the publicity against Joe seemed to react in his favor, giving him an underdog appeal. He was admired as a slugger, and the relentless campaign against him carried on by the major newspapers and nationally circulating magazines inspired resentment.

And reelected McCarthy was, on November 4, in an Eisenhower landslide, although for weeks he had virtually turned his back on his personal campaign, working in other states for the national ticket. The results generally were impressive. Eisenhower and Nixon won. In Connecticut Senator Benton was defeated; and so was Senator McFarland in Arizona. These defeats brought Joe's string of victories, real or credited, to eight at least—eight senators to whose defeat since 1950 he had contributed, in some instances primarily. His work in the campaign was said also to have helped the Republicans materially in regaining control of Congress.

Joe's antagonists sucked what consolation they could from the circumstance that he had finished well behind the head of the Republican state ticket, Governor Kohler, and also behind Eisenhower, coming in a lagging third. But this was cold comfort: Joe had coasted in by a handsome margin over his Democratic opponent, and he was sure of six more years in the Senate—where his party, at least for the next two years, would be in control.

In December McCarthy appeared as guest of honor at a luncheon in the Hotel Astor in New York and received a plaque in recognition of his "historic and sacrificial battle against subversion in high places." The honor was bestowed by the Joint Committee Against Communism. Rabbi Benjamin Schultz presided, and in his speech of acceptance the senator stressed the need for unremitting vigilance. Already "Communist thinkers," he warned, were scheming to burrow into the new administration.

At the end of that month McCarthy was awarded six military decorations for "heroism and extraordinary achievement" as a Marine Corps officer in the Pacific—the Distinguished Flying Cross and the Air Medal with four Gold Stars. The presentation was made by Colonel John R. Lanigan, commanding the Fifth Marine Reserve District, in the senator's office, and inquisitive reporters were assured that no significance could be attached to the tardiness of the awards; records had to be checked, and the process took time. Asked how many combat missions he had flown in the war, Joe replied offhand, "Thirty."

All in all, 1952 was ending dishearteningly for the enemies of Joe McCarthy. But the battered losers, nursing their bruises, were consoled by two of their more eminent prophets, Walter Lippman and Joseph Alsop. Both these sentinels upon the watchtowers of enlightened liberalism advised the dispirited to pluck up and take heart, for as soon as Dwight D. Eisenhower entered the White House, the reign of McCarthy would end.

PART FOUR

The Power and the Glory

"Is it not brave to be a king, Techelles!—
Is it not passing brave to be a king,
And ride in triumph through Persepolis?
To ask and have, command and be obey'd . . ."
                              —*Tamburlaine the Great*

Corsair at Large

"There are those who voted Republican on November 4 in the belief that Eisenhower's victory would mean Senator McCarthy's demise. The Wisconsin senator was not among them."

With this laconic reflection the *New Republic* greeted 1953 and the new Congress. To the *New Republic*'s readers the prospect looked dismal: as a result of the Republican takeover of the Senate, Joseph McCarthy had been elevated to a position which (in the freely expressed opinion of *Newsweek*) made him "one of the most potentially powerful men in the Congress and the country." He was determined to prove *Newsweek* right.

Yet paradoxically, just twenty-four hours before his promotion, McCarthy had been the target of a blistering denunciation by the Gillette subcommittee, reporting on its fifteen-month, off-and-on investigation of Benton's charges against Joe, and Joe's reciprocal accusations against Benton.

The subcommittee filed its report with its parent Rules Committee on the last day of the expiring 82nd Congress. Actually the subcommittee no longer bore Senator Gillette's name as chairman, although it would continue to be referred to popularly by that label. The statuesque Iowan, who disliked brawling, had withdrawn from the subcommittee the day after McCarthy's Wisconsin primary victory. His departure had been preceded by the resignation of another investigator, protesting against what he felt was a prejudice against McCarthy, and the walkout of Senator Welker for the same reason. Meanwhile Senator Monroney had eliminated himself for all practical purposes by taking a protracted vacation abroad. Left to stumble along were Senators Hennings and Hendrickson. In order to maintain a Democratic majority, Senator Carl Hayden of Arizona, chairman of the Rules Committee, had rather desperately

281

assigned himself to the investigating group. At the same time Senator Hendrickson, who had been threatening to quit, was persuaded to stay on in order to preserve bipartisanship. He had been helped to make up his mind by McCarthy's constant needling of the subcommittee members. For instance, Joe had written to Senator Hennings:

"Dear Tom—I should have thought perhaps the election might have taught you that your boss and mine—the American people—do not approve of treason and incompetence and feel that it must be exposed."

Instead of which, he complained, the subcommittee was "dishonestly" investigating people who exposed treason and incompetence in the government. This taunt was more than Hendrickson was willing to take, and he sat tight.

The subcommittee was in a quandary because Joe had declined to comply with an "invitation" to appear and be questioned; he said he would accept a subpoena. But his fellow senators shrank from taking that step; besides, nobody could be certain what would happen. Investigating McCarthy was turning out to be like Russian roulette: prudence counseled against it. So the subcommittee's report was filed on January 2, 1953, without Joe's having been questioned or entering any formal defense. It bore the signatures of Hayden, Hennings, and Hendrickson.

Its main emphasis was on two aspects of the inquiry. In a long preamble it traced the tortuous course of the investigation, alleging that McCarthy had turned down six invitations to appear and answer questions, and interpreting his conduct as "disdain and contempt for the rules and wishes of the entire Senate." This, in turn, led to the "inescapable conclusion that Senator McCarthy deliberately set out to thwart any investigation of him by obscuring the real issue and responsibility of the subcommittee by charges of lack of jurisdiction, smear, and Communist-inspired persecution."

Then substantively the report delved into McCarthy's checkered financial record. The Lustron fee, speculation in soybean futures, stock gambling, the wandering course of monies donated to "fight communism" through a dense thicket of bank accounts—these and other subjects were explored in detail. No conclusions were reached, but six questions were posed, some of which pointed toward possible violations of banking and other laws. No recommendations were made, and since Senator Jenner, a fervent admirer of McCarthy, was assuming the chairmanship of the Rules Committee the next day, it seemed clear that the indictment was headed for oblivion.

McCarthy dismissed the report as "a new low in dishonesty and smear"; called Hennings and Hayden administration "lackeys"; and pilloried Hendrickson as "a living miracle in that he is without question the only man in the world who has lived so long with neither brains nor guts."

Hayden was so angered by this gratuitous attack that he tried to block Joe from taking his seat. McCarthy got wind of the attempt, and sent back word that if he were challenged, he would challenge the right of Senator Chavez to another term; rumors of wholesale irregularities in Chavez's reelection had reached Washington. The Democratic caucus "played it safe," and when the roll was called on January 3, Joe strode down the aisle on Senator Wiley's arm and not a voice was raised against him. As he passed Senator Hayden, he gripped the Arizonan's shoulder in friendly greeting and grinned. Ignored was the bitter observation in the "three H's" report, that the issue raised by the facts disclosed, namely, McCarthy's fitness to sit in the Senate, "transcends partisan politics and goes to the very core of the [Senate's] authority, integrity, and the respect in which it is held by the people of this country."

"A Senate sell-out!" cried *The Nation;* and the *New Republic* found the silence maintained by the Senate's "cowed children" frightening, for such a silence "McCarthy may impress upon this nation forever if he has his way."

Hennings sent copies of the report to the Justice Department, Internal Revenue Service, and Reconstruction Finance Corporation for study, and certain critics of McCarthy employed attorneys privately to prod the government into undertaking a prosecution; but the consensus of counsel, it developed, was that no basis for a successful prosecution had been established, and eventually the whole matter, except for periodic resurrections for political effect, would be shelved. *The New York Times* reported that "any attempt to discipline McCarthy may be considered almost inconceivably remote."

"They should know by this time that they can't scare or turn me aside," was Joe's unconcerned comment.

[II]

In the reorganization of the Senate, McCarthy moved into the
chairmanship of the Committee on Government Operations, with
its permanent subcommittee on investigations. This committee was
not regarded as of first rank; nevertheless, it held a mandate which
in many directions stretched virtually without limit. It was empowered to look into anything connected with the "operation of
the government at all levels with a view to determining its economy
and efficiency." This might be stretched to authorization to investigate every person, group, school, institution, industry, business,
or activity whatsoever which directly or indirectly touched the
government or benefited from federal funds, whether by grant,
subsidy, payment, tax exemption, or otherwise. In fact, it was
difficult to name any activity that did not come under the heading.

Armed with this authority, McCarthy sketched out his intended
plan of action. He would keep after the State Department, he said,
because although Acheson was out as Secretary of State and John
Foster Dulles was in, "Communist thinkers and fellow travelers"
were still there. "They're still following the same line of thought,
so obviously it hasn't been cleaned up." Of the eighty-one individuals whose names he had given to the Tydings Committee, "we
have gotten rid of fifteen or sixteen," he said, but much remained
to be done.

The educational system, especially certain colleges, was in line
for scrutiny also, he said, and he predicted that this task would
be nasty because "the minute you expose Communists and Communist thinkers in your educational institutions, all hell breaks
loose. From coast to coast you hear the screaming of 'interference
with academic freedom.' So it will be an awfully unpleasant task,
and you will hear me called a lot worse names than I've been called
before—if they can think of any new ones."

A radio interviewer asked whether McCarthy felt he might be
"pushed out of the anti-Communist picture" by the incoming administration, but Joe had no fear. "No one can push me out of
anything; I'm not retiring from exposing Communists."

(The *New Republic* shuddered, "What killings lie ahead!")

Some of his projected inquiries wouldn't be ready for public
hearings for six or eight months yet, the senator cautioned. "Until

just before election time?" came the sardonic suggestion. "You go to hell!" Joe said and grinned at the reporter.

The makeup of the Government Operations Committee could not have made McCarthy happier if he had selected it himself. His complete freedom of action would hardly be hampered by such associates as Mundt of South Dakota, Dirksen of Illinois, Dworshak of Idaho, Butler of Maryland, and Potter of Michigan. Mundt was a veteran of the House Un-American Activities Committee, largely instrumental in uncovering Alger Hiss; Dirksen had been haranguing the voters on the "lavender lads" in the State Department; Dworshak was in McCarthy's political debt; Butler was eminently the creation of McCarthy; and Potter, a combat veteran who had lost both legs in the Battle of the Bulge, also owed something to the McCarthy influence. The fact that all these senators were under personal obligation to him gave the new chairman extraordinary political muscle, all the more formidable because he was not dependent upon the favor of the party leaders; McCarthy had his own center of senatorial prerogative in which he was kingpin. The only Republican member of his committee who was not in his corner was Margaret Chase Smith, and she could be ignored, especially since she was not assigned to the subcommittee on investigations, the active branch; that group included Mundt, Dirksen, and Potter, with McCarthy himself chairman.

The Democrats on McCarthy's investigations subcommittee had been chosen cannily by the new minority leader, Lyndon Baines Johnson of Texas, succeeding Arizona's McFarland, unseated by Barry Goldwater with an assist from McCarthy. These Democratic members were John L. McClellan of Arkansas, Stuart Symington of Missouri, and Henry M. Jackson of Washington. McClellan and Jackson had served in the House of Representatives, while Symington had filled appointive offices under President Truman, notably Secretary of the Air Force in the new Defense Department. All had had experience in government, and none was facing immediate election problems; hence they would be relatively immune to rumblings about voter reprisals.

Furnished with a $189,000 budget and a staff of trained investigators, armed with broad powers and boundless audacity, McCarthy proceeded to show what a determined raider could do. Up to now he had been what *The New York Times* described as "an arm-swinging outsider trying to break in"; now he was on the inside; and what he accomplished in the next ninety days brought his dazzled antagonists to the point of believing that he held the State Department in thrall, was throttling free speech, had the press and radio jumping to serve him, and was compelling even his inveterate enemies to play the game of glorifying Joe.

[III]

McCarthy had predicted that for "the first three, four, five, six, or seven months" his work would be easy, because he would be investigating "what happened in the past. The time will come, however, when we won't be any longer investigating what the Truman administration did—we'll be investigating what our own administration is doing," and he would expect cooperation. "We're not going to take the answer from a witness, 'My superior officer told me not to tell you.' " And he flatly stated his belief that nobody, President or not, could "order someone to refuse to answer legitimate questions before a Senate committee any more than they can order them to commit perjury or any other crime." This had been a bone of contention between McCarthy and the White House under President Truman; and apparently President Eisenhower took note, for in his State of the Union message he in effect took issue with Joe, saying:

"Primary responsibility for keeping out the disloyal and dangerous rests squarely upon the executive branch. When this branch so conducts itself as to require policing by another branch of the government, it invites its own disorder and confusion."

This plain staking out of areas of jurisdiction was welcomed by liberals as the promise of a new day. But almost before the new tenant of the White House had got fairly settled, McCarthy was conducting hearings on the operations of the Voice of America, a State Department activity, and was reaping sheaves of sensational publicity.

The government's overseas radio service actually was run by the International Information Administration, a division of the State Department. The hearings were launched in New York City, and McCarthy had announced that the inquiry would focus on "mismanagement, waste, and subversion." Subpoenas were issued for more than fifty present and former employes of the Voice, and everyone desiring to present information was invited to appear.

"We want to hear everybody who is accused and give them a chance to answer before we do anything publicly," the senator explained, adding that he foresaw a lengthy inquiry. "Some persons in the Voice of America are doing a rather effective job of sabotaging Dulles' and Eisenhower's foreign policy," he said, and the ructions started immediately.

The day before McCarthy and Senator Jackson held the first hearing, a directive was issued at the New York office of the Information Administration, instructing Voice writers that in preparing broadcasts they might make use of material from the works of "controversial" writers, even if the author happened to be a Communist or a fellow traveler, or "if—like Howard Fast—he is known as a Soviet-endorsed author."

As a writer thus described officially as "Soviet-endorsed," whose works were or might be used in Voice of America broadcasts, Fast was called to testify in executive session. Afterward McCarthy told the press that Fast had refused to say whether he was a Communist, or whether he knew of any Communists working for the State Department or the Voice of America. When faced with such questions, McCarthy said, Fast had taken refuge in the Fifth Amendment, which safeguards one against possible self-incrimination.

But news of McCarthy's delving into the Voice of America's policy on "Soviet-endorsed" books reached Washington, and instantly a fresh directive was issued, rescinding the New York order, and laying down the rule that nothing whatever from "controversial" writers could be used.

This about-face, it was learned, had been executed at the insistence of the Secretary of State himself, and the press interpreted it as knuckling under to Joe. But a more resounding backdown came the next day when McCarthy summoned reporters and angrily denounced the "reprisal action" that he said had been taken against a State Department clerk named John E. Matson, who had told McCarthy investigators that the department's loyalty files were in a "deplorable condition." Matson thereupon had been questioned for hours by John W. Ford, the department's security chief, McCarthy said, and had then been transferred to a "beat-pounding job ringing doorbells."

In the midst of this outburst, the senator was informed that still another directive had just been issued to all State Department

employes, advising them that they might decide for themselves
whether they would answer questions put by subcommittee investigators, when no senator was present. So, exclaimed Joe, prospective
witnesses were being notified in effect that what had happened to
Matson might happen to them if they dared to report any wrongdoing!

"This committee is not going to be hamstrung by the State Department or any other department," McCarthy fumed. Reaching
for a telephone, he called General Walter Bedell Smith, Eisenhower's newly appointed Undersecretary of State, and ordered
him to hustle over to the senator's office for an "informal conference." General Smith hustled, and he and McCarthy went into
a private conference for three-quarters of an hour. When they
emerged from the inner office McCarthy was grinning. He had a
statement to make, he told waiting reporters, and while he made
it Bedell Smith, extremely pale, sat beside him in silence. The
difficulty had been resolved, the senator said: "We have everything worked out. The department will appoint a liaison man to
work with the committee and get us the witnesses we want. The
general agrees that the first directive, which we praised, should be
in force. He never intended that it should be canceled."

Smith declined to say that the second directive, found so offensive
by McCarthy, had been rescinded, but it was obvious that it had
become a dead letter.

Then McCarthy took up the Matson matter, and Donald B.
Lourie, the new Undersecretary of State for Administration, meekly
announced that Matson had been reinstated in his old job.

The rapidity and ease with which McCarthy had wrung these
humiliating reversals of policy from the State Department (all on
questions of its own internal administration) stunned the senator's
critics. It had been accomplished so effortlessly—by the simple expedient of figuratively holding a pistol to Dulles' head, and inferentially to the head of the President. Capitol correspondents were
dumfounded. Joe had served notice that he would not be elbowed
out of the spotlight, and that he would investigate the high and the
low, in or out of office, as he deemed proper. And his promised
investigations had hardly begun!

"No greater series of victories by a Congressional body over a
senior executive department in so short a time is recalled here,"
read the astonished report of William S. White to *The New York*

Times; while *The Nation* reported that such seasoned observers of the Washington scene as the Alsop brothers, Doris Fleeson, Thomas L. Stokes, and Marquis Childs were "stunned by the ease with which McCarthy, with a few cracks of his whip, brought John Foster Dulles, Walter Bedell Smith, and Donald Lourie into line. After only a month in office, the Eisenhower administration is being warned from all sides that a day of reckoning . . . with the town tough and prize soy-bean speculator of Appleton, Wisconsin . . . cannot be avoided much longer."

The *New Republic* went further. Although the country seemed to be taking the drama in stride, that delineator of disaster said that McCarthy was already installed as the "shadow Secretary of State" and implored the President to halt the ignominious knuckling under to a bully. Otherwise, the Cassandra voice croaked, Eisenhower might "look back on his electoral excursion to Wisconsin as a point of no return on the road to hell."

"Too Bad It Isn't Poison"

The Voice of America hearings were being held in the United States courthouse in Foley Square, in downtown New York City, the public sessions televised. Network sources estimated that the viewers who tuned in regularly numbered millions; Joseph McCarthy was the nation's most talked-about politician, and his personality caused as much excitement as the disclosures being made. It was widely sensed, however, that the real drama was not the one being played in the stifling hot hearing room, but the behind-the-scenes struggle in Washington between the senator and the executive branch of the government.

President Eisenhower was being badgered by the press to clamp down on the Wisconsin roustabout, while other advisers were equally vehement in urging the President to humor Joe, because his value to the party was too great to risk losing his good will. In the end Eisenhower did nothing. When asked point-blank in a press conference whether he thought the senator's digging into the Voice of America was helping the fight against communism, he glided off into evasive tactics. Well, he said, he didn't know exactly what Senator McCarthy was aiming at. Of course, it would be extremely dangerous to try to limit the power of Congress to investigate, and he supposed that any methods being used were approved by Congress or they would not be allowed. From that opaque smudge-cloud of words the President declined to emerge.

Secretary Dulles issued his own declaration of policy, placating but noncommittal. The State Department, he said, would welcome any disclosures that would help to render it "more competent, loyal, and secure"; but the responsibility for running the department was his, and he expected to exercise it. Unfortunately, Dulles coupled this statement with an action that duplicated Acheson's manner of handling the elimination of Edmund Clubb. The loyalty review board had found a reasonable doubt of loyalty in the case of John Carter Vincent, and he was in line for dismissal. Then Dulles stepped in, overruled the review board, reinstated Vincent and accepted his resignation, thereby preserving his right to a pension of $8,000 a year.

Needless to say, this action did not sit well with Senator McCarthy. A pension, he grumbled, was awarded "for having served well"; but his strictures were limited to growling. Meanwhile he did not fail to point out that Vincent's name had been on his 1950 list, so here was another one dug out of government. Nor did Dulles' magnanimity earn him any favor in the camp of Joe's enemies. The *Washington Post,* foremost in the throng of McCarthy's adversaries, disgustedly called the Secretary the "inert tool" of Joe's malevolence, and *The New York Times* castigated both the "supineness" of the State Department and the "television carnival" being staged by Senator McCarthy. Such a "spectacular, free-wheeling assault," it was said, certainly was no way to improve the Voice of America; already the continued "caving in" to the senator's demands had reduced the demoralized State Department to a condition of "near panic."

But the public kept watching the show as witness after witness, some cooperative, others hostile, was caught in the camera's focus. There was testimony regarding gross mismanagement in Ceylon, and waste amounting to millions of dollars, with technical incompetence. Plans that had been approved for the construction of two relay stations, one near Seattle, Washington, and the other near Wilmington, North Carolina, indicated sabotage, McCarthy charged, because atmospheric interference at those sites was excessive, resulting in the estimated costs shooting up to $29,000,000 or $31,000,000, ten times the figure originally submitted.

Others besides McCarthy were angered by the evidence. Senator McClellan felt that there was "a whole lot more than incompetence and stupidness attached to this affair. The whole thing looks rotten on the face of it." The State Department ordered the construction halted.

In a public hearing McCarthy and Howard Fast locked horns in what the newspapers described as a "shouting match," when Fast, who had served time in jail for contempt of the House Un-American Activities Committee and who was appearing under subpoena, refused to say whether he was a Communist. When he repeatedly insisted on "explaining" his responses, McCarthy cut him short, refusing, he said, to let the hearing be used as a "transmission belt" for the witness's views. Senator Potter, sitting with McCarthy, asked Fast whether he would fight the Communists in Korea, and the witness retorted that he had given his life to serving his country and would "respond to the draft," but he would not say that he would fight. Through McCarthy, the subcommittee demanded and was promised by Voice of America authorities that all of Fast's works would be removed from their libraries forthwith.

Staff writers for the Voice testified, one asserting that anti-Communist content had been cut out of his broadcasts to Latin America, and a former employe, Miss Nancy Lenkieth, stated that she had been fired after she wrote a favorable review of Whittaker Chambers' autobiography, *Witness*. She also said that after being hired, her superior officer had suggested that she join a commune and "start bearing children," a proposal that left her "a little bit stunned."

The chief of the Voice's Hebrew section testified that at a time when the American embassy in Tel Aviv was urging a stepping-up of Hebrew language broadcasts, he had been ordered by Reed Harris, acting director of the Information Administration, to drop them. The order had finally been canceled, but only after an appeal had been carried to the then head of the agency, Dr. Wilson M. Compton, who was on an inspection trip abroad. Dr. Compton since had resigned.

Another section manager told how anti-Communist material was taken out of the broadcasts in Turkish. And another witness testified that when the Voice took over the radio facilities in Vienna from the Army, the transmitter tower was cut down from 900 to 450 feet, so that the broadcasts no longer penetrated deep into Russia but were confined to Austria.

Reed Harris was questioned, and in an excitable manner accused McCarthy of dealing in "innuendoes," "distortions," and "aspersions." Saying he had been investigated six or seven times, twice by the FBI, and had been cleared on security grounds every time, he insisted that the views he had held as a callow youth were no longer his in maturity. But it was clear that not all members of the subcommittee were convinced that he had cut loose entirely from his student-days flirtation with the ideological left.

McCarthy then produced a consulting engineer who had worked for the Voice of America for two years "in the wrong building"; he had been engaged to advise on policy, but was put to work writing pamphlets. Senator Taft, commenting on this sort of thing, praised McCarthy's work as "helpful and constructive," adding that if he had the power, he would "fire the whole Voice of America setup."

And so it went, against a background of criticism and objections by the press and others that the persons being accused in televised testimony were given no chance to reply—or were called on such short notice they had no time to prepare a proper defense. Senators Jackson and Symington also complained of the procedure, saying they were receiving much mail along the same lines. Thereupon McCarthy spelled out publicly the rules that would be observed henceforward: each person accused publicly was to be given an opportunity to reply, at once or later, as he might prefer; if the accusation was made in closed session, the accused was to be informed at once and invited to appear in rebuttal at once. The Democrats thought this was fair, and *The New York Times,* which had started by being sharply critical, commended McCarthy for adopting a "relatively restrained" manner, for his scrupulousness in explaining the rules to each witness, and for allowing witnesses to consult with their counsel during examination.

[II]

In the midst of the Voice of America hearings, a fresh test of strength between the senator and the executive branch was precipitated by the President's nomination of Charles E. Bohlen to be ambassador to Russia, and of Dr. James B. Conant, president of Harvard University, to be high commissioner to Germany. Both nominations drew fire from a group of conservative senators, led by Styles Bridges of New Hampshire, Dirksen of Illinois, and McCarran of Nevada. Conant was objected to because of his "naiveté" in doubting that such a thing as a Communist cell could exist among the Harvard faculty, an opinion he clung to even after two Harvard professors—Granville Hicks and Robert Gorham Davis—had told the Un-American Activities committee about such a cell to which they had belonged in the 1930's, and had named other faculty members. Other educators were less cooperative. Barrows

Dunham, of Temple University, refused to say whether he was a Communist or to give any information beyond his name and date of birth, pleading possible self-incrimination. And Wendell Furry of Harvard similarly refused to say under oath whether he was or ever had been a Communist, although outside the hearing room he assured reporters that he was not at present a member of the party.

Under White House pressure, Conant's appointment was confirmed by the Senate, but a real fight developed on Bohlen's nomination. Although he had not started it, McCarthy soon took the lead in this attack, although he candidly admitted that he had no expectation of winning it. The episode illustrated perfectly Joe's love of a shindy, and also his dexterity in crystallizing an issue and dramatically focusing it upon himself.

This time the issue was important, because skillful strategists behind the lines were sweating to stave off a defeat for the administration so early in its career. Eisenhower himself was still bent on staying aloof from McCarthy; he told his advisers, "I just will not—I refuse to get into the gutter with that guy." But publicly he left the door ajar for conciliation.

Bohlen, a career diplomat, was acknowledged to be the State Department's foremost authority on Soviet Russia; the difficulty lay in the fact that he had served as adviser to President Roosevelt at the Yalta conference. That damned him in the eyes of McCarran, Bridges, and their allies. When questioned by the Foreign Relations Committee, Bohlen had refused to subscribe to any blanket condemnation of the Yalta agreements; but he denied, convincingly, having any sympathy with Soviet aims or philosophy. The committee reported the nomination favorably to the Senate by unanimous vote; then it was that McCarthy joined in the battle, the floor of the Senate being always his most congenial forum.

The basis of his opposition, McCarthy said, was the ignoring by Secretary Dulles of sixteen closely typewriten pages of derogatory information found in Bohlen's file by Scott McLeod, the State Department's new security chief. McLeod, a former FBI investigator, was a friend of McCarthy, at whose appointment the senator had remarked that he would no longer have any difficulty in getting loyalty data; McLeod would see that he got the files.

According to McCarthy, Dulles had examined McLeod's report and had dismissed the derogatory data; whereupon McLeod had carried the matter to the White House and had laid the file before President Eisenhower. Dulles, McCarthy went on, was called in and the President listened to both men, then upheld Dulles. Whereupon Dulles issued a statement saying there was no basic disagreement between himself and McLeod. This statement, McCarthy told the Senate, was untrue; "certain aspects" of the case had not been brought to Eisenhower's attention; and while Bohlen's file did contain much in his praise, "in our opinion he is a bad security risk." He had tried to get McLeod before his subcommittee for questioning, he said, without success, because, he suspected, McLeod had been ordered to stay away.*

The debate grew rancorous. Senator Tobey suggested that McCarthy's theme song was "I'm Forever Chasing Rumors," and the galleries laughed. On the floor everybody was too angry or too excited to giggle—everybody except Joe. Senator Taft's aid had been enlisted by the White House, and he led a counterattack on McCarthy, rejecting with open expressions of contempt the latter's suggestion that Bohlen either submit to a lie detector test, or testify under oath on "how he got his clearance." McCarthy fought back, and of several bursts of applause that came from the galleries, the loudest was for Joe. So hard did he press that in a rare conciliatory move the President consented to open Bohlen's file to any two members of the Senate whom the senators themselves should designate. Senators Taft and Sparkman were selected, and for three hours they studied the data and found nothing, they reported, to indicate that Bohlen was a security risk.

The debate carried over to a second and a third day, marked by intense anger on both sides. Senators heretofore friendly toward McCarthy turned on him savagely. When Senator Knowland, usually close to McCarthy, held up a letter and memorandum which he said had been transmitted by Dulles, showing that three veteran diplomats—Joseph Grew, Hugh Gibson, and Norman Armour—all had given Bohlen's nomination their entire approval, McCarthy looked dubious. Might Senator Dirksen be allowed to verify the signatures? he asked. Knowland flushed purple. "I don't want to be required to get a handwriting expert in here when a letter comes from a responsible official like the Secretary of State!" he shouted. "If we have so destroyed confidence in men in the government of the United States, then God help us!"

Again the galleries burst into applause, and McCarthy chided

---

* Long afterward a former Eisenhower adviser disclosed that a White House representative, or "bodyguard," had been assigned to McLeod to keep him out of McCarthy's reach.

Knowland for treating a matter of such gravity with "ridicule and levity." Again came applause, and McCarthy went on to take swipes at the President, whom he accused of apparently taking a different line since election from the one he had taken in the campaign. "The Republicans are in control of the Senate because in November the voters repudiated the Acheson-Hiss sellout of America," he reminded his colleagues. "In November 31,000,000 people told us to clean house. This means get rid of Acheson's lieutenants—including all the Bohlens. If we don't, we're not entitled to control."

In a news conference on the eve of the vote, the President again refused to be drawn into a direct confrontation with Joe. He repeated his belief that Bohlen was the best choice for the Moscow post, and expressed sadness that the attacks were coming from the ranks of his own party. He alluded to the danger of investigations reaching a point where they imperiled the national interest, but he firmly refused to discuss McCarthy.

That evening, at a party given by Senator and Mrs. Taft in honor of Mrs. Eisenhower, McCarthy and Eisenhower met face to face. As the crowded room watched, they shook hands and exchanged a few polite words. Such token courtesy was not for caustic-tongued Lady Nancy Astor, standing nearby, and as Joe sipped his cocktail, she sniffed audibly, "Too bad it isn't poison!"

[III]

On the day of the vote, the Democrats sat in smug silence while the Republicans tore into each other again. At the close, one voice was raised on the minority side, that of Senator Lehman. He made the last speech. His voice quavering, close to tears, he asked what was happening. "Men blasted without hope of defense and without cause! I think it is about time the American people call a halt to these vicious attacks!" He had come to doubt his very right to encourage men to go into public service, he said, when "all they can expect to receive is calumny and accusations of treason."

The speech drew no applause, and no one except the sincere old man appeared to be affected. Then, in an atmosphere of scowling animosity, the roll was called and Bohlen was confirmed, 74 to 13. A bare majority of 44 would have been sufficient. The count was more than five to one against the cause that McCarthy had made his own. Voting with him against confirmation were Senators

Bricker, Bridges, Dirksen, Dworshak, Goldwater, Hickenlooper, Malone, Mundt, Schoeppel, and Welker, all Republicans; and two Democrats, McCarran and Edwin C. Johnson of Colorado.

Jubilant over this reasounding setback for Joe, *The New York Times* fervently hoped that the administration had learned its lesson —that "McCarthyism can be beaten by standing up to it." But then second thoughts obtruded. Was it really a defeat for McCarthy? The number of senators who had voted with him was impressive, in view of the Senate tradition that an incoming administration be allowed wide latitude in making its first appointments. And the flood of publicity that McCarthy had generated by quixotically jumping into a hopelessly wrongheaded fight was disheartening to his opponents. Dislike, even loathe, him as an important segment of the nation's press did, such newspaper coverage was the meat on which McCarthy fed. The newspapers knew this, claimed to deplore it, and pleaded that they could not prevent it. Joe was news; in everything he said and did there was public interest—this was their exculpation. And he had the telling issue—the Communist peril.

No newspaper despised and fought Senator McCarthy more heartily than the *Washington Post,* whose brilliant cartoonist, Herblock (Herbert Block), lampooned the senator in countless shapes and guises. The publisher's wife, Mrs. Agnes Meyer, carried on a personal vendetta, tirelessly preaching the menace of "McCarthyism." Yet in a single issue, during one of McCarthy's periodic eruptions, the *Washington Post* carried three front-page stories about the senator, all hostile; a Herblock cartoon; an editorial denouncing him; mentions in the syndicated columns of Drew Pearson and others; and numerous secondary allusions. In all, the name McCarthy appeared in that one day's issue forty-three times.

If the outcome of the Bohlen fracas was really a defeat for the senator, he gave no sign of realizing it. Instead, piling audacity on audacity, two days later he rounded on the administration with a new salvo that exploded in more headlines and threw the Eisenhower forces into fresh turmoil. This time the cry arose that McCarthy was defying the Constitution by attempting to usurp the treaty-making powers of the President.

Those Semantical Greek Ships

During recent weeks, a succession of events had occurred that lent urgency to the new activity McCarthy announced. In January, William Remington had been convicted a second time and sentenced to prison for denying Communist connections. Julius and Ethel Rosenberg, the convicted atomic spies, had been much in the public mind because of the worldwide agitation being carried on to prevent their execution. This had attained such proportions, and was so blatantly Communist-inspired and manipulated, that some strongly liberal elements were cautioning opponents of the death penalty on humanitarian grounds not to be taken in by the campaign of mendacity and vilification of America. The American Committee for Cultural Freedom, a group of public-spirited citizens equally hostile to McCarthy and to the Communists, pointed out repeatedly that the Rosenbergs had received a fair trial and had been convicted on evidence "so incontrovertible that the *Daily Worker* did not even bother to inform its readers that the trial was taking place." *

As one of the last acts of his administration, President Truman had granted the Rosenbergs a stay of execution, and President Eisenhower, while denying their plea for clemency, had extended this at least until March. Meanwhile the hectic agitation went on.

Owen Lattimore was making the headlines as he fought through the courts to have his indictment quashed.

Amid all this, Joseph Stalin died, and the world waited tensely to see what shift in Soviet policy would develop with the removal of the dictator.

Wherever one turned, one was confronted with the issue that was

---

* At the same time the committee accused McCarthy of "smearing reputations," "sensationalism," and "goading public officials into issuing absurd instructions."

the cause of constant irritation and anxiety—the issue with which McCarthy's name had become synonymous—Communist penetration and aggrandizement, aimed for the most part at the United States. This was the "fifth ace" that gave the senator an unbeatable hand and won him support from Americans who would hesitate to justify all his actions but did endorse his objectives unreservedly. A feeling widely shared was that the Communist menace was something new in international relations and that it would be foolish to quibble over the means used to defeat it. The times would not admit of hairsplitting.

When McCarthy announced his new venture he expected to be praised for a patriotic action daringly performed. Instead he ran into a storm of denunciation.

Two weeks before the Bohlen blowup, the senator had let it become known that his committee was studying the use of merchant ships purchased from the United States, and flying the flags of various friendly nations, to carry strategic materials behind the Iron Curtain, where at least a portion of the cargoes were being used "to kill Yanks in Korea." Ninety-six ships were engaged in this "blood trade," McCarthy said. They had been sold as war surplus, and the United States still held mortgages on them to the extent of $25,000,000. Forty-five of these ships, still technically American property until they should be fully paid for, were carrying war cargoes to Red China, he specified, although the Chinese were our enemies in Korea. A principal witness who would testify regarding this shady condition of affairs, McCarthy added, would be Harold Stassen; as head of the Mutual Security Administration, Stassen would know all about the matter.

Two weeks went by. Then McCarthy announced triumphantly that he had negotiated an agreement with a group of Greek shipowners which would reduce shipments to Red China by 45 percent. The agreement covered 242 ships whose owners had agreed to cease all trade with Red China, North Korea, and Far Eastern Soviet ports. The senator explained that the agreement would have "some of the effect of a naval blockade . . . and should hasten the day of a victorious and honorable conclusion of the Korean war." Furthermore, his subcommittee was negotiating with the Greek shipowners' London committee to extend the agreement to 100 or 150 more ships. He added with satisfaction that the agreement had been negotiated without the assistance of the State Department, and stressed that it would remove from Communist trade "more tonnage than all the Communist countries, including the USSR, own themselves."

When asked cynically what return he had given the shipowners, McCarthy said no return, but those cooperating would not figure in his pending investigation of postwar tanker sales to foreign nationals.

[II]

The State Department was furious. McCarthy's agreement was "phony," said officials there, and his intrusion into diplomatic business was, to say the least, "highly irregular." The department had been closing in on Greek and other shipowners for a long while, it was explained, and already had succeeded in imposing so many obstacles and restrictions on the trade to Communist countries that it was no longer profitable. In 1951, they had secured agreements with the governments of Panama, Costa Rica, and Honduras blocking the trade under their flags; in 1952, they had obtained a similar agreement with Liberia; and a week ago, they had signed one with the Greek government and had also concluded a deal with the French and British governments prohibiting vessels engaged in the China trade from touching at British or French ports.

What really incensed the department, however, was that Senator McCarthy was using a congressional committee to negotiate with foreign nationals, in violation of the Constitution, which reposes the conduct of foreign relations in the executive department.*

Proud of his accomplishment, McCarthy set up a public hearing, with Stassen as chief witness, and invited television crews to record what he confidently expected would be Stassen's wholehearted endorsement of this demonstration of patriotic hustle. Instead, Stassen angrily reprobated the action and accused Joe of hampering the administration's efforts to restrict trade to Red China by agreements with foreign governments. "You are in fact undermining and are harmful to our objectives," Stassen charged.

---

* James Reston, in *The New York Times,* remarked that the officials at the State Department who were the most bitter against McCarthy showed the greatest reluctance to come into the open and be quoted. The inference was that they dreaded provoking the senator to a personal showdown.

Taken aback, McCarthy explained that he had not kept the State Department informed of his negotiations because of their "extreme delicacy. . . . I frankly feel that we are helping you," he insisted.

With cold acidity Stassen asked whether "this agreement was accompanied by a promise that those Greek ship owners who joined it would not be investigated?"

The insinuation of blackmail was clear, and McCarthy snapped angrily, "That is no concern of yours, Mr. Stassen," while the subcommittee's counsel, Francis D. Flanagan, exclaimed loudly, "Absolutely not!" Later both Flanagan and McCarthy denied that there had been any promise of immunity.

The situation was so tense—and was being exploited so sensationally by the press, whole pages being given to the pros and cons—that Vice-President Nixon moved in as mediator and suggested a Dulles-McCarthy meeting. The senator was agreeable, requested an appointment, and was invited to join the Secretary at lunch the next day. The Secretary lunched at his desk, and the discussion ranged amicably from tomato juice through ice cream and coffee, each man expounding to the other the facts of governmental life as he comprehended them. McCarthy said he was only trying to help, and because of the intricacies of ship registry many vessels engaged in the so-called scavenger trade would not be affected by agreements between governments. Dulles responded by stressing the dangers—not to mention the illegality—of interference by private citizens or congressional committees in the conduct of foreign affairs.

At the close a joint communiqué was given out, lacking only the formality of red ribbon and sealing wax to constitute a treaty between sovereign powers, stating that it had been mutually agreed that foreign relations were "in the exclusive jurisdiction of the chief executive," but that both parties felt that the subcommittee's actions had been "in the national interest." Joe told reporters he had promised to keep Dulles informed of any future deals, and he conceded that perhaps "negotiate" had been the wrong word for him to use to describe his overtures to the Greek shipowners.

How little outsiders agreed on what had been agreed was made plain by the headlines in two Washington newspapers, reporting the same event. The *Times-Herald,* generally favorable to McCarthy, headed its account of the luncheon parley:

DULLES LAUDS McCARTHY SHIP AID CURB.

The rival *Post,* bitterly anti-McCarthy, read the facts in a different light, and headlined its account:

DULLES WARNS McCARTHY ON SHIP DEAL.

This led McCarthy to write to Dulles protesting the distortion of the news by certain elements of the press-radio-television media, in the hope, he said, of provoking "a split in the Republican party over matters where there can be no disagreement. As I recall, there was not even the slightest indication . . . that my committee was interfering in foreign policy or in any way with your department, and therefore no occasion for any 'warning.' "

Still, the press devoted page after page to the incident, and Eisenhower's reaction was tensely awaited. Would he seize the weapon that Stassen had held out to him to strike back at McCarthy, as so many of his advisers were urging? Or would he continue to impersonate the reluctant lion and avoid conflict?

The mild tone of the President's next press conference ended the suspense. He had not been upset by all the flak, he said, and he thought that maybe Stassen had meant to say "infringing" instead of "undermining" the administration's efforts; and while the subcommittee might have been misguided, no attempt had been made to raid the jurisdiction of the executive to transact foreign affairs.

This meander through semantical distinctions was followed by a statement issued at the White House, over Stassen's signature, in which the mutual security chief meekly echoed his commander and conceded that, yes, he might well have employed the word "infringe" instead of "undermine." Lest there be any doubt about the authority backing this statement, the press was told that it had been thoroughly discussed and approved in advance at a cabinet meeting. Thus harmony and cordiality were preserved, and (as some observers could not refrain from quoting) all went merrily as a marriage bell.

Later in the week, in a television interview, Stassen seemed less mellow. Only future events, he said inscrutably, could "determine the lasting effects of this week's happenings."

[III]

In public speculation over who had won this round in the developing test of strength between the President and the senator, the consensus awarded the decision to McCarthy by a wide margin. Liberals were in despair over the way the administration which they had helped to bring into power had jumped when McCarthy whistled. Obviously rational thought in politics had been replaced by "sulphurous invective" and "the fumes of McCarthyism," said *The Nation* gloomily.

For his part, McCarthy merely laughed at the idea that he was fighting the White House. Patiently he repeated that he was simply trying to "clean out the leftwing debris" left by the "Acheson-Hiss crowd." But some Republicans, in and out of office, suspected that he was deliberately disrupting Eisenhower's orderly reorganization of the government in the hope of supplanting Ike as the party's Presidential candidate in 1956. Taxed with this rumor, Joe replied that such talk was nonsense. But his critics continued to speak darkly about "incipient Fascism," and writers in left-wing periodicals drew what they construed as parallels between McCarthy's tactics and those employed by Hitler when he was strong-arming himself into power.

But why should Joe look ahead when things seemed so pleasantly to be coming his way? There was the settlement of his libel suit against the *Syracuse Post-Standard;* it came about just now, and Joe said the payment was "of less importance than clarification of the facts"; the editor-publisher acknowledged that he had erred through carelessness.

A majority, a large majority, of the nation's intellectuals, particularly those having access to the channels of public communication, remained unshakeably hostile to McCarthy. To judge by the printed matter available, McCarthy was universally condemned and rejected among thinking, articulate Americans.*

---

* The *New Republic* at about this time published a list of writers, publicists, and others who were said to have been "mentioned unfavorably" in testimony before the House Un-American Activities Committee, or cited by the committee as belonging to one or more Communist fronts. Not a person on this list was, or ever would be, a pro-McCarthyite. The list offered a striking cross section of the forces, mostly in the intellectual field, arrayed against McCarthy. There was no suggestion, either, that this list was exhaustive or complete. It follows:

James Truslow Adams	Ernest Hemingway
Sherwood Anderson	Stanley High
Roger Baldwin	Sidney Hillman
Charles Beard	John Hays Holmes
Leonard Bernstein	Sidney Hook
Van Wyck Brooks	Fannie Hurst

(Continued overleaf)

Gratifying to the senator, therefore, was a "Declaration of Conscience" subscribed by twenty-eight writers, actors, journalists, and others, and sent by them to 700 newspapers, protesting against the "unfair treatment" accorded to McCarthy by the news media. This manifesto read in part:

"Some of our colleagues in newspapers, magazines, on the radio and television have enjoyed a virtually unchallenged forum of loose talk on the subject of 'McCarthyism.' We feel that they owe to their readers, their listeners, and their consciences an accounting." For example, hardly any book reviewers had paid the slightest attention to McCarthy's book *McCarthyism,* in which his record and his motives were treated in question-and-answer form, "forthrightly discussing every significant charge made against him. How many reviews has it had? The answer—hardly any—is a blight on a profession supposedly objective and courageous." By contrast, Owen Lattimore's *Ordeal by Slander* had received the "widest acclaim" and the "most extravagant and uncritical praise" when it was published in 1950.

Pearl Buck	Harold Ickes
James Branch Cabell	Alvin Johnson
Erskine Caldwell	James Weldon Johnson
Stuart Chase	Matthew Josephson
Marc Connolly	Oliver LaFarge
Aaron Copland	Harold Lasswell
Norman Corwin	Max Lerner
Clarence Darrow	David C. Lilienthal
Eugene Debs	Robert and Helen Lynd
John Dewey	Archibald MacLeish
John Dos Passos	Norman Mailer
Olin Downes	Thomas Mann
Theodore Dreiser	Burns Mantle
Max Eastman	Reginald Marsh
Sherwood Eddy	Lewis Mumford
Irwin Edman	Reinhold Niebuhr
Albert Einstein	Dorothy Parker
Morris Ernst	Arthur M. Schlesinger
Clifton Fadiman	Budd Schulberg
Louis Fischer	Upton Sinclair
Lewis Gannett	Norman Thomas
George Gershwin	Virgil Thomson
Frank Graham	Henry Wallace
Louis Hacker	Frank Lloyd Wright
Roy Harris	Richard Wright
Arthur Garfield Hays	Gregory Zilboorg

What did McCarthy's critics mean when they said his aims were fine but his methods were wrong? the statement asked. "What methods have his critics used to remove traitors and subversives and security risks from the government? How adequate is the substantiation of the charge that McCarthy has attacked and injured innocent people? Are McCarthy's specific charges weighed before concluding, as with Owen Lattimore, that McCarthy is wrong?"

The signers of this "recall to reason" alleged that they were speaking for themselves, and not on behalf of any organization or stratum of society. They were: Ward Bond, actor; William F. Buckley, Jr., author; Oliver Carlson, biographer; John Chamberlain, author; John B. Chapple, editor; Charles Coburn and Adolph Menjou, actors; Kenneth Colegrove, professor of political science, Northwestern University; Frank Coniff, columnist; George Creel, authority on the Far East; Ralph de Toledano and John T. Flynn, authors; Devin Garrity, publisher; Frank Hanighen, editor of *Human Events;* Karl Hess, press editor of *Newsweek;* Rupert Hughes, author; Robert Hurleigh, commentator; Suzanne LaFollette, journalist; Victor Lasky, author; Fulton Lewis, Jr., commentator; William Loeb, publisher of the *Manchester* (New Hampshire) *Union-Leader;* Eugene Lyons, author; Rabbi Max J. Merrit, of Los Angeles; Felix Morley, author; J. C. Phillips, editor, the *Borger* (Texas) *News-Herald;* Morrie Ryskind, playwright; Frank Chodorov, author; Henry Regnery, publisher.

In instant retort to this statement, former Attorney General Francis Biddle, national chairman of Americans for Democratic Action (ADA), called on Attorney General Herbert Brownell to open a thorough probe of McCarthy's personal affairs, on the basis of the pigeonholed report of the Gillette-Hennings subcommittee, suggesting income-tax cheating, embezzling, illegal use of classified documents, bribery, kickbacks, and other offenses, directly charged or implied.

The Justice Department replied that the matter was "still under active consideration," and McCarthy hit back:

"The *Washington Star* of June 9, 1950, quotes Biddle as having told the AMVETS [veterans organization to which McCarthy himself belonged] that the dismissal of William Remington [from his Commerce Department job] was 'outrageous' and he blamed 'the hysterical obsession in this country.' This is only one of many items in his long record of defense of Communists and Communist causes."

This was the open-palm slap. Joe followed with his haymaker:

"It should be recalled that the ADA, of which Biddle is national chairman, has viciously attacked the FBI; has attacked the Smith Act, which makes it a crime to 'conspire to teach and advocate the overthrow of this government by force and violence'; has urged the recognition of Red China; and in many other respects has followed the Communist party line. . . . I am too busy with work of much greater importance to take time out to waste it on a man who has been as thoroughly discredited and who is as well known for what he is as Biddle."

Twelve Weeks in Spring

[I]

When Senator McCarthy took over the chairmanship of the Government Operations Committee at the start of 1953 it was meant to be a dead end for him. The intention of the Republican leaders who made the committee assignments had been to shunt him into a corner where he could cause no disruption of the incoming administration. Under the Democrats, the Operations Committee and its police arm, the Permanent Subcommittee on Investigations, had plodded along inspecting accounts and performing other dull chores possessed of no headline glamor. In a few weeks Joe had changed all that, so much so that just a month and a day after taking office, President Eisenhower was seen by *The New York Times* as faced with the necessity of "making an accommodation with McCarthy, or colliding heavily with the most feared and powerful investigator in Congress." The Senate leadership had committed the folly of once more underestimating the senator's audacity and his uncanny ability to spring surprises in unlikely places. Joe was not an accommodating man.

His first step had been to organize a task force, and that involved replacing the committee's chief counsel, Francis D. Flanagan, with one more suited to McCarthy's temperament and temerity. His choice fell on a "whiz kid" prosecutor whose legal exploits at twenty-six had attracted much attention—Roy Marcus Cohn.

The only child of a respected New York judge, high in Democratic circles, Roy Cohn had been indulged in every whim by his adoring parents. Them he revered but did not emulate. After expensive private schooling and law study at Columbia University, he had been graduated at twenty, a year too young to be admitted to the bar. Time had removed that handicap, and through his father's influence he had been placed at once in favored legal positions. Politics interested him more than law practice. Apprenticed to the Justice Department in Washington, he had helped to draw up the indictment against Owen Lattimore. More spectacularly, he had been prominently associated with the prosecution of the Rosenbergs and Remington, and took credit for obtaining the latter's conviction by a legal maneuver that startled more staid counsel.

In December, 1952, when McCarthy was in New York to attend a luncheon in his honor, he invited young Cohn to drop around to the Astor Hotel, where he was staying, at eleven that evening. Cohn found the senator's suite crowded with men and women in formal dress, everybody talking at once. The senator had shed his tuxedo and vest and stripped down to a T-shirt, over which suspenders held up his dress trousers.* McCarthy looked the chubby, cherubic-faced youth over, saying he just wanted to see if Cohn was one-tenth as smart as people were making him out to be. He told Cohn he would hear from him.

Some time later Cohn was offered the job of chief counsel of McCarthy's subcommittee, and against the advice of political friends who knew the pitfalls of Washington for the overambitious, he accepted; his self-confidence was boundless. Shortly thereafter, he brought to the subcommittee staff a young man whose name was destined to ring around the world, albeit somewhat sourly— Gerard David Schine.

Schine was twenty-five, the pampered child of wealthy parents, who also had indulged him to excess. His family owned movie theaters and luxury hotels from Miami to Hollywood, and of that sybaritic empire of folding chairs and downy beds David, despite his juvenility, was nominally president and general manager. His education had been erratic but expensive; at Harvard he was remembered for such chitchat as his remark to a classmate: "I just signed a check for $3,000. Did you ever sign a check for that amount?" His hobby was collecting cigars, and he claimed to possess the largest museum of unusual specimens in the world.†

---

* "There were always people around McCarthy," Cohn would recall, and the record contains hardly an allusion to McCarthy as ever appearing except in a crowd, at least until the final bleak days.

† In a sketch published in the *Saturday Review,* Cleveland Amory quoted an article in the Harvard *Crimson* as remarking, "Wealth, of course, is not out of place here, but Schine made it so." Among other peculiarities, he was said to have had a valet and a secretary, who attended his classes and took his lecture notes, and also, via a dictaphone, transcribed his reading notes. According to

Somewhere along the line he had become aware of communism, and deduced that it posed a threat to his way of living. Forthwith he had composed a monograph upon the subject. Entitled *Definition of Communism,* this six-page treatise was published under the imprint of "Schine Hotels—'Finest Under the Sun,'" and a copy was placed in every room—bed, rest, dining, or ante—of the Schine domain.

This critique of Marxism has been described with more clarity than charity by Richard Rovere: "In a couple of thousand of deplorably chosen words, the author managed to put the Russian revolution, the founding of the Communist party, and the start of the first Five-Year Plan in years when these events did not occur; he gave Lenin the wrong first name, hopelessly confused Stalin with Trotsky, Marx with Lenin, Alexander Kerensky with Prince Lvov, and fifteenth-century Utopianism with twentieth-century communism."

This "bedside treasury of wrong dates and mistaken identities and misunderstood principles" having come to the attention of Roy Cohn, he introduced the author to Senator McCarthy, and G. David Schine became "chief consultant" (unpaid) to the Senate's Permanent Subcommittee on Investigations—presumably relieved for the nonce of the obligation to preside over so many Schine hotels. Soon Cohn and Schine were industriously screening prospective witnesses in the stimulating atmosphere of a penthouse apartment in the Waldorf Towers.

To have two such scions of wealth and political influence as aides may have flattered Joe McCarthy for a while, and he gave the eager pair a relatively free hand.

Joe was acquiring political muscle elsewhere, including support from an important Democratic source, Joseph Patrick Kennedy, millionaire former ambassador to Great Britain. Kennedy was pushing the career of his son, John Fitzgerald Kennedy. In 1952, JFK, after serving two undistinguished terms in the House of Representatives, had been entered by his father in the Massachusetts race

---

Amory, "At one time the housemaster of Adams House begged Schine's roommates to be nicer to him. 'We tried,' said one of them, 'but Schine made it impossible.'" Schine was musically ambitious, according to Amory, and played the cymbals in the college band. He also composed songs, and went to New York in an attempt to get two of them published. They were titled "All of My Loves," and "Please Say Yes, or It's Good-bye." Tin Pan Alley said "no" and "good-bye."

for the Senate, bucking blueblood Henry Cabot Lodge, who was seeking a second term. Kennedy's chances looked slim: Lodge was popular, blessed with a name famous in his state, and he had just scored a great success in managing Eisenhower's successful bid for the presidential nomination. But the Kennedys went to work, and among other stratagems, the father prevailed upon McCarthy to stay out of the state during the campaign. Joe was highly popular with the Irish Catholics of Boston, and his failure to speak for the Republican ticket was credited with causing Lodge's defeat. McCarthy had been friendly with the Kennedys for some time, had been a guest at Hyannis Port and Palm Beach, and Joseph Kennedy had contributed to McCarthy's campaign chest in Wisconsin. With the election of John Kennedy to the Senate, however, Joseph Kennedy became a constant behind-the-scenes adviser and financial supporter of McCarthy, and John F. Kennedy's younger brother, Robert Francis Kennedy, who at twenty-seven was itching to get into the political swim, was placed on the investigations subcommittee's staff. With so much youthful energy at his service McCarthy looked forward to getting results.

Between Bobby Kennedy (as he was generally called) and Roy Cohn—two ambitious young men with conflicting interests—dislike was kindled immediately; but for the time being, Roy had the authority and Kennedy could only chafe and bide his time.

Once Cohn had been engaged as chief counsel, McCarthy demonstrated his personal softness by the way he eased out Flanagan. He could not bring himself to fire him out of hand, but put out a press statement announcing Cohn's appointment and saying that Flanagan would stay on as "general counsel." When reporters asked what was meant by "general counsel," Joe admitted that he didn't know. Flanagan remained for a while, found employment elsewhere, and McCarthy's "new broom" was ready to sweep clean. The senator posed for photographs on Capitol steps with a broom in hand to point up what he intended to do.

[II]

Senator McCarthy has been described by some commentators as a "lazy demagogue." Slipshod and superficial in the preparation of his material McCarthy could be, stupendously so on occasion;

but personally lazy, no. A curious impression conveyed by this always hurrying man, dashing from here to there without rest, was that each pause in the rushing forward seemed a crouch, a tensing for a fresh leap ahead. In his few moments of inactivity there was no repose. The sum total of McCarthy's actions during 1953 fatigues the mind to contemplate. The record of twelve weeks in the spring of that year is typical—a chaotic drama of ceaseless declamation and movement reaching no conclusion. Let us pick up the record in April. The Bohlen nomination has been confirmed, and McCarthy has humiliated the State Department by usurping its prerogative in the matter of the Greek ships. The senator is simultaneously pursuing his inquiry into the Voice of America and the State Department's overseas libraries, trying to determine, he says, who in the previous administration was responsible for purchasing the books of Communists and apologists for Soviet Russia with taxpayers' money, and for placing them in the libraries set up to give people in other lands a true notion of American ideals, history, and institutions. Under the new administration, the State Department has affirmed that the policy has been changed.

McCarthy will question authors whose books have been found in the overseas libraries, and whose "tainted ideas" have incurred his anger. Among these will be Earl Browder, Dashiell Hammett, Langston Hughes, Sol Auerbach (who wrote under the pen name James Allen), Lawrence Rosinger, and William Marx Mandel. Browder refuses to answer anything. Auerbach, Hammett, and Rosinger stand on the Fifth Amendment. Hughes says he was once a Communist sympathizer, but is so no more, and he agrees that his "Communist-slanted" books should not be in the overseas collections. Mandel merely shouts, "I am a Jew!" and insists that he is being persecuted because of his faith.

April 7—The headlines concern Cohn and Schine. Traveling as emissaries of the McCarthy committee, they arrive in Bonn "to investigate the U.S. information program in West Germany and West Berlin." Meeting correspondents in the office of the American High Commissioner, Cohn says that he and Schine hope to "talk with hundreds of persons on the trip," and then Cohn and Theodore Kaghan, director of the information service in Germany, have a private talk.

The next day, in Washington, McCarthy calls on Secretary Dulles to assign somebody to "run down the purchase orders" for the objectionable books or, if the books were gifts, the names of the persons who accepted them. From "lieutenants of Acheson" who are still in the department, he complains, he has elicited only "bad memories, evasion, and no cooperation whatever." He says that he expects the "new team" to do better.

That same day, in Berlin, Cohn says, "a top American official" in Germany (speedily identified as Theodore Kaghan) will be recalled shortly to testify about some plays he wrote in the 1940's that show Red tendencies. Kaghan says he will be delighted to testify.

April 13—*The New York Times* starts a three-part report by a staff writer on what it maintains is a "breakdown of morale" among government workers, caused by fear of Senator McCarthy. The series is launched with front-page display, and will be continued for two days more.

April 15—Reed Harris quits as deputy director of the Information Administration, charging "persecution" by Senator McCarthy. "It is my public neck you are trying very successfully to wring," he tells the senator, but McCarthy sees the matter differently; he thinks "resigned" is the wrong word to use, and he considers Harris' exit "the best thing that has happened in a long time. I only hope that a lot of Mr. Harris' close friends will follow him out."

The same day in Vienna the Socialist *Arbeiter Zeitung,* usually friendly to the United States, asserts that McCarthy's "terror methods" differ in no essential from those of the Nazis or the Russian GPU, and the paper takes President Eisenhower to task for his "cowardly surrender" to the "GPU senator." A day-and-a-half visit of Cohn and Schine to Vienna the paper belittles as "exactly long enough to receive denunciations," and McCarthy's televised hearings are compared to the Soviet "purge trials" of the 1930's.

A dispatch from Belgrade this day quotes Cohn as saying, during a rapid survey of information facilities there, that the McCarthy committee has made no distinction "so far" between Russian and Yugoslav communism.

In still another dispatch, this one from Munich, Cohn reports that he and Schine have found books in the libraries by authors who have refused to say whether or not they were Communists, and "despite obstacles put in our way by many people," their nine-day tour of Germany and Austria has proved "most successful" and they have gathered documents filling three briefcases.*

April 16—The headline, page one, reads: McCARTHY CHARGES STASSEN THWARTED NEW PACT ON SHIPS. In effect, the senator accuses the Mutual Security Administrator of torpedoing efforts to get a London group of Greek shipowners to withdraw from the trade with Red China, after most of the group had pledged cooperation. "An apparent misunderstanding as to the policy of the United States government" had queered the agreement at the last minute, he says, and the *Times* emphasizes that the statement was made at a "Klieg-lit television" press conference. The effect, the *Times* adds, is to throw down the gauntlet to the administration in the most direct manner by bluntly asserting that "more Americans will die because of the decision of those Greek ship owners in London."

The following day McCarthy calls another press conference and announces that the owners of 53 Greek ships have promised to halt their trade with Red ports, bringing to 295 the number of cargo carriers now denied to the Communists. He adds that he had forwarded a copy of the new agreement to the State Department, in keeping with his promise, although actually the so-called agreement is only a "voluntary pledge" by the shipowners.

This day the public is reminded of Hiss once more when he writes from prison to Representative Kenneth Keating of New York, denying that he ever recommended anybody for employment by the United Nations; he says he submitted lists of qualified persons, but made no recommendations.

April 19—From Paris comes a dispatch reporting a hostile encounter between Cohn and Schine and British correspondents, who "scent a McCarthy investigation of the British nation." The Americans were peppered with questions such as: "Will you investigate British subjects?" "Where do you get authority to question people?" "Do you think it fitting for persons as young as you to be investigating seasoned employes?"

---

* This day *The New York Times* carries five separate stories on McCarthy, including one set prominently on page one. The rumors and gossip that are flying around Washington about the senator's "Rover Boys" abroad are far more numerous. An example is the report of their display of boyish high spirits as Schine chased Cohn through a hotel lobby swatting him with a rolled-up magazine, both "laughing like crazy."

April 21—From London comes word that Cohn and Schine have concluded their whirlwind tour with a five-hour visit to London, a pat on the back for the American ambassador, Winthrop W. Aldrich, and a verbal mauling by the British press. Schine gives his judgment that "for a man who has been here only two months," the ambassador "seemed to have grasped the problem very well," and the President had made "a very wise choice" in filling this important post. Besieged at the airport by sixty bitter reporters, Cohn scoffs at the supposition that he and Schine want to investigate the British Broadcasting Corporation or introduce "McCarthyism" into England. They are lampooned in a song to the tune of "Mister Gallagher and Mister Shean:"

> "Oh, Mister Cohn, oh, Mister Cohn?"
> "Yes, Mister Schine?"
> "Do you really think these true-blue
> English really Red?"
> "They are definitely rude—
> I heard Lady Ermyntrude
> Quite clearly and distinctly
> Shout, 'Drop dead!' "

April 23—Front-page headlines report the dismissal of 830 Voice of America employes in a "retrenchment program." Dr. Robert L. Johnson, former president of Temple University and now head of the information service, announces the cutback and says it will save $4,300,000.

April 26—An article by Bertrand Russell in *The New York Times Magazine* gives his concept of the inevitable shaping-up of history, based on current trends. The article is written as if by some future historian looking back on the 1950's. The imaginary writer recounts that "after Senators Taft and McCarthy had gradually taken control of the Eisenhower administration," McCarthy was elected President by a landslide in 1956. Georgi M. Malenkov meanwhile had succeeded Stalin as the Soviet dictator, and this led to the "McCarthy-Malenkov Pact," which divided the world between the United States and Russia. In America vast reforms were carried out: only the Republican party was tolerated, and the press and literature were severely censured; all political criticism was held to be subversive and subject to penalties; indoctrination became the main purpose of schooling. Some of these changes were regrettable, of course, but they had reduced the possibility of world war and had opened the way to drastic tax cuts.

In Russia, no anti-American criticism was allowed, and no anti-Soviet criticism was permitted in the United States. No one in Russia was allowed to contradict the "historical truth that Peter the Great was an American," and no one in the United States was permitted to question the "historical truth that Columbus was a Russian." No one in Russia could allude to racial conflict in the United States, and no one in the United States could mention slave labor in Russia. In Western Europe the pact had not been popular, because it relegated that region to the unimportance it had brought upon itself by continual wars. Discontented Europeans were not allowed to travel in the United States for fear of their infecting the inhabitants with their quaintly outmoded beliefs in free speech, party government, and a free press.

"There were doubts at first whether the pact would be observed," this historical projection concluded, "but McCarthy and Malenkov found each other so congenial and so united in their aims that they had no difficulty about genuine cooperation. Each designated as his successor a man with the same aims, and the remaining years of the Twentieth Century persuaded all but a peevish minority that the pact is as permanent as it is beneficial. All honor to the memory of the two great leaders who brought peace to the world!"

April 29—After this peep into the future, today brings hard news. Theodore Kaghan, summoned from Germany, is questioned by Senator McCarthy in closed session and is promised a public hearing quickly. The papers also tell how Lincoln White, State Department press officer, cooled his heels outside a hearing room of the Senate Appropriations Committee for an hour and forty-two minutes, waiting to be questioned by McCarthy. Then the senator's office brought word that he had left for Philadelphia to receive a citizenship award. The Appropriations Committee, meanwhile, is treated to a display of listening devices used to spy on American diplomats behind the Iron Curtain. Some of the gadgets had even been pried out of embassy walls.

April 30—Two front-page stories about McCarthy. In New York, Democratic party bigwigs attended a $100-a-plate dinner at which Senator Lehman defines "Creeping McCarthyism" as a disease threatening to annul the Bill of Rights by means of "inuendo, smear, and indirect attack." This speech will be printed and distributed in thousands of copies.

In Washington, Theodore Kaghan is questioned in a public hearing regarding his having called Cohn and Schine "junketeering gumshoes." Kaghan denies he had the pair shadowed in Europe, explaining that he had merely assigned the pair an escort officer, as was done with "all VIPs." McCarthy contends that the "escort" was a "tail," who snooped on what they said and did and reported it all to Kaghan. The latter denies he received such reports, and defends his interference by saying he was prompted to it by "a raft of cartoons and dispatches" in the German press about the two investigators and their antics, and "I felt it was time I became interested in it." He admits that back in the 1930's he had seen no reason to fear communism, but contends that his ideas have changed since then.

Another thorny witness before McCarthy is James Wechsler, editor of the *New York Post,* which has violently opposed the senator. Several of Wechsler's books had been found in the overseas libraries. The session is closed, and immediately after it is concluded Wechsler demands a public hearing and the release of the transcript of his testimony, charging "attempted assassination of the *Post.*" He had testified freely about belonging to the Young Communist League in his youth, and had cited his long record of militant anticommunism since then. Alluding to Wechsler by his long-ago Communist pseudonym, McCarthy promises a public hearing if the witness will submit the names of "all you know to be Communists," including any presently working for the *New York Post.* Wechsler agrees to this condition, and at the same time brings the matter to the attention of the American Society of Newspaper Editors, asking that this "clear and present threat to all newspapers" be condemned, for in his opinion he is only "the first in a long line of editors who are going to be called . . . because they refuse to equate 'McCarthyism' with patriotism."

[III]

Above is the partial record of Senator McCarthy's activities, with related developments bearing on the issue as these were reported in the daily press, during three weeks in April. The pace would quicken in May.

May 1—McCarthy announces he has established that some ships carrying cargoes to Red China "under the protection of the British navy" are actually owned, at least in part, by Chinese Communists. And the French government has at least three ships in the China trade which were acquired from the United States but have not been paid for, he says. He promises to disclose details shortly.

May 2—Front pages carry long accounts of the action of Judge Luther Youngdahl, in United States District Court, in throwing out four of the seven counts of the Lattimore indictment. The judge rules the four counts are "violative of the First and Sixth amendments" and "so nebulous and indefinite that a jury would have to indulge in speculation" to arrive at a verdict. Judge Youngdahl refuses to dismiss the remaining three counts, but casts doubt on their validity by ordering the prosecution to submit a bill of particulars. At the same time he rejects Lattimore's contention that he cannot receive a fair trial in Washington.

This politically explosive decision arouses much excitement in the capital. Senator Arthur Watkins, a former Utah judge, dissents, maintaining that "when Youngdahl talks about the Constitution and free speech, he is entirely missing the point." The issue, Watkins says, is simply whether Lattimore lied to a Senate committee and, if so, whether he lied about a material matter. Watkins is a member of the committee before whom Lattimore is accused of lying.

With Owen Lattimore preempting *The New York Times'* front page, as well as two pages inside, McCarthy is relegated to a "sidebar" description of the senator in action. He is pictured as "cold and calm" during interrogation. "His eyes narrow as he sizes up his customer. He talks with hardly a movement of his lips. At times he is so quiet in his feeding of inquiries that the witness has them repeated. While answers are being given, he usually gazes at the ceiling. At frequent intervals he sums up the testimony. The summations as a rule are blunter than the actual answers, and not always in strict conformity with them. Often they bring protests from the witness. But the summations stand in the record."

May 5—Ships are in the news again, with McCarthy angrily cutting short the testimony of a State Department spokesman. Assistant counsel Robert Kennedy reports for the subcommittee that in 1952, 193 vessels owned by 19 companies of Allied nationals made "at least" 445 voyages to Red China, and possibly 600.

Eighty-two of the ships were owned by Allied nationals who not only put their ships into Communist trade but were earning good profits transporting American cargoes designed to strengthen the Allies against the Communists. The Wilh Wilhelmsen Company of Norway had seven ships delivering Mutual Security Administration cargoes to allies, and nine in trade with Red China. The Blue Funnel Line, British-owned, had twenty-eight vessels trading with Communist countries since the start of hostilities in Korea, while some of the line's ships were hauling MSA cargoes to help the Allies. There is much more, and spokesmen for the Defense and Agriculture Departments and the mutual security program are unanimous in agreeing that cutting off all trade with the Chinese Reds would produce good results. But John M. Leddy, acting Deputy Assistant Secretary of State for Economic Affairs, demurs and makes clear that his department is not "seeking at this time the discontinuance of all trade and all shipping to Red China" because a total embargo would work hardship on our allies. Exclaiming that it is "inconceivable" and "unbelievable" that the State Department should recoil from "hurting the feelings of our allies" by calling a halt to this "unholy dual trade," McCarthy abruptly ends the hearing and strides out of the room. As he passes Assistant Secretary of State Thruston B. Morton, he raps out a demand that Secretary Dulles produce a "clear-cut statement" on the subject quickly.

The next day W. Averell Harriman, a former director of the mutual security program (McCarthy had considered calling him for questioning), denounces the Wisconsin senator before a meeting of Democratic women as an "evil influence"; and Dr. Lester Granger, executive director of the National Urban League, assails McCarthy, contending that the statements put out by the senator "virtually every day" are doing more to build up Communist influence in Asia than Communist propaganda could ever do.

This day Wechsler gives McCarthy a list of all the persons he had known to be Communists from 1934 to 1937. He requests that the list be kept secret, and McCarthy agrees "at least for the present." A long and eloquent statement blasting McCarthy with which Wechsler accompanies his list is printed at great length in the newspapers.

May 7—McCarthy instructs a witness, Harvey Matusow, who

testified that he joined the Communist party in Germany in 1947 and got out in 1951, to draw up a list of all the Communists he knows about in the communications field—press, radio, television. Matusow counters that it will be a "monumental task," but McCarthy tells him to take his time and do a thorough job.

In a televised hearing, three writers and an artist—Millen Brand, Philip Foner, Herbert Aptheker, and William Gropper—invoke the protection of the Fifth Amendment in refusing to answer questions about Communist party membership.

(So here we are, through the first week of the month ushered in by that day of affirmation dear to international socialism, May Day.)

May 8—Transcripts of a five-hour battle waged in two hearings between Senator McCarthy and James Wechsler are released, containing a remark by Senator Symington, sitting with McCarthy, that the editor was "the most forthright witness yet to appear." Wechsler introduced a mass of articles and editorials showing his fight against Communists over the years, including a letter from Vice-President Nixon praising his activity in this field, and charged boldly that he would never have been called before the subcommittee if the *New York Post* had not assailed the senator. Countered McCarthy: "You have been shouting that this inquiry is interfering with the freedom of the press. It puts me in mind of so many people screaming that their right to scream has been denied. I have not found that your right to scream has been denied you at all. I have not found that your right to twist and distort the news has been interfered with since you have been here."

The same day a dispatch from Boston reports that an advertisement had appeared in the *Boston Herald,* signed by fourteen Bostonians, mostly academic and religious leaders, headed by the Episcopal Bishop of Massachusetts, terming current anti-Communist inquiries, including McCarthy's, a peril to democracy and bearing all the characteristics of police-state methods.

May 10—The *Times* agrees editorially with Wechsler that McCarthy has embarked upon an attempt to "harass and intimidate the press." The *New York Herald Tribune,* staunchly Republican, also believes that the McCarthy committee is using its power of investigation as a cover for "a general inquisition into the politics and practices of a newspaper."

The next day the American Society of Newspaper Editors instructs its committee on freedom of information to look into McCarthy's questioning of Wechsler.

May 11—The State Department accepts the resignation of Theodore Kaghan and calls off a security check begun on him. It is reported that Kaghan never had a security check until McCarthy brought up his name. In Bonn, Kaghan says he received word from Scott McLeod that his resignation was desired, and realized that "when you cross swords openly with Senator McCarthy you can't expect to stay in the State Department." Retorts McCarthy: "Good riddance! I congratulate the new State Department team for sending home these Acheson lieutenants."

May 15—The Senate rings with McCarthy's bristling jibe at Clement Attlee's speech in the House of Commons cautioning Britons that in the event of a summit meeting with the Russians, a factor to be taken into consideration is the question: "Who is more powerful—President Eisenhower or Senator McCarthy?" McCarthy says that "we need no advice from Comrade Attlee," who, he contends, had joined Acheson in "compromises with treason." During the Spanish Civil War, he added, Attlee had given the Communist raised-fist salute to British volunteers fighting in Spain.

That day two editors of the harshly anti-McCarthy *National Guardian,* a publication designated in previous hearings as a Red front, appear before the senator. They are Allen J. Aronson and Cedric Belfrage, a British subject. Both take refuge in the Fifth Amendment on the question of their being Communists. An Immigration Service official attends the hearing and is told by McCarthy that he hopes Belfrage's status will be "studied expeditiously," and he will expect progress reports on the matter.

May 16—Belfrage is arrested and taken to Ellis Island pending deportation proceedings. In Washington a tremendous outcry against Attlee arises from the Republican leadership; Senator Dirksen threatens to cut United States aid to Britain. The *Times* reprints Attlee's speech in full, and a commentary from Paris saying that the Communists there are stoking the fires of American hatred with the dispute.

May 17—*The New York Times* quotes McCarthy as charging that "ships flying the British flag and trading with Communist China are actually owned by British Communists. Let's sink every accursed ship carrying materiel to our enemy!" The *Times* of London states that Senator McCarthy is no longer an internal United States affair; "he has become the direct concern of the United States' allies." And *The New York Times* reports that Europeans are so aroused by McCarthy, whose power they exaggerate, that widespread astonishment was felt abroad when he failed to block the Bohlen appointment.

May 18—The McCarthy story is continued in a long report of James Wechsler's appearance before a panel of newsmen, in which he asserts that the senator is trying to bully the press, with other editors in mind "who aren't so tough and who scare more easily." The questions put by the panel are not very pointed.

May 20—Raymond Gram Swing, veteran Washington correspondent, resigns as political analyst for the Voice of America in protest against the treatment of Kaghan and "the spineless failure of the State Department to stand by its own staff." The Voice, he says, has been "crippled, perhaps beyond recovery, by slanderous attacks on its integrity."

May 22—Before the Jenner Internal Security subcommittee, witness after witness refuses to say whether he is or was a Communist at the time he took an oath of loyalty to the United States, required for employment by the government. One such witness is Edwin S. Smith, former member of the National Labor Relations Board and former Massachusetts Commissioner for Labor and Industry, now a registered agent of the Soviet Union. Smith took four loyalty oaths between 1934 and 1937, affirming that he was not and never would be, as long as he was in the government service, a member of an organization that advocated the overthrow of this government by force and violence. Since in regard to that period Smith is in the clear, under the statute of limitations, even if perjury had been committed, Jenner wonders what may be the reason for his and similar witnesses' present silence?

May 24—Senator Lehman tells the convention of Americans for Democratic Action that "the issue is not between Russia and the United States, but between 'McCarthyism' and America's role of leadership in the free world. The two are inconsistent. To attempt to reconcile them is to invite disaster."

May 25—A B'nai B'rith committee appeals to President Eisenhower to halt the "needless imposing upon the American people of a climate of suspicion, anxiety, and fear," and the "destruction of reputation by rumor, defamation, and intimidation of critics." McCarthy is not mentioned, but it is accepted that he is the target.

The same day, in a "Call to Sanity," officials of Freedom House rebuke McCarthy for his "irresponsible attack" on Attlee, saying the senator had shown himself 'once more as a man ever ready to stoop to false innuendo and commit as dangerous an assault upon democracy as any perpetrated by the Communists." The statement is signed by Harry D. Gideonse, chairman of the board of Freedom House; Ralph J. Bunche, Leo Cherne, and Father George B. Ford, vice-presidents; Herbert Bayard Swope, treasurer; and George Field, secretary.

At the same time another critic—the left-wing Council of the Arts, Sciences, and Professions—denounces McCarthy's questioning of Wechsler, Belfrage, and Aronson as "a calculated attack on the traditional American freedom of the press."

Senator McCarthy is in Bethesda Naval Hospital for a checkup, but remains in touch with his office by telephone.

May 31—The State Department releases "the facts" about two of the British ships which McCarthy charged were carrying cargoes to Red China, and in part he is vindicated. Both ships transported Chinese troops, but only under coercion, the owners contend. British Ambassador Sir Roger Makin announces in the muffled phrases of accredited diplomacy that at the time of the "alleged incidents" the ships did "appear to have been under the effective control of the Chinese Communists."

This day the Rosenbergs' execution is set for the week of June 15, their third appeal having been denied by the Supreme Court. Clemency now hinges on their consenting to "talk" and reveal all the details of their treason.

[IV]

A momentary shift in accent starts off the month of June, the newspapers being absorbed in the coronation of Queen Elizabeth II. But this diversion is of brief duration; two days after the ceremonies the *Times* of London urges its readers to "get back to reality" after their "coronation spree," and in Washington "reality" means McCarthy.

June 6—In a televised hearing filled with bitterness and taunts of "lie," "persecution," and "intimidation," Senator McCarthy requests the State Department to keep Frank Coe, former secretary of the International Monetary Fund, from leaving the country. Coe invokes the Fifth Amendment on the question of whether he is or has been a Communist, or whether he had engaged in espionage while an official of the fund. He says he is not engaged in espionage now and was not last December 2, but will say nothing about before that time. Months ago Coe balked at answering questions before the Internal Security Committee and was dropped from his $20,000 job with the fund.

June 11—A roundup story on the purging of United States libraries in Germany of the works of authors who refused to answer questions in the McCarthy and other hearings.

June 12—Senators McCarthy and Lehman tangle in the Senate when the former accuses Lehman of "gross abuse" of the free mailing privilege by attempting to send out 100,000 copies of his speech, "Creeping McCarthyism—Its Threat to Church, School, and Press," under his Senate frank. Lehman retorts hotly that only a few copies had been sent out, and those by mistake, and he offers to make a full disclosure of his use of the franking privilege if Senator McCarthy will do the same.

This page-one story in *The New York Times* is twinned with a report that Albert Einstein has urged every intellectual to refuse to answer questions in any congressional inquiry and to be prepared to suffer jail and obloquy, if necessary, in the defense of free thought. *The Nation* is "appalled" by the flood of press editorials, inspired by this report, bitterly castigating Einstein. *The Nation* considers this manifestation a clear sign of the "demoralization of McCarthy's opposition."

June 14—The *Times* speculates that the purging of our overseas libraries "must really set the Germans—and all free Europeans—to wondering about our stability if not our sanity."

June 15—Front pages blossom with reports of President Eisenhower's Dartmouth College commencement speech, in which he exhorted: "Don't join the book burners! . . . Don't be afraid to go to the library and read every book so long as it does not offend our own ideas of decency."

Asked about this, Secretary Dulles says that a few books have actually been burned by overzealous employes—eleven copies out of the two million on the shelves of the overseas libraries. The

Times says the incinerations took place in Sydney and Singapore, although officials there deny it. Dulles becomes wearied by the pertinacity of the reporters and ends his press conference abruptly.

June 18—On the eve of execution, the Rosenbergs are granted another stay by Supreme Court Justice Douglas, and the court is at once called into special term to review the point of law that has been raised.

June 19—President Eisenhower in a news conference disclaims knowledge of any directives having been sent to the U. S. overseas libraries to ban certain books. At Dartmouth, he says, he was not talking about books by Communists, or about books that advocate the destruction of the government. And again he refuses to discuss McCarthy, repeating that he never deals in personalities.

Also on the front pages this day is the report of the dismissal of a high-school teacher of English in Brooklyn who had sought Einstein's advice on testifying before Jenner's Internal Security Committee and, acting on that advice, had invoked the Fifth Amendment. He was dropped from his teaching job, along with five others, by order of the New York Board of Education.

A sensation along another line, this day, is testimony before McCarthy's committee regarding a plot to kill the senator. The hearing is conducted by Senator Mundt, and the witness is Joseph P. Mazzei, a Pittsburgh theater operator, who says that for twelve years he acted as an FBI undercover agent in the Pennsylvania Communist party. Mazzei says he had been intimately associated with Lou Bortz, party leader and trainer of "goon squads" in the techniques of sabotage, bomb-making, and marksmanship. At a party meeting last December, Mazzei states, Bortz had announced that he had been selected by the party "to do a job in the liquidation of Senator McCarthy. He said it was very gratifying . . . and that when the time came, he would carry it out."

Bortz is called and sullenly invokes the Fifth Amendment on questions regarding bomb-making, instruction in the handling of firearms, and a house in Pittsburgh in the basement of which was a pistol range.

June 20—Somber accounts of the execution of Julius and Ethel Rosenberg, the atomic spies. In New York's Union Square, 5,000 persons listen to denunciations of President Eisenhower for turning down a last-minute clemency plea. Thousands wept, and *The Nation* reports that a Russian-born pamphleteer, who had instigated the last court review, was chased by an angry crowd and took refuge in a coffee shop, shouting at his pursuers, "If you are happy about the execution of the Rosenbergs you are rotten to the core!" *The New York Times* reports that the small crowd gathered in Times Square appeared listless and indifferent to the speakers, but reports come in of protests and demonstrations in many cities abroad. In Paris one person was shot and 400 were jailed in an anti-American demonstration. American embassies generally were picketed.

McCarthy marks the day by tangling with a teacher from Brooklyn College, Dr. Naphtali Lewis, and his wife, Helen B. Lewis. Dr. Lewis' Fulbright scholarship has been canceled by the State Department, the senator announces at the conclusion of the thirty-seven-minute inquiry into the background of the pair. The wife, who also had taught at Brooklyn College, invokes the Fifth Amendment when she is asked about Communist party membership, and whether she had held party meetings in her home at which the overthrow of the United States was freely discussed. Her husband swears that he is not a party member and has never attended Communist meetings with his wife; but on the advice of his lawyer he refuses to say whether she is or was a member. Lewis protests his "astonishment" at McCarthy's inquiring into his own and even his wife's "political beliefs." McCarthy reminds him that since the couple were planning to live abroad for a year at the expense of American taxpayers, his questions were pertinent, and "I think the cancellation an excellent idea."

June 21—Much space is given in the newspapers to a verbal tussle between McCarthy and Dr. Conant of Harvard, currently serving as High Commissioner in Germany, over the "book burning" issue. What would Conant do with the books being removed from the libraries? the senator asked. How dispose of them? Pay for storing them? Give them to somebody? Conant thought some harmless disposition could be made without actually destroying them. The colloquy went on hour after hour, and "More Faggots on the Fire" ran the *New Republic*'s incendiary headline.

June 22—McCarthy gets much space in the press with his televised debate with Paul Scott-Rankine, correspondent for Reuters, the British news agency, on the practice of witnesses taking refuge in the Fifth Amendment when questioned about Communist associations. Says McCarthy: "If you ask a man whether he's a Communist, and he's under oath, if his answer were to be 'no'—a truthful answer—that would not incriminate him. The only way he could be incriminated would be if he is a Communist. So, when a man comes before our committee and says, "I won't answer because if I told the truth I might go to jail,' it means, of course, that obviously he's a Communist."

Scott-Rankine contends that in the view of most Europeans the "McCarthy controversy" has made the United States a country in which people are afraid to speak freely, or to "confess mistakes," lest they lose their jobs or be "incriminated or intimidated."

Rejoins McCarthy: "I get rather amused each week when I hear so many of the bleeding hearts screaming to high heaven that their right to scream has been curtailed. As far as I know, there has been no one yet who has been afraid to talk in this country." Condemning Einstein for his advice to intellectuals not to testify, he says there is "nothing new about that advice. We have had Communist lawyers appear before our committee day after day, and the advice is always the same: don't tell the committee what you know about espionage and sabotage. I may say that any American, I don't care whether their name is Einstein or John Jones, who would advise American citizens to keep secret information which they may have about espionage and sabotage—that man is just a disloyal American. I may say now that a witness is entitled to refuse to testify under our Constitution if his testimony would incriminate him. He is not entitled to refuse to testify if the testimony will incriminate some other spy or saboteur."

June 25—The books issue blazes up again as Robert B. Downs, president of the American Library Association, denounces "McCarthyism" at the association's annual conference in Los Angeles. Meanwhile, from The Hague comes a satirical report that word has been received that the works of Mark Twain, Emerson, Hawthorne, Thoreau, and Henry James have been cleared by the State Department for use overseas. "The communication does not indicate what tests Mark Twain has been submitted to, but it does explain that he has been 'cleared' under Infoguide Bulletin 303," the dispatch reads. A *New York Times* survey indicates that in twenty capitals several hundred books have been removed from the libraries, although in Copenhagen only seven out of the eight thousand on the shelves had been banished.

On the same page of the *Times* Senator McCarthy is quoted as answering a threat made by nine Germans on the staff of RIAS, the

United States radio station in Berlin, to resign if he should call Gordon A. Ewing, the deputy director of the station, before his committee: "We don't need the advice of any foreign nations on running the affairs of this committee or this country."

June 26—McCarthy raps the welter of conflicting directives coming from the State Department on the subject of undesirable books; he says it begins to look like a deliberate attempt to make the department look silly by banning books wholesale. He is upset by a report that Whittaker Chambers' book, *Witness*, has been banned, and says if that is true, it indicates sabotage of the needed housecleaning in the department.

This day the newspapers reprint excerpts from an article by Mrs. Franklin D. Roosevelt appearing in *McCall's* magazine, saying she would like to see McCarthy's committee "done away with," while the House Un-American Activities Committee, she thought, was "ruining our reputation in the rest of the world."

This day the Communist party officially charges that the Rosenbergs were "foully murdered' by the joint forces of President Eisenhower, Attorney General Herbert Brownell, and J. Edgar Hoover, head of the FBI. The wording of the denunciation duplicates the language used by the Rosenbergs' lawyer at their funeral. The three American leaders are described by party spokesmen as working hand-in-glove with "swastika-minded McCarthy and his goons." The *Times* comments that the outburst is exceptionally vitriolic, even for the Communists. The pronunciamento is signed by William Z. Foster, Elizabeth Gurley Flynn, and Pettis Perry, members of the national council.

The emotional storm raised by the symbolic phrase "book burning" continues, and the American Library Association promulgates a "Declaration of Principles," calling for free expression and assailing the State Department's book purges as a threat to liberty and democracy. In Washington, the department states that about 300 titles, and some 18 authors, have been weeded out. But *The New York Times* estimates that some 40 authors have been banned outright. And the American Civil Liberties Union petitions the Senate to look into McCarthy's attack on the overseas libraries. In some papers these combined developments take up nearly a whole page of type.

June 27—Big play given in the press to a letter from President Eisenhower that is read to the librarians' convention. The President in his letter reaffirms the sentiments of his Dartmouth speech, and condemns "zealots" who would go to extremes.

June 30—McCarthy launches a diversionary raid and sends the newspapers off on a new tack by revealing that he is in search of a list of more than 100 atomic spy suspects, which he understands was given to President Truman in 1945 or 1946, after the Igor Gouzenko revelations in Canada. McCarthy stresses that he wants to find out whether the list ever reached Truman, or whether it had been turned over to the Justice Department; and if so, what had been done about it. He may call the ex-President as a witness, he says. Which is sensation enough for one day, opening up a completely new line of speculation. Truman, asked about it all, smiles grimly and replies: "What I could tell you the press wouldn't print. Therefore I say, 'No comment.'"

So July and the dog days rolled in, with the opposing factions firing away at each other without respite, while millions of sweltering citizens watched the ebb and flow of the battle with increasing tension and anxiety on all sides.

Joe Stubs His Toe?

Just what goal was Senator McCarthy aiming at? That question bedeviled the press, the liberals, and his fellow senators during 1953 as he harried his opponents and outmaneuvered them in a display of tactical audacity which even his enemies marveled at. As soon as the battle against Bohlen went against him, he brought up the matter of trade with Red China, and in the midst of that commotion he shifted back to the "book burning" controversy. Foreign and domestic criticism he had blanketed by counterblasts, and he had never been pinned down in a position of last-ditch defense.

There was a growing suspicion that his goal was the Presidency, although he scoffed at the suggestion. The *New Republic* thought he simply craved power and would stop at nothing to attain it. *The Nation*, animadverting upon his "calculated campaign of confounded and confounding idiocy," also suspected that power was his objective, although in what form it was hard to say. And then, as soon as he arrived at power he seemed determined and even eager to risk losing it by fresh hazards; his recklessness was becoming proverbial.

Comparisons between McCarthy and Hitler were by now commonplace, although the basic differences between the two were sometimes pointed out. McCarthy seemed to present none of the traits of a revolutionary. He expressed no wish to change the system, but was quite satisfied to work within it; he offered no far-reaching political program, but only his one issue, and that was merely negative and limited, contemplating no new order of things, but only the remedying of what he perceived as a current and removable defect.

Writing in *Look* magazine in mid-1953, William S. White

329

guessed that McCarthy's strategic plan was to "contrive to alter the views, actions, and tone of the Republican party. With its consent, preferably; without its consent, if necessary." This would place the test of strength plainly between the President, as leader of the party, and the rebellious senator, and the alternatives facing Eisenhower were seen as three: (1) He could avoid any open breach, in the interest of party harmony; (2) he could "take on Joe," so as not to forfeit the party leadership; (3) he could rely on the "enough rope" theory in the belief that sooner or later Joe would hang himself and thus bring about his own elimination.

At the Capitol the feeling was that McCarthy would stand or fall on the extent of his political appeal, rather than on his moral strength or vulnerability. The moral aspects had been served up by his opponents ad nauseam without producing any noticeable political effects. The Gillette-Hennings report delving into McCarthy's financial dealings had been distributed in hundreds of thousands of copies (the *New Republic* claimed to have sold some 150,000 reprints) without making a dent in the senator's popularity. His supporters obviously simply did not care about any moral issue; they were worked up over communism, and on that score his support was plainly widespread and deep. Favorable mail flooded into his office, and wherever he spoke he was applauded. In the face of continuous press condemnation he gained sympathy. Some New Deal Democrats in the Senate longed to take him on, but were dissuaded by the leadership, which for the most part was in the hands of Southern conservatives from states where communism was not a live issue and which McCarthy had invaded very little. The safe policy for the Senate's Democrats, therefore, seemed to be one of ignoring him.

[II]

All was not cooperation among the members of the McCarthy committee's staff; Cohn and Bobby Kennedy bickered, and some of the investigators were inclined to run wild. The placing of a mature overall director in charge of the backstage operations, therefore, seemed a wise administrative policy; but the man Joe picked for this job turned out to be as grave a mistake as any the senator had made in his whole career. The man was J. B. Matthews, a one-time fundamentalist Methodist preacher and assiduous fellow traveler, who had abjured his Communist ways and since 1938 had been a professional anti-Communist and investigator for the House Un-American Activities Committee. Since he had helped to organize several Red fronts in his wayward days (including the American League Against War and Fascism), he knew the party's methods of infiltration, and should be of immense help in ferreting out those members of the conspiracy who had infiltrated. So ran McCarthy's reasoning as he named Matthews executive director of the investigations subcommittee. In his capacity as chairman, McCarthy made the appointment without consulting his colleagues. The date of the action was June 22.

On July 3, the storm broke. A reporter for the *Washington Post,* picking up a copy of the current issue of the *American Mercury,* noticed an article by J. B. Matthews.* The article was titled "Reds and Our Churches," and the opening sentence read, "The largest single group supporting the Communist apparatus in the United States today is composed of Protestant clergymen."

The author went on to stress that only about 2 percent of the Protestant ministry was wittingly or unwittingly peddling the Communist line. This statement in itself was not new; here and there similar charges had been preferred, and they had always provoked a violent reaction. McCarthy had noticeably steered clear of becoming involved in religious controversy. He was a Catholic, although not an ostentatious one, and nobody yet had suggested that he was religiously prejudiced. But Matthews blew the lid off, and for the first time in his free-swinging career McCarthy was seriously embarrassed.

Unluckily, Southern Democrats were brought into the fray by this accusation. Senator Harry F. Byrd of Virginia demanded angrily that Matthews "give names and facts to sustain his charge or stand convicted as a cheap demagogue, willing to blacken the character of his fellow Americans for his own notoriety and personal gain." Byrd was the most prestigious Southern conservative in Congress, and he was joined by all three Democratic members of McCarthy's subcommittee, Senators McClellan, Symington, and Jackson, in denouncing this "libel" on the clergy. In vain Matthews explained that the article had been written months previously, long

---

* The *Mercury* had fallen from its high estate under the editorship of H. L. Mencken, and had degenerated into a vehicle for the views of the far right politically. Editorially it carried little weight.

before there had been any question of his joining the committee staff. McCarthy tried to stall, but secretly knew he was licked; the issue was far too inflammatory. The Democrats demanded that Matthews be dropped immediately; McCarthy met with the full subcommittee but was outvoted, 4 to 3, on retaining the new director, Senator Potter lining up with the three Democrats on this point and demanding Matthews' instant discharge.

Potter had grown increasingly restive over the behavior of Roy Cohn. In his opinion (and in this he was strongly seconded by the Democrats) the mad gambol of the two "boy sleuths" through Europe, together with Cohn's arrogance and attempts to set the course of investigations, had brought discredit upon the entire committee, and he wished to get rid of Cohn as well as the new incubus, Matthews.

In answer to the vote demanding Matthews' instant discharge, McCarthy replied that he, as chairman, alone had the power to hire and fire committee staff; and he assured reporters that he had "not the slightest intention of investigating the clergy under any circumstances."

At this point, Vice-President Nixon stepped in as mediator, suggesting to Senator Potter that he reverse himself and confirm the chairman in his authority to hire and fire, in return for which McCarthy would shortly accept Matthews' resignation.

But the anti-McCarthy advisers around the President had no wish for a peaceful solution; to them this opportunity to bring the controversy within the party to a head seemed heaven-sent; and immediately they set in motion an intrigue to jockey the President into coming out publicly against the senator.

Protestant ministers had taken to their pulpits to denounce Matthews' slur. In New York, the Reverend Jame A. Pike, dean of the Cathedral of St. John the Divine, declared that "if this smearing of our fellow citizens continues to go on, more than the Rosenbergs will have died in our land." The Reverend Adam Clayton Powell said flatly that Matthews "lied," and preached that "this is the hour of anti-Christ." At New York's Broadway Tabernacle (Congregational) the Reverend Joseph D. Huntley deplored that "the land of the free and the home of the brave has suddenly been seized with hysteria."

The White House clique anxious to "stop McCarthy" moved to bring these and numerous similar protests into powerful focus by procuring from the leaders of the National Council of Christians and Jews a statement of indignation, which they would embody in a telegram to the President. The latter then could seize upon this telegram as a cue to express his own resentment of the Matthews slander. Emmet John Hughes, a speech writer for Eisenhower, and Sherman Adams, the President's chief of staff, drafted a statement for Eisenhower's use while waiting for the message of protest to arrive from New York.

Meanwhile McCarthy met again with his subcommittee and refused to surrender his authority to do the hiring and firing of staff. No vote was taken, although Potter was ready to side with the Democrats again had the issue come to a vote. And McCarthy stubbornly insisted that he had no intention of accepting Matthews' resignation, although it had been offered. Matthews, he contended, was "a free-lance writer projecting his own views and conclusions. What he wrote in the article has nothing to do with the committee."

At the White House, the plotters of Joe's downfall were in suspense as the promised message from the clerical leaders in New York still did not arrive. Telephone calls were put through urging speed, because word was leaking from the Capitol that McCarthy might reverse himself and bow to the inevitable at any minute by announcing Matthews' resignation. This would undercut the President's rebuke, robbing it of much of its moral effect. On the other hand, if the resignation were announced after the President spoke out, the action would look like a knuckling under by McCarthy to the President's demand.

At last the message came through, terming Matthews' attack on the Protestant ministry "unjustified and deplorable," although the right of Congress to investigate the loyalty of any citizen was acknowledged. The statement was signed by Monsignor John J. O'Brien of Notre Dame University; Rabbi Maurice H. Eisendrath, president of the Union of American Hebrew Congregations; and the Reverend Dr. John Sutherland Bonnell, pastor of New York's Fifth Avenue Presbyterian Church. At 5:29 P.M. the President's reply, drafted in advance, was handed to reporters, expressing Eisenhower's feeling that such attacks were "alien to America" and betrayed "contempt for the principles of freedom and decency."

McCarthy was actually on his way to a press conference to announce Matthews' resignation when the White House statement was released. According to Hughes, he was waylaid by Nixon and

Deputy Attorney General William Rogers and kept engaged in conversation until the presidential rebuke could be handed to the press. Then, at 6:35 P.M., he announced that Matthews had been dumped. But the headline play had been taken away from him; for once he had been beaten to the punch.

[III]

But this apparent retreat he covered brilliantly. Striding into the Senate, he opened fire on Allen W. Dulles and the Central Intelligence Agency, demanding that they be investigated because of a "most blatant attempt to thwart the authority of the Senate." He had tried vainly, he said, to question William P. Bundy, a CIA official who had been promoted to liaison duties between the National Security Council and the Atomic Energy Commission, and whose fitness for the job McCarthy doubted because he had contributed $400 to Alger Hiss's defense fund. Allen Dulles, head of the CIA, was the brother of the Secretary of State. Bundy was Dean Acheson's son-in-law.

McCarthy told the Senate that Bundy had "suddenly disappeared" when it became known that the committee wished to question him. At eleven o'clock that morning the CIA had telephoned to say that they did not know the whereabouts of "one of their top men," the senator related. Later they had telephoned to say that Bundy had "gone on vacation." Then at 3 o'clock that afternoon the CIA's liaison man with Congress had telephoned to say he "had talked with Bundy and that the policy of the CIA was to refuse to allow any employe of the CIA to appear before any Congressional committee." To McCarthy this was outrageous. "I can't believe that one of the most important officials in the executive branch of the government would take it upon himself to say that," he exclaimed. And he demanded that Allen Dulles be subpoenaed.

Joe had executed a familiar tactic with perfect success. His blast at the CIA's "defiance of Congressional authority," always a sensitive point on Capitol Hill, had followed immediately the Matthews resignation developments. Eisenhower's censure had come too late to catch the afternoon newspapers, but was bound to get major front-page display in the editions the next morning. Then McCarthy's sensational call for an investigation of the CIA—the nation's supersecret spy-and-counterspy agency—capped the Matthews matter in the next morning's newspapers, all but smothering Eisenhower's rebuke and the senator's humiliating acceptance of the resignation. It was the tactic of a raider, which McCarthy would use time and again with brilliant effectiveness—while he was being repelled on one front, he would throw the enemy into disarray by striking without warning at a totally different point.

The next day the three Democrats resigned from McCarthy's investigations subcommittee. The reason they gave was that the chairman's sole control of the staff placed them in an "impossible situation, having responsibility but no voice, right, or authority," but Joe detected an odor of politics in their walkout. "It's the old Democratic policy of either rule or ruin." He shrugged. "If they don't want to take part in uncovering the graft and corruption of the old Truman-Acheson administration, they are, of course, entitled to refuse. The subcommittee will continue to function whether or not it has any Democrat members."

That same day Joe's threatened investigation of the CIA was discreetly sidetracked, for the time being at least. Allen Dulles visited the Capitol and talked with McCarthy privately; then the senator announced that Dulles had requested and had been granted "time to think over" their discussion, and he would be back.

Looking back on the events of the week, observers guessed that McCarthy had suffered a real setback—his first important one— in the Matthews affair. But he had covered his retreat superbly, and if he should push the CIA matter, it was agreed that it would be the most audacious challenge yet to the President's authority, and might compel Ike to "come out fighting" at last. But this analysis of the potentialities had a wishful undertone, especially since no one knew how serious McCarthy had been in rounding on Allen Dulles.

There had been some humor connected with his unheralded blast at the CIA: he had taken the Senate floor in the midst of debate on a cattle drought relief bill. For half an hour he had fulminated against the arrogance of the CIA, while the senators listened calmly but attentively; where this would all lead, nobody could even guess. Then Joe sat down, and the senator whom he had interrupted resumed, in a dry tone, "As I was saying . . . "

The galleries burst into laughter, and on the floor Joe shared the laugh.

[IV]

McCarthy of course had not neglected the other irons he had in the fire. There was the "book burning" issue. While he was burning no books himself, he commented, he felt there were some that he would consent to commit to the flames. When Doxey A. Wilkerson, author and former professor at Howard University, refused to tell the subcommittee whether he was a Communist or in the pay of the Communist party, the chairman and Mundt agreed that Wilkerson's book on Negro problems in the United States ought to be removed from the overseas libraries. And Joe added pointedly, "I don't care what they do with this book—whether they burn it or not. Certainly it should not be stored at government expense." Wilkerson testified that he didn't know of any Communists who had been "properly convicted," and that went for the Rosenbergs, too; also, he shared "the doubts of a lot of people" that the Reds were the aggressors in Korea. The law had no right, he held, to interfere with the "teaching and advocating" of communism: "I think I have a right to teach and advocate anything I please."

When Rockwell Kent, the artist, appeared before McCarthy sitting as a one-man committee, he refused to say whether he was a Communist, but attempted to read into the record a prepared statement. This accused the senator and other congressional investigators of leading a movement to overthrow democratic government by force and violence, if necessary, and replacing it with a form of Fascism or Nazism. McCarthy told the witness he might insert his statement if he "had the guts" to say "yes" or "no" to the question of whether he was a Communist. The statement did not go in.

President Eisenhower, meanwhile, somewhat amplified his views on the subversive books issue by giving his opinion that exclusion from government libraries of Dashiel Hammett's detective novels was going too far; but when prodded directly about McCarthy, he stood on his refusal to "deal in personalities." At the same time the welter of directives being sent out by jittery policy-makers reached a climax with a piteous plea from the American ambassador to Burma, inquiring why the textbooks on sanitary plumbing that he had requisitioned were being held up for "State Department clearance." Then the four-month tenure of Dr. Johnson as director of the information service came to an abrupt end with the promulgation of a tenth and "authoritative" directive regarding the use of "controversial" works which went right back to the first one issued, namely, the one sanctioning the use in Voice broadcasts of material taken from Communist sources if it would "affirmatively serve the ends of democracy." This new directive had been written by Johnson himself and approved by Secretary of State Dulles. It coincided with Dr. Johnson's resignation, "on the strict orders of his doctor."

McCarthy, who had praised Johnson for his cooperation at first, angrily changed his tune when the State Department followed with a statement of policy denouncing the burning of any book as "a wicked symbolic act"; Johnson's outgoing directive the senator berated as "ridiculous, completely ridiculous," and he released testimony taken in previous hearings exposing the total chaos that had been produced by the State Department's contradictory orders. One librarian, this testimony showed, had tried to throw out books by Dwight D. Eisenhower, Judge Learned Hand, and Abraham Lincoln. The newspapers carried columns of wordage on the confusion, and the American Committee for Cultural Freedom laid the blame squarely on McCarthy for driving the State Department to the point of making itself look silly.

Floodgates of vituperation were opened against the departing Dr. Johnson when he harshly criticized McCarthy's appointment of Karl Baarslag, a former director of anti-Communist activities for the American Legion, as his research chief. Baarslag, Johnson asserted, had made "flagrantly inaccurate" statements about the overseas libraries, alleging that "they just don't go in for anti-Soviet literature." In reply, McCarthy accused Johnson of a "completely dishonest attack," saying: "If you had deliberately set out to sabotage any possibility of getting adequate funds to run a good information program, you could not have done a better job. . . . Clearly, Mr. Johnson, one good way not to fight communism is for men like you to direct your energies to trying to smear such ardent anti-Communists as Karl Baarslag. Such attempts at character assassination can only help the cause of communism."

McCarthy's outburst, in the form of an open letter, had point, because the Senate Appropriations Committee was about to consider the allocation of funds to run the information service, and

McCarthy was a member of that committee. Musing on his former pleasant relations with Dr. Johnson, Joe wondered whether somebody at the State Department was "using" him.

Meanwhile, the Reds-in-churches issue was being kept bright, if not illuminated, by conflicting statements made by two eminent clergymen. In New York, the Right Reverend James P. De Wolfe, Protestant Episcopal Bishop of Long Island, called on the churches to cleanse their houses of subversive elements. Interviewed on his return from Europe, Bishop De Wolfe said he felt that there indeed were subversives in the churches and in education, although "97 percent" of the clergy with whom he came in contact in his diocese were loyal. Three percent of disloyals was one greater than the two percent alleged by Matthews in his disputed article.

Conversely, in an address at Hamilton, New York, the Reverend Robert C. Harnett, S. J., editor-in-chief of the Jesuit magazine *America*, said that McCarthy was much more open to criticism than other congressional investigators, and cited as an example of intolerable behavior the senator's saying about Theodore Kaghan, "We put him on public exhibition; we picked him up by the scruff of the neck and brought him over and questioned him." Said Father Harnett, "No senator exercising the authority delegated to him by the American people has any business talking about an appointee of the executive branch, or any other person convicted of no crime, as if he were some lower species of animal."

The CIA investigation issue was muffled further after a conference between Allen Dulles and three subcommittee members, McCarthy, Mundt, and Potter. Backed by the approval of the White House, Dulles explained that the rule against allowing anybody from the CIA to testify before a congressional committee was necessary because of the tight secrecy surrounding the agency's work. After the talk, a joint statement was handed out calling off the Bundy matter but upholding McCarthy's right to subpoena witnesses to "uncover graft, corruption, and subversion" in any branch of the government. McCarthy himself further explained that his subcommittee would relay to the CIA the information it held on Bundy, and the CIA would reevaluate his security standing. Asked whether he felt he had won a victory or taken a defeat, Joe replied, "Neither; it's just an agreement."

In another direction, McCarthy released for the Sunday papers, knowing that there it would receive the most generous amount of space, his report on trade with Communist China. This was highly critical of both the State Department and Great Britain. The hearings had disclosed, the report stated, that since the start of the Korean war, 450 merchant ships had carried 2,000 cargoes to Red China for a gross trade of more than $2,000,000,000 and more than half of these ships had flown the British flag. "It is known that China is on a full war economy and carries on trade only in those items which assist her war effort," ran McCarthy's comment. The cleavage between the State and Defense Departments on this issue was brought out, with Defense Secretary Charles E. Wilson being quoted to the effect that the traffic had definitely helped the Communists in Asia to wage war on the free world. McCarthy rebuked the State Department for "this shocking policy of fighting the enemy on the one hand and trading with him on the other" and for its failure to exercise "the forcefulness and vigor necessary to convince our allies that they should ban this trade."

This was taking issue openly again with the administration, and Stassen hit back. "You just don't throw your allies in six different directions," he complained; "some of them live by this trade."

Abroad, the report received varied official reaction. In London the government reaffirmed its policy of limited trade; Norway was silent; Paris had no comment; the Rome press ignored the charges; Bonn deferred comment; and two papers in Holland carried brief mentions of McCarthy's findings. But confidential advices to the State Department represented Europe as in an uproar over Senator McCarthy and the "reign of terror" which he obviously was inspiring in the United States. This impression was borne out by Americans traveling abroad. In Athens, Mrs. Eleanor Roosevelt told reporters that in her opinion Senator McCarthy had done "a great deal of harm" to her country, but added that "I am speaking as a Democrat, of course. One must feel very free in the United States these days to differ with Senator McCarthy," she continued. "He has made the great mass of people blindly afraid." She did give the senator credit for one thing—for "perhaps creating something that is essential— public realization of the danger of communism."

Another Democrat who opened fire on McCarthy at this time was Senator "Mike" Monroney of Oklahoma. In a speech that appeared to take his party colleagues by surprise, Monroney belabored Joe for daring to suggest investigating the CIA, whose secrets were not given even to cabinet members or to the committees of Congress passing on its applications for funds. Without mentioning names, the Oklahoman jeered at the antics of the senator's "Keystone Cops" associates, Cohn and Schine, during their European jaunt.

McCarthy was not on the floor when Monroney unleashed his attack, but promised to "take time to read it." The anti-McCarthy press gave fulsome coverage to the speech, *The New York Times* devoting two columns to it. In the Senate, however, no one rose either to defend McCarthy or to second Monroney. Three days later, the latter renewed the attack by reading to the chuckling senators the "pan mail" he had received—more copious than his "fan mail." He explained that he simply wished to give the senators "a true picture" of the "Keystone Cops Club."

McCarthy struck back in a television interview, hinting at anti-Semitic bias in Monroney's "Keystone Cops" ridicule. Senator Lehman arose in the Senate to chide McCarthy for having the effrontery to impute religious prejudice to their colleague.* McCarthy then turned on Lehman with the introduction of a letter Lehman had written in 1948 to Alger Hiss, expressing sympathay and "complete confidence" in Hiss's loyalty and condoling with him on being "very badly treated." Said McCarthy:

"After the junior senator from New York had set himself up as an evaluator of who is a good anti-Communist and who is not, I took the trouble to check some correspondence in the Hiss case . . . which will perhaps give a better picture of the great authority who sets himself up to attack the staff of my committee." And he read the letter, dated August 6, 1948, the day after Hiss first denied Whittaker Chambers' accusations publicly. He continued: "I cannot help wondering why the junior senator from New York spends so much time, not naming a single Communist, but in going about through the country and in taking the time of the Senate and space in the *Congressional Record* to criticize and condemn anyone who is talking out and is prosecuting the traitors to the United States. I have given the record of the junior senator from New York not because I am concerned with the senator, for I think he is completely unimportant in this body, but I have done so in order that the country may better know why he springs to the de-

---

* An alert reader of the *New York Post*, suspecting a misprint, wrote in that surely McCarthy must have meant to accuse Monroney of "anti-Sennettism" instead of "anti-Semitism." McCarthy jokes were about as plentiful as Ford jokes in the Model T days, but far more bitter.

fense of men like Alger Hiss, why he starts a prolonged program of character assassination against my very able staff, who are doing such an excellent job in digging out the truth."

In an emotional response, Senator Lehman retorted that his letter had been written before there was any "real evidence" against Hiss, and "I did what I felt was the human thing to do . . . I sent him a line to express my sympathy in a difficult situation in which he was placed." And he accused McCarthy of a "despicable smear." Why did not this "great enemy of communism," he demanded, explain why he "accepted the support of the Communist party when he was a candidate for the Republican nomination for the Senate? Oh, Mr. President, he has so many questions to answer—questions raised in an official report of a Senate committee, which he has refused to answer, thereby showing his contempt for the Senate. He does not want to answer those questions. He does not dare to. So he makes charges and pretends to expose Communists and charges his fellow senators with religious bias and high crimes. . . . How long are we going to be vilified and misrepresented and blackened? How long are we going to continue to be blackened by a man charged with misdemeanors, one who has not even the guts to answer to the Senate and the American people?"

Senator Monroney joined in to express outrage at the "implications made as to the loyalty and patriotism of the distinguished senator from New York." McCarthy merely replied that he felt no need to repudiate Communist support "because the Communists did not support me." Lehman's other taunts he ignored.

The senators present listened intently but uttered no sound.

The emotion-packed exchange epitomized the temper of the country, summing up the wrathful confusion which this "irrepressible conflict" of radically opposed ideas, personalities, prejudices, and concepts of loyalty, truth, and honor had attained. The spectacle of angry men locked in mutual crimination had grown wearisome; the hackneyed accusations had been heard time and again; the country was edgy, nervous, irascible. The all-engrossing controversy could only grow greater—reach some climax—or die out.

Then Congress adjourned. But Joe did not.

High, Wide, and Handsome

Unlikely as it seemed, neither the pugnacity of McCarthy nor the stubborn resistance of his antagonists had been extended to their limits yet, and how the struggle would end was anxiously debated. From the sidelines, it still appeared to be "anyone's ball game." A peaceful ending of the conflict seemed improbable: Joe felt himself on the upswing and was bursting with daring and energy, and President Eisenhower, on his side, gave no hint of abdicating his leadership. The President's problem was to find a way to defuse the time bomb represented by McCarthy before the senator, whether by intention or the drift of events, should take over control of the Republican party.

Eisenhower was still publicly holding aloof, in spite of constant pressure to intervene. And McCarthy and his subcommittee, although shorn of bipartisanship by the walkout of its Democrat members, went ahead with scheduled inquiries. Overtures were made periodically to the decamping three, but Senator McClellan said firmly that "my resignation is final," and Senators Symington and Jackson concurred. McCarthy contended that the three had walked out on a "phony issue," their real reason being that the committee was turning up graft and subversion in the Truman administration, and, as one of the bolters was said to have put it, "the better job the committee does, the more abuse we Democrats will have to take." McCarthy reminded a television audience that McClellan would have a reelection fight on his hands in 1954, and that Symington was being actively boomed as presidential timber. He termed the walkout "the sort of thing that small boys have been doing since the beginning of time, but it never happened in Congress before." It was like the Russians' walking out of the United Nations debates when they couldn't get their own way, he said. Certainly he would like to have the Democrats back, but if they preferred to "draw their pay and not do their work," he wouldn't try to compel them.

The fascination of periodically rating Joe's gains and losses by now had become a national pastime. Newspapers ran their "box scores" week by week, but always with qualifying provisos, because nobody knew where McCarthy was going, except that it seemed to be straight ahead. Latest losses chalked up against the embattled senator were Matthews, the Democrats' walkout (maybe), and the CIA (unclear). On the side of gains stood the withering report on trade with Red China, and the forcing of the State Department to propose a whole new agency for psychological warfare in place of its shell-shocked Information Administration.

All, or nearly all, of Joe's critics appeared to agree that his strength nationally was growing steadily. In June, *The Nation* had said flatly that "events of the last four months have changed 'McCarthy the Irresponsible Bounder' into 'McCarthy the Serious Contender for Power.' " And even while counting up the recent rebuffs the senator had sustained, *The New York Times* could detect no inclination in Washington "to count McCarthy out." Even Hanson W. Baldwin, the *Times'* authority on military affairs, conceded that while McCarthy's approach had been wrong, he had pointed up the need of more careful scrutiny and control of the CIA by Congress.*

Despite the "agreement" with Allen Dulles, McCarthy did not drop his suspicion of Bundy, and three weeks later he released— with appropriate noises of honest indignation—several letters he had received from Dulles, clearing Bundy of political motives in having contributed to the Hiss defense but refusing to give the subcommittee the evidence on which the clearance was based. Unwilling to let the matter rest, McCarthy demanded that the State Department withhold a passport from Bundy, who was planning a vacation trip abroad, on the grounds that he was technically under subpoena to appear before the subcommittee. No written subpoena had been issued, McCarthy admitted, but he argued that notice to Bundy of the subcommittee's intention had the same legal effect.

At the same time, McCarthy took time out to renew his feud with his press critics. The committee directed by the American Society

---

* In the light of revelations much later about the part played by Kim Philby, Soviet master spy in the British Secret Service, in setting up the CIA, this 1953 veiled reference to something amiss in the intelligence agency takes on sharp significance. McCarthy's interest apparently was not unjustified.

of Newspaper Editors to study James Wechsler's charge of attempted intimidation had reported its inability to reach any unanimity of opinion. Its conclusion therefore was that it was the responsibility of every editor to read the transcript of the Wechsler questioning and decide for himself whether it amounted to infringement of the freedom of the press. Four members of the committee presented a minority report blasting McCarthy outright, while opinion among the others ranged from doubt to vindication of McCarthy. Editors generally did study the transcript thereafter and came to no more united conclusion than had the committee. Joe kept the feud going for a while, then wearied of it and dropped it.

[II]

In the Senate McCarthy was at loggerheads with Senator Fulbright of Arkansas. During an Appropriations subcommittee hearing on State Department expenditures, Fulbright appeared on behalf of funds for the scholarships bearing his name. Could Communists benefit from this program, McCarthy demanded, or people who "took the Fifth" before congressional committees? Fulbright said that he could "well imagine intelligent people refusing to testify because they have been the object of indignity." Senator Mundt tried to head off Joe by reading the law requiring all persons assigned to federal missions to be examined by the FBI. Snapped McCarthy, "That law has not been followed. I have called this the 'half-bright' program—no reflection on the senator intended."

Fulbright was so insulted that he refused to answer any questions put by McCarthy, "who obviously is out to destroy my testimony."

The anti-McCarthy press made the most of this display of McCarthy's peevish temper and also quoted with gusto a remark attributed to Arthur Eisenhower, the President's elder brother. Interviewed in Las Vegas by a McCarthy-hating newspaper, the Tacoma banker was quoted as saying that he considered Senator McCarthy "the most dangerous menace to America; when I think of him I think of Hitler." The words stirred up ripples from coast to coast, and at his next press conference the President was pressed to comment, but adhered to his principle of "not discussing personalities," and persistent prodding could not draw him out.

Beginning to bear fruit at this time, although not mentioned much in the press, was the functioning of a newly organized agency aimed at counteracting and hopefully eliminating Senator McCarthy from public life. This was a privately financed "lobby," set up on a hard-boiled, practical basis to provide ammunition and expert guidance for anyone who would take on Wisconsin Joe. The man who promoted the idea was a Washington lobbyist named Maurice Rosenblatt. In McCarthy, Rosenblatt saw foreshadowed an American Hitler, and he was deeply concerned. Back in 1948, Rosenblatt had helped to found a political group calling itself the National Committee for an Effective Congress, whose purpose had been to raise campaign funds for liberal candidates anywhere. Rosenblatt had become disenchanted by the amateurishness of McCarthy's critics, who wasted their breath in pointless denunciation. Calling names would never stop McCarthy, Rosenblatt argued; what was needed was a professional, full-time anti-McCarthy lobby, which would use the same methods in fighting him that any "God-damned power company" would employ to push a favorable tax bill through Congress.

Rosenblatt and a few friends succeeded in raising funds (although not much) and set up a modest "clearing house" of information on McCarthy's activities, past and present. The NCEC name was utilized, and professional research and speech-writing assistance was offered. More subtly, contacts were made with influential citizens in the home states of key senators, men whose word carried weight politically; these sources of indirect pressure were cultivated and encouraged to take a stand against "McCarthyism." By mid-1953 this organization was beginning to show results. When Dr. George N. Shuster, president of Hunter College in New York, spoke out against McCarthy, it was remarked that he eschewed invective, but called on the academic community of the nation to undertake a systematic study of the senator, marked by "utmost objectivity and calm and chilly resolution," so that an authoritative report could be made to the public. Dr. Shuster's position as a prominent Catholic layman lent force to his proposal, as did also the care he observed not to dignify McCarthy by exaggeration; most of his speech was a plea to outlaw the Communist party and end the legal ambiguity shielding this "international conspiracy."

McCarthy's reaction was terse and characteristic. "Every Communist and leftwinger in the country has been investigating me," he said. "This gentleman is welcome to join the pack if he wants to."

Certain elements of the clergy, too, were becoming bolder in their opposition to McCarthy and his "satellites," Senator Jenner and Representative Harold H. Velde, chairman of the House Un-American Activities Committee. The Very Reverend Francis B. Sayre, Jr., dean of Washington Cathedral and grandson of Woodrow Wilson, saw these three as "demonstrating that they believe God and the nation are best served by the frightened and credulous collaborators of a servile brand of patriotism." The pastor of All Souls Unitarian Church in Washington, Dr. A. Powell Davies, in a sermon titled "Study in Tyranny," denounced the same three legislators; and energetic Methodist Bishop G. Bromley Oxnam declared that "men who say that in every little red schoolhouse there is a little Red teacher lie!'

In a different tone, Francis Cardinal Spellman, Archbishop of New York, speaking in Brussels, Belgium, decried the hysteria prevailing in Europe over events occurring in the United States, including the reaction to Senator McCarthy. Assailing the "tired, jaded charges" which he found being repeated against Americans, he contrasted the outbursts in European countries against the execution of the Rosenbergs with the silence of the same elements on the purge of Lavrenti Beria, the Soviet secret police chief, in Russia. The Cardinal found it ironic that Tito's Yugoslavia ("a country which has bullied and threatened continually those who do not share its totalitarian concepts") should regard "McCarthyism" with such frenetic alarm. To judge by the criticism he had heard, Spellman went on, "one would imagine that it is no longer possible in America to keep one's good name. Nothing could be further from the truth. No American uncontaminated by communism has lost his good name because of Congressional hearings on un-American activities."

When the General Council of the Presbyterian Church in the U. S. A. addressed a letter to its 8,000 ministers directing their "sober thought" to the growing tendency to "combat communism with fanatical negativism" and to turn congressional investigations into "inquisitions," the action was construed as an attack on Senator McCarthy and aroused resentment. One Presbyterian layman protested in letters to the newspapers that even if one held no brief for McCarthy, it "is un-American, not to speak of un-Christian, to 'smear' him by withholding his name but describing his activities— inaccurately. He has done considerable cleaning-up that needed to be done."

On the academic level, George Kennan, diplomat and scholar,

warned at Princeton that "witch hunts are whipping our established institutions about like trees in a storm." No less dolefully, Edward R. Murrow cried out on television at "pompous, posturing practitioners of terror, who would ride down those who are searching for truth."

That this public outcry, widely aired by all branches of the news media, was really sapping the foundations of McCarthy's popularity certainly seemed belied by the enthusiasm with which he was received at every public appearance. Invited to address the convention of the Marine Corps League in Cleveland, he chose as his theme the "tarnishing of our nation's honor by the defeatist truce agreed to in Korea and by the Communists' shameful treatment of American prisoners there.

"We cannot have a peaceful, stable world unless we have the friendship and respect of the people of the Orient," he told his audience. "And we cannot have their respect if the rights of American fighting men are trampled upon." The action of the Reds in sentencing American officers to prison "before the ink was dry on the truce agreement," he said, was "for the simple, sole purpose of disgracing and degrading us before the Asiatic people. In the past, when an unfriendly hand was laid on a Marine or other fighting man, this nation stepped in and removed that hand. In the past, brutalitarians walked softly in the presence of American Marines, soldiers, and sailors. How free are we when a single Marine private rots in jail? Our message to the Chinese Communists should be: 'You return those men, not next week, not next month, you will do it immediately, or we will wipe your accursed Communist leaders who are responsible from the face of the earth!' " The crowd stood up and cheered, and he concluded: "We can and must recapture our national honor. The price may be high, but we need pay it only once."

[III]

Amid all this, Joe seemed to be striking pay dirt in his investigations. One taunt that had been flung at him innumerable times was that for all his bluster, "Joe McCarthy never uncovered a single Communist." In the middle of August, while most senators were mending fences, junketing abroad, or working on future legislation, McCarthy flew back to Washington from a brief vacation in Wisconsin and went into a closed hearing before his committee. Four witnesses were heard, three men and a woman, and after the hearing Senator Dirksen, who sat with McCarthy, said the testimony "would appear to involve national security."

It quickly became evident that the senator's new inquiry centered on the Government Printing Office with its 7,300 employes, all of whom were supposed to have passed rigid loyalty tests. McCarthy said the testimony indicated that a Communist party member, identified as Edward M. Rothschild, a bookbinder, had had access to highly confidential government secrets. Rothschild, employed by the GPO for twenty years, had been cleared by the agency's loyalty board in 1948 in the face of FBI reports warning of his Communist involvement, McCarthy indicated.

Open hearings followed. Rothschild and his wife, Esther, both invoked the Fifth Amendment when asked about Communist activities.* Rothschild admitted having had access to secret and confidential material, but when accused by another witness of having pocketed a Merchant Marine code book during the war he refused to answer questions about it. "Your refusal," McCarthy told him, "is telling the world that you have been selling secrets and that you have been engaged in espionage." Rothschild remained mute. So did Mrs. Rothschild when a witness, Mrs. Mary Stalcup Markward, who had joined the party in Washington and had remained in it for twelve years as an undercover agent for the FBI, positively identified her as an active Communist. McCarthy instructed Roy Cohn, the subcommittee counsel, to notify the Printing Office of Rothschild's silence, and within one hour the man was suspended from his job.

What drew attention to this episode was the scrupulous care that McCarthy took to respect all constitutional guarantees and hearing rules. Those accused were allowed to face their accusers. Every witness whom an accused person asked to have called was summoned, if he could be found, and the accused persons were permitted to consult counsel freely and were given every opportunity to present

* So continually was the Fifth Amendment mentioned in the daily McCarthy story that *The New York Times* had adopted the precaution of printing, immediately after every such mention, the following statement of what this meant: "The Fifth Amendment to the Constitution provides that 'no one shall be compelled in any criminal case to be a witness against himself.' This has been interpreted by the courts to mean a witness is not required to give testimony that is liable to incriminate him in a criminal case." Day after day this explanation was printed, the wording never varying.

a defense. They presented none. McCarthy repeatedly asked the Rothschilds' counsel, Charles E. Ford, a well-known Washington criminal lawyer, to submit any questions that he wished the sub-committee to ask of the witnesses against his clients. Ford wrote out sixteen questions to be asked of Mrs. Markward, and she answered all but one, which dealt with her income; Senator Dirksen advised her that she need not answer that because it was not relevant.

At the close, McCarthy asked Ford whether he had any complaint to make about the conduct of the hearing, and the attorney replied that he had none; he thought it had been conducted in a "most admirable" and "most American" way.

McCarthy later called in the two GPO officials responsible for security procedure, trying to find out why Rothschild had been cleared in the face of available testimony by his fellow workers, in the face of repeated alerts from the FBI that Rothschild was a Communist, and without any steps being taken except to ask the man himself whether he was a Communist, and to accept his unsupported word that he was not. From the officials the senator was able to educe only that they had acted to the best of their knowledge at the time. To McCarthy this was "the most fantastic thing I ever heard of, not even remotely intelligent!" How could they have managed to ignore the FBI reports that Rothschild was a Communist and an associate of Communists when the file contained the names of forty persons who would testify to that effect? One official protested that he could not "plead guilty to complete stupidity," whereat the senator exploded:

"The FBI reports showed that the Rothschilds were Communists. They showed that he was stealing papers. They gave the membership card in the Communist party of Mrs. Rothschild. They gave the name of a witness who saw him steal a secret code book in wartime that enabled the enemy to break our code. Why was he working in the Government Printing Office until yesterday? Man, you had the FBI report! What more did you need? This is the most fantastic picture—for the last three years I've been talking about the complete incompetence of the loyalty boards. Here is an example!"

Off the record, the senator described the security officials as "nice, well meaning people, but inconceivably incompetent in loyalty matters." And he expressed further shock upon learning that the penalties at the Printing Office for violating the secrecy of classified documents ran from thirty-day suspensions to dismissal. In the Army, he pointed out, similar violations could lead to court-martial and perhaps shooting.

It was noted by the press that throughout these hearings sustained applause came from the two hundred spectators, and usually it was when McCarthy scored a telling point.*

A few days after the hearings, the new Government Printer, Raymond C. Blattenberger, announced that the Printing Office was being returned to a "wartime security status pending completion of its own checkup on the safety of its secret documents from delivery to the Reds," and McCarthy was credited with a decided victory. True, *The Nation* dismissed the investigation as a "thundering dud."

McCarthy himself had flown to Los Angeles to hold hearings there which he intimated might prove to be "tremendously more important than the Alger Hiss case."

At nearby La Jolla, Joe found himself in the same hotel with J. Edgar Hoover, who was vacationing there. The day before, a San Diego newspaper had carried an interview with the FBI chief in which Hoover said he considered Senator McCarthy a friend, and described him as earnest and honest, "a vigorous figure who won't be pushed around." While declining to pass judgment on the techniques used by the McCarthy committee, Hoover did say that in his opinion it and other congressional investigating committees were doing "a valuable job."

This apparent endorsement of Senator McCarthy by the director of the FBI was to produce instant, strident echoes in Washington.

---

* A bit of lagniappe produced by the hearings was the uncovering of a bookie ring. Carl J. Lundmark, a printer, invoked the Fifth Amendment—not on the question of communism, but as to whether he had netted $25,000 the previous year from a betting operation he ran in the GPO with the help of two full-time runners, or bet collectors. Lundmark's swift suspension followed.

Mellow but Not Mild

[I]

John Edgar Hoover was an employe of the Justice Department, whose head, Attorney General Brownell, was a spokesman for the Eisenhower administration. Reporters at once jogged Brownell to explain just what Hoover's statement meant. Did it mean that the Justice Department was dropping its investigation of the charges of peculiar financial dealings filed against McCarthy by the Hennings Committee months before? No, that subject was "still under study," Brownell replied; whereupon certain sections of the press speculated that the words were intended to serve as an oblique warning to the senator not to antagonize the administration further.

At the same time, a rumor was circulated that the National Security Council planned an official review of the effect of "McCarthyism" on American prestige abroad. Travelers returning from Europe reported a growing conviction there that the United States was headed down the road to Fascism. Walter Lippmann on a recent tour had found American influence "declining precipitately." Walter Reuther, of the United Auto Workers, CIO, and ADA, brought back word that on his six-week swing around the continent he had met "not one person who wasn't willing to admit privately that Joe McCarthy has done more to strengthen the Communist movement than any other one person in history."

The State Department, meanwhile, continued to be worried by advices coming from our embassies in Europe warning of a violent reaction to the "fact-finding revels" of the "Rover Boys," Cohn and Schine, on their uninhibited tour of the overseas libraries.

In Los Angeles, the hearings that Joe had hinted might be sensational proved unimpressive. The first witness called was William C. Taylor, who described himself bluntly as a Communist party functionary and refused to give any other information. The hearings, he said with a sneer, were "the same old 'McCarthyism.' "

351

Sensing that nothing was to be gained, the senator abandoned this inquiry with characteristic nonchalance and flew back east to launch an investigation into another executive arm of the government, the Army's Quartermaster Corps. Brownell's covert warning, if it had been such, obviously was not going to be heeded. Since taking over the chairmanship of the Government Operations Committee, Joe McCarthy had investigated the State Department, Voice of America, overseas libraries, Allied trade with Red China, and the Government Printing Office; he had made threatening gestures toward the General Accounting Office, a special preserve of the President, and the Central Intelligence Agency; and he was preparing to take on the staff of the United Nations. Now he was elbowing his way into a vital branch of the United States Army.

The first hearings, held in the federal courthouse in New York, were closed, but McCarthy gave the press a daily rundown on the testimony. Present with him during the questioning were Cohn and consultant Schine. The first day two Army civilian employes, a woman and a man, admitted Communist ties, the senator reported; they had had access to classified information regarding shipments of food and supplies that would tip them off to movements of troops in Korea and about the United States. The woman admitted having once accepted a Communist party membership card, but denied knowing what this meant. She had been advised by the chairman to consult her lawyer before appearing again. McCarthy was perturbed by the circumstance that she had been cleared as to loyalty by Army authorities.

The next day ten witnesses were questioned. Names were withheld, but McCarthy said one, whom he called "Mrs. Commissar," had been so powerful in the party that she had given orders to another witness (designated as "Miss Q") at a time when the latter held membership in the party's national committee. Both women had invoked the Fifth Amendment. On the other hand, an Army security guard had denied that he had ever joined the party formally, but admitted he "hadn't decided that communism was bad." Three Army officers, a colonel, a lieutenant colonel, and a captain, were questioned, and McCarthy instructed them to bring in the personnel files of "Fifth Amendment Communists" whom he named; he wanted to find out who had cleared them. The officers respectfully refused to comply, saying they were bound by orders.

The next morning McCarthy became definitely irked when it

developed that neither of the accused women employes had been
suspended pending a fresh loyalty check, although the guard had
been summarily fired. The record of "Miss Q," McCarthy said, was
so flagrant he couldn't understand how she could have been cleared,
unless the people granting clearance were "incompetent beyond
words, or in sympathy with Communists." His mystification grew
greater when he received the personnel files of the accused employes, but no records on their clearance, these having been withheld in compliance with the executive order issued by President
Truman in 1948.

This defiance of the subcommittee was followed a day later by
the flat refusal of the First Army, in New York, and the Army chief
of legislative liaison, in Washington, to release the names of the
persons responsible for clearing Army employes. McCarthy protested that he was having "more trouble with the Army than with
any other department," and he berated "Miss Q's" superior officer,
Col. Robert A. Howard, Jr., for failing to suspend the woman immediately; the colonel, he said, had "done a tremendous disservice
to the Army by discrediting it so badly, and thereby to your country. So far as I know," he added, "this is the first time any government department under any administration has failed to suspend an
employe who invoked the Fifth amendment."

Colonel Howard, visibly shocked by this dressing down, responded that he was bound by Army regulations, and the stage was
set for a showdown when Colonel Wendell G. Johnson, First Army's
assistant chief of G-2 (Intelligence), notified Senator McCarthy
formally that "it should be made as clear as possible to the committee that the names of individuals responsible for the granting or
withholding of loyalty or security clearances will not be made available to the committee. This is in accordance with presidential directive of 13 March 1948."

Faced with this ultimatum, McCarthy threatened to carry the
issue to the White House, and tempers grew short on both sides. Not
entirely incidental was the fact that New York City was sweltering
under an almost unprecedented heat wave; on September 3, the
ninth day of the scourge, the temperature hit 99 degrees, and rain
and cool winds did not bring relief for another three days. The
break in the weather coincided with a luncheon meeting between
Senators McCarthy and Dirksen and the Secretary of the Army,
Robert T. Stevens, during which an attempt was made to smooth

matters out. Afterward, Stevens said that while he felt bound by the 1948 directive, he could promise that there would be no "whitewash" or "coverup" of any action taken by the Army.

The press reaction to this meek pledge of cooperation was shown with painful clarity in the captions that appeared over a photograph distributed by the Associated Press, taken just after the luncheon. Stevens, making his statement to reporters, was flanked by Dirksen, who looked severe; McCarthy stood behind the secretary, hovering over him, watching him narrowly. "Watchful Eye," read the caption in *The New York Times,* while *The Nation* blazoned, "McCarthy: Commander-in-Chief." McCarthy was further described by the ever-hating *Nation* as "a coldly aloof background figure" in the scene—"tough and hard-boiled as a Mickey Spillane private eye," proving that he could "make the colonels talk."

[II]

But the issue was not laid to rest by Stevens' placating words, and more heat was generated when McCarthy made public a "restricted" Army pamphlet which he called "the best Communist propaganda I've seen in some time," and demanded the names of those responsible for putting it out. Titled "Psychological and Cultural Traits of Soviet Siberia," it had been distributed in limited quantities among intelligence officers of the Far Eastern Command for the purpose of giving them an insight into the viewpoint of the average Soviet citizen. The bibliography listed a book by Corliss Lamont, long identified with extreme left-wing activities and an apologist for Russia. In 1947, Lamont had even been called a "self-professed Russian spy" whom the Communists considered "one of themselves."

This time the Army struck back by declassifying the document "as a result of prior disclosure" and accusing McCarthy of violating the espionage laws, conviction under which could bring fines of up to $10,000 and imprisonment of up to ten years. Furthermore, the Army charged that McCarthy had deliberately withheld five pages of the pamphlet which showed it to be anti-Communist, even comparing the life of a Russian with that of a convict. McCarthy retorted that he had not released the five pages because he did not have time, and he served notice that neither the Army "nor any other branch of the government is going to hide dishonesty, corruption, or communism by putting a 'restricted' or 'secret' label on a document.

"This subcommittee has been very careful not to release anything that would jeopardize the security of this country," he went on pugnaciously. "We have leaned backwards on that. But I find that unfortunately the Army is doing what they did under the Truman administration. The pattern is the same. The document is ninety-five percent Communist propaganda, and two or three or five percent is a slap on the wrist for communism. Whenever they are called to task, they quote the small percent that lightly condemns communism."

Plainly a collision was building up between the belligerent senator and the Pentagon; but for the time being McCarthy sidetracked this line of questioning in order to quiz before the television cameras numerous employes of the United Nations, not a few of whom invoked the Fifth Amendment amid scenes of great confusion and bitterness. The senator showed marked restraint during these hearings, allowing the witnesses every leeway compatible with the rules. He assured the lawyer for one balking witness that he might offer rebuttal to the allegations at any time, so there need be no repetition of the charge, often heard, that "the retraction never catches up with the accusations." When witnesses objected to the TV lights, he ordered the cameras to be turned aside.

A major disturbance was created by Abraham Unger, who had been a defense attorney in the conspiracy trial of eleven top Communist leaders. As Unger was called, the chairman announced: "We heard this witness yesterday [in closed session] and asked him two simple questions. One was whether he was a member of the Communist party, and the other was whether he had organized a professional group within the party. He spoke for seventy minutes without answering either question. I am not going to waste time on him this morning unless he wants to deny the testimony we have received about him. I'm not going to listen to his type of filibuster."

Unger stepped toward the witness chair, saying, "You will have to decide for yourself, Mr. Senator, whether you want a witness or not."

"Remove that man," came the curt order, and two uniformed bailiffs caught Unger by the arms and hustled him out, struggling slightly, while the cameras rolled. Hisses and a shout, "Throw him out!" came from the spectators, and McCarthy turned to Unger's counsel, repeating that he would permit the witness to testify if he wished to reply to testimony that he and a law partner were Communist functionaries who had helped in expelling Dr. Bella V. Dodd from the party.

"I am not going to let Mr. Unger repeat what he did yesterday," McCarthy made clear. "If he wants to testify he can do that, but I won't have him come in here and raise objections to answering questions. He can testify yes, no, or claim the Fifth amendment. I am giving him the privilege of not answering anything he considers unfair or untrue. But I don't want to hear any lecture from him today."

Unger's law partner was called, and when he took refuge in the Fifth Amendment, the chairman explained patiently that he was inquiring into the "Communist conspiracy" and not into anyone's "political beliefs." And he reminded the witness that when he refused to answer the simple question of Communist party membership, "you are signifying to the world that you are a Communist, because a truthful answer would not tend to incriminate you in any way." When the witness objected to the television cameras, the chair ordered them turned away, and also forbade the taking of still pictures.

A new situation developed when Corliss Lamont was called and calmly refused to answer questions but did not invoke the Fifth Amendment. Lamont, a professor of philosophy at Columbia University and writer on political subjects, rested his refusal on the First Amendment to the Constitution, guaranteeing free speech. Lamont contended that since he was not in the government service, held no public office, and had no access to classified information, what he thought, said, or wrote was his affair and he was under no obligation to submit to interrogation. To clear the air, however, at the very outset he stated voluntarily, "I am a loyal American and I am not now and never have been a member of the Communist party." Then he retreated into stubborn silence, although the long statement explanatory of his reasons for denying the subcommittee's right to question him was placed in the record with the chair's consent and was also given to the press. The confrontation came in a closed session, but at the end McCarthy gave the press his version of what had taken place. This version later would be disputed by Lamont when McCarthy moved to cite him for contempt and eventually procured an indictment. Lamont welcomed the legal test of the senator's authority to delve into private actions, and the battle would drag out slowly through the courts to a surprising conclusion.

The McCarthy "new look" of reasonableness and fairness caught the eye of at least one presumably impartial observer, Alistair Cooke, correspondent for the influential liberal journal, the *Manchester Guardian.* Cooke noted a "developing discrepancy between 'McCarthyism' and McCarthy." In all his recent investigations, Cooke reported, the senator had moved "with careful planning and masterly discretion. He is patient with witnesses whose FBI file would give innocent citizens the creeps. He has consistently protected the anonymity of highly suspect witnesses. In short, Senator McCarthy is working well within the sanction of legislative investigations. . . . This is a new turn which liberals are loathe to acknowledge." *

[III]

Such unwonted mellowness in the "fighting Marine" may have stemmed from a major change in his personal life at this time. On September 12, a friend and colleague, Senator John Fitzgerald Kennedy, had married Jacqueline Lee Bouvier in a wedding of high fashion at Newport. A crowd of 3,000 outside St. Mary's church had broken through police lines in the rush to glimpse the couple.

A week later, Senator McCarthy and Jean Fraser Kerr were married in St. Matthew's Roman Catholic cathedral in Washington. Joe was forty-five, and his tall, auburn-haired bride was twenty-nine. In her student days at George Washington University Jean Kerr had been voted the "most beautiful girl on campus." She had been on

* How little some avowed "journals of opinion" at this period (and often at others) reflected the opinion of the bulk of citizens then prevalent was shown by their circulation figures. From 1950 to 1957 (the year of Joseph McCarthy's death) the paid circulation of *The Nation* sank from 39,000 to 28,000. In the same period the *New Republic* lost half of its subscribers, the figure falling from 52,000 to 24,000. These journals of opinion, which had a very low opinion of Joe McCarthy and at times betrayed almost obsessive hatred of him, lost the attention of their readers as their detestation of the senator grew; yet during McCarthy's six most active years, the population of the United States increased by 10,000,000.

By contrast, *U.S. News & World Report,* a news magazine pronouncedly conservative, paid little attention to McCarthy until 1953, but from then on reported the senator's doings with some degree of sympathetic comprehension; and between 1950 and 1957 its circulation rose from 373,000 to 820,000. *Time,* which after initially turning thumbs down on McCarthy adopted the safer course of passing him by as often as possible, pushed its circulation from 1,500,000 to above 2,000,000 in the same seven years; and *Newsweek,* which endeavored to preserve impartiality in its reporting of McCarthy, also gained subscribers—from 830,000 to more than 1,000,000.

McCarthy's staff as a research assistant since 1948 and had helped actively in his anticommunism work from the start. Their courtship had been stormy, with Joe shying away from marriage, believing that he was incapable of domestication. He had always kept irregular hours; ate, slept, relaxed when the mood struck him; and was always on the go, always in a rush. Married life, to his mind, meant adhering to a steady schedule and forming regular habits.

The wedding was Washington's biggest social event since the inaugural ball. The political elite of the capital filled St. Matthew's during celebration of the nuptial mass, and in the street outside 3,500 "ordinary folks" collected to sing out good wishes and yell, "Kiss her, Joe!" as the senator led out his lovely bride. Reporters noticed with a start his attire—the full diplomatic panoply of striped trousers and morning coat; it seemed hardly compatible with "good old Joe."

The guests included Vice-President and Mrs. Nixon, Secretary of the Army Stevens, Postmaster General Summerfield, Harold Stassen, Allen Dulles, presidential assistants Sherman Adams and Major General Wilton Persons, Representative Velde, Senators Ives, Hickenlooper, Chavez, Goldwater, Green, and Kennedy, and Jack Dempsey, the ex-heavyweight champion. Joe McCarthy had come a long way from the chicken farm, and Washington paid him homage. Two wedding gifts that came shortly were particularly gratifying.

First, Attorney General Brownell, after months of studying the Tydings-Maryland election report and the Hennings report blasting Joe's financial record, announced that no evidence of law violations had been found, and the complaints were dismissed.

Then Joe was awarded the Bill of Rights gold medal given annually by the Wall Street post of the American Legion to a citizen or group "whose outstanding Americanism has provided exceptional protection to our way of life."

McCarthy went to New York to accept this honor and spoke to a noonday crowd of 5,000 from the steps of Federal Hall at Nassau and Wall Streets. He revealed that his subcommittee, under Senator Potter, was conducting an inquiry into North Korean war atrocities; and he hoped the findings might "do something to prevent any more experts from making one trip around the world and then coming back to tell us that you can beat the Communists at the conference table. They will never surrender there."

This was a slap at Adlai Stevenson, who had just completed a world tour and at that moment was being given a red-carpet welcome at the White House, while dispensing Democratically acceptable counsel on how to fight communism abroad.

Attacking Great Britain's trading with Red China, McCarthy enjoined the Wall Street crowd: "It's up to you people to call a halt to the cringing, whining, crawling appeasement of the last twenty years and to tell our great President Eisenhower that you do not want any more of it. Some eggheaded elements of the press, radio, and politics will say that means going it alone. If we must go it alone, we will, and so help us God, we will win it alone if we have to!"

Then the senator and his bride took off for a honeymoon on an island in the Bahamas, cut off from all communication except by radio telephone.

The honeymoon was brief. In October, an urgent summons from his staff brought Joe back to look into an alarming situation that had been uncovered, he was told, in the Army's supersecret radar research laboratories at Fort Monmouth, New Jersey. And confidently the raider sailed into waters more perilous than any he had navigated before.

PART FIVE
Fugue on an Army Theme

"Now, now you stars, that move in your right spheres,
   Where be your powers? Show now your mended faiths,
   And instantly return with me again,
   To push destruction, and perpetual shame
   Out of the weak door of our fainting land. . . ."
                                    —*King John*

"I Spy" at Monmouth

A belief had spread, encouraged not altogether by people who saw the nation in the grip of a "reign of terror," that Senator McCarthy was served by a scattered network of spies and informers, constantly prying into the most privileged sanctuaries of privacy. This was a misapprehension; no such intelligence network existed, nor was Senator McCarthy capable of organizing and minutely supervising so complex a machine. Roy Cohn, who as chief counsel of the investigations subcommittee was in a position to know, has described how the senator got most of his information—through the mail, from voluntary informers, by telephone and personal interviews. While most of the tips thus received were worthless or trivial, here and there a solid lead would be uncovered, and the staff would follow it up.

The standard method of procedure was to question witnesses privately. Most of these were dismissed at once, without any public notice of their appearance. Witnesses whose testimony might be material then were brought into a public hearing, and of the hundreds interviewed only a few ever reached this stage. Even then the objective of the committee was not to convict or punish anybody—that was the function of other branches of the government—but rather to expose a dangerous situation or instance of misconduct before the public and refer it to such agencies of the government as were empowered to correct it.

The Committee on Government Operations and its Permanent Subcommittee on Investigations had been created by the Senate for the express purpose of overseeing the activities of other branches of the government, and naturally, charged with that kind of mission, it could hardly expect to win favor, least of all from individuals or departments coming under its scrutiny. The fight against congres-

363

sional investigations consequently was almost continuous, and Mc-Carthy's committee came under especially bitter fire. In a manual for internal security put out by the Senate Foreign Relations Committee at this time, Senator Wiley, the chairman, noted that behind the passing of resolutions authorizing congressional inquiry into internal security matters lay "some of the most dramatic controversies in legislative history," while efforts toward the "continuation of these investigations have been the subject of some of the bitterest battles in the Senate and House, and in the forum of American public opinion"; and the principal figures in such inquiries, especially the committee chairmen, had often been subjected to "personal attacks of unprecedented proportions." In spite of this, Wiley found that the nation's security would be "infinitely more endangered today" had not congressional investigators sought out and exposed subversion. "How many espionage agents, how many subversive government employes, might still be engaged in their nefarious work had it not been for Senate and House committees courageously flushing these enemies out from the darkness so necessary to their success?"

Although Senator Wiley did not mention McCarthy, many newspapers did, in publishing these remarks, and for the most part derogatorily.

Joe was busy putting out his own summary of the testimony his subcommittee had taken regarding the "deplorable" confusion existing in the State Department's personnel files and the laxity of their supervision. Three to four hundred persons had access to these, witnesses had testified; keys to the file rooms were handed out to persons who entered after hours and spent as much time as they pleased with the files; there was no page-numbering, cross-indexing, or other means of indicating whether a file was complete; files had been withdrawn and shunted about for as long as eighteen months before being returned—these and other derelictions were cited, calling for a sweeping reorganization.

McCarthy's report drew comparatively little public attention at this time because of the greater interest in the testing of a hydrogen bomb by the Soviets, heightening the external threat to the United States. High administration spokesmen were warning of the menace, and Representative W. Sterling Cole, chairman of the Joint Congressional Committee on Atomic Energy, pleaded for a budget of ten billion dollars as absolutely essential for the national defense.

Minor attention also was paid to a statement at this time by the Army saying that several civilian employes at the Fort Monmouth radar laboratories had been suspended "for security reasons." The *Chicago Tribune* said that five had been suspended and that thirty more were under scrutiny by the Army after a preliminary inquiry conducted by the Senate investigations subcommittee. The announcement said that the Army had "complied with the request of the subcommittee to question individuals employed at Fort Monmouth," but had given "no agency outside of the executive branch of the government any . . . material which it has developed [regarding] the suspension of employes at Fort Monmouth."

This official disclosure was what brought Senator McCarthy racing back from his honeymoon, and three days after his arrival in New York he opened his own investigation of what he at once labeled "extremely dangerous espionage." He intimated it might envelop the entire Signal Corps. In a closed session he examined five witnesses, one a former radar specialist at Monmouth, the others still employed there. The former employe, the senator told reporters after the hearing, had taken refuge in the Fifth Amendment when asked whether he had passed top secret information to Julius Rosenberg during the war or whether he had given any radar screen data to the Communists.

This statement *The New York Times* and other leading newspapers judged unworthy of the front page; but twenty-four hours later the sensations that began to tumble out of McCarthy's sleeve did land on page one, and there they would stay for weeks to come.

[II]

Radar had been one of the most valuable of the United States' "secret weapons" during World War II, and it had taken on further importance as an indispensable component of the nation's missile defenses. Research being carried on continuously at the Signal Corps laboratories at Fort Monmouth was not much talked about; but intimations of espionage there were sure to generate public alarm.

The excitement started when Senator Dirksen, who had sat with Senator McCarthy in the first Monmouth sessions, told the Desk and Derrick Club in Chicago that a former Army officer had testified that a "sizable amount" of "top secret documents" of the Signal

Corps was missing. Some of the documents contained radar secrets, the witness had added, which, if they "got into the hands of an enemy, could be extremely dangerous to this country." Twenty-six of the missing documents had been found in the Russian zone in East Germany "recently," and they dealt with radar defenses; "more than that I dare not say," Dirksen concluded. "The real tragedy is that the whole secret of our radar defenses may have been peddled away. That would be colossal treachery."

In Washington, Secretary of Defense Charles E. Wilson was deeply concerned. "It looks like it might be worse than just a security leak," he admitted to reporters; however, Secretary of the Army Stevens was attending the hearings, and Wilson was sure he would handle the matter properly.

As the inquiry progressed, invoking the Fifth Amendment became a set pattern before McCarthy. Five more scientific workers were suspended, bringing the total to ten. The name of Julius Rosenberg, the executed atomic spy, kept cropping up. Rosenberg had worked at Fort Monmouth during the early years of the war, and the reports being given to the press by McCarthy indicated that he might have set up a radar spy ring at Monmouth which might still be operating.

It was disclosed that in January, 1952, three Army officers and seven civilians had petitioned Congress to investigate what they charged was the lax security setup at Fort Monmouth. They had stated that secret documents were missing. In June of that year, the Army announced that no documents were missing. Now, more than a year later, the Army stood pat on its 1952 conclusion, despite the statements that McCarthy was passing to the press making that stand look suspect.

There was the story of an East German scientist who defected to the West and told about the missing documents, describing them and insisting they were in the hands of the Russians, who had laughed at the ease with which they had been stolen. The defector was being guarded in Germany, it was said, and McCarthy dispatched a subcommittee investigator, James Juliana, to get his statement directly.

Another witness testified that during the war it had been "common practice" for scientists at Monmouth to take secret material home for after-hours study, with little or no checking. Other witnesses, most of them former employes in the radar laboratories, took refuge in the Fifth Amendment repeatedly when asked about associations with Rosenberg or membership in the party. One witness broke down, wept, confessed he had lied and offered to tell all, according to McCarthy's hurried report; amid much drama he was rushed to a Manhattan hotel. The whole week reeked of drama, with witnesses scuttling in and out furtively, no names being revealed, and the press being barred from the closed sessions. Periodically McCarthy would emerge and pass along his account of what was happening inside the hearing room.

After seven days of tension and building excitement, *The New York Times* expressed the "big question" which it said was forming in the public mind: When would the "full story" of Fort Monmouth be revealed? In the *Times'* opinion, "The feeling is that too many questions have been raised . . . for the lid to remain on much longer."

During a weekend lull, McCarthy attended a communion breakfast of the alumni of Cathedral College in New York, at which the Reverend Florenz D. Cohalan, professor of history, paid tribute to the senator for fighting communism in a "consistent, sensible manner, in strict accord with the American tradition." McCarthy's antagonists the speaker described as mainly persons of "some degree of influence," who were now "a bit embarrassed because they have been caught leading their followers up the wrong hill," and consequently they had built up McCarthy as the "bogey man" to distract attention from their own delinquencies. The Most Reverend Joseph F. Flannelly, auxiliary bishop of the archdiocese, thanked Father Cohalan for having spoken "the truth about a vital subject."

Just at this time the senator was seen as deriving some degree of vindication, even though indirectly, by the White House's release of the first official figures on the number of employes who had been separated from the government service as security risks under the tighter procedures ordered by President Eisenhower. A total of 1,456 had been dropped, 863 of them dismissed and 593 forced to resign. The report was presented as evidence of Eisenhower's making good on his promise that the executive arm would do its own policing. At the same time, it lent credence to McCarthy's contention that security risks did exist in the public service. All but five of the 1,456 ousted workers had been holdovers from the

Truman regime. Critics of the new procedures demanded a breakdown on the figures to show how many of those dismissed had been
let out because of communism, but none was forthcoming.

[III]

The second week of the Fort Monmouth investigation began with
a tour of the sprawling Evans laboratories there by McCarthy,
Stevens, and Major General Kirke B. Lawton, commander of the
base. Roy Cohn and the administrative assistants of Senators Potter
and Dirksen flew to the site with the senator but were not admitted
to the laboratories because they lacked clearance. This caused some
altercation at the gate, Cohn especially appearing to be incensed
by his exclusion; but the visit ended with mutual expressions of
harmony and pledges of cooperation. Incidentally McCarthy revealed that more than a dozen workers at the highly sensitive laboratories had been suspended, and said that his investigation would
continue.

"I have been very favorably impressed with the forceful and
aggressive steps taken by Secretary Stevens and General Lawton
to clear up this situation," the senator said, beaming. "I was more
than impressed, I was surprised, to find General Lawton, instead
of resenting the exposure of facts which should be exposed, helping
out in this housecleaning. An extremely bad and dangerous situation has existed here over the years. Some past and present—until
recently present—employes have been very unfaithful. But I am sure
that the great majority here are loyal, true, and doing an outstanding job for their country. . . . They are just as happy as we are
to see the few bad apples thrown out by Mr. Stevens and General
Lawton. After seeing the Evans laboratories I am impressed with
the tremendous damage a spy could do if he had access to its classified information."

Not to be outdone in cordiality, Secretary Stevens responded that
"this is the kind of teamwork between the executive and legislative
branches of the government which will clean up any situation which
needs cleaning up. We have had the complete cooperation of the
commanding general and his staff. . . . I said recently that if any
person was unwilling to answer the question of whether he was a
Communist, there was no place for him in the Department of the
Army."

Two days later McCarthy announced that three more Fort Monmouth specialists had been suspended, and the day after that the total rose to twenty. Then the senator took off on a speaking tour of the Midwest. By the time he got back to Washington the whole country would be caught up in a controversy that quite overshadowed his veiled intimations of skullduggery through betrayal of the nation's radar secrets.

[IV]

The furor had been raised by Attorney General Herbert Brownell's blunt charge that Harry Truman, while President, had retained in the government service and had even promoted the late Harry Dexter White, although knowing that White was a Soviet spy. Addressing the Executives Club at a luncheon in the Palmer House in Chicago, Brownell tossed his bomb in these words:

"I can now announce officially, for the first time in public, that the records in my department show that White's spying activities for the Soviet government were reported in detail by the FBI to the White House by means of a report delivered to President Truman through his military aid, Brigadier General Harry H. Vaughan, in December of 1945. In the face of this information, and incredible though it may seem, President Truman subsequently, on January 23, 1946, nominated White, who was then Assistant Secretary of the Treasury, for the even more important position of executive director for the United States in the International Monetary Fund."

This sensational accusation hit Washington harder than anything since the Alger Hiss case. Democrats were enraged that the loyalty of the ex-President should be impugned. Cried Adlai Stevenson, the administration had "taken 'McCarthyism' away from McCarthy!" Truman, reached by telephone, insisted that "as soon as we found White was disloyal we fired him." The White House said White had "resigned." General Vaughan, not unpredictably, could remember nothing. Former Secretary of State James F. Byrnes, now Governor of South Carolina, said that Truman had received and discussed the FBI report on White, although Truman denied having seen it. The House Un-American Activities Committee subpoenaed the ex-President and released several pages of the famous "pumpkin papers" produced by Whittaker Chambers that were clearly in

White's handwriting. Decrying the "hysteria," Truman ignored the subpoena, saying it was his duty as a former President to do so.

The incontrovertible evidence of secret memoranda prepared for transmission to Moscow, in White's own handwriting, did bring about a significant change in the attitude of many liberals who had long complained of the "Washington witch-hunts." For years they had accepted White's vehement denials of espionage and had represented him as "hounded to death" by unproved slanders. Now, even so inveterate a critic and doubter as the *New Republic* conceded that the evidence "seems to us to be convincing." Mrs. Eleanor Roosevelt, it is true, dismissed the new developments with an airy, "I don't know that Mr. White was ever convicted of any crime."

At a stormy press conference President Eisenhower explained that he had given Brownell the green light to go ahead without knowing all the facts, although it was inconceivable to him that Truman could knowingly have done anything to harm the United States. Under the hail of questions Ike grew annoyed, and he repeated sharply that he had not looked into the facts—no, not even since the matter had become a nationwide controversy.

This attitude satisfied nobody; the scandal was too great to be quieted by anything less than a thorough ventilation. All segments of the press clamored for this, and abroad the fracas astonished and dismayed our allies. The *London News-Chronicle* called the uproar "an exhibition of political rowdyism," and the *London Daily Express* carried a cartoon showing two senators standing under a bust of George Washington, one saying, "Personally, senator, I'd like to reopen the whole cherry tree inquiry. I figure he was shielding someone."

Then Truman announced that he would answer all questions in a radio and television broadcast from Kansas City. And he did so in an "address to the nation." Brownell he accused of lying. The FBI, he said, had known and approved his action on White. The attack he deplored as tending to degrade the Presidency, and he irately accused the Republican party of "embracing 'McCarthyism.'"

But this reply did not clear the air. It was felt that some questions remained unanswered; that in dogged determination to protect his party, Truman had slurred over aspects that would have given comfort to those who accused the Democrats of culpable carelessness, if not worse, in dealing with Communists. In Washington, Brownell's attack was interpreted as an administration counterattack on McCarthy, aimed at snatching his issue from him, while salvaging for the party whatever vote-getting value it might possess. McCarthy's reaction, when he should find himself pushed into a "me-too" position on the issue of Reds in government, was tensely awaited.

At first he appeared to be oblivious of any competition. He returned from the Midwest and picked up the Fort Monmouth hearings, day by day releasing to the press sensational bits of the testimony assertedly being heard in secret sessions; but now his disclosures wound up on the inside pages, the big headlines being preempted by the Brownell-Truman battle royal.

Moving into a new area of inquiry—Communist infiltration of industrial plants holding defense contracts—he conducted hearings in Albany, questioning eleven witnesses, most of them members of the United Electrical Workers Union, which had been expelled from the CIO because of its Communist tinge. One witness spat insults at the senator and his staff, calling them "a bunch of Fascist agents" lacking only a swastika, and the hearings grew rowdy, but McCarthy observed exemplary restraint.

Coincidentally, Army Secretary Stevens reported that the Army had been unable to turn up any evidence of current spying at Fort Monmouth, although there may have been some at one time. In all, thirty-three workers there had been suspended, but several of these had been cleared and restored to their jobs; the others would get speedy hearings. While amicable in tone, the statement took issue with McCarthy on several points. However, the senator said that he would let his hearings "speak for themselves"; it was not his job to evaluate testimony, his job was to produce it.

Then J. Edgar Hoover, in an unprecedented appearance as a witness before the Un-American Activities Committee, stated before a nationwide television audience that he had never agreed with Truman to the promotion of White and that both Tom Clark, then Attorney General, and Fred M. Vinson, then Secretary of the Treasury, had tried to get rid of White, implying that Truman had overruled them. Hoover also denied that he had ever asked any government employe to help the FBI in its work.

This testimony cast doubt on Truman's version. At the same time, the line of questioning alarmed President Eisenhower, who feared it might impair the confidential operations of the government; and in spite of apparent tactical gains scored by the Republicans, he backed away from Brownell, letting it become known that he had not seen the text of Brownell's speech in advance and had never even met Harry Dexter White. Brownell retreated a little, too, without retracting in full; evidently he was being muffled.

While this storm raged, McCarthy kept at his defense plants inquiry, hearing from an FBI undercover agent who had infiltrated United Electrical Workers that there were Communist cells active in several General Electric plants in Massachusetts and New York. The witness identified as Communists two men sitting in the room who the day before had invoked the Fifth Amendment on that question. Both demanded loudly to be heard, but McCarthy shut them off, saying, "This committee will hear no speeches from Fifth amendment Communists." When they continued to shout, he had them and their equally unruly lawyer ejected.

Eisenhower's ambiguous course in the absorbing White controversy continued to overshadow the senator in the news until November 24. On that day, in a nationwide radio and television broadcast, Joe turned on Truman and on his own would-be supplanters, and in half an hour reinstated himself as the one authentic chief Red hunter in the Republican ranks. It was a demonstration of audacity that left both his rivals and his enemies reeling.

"A Declaration of War"

When Truman replied to Brownell he repeated Adlai Stevenson's anguished taunt that the Eisenhower administration had "taken 'McCarthyism' away from McCarthy"; and then defined "McCarthyism" as "the corruption of truth, the abandonment of our historical devotion to fair play . . . the use of the technique of the big lie and unfounded accusations."

At his next press conference President Eisenhower said he would leave it to the White House correspondents to decide whether he had embraced "McCarthyism." A poll of eighty reporters showed that most of them absolved Eisenhower personally of the charge, but felt that Brownell and some elements of the administration were using the Wisconsin senator's alleged methods. But the poll also revealed much muddled, vague, and partisan thinking on the subject.

McCarthy reacted to Truman's jibe characteristically—he instantly demanded that the networks grant him equal time to answer this "smear." He accompanied his request with a warning that he would urge the Federal Communications Commission to review the license of any station that might fail to carry his rebuttal. The networks did not quibble: they allotted him free radio and television time on a national hookup estimated to be worth, at going rates, $300,000.

The script had called for a reply to Truman's "personal attack" on the senator, and Joe did wade into the ex-President in the first sentence, "Good evening, fellow Americans," he began, and went on without a break. "Last Monday night a former President of the United States, while attempting to explain away his promotion of a Communist spy, made a completely untruthful attack upon me. Tonight I shall spend but very little time on Harry Truman. He is of

373

no more importance than any other defeated politician. . . . The other night Truman defined what he calls 'McCarthyism.' The definition was identical, word for word, comma for comma, with the definition adopted by the Communist *Daily Worker,* which originated the term."

By contrast, he gave his own definition of "Trumanism," which meant "the placing of your party above the interest of your country, regardless of how much the country is damaged thereby, on the theory that no matter how great the wrong, it is right if it helps your political party. 'Trumanism' also in effect says to the head of a household that if you catch a criminal looting your safe, kidnapping your children and attacking your wife, do not dare turn the spotlight on him, do not get rough with him, or call for the police, because if you do, the criminal will have you arrested for disturbing the peace."

The senator then examined five "misstatements" with which he charged the ex-President, and concluded:

"Now, having been caught five times red-handed, Truman comes up with the granddaddy of them all. Here's what he says. He says: 'It's all McCarthy's fault,' he says, 'all the fault of 'McCarthyism,' and isn't that Senator McCarthy an awful man?' Now, my good friends, there is no reason on earth why the fight to expose and remove Communists and traitors from positions of power should be a contest between America's two great political parties. Certainly the millions of loyal American Democrats love America just as much, they hate and despise Communist spies just as much, as the Republicans do. Certainly there is no division along party lines among the mothers and fathers and wives of the 140,000 Korean casualties whose miseries have come to them from the trickeries and betrayals of an administration whose foreign policy was so carefully shaped by the Alger Hisses, the Harry Dexter Whites, the Owen Lattimores, the Dean Achesons, the John Carter Vincents. . . . It is all a matter of cold record. . . .

"The most amazing and disturbing thing about this incredibly unbelievable picture is that, as the danger to the nation is slowly and laboriously exposed, instead of an admission of guilt, of stupidity, cheap politicians from coast to coast join the chorus of the Communist *Daily Worker* and shout, 'Oh, isn't this "McCarthyism" an awful thing! Isn't it terrible to dig out these Communists!' How many American young men have died and how many will die because of stupidity, blindness, and treason none will ever know. But what answer do we get when it is exposed? The leader of the Democratic party—Harry Truman—in the most intemperate language condemns Attorney General Brownell for giving the nation the facts. He then, of course, proceeds to damn McCarthy, drawing heavily upon his repertoire of dirty names, because I took some part in the exposure of the Communist infiltration of his administration. I would not be concerned about what a discredited politician has to say, except that his leadership on the Communist issue is being followed by so many Democrats."

That took care of Harry Truman. Now Joe turned to his real objective and flung down the gauntlet to the Eisenhower administration on the question of what the issue would be in the coming congressional elections—and who would embody that issue.

"A few days ago," the metallic voice went on, "I read that President Eisenhower expressed the hope that by election time in 1954 the subject of communism would be a dead and forgotten issue. The raw, harsh, unpleasant fact is that communism is an issue and will be an issue in 1954. Truman's diatribe against those who fight communism is the best proof of that. Democrat officeseekers from the Atlantic to the Pacific have been proclaiming that 'McCarthyism' is the issue in this campaign. In a way, I guess, it is, because Republican control of the Senate determines whether I shall continue as chairman of the investigating committee. Therefore, if the American people agree with Truman, they have a chance to get rid of me as chairman of the investigating committee next fall by defeating any Republican up for election."

This was making himself the issue, and he made his defiance all the bolder by going on to point up the shortcomings of his party's leadership.

"Let's take a look at the Republican party," he said. "Unfortunately in some cases our batting average has not been too good. Before looking at some of the cases in which our batting average is zero [here the anti-McCarthy wing of the party really sat up], let me make clear that I think the new administration is doing a job infinitely better than the Truman-Acheson regime, that there is absolutely no comparison. For example, the new administration in the first ten months in office has gotten rid of 1,456 Truman holdovers who were all security risks . . . an excellent record for the time President Eisenhower has been in office. However, let us glance at a few cases where we struck out." And he brought up the case of John Paton Davies, Jr., a career diplomat whom he called "part and parcel of the old Acheson-Lattimore-Vincent-White-Hiss group which did so much toward delivering our Chinese friends into Communist hands. Why is this man still a high official in our State Department after eleven months of Republican administration?" *

Then the speaker turned to "the failure of my party . . . to liquidate the foulest bankruptcy of the Democrat administration. On September 12, 1953, the Chinese Communists announced that they would not treat as prisoners of war American fliers who were shot down during the Korean war over Manchuria. On September 10, 1953, the Army had announced that some 100 American young men known to have been prisoners of the Communists in Korea were still unaccounted for. Unaccounted for as of tonight, my good friends.

"Well, why do I bring up this situation tonight in talking about the Republican party? The Republican party did not create the situation, I admit. We inherited it. But we are responsible for the proper handling of the situation as of tonight. Now, what are we going to do about it? Are we going to continue to send perfumed notes, following the style of the Truman-Acheson regime? Or are

---

* John Paton Davies, Jr., was the center of a storm over his motives in the so-called "Tawny Pippit Case." This revolved around a memorandum submitted by Davies to the State Department in 1949, proposing to utilize a mixed group of Communists and liberals in the cold war. The points at issue in the ensuing controversy were why these Communists or open Soviet sympathizers were to be used, how, and in whose interest. Had Davies proposed that they be placed in a position where they might perhaps aid the Communist conspiracy because he himself was "soft on communism"? Or did he envisage their use, without their knowledge, in an ultra-secret psychological warfare operation to "subvert the subversives"? The case, which rivaled in mystery the Hiss and Dexter White cases, had brought into focus the long-smouldering dispute over the loss of China, State Department infiltration, and the schism in Republican ranks between the liberal and the conservative wings. The tawny pippit, a small singing bird admired in England, was picked as a code name for Davies' proposal.

Davies had played a part in another famous dispute regarding the origin of the term "agrarian reformers," widely used in the 1940's to designate the Chinese Communists, usually coupled with firm denials that the Chinese Reds were Communists at all. While serving as State Department advisers in China in 1945, Davies and John Stewart Service jointly signed a dispatch, dated February 14, referring to the forces of Mao Tse-tung as "so-called Communists," who actually favored a program of "agrarian reform, civil rights, the establishment of democratic institutions."

At the time of McCarthy's 1953 speech, Davies was on assignment in Peru, where he had been transferred by friends in the department, it was whispered, to keep him out of sight.

we going to take the only position that an honorable nation can take—namely, that every uniformed American packs the pride and the honor and the power of this nation on his shoulder? . . . I realize, of course, the low ebb to which our honor has sunk over the past twenty years. But it is time that we, the Republican party, liquidate this blood-stained blunder of the Acheson-Truman regime. We promised the American people something different. It is up to us now to deliver—not next year, next month—let us deliver now, my good friends. How are we going to do it?" Without a pause, headlong, he hurled a challenge to the policy-makers of his party:

"Once a nation has allowed itself to be reduced to a state of whining, whimpering appeasement, the cost of regaining national honor may be high. But we must regain our national honor regardless of what it costs. . . . Let us be specific. As you know, we have been voting billions of dollars each year to help our allies build up their military and economic strength, so that they can help us in this day-to-day struggle between the free half of the world and the Communist slave half. If that money we give them is being used for that purpose, it is well spent. If not, then those allies are defrauding us.

"How does that affect you? As of today, some money was taken out of your paycheck and sent to Britain. As of today, Britain used that money from your paycheck for the shipment of the sinews of war to Red China. What can we do about that? We can deal a death blow to the war-making power of Red China. We can, without firing a single shot, force the Communists in China to open their filthy Communist dungeons and release every American. We can blockade the coast of China, without using a single ship, a single sailor, or a single gun. . . . We can handle this by saying to our allies: if you continue to ship to Red China, while they are imprisoning and torturing American men, you will not get one cent of American money. If we do that, my good friends, this trading in blood-money will cease. No question about that."

[II]

The reaction to this unabashed defiance of administration policy was volcanic. The members of the anti-McCarthy clique at the White House, who had helped to plot the counterattack against Joe, were described as "fit to be tied," seething with anger. The speech, they cried, was "a declaration of war" against the Eisenhower administration; and what had heretofore been a latent suspicion became an ineradicable conviction, namely, that the senator had opened his campaign to seize the presidential nomination in 1956. McCarthy's opponents' fury was intensified by the realization that their strategy had backfired: Joe was prepared to slug it out, and the President was not ready to go to the same length. Privately Eisenhower was being reported to have told a friend, "Why should I take on McCarthy to please the intellectuals and pundits? When I do, it will be for something that 160,000,000 Americans know is right."

Brownell and his charges receded in the public view, and in a few days the Attorney General, in a roundabout jab at his Wisconsin "defender," gave his opinion that all Communists had been routed out of the government. McCarthy did not agree.

Then the senator was placed officially on the administration's index expurgatorius (not read out of the party but sternly censured) by Secretary of State Dulles. McCarthy's brash proposals regarding United States foreign policy were rejected and the senator implicitly rebuked in a statement that Dulles made clear had been endorsed by the President. While no names were mentioned, the target was obvious. The statement was read by Dulles to attentive reporters:

"Since I met with you last week there has been a widely publicized criticism of this administration's foreign policy. The burden of that criticism was that we spoke too kindly to our allies and sent them 'perfumed notes' instead of using threats and intimidation to compel them to do our bidding. I welcome constructive criticism. But the criticism I refer to attacks the very heart of American foreign policy."

The expedients proposed by McCarthy then were rejected out of hand. Asked about Davies, the Secretary said that two investigations of Davies were under way, by the State and Justice Departments, and that Davies himself had asked for a third as soon as McCarthy uttered his blast.

McCarthy was in Wisconsin when Dulles announced the break. Later in the day he flew back to Washington, where he was handed a copy of the Secretary's statement. He read it, and asked jocularly, "Do you think he was referring to me?" Then he said he would hold a press conference of his own in a day or two.

President Eisenhower had been urged to cancel his scheduled meeting with correspondents on the day after Dulles spoke out, for sharp questioning could be expected; but Ike faced up to the barrage and backed Dulles fully. He, too, rejected McCarthy's program for "getting tough" with our allies, and took issue with other portions of the senator's speech. The winning issue for the Republicans in 1954, Ike insisted, would be their record of having enacted a legislative program "enhancing the welfare of the people," not communism. He did not mention McCarthy by name, but the object of his irritation and displeasure was unmistakable, and the anti-McCarthy press played up that fact. The *Times* charged that McCarthy was trying to convert the struggle against communism into "a vehicle on which to ride to personal power," and James Reston felt that the President was reminding the party that—in the words of Winston Churchill—"if we open up a quarrel between the past and the present, we shall find we have lost the future." But Reston could not see how Eisenhower could stop the party quarrel. "Attack and attack, investigate and investigate, elect and elect," seemed to be the senator's formula for victory in 1954, and apparently he had the power and the allies to keep the investigations going, regardless of the President. "About all we can hope for is that he and his colleagues will investigate the right things."

McCarthy gave little encouragement to this hope. In a rebuttal delivered in a press conference that was as well attended as any at the White House, he said that some political enemies of all Republicans had suggested that he was challenging the President for the party's leadership, but "that suggestion is both ridiculous and untrue." He pledged his full support of all Republican candidates running in 1954, "because it is so important to this nation that the Republicans retain control of Congress." But he would not stop criticizing and exposing the party's mistakes because "one of the reasons why the Democrats were removed from office was their failure to recognize their own errors." Repeating his attack on the "very heart" of United States foreign policy, he said that "on this matter Secretary Dulles and I are in complete disagreement. In a republic such as ours there must be room for honest differences of opinion. I respect the honesty and sincerity of purpose of Secretary Dulles. However, I have such deep convictions on the subject that I shall continue to discuss the matter at every opportunity."

In reading this statement for the newsreel cameras, Joe added a suggestion that listeners might like to let the President know how they felt on this issue. "Now, I think President Eisenhower is an honorable man," he said. "I think he will follow the will of the

American people, if that can be made known to him. I should like
to urge every American who feels as I do about this blood-trade
with a mortal enemy to write or wire the President of the United
States and let him know how they feel so that he can be properly
guided in this matter."

The *Chicago Sun-Times* detected in McCarthy's statement an
echo of Marcus Antonius' funeral oration, designed to inflame the
mob against Caesar's murderers while ostensibly praising them—
"all, all, honorable men." And Joe's appeal did have an effect.
Letters and telegrams poured into the White House, although there
was disagreement on the number. By the third day, with telegrams
coming at the rate of 300 an hour, it appeared that at least 50,000
letters and wires had been delivered, although McCarthy claimed
the count was considerably higher. No breakdown on those "for"
and "against" was given, and McCarthy's critics claimed that the
co-called deluge was a flop: *Christian Century* pointed out that
Father Coughlin, the rabble-rouser of the Depression years, "could
bring an avalanche of a hundred thousand wires and letters down
on Washington with a single sentence in a Sunday afternoon broadcast." Nevertheless, the same commentary cautioned that it would
be rash to draw the conclusion that McCarthy was beginning to
lose his appeal, and a national poll conducted at this time seemed
to carry the same implication: sixty-five percent of those polled put
down "getting Communists out of government" as the top problem
they should like to see the administration tackling harder.

The *Toledo Blade* made its own sampling of the direct support
Eisenhower might count on in the showdown. An invitation printed
on the front page suggested that readers who wished to add their
names to a letter of endorsement to be sent to the White House
should telephone and say so. The letter read: "Dear Mr. President:
We supported you before and we do now. We still like Ike." After
a seven-hour struggle to handle the response, the *Blade* shut off
its switchboard and sent forty exhausted operators home. The
count was 10,194 calls received—9,870 for Ike, 324 for McCarthy.
But Joe himself said that in such a "popularity contest," Ike would
win by 40 to 1 every time.

[III]

Not all Joe's opponents believed that he had lost ground by
forcing the administration to the brink of a party schism; on the

liberal side, many thought he had actually gained strength. The comments of these critics were bitter. Said *The Nation*: "It should have been obvious to all not blinded by paranoia or bewitched by the cynical concentration on 'smart political tactics' that the administration's attempt to preempt the anti-Communist hoax would boomerang. Since Senator McCarthy's reasseveration of his monopoly of genius . . . even Brownell must be smarting, if not smarter. There are dangers for the uninitiated in gargling poison."

A week later, having pondered the situation more profoundly, *The Nation* came up with its final reasoned analysis and conclusion, namely, that Joe McCarthy was "driving for the White House," and there was a good possibility that he might succeed. "He has the weapons, the skill, the ruthlessness, and the total amorality to exploit his opportunities. For the first time in American history we are confronted by a demagogue with national appeal, whose tactics cut across all the barriers of race, class, religion, and income which have previously served to frustrate the pursuit of absolute power. Furthermore, his tactics have been strengthened—more than that, they have been prepared for him by the high priests of the mass media. Attempts to answer McCarthy by reliance upon reason are undercut by the cultivation of unreason and the destruction of critical intelligence by habits inculcated by the hucksters. This corruption is further underlined by the weak-kneed capitulation of the radio-television moguls in conceding to the Wisconsin senator the use of a full half-hour on a national network. Mr. Truman did not attack McCarthy. He took at the most a minute to explain the contemporary meaning of 'McCarthyism.' Does this imply that Senator McCarthy is the acknowledged spokesman for Mr. Brownell and the Eisenhower administration, which were, after all, the primary objects of Mr. Truman's attack?

"Those who voted for President Eisenhower in good faith must recognize this as the showdown. McCarthy has challenged both the President's policy and his position as leader of his party. If Eisenhower does not assume leadership now, if he does not accept this challenge and go to the people with a forthright declaration of independence and responsibility, McCarthy will boss the G.O.P."

Commonweal, which had consistently fought the "virus of 'McCarthyism,'" yielding neither to the hysteria of fear nor the shrill, surging demands for retribution, was outspoken. The date of McCarthy's broadcast might assume historical importance, *Common-*

weal surmised, because McCarthy's words on that day "actually contained [his] public declaration of war on the present administration, and perhaps his first public bid for the Republican nomination for the Presidency in 1956. . . . The battle lines are drawn. . . . In the past, many observers have consistently underestimated Senator McCarthy. We hope President Eisenhower and his advisers will not make that mistake now."

[IV]

There was no doubt that the President and his party faced a crisis of leadership; yet Eisenhower seemed diffident to act. The risk of provoking a party schism that would allow the Democrats to sweep back into power was always in his mind, although Joe's extremist critics, being mostly Democrats anyway, cared nothing for that factor; they urged, begged, beseeched, and belabored Eisenhower to make a stand against the arrogant encroachments of the senator. The *New Republic* regretfully reflected that "it takes two to make a fight," and only one of the parties in this instance seemed ready to do battle. McCarthy had outflanked his would-be supplanters, *New Republic* believed, by plain audacity—"restating his issue in terms so harsh and inclusive as to place it beyond his rivals' present reach." Brownell and those acting with him had said that, given time, they would solve the problem of Red infiltration; McCarthy had declared in his radio address that the threat "will be with us until our civilization wins or is destroyed." Brownell had said the problem of subversion was immense, but there were other problems, too; McCarthy answered, "No," all the nation's woes— high taxes, the draft, internal unrest, educational erosion—stemmed from this one cause, and all those who opposed taking any counter-measures necessary to meet this dire national emergency he denounced as "phony, deluded, fuzzy-minded, eggheaded liberals." The Eisenhower administration, McCarthy said, by dealing in "perfumed notes," had reduced the nation to a condition of "whining, whimpering appeasement," and only the utter destruction of the source of the threat would bring security; he had invoked the vengeful cry of Cato in the Roman Senate, "Delenda est Carthago!" (Carthage must be blotted out) as the only policy capable of insuring national survival.

Here and there a cautionary voice arose, warning against inflating McCarthy beyond his true dimensions by the very intensity of the attacks upon him. In *Newsweek,* Raymond Moley devoted an editorial to the subject, prefacing his remarks with a plain statement of his personal attitude toward McCarthy and "McCarthyism." He approved of McCarthy's objectives, he stated, and he did not disapprove of his methods. It was his own opinion that no innocent person had been harmed permanently by anything the senator had done, although if "innocent people" meant "the fools who entered the Communist party before 1939,* I do not think we should bemoan the fact that their foolishness has found them out. Some of them have repented their foolishness. They should be forgiven but not exalted. They should be excluded from places of trust in government or education."

Having taken this stand, Moley continued editorially:

"The eminence of a McCarthy . . . is a product of the fright and anger of a deceived and injured public. . . . And the pre-eminence of McCarthy over other useful investigators is due as much to the attacks of his enemies as to his own efforts. But the attacks upon him are creating in him something more than an instrument for an unpleasant job or the symbol of the anger of an outraged nation. These attacks are making him and his work not only *an* issue but *the* issue. . . . To elevate 'McCarthyism' to a national and international issue is to drive to McCarthy's support and defense many people who regard him as a useful worker in a limited field, but not a towering national figure. . . . His scope of interests is too narrow and his mind too circumscribed for the tasks of high statesmanship. But his enemies may make him think he is the savior of the nation.

"Let us not be silly," concluded this warning against "building up" McCarthy. "When a Congressman is out there fighting for his political life, he isn't going to let Eisenhower or Stevenson or us pundits of the press define the issues of 1954. He is going to say what will get him votes. And if the fever of the nation is aroused by screams against 'McCarthyism,' that is what the voters are going to want to hear about."

* Date of the Hitler-Stalin pact.

Ruffles and Skirmishes

Conciliation was still in the President's mind, and during the closing weeks of the autumn of 1953, with tension mounting steadily between the rival factions, the peace-at-any-price advocates in the White House instigated two behind-the-scenes attempts to come to terms with the rambunctious senator. Both revealed a total lack of understanding of McCarthy's character.

The first overture was undertaken by the President's brother, Dr. Milton S. Eisenhower, president of Pennsylvania State University, who often carried out delicate missions for the White House. A luncheon meeting in New York was arranged with George E. Sokolsky, syndicated right-wing columnist and close adviser of Senator McCarthy. Over the luncheon Sokolsky was sounded out as to whether there might not be some way by which "things could be worked out" satisfactorily to both sides. Sokolsky doubted it. The senator, he said, was not in a conciliatory mood; feeling sure of his footing, he intended to push ahead. Also, the White House had nothing to offer that McCarthy wanted: social recognition meant less than nothing to him, for he detested social functions and appeared at them only when he could not avoid it, and patronage had never been a primary concern with him.

Presumably this reply was relayed to the President, and a short while later, during the same month, a direct approach was tried. Senator Taft had died recently, and his administrative assistant, I. Jack Martin, had joined the White House staff as a contact man with the conservatives on Capitol Hill. Martin sent word that he would like to talk with the senator privately, without any press interference, somewhere away from the Capitol. The home of Mrs. Ruth McCormick Tankersley (the former Ruth McCormick Miller), publisher of the *Washington Times-Herald,* was chosen. McCarthy drove there one evening with Roy Cohn, as if paying a social call. Martin was on hand, and he and the senator adjourned to the basement den.

After about twenty minutes, they reappeared, McCarthy looking grim and Martin crestfallen. Taking Cohn aside, the senator said: "Poor Jack! He has got to give blood or he'll be out of a job. Listen to the deal they offered me—this one really takes the cake! Stop all public hearings and hold only executive sessions. The minutes of the executive sessions will be taken to Ike personally. He will read them closely and take what they call 'appropriate action on an administrative level' against the people named in the testimony." He had spurned the proposal out of hand, of course, although Martin had pleaded that he "think it over." He had thought it over, for almost a whole second, Joe had replied, and the answer was still "No!" Not only did the proposal amount to unconditional surrender on McCarthy's part, it was ridiculous on its face. McCarthy's committee had been set up for the precise purpose of keeping an eye on the executive branch; and what could be sillier than to hand over its findings to the people being investigated and trust them to take disciplinary action against themselves? What assurance was there that the findings wouldn't wind up in the Presidential wastebasket?

The sheer absurdity of this overture convinced McCarthy that the liberals were panicky, and were now determined to rule or ruin; his scornful rejection therefore would infuriate them and lead to an all-out attempt to destroy him politically. Personally he rather relished the prospect of a knockdown fight. Riding home after that unproductive evening, Joe told Cohn his view of the situation and said, grinning, "I guess I'll just have to lead a life deprived of tea and watercress sandwiches on the White House lawn!"

[II]

The senator's strength lay in the fact that he really was independent. He was running for no office at the moment, and the lure of the White House did not tempt him. The Presidency was cramping, and like the corsair he was, he needed to be free to fire on any unfriendly sail that hove into sight, and either capture a prize or, if the contest grew too hot, make all sail away and try elsewhere. He was already a national force; people told him so and he knew it.

The ease with which he had commandeered $300,000 of free broadcast time had proved the reality and magnitude of his power. Politically he was effective for the very reasons that made him an enigma to some of the astute politicians around him. These men were baffled by his recklessness; his audacity was beyond their comprehension, and they marveled at his extraordinary sense of timing. Again and again he had taken his opposition by surprise.

Doubtless a contributory element in McCarthy's cold-shouldering "the boys in Ike's camp," as he called the White House group trying to neutralize him, was his personal low estimate of the President. He rated Eisenhower a lightweight, easily manipulated by a coterie of liberals. For Ike's performance in office McCarthy generally had contempt, although in public he preserved the attitude of loyalty that party unity required. Joe had no idea of leaving the Republican party; he was perfectly content to work inside it. His following, while large, was amorphous to the extent that it lacked any firm nucleus or central organization. Nor did McCarthy make the slightest gesture toward mobilizing this support in a clearly defined group, party, or association. He offered no comprehensive political program, but except for details accepted the platform of his party. In the Senate he stood basically for the same things as at least those of his colleagues who were in the conservative camp, his only point of difference being the greater intensity with which he embraced the issue of communism. Politically a maverick, he was now in a position where he might be driven into radical measures by the increasingly direct efforts of the liberal wing of his party to force him to conform to their policy; and this he would never consent to, for it would mean giving up the one issue on which he had risen to eminence, and which by now had become inseparably associated with his name. On the durability of that issue would depend his own political prestige and his rise to greater influence, or his decline.

[III]

During the next few weeks, attacks rained on McCarthy from all sides. He was challenged in the courts by witnesses who denied his right to question them about subversion; the courts upheld Joe. He was blasted by politicians and educators. He maintained a running feud with Dr. Nathan M. Pusey, president of Harvard University, after Pusey took umbrage at McCarthy's calling the Harvard faculty "a mess" because of Communist infiltration. The exchange of asperities had special piquancy because Pusey, like Joe, hailed from Appleton, Wisconsin.

Senator Lehman, never wavering in his crusade against McCarthy, told the Friends Committee on National Legislation that the Soviets had gained more from the "paralyzing influence of 'McCarthyism' " than they could have gained from a knowledge of all the nation's vital secrets. Assailing the "cultivated frenzy and hysteria of today," the New York senator warned that what had started as a "guerilla activity" conducted by McCarthy had become a "full-scale assault on the government service, the schools, the stage, the publishing world, and even the churches."

In Pittsburgh, Methodist Bishop Lloyd C. Wicke told a ministerial conference that Senator McCarthy and Representative Velde, chairman of the House Un-American Activities Committee, were using the "techniques and practices of our enemies in the name of national defense and vigilance." He called them "rightwing subversives." *

The same general view led to a student rag at the University of Toronto, when hundreds of youths, draped in Ku Klux Klan hoods and bedsheets, romped around the campus chanting "Burn McCarthy!" and "Down with Joe." While speakers inveighed against his "terror tactics" the senator was burned in effigy. Although the Canadian press by and large heartily opposed McCarthy, the *Toronto Globe and Mail* denounced the students' "depraved mumbo-jumbo" and called the gambol an imitation of mere "boll-weevil decadence." Yet oddly enough, a Gallup Poll conducted in Canada at this time produced results which indicated that the Dominion's press was not representative of the public mind. Of those polled, 43 percent were able to identify the senator and his issue, an extraordinarily high percentage for a foreign political figure. Thirty-three percent approved of him; thirty-five percent disapproved; and the remainder held no strong opinion either way. In French-speaking, Catholic Quebec province, the vote was 4 to 1 in Joe's favor. It was lightest in extreme western Canada.

The senator meanwhile kept on with his probing of conditions both at Fort Monmouth and in General Electric defense plants.

---

* Long before this *The Nation* had "proved," by strict logical deduction, that Senator McCarthy was a concealed Communist, "boring from within."

There the management announced that any employe who refused to tell any congressional authority whether he was a Communist would be suspended automatically and, if persisting in the refusal, would be fired. The order applied to 131 plants and 230,000 employes.

In the Fort Monmouth hearings, witness after witness refused to answer questions about espionage or Communist ties. One radar expert, Aaron H. Coleman, was suspended after being identified as a member of the Young Communist League, although he denied it. Outside the hearing room he admitted that he had attended one meeting of the league, at Julius Rosenberg's request, going with "an open mind." The chief intelligence agent at Fort Monmouth, Andrew J. Reid, however, testified that when he asked Coleman whether he had taken some forty restricted and confidential documents to his home, the latter "at first denied it; then he said maybe; finally he said yes." Coleman argued that he was authorized to take the documents off the base, but agreed that the Russians would have got "a pretty clear picture" of our radar secrets if they had seen the papers. Reid testified that in thirteen years at Monmouth he had never encountered anything "as serious as this," and McCarthy threatened to seek Coleman's indictment for espionage as well as perjury.

Since this threat could relate only to recent or current espionage (not to wartime spying, on which the statute of limitations had run), reporters wondered whether fresh evidence had been found that would shatter the harmony thus far prevailing between the committee and the Pentagon. Secretary Stevens, after all, had stated formally that the Army had been able to find no evidence of recent espionage at Monmouth, and the question arose whether McCarthy might not be jabbing deliberately in an effort to provoke the administration into showing its hostility to him more openly. A clue to this seemed to be intimated in the removal of General Lawton from his Fort Monmouth command.

The action attracted little attention at the time, but afterward it was recalled that Lawton had been complimented by McCarthy on his splendid cooperation with the subcommittee. Lawton had testified in two executive sessions and attended others. His testimony in part had related to what he construed as the apathy which he had encountered when he attempted to clear up lax security conditions throughout the installation. Repeated warnings from the FBI apparently had been ignored, he said, and he himself had been hampered by military regulations, so that he had been able to accomplish little. At one point McCarthy had asked the General: "Would you say that since you have taken over . . . you have been working to get rid of the accumulation of security risks?"

Lawton had replied: "I have been working for the last twenty-one months trying to accomplish what is being accomplished in the last two weeks."

McCarthy: "So that you would say that in the past weeks you are getting some effective results?"

Lawton: "Absolutely, that we have not gotten in the last four years."

Then McCarthy probed deeper: "Could you tell us why it is only in the last two or three weeks that you are getting these effective results?"

"Yes, but I had better not," was Lawton's cautious answer. The inference drawn, of course, was that obstruction, resistance, or just plain apathy at higher levels had stymied Lawton's efforts to "clean house," and McCarthy had alluded to this in conversation with Secretary Stevens. The Secretary, in turn, had asked McCarthy whether McCarthy would object if General Lawton were transferred to another command. The senator had replied, bearing in mind the circumstances, that he certainly would take such a transfer amiss, and the subject had been dropped.

Some time thereafter General Lawton was ordered to Walter Reed Hospital for a periodic physical checkup, and soon after that a rumor circulated in Washington that the General had been found to be suffering from a physical disability that would require his remaining in the hospital for treatment. Further rumors alleged that the patient had been installed in a luxurious suite and provided with every comfort, but sealed off from further cooperation with McCarthy. Nor would General Lawton return to Fort Monmouth. That was his last command, as he was retired.

Was this an indication of stiffening Army resistance to McCarthy's brash invasion of their closely guarded preserve? With an old soldier in the White House, perhaps the Army was drumming up courage to oppose the senator in a way the State Department had never done. To onlookers the situation was puzzling, and no clarification was thrown on the problem when a speaker at West Point Military Academy sharply rapped McCarthy and his activities.

The speaker was Telford Taylor, a reserve brigadier general and former chief American prosecutor at the Nuremberg war crimes trials. Taylor, now a lawyer practicing in New York, told the cadets that Senator McCarthy was a "dangerous adventurer" making "an unscrupulous grab for publicity with his accusations and undermining Army morale by his action at Fort Monmouth." The hearings, Taylor said, were "calculated to create panic, destroy public confidence in the Army, and undermine military morale." Nothing, he contended, had been disclosed to give substance to the accusations, and the device of excluding the press from the closed sessions and then giving reporters the senator's own version of the testimony was an "outrageous procedure, designed for the sole purpose of publicity." Taylor also criticized Stevens and the Army high command for their "failure to stand up against this shameful abuse of the Congressional investigating power."

The prominence of the speaker gave his remarks wide acceptance, and McCarthy was not slow to respond. His immediate reply was in the form of a letter to Major General Frederick J. Irving, superintendent of West Point, demanding an explanation of why General Taylor had been invited to address the cadets and "spend most of his time in an emotional tirade against Congressional committees, especially our investigation of Communist infiltration and espionage at Fort Monmouth." He stated also that Taylor's civil service file had been "flagged" on a question of loyalty, which, he wrote, "as you know, is for the purpose of preventing his employment by any other government agency on the grounds stated in the 'flag.' You will note that the 'flagging' was not on security grounds, but on loyalty grounds. . . . If the loyalty grounds on which his file was 'flagged' are valid, I assume the Army will take the necessary steps to have his reserve commission revoked."

McCarthy showed reporters a photostat of Taylor's file which did have a check mark in the "flag" square and the notation: "Unsolved question of loyalty."

General Taylor was quick to strike back. A "flag," he said, merely indicated that the file contained derogatory information, which should be taken into consideration, and "anyone who has held important public office and taken positions on public issues" was likely to have critical letters written about him, as Senator McCarthy should know. As for the senator's investigations, in Taylor's opinion they had achieved "very little, if anything, of value. They have done a great deal of harm."

Sought out for a comment on this, McCarthy quoted some of Taylor's fellow prosecutors at Nuremberg, British and American, as accusing Taylor of "moral fraud" and grossly improper conduct. ("Of course, the *Daily Worker* praised him," was McCarthy's aside.) As for his own investigative methods, the senator pointed out that "the fairness of the subcommittee's procedures has been complimented repeatedly, not only by witnesses who have appeared, but also by attorneys who have defended Fifth amendment cases." As for having allegedly damaged Army morale at Monmouth, Joe said he was "happy to plead guilty to damaging the morale of Communists and espionage agents, regardless of whether they are at Fort Monmouth or any other place in this country."

Meanwhile, Eisenhower remained mum. Senators returning for the reconvening of Congress directly after Christmas deplored the deep division in Republican ranks; nevertheless the returning Republicans were by no means unanimous in pledging unqualified support for the President. Senator Alexander Smith of New Jersey believed that on foreign policy there was "a lot to be said for McCarthy." Senator Knowland of California, since Senator Taft's death the Senate majority leader, also gave support to McCarthy's position on trade with Red China, and he disagreed absolutely with the President on what would be the big issue in the 1954 elections; he was sure it would be communism, and he felt that would be the chief issue in 1956 also.

Joe continued to scoff at the notion that he was aiming at the White House. Interviewed on the radio, he said emphatically that he had "no intention of ever running for the Presidency, no desire to run." Asked whether he would respond to a draft, he retorted that "nobody was ever drafted for the Presidency unless he started the wind himself," and any talk of a man's being nominated "without going out for the job" was nonsense.

At the same time, he went out of his way to allay talk of friction between himself and the Pentagon. He prefaced a public hearing by explaining that the purpose of his investigation was to "expose potential espionage," not to "take over the job of the Justice Department and prove espionage beyond a reasonable doubt." But in a jab at Army security procedures under President Truman, he added that "it becomes more and more clear that, up to at least the first of this year [the incoming of the Republicans] there apparently was no concern for the security of our secrets." Under the new administration, all that had been changed; Secretary Stevens and "those who are now in charge" had been cooperating fully with the committee, and "I think they are just as concerned as we are about the very, very unusual picture unfolding. More and more they are doing something about it."

This spirit of sweet concord apparently extended even to the White House. On the eve of the new session of Congress, the President met for three days with congressional leaders to consult on the legislative program. A tougher fight against subversives was included. The consultations on security problems brought Eisenhower and McCarthy face to face, and on leaving the executive mansion Joe told the press that he was "not displeased with anything I heard."

Upon getting back to his office he seemed to think this was a grudging comment, and he telephoned an amplification of his statement. "This is the first time I have had an opportunity to watch the President in action over a period of time," he added. "I was tremendously impressed with his handling of the conference and his detailed knowledge of every subject or piece of proposed legislation that was discussed."

Plainly it was the season of good will. The White House tree was lighted with traditional ceremony, and reporters observed less heavy drinking at holiday parties than in recent years.

The McCarthys had flown to Miami for three days at the invitation of Vice-President Nixon. Besieged there by reporters, Joe extended a sprig of mistletoe to the old soldier on the Potomac by intimating that his investigations in the new year might take a different turn, away from the Army. For one thing, he wanted to look into some tax cases that had been compromised "at ridiculously low figures—as low as twenty cents on the dollar." Some of the settlements, he said, were "inexplicable on the surface." This would bring the Treasury Department under Joe's watchful eye, and the Army might get a respite.

In keeping with the spirit of the season, one reporter asked genially, "How's married life, Joe?" With an arch glance at his wife, the senator asked dutifully:

"Can I hide behind the Fifth Amendment on that one, Jeanie?"

"George Washington
with a Running Sore"

Underneath the surface benignity of the Christmastide, currents of hatred, suspicion, and lust for power were flowing with mounting intensity. The Democrats were swarming back to the capital in an angry mood. They were furious with McCarthy for labeling theirs the "party of treason"; Attorney General Brownell's treatment of former President Truman had sent their blood pressure spurting to new heights of indignation; and Governor Dewey of New York had triggered a fresh eruption by remarking that the Democrats were afraid the American people would discover "what a nice feeling it is to have a government which is not infested with spies and traitors." As a result, powerful Democratic senators were reported to be preparing to raise a partywide challenge to McCarthy in the new session, and were enlisting the help of liberal and anti-McCarthy Republicans. The plan was to force the equivalent of a Senate vote of no confidence in the Wisconsin terror by one of three methods: (1) denying his subcommittee further authority unless he took back the three bolting Democrats on their own terms; (2) bringing the subcommittee's work to a halt by withholding funds; (3) creating a joint Senate-House committee to take over all investigation of subversion.

But wherever McCarthy entered, confusion followed, and the above proposals were no sooner bruited than one powerful Democrat, Senator McCarran of Nevada, served notice that he would never vote for a joint committee, because "they never get anywhere and I'm opposed to them." Besides, there was plenty of room for committees of both houses to operate in the field of subversion, he felt, although he also thought that McCarthy had "stepped over into a field where he was not intended to function at all." Much as he liked Joe, and although Joe had done good work, McCarran was of the opinion that the Senate's internal security committee, of which he was ranking minority member with Senator Jenner as chairman, was able to do all the work necessary on the Senate side in probing subversion. Also, McCarran demanded, if McCarthy had to be curbed, why didn't the Republicans do it? After all, he was a Republican, not the responsibility of the Democrats. The Senate minority leader, Lyndon Johnson, shared this feeling: let the quarreling Republicans handle their own problem.

From Miami, McCarthy signified that he had no quarrel with Senator McCarran, but he felt his committee was authorized to "dig out communism" too, although that was not its sole area of jurisdiction.

Washington, which at all times is one vast echo gallery, suddenly seethed with a rumor that Joe had given private assurances to the administration that he would concentrate on other fields in the new year, and the administration was said to have promised in return to furnish him with leads rich in headline appeal—juicy tax files, for instance. Senator Ellender of Louisiana refused to believe the rumor, and besides, McCarthy wouldn't keep such a promise. Ellender had long fought to curtail the outlay of taxpayers' money on investigations, and he called for a halt to voting big budgets for such activities. What had McCarthy done with the $200,000 he had received a year ago, Ellender asked, except to support a horde of "professional snoopers" who were more interested in "glorifying their bosses," the investigating committees' chairmen, than in doing productive work?

McCarthy bounced back to Washington full of vim, and in a fine fit of outrage denounced the appeasement rumor. Whoever spread the story that he had promised the administration to pull in his horns "was either lied to, or he was deliberately lying," he exclaimed, banging the desk. Certainly he would investigate in other fields, but no "men of little minds and less morals" were going to limit his scope. One big investigation he was working on involved graft, inefficiency, corruption, and mismanagement, with communism a sideline; he wouldn't identify the target yet, saying he wouldn't be ready to start public hearings for another six months.

"Just before the election?" sniped a reporter, and Joe said, grinning, "You go to hell."

Later the target was identified as Alaska, but McCarthy said he didn't plan to go north for a while—"at least not during the winter."

The *Washington Star* said the source of the McCarthy "peace gesture" story was the Vice-President. Nixon said nothing, but it was recalled that he and Joe had been hobnobbing in Miami recently.

In this way the confusion multiplied, until Republicans and Democrats alike began to doubt that any attempt to curb McCarthy could succeed; too many persons were taking a hand. Some Democrats still hoped to deny him funds, but these were thrown into a panic when word leaked out (inspired by Joe himself) that he was going to present an operating budget of $300,000, instead of the $200,000 he had been granted a year before, contending that he needed to double his staff of eleven investigators to cope with the load of work already assumed. Right away, on the Democratic side, talk of refusing any money changed to prayerfully expressed hope that the senator could be induced to accept just what he had received last year.

Joe dared the Democrats to slash his funds. If they tried it, he said, he would brand them again as the party that favored "covering up spies and traitors." Furthermore, he intended to fight Communists "just as roughly as before," and he denied that he was being pressured to shift his targets. "No administration official, from Eisenhower on down the line, has ever remotely suggested how our committee should operate or what our field of investigation should be," he told reporters; and he predicted that on the matter of cutting his committee's funds, if the Democrats should "win that one, I guarantee it will be the most Pyrrhic victory in history." A newsman asked what he meant by "Pyrrhic." That, said Joe, was a victory in which "you destroy yourself." Then he dashed away to address a conference where he called for a full-scale investigation of communism in colleges. Red agents, having students as a "captive audience," could do even greater harm than radar spies, he charged, and he personally assailed Harvard president Pusey for his refusal to dismiss Professor Furry, who had invoked the Fifth Amendment when questioned about Communist activities before McCarthy's committee. The senator repeated that he planned to introduce a bill to deny tax exemption to foundations and educational institutions "which insist upon employing Fifth Amendment Communists. Touch their pocketbooks and they get religion."

A score for Joe came from the judiciary when United States Judge Irving R. Kaufman refused an injunction to two witnesses before

McCarthy's subcommittee which would have prevented McCarthy from forcing them to produce records of their suspension as workers in the Fort Monmouth radar laboratories. In a decision affirming the rights of congressional committees of investigation, Judge Kaufman ruled that it appeared entirely clear that "neither this nor any court may prescribe the subjects of Congressional investigations. Were a court empowered to limit in advance the subject matter of Congressional investigations, violence would be done to the principle of separation of the powers upon which our entire political system is based. Justice Brandeis warned of the danger of encroachment by one department of the government upon another, when he spoke of the dangers of 'usurpation, proceeding by gradual encroachment rather than by violent acts . . .' If a prior restraint is to be imposed upon the defendant, it must come from the Congress, not from the courts. . . . The legislature cannot be compelled to submit to the prior approval and censorship of the judiciary before it may ask questions or inspect documents through its legislative committees, or even before it enacts legislation, any more than the judiciary can be compelled to submit its rulings or decisions to the legislative approval."

This placed the matter of curbing McCarthy, if that was really desired, squarely up to Congress, and specifically the Senate. But the real temper of both houses was shown when, on January 7, President Eisenhower read his State of the Union message, containing his legislative recommendations, before a joint session. As the President mounted the rostrum every eye was on him and on Senator McCarthy, placed near the front at Eisenhower's left. The senator appeared confident and at ease. The President first turned toward the visitors gallery, on his left, where Mrs. Eisenhower was seated, and bowed; as he did so, McCarthy caught his attention with a wave of the hand. Ike smiled and waved back. Then he turned toward the other side of the chamber and acknowledged the applause there.

The President's program included a call for reduced spending to assure the continuance of the nation's prosperity and defense, and a revolutionary proposal to strip persons convicted of advocating the overthrow of the government by force or violence of their citizenship. Calling the Communist conspiracy "akin to treason," the President said that any American conspiring for the forceful overthrow of the government should be treated as "having, by such act, renounced his allegiance to the United States and forfeited his United States citizenship."

The proposal surprised and delighted the Congress, and it was greeted with yells of approval. Throughout the speech the speaker was applauded forty-five times, for the most part perfunctorily; but the citizenship-loss proposal brought a thunderclap of applause. The next noisiest demonstration followed the announcement that the United States would continue to give military and economic aid to Chiang Kai-shek. The President's statement that the United States ought to share some atomic secrets with its allies was greeted with stony silence.

Settled beyond all further question was who had been correct in predicting that communism would be the paramount issue in the coming elections—Eisenhower or McCarthy. A bill to enact the punitive citizenship measure was introduced at once by Senator Margaret Chase Smith. It was a time of fear and suspicion, and the fear and suspicion were growing more intense every day.

[II]

Oddly, Senator McCarthy now backed away from his earlier guess on the winning issue for 1954. When polled by *U.S. News & World Report*, he placed the restoration of farm prices at the top of the list. "Prices must be put back to where they were when they started to toboggan two years ago," he said. "If you give people good farm prices, and show how the opposition played with Communists, there will be no question of a victory equal to or greater than 1952. But the Communist issue will not win the election if farm prices are low. It is just as simple as that."

There was no doubt about the nationwide revulsion against Communists and the Soviet threat. Almost daily reports came from all over the country of schoolteachers dismissed for refusal to testify regarding asserted Communist links, and almost without exception the courts were sustaining these dismissals. Loyalty oaths burgeoned; state and local authorities prescribed them for employment, and many industrial firms followed suit.*

* Even the "good, gray" *New York Times* was not impervious to the general urge, although its formal surrender would take place only in 1955, after specific accusations of being "soft on Communists" had been made by the Senate internal Security Committee, then under Democratic control. The policy adopted there-

In California, the entire state service, including the educational system, was thrown into turmoil by stringent loyalty oath enactments. The cry arose that the right of intellectual inquiry was being denied and free speech threatened, although a contrary, and probably larger, faction thought that if a person was loyal to the United States, why should he object to saying so? And if he had never been a Soviet spy, why should he hesitate to proclaim that fact, but by invoking the protection of the Constitution against possible self-incrimination in effect plead guilty by inference? The storm echoed throughout the nation, to the detriment of orderly process and of real education. A vindictive spirit seemed to permeate all public discussion. Tempers were inflamed. The *New Republic* raged at President Eisenhower's "degrading refusal" to break with McCarthy, contending that the action "bewildered" the President's friends and rendered his own vaunted nobility of character suspect: He is George Washington with a running sore . . . still firing salvos over Joe's head, not at Joe himself."

The United States court of appeals, in denying William Remington's appeal against his perjury conviction, jabbed at his contention that he had been "entrapped." He had indeed, the majority decision read, but "not by devious means and methods employed by the government, but by his own acts. He is caught in a web of his own duplicity."

In a talk before the Speech Association of America, Barnet Baskerville, of the University of Washington, bracketed Senator McCarthy with "other prominent misleaders of the people," although differing from them in the nature of his appeal. Other demagogues, said the speaker, had appealed to selfishness and greed—

---

after by the *Times* was this: any employe who refused to cooperate with the management's own screening process (i.e., answer questions regarding Communist involvement) would be dismissed; but an employe who cooperated with the management on this score, although defying a Congressional inquiry, would be retained. The *Times* reported that of twenty-three employes who were called before the Senate committee, three refused to cooperate with either management or the committee and were fired. Seventeen who cooperated with management, but defied the committee, were kept in their jobs. Also retained were three who, although cooperating with the *Times,* defied the Senate and were cited for contempt. Testimony before a congressional committee was under oath, rendering the witness vulnerable to perjury prosecution, whereas statements made before an employer carried no such risk. For this reason some criticized the *Times'* loyalty procedure as a "hollow sham."

"to the desire to get something." But McCarthy appealed "to the desire to get somebody." The attack received wide coverage in the press.

As if in response, Joe headed into the educators' preserve and held a televised hearing in Boston, during which Professor Furry and Leon J. Kamin, a research assistant in Harvard's department of social relations, admitted former membership in the Communist party. But they defied McCarthy when he demanded that they name others who were in the party with them. Both witnesses had previously invoked the Fifth Amendment, and McCarthy questioned whether either had really left the Communist ranks. He expressed his hope that Eisenhower's citizenship proposal would become law, because such persons, "responsible for the deaths of thousands of American boys," did not deserve the protection of their country. He heaped scorn on "Pusey's Fifth Amendment Communists" and said of Furry that it was "inconceivable that a university which has had the reputation of a great university should keep this kind of creature teaching young Americans."

Asked if he intended to call Dr. Pusey to testify, the chairman snapped: "I didn't see why. He has already made his position quite clear that he will go on maintaining a privileged sanctuary for Fifth Amendment Communists."

The next day, in a hearing on Communists in defense plants, Joe paid his disrespects further to Harvard and his fellow Appletonian, Dr. Pusey. A witness who had "taken the Fifth" asked to have a question repeated; he had mentioned that he had studied law at Harvard. Sneering, Joe said, "I should think that a Harvard law student could understand a simple question." When that witness and two others noisily "invoked the Fifth," McCarthy had them ejected from the room; it required five marshals to remove one shouter who had been identified by an FBI undercover agent as a Communist.

In Baltimore, meanwhile, a man who had given McCarthy testimony supporting the senator's charge of security breaches at Fort Monmouth pleaded guilty to failure to disclose his former membership in a Communist-dominated labor union when applying for a defense plant job. Both the prosecutor and Senator McCarthy urged a suspended sentence, saying that the man had been extremely co-operative, but the judge swept aside their pleas and handed out a sentence of four months in prison.

[III]

On another level, five distinguished former ambassadors sternly
indicted the "flimsy attacks" being made on the nation's diplomatic
corps. The five—Norman Armour, Robert Woods Bliss, Joseph C.
Grew, William Phillips, and G. Howland Shaw: all veterans of the
foreign service, all retired—in a letter to *The New York Times*
deplored the current personnel and security policies of the State
Department and expressed alarm over the "sinister results." The
department's present course, they warned, was "laying the foundation of a foreign service competent to serve a totalitarian government rather than the government of the United States as we have
heretofore known it."

Although not named, the targets of this blast were clearly Senator
McCarthy and his reputed "man Friday" in the State Department,
Scott McLeod, who as head of both the security and personnel
offices had stirred up bitter resentment by his control of advance-
ment and promotions. Much of the criticism contained in the letter
had been voiced before, but not by such eminent citizens. "Fear,"
the five retired envoys wrote, "is playing an important part in American life at the present time," and, as a result, "self-confidence, confidence in others, the sense of fair play, and the instinct to protect
the rights of the nonconformists are—temporarily, it is to be hoped
—in abeyance."

McCarthy ignored this development, and Secretary Dulles suggested that the five critics "didn't have quite a clear picture" of the
department's security setup. But some support for the expressed
alarm was seen in a remark by a former Assistant Secretary of State,
Edward J. Barrett. In the course of briefing a delegation of visiting
European newsmen, Barrett cautioned the group against misreading
the political signs. "The people of Italy, France, Great Britain, The
Netherlands, Belgium, Portugal, Iceland, and Denmark," said Barrett, "see us as a nation that has gone off on an emotional binge of
witch-hunting, book-burning, and the like"; but such impressions,
he advised, were "vastly exaggerated." Unfortunately, the remark
coincided with what became known as the Norwalk Incident.

As a feature of a national membership drive being conducted by
the Veterans of Foreign Wars, the Mulroy-Tarlov-Aquino VFW
post in Norwalk, Connecticut, became involved in some amateur

"spy-hunting," the exposure of which stirred up angry resentment in the town and elsewhere. Members of the post had been turning in to a special, secret committee the names and addresses of residents whose behavior seemed in one way or another to be "Communistic." The committee was said to be made up of men "from all walks of life." They sifted the reports received and, if they judged there was sufficient weight of evidence, passed the information along to the FBI. The committee was so secret that no member knew who all the others were.

A public outcry was raised against this instance of what the state office of Americans for Democratic Action denounced as use of "police state methods of secret smear." Officers of the post defended the activity. Said Charles J. Post, a member: "There is nothing fly-by-night about it. It is designed to wake up our own people in this town. We have more or less been alerted by the national organization to keep our community active and wise. I won't say that we received a directive to do this; it's not exactly that. But it's the sort of thing that's being done in other towns across the country."

The post commander, Albert A. Beres, owner of a service station in nearby Darien, maintained that the policy authorizing the campaign had been laid down in a resolution at the VFW encampment in El Paso, Texas, in 1926, charging the membership with the duty of reporting any persons believed to be engaged in subversive activities.

Beres resented the suggestion that the veterans were "snooping behind bushes, watching houses, and acting like totalitarians. I can't tell you whether I have personally turned in the names of Norwalk people," he told a reporter. "But you can say that sources close to the officials of the VFW have done so. We aren't judges. A man with a tendency to be leftish may be all right. It doesn't mean that every name turned in is that of a Communist or subversive person; lots of good Americans might have been pushed into such activities long ago. If a man has a good conscience, why should he worry?"

This was merely the beginning of the affair. Protests in Norwalk were loud, and the national commander of the VFW, Wayne E. Richards, denied that the organization was engaged in a "witch-hunt"; he stressed that the names of suspects were not published. Senator Potter, of McCarthy's committee, said there was nothing new in the activity, but advised that it should be carried on with caution. Senator McCarthy thought the program was "excellent." At a meeting of another Norwalk post, the practice was ratified after three hours of heated debate. The Americanization director of the VFW criticized the action in Norwalk, and the adjutant of the Iowa department of VFW made clear that the members in his state would never adopt the practice. In places as far apart as Albuquerque and Boston, VFW revealed that they had been cooperating quietly with the FBI for years; the American Legion in Boston, it was learned, had been giving its files regularly to Massachusetts investigators of Communist infiltration.

Even President Eisenhower was challenged at his next press conference to say whether he approved what was going on in Norwalk. Well, the President guessed, he didn't see how anybody could be prevented from reporting Communist suspects to the FBI, and there were libel and slander laws to cope with false charges. But didn't he realize that the names of persons secretly denounced were not published, so they could not have recourse to the libel laws? "Don't you think this is a threat to civil liberties?" Ike stuck to his point: there was no way to prevent a person putting something down on paper and sending it to somebody else, and the libel laws covered that.

Then it came out that what the Norwalk veterans were doing was in strict compliance with numerous Presidential directives, beginning with one issued by President Franklin Delano Roosevelt on September 6, 1939, directing the FBI to assume the task of assuring internal security against espionage and sabotage. There had been renewals by Roosevelt, President Truman, and Eisenhower himself a few weeks back. Each directive had been accompanied by an appeal to the public, to patriotic organizations, and to local police to report suspicious persons and activities to the FBI. And J. Edgar Hoover had followed up with his own appeal to the public, with suggestions in detail. He had stressed that one purpose of the appeal was to discourage local vigilante groups and channel all information to a single responsible source.

Norwalk did not see it that way. The town was torn by lasting bitterness. Stories of harassment became commonplace. A couple moving there from another state, for instance, found themselves subjected to spiteful annoyances, they did not know why. Their telephone rang at all hours, anonymous callers mumbled threats and spat obscenities. One morning they found a sign driven into their front lawn, "This House for Sale," by whom and for what reason they never found out. The malaise seemed universal, for what was happening in Norwalk was happening elsewhere. In the metaphor preferred by *The Nation,* the virus of "McCarthyism" had spread until it had become a plague.

[IV]

Events in Washington crowded upon each other. The three bolting Democrats—Senators McClellan, Symington, and Jackson—at length agreed to return to McCarthy's subcommittee, although only after they had wrung concessions. Hiring and firing of staff was taken out of the hands of the chairman and placed under majority control; the minority were assigned a counsel and clerk of their own; and the parent Government Operations Committee was given authority over the public hearings, when such were opposed by the Democratic minority. The "surrender" was definitely a setback for McCarthy; but the terms were announced in a spirit of joviality, with Symington and Joe laughingly agreeing to "bury the hatchet." Where was not stated.

The Democratic "walk" had lasted six months and sixteen days, and the truce had been effected under extreme pressure from both Republican and Democratic leaders. McCarthy had been in an unusually placable mood, perhaps because the Senate had not yet approved his request for funds. One week later this matter came to a vote, and although no serious doubt existed that the money would be granted, the Senate galleries were crowded with correspondents and spectators in anticipation of fireworks.

The three-hour debate was dominated by Senators Ellender and McCarthy. Ellender was making his annual pitch to economize on funds for all committees. He conceded that there had been "lots of laxity" about communism under previous administrations, and he thought that McCarthy had done "a lot of good in dramatizing the Communist issue before the country." But he was against duplication of effort and expense, and the job of fighting Communists belonged to Senator Jenner's Internal Security Committee.

McCarthy denied that there had been any duplication during the past year, but he declined to give any guarantee about the coming year; he just refused to set a limit to his committee's jurisdiction, and said flatly that he would look into anything that he thought needed looking into, whether some other committee was investigating it or not. He threatened to reopen the *Amerasia* case, "one of the foulest coverups in history," and pugnaciously repeated his claim that he had turned up evidence of "very, very current espionage" at Fort Monmouth, denials by the Army notwithstanding. It was a belligerent speech, and at the end the Senate voted his committee every dollar he had requested, $214,000. The vote was 85 to 1. The lone objector was Senator Fulbright.

"Who Promoted Peress?"
—Act One

The debate on McCarthy's budget request took place on Tuesday, February 2, 1954. A little backtracking is necessary at this point to account for the persuasive vigor of Joe's tone as he pugnaciously declined to give any pledges regarding his future course. The fabric of causes and consequences that had been weaving around McCarthy more or less continuously for months, and which he had repeatedly ripped apart before it could enmesh him, in recent weeks had been marked by the introduction of threads of a new color and a tougher fiber. One of these filaments led back to Roy Cohn, the cherubic chief counsel of the investigations subcommittee.

Cohn fascinated the politician-watchers of the capital. With his baby face and artless air, he suggested a choirboy thrust into the gladiatorial arena where Washington fought its knockdown battles. But his capacity for taking care of himself had quickly become evident; he was conceded to be devilish clever. It was true that his brashness galled some, and the very excessiveness of his ingenuity made some people uneasy in his presence. Generally he was judged to be a trifle too cocksure to wear well. Like his boss, the senator, he did not disdain to cut a corner if it would help to flatten an opponent, or would bring him faster toward his goal. Yet for all his pushing assertiveness, he conspicuously lacked the seasoning of experience that provides restraint.

Moon-faced Frank Carr, the FBI alumnus who held the position of administrative director, was technically Cohn's superior on the subcommittee staff, but nothing was plainer than that Cohn gave the orders and Carr obeyed.

McCarthy, who shunned detail work, allowed his counsel a free hand in plotting investigations, and Cohn coveted the responsibility and frequently shone at it. Like McCarthy, he worked hard.* But Cohn played, too, and his most congenial playmate was his fellow investigator, G. David Schine. In stylish night spots of Manhattan the two were frequently seen with their girls (Schine seemed partial to a brassiere model), two well-heeled blades likably enjoying a young man's fling.

Since November this happy association had been interrupted, for on November 3, David Schine had been drafted into the Army. After gaining a week's delay in order to wind up his subcommittee work, on November 10 he had been inducted and sent to Fort Dix for basic training. Army officials made clear that Schine would receive the same treatment accorded to every inductee.

Shortly after this, rumors trickled into Washington alleging the oddest sort of goings-on at Fort Dix, the training center in New Jersey. Insiders didn't know whether to laugh or be scandalized, although they inclined to the latter, for not only was Schine involved, but Roy Cohn, too, and perhaps even Senator McCarthy.

At about the same time a rumor went the rounds that some members of Senator McCarthy's subcommittee were urging that Cohn be got rid of. The matter had been brought into the open on January 22, when a reporter asked McCarthy whether Cohn had resigned, or whether the still-holding-out Democratic senators had demanded Cohn's dismissal as their price for returning. Joe answered that Cohn had not resigned, and he had heard no requests for his resignation. "Roy is one of the most brilliant young men I have ever met," he added. "He is extremely valuable to the committee. I should be very disappointed if he left."

With this the matter rested for seven days. Then *The New York Times* printed a Washington dispatch, unsigned, saying that G. David Schine, heir to hotels and motion picture palaces, was the object of an Army investigation to determine whether he had received special consideration at Fort Dix. The inquiry was said to have been ordered by the camp commander, Major General Cornelius E. Ryan, and it was being conducted by the Inspector General, James J. Fogarty. The alleged infractions of rules were said to include getting weekends and holidays off, skipping guard duty and target practice, serving a single short stint at kitchen police, chat-

---

* When in the U.S. attorney's office in New York, Cohn had attracted attention by carrying a walkie-talkie as he roamed the corridors of the courthouse so that his secretary might reach him at any moment.

ting with officers, and hinting that he was on a hush-hush mission to check morale at the camp.

Cohn and Schine, the inseparables, were back in the news, and although no one realized it then, it was bad news for McCarthy.

[II]

From this point on, dates were to become all important. The question about Cohn's resignation had been raised on January 22, 1954. First word of the reported Schine inquiry had come on January 29. That same day McCarthy was the target of an attack by a panel of scientists reporting on their study of the senator's much headlined Fort Monmouth investigation. The scientists found that no spies had been uncovered, and no charge of "actual espionage or real subversive activity" had been brought against any of the twenty-nine scientists who had been suspended or transferred to unclassified work. The report, read before the joint annual meeting of the Federation of American Scientists and the American Physical Society, at Columbia University, castigated the senator for causing a "serious disruption" of the scientific program at Fort Monmouth. This stricture, from the camp of the intellectuals, McCarthy ignored; he was otherwise preoccupied with the necessity, as he saw it, of taking out of the hands of the Army the torturous case of Major Irving Peress, an Army dentist. The senator had come to the conclusion that despite their full knowledge of the facts of this case, the Army had no serious intention of doing anything about exposing the dangerous situation it epitomized.

McCarthy had been concerned with this case, in a desultory way, since early in December. Roy Cohn would recount later how it had been brought to the senator's notice. A "high ranking general," who was never publicly identified, this story ran, had telephoned to the senator and had asked him to ring a certain number at a certain time. The number was that of a pay station. McCarthy called and the General answered. Speaking urgently, he told briefly of an "explosive situation" and asked McCarthy to send a representative to the Sherry-Netherland Hotel in New York the next day. Cohn was sent, and in the bar he met a young lieutenant attached to the General's staff. The full story followed. It was this:

At the outbreak of the Korean war, the Army suddenly needed doctors and dentists, and in the emergency resorted to the draft.

Irving Peress, a slightly balding New York dentist, about forty years old, living in Queens but maintaining an office in Manhattan, had registered with his draft board as the law required and applied for a commission. He was handed a form to fill out (Defense Department Form 390), which he completed, signed, and returned. One of the statements to the truth of which he had attested read: "I am not now and have not been a member of any organization . . . seeking to alter the form of the government . . . by unconstitutional means." (This was a legal definition of the Communist Party U.S.A.) The form was dated August 11, 1952. On October 15, 1952, Peress was inducted into the Army as a captain in the reserve, assigned to the Dental Corps.

On October 28, 1952, the newly commissioned captain was given a loyalty form to fill out, Defense Department Form 398. Three questions on that form Peress answered by invoking the protection of the Fifth Amendment. The questions were: Was he now or had he ever been a member of the Communist party or any Communist organization? Had he ever been a Fascist? And, "Are you now, or have you ever been a member of any organization which advocates the overthrow of our constitutional form of government . . . by unconstitutional means?"

After each of these critical questions Captain Peress had written: "Federal constitutional privilege claimed"—a formula for invoking the Fifth Amendment.

Two months later Captain Peress was ordered to active duty, effective January 1, 1953. He was sent to Fort Sam Houston, Texas, for basic training; thence to Fort Lewis, Washington, for assignment to Yokohama, Japan. While at Fort Lewis he obtained emergency leave to return to New York because of the illness of his wife and six-year-old daughter. He then applied for and received a "compassionate" reassignment to Camp Kilmer, New Jersey, about thirty miles from New York City.

Meanwhile, G-2 (Intelligence) of First Army, headquartered in New York, had checked Captain Peress' loyalty forms, noted that he had claimed the constitutional privilege on the vital questions, and ordered an investigation. The entire file was forwarded to the Pentagon with a summary stating that the evidence warranted Peress' discharge as a security risk.

This recommendation retraced Captain Peress' journey to the western ocean and back, stage by stage, but never catching up with him. Seven high Army officials added their recommendations for dismissal during this nine-month hegira.

Meanwhile, Congress had passed legislation providing that any reserve doctor or dentist called to active duty should be promoted to "such grade or rank as may be commensurate with his professional education, experience, and ability." On the strength of this law, Captain Peress applied for promotion, and on September 23, 1953, First Army approved the application. On October 23 the captain was promoted to major, although two days before (on October 21, 1953) Brigadier General Ralph W. Zwicker, commanding at Camp Kilmer, where Peress was stationed, had written to First Army, outlining the case against Peress and recommending that he be gotten out of the Army at once.

Thereafter weeks passed, and it was not until January 18, 1954, that the Department of the Army directed that Major Peress be given an honorable discharge, allowing him to set the date any time within the next ninety days. He selected March 31.

This was the situation which had so exercised the "high-ranking general" that he took the matter to McCarthy, according to Roy Cohn's subsequent version. The General was wroth at the lethargy shown in the case, and he feared that the startling series of blunders would be discreetly glossed over, leaving the door open to further, and possibly much more serious, breaches of the nation's security safeguards.

At McCarthy's direction, Cohn relayed the facts to John G. Adams, the Army's counsel, and Adams promised to take action. McCarthy was content to let the Army handle its own problem, because he wished to get along with his investigation of defense plants infiltration. But time went by and no action was taken. Finally the senator's patience, never very elastic, snapped. "I don't believe the Army is going to do a damn thing!" he exclaimed to Cohn, and called Peress for questioning.

[III]

The hearing took place in New York, in the federal courthouse in Foley Square, on Saturday, January 30. The session was closed, the press excluded, but the testimony would be released to the public later.

Major Peress had not been under subpoena; he had simply been requested to appear. Other Army representatives had been invited to attend the hearing if they desired, but none showed up. Peress was accompanied by his counsel, Stanley Faulkner, of New York. The session got under way promptly at 10:30 A.M., with McCarthy presiding and Cohn doing most of the questioning. No other member of the subcommittee was present. After being sworn, Peress gave his name and rank and military history. At one point Cohn volunteered: "By the way, any time that you want to you can consult with counsel. He can talk to you or nudge you and you can do likewise." The first interruption by the chairman came as Peress was recounting the circumstances of his entering the Army.

"Apparently, Major, the situation was—see if I understand you correctly," McCarthy broke in. "Correct me if I am wrong. You did register for the doctors' draft?"

The witness nodded. "Every physician and dentist had to register under the 1951 law."

McCarthy: "Then there came a time when the draft board notified you you had been called up. . . . You attempted to enlist in the Army. They told you that due to the proximity of enlistment to your classification, they hadn't recognized your enlistment and you were about to be inducted. . . . In effect, you attempted to volunteer in the service. Is that correct?"

"In effect, yes, sir."

Peress then told of being shifted to Fort Lewis under assignment to Japan, and of obtaining leave and then the "compassionate" reassignment to Camp Kilmer because of family illness. McCarthy was curious about how this had been brought about. Peress said he had applied for it, and his wife had sought advice from their congressman and had been told to try the Red Cross.

"In other words," said McCarthy, "no congressman, no senator, no one to your knowledge intervened in your behalf to promote your change of orders?" The witness agreed that was so, and then came the crucial question: "Did anyone in the Army ever ask you whether you were a member of the Communist party or a Communist party organizer?"

Promptly came the answer: "I decline to answer that question under the protection of the Fifth Amendment on the ground it might tend to incriminate me."

That was the first of twenty-four refusals by the witness to answer questions regarding Communist activity. Was he at present a mem-

ber of the party? "I again claim the privilege." Had he been a
member when he was inducted? "I again claim the privilege." Did
any Communists intervene to help him get his orders changed so
he would not have to leave the country? "I again claim the privilege." Was his wife a Communist? "I again claim the privilege."

The chairman appeared baffled. "I am curious to know," he said,
tapping the table with a pencil, "how Communists can get their orders changed so easily. The average man would be sent to Yokohama. You can suddenly have your orders changed and keep in
this country. . . . Every day in my office I have young men writing in saying their wives are sick, very ill, asking to have their orders
changed so they will not have to go overseas. They are sent overseas. I just wonder how you Communists have such tremendous
luck day after day. . . . There is no consideration too great. I
want to find out how you stopped at the port of embarkation; who
stopped you when he knew you were a Communist, and whether
another Communist did it for you, and I am going to order you to
tell us what the alleged illness [of your wife] was."

"My wife and daughter were undergoing psychiatric treatment."

"In other words . . . some emotional disturbance," said Mc-
Carthy, and the questioning was picked up by Cohn:

"Now, Major, you are a graduate of the leadership training school
of the Inwood Victory Club of the Communist party, are you not?"
The litany—"I again claim the privilege"—was resumed and went
on monotonously, the witness refusing to say whether he had delivered talks at Communist discussion meetings; had attempted to
recruit soldiers into the Communist party at Camp Kilmer; had attended Communist meetings in his home with soldiers; had taken
orders from Communist functionaries while at Kilmer; how much
of his salary, if any, he contributed to the Communist party; whether
he had attended a Communist meeting within the current week;
whether there existed a Communist cell at Camp Kilmer, or whether
he had tried to organize one.

The witness declined absolutely to discuss the Defense Department forms he had filled out. He had never been questioned by any
security board or officer in the Army, he said; after handing the
completed forms to an intelligence officer whose name was "Smith
or something like that," he had never heard from him.

McCarthy was incredulous. "You say you were never before a
board of inquiry or questioned about your background by any offi-

cer of the Army?" he asked. Peress confirmed the fact, but the senator dwelt on the point, demanding:

"After you refused to answer questions concerning Communist party affiliations, claiming the Fifth Amendment, in this questionnaire, you heard nothing more about the matter from any Army officials and you were subsequently promoted? Is that correct?"

"That is correct," Peress repeated.

"You haven't been asked to resign, have you?"

"Yes, I have."

McCarthy: "Who asked you?"

Peress: "Colonel Moore. I am not sure of that name, it may be some other."

McCarthy: "Did you refuse to resign?"

Peress: "No, I accepted the request. I have a date of termination . . . the 31st of March, but I can move it up if I so desire."

McCarthy: "You are being given an honorable discharge?"

Peress: "I haven't been given——"

McCarthy: "So far as you know, you are being allowed to resign with no reflection on your record?"

Peress: "There was no discussion of that."

McCarthy: "Why were you asked to resign?"

Peress: "They wouldn't tell me the reason."

McCarthy: "When were you requested to resign?"

Peress: "A week ago this morning at eleven o'clock."

"O. K., you may step down," the chairman finally said, and the witness was told to return for public questioning on February 18, same place, same hour.

[IV]

At the moment, the public learned nothing about the above colloquy except what McCarthy told reporters after the session, but this was startling enough. He said he intended to ask the Army to court-martial a major who had refused to answer questions about his "Communist party membership and activity," and he laid stress on the point that the major had been promoted after his refusal to talk. The officer was not named, but was described as a graduate of City College of New York and a dental officer at Camp Kilmer. The senator cited a few of the questions that the witness had declined to answer and said that he had notified Army authorities that he intended to question the man; following which, the Army had asked the major to resign and the latter had agreed to step out by the end of March.

McCarthy had other business in New York that day, namely, acceptance of Americanism awards from two veterans' groups, the Theodore Roosevelt, Jr., post of the American Legion, and the Catholic War Veterans of New York County. Addressing two hundred Legionnaires at the Press Box restaurant on East 45th Street, he urged them to defeat any congressional candidate in the coming elections who favored giving aid to countries that traded with Communist China. Mentioning his morning's experience, he said he would press for the officer's court-martial, so that he would not leave the service with a clean record.

The senator also went on record as opposing any weakening of the constitutional safeguards provided by the Fifth Amendment, even though it was being abused to "protect a criminal conspiracy rather than the individual."

Another speaker was Archibald Roosevelt, only surviving son of President Theodore Roosevelt. He urged the veterans to support any proposition that was opposed by the *Daily Worker, New York Times,* and *New York Herald Tribune.* When those three newspapers, he said, "my cousin, Eleanor Roosevelt, and my cousins, the little Alsops, are all lined up together, you can be sure something really good is cooking." McCarthy laughed heartily at the dig against his critics the Alsops, whom he himself had long since ceased to call anything except the "Allslops."

Later, accepting a plaque from a hundred and fifty Catholic Veterans at the New Yorker Hotel, the senator pledged that "a sizable number" of Communists would be jailed for contempt of Congress.

That evening he returned to Washington, and on Monday, February 1, he wrote to Secretary of the Army Stevens urging that the Army deny Major Peress an honorable discharge. A thorough investigation of the case was indicated, he said, to "disclose the names of those responsible officers who had full knowledge of [Peress'] Communist activities and either took no steps to have him removed or were responsible for his promotion thereafter." Such gross neglect, or connivance, he said, "without question should subject them to a court-martial."

The letter went to Stevens' office my messenger that same day.

The Secretary was on his way home from an inspection tour in the Far East, and in his absence the letter was received by the Army counsel, John Adams.

(That same day, Monday, February 1, the Army announced that Colonel Fogarty, Inspector General, had begun the inquiry into alleged preferential treatment accorded to Private Schine at Fort Dix, and newsmen were permitted to interview soldiers returning from furlough who had trained with Schine in Company K of the 47th Regiment. The men, interviewed in twos and threes, seemed divided in their feelings, but all agreed that Schine had been recognized as a special character in the camp, and had been a prime subject of argument. Schine himself had been transferred to the CID school at Camp Gordon, Georgia, but authorities said he would be questioned.)

Several times on that Monday, and also on Tuesday, February 2, Frank Carr telephoned Adams on McCarthy's behalf, strongly urging that Peress' discharge be held up, at least until Stevens returned and could act on it personally. Adams was noncommittal. But on Tuesday morning Major Peress spoke with General Zwicker at Camp Kilmer and requested that his discharge be made immediate. The request was unusual; but Zwicker's orders said that Peress could set his own time, so at 1 P.M. that same day the dentist was handed his walking papers in the form of an honorable discharge and he reverted to civilian life. The Army hoped that it had seen the last of Major Irving Peress.

By coincidence, McCarthy's budget request had come up for a vote in the Senate that day, and although Joe was not aware of Peress' discharge when he defended his investigations, he was exercised by the affair, and told the senators that he was going to demand that the Army court-martial a major who, in an executive hearing three days before, had refused to say whether he had tried to recruit soldiers into the Communist party. And he added that he would demand punishment of any officers who had failed to expose this major, or who had had a hand in promoting him from captain to major. "This is the only way to notify every Army officer that twenty years of treason are past, and that this really is a new day," he had said, bristling, and the Senate had voted him funds to carry on.

Before evening, McCarthy's major had been identified publicly as Peress, and Camp Kilmer authorities revealed that he was no longer in the Army, having been discharged one hour after noon that day.

McCarthy was infuriated. "When they want to move fast, they can shuffle those papers faster than you can see them!" he cried bitterly and, telephoning Adams, he told him explicitly and profanely what he thought of the Army's action. It was a clumsy attempt to hush up a scandal, he charged, but it would never wash, because he was going to make it his business to get to the bottom of the mess, and before he got through the Army would be sorry that it had ever tried to buck him, he promised them that. And Joe meant it.

"Who Promoted Peress?"
—Act Two

[I]

For the moment, however, Senator McCarthy had other fish to fry—Democrats generally. Electioneering was under way, and he took off on a ten-day speaking tour on behalf of Republican candidates in seven states: Ohio, West Virginia, Michigan, Wisconsin, South Dakota, California, and Texas. Politicians in both camps were in an angry mood and name-calling was general, in spite of pleas by Vice-President Nixon to end the mutual vituperation. Each party had found the other's raw nerve: the Democrats were shouting "recession" in an attempt, the Republicans said, to create one; while the Republicans were dubbing their rivals "the party of treason" through the Democrats' long supposed complacency toward subversion. The Democrats were handicapped by President Eisenhower's personal popularity; most people continued to "like Ike." Therefore the Democrats concentrated their attacks on the McCarthy wing of the G.O.P., charging that it was the tail that wagged the dog. "Political sadists," Sherman Adams, the White House chief of staff, called the Democrats, saying they were trying to panic the country into a depression, and McCarthy went one better. Speaking in Canton, Ohio, he not only denounced the Democrats for their attempt to whip up a "depression scare," but labeled the Franklin Roosevelt and Truman administrations once again as "twenty years of treason." To the whoops of his audience he declared that the "hard fact is that those who wear the label 'Democrat' wear it with the stain of an historic betrayal." There were some outstanding Democrats in Congress, he conceded, but they had no control over their party. Adlai Stevenson he mocked as the "grand mogul" of the "fear camp," trying to "talk the country into a depression" in order to win an election. Stephen Mitchell, the Democratic national chairman, he ridiculed as a "little forgetter"

416

who "thinks it is completely immoral to remind the American people that the Democratic party has time after time and irrevocably labeled itself the party which stands for government of, by, and for Communists, crooks, and cronies."

In self-defense the Democrats distributed to the news media in the cities where Joe spoke "truth kits," containing the asserted facts of the senator's career and reminding local editors and others that Joe was "considerably more careless of the truth when speaking away from Washington" than he was in the capital, "where he is under the scrutiny of reporters who have facts readily available to check on his claims." These "truth kits" in no way cut down the press and radio coverage given to Joe on his tour. Party strategists in Washington reported happily that McCarthy was getting under their opponents' skins as no other Republican had for a generation; even the Southern conservatives, who had been relatively untouched by the senator's activities, were said to be "hopping mad."

That made no difference to Joe. In Madison, Wisconsin, he told an overflow crowd that "the Democratic leadership has betrayed the confidence of millions of loyal, decent Americans." In Los Angeles he called Harry Dexter White "worse than a Soviet spy; he was a policy maker in the Truman administration."

So bitter was the reaction that President Eisenhower appealed to all to tone down their speeches; but the disunity prevailing in Republican councils was shown when the party's national chairman, Leonard Hall, assumed full responsibility for McCarthy's tour and called the senator an asset to the campaign. Asked on television whether the party endorsed McCarthy, Hall replied, "We pay the expenses of every Republican speaker who goes out, and if that is an endorsement, yes." The senator was in demand all over the country, Hall reported, and he made his own choice of where to go.

At the President's next press conference, he obviously came prepared for a barrage of questions. A reporter read a sample quotation from a McCarthy speech and asked for comment. Eisenhower said he would not comment on personalities. Asked whether he approved of the party's underwriting McCarthy's tour, and agreed with Hall that the senator was an asset to the party, Ike gave the same answer. And so with other questions regarding McCarthy's rampage; the President fended off all queries, growing impatient finally and ending the conference abruptly.

Expressing keen disappointment at Eisenhower's failure to declare himself, *The New York Times* pointed out editorially that accusations of treason went far beyond ordinary political warfare and, if allowed to go unchecked, would sap the very foundations of political life in America.

McCarthy took notice of the President's advice to moderate one's language in a speech in San Mateo, California, but didn't think it applied to him. "I have no plans for a major change in my line of speeches," he said. "I don't think the President is advising that we whitewash and cover up the truth. It's not abuse to expose what's going on. The people of the country have the right to know. I intend to continue giving the cold facts to all the audiences I address." Asked whether he was "defying" the President, he said, "No; I think he is doing a fine job."

In Riverside, California, he told a crowd in the municipal auditorium that he thought the President was "grossly in error' in not cutting off aid to nations trading with Red China, particularly Great Britain. And in Dallas the senator assured 1,022 persons attending a $100-a-plate dinner that the United States should blockade China and halt the "blood trade" with the Communists. "I know that I don't agree with our administration on trade with Red China," he said "but that doesn't mean that I don't support the administration."

Nor was McCarthy the only irritant exacerbating the Democrats. Scott McLeod, on leave without pay from the State Department, was stumping the West, telling audiences that the Democrats were "playing the old numbers game, the game they started in 1950 with Senator McCarthy," by demanding a breakdown of the administration's 2,200 dismissals from the government service, contending that the administration was deliberately giving the impression that most of the dismissals were for Communist activity, whereas the truth was that no Reds whatever had been found. On this issue Truman had accused the Republicans of perpetrating "one of the greatest hoaxes ever attempted in American history," while Senator Morse had accused Eisenhower of using the "big lie" technique. McLeod retorted that people "aren't interested in whether loyalty risks are drunks, dope fiends, sex perverts, or Communists—they are interested in getting them out of government."

The air, the press, and everyday conversation echoed the bitter exchanges. Democrats assailed Republicans as "blabbermouths." Attorney General Brownell cautioned the Democrats to curb their "loose talk." Senator Knowland and House Speaker Joseph Martin became so alarmed they tried to soften the speeches, with little effect. In Columbus, Ohio, Senator Jenner announced that he would "continue to tell the people the truth regardless of politics," and went on to charge that "the Fair Dealers sent our young men to Korea to fight in a country they had stripped bare of American troops. . . . Our brave fighting men didn't know they were supposed to be defeated. They went ahead and won the war with one hand tied behind their backs. Don't let anyone tell you that communism will not be an issue in the coming campaign. It must be and will continue to be until we get the rats out of the government." McCarthy sounded the same theme, and others wove variations on it. The temper of the country seemed verging on the psychotic, and Senator Lehman merely reminded people that he was a relic of a discarded era when he ripped into Senator McCarthy and Governor Dewey of New York as "the newly formed team of Smear & Run," and then, reviving the well worn phrase of FDR, forecast that their accusations would "long live in infamy."

In this atmosphere, ominous with ill-feeling, McCarthy flew back to Washington bent on getting to the bottom of what he regarded as the disgraceful Peress affair.

[II]

Dr. Peress had been ordered to return for public questioning on Saturday, February 18, directly after the senator's return from his Western trip. A disagreeable prelude to the session occurred when the taxicab in which McCarthy and his wife were riding to their hotel in New York was hit by another car and Jean's right ankle was broken. Joe escaped with a bump on the forehead. His equanimity was not improved by the accident and the driver of the other car eventually would be fined for drunken driving and driving the wrong way on a one-way street. Jean McCarthy was taken to Flower-Fifth Avenue Hospital.

General Zwicker had been invited to attend the morning session, and he arrived with a medical officer who was treating him for a mild virus infection. John Adams, the dapper Army counsel, also was on hand.

Before introducing the first witness, a woman, the senator asked the photographers to move back from the table and take no pictures, even putting their cameras out of sight, because the witness had had some "bad experiences with the Communist party" and was very nervous. The television lights also were ordered turned off.

The witness proved to be Miss Ruth Eagle, for the last eleven years a member of the New York City police force. For two and a half years she had been on special assignment, posing as a member of the Communist party. As such she had attended party meetings and indoctrination courses, concerning which she had submitted written reports regularly to the police. In these reports both Irving Peress and his wife, Elaine, had been named as active "comrades."

Here McCarthy interrupted to express the "tremendous respect" his committee felt for "individuals like yourself," who were willing to accept the opprobrium and unpleasantness "incident to being a member of the Communist party." Miss Eagle, he said, deserved the "undying gratitude of the American people."

More to the point, the witness in resuming her testimony said that she had continued to submit reports on Peress, whom she judged to be a party functionary, until the secret of her being a policewoman leaked out. Thereafter she had suffered some "very unpleasant experiences" in retaliation.

Then Peress was called. His lawyer announced that his client refused to be photographed or televised; he was not "on exhibition." McCarthy pledged that no photographs would be taken in the courtroom, although stipulating that "we have no jurisdiction over the corridors, you understand." When the senator addressed the witness as "Major Peress," the latter called attention to his civilian status, saying, "I am not a major . . . I stopped being a major February 2, 1954." Then he requested permission to read a preliminary statement. McCarthy reminded him that under the rules (of which Peress' counsel had been fully advised) such statements were to be submitted twenty-four hours in advance; but after glancing over the document he told the witness he might proceed.

The statement started with a blank defiance: "I have been subpoenaed to appear before this committee presumably to answer certain questions concerning my political beliefs, both past and present. So that there may be no mistake about my position in this regard, I shall decline to answer any such questions under the protection of the Fifth Amendment to our Constitution."

"May I interrupt you there?" came from the chair. "You are not being subpoenaed to answer in regard to your political beliefs. You are here to answer to the part you played while an officer in the United States Army in the conspiracy designed to destroy this nation. That is what you are being called about. You are not being asked about any of your political beliefs. You will not be asked about any of your political beliefs."

The reading proceeded, down to the closing words, taken from the Old Testament. "I highly recommend to you, senator, and your counsel," said the witness, "Book 7 of the Psalms, which reads: 'His mischief shall return upon his own head and his violence shall come down upon his own pate.'"

The next words were the chairman's: "Major, you just heard a policewoman for the City of New York testify that you attended a Communist leadership school. Is that testimony on her part true or false?"

The answer was unhesitating: "I must decline to answer that question, senator, under the protection of the Fifth Amendment, on the ground that it might tend to incriminate me. I would also like to say, senator, that I am not a major. The title is Dr. Peress, not Major Peress."

McCarthy's eyes narrowed as he retorted: "Let me make this very clear. You have been accused, *major,* of the most dishonest, the worst conduct that anyone in the Army can be guilty of. You have been accused under oath of being a member of a conspiracy designed to destroy this nation by force and violence. You are here this morning, you are given an opportunity under oath, to tell us whether or not those charges are true or false. If you are a part of this treasonous conspiracy . . . obviously you will take the protection of the Fifth amendment. If you are innocent, you will tell us that. Now, let me ask you this question: is it true that as of this moment and during all the time that you were an officer of the United States Army, you were a member of the Communist conspiracy?"

The witness consulted with his counsel. McCarthy repeated: "At the time you received your commission in the Army, were you a section organizer for the Communist conspiracy?"

More whispering between the witness and his legal adviser; then Peress said, "I claim the privilege."

"What privilege?" demanded the chair.

"The privilege to decline to answer under the Fifth Amendment."

"On the ground of self-incrimination?"

"On the ground that it might tend to incriminate me."

That started the refrain. For more than an hour McCarthy and Cohn bore down on Peress' activities and especially the circumstances of his promotion in spite of his having refused to complete a loyalty questionnaire. The Army officers responsible for the promotion should be court-martialed, the senator repeated; and he got into the record the fact that Peress had been handed his honorable discharge *after* the Pentagon had received the senator's letter requesting that the discharge be held up pending investigation of the circumstances. From this point on, it was apparent that the focus of the inquiry had shifted, in McCarthy's mind, from Peress himself to the broader matter of a blunt refusal by the Army Department to comply with a legitimate request made by a properly authorized congressional committee.

Peress was of little help; he said he had asked for his discharge and a few hours later a sergeant handed him the papers, all properly executed. McCarthy appealed to John Adams, sitting in the audience, as to whether the Army considered that since his discharge Peress was beyond the reach of the military for the purpose of a court-martial. Adams said that was the Army's interpretation of the law, and in addition, "the Army is not aware of any offenses which have been brought officially to its attention under which he could be tried."

Why, exclaimed McCarthy, "you have the evidence, the sworn testimony, that this man was part of the Communist conspiracy. You have the information that he took a false oath when he swore that he was not a member of the Communist party. You have his refusal to answer questions before a Senate committee. I don't think you want the record to stand, John, as saying that you were not aware of any offense. . . . I do not want to put you on the stand and cross-examine you, but I am just curious about this fantastic procedure, where we have this man before us, and we invited the legal counsel for the Army to sit in, listen to all of his testimony. He refused to answer, invoking the Fifth Amendment. I wrote to the Secretary of the Army and asked for his court-martial. Before Secretary Stevens could get back to the United States, somebody in the Army—I cannot conceive they were acting in good faith— gave him a hurry-up honorable discharge."

By now the senator's upper lip was drawing taut, always a sign of rising anger, and he admonished Adams: "I am going to ask that you give us the names of every officer, every member of the military personnel or any civilian who had anything to do with this man's promotion, knowing that he was a Communist; anything to do with his honorable discharge, knowing he was a Communist, knowing I had suggested a court-martial for him. . . . Will the information be forthcoming without subpoena? If not, this is something that will not be allowed to drop. I want to assure everyone concerned, if it is humanly possible I intend to get to the bottom of it. . . . I intend to take this right to the very limit to get the names of all those individuals, John."

Adams broke in to say that Stevens had sent McCarthy a letter "which discussed the facts of the case as he now knows them. He is investigating."

McCarthy would not be put off. "John," he warned, "I will not take any double-talk, any evasion on this. Either the Army is going to give me the names of individuals responsible for coddling and honorably discharging a known Communist . . . or the Army is going to refuse. . . . If the Army refuses, I intend to take this to the floor of the Senate, and I intend to try to have cited for contempt any man in the military—and I do not care whether he is a civilian or an officer—who tries to cover up those responsible for this most shameful, most fantastic situation. . . . I will want to know within twenty-four hours whether or not the Army is going to give us the names of those whom I just indicated. We will ask for that information by tomorrow night."

Adams was silent, and McCarthy resumed the questioning of Peress, only to get the monotonous response: "I decline to answer . . . I claim the privilege . . ." At 12:15 the hearing was recessed until after lunch.

[III]

General Zwicker lunched pleasantly with McCarthy, and all seemed cordiality when the hearing was resumed, this time in executive session, without television cameras, photographers, or reporters. Zwicker was called to testify. About the distinguished record of Ralph W. Zwicker there could be no disagreement. He was fifty, had been born in Madison, Wisconsin, and was a West Point graduate, class of 1927. During the Normandy invasion in World War II he had led a reconnaissance detail ashore, and later he commanded the 38th Regiment of the Second Division. He had received many decorations, including the Combat Infantryman's Badge, the Silver Star, the Legion of Merit with cluster, the Bronze Star with two clusters, and the Croix de Guerre with palm. General Eisenhower had personally extolled his holding of the vital "north shoulder" during the Battle of the Bulge.

Five days before, Zwicker had discussed the Peress case with James Juliana, an investigator of the McCarthy committee, and had seemed entirely cooperative. Subsequent to that talk, the General had spoken with John Adams. The surprise of both McCarthy and his counsel, Cohn, therefore, was extreme when, almost from the first question, Zwicker assumed an attitude which he himself would describe (three years later) as one that "would certainly tend to give a person the idea that perhaps I was recalcitrant, perhaps I was holding back, and perhaps I wasn't too cooperative." He shied away from giving a connected account of the Peress case as it had unfolded at Camp Kilmer—not because the circumstances would reflect unfavorably on himself, he stressed, although how they might affect others he couldn't say, he just didn't know. The colloquy became acidulous.

"You know that somebody signed or authorized an honorable discharge for this man, knowing that he was a Fifth Amendment Communist, do you not?" McCarthy pressed.

"I know that an honorable discharge was signed for the man," was the cautious reply.

"The day the honorable discharge was signed, were you aware of the fact that he had appeared before our committee?"

"I was."

"And had refused to answer certain questions?"

"No, sir, not specifically on answering any questions. I knew that he had appeared before your committee."

"Didn't you read the news?" The chairman's tone expressed astonishment.

"I read the news releases."

"And the news releases were to the effect that he had refused to tell whether he was a Communist, and that there was evidence that he had attended Communist leadership schools. It was all in the wire service stories, was it not? You knew generally what he was here for, did you not?"

"Yes, indeed."

"And you knew generally that he had refused to tell whether he was a Communist, did you not?"

"I don't recall whether he refused to tell whether he was a Communist."

The senator took a minute to digest this. Then he tried a different tack.

"When an officer appears before a committee and refuses to answer, would you not read that story rather carefully?"

"I read the press releases," was the stubborn reply.

"Then, general, you knew, did you not, that he appeared before the committee and refused, on the grounds of the Fifth Amendment, to tell about all of his Communist activities? You knew that, did you not?"

"I knew everything that was in the press."

McCarthy's temper was rising. "Don't be coy with me, general."

"I am not being coy," Zwicker responded, and then backtracked cautiously: "I believe I remember reading in the paper that he had taken refuge in the Fifth Amendment to avoid answering questions before the committee."

"About communism?"

"I am not too certain about that."

"Do you mean that you did not have enough interest in the case, general, of this major who was in your command, to get some idea of what questions he had refused to answer? Is that correct?"

Zwicker didn't think that was "putting it quite right," and McCarthy told him, "You put it right, then."

"I have a great interest in all of the officers of my command, with whatever they do," the general began, but McCarthy broke in; "Let's stick to Fifth Amendment Communists. Let's stick to him. You told us you read the news releases."

"I did."

"But now you indicate that you did not know that he refused to tell about his Communist activities. Is that correct?"

"I know that he refused to answer questions for the committee."

McCarthy would not accept this by now threadbare answer, and the blood pressure of both men was rising.

"Did you know that he refused to answer questions about his Communist activities?" the chairman repeated.

"Specifically, I don't believe so," came the response.

"Did you have any idea?"

"Of course I had an idea."

"What do you think he was called down here for?"

"For that specific purpose."

"Then you knew that those were the questions he was asked, did you not? General, let's try and be truthful. I am going to keep you here as long as you keep hedging and hemming."

"I am not hedging."

"Or hawing."

The General's back was up. "I am not hawing, and I don't like to have anyone impugn my honesty, which you just about did," he retorted angrily, and McCarthy shot back with both barrels: "Either your honesty or your intelligence!" With anger matching Zwicker's he went on: "I can't help impugning one or the other, when you tell us that a major in your command who was known to you to have been before a Senate committee, and of whom you read the press releases very carefully—to now have you sit here and tell us that you did not know whether he refused to answer questions about Communist activities. I had seen all the press releases and they all dealt with that. So when you do that, general . . . I cannot help but question either your honesty or your intelligence, one or the other."

Once more the question was put, but Zwicker would not budge, and the inquiries turned to the General's failure to hold up Peress' discharge at least until the matter of his reported standing on loyalty grounds could be looked into. Zwicker contended that under his orders he had no authority to interfere. Not even if, for example someone had come in at the last minute and reported that the man had just stolen $50? Well, certainly he would look into such an accusation before letting the man out of Army jurisdiction, the General agreed. But he wouldn't hold up the discharge of a man accused of being a traitor? McCarthy asked. Zwicker replied that he had never been "officially informed by anyone that [Peress] was part of the Communist conspiracy, Mr. Senator."

"Would you tell us, general, why $50 is so much more important to you than being part of a conspiracy to destroy a nation that you are sworn to defend?

Zwicker was indignant. "Mr. Chairman, it is not, and you know that as well as I do."

Then why couldn't he have held up Peress' discharge? The General blurted that everything he had read in the press, everything he had heard that morning, had been known to "plenty of people long prior to the time that you ever called this man for investigation."

But McCarthy stuck to his question, asking Zwicker whether he thought that a person responsible for giving an honorable discharge to a man named under oath as a Communist should be removed from the military service.

If that person was acting under orders, Zwicker replied, no, he should not.

But if he were, say, the General who originated, who first gave, the order, McCarthy persisted. Zwicker hedged. That was not a question for him to answer, he said.

"You are ordered to answer it," McCarthy said sharply. "You are an employe of the people. . . . I want to know how you feel about getting rid of Communists."

"I'm all for it!"

"All right. You will answer the question, unless you take the Fifth Amendment. I don't care how long we stay here, you are going to answer it."

"Do you mean how I feel toward Communists?"

"I mean exactly what I asked you, general, nothing else. And anyone with the brains of a five-year-old child can understand that question."

Zwicker requested that the question be repeated; he had already had it read back once.

"The reporter will read it to you as often as you want to hear it so that you can answer it, and then you will answer," McCarthy said stonily.

The reporter read the question, and there was a tense moment of silence. Then General Zwicker answered, "I do not think he should be removed from the military."

At this McCarthy's temper flew completely out of bounds, and without raising his voice he tongue-lashed the witness:

"Then, general, you should be removed from any command. Any man who has been given the honor of being promoted to general and who says, 'I will protect another general who protected Communists,' is not fit to wear that uniform, general. I think it is a tremendous disgrace to have this sort of thing given to the public. I intend to give it to them. I have a duty to do that. You will be back here, general."

There was more questioning to follow, and at one point, where McCarthy was endeavoring to get the General to say whether he had done anything to prevent the issuing of an honorable discharge to Peress, after he became aware of the major's behavior before the committee, Zwicker respectfully took refuge in the Presidential directive forbidding the release of confidential information.* "The President says don't do it and therefore I do not," he said, and McCarthy accepted that explanation, after Zwicker had made clear that he was expressing no opinion as to the propriety of that directive, "because I will not criticize my commander-in-chief."

Finally the senator banged an ash tray on the table and curtly ordered the witness to stand down. The hearing continued in private; but when John Adams refused to be sworn as a witness, on the ground that he was the Army's legal adviser, McCarthy ordered him and Zwicker to leave the room. Later he told reporters that he had shut out the two "because I thought it was a good idea." He also told the press that a lieutenant colonel from Camp Kilmer had refused to give certain information, pleading that he would be subject to court-martial if he did.

At day's end McCarthy had not established to his satisfaction "who promoted Peress"; but he had fired the first rounds in a controversy that would spread until it involved the entire nation.

* President Truman's directive of 1948 was still in effect.

That Chicken Luncheon

Secretary Stevens had returned from the Far East while Senator McCarthy was on his Western speaking tour. On February 16, two days before the clash with General Zwicker, Stevens had sent McCarthy a conciliatory letter, conceding that a mistake had been made in the Peress case, where the Army's screening system had broken down, and assuring the senator that orders had been issued that no officer taking refuge in the Fifth Amendment should be given an honorable discharge. Meanwhile the Peress mix-up was being studied, but there seemed to be no practical way to recall his discharge. John Adams had mentioned this letter during the Zwicker exchange, and McCarthy had jabbed back that he wasn't going to take any "double-talk."

Secretary Stevens, an able business executive heading a family textile firm in New Jersey, was earnest, honest, loyal, and well-meaning. He was a graduate of Yale, and in the First World War he had served as a lieutenant; in the second, as a colonel. He had been decorated with the Legion of Merit and the Distinguished Service Medal. He had held office less than two months, and he was quite unversed in the ways of Washington's political jungle, where warfare went on incessantly under the primitive "rule of tooth and claw." It chanced, too, that at this very moment he was under extra responsibility, acting as Secretary of Defense also during the vacation absence of Secretary Wilson. Stevens' obligation toward the entire defense establishment was therefore felt by him to be immediate and personal.

General Zwicker had returned to Camp Kilmer in a wrathful mood, and the more he mentally chewed over the verbal mauling to which he had been subjected, the more indignant he became. Finally he wrote out an affidavit account of the episode and sent it to his superior at the Pentagon, Lieutenant General Withers Burgess. "I don't have to take this sort of thing," he told Burgess. "I'm quitting." Burgess persuaded him to do nothing until the matter had been laid before the Army Chief of Staff, General Matthew Ridgway.

Ridgway was almost as incensed over McCarthy's telling Zwicker he was "not fit to wear that uniform" as was Zwicker himself. Bursting into Stevens' office with Zwicker's affidavit, he declared that McCarthy was destroying Army morale. Officers shouldn't be treated like common criminals, he expostulated, and Stevens, after reading Zwicker's account, boiled up in his turn.

McCarthy, meanwhile, speaking before 2,500 persons at a dinner of the Traffic Club of New York in the Hotel Commodore on the evening of the Peress-Zwicker testimony, had made clear that the incident was not closed. "There was a disgraceful performance today," he had reported, "but I intend to find out who was responsible for covering up a Communist who was an officer in the Army. I have asked General Zwicker to return for an open hearing Tuesday morning. I have also asked the Army to produce its adjutant general, Major General William E. Bergin, as a witness. It is up to Secretary Stevens to correct this situation quickly. He should take a new look at the top of the team to see whether this type of coddling of Communists will continue."

The newspapers carrying this front-page challenge also reported in detail Peress' invoking of the Fifth Amendment more than fifty times on questions regarding communism.

On the morning of Saturday, February 20, Secretary Stevens issued an order forbidding Army officers to appear before the McCarthy subcommittee. This he did on his own authority without consulting the White House. He then telephoned McCarthy, who had gone to Albany to conduct a hearing on Red infiltration in defense plants in that area, reporting what he had done and warning that "I'm not going to stand for having Army officers pushed around." He called the treatment of Zwicker "outrageous."

At first McCarthy thought the call was a gag, that some joker was on the wire; but when he became convinced that it really was the Secretary speaking, he exploded. In sulphurous language he told Stevens that he was going to make him repeat in open hearing his defiance of a duly constituted congressional committee. Stevens said that would be fine; if McCarthy wanted to find out anything, just call him, but "leave my officers alone." To which McCarthy barked that he would go right ahead and "kick the teeth in of anyone caught coddling Communists. You're subpoenaed now!" Then he slammed down the phone.

This set the stage for a head-on collision between the senator, representing congressional authority, and the Pentagon, representing the executive department. Stevens moved quickly to get in the first blow by preparing a memorandum account of the episode and giving it to the other members of McCarthy's committee. Then on Sunday the Secretary issued a public statement charging that McCarthy had "insulted" General Zwicker and making clear that the Army would not stand for it.

"In a closed hearing in New York last week," the statement read, "General Zwicker suffered humiliating treatment only because he carried out actions which were his official duty and executed an order he had received from high headquarters which he was required to execute. I cannot permit the loyal officers of our armed forces to be subjected to such unwarranted treatment. The prestige and morale of our armed forces are too important to the security of the nation to have these weakened by unfair attacks on our higher officer corps."

High-ranking officers told reporters that although Stevens had gone along with McCarthy's Fort Monmouth investigation, he had concluded after the Zwicker incident that "this is the end of the line for us."

McCarthy, who was spending the weekend in New York, where his wife was still in Flower-Fifth Avenue Hospital, covered Stevens' statement with one of his own. He met reporters in Roy Cohn's home at 1165 Park Avenue and announced that he had postponed the appearance of Stevens until Thursday at the request of Senator Dirksen, who would be out of Washington until then; and also that the hearing would be held in the capital because of the "tremendous importance to the country of the Army's attempt to coddle and promote Communists and then claim special immunity," and "so that this issue cannot be beclouded by unwarranted complaints that development of unfavorable facts constitutes abuse of the witness." What Stevens was trying to do was "simply unfair to good and loyal officers in the Army," the senator emphasized, adding, "He's got to clear this up. He must realize this about his position: that, in effect, he served notice on officers that

they can cover up any conspiracy under them. This action is undoubtedly the result of bad advice. I think Bob Stevens is a good
loyal American, and that he is man enough to change his mind
and his position." And he hoped the Democratic members of the
subcommittee would attend the hearing Thursday.

The underlying issue raised was chiefly in the minds of official
Washington—the defiance by a branch of the executive of the
power of Congress. This basic conflict of interest had been written
into the Constitution intentionally, as part of the "checks and bal-
ances" aimed at containing each branch of the government within
certain limits, and preventing any one branch from gaining absolute
control. As one senator put the issue, it was simply "whether the
Army is supreme over Congress, other agencies, and the American
people, and can enjoy special dictatorial immunity in covering up
its own wrongdoing." On this issue McCarthy could count upon
the solid support of the Senate, which, with the House, had again
and again rallied to the defense of its right to investigate the executive.

[II]

President Eisenhower, vacationing in Palm Springs, got first
word of the dispute from the news ticker. He told his press secretary, James Hagerty, to keep hands off, and Hagerty made known
this decision to the press.

In Washington, however, the party leadership was deeply
troubled. The spectacle of the Republican Secretary of the Army
and a Republican senator in a cat-and-dog brawl, with an election
in sight, was poisonous, they felt—especially considering who the
senator was. Stevens was bombarded with telephone appeals to
avoid "splitting the party," and the President's congressional liaison
officer, General Wilton B. Persons, had got Senator Dirksen to
request that postponement of Stevens' appearance before the committee to allow time for smoothing over the dispute.

On Monday, February 21, Stevens and Senator Mundt had flown
to Willow Grove, Pennsylvania, to receive Freedom Foundation
awards at Valley Forge the next day, Washington's Birthday.
Mundt, a former schoolteacher with a patient, soothing manner,
talked frankly on their flight.

"Look here, Bob," he said, "you can't go before that committee and say you won't allow your generals to respond to a committee subpoena. You can direct them not to answer certain questions that violate presidential directives, but you can't keep them from appearing. Besides, after all, you and Joe are friends. You went to his wedding. You're against communism and so is Joe. I think we should work something out." And he explained to the politically naive Stevens the weakness of his position.

There were two quite different subjects involved, he pointed out —the Peress case, and the Zwicker incident. On Peress, Stevens had already admitted that the Army bungled, and bungled badly; on that issue public opinion would side with McCarthy. In regard to his treatment of Zwicker, Joe was vulnerable, yes; but Joe would control the questions put to Stevens and he would hammer on Peress, never letting Stevens get started on Zwicker. "Joe will murder you," Mundt warned.

Stevens, however, was determined not to back down. His responsibility to the Army was on his conscience. "I've got to do something, Karl," he protested. "Zwicker was abused and Army morale is badly hurt. I've got to do something to restore morale."

Mundt was sympathetic. He said he would try to work out some compromise that would get both the senator and the Army back on the track.

On Washington's Birthday Senator McCarthy accepted a good citizenship medal from the Philadelphia chapter of the Sons of the American Revolution. A heavy police guard watched over McCarthy in consequence of death threats received. Although the chapter's president, David L. German, had boycotted the ceremony as a "desecration," all but a few members attended. They heard McCarthy read excerpts from Zwicker's testimony, then comment:

"As I look it over today, I was too temperate in what I said. If I were doing it today, I would be much stronger in my language. There is nothing disloyal about Bob Stevens. He is one of the finest dupes I have ever met."

[III]

That was on Monday, and the showdown was set for Thursday. At the demand of both the Republican and the Democratic members of McCarthy's subcommittee, the transcript of General Zwicker's testimony had been released and the front pages nationwide sizzled with the asserted "abuse" of the fencing general. Almost all editorial comment was hostile to the senator, and relief was expressed that the Army had decided to fight back. Stevens was a hero, and Joe was pictured as having lost ground by the encounter.

In the Peress tangle, however, the press for the most part lined up with Joe, as Mundt had predicted. The *Brooklyn Eagle* said that the senator deserved "a vote of thanks for his inquiry, despite his resort to tactics which can at the very least be described as offensive." The *New York Daily News* felt that "the nation as a whole should be thankful that, somehow, details of the Peress case are going to be made public." The *Washington Star* found it "hard to believe" that Peress' discharge "was a routine move, made in a routine way. It is hard not to believe that someone at a high level made a decision to get rid of Major Peress before the McCarthy group could complete its investigation. . . . The Army ought to reveal the identity of that official."

Public interest was intense as the press reported the feeling that this would be an all-out, no-holds-barred test of strength, in which Stevens apparently had administration backing. The television networks announced that they would be carrying the hearing coast-to-coast. And McCarthy brought into the open the constitutional issue by contending that Stevens' "gag" order struck at the heart of the right of Congress to investigate and, if sustained, would "mean an end of all investigations of dishonesty, corruption, and communism in government. If Bob Stevens can do it, then any department head can pick the committee he wants his people to go before."

The senator was in a buoyant mood. He had met the press in his office directly after returning from Philadelphia and had announced with many a chuckle that he had summoned his subcommittee to a closed session at 10 A.M. on Tuesday, to be followed by a public hearing to expose "a new Red link to the Army." He was evasive about the identity of the witness, but laughingly said that "this is principally for Stevens' benefit . . . another matter that should be spread on the public record and made known to Stevens before he testifies under oath. I don't want him to be in the embarrassing position of not having the full picture. I feel he has been badly misinformed, and in fairness he should be aware of these facts."

General Zwicker got into the news with a gruff denial that he was suffering from a serious heart ailment, which was why the medical officer had accompanied him to the McCarthy hearing. Zwicker was concerned because a rumor had spread that McCarthy had "browbeaten a sick man," and it would certainly look bad if the Army kept in active service an officer suffering from heart disease to the extent of requiring constant attendance by a physician. But nobody seemed to be thinking clearly any more.

The new "Red link" was duly disclosed on Tuesday, in the person of Mrs. Annie Lee Moss, a civilian employe of the Signal Corps, who McCarthy said was listed as a Communist party member in FBI reports dating back to 1944. He asserted that Mrs. Moss was still employed by the Army in "coding and decoding top secret messages." The Army promptly denied this and said a reexamination of her file for possible security risk had begun "prior to any action by the subcommittee."

Mrs. Moss already had appeared before the House Un-American Activities Committee with her lawyer and had answered all questions, denying she was ever a Communist and not invoking the Fifth Amendment. Before the McCarthy committee, Mrs. Mary Markward, the FBI undercover agent, who had previously appeared before it, had testified that she knew Mrs. Moss from party lists as a dues-paying member until 1945, when her name disappeared from the lists. She said she had reported this to the FBI at the time and she made clear to the senators that she was not aware of ever having seen Mrs. Moss and was not certain that she would be able to recognize her.

After the hearing Senator Potter expressed some doubt about the evidence and suggested a case of mistaken identity. Mrs. Moss was reported ill at home. The returned Democratic members of the subcommitee, Senators Jackson and McClellan, attended the session with their new minority counsel, Robert Kennedy, but offered no comment. Senator Symington, the third Democratic member, was in Europe.

[IV]

Meanwhile, the wheels had been grinding behind the scenes to head off a knockdown struggle between Stevens and McCarthy on nationwide television on Thursday. The administration's dilemma was outlined tellingly by columnist Arthur Krock in *The New York Times*. The stage was set for a dramatic meeting, only twenty-four hours hence, he wrote, at which Stevens, substituting himself for the officers whom he had ordered not to appear, would lock horns with McCarthy and "at last the senatorial bully [would] meet an executive official who would not give way to threats or abuse, and who, under the aegis of the President, would champion witnesses subjected to the third-degree tactics of McCarthy."

But Krock went on to point out a difficulty facing the Army, namely, its vulnerability in regard to Peress. "The facts demanded by McCarthy, though in his brutal way, are legitimate matters of public information. . . . From the beginning it was obvious . . . that the facts . . . must be given to a Senate group authorized to make such inquiries." Stevens had a good case in regard to Zwicker, but would he be allowed to present it? "Confronted by a showdown of such indicated violence between the executive and legislative branches," a decision had been reached "on high administrative levels," Krock reported, that it must be averted.

And this was correct. President Eisenhower had returned from California determined to avoid a humiliating brawl. Personally he believed it beneath the dignity of his office to engage in name-calling with Senator McCarthy or any other congressional committee chairman. As a soldier he was prepared to back up General Zwicker to the limit, but he feared that the Army would suffer most from a public slugging match.

Acting in line with this privately expressed view, liaison man Persons had telephoned Stevens on Tuesday afternoon, asking him to meet with the Vice-President. Persons attended this talk, during which it was agreed that Army morale had been injured, but an attempt was made to make Stevens appreciate the weakness of his case in respect to Peress. Stevens admitted that that matter had been mishandled, but insisted that was not the issue—the issue was the treatment of General Zwicker.

Although no conclusion was reached, Stevens came away from the conference elated, interpreting it as a clear indication that he had White House support. Back at the Pentagon, he and his aides worked far into the night drafting a fighting statement which he intended to read at the hearing on Thursday.

In the midst of this, Senator Mundt called and suggested a meeting with the Republican members of the subcommittee to work out some way "to save the Republican party." Stevens said he was "always willing to talk," and Mundt replied that he would call back.

Early on Wednesday, Mundt tackled McCarthy, but found Joe bent on a showdown. Mundt pleaded: "Gee whiz, Joe, Bob Stevens is your friend. He has got a morale problem on his hands. You used some pretty extreme language to Zwicker, but that's not the point here. The party's being torn apart and the country's being torn apart. We've got to stop that hearing."

Finally McCarthy agreed reluctantly to meet Stevens at lunch, if Mundt could arrange it. Then he went off to interrogate Annie Lee Moss in a public hearing.

Mrs. Moss, a black woman who kept either shivering or trembling, came in on the arm of her lawyer. She seemed to be suffering from a bad cold and frequently lifted her spectacles and wiped her eyes. She was neatly but shabbily dressed, and seemed extremely nervous. The chairman confronted her with the testimony that she was a Communist, or had been one, and warned her that he would cite her for perjury if she denied the fact. He said she needn't testify if she was ill, and when her counsel objected that she had answered all questions before the House committee, withholding nothing, McCarthy said he was not interested in her as a person, but in finding out "who in the military, knowing that lady was a Communist, promoted her from cafeteria waitress to coding clerk although she had no ability at all." He then ordered her to return the next day, or to present a medical certificate that she was too ill to testify.

Another witness, also a woman, "took the Fifth" when asked if she had recruited Mrs. Moss into the party, and again when asked if she could identify Mrs. Moss. And still another woman, who had been identified by Mrs. Markward as a former membership director of the party, also invoked the amendment on several questions, but stated that she did not know Mrs. Moss and had never heard her name until the senator brought it up.

Mrs. Markward was in the hearing room, but was not called; she told reporters that she would have been unable to identify Mrs. Moss.

Going from the hearing to Senator Mundt's office, McCarthy found Senator Dirksen there. Mundt telephoned to Stevens: "Bob, I've got Ev Dirksen and Joe right here in the office with me. Will you have lunch with us so we can talk the situation over?" Stevens said he would come right over, and Mundt told him to come to room P-54 in the Capitol, an inconspicuous room in a corridor off the rotunda, used by the Senate Republican campaign committee. The meeting was to be kept secret.

Before he set out from the Pentagon, Stevens called the White House, but could reach no one in authority there. He then checked with the Defense Department's counsel, H. Struve Hensel, and tried the White House again, with no better luck. So he set out alone.

[V]

Somehow, word of the "secret" luncheon had leaked out, and Stevens had to push through upwards of fifty reporters and photographers outside room P-54. Waiting he found McCarthy, Mundt, and Dirksen. Senator Potter, the fourth Republican on the subcommittee, had sent word he was otherwise engaged. Stevens put out his hand and said, "Hello, Joe, how's Jeanie feeling?"—alluding to McCarthy's wife, recovering from her broken ankle. McCarthy grunted a reply and the four men sat down to the luncheon already spread on a table—fried chicken, with potato, peas, salad, and coffee.

The chicken was tasteless and the conversation was strained. Stevens and Joe sparred grumpily. Finally Mundt came to the point: "Let's get down to business. Bob, I've asked Joe and Ev here to see if we can't avoid a public brawl tomorrow." He lit a cigar and sitting down to a typewriter tapped out the heading:

"Memorandum of Understanding, February 24."

"Look here," he said, "I'm going to try to hammer out a statement that we can give to those reporters outside. Now then, we all agree that Commies should be rooted out, don't we?"

The dickering and arguments began. McCarthy said little. Dirksen's mellifluous sincerity was poured over the Secretary from one side, and Mundt's homely common sense from the other. Party loyalty demanded that both sides give; party unity must be preserved, the party's interests placed first; the situation called for peace. Sentence by sentence the memorandum was beaten out. The task took two hours, but at length it was completed, and at 2:55 P.M. the door was opened and the press swarmed in. A glance showed the tough chicken hardly touched. Stevens, seated on a green leather couch, maintained a blank silence as Mundt prepared to read the statement. To some of those present the Secretary looked like a man in a trance.

The TV lights were turned on and Mundt read the memorandum through rapidly. Still Stevens said nothing. To the *New Republic*'s reporter he seemed "in shock; like a man who has been in an auto accident. . . . He wore a blue suit, silver hair, and red face. Cameramen said 'Smile!' and he turned on a sickly grin, with Joe's hairy hand on his shoulder." Crucially, Stevens agreed to stop telling officers to resist subpoenas. As the memorandum phrased it:

"There is complete agreement . . . that the Secretary of the Army will order the Inspector General to complete the investigation . . . in the Peress case as rapidly as possible; and he will give the subcommittee the names of everyone involved in the promotion and honorable discharge of Peress; and that such individuals will be available to appear before the committee."

And of course Stevens' appearance before the committee the next day was canceled.

To those who heard Mundt rattle off this "understanding," it appeared that Stevens had handed Senator McCarthy everything the latter could ask for; in fact, as one reporter put it, "everything short of a ninety-nine-year lease on the Pentagon."

Brusquely refusing to answer any questions, muttering, "I've had enough of this," the Secretary hurried from the room. Back at the Pentagon, he informed his staff that he had successfully defended the dignity of the Army and was congratulated on his victory. Some time later top officers got copies of the memorandum; they were appalled. Stevens and the Army were in deep trouble, it was plain to see, but nobody ventured to break the news to the Secretary.

His euphoria lasted about two hours. Then the ticker began reporting the reaction, and it showed every newspaper, every commentator, in this country and overseas, interpreting the memorandum as unconditional surrender to McCarthy.

(Cynics among the reporters who had waited outside the conference room had offered to bet that Joe would "take Stevens' vest without even unbuttoning his coat." They were said to be chuckling now that Joe had taken Stevens' pants and reputation, too!)

The Secretary himself was more than aghast, he was horror-stricken. At first he tried to discount the reports, but his nerves gave way completely when he heard that McCarthy had told a friend, "I'm having a hell of a time to keep from laughing; Stevens couldn't have surrendered more if he crawled on his hands and knees!" And when a reporter asked whether he "considered the memorandum a surrender," Joe had said, grinning, "Of course not! It's just an agreement!" at the same time surreptitiously kicking the reporter's shins. "Want a commission? I can fix it up!"

In despair, Stevens rang the White House and reached Hagerty, Ike's press secretary. What should he do? he pleaded. "Wait," Hagerty told him. Stevens then called Mundt and sobbed: "Yesterday I was a hero; today I'm a heel! I'm going to call a press conference at eleven tomorrow morning and announce my resignation!"

Mundt tried to calm him, urging him to wait and take a philosophical view. "Look," he said, "all of us in politics have been beaten over the head sometimes."

Stevens would not be pacified. Alternately he raged and despaired. He telephoned several senators, and sobbed that his career was finished. Toward midnight he bucked up, and backed by his aides he decided to fight back. As a first step, he released to the press the belligerent statement he had expected to read at the canceled hearing. It began:

"I am here today to defend an officer of the United States Army . . . who was humiliated before this committee . . . because he was carrying out my orders. I am here because I feel that the integrity of the entire Army is involved. . . . Peress is not the issue here. The issue is the treatment given a distinguished combat soldier who followed official orders."

But this tardy defiance sounded somehow thin and vain.

At the White House, word of the memorandum caused consternation. "Oh, no!" Nelson Rockefeller was quoted as groaning. The President was furious. He called for the transcript of Zwicker's testimony and read it through. At the end he was boiling. Slamming his fist on the desk he called McCarthy's treatment of Zwicker nothing short of disgraceful; the staff had never seen Ike in such a rage. And the situation grew steadily worse as the headlines poured in from all over the country and abroad, all using the word *surrender.* McCarthy's stock was never so high.

For days the stunned, indignant commentary would keep up. The Washington correspondent of *The Times* of London began his report:

"Senator McCarthy this afternoon achieved what General Burgoyne and General Cornwallis never achieved—the surrender of the American Army."

Throughout the United States newspaper offices reported receiving more excited telephone calls about the incident than about any news happening since the dismissal of General Douglas MacArthur from his Far East command.

The *Washington Post* rushed out a cartoon showing Stevens handing his sword to McCarthy, and the latter snarling, "Okay, bud, when I want you again I'll send for you."

At the Pentagon an officer said disgustedly: "Stevens didn't mean to surrender to McCarthy, Mundt, and Dirksen; he merely thought they wanted to look at his sword!"

Eisenhower was treated with the same bitter scorn. Commented the *New York Post:* "Secretary Stevens, after a two-hour brain-washing session with Joe McCarthy, surrendered to the Piltdown politician. . . . Perhaps the President can truly say he never surrendered; he never took command."

The *Detroit Free Press:* "We think that in the annals of the Army, February 24, 1954, can be appropriately set down beside July 21, 1861. That was the date of the first Battle of Bull Run."

The *Chicago Sun-Times:* "Secretary Stevens' unconditional surrender to Senator McCarthy is shocking and dismaying."

The *Milwaukee Journal:* "Not a retreat, a collapse. . . ."

The *Washington Star* said that Stevens "beat a retreat from his earlier position, and no denial can conceal the fact that it was a retreat."

The *Chicago Tribune,* which had consistently supported McCarthy, contented itself with mildly taking issue with the senator over his treatment of General Zwicker and advising: "It seems to us that Senator McCarthy will better serve his cause if he learns to distinguish the role of investigator from the role of avenging angel."

But the *Richmond News-Leader* was blunt: "Secretary Stevens might just as well submit his resignation . . . and be done with a sorry job. . . . Mr. Stevens has merely contributed to the delusion that McCarthy bestrides this nation like a Colossus, while petty men walk about under his huge legs."

And the *St. Louis Post-Dispatch* struck with deadly bluntness: "Dwight D. Eisenhower still is President under the Constitution, but he is not in full command of the Department of the Army today. Control of that vital element of our national defense has passed, in part at least, from the White House to the unscrupulous hands of Senator McCarthy. No matter what he does, no matter what he says, no matter whom he attacks, the White House apparently will avoid a break with the wild man of Wisconsin."

The London *Spectator* had the same feeling. Drawing the moral that public indignation against McCarthy was virtually useless, it declared that what was needed was "a plan to end his public life." But who would do it? Senator Lehman might proclaim his "abhorrence" of McCarthy's tactics, but his own party held virtuously aloof; Joe was a Republican problem, the Democratic leadership of the Senate said; let the Republicans deal with him. Bishop Oxnam might warn that "fear rides the nation." The liberal press might cry that the President could and must end the rampage. *The Nation* might exclaim that McCarthy did not need to prove a charge. "All he needs to do is whisper 'communism' and even men sworn to uphold and defend the Constitution will act like so many sheep." *The Nation* saw the Eisenhower wing of the Republican party nearly encircled and abandoned hope: "Today the President's advisers tell him that it is inexpedient to oppose McCarthy; tomorrow they may tell him it is too late."

In whom could Americans place their faith—Eisenhower or McCarthy? Amid the uproar probably few newspaper readers noticed an announcement by the Post Office Department of a new stamp that had just gone on sale—an eight-cent stamp, unique in being the first postage stamp to carry the motto: "In God We Trust."

"Point of No Return"

Plainly it was time for the commander-in-chief to take command and stem the rout. And Eisenhower did assume command, with a result that was stated by the *New Republic* with all too cruel brevity:

"Ike turned the other cheek last week, and Joe slugged it."

It started on the morning after Stevens' ignominious "surrender." Senator Mundt was alarmed. He called General Persons at the White House and pleaded with him to "calm Stevens down; he's going to blow his top. You folks must stop him."

Persons relayed the alarm to Sherman Adams, the President's chief of staff, who telephoned Stevens and told him to sit tight, that the White House was reviewing the situation.

Overnight the President's choler had evaporated. After listening to the doleful report of Stevens' calls to Capitol leaders, he sent quietly for Senator Dirksen. Apparently in a cheerful mood, the President explained to the senator that Stevens had worked himself into a corner and suggested that anything Dirksen might be able to do toward extricating him and restoring harmony would be appreciated.

To good soldier Everett (even though he had done his part in cornering Stevens) this hint was a command. Posting back to the Capitol, he conferred with Mundt and Senator Potter on an "explanatory statement" which Stevens might make. Potter had been causing difficulty on his own account because he was fiercely loyal to combat veterans, and he resented McCarthy's pushing Zwicker around. But finally the three senators agreed on a text. But McCarthy refused to accept it without changes. Dirksen referred these to the White House and was told they wouldn't do; there must be a promise by McCarthy that witnesses would not be abused in the future. Joe refused to admit that any had been abused, and on this point Dirksen backed him up.

443

At the Pentagon, the corridor outside Stevens' office was jammed. Television cameras were in place there and at the Mall entrance, but not one of the throng of correspondents got through the Secretary's door. Mrs. Stevens arrived with an armful of roses for her husband's desk, and was admitted.

At about 3 P.M., Roger M. Kyes, Assistant Secretary of Defense, called Stevens and said the President wanted to see them at once. At 3:25 the Secretary emerged from his fortress, brushed past the clamoring newsmen with a curt, "Sorry, boys, but I've got work to do," and escaped through a side entrance with Kyes and Fred Seaton, Defense Department public relations adviser. Behind them the brushed-off reporters voted Stevens' wording the understatement of the week.

At the White House the Pentagon three joined a huddle of top-level officials in Hagerty's office. Among those participating were Sherman Adams; William P. Rogers, Deputy Attorney General; Bernard M. Shanley, White House counsel; and three Presidential assistants, Persons, Martin, and Gerald D. Morgan. Eisenhower remained aloof and unruffled while his staff sweated out the tactical problem he had presented them. At 4:45 he changed into golfing slacks and went out on the back lawn to practice pitch shots.

At 5:30 P.M. the diligent golfer was informed that a statement had been achieved. Going to his second-floor study, he there found Adams, Kyes, and Vice-President Nixon with the draft statement. Ike read it, discussed it for about half an hour, then gave it his approval and instructed that it should be read to the press by Stevens in Hagerty's office in the east wing, to emphasize that it carried full Presidential endorsement. In addition, Hagerty was to say plainly that the President had seen the statement and approved it "one hundred percent."

At six o'clock the statement was read over the telephone to Dirksen and McCarthy. Both senators rejected it, and Dirksen thereupon told newsmen that there was no "meeting of minds" yet. Nevertheless, at 6:15 Hagerty called correspondents into his office, and Stevens read the statement aloud.

It was a total repudiation of the chicken-luncheon "understanding." That memorandum had been misconstrued, the Secretary said, and he had not receded from "any of the principles upon which I stand. I shall never accede to the abuse of Army personnel under any circumstances, including committee hearings. I shall never accede to them being browbeaten or humiliated. I do not intend them to be deprived of counsel when the matter under consideration is one of essential interest to me as secretary, as was the case with General Zwicker. From assurances which I have received from members of the subcommittee I am confident that they will not permit such conditions to develop in the future."

At the close, Hagerty said the President had seen the statement and approved it completely. Asked whether Stevens would resign, Hagerty said, "No."

The Secretary was jubilant; all his self-confidence was restored. "We certainly have a commander-in-chief," he said, beaming. "He stepped up to the plate and knocked out a home run!"

This elation was premature. Over in the Capitol outfield, the senators' McCarthy scooped Ike's sizzler out of the air and hurled it back red-hot. He accused Stevens of making a "completely false statement." Not only had nobody been "browbeaten and humiliated," he said, but "Stevens knows that Zwicker did not demand counsel. Witnesses in the past have been allowed counsel whenever they want. That condition will continue in the future." And he thought the committee ought to recall Zwicker to tell about "this affidavit he signed giving a false version of his testimony. I want to know whether he was mistaken, or whether the secretary was purposely misinformed." Finally, no assurances about the future had been given; on the contrary, "if witnesses are not frank and truthful," they would be "examined vigorously to get the truth." Joe was fighting mad.

But the next day, repeating his comments before fifty reporters and newsreel and television cameras, he toned them down somewhat. He couldn't have given anybody assurances against "browbeating" witnesses, he said, because none had ever been browbeaten: "Eisenhower has said he is against browbeating witnesses. I am, too." No Republican leader, from the President down, the senator insisted, had ever suggested that he soft-pedal or call off any probe of communism or corruption, and he would continue to "expose Communists and crooks, even if it embarrasses my own party." So far as he was concerned, this present incident was closed, and he had no further differences with Stevens.

That day the Secretary visited the Capitol and talked with Senator Margaret Chase Smith, but not with McCarthy. At the White House, it was said that "lots of telegrams" were coming in about the controversy, but no breakdown was given. The atmosphere at the Pentagon was one of gloom and bitterness; the unspoken question in most minds was whether Stevens, despite his recovery of firmness, could ever regain the confidence of the Army.

Reviewing the whole snarled skein of events, Arthur Krock dwelt on one source of wonder to him—that so many of those "who take on McCarthy play into his hands. The Army let him disclose the [Peress] story that it had kept secret. General Zwicker tried to fence with the senator . . . and this fencing got him into the silly trap about the hypothetical theft of $50. Secretary Stevens . . . while outraged by McCarthy's manhandling of a helpless witness, lost much of [his] advantage . . . by taking a position which McCarthy could attack as . . . disregard of the legislative function of Congress." To Krock the moral was clear:

"Officials who get into a slugging match with McCarthy had best be sure in advance that they have loyal seconds in their corners, a Sunday punch in both fists, and stamina to stay to the finish."

In Krock's estimation the President's reputation had been "plainly impeached."

[II]

This view was shared by many critics of both McCarthy and Eisenhower, and it led to their transposing the struggle into a different key. In immediate reaction, the Republican command was shocked into realizing that a party split was not only possible but entirely likely, unless somehow McCarthy were curbed. But it was the old dilemma of who would bell the cat. Senator Homer Ferguson, chairman of the Senate Republican policy committee, called a meeting at once to consider changes in the rules governing all investigative committees, the avowed object being to devise safeguards that might protect McCarthy from his own excesses. Joe expressed a lack of interest in the subject, saying that no matter what rules were adopted, "if a committee chairman is competent and thorough, you will have a good investigation; but if the chairman is incompetent, the rules won't help him."

The problem, as Republican strategists saw only too clearly, was to keep McCarthy within bounds, without forfeiting the benefit they expected to reap from his vote-getting strength in the coming election. The Democrats were nervous for the same reason: they *feared* Joe's popularity with the voters. And about that popularity there was no division of opinion. *Newsweek* conducted a survey of Wisconsin voters and found that if Joe were running again, he would be reelected easily. Beyond all question, McCarthy was in a strong position. *America,* the magazine of liberal opinion edited by Jesuits, in an extended article traced the "incredible events" of the week and pointed out that, whereas both Stevens and the administration had retreated and misfired, McCarthy had successfully stood his ground—"which, considering the odds against him, took some doing." It was undoubtedly McCarthy's greatest victory, the writer believed, because it had brought into play the constitutional principle of the separation of governmental powers. The battle over the mutual independence of the executive and the legislative branches had been fought sporadically ever since the administration of George Washington; Presidents had clashed with Congress on that issue again and again; but never had they been challenged so boldly and on the whole so successfully as they had been by McCarthy. By wringing from Stevens (in the "surrender" memorandum) the right to question Army officers at will, the senator had acquired a preponderant influence over that branch of the executive, for officers under fire would be strongly tempted to adapt their ways, not primarily to fidelity to the Army's interests, but rather to "looking good" before their inquisitor. And this would mean letting a single senator dictate Army policy—a situation frightening in its possibilities. Stevens' retraction, followed by McCarthy's unyielding defiance, brought this threat to constitutional government clearly into focus.

The same article, signed by *America*'s editor-in-chief, the Reverend Robert C. Hartnett, S.J., and rather forbiddingly titled "Presidential Leadership vs. Senate Hegemony," went on to note that Eisenhower had been endeavoring to "get along" with McCarthy ever since the 1952 election. He had taken issue with the senator on a few specific issues, such as the Bohlen appointment, but he had never faced up to a direct, personal challenge to his constitutional prerogative. Now, however, the issue was no longer one of "Ike versus Joe," but of the invasion of executive autonomy by the legislative branch, represented by one senator—a shockingly successful invasion, too, carried out in a typically audacious manner. This issue was serious; history held many warnings of its gravity and of the harm it could do to the nation's liberties; and *America* fervently hoped that the President at last would provide the leadership in this crisis that he had promised.

"It is depressing," Father Hartnett concluded not unprophetically, "to wonder how we can keep Indo-China out of the hands of Red China when doubt is thrown on the ability of the President to keep control of his own branch out of the hands of Republican senators."

And the issue thus fundamentally stated was echoed elsewhere. Writing in *The New York Times,* W. H. Lawrence pointed out that each of McCarthy's successive defiances of the administration had brought him greater power; and Lawrence traced the senator's successful belligerency back to the accommodation Ike had reached with the senator in the 1952 campaign, when Eisenhower had stricken from his Milwaukee speech his proposed defense of General Marshall. "From that time on," Lawrence wrote, "McCarthy had little fear of Eisenhower. There is little doubt that McCarthy is a powerful influence in and out of the Senate. Now the question is: when, if ever, will the administration have a genuine and decisive showdown with him? Time alone can tell whether McCarthy's greatest victory may turn out to be a prelude to the big defeat; but the road that has been traveled from Peoria to the Pentagon contains no evidence that such will be the case."

[III]

The issue would not be exorcised by scholarly analysis, and reporters prodded Joe about rumors that were becoming persistent to the effect that "one last effort" was being made to bring him and Eisenhower into harmony, or even directly together. How would he like to go to the White House, Joe was asked.

"Permanently?" he shot back.

"Permanently or temporarily."

"Permanently, no. Temporarily, I wouldn't mind." He smiled. And in New York, preparing to take his wife home from the hospital, he told the press that he didn't think the President wanted to curb his power.

"I see some stories one day, and I see them changed on another," he commented offhandedly. "But I doubt whether the President intends to prevent me from digging into Communists. His campaign promises and mine were the same—to dig out the Communist menace in this country."

Leonard Hall, GOP national chairman, emerged from a conference with the President and agreed with newsmen that the dispute indeed was hurting the party. When it came to fighting communism, Hall said, he went along with Joe, but not when it came to attacking generals and others who were just as anti-Communist as himself.

Some vivid retort from Joe was expected; but Hall called the senator to his hotel secretly and begged him not to make any rejoinder, for the sake of the party, and Joe consented. His only comment on the visit, when reporters found out about it, was that "Len and I are good friends," although they had a right to differ. Personally, he added, he was "about ready to call a moratorium" on exchanging barbs with his critics.

For a day or two the headlines were preempted by a topic other than McCarthy when several Puerto Rican fanatics opened fire from the visitors gallery in the House of Representatives, wounding five congressmen. The assailants wanted independence for Puerto Rico. This sensational flurry momentarily distracted attention from the struggle for political dominance taking place in Washington. But the pressure on the President not to let McCarthy's latest defiance pass without rebuke was incessant. If he failed to assert his authority, not only the liberal press was saying, there would be nothing to halt the drive of McCarthy, the "neo-Fascist," toward total power, and for Eisenhower to maintain silence would be a surrender to egregious Joe even more glaring than Stevens' capitulation.

The alarmists overlooked several factors in the equation, but the time was inimical to clear reasoning. It was evident that in his party McCarthy was tolerated rather than accepted; he still held no post of leadership and was not admitted to policy-making councils. He had supporters, yes, but they were dispersed, undisciplined, unorganized, effective only at intervals, at the ballot box; between elections they were a rumble of opinion only, committed to no economic or social program, focused on no basic political reform. He had no private army, no "shirts," black, brown, red, or motley. Joe, in a word, was not a wager of strategic warfare; he was a pirate, a raider, who fought by sudden attack, by ambushes and skirmishes. Mobility was essential to his style of fighting. Politics was a game, and he played it with the same concentration and gusto with which he played poker—ruthlessly, to win. Each deal was separate, a new hand, a fresh encounter with an adversary, and all his energies would be bent on taking that immediate round. As the stakes inevitably grew higher the fascination of the game increased; yet although the payoff was in personal power, he seldom gave any indication of knowing what to do with the power that he gained. Such a corsair, supremely independent, darting in or sheering off as luck and daring dictated, had little concept of any ultimate victory; he lived from day to day, temperamentally all but oblivious of tomorrow. Taking chances was his way of life; his chief weapons were surprise and audacity; his only counsel of prudence, to attack. *The Nation* erred in ascribing to him a Hitlerian ambition—"a good showman and astute politician . . . who, while he plays by ear, also follows the score" and thoroughly understood "the blueprint by which European Fascists undertook the conquest of power." *The Nation* was correct, however, in estimating that "no matter how reckless or desperate the particular gamble may be, [McCarthy] has no choice now but to take it, for he has reached the point of no return."

That position suited Joe exactly: it left him no choice but to win.

[IV]

On the Wednesday after Stevens' "recovery operation" at the White House, the President was to hold his regular press conference. The day before, reporters prodding Hagerty to say whether the President would take up McCarthy's challenge were told impressively, "Wait until tomorrow." This set off intense excitement at the Capitol. It also alerted Joe, and he announced that he would hold a press conference of his own immediately after the President had spoken; television coverage was invited.

On Wednesday morning, correspondents lined up early for admission to the Indian Treaty Room of the old State Department building, where Eisenhower was to appear. The Treaty Room was known throughout Washington for its ugliness ("the ugliest room in Christendom"). It was a pretentious Victorian monstrosity, with immensely high ceiling, cast-iron gallery, walls paneled in green and purple marble ("the colors of mildew and clotted blood"), and in each corner cast-iron angels holding aloft "a set of pawn-shop lights." At conference time 256 reporters were crowded into the ungainly chamber.

On the dot of 10:30, the President arrived, spruce and ruddy. He spoke at ease as he extended his sympathy to the men wounded in the House of Representatives shooting. Then he read a prepared statement—the keenly awaited chastisement that was to tame the Senate's incorrigible Joe. What the reporters heard was a letdown.

The President led off with mild criticism of the "disregard for standards of fair play" shown by some congressional committees. The Peress case he conceded had been mishandled, but the Army was "correcting its procedures to avoid such mistakes in the future," and neither in this case nor in any others would the executive department allow any witness to "submit to any kind of personal humiliation when testifying before Congressional committees or elsewhere." Furthermore, the ultimate responsibility for the conduct of the executive branch lay with the President of the United States, and "that responsibility cannot be delegated to another branch." The right of Congress to investigate must be upheld, but real cooperation could be achieved "only in an atmosphere of mutual respect," and employes of the executive branch appearing as witnesses would have "unqualified support" in insisting that they be treated fairly.

The statement wound up with warm praise of the Army and specific praise of General Zwicker, and the relaying of assurances received from Senator Knowland, the Senate's majority leader, that new codes of procedure were being worked out for committees. Not once was McCarthy mentioned, and the total lack of belligerency or indignation in the statement acted on the press corps like a wet blanket. Inviting questions, Eisenhower remained unruffled, laughed readily at some allusions, but declined to add anything material to his formal statement or to attack McCarthy directly, merely expressing the hope that the average American's love of fair play would bring about fair play in all investigations.

The conference lasted twenty-six minutes, and as soon as it ended, McCarthy met the press in Room 155 of the Senate Office Building and read his own prepared statement before the television cameras, stopping often to let the photographers catch all the angles. At the close of the reading, but not before, he handed mimeographed copies of the text to newspaper reporters.

About the belligerency of *his* statement there was no possible misunderstanding. He not only defied the President again, he patronized him.

"It is important to remember that this silly tempest in a teapot," the senator read, "arose because we dared to bring to light the bold, unpleasant facts about a Fifth Amendment Communist officer, who was promoted, given special immunity from duty outside the United States, and finally given an honorable discharge with the full knowledge of all concerned that he was a member of the Communist party. It now appears that for some reason he was a sacred cow of certain Army brass."

(Here, in the typed statement but mraked out in pencil and not read to the cameras, appeared: "Too much wind has been blowing from high places in defense of this Fifth Amendment Communist officer.")

"A continued exchange of statements about our exposure of this Fifth Amendment Communist Army officer is worse than ridiculous," the senator's crisp, nagging voice went on. "I stated last night that I will take no part in this pointless waste of time. Rather, I shall spend my time in action—in the continued exposure of those who are dedicated to the Communist enslavement of the world."

Then Joe clouted General Zwicker with both fists:

"If a stupid, arrogant, or witless man in a position of power appears before our committee and is found aiding the Communist party, he will be exposed. The fact that he might be a general places him in no special class so far as I am concerned."

Next it was Eisenhower's turn for a backhand swipe:

"Apparently the President and I agree [here the word *now* had been deleted, with a reminder to the press to take note] on the necessity of getting rid of Communists. I hope that the President realizes the reason for the gleeful shouting of every un-American element over what they consider a fight between those who honestly oppose communism. I think their joy will be shortlived. When the shouting and the tumult dies, the American people and the President will realize that the unprecedented mudslinging against the committee by the extreme left wing of the press and radio was caused because another Fifth Amendment Communist in government was finally dug out of the dark recesses and exposed to the public view."

As the television lights were snapped off, a sardonic reporter commented, "Pretty conciliatory statement, Joe."

"You should have seen it before they changed it!" was Joe's comeback.

And the headlines that afternoon and the next day were something to see, too. The heading on James Reston's account in the *Times* was a fair sample:

OTHER CHEEK IS STRUCK—EISENHOWER WOULD
TURN IT TO McCARTHY, AND THE SENATOR,
HE JUST UP AND OBLIGED

Reston could not get over his astonishment at this brilliant demonstration of McCarthy's mastery of mass communication techniques. "He knows the importance of timing and of violence and of brevity in a political fight. In the first place, he produced his statement soon enough after the President's to insure that it would be displayed alongside the President's. He concentrated on getting it out on television, with the result that the McCarthy image and melody lingered on the TV screens long after the President had gone to bed."

Then again, only after he had read his statement to the television audience did the senator release the text to the wire services, which then flashed it to the press nationwide. Under these conditions, Joe's rebuttal had to be included in the main, page-one reports of the President's remarks, because it ran directly counter to numerous points in the President's text. This insured Joe equal coverage on the front pages, as well as separate coverage inside. *The New York Times,* for instance, carried a full page of questions and answers at Ike's conference, half a dozen news stories, texts, and comment, which the two principal figures shared about equally—even though one was the President of the United States. It was indeed a masterly exercise of McCarthy's peculiar skill and incredible daring, and the reaction of all who had been banking on Eisenhower to stop the senator was one of dismay.

This feeling was aptly expressed in a cartoon showing a martial Ike drawing his sword with a stern, "Have a care, sir!" Second glance showed that what was emerging from the scabbard was a feather, while black-jowled Joe stood grinning, clutching a dripping butcher's cleaver.

Eisenhower definitely was the loser in the encounter. The *Washington Post* recalled despairingly that in 1952 it had predicted that if Eisenhower were elected President, " 'McCarthyism' would disappear overnight." But now the *Post* had waited "some four hundred nights for the President to exert the kind of leadership that would bring that happy result," and the prophecy remained unfulfilled.

The *New York Herald Tribune* declared that McCarthy grew "increasingly insolent" in his unchecked resort to "reckless demagoguery and irresponsible power."

The officers of Freedom House and the American Civil Liberties Union wired the President urgently to muzzle McCarthy. Mrs. Agnes Meyer told the Ohio chapter of the American Association of University Professors that McCarthy was "our number one Fascist." And Democratic National Chairman Stephen Mitchell refused to appear with the senator at a St. Patrick's Day dinner given by the Irish Fellowship Club of Chicago, saying, "I will not break bread with a man who has borne false witness against 30,000,000 Americans." (The club reported "a tremendous boom" in the demand for tickets following Mitchell's statement, and the dinner, at which McCarthy was to be the guest of honor, was sold out.) A faculty adviser of Cornell University's Republican Club resigned when the club invited Senator McCarthy to speak on the campus. And in Washington, John F. Kane, special assistant to Army Secretary Stevens, resigned because the Secretary was not getting the "energetic support" he needed in his fight with McCarthy.

In *The New York Times,* military affairs writer Hanson W. Baldwin said, under the headline, "Who Commands the Army?" that both Stevens and Eisenhower had lost face in the showdown, and "whether President Eisenhower realizes it or not, Senator McCarthy is now sharing with him command of the Army."

And still the storm did not abate. Preachers took to their pulpits to denounce the senator with fresh ferocity. In New York the pastor of the Broadway Tabernacle branded McCarthy "a menace to our society and way of life. . . . His arrogance, his methods of investigation, his publicity seeking, his disregard of truth, his seeking after power, his contempt for all who come within his grasp are a travesty of Americanism."

At the Riverside Church, Dr. Robert J. McCracken mourned that "Senator McCarthy goes his way undeterred, bullying and browbeating witnesses, smearing reputations, claiming in the sacred name of patriotism to be exposing Communists, but in point of fact undermining the principles which brought this nation into being." Nor did this preacher recoil from stirring the waters of religious strife; pointedly he reminded his congregation that the senator was "a member of a church that has never disavowed the Inquisition, that makes a policy of censorship, that insists upon conformity."

Overseas, British Conservatives, Liberals, and Laborites joined in an acid chorus of condemnation and alarm: McCarthy was compared to Hitler, and President Eisenhower to the senile and inept Field Marshal von Hindenberg, who had been Hitler's unwitting stalking-horse. The cry arose that by his "moral paralysis" Eisenhower was threatening to "betray the peace." The *Spectator* promulgated the doctrine that "to be pro-American and anti-McCarthy are the same thing." Herbert Morrison, the Labor party's deputy leader and former Foreign Secretary, told a party rally that McCarthy above all others was injuring his country's reputation, and called on the people of the United States to "deal with him." (Joe fluffed off Morrison's attack as inconsequential, saying, "We don't need the advice of Herbert Morrison—not right away, anyway.")

At home, the tumult grew louder when Defense Secretary Wilson, back from vacation, was questioned about McCarthy's charge that the Army "coddled" Communists. "That's just plain damned tommyrot!" Wilson scoffed. The way the Peress case had been handled was wrong, he agreed, but steps were being taken to prevent a repetition, and Stevens would take care of all that. But Wilson had to be nudged before he would criticise McCarthy, and on the whole he applauded the senator for "bringing to the attention of the country the fact that we have this Communist business and we have to deal with it. I know the American people are fed up with the consideration the Communists had in the past. There has been too much footsie-playing with them."

McCarthy was talking with reporters when word was brought of Wilson's "tommyrot" remark. At first the senator shrugged it off, saying that "a healthy fight clears the air," and all the public uproar didn't mean a permanent split in the Republican party. Later he replied specifically that "no one ever charged that the Army as such was coddling Communists," and he recommended that Wilson read the record on the "last three Fifth Amendment Communists."

But speculation on a lasting division of Republican ranks was heard everywhere. Leonard Hall decried the possibility; all this exchange of views, he said, was "just a family difference." But independent observers like Arthur Krock said bluntly that the Republicans now faced an inevitable choice—Ike or Joe. And the *Washington Post* regretfully conceded that McCarthy held the initiative and had "given much evidence that he will continue to use it." Eisenhower was the liberals' last hope, and that was a fading one. A bitter Herblock expressed this feeling of near despair: a voter wearing an "I Like Ike" campaign button sat facing a glum Eisenhower, saying, "And I would *still* like to see you President of the United States."

No one in Congress was willing to act, that seemed certain. The Democratic leadership in the Senate, from Lyndon Baines Johnson down, was determined to sidestep any open clash with Joe: let the Republicans tear each other to pieces over him. And the Republicans were circumspect: few of them would desert Eisenhower, if matters came to a test, but they skidded away from going on record as opposed to McCarthy.

The liberal wing of the Democratic party, however, believed that an opportunity had been opened to carry the fight directly into the Eisenhower camp and pin on the President himself the responsibility for letting McCarthy run riot. The decision to mount such an attack was reached at a conference of party leaders in Miami, to the distress of conservative Southerners. But as Chairman Mitchell put it, the issue now was "not whether the Army was coddling Communists, but whether the Republicans were coddling Joe."

[V]

On the day of Wilson's incautious expletive, word leaked out that two Democratic senators, McClellan of Arkansas and Richard Russell of Georgia, had asked the Pentagon for a "full report" on the rumored interference by Roy Cohn with the military career of his friend, Private G. David Schine. This development opened up a new line of speculation as to whether the Army, with the help of some Democrats, had decided to fight back.

Then three days after the President's even-tempered press conference, Adlai Stevenson delivered a slashing attack on the President personally. This was a new tactic, since hitherto Eisenhower's popularity had been simply too overwhelming for the Democrats to risk a direct assault; in recent polls Ike's favorable ratings had ranged as high as 75 percent. Reviewing the ills that supposedly had been brought about by "McCarthyism," the 1952 Presidential standard-bearer charged that the Republicans ("half McCarthy and half Eisenhower") had embarked on a campaign of "slander, dissension, and deception to win elections," and called over the list of disastrous effects as he perceived them:

"Our State Department has been assailed and demoralized; the American voice abroad has been enfeebled; our educational system has been attacked; our servants of God impugned; a former President maligned; the President himself patronized; and now the integrity, loyalty, and morale of the United States Army have been assailed."

The issue in the coming election, Stevenson asserted flatly, was and would be "McCarthyism."

All these mischiefs wrought by the junior senator from Wisconsin—a man without party authority, heading no united, organized support, a maverick politician as quick to offend a friend as a foe? The spirit of hysteria indeed was abroad in the land, so much so that some staunch elements of "anti-McCarthyism" were moved to protest against Stevenson's overmagnification and oversimplification. *Commonweal* reminded its readers that it was important to note that "McCarthy has not killed the country; he has only made it mildly sick."

Similar cautions were offered abroad, where some competent observers warned Europeans that the picture they were receiving was at least partially distorted. Writing in the *Spectator,* Denis W. Brogan reported that there was something to the anti-Red zeal of Americans "besides 'witch-burning hysteria.'. . . There *were* secret Communists in high places. The Tydings committee *did* lean over backwards in giving the Department of State a clean bill of health. If it is a fault in Americans to shout 'We were betrayed!' so loudly, it is a fault to forget that there *were* betrayers, and that the charges of Communist penetration were not merely a campaign 'red herring.' "

The New York correspondent of the *London Daily Telegraph* also cautioned, in an article entitled "McCarthy's Other Side," that Britishers might not realize "what dismay was caused by the evidence of quite large-scale Communist penetration into top government positions." Penetration of the government by Soviet Russia, the article continued, "worries Americans concerned for the safety of their country, and many are prepared to put up with some abbreviations of civil liberty if they think it is the only way to root out what they are now convinced is a threat to all liberty."

McCarthy was in Miami for a weekend of fishing when Stevenson spoke, and instantly he demanded equal free time to answer "this good police court lawyer's job of attacking me." He told reporters confidently that he had no doubt the networks would grant the request. This brought the savage comment from Mitchell, "Now we'll see whether McCarthy controls the FCC and the broadcasting companies."

On all sides it was pointed out that Stevenson's target had not been McCarthy personally, but the President and the Republican party for allegedly embracing the senator's methods, and furious protests arose against McCarthy's replying, thus implying that he was the party's spokesman. This was intolerable to the Eisenhower wing; it would mean the virtual abdication of party leadership by Ike. Joe said his request offered a test of whether free speech prevailed, and such bellwethers as *The New York Times* agreed that it provided a test, "but not of free speech. Mr. McCarthy has that. It is a test of the control of the Republican party. Mr. McCarthy hasn't that—yet. And it is up to President Eisenhower and his advisers to prevent him from getting it."

In Stevenson's eyes, control of the Republican party by Joe McCarthy was a *fait accompli;* to *The New York Times* it seemed impending unless vigorous steps were taken to prevent it. And what would control of the Republican party mean? Why, control of the government, which in turn exercised majority control over the most powerful nation the world had ever seen. Magnifying either the conscious ambition, or the potentialities, of the junior senator from Wisconsin to such awesome proportions was as delusive as were the underestimates of his abilities and effectiveness by which he had been so pertinaciously discounted.

The clamor over the reply to Stevenson swelled to a din, drowning out, for the moment, all other issues, foreign and domestic; Washington seemed at a standstill. The spectacle bewildered many an unhysterical and seasoned observer of the capital's moods. Anne O'Hare McCormick, *New York Times* writer on foreign affairs, was appalled. Secretary Dulles had just returned from a meeting of foreign ministers in Berlin where questions of worldwide import had been discussed; a summit meeting of the big powers at Geneva was in preparation; yet, in the turmoil over McCarthy, vital events like these, and the urgently pressing problems which they presented, were being pushed into the background and positively ignored.

"Ever since the storm [the McCarthy-Stevens issue] broke over this shaken capital," wrote Mrs. McCormick, "Berlin is all but forgotten . . . even the controversy over the Geneva conference as the opening wedge to the recognition of Red China is reduced to a murmur by the thunderous repercussions of the latest episode in a cumulative story. The story begins to be frightening. . . . It is serious enough that Senator McCarthy's success in monopolizing the headlines distracts public attention from more important matters. It is more serious when a legislator can challenge the executive branch of the government and sow discord, bitterness, and fear among the American people at a time when national unity is imperative. The truth is that the country cannot concentrate upon the great problems of our time, cannot give due thought to the crucial questions . . . while the McCarthy issue continues to poison the atmosphere."

In plain words, the nation could no longer afford McCarthy.

When matters reach such a pass, reaction—or revolution—is inevitable. To either of these possibilities the senator paid no heed. He was living in the moment, and the moment was satisfyingly heady—giving and taking blows, a melee of highly agreeable risks and encounters.

The Bursting of the Dam

But this was only the beginning of what would go down in Washington annals as the city's most tumultuous week since the Republicans had come to power.

Stung by having been beaten to the draw by McCarthy, Leonard Hall, at Eisenhower's direction, one day later asked the networks for free time to answer Stevenson in the name of the party, emphasizing that this was not a matter "for personal rebuttal by any individual," but for a person designated by the party to speak for it. Relieved to be extricated from their dilemma, CBS and NBC granted Hall's request immediately, and it was announced that Vice-President Nixon would make the party's reply. McCarthy's request was turned down.

Arriving in New York from Miami on that day, the senator agreed that Hall should have the free time, but insisted he should have time, too, to answer "a lengthy and vicious attack on me personally. I am delegating no one to answer the attack on me. Nixon is speaking for the party; I am speaking for myself." And he promised that the networks would either grant him time "or learn what the law is—I guarantee that."

The senator was met at La Guardia Airport by an escort of ten city policemen under command of a captain. The latter shook McCarthy's hand cordially and explained that the escort had been assigned as a result of telephoned threats. "Everybody in the crowd has got to be watched," he said. Joe and his wife taxied to the Waldorf-Astoria for their overnight stay. At the same time word leaked out that one reason for Hall's swift request for air time had been the administration's want of confidence that Joe wouldn't start out attacking Democrats and wind up attacking the White House. These events happened on Monday.

On Tuesday, McCarthy spent forty-five minutes privately with Bernard Baruch, the "elder statesman," in the latter's apartment at the Drake Hotel, and attended a luncheon of the Dutch Treat Club, where he spoke off the record and accepted an award. He repeated the speech in a press conference, during which he deliberately turned his back on the NBC and CBS television cameras, saying, "I'll do nothing for them." The cameramen pleaded, but he was unyielding; about the law governing free time he conceded he was not entirely clear, but he intended to find out, and meanwhile, NBC and CBS would be boycotted.

In Washington, meanwhile, two developments were occurring, both in the Senate. Senator Ralph Flanders, the whimsical, crotchety Vermont Republican who had entered the Senate simultaneously with McCarthy, attacked Joe in a speech filled with biting ridicule. It was the first direct attack from the Republican side and caused immense excitement, with speculation as to what lay behind it. Actually it was a purely impulsive and independent action.

"The junior senator from Wisconsin interests us all, no doubt about that," Flanders began in his homely twang. "But also he puzzles some of us. To what party does he belong? Is he a hidden satellite of the Democrat party, to which he is furnishing so much material for quiet mirth? It doesn't seem that his Republican label can be stuck on very tightly, when by intention or through ignorance he is doing his best to shatter that party whose label he wears. He no longer claims or wants any support from the Communist fringe. What is his party affiliation? One must conclude that his is a one-man party, and that its name is 'McCarthyism,' a title which he has proudly accepted.

"The junior senator from Vermont," Flanders went on with puckish humor, "finds much to admire and much to deplore in 'McCarthyism' as he sees it displayed on the national scene. That which is praiseworthy is the vigorous and effective housecleaning which it undertakes. In January of last year the Republican family moved into quarters which had been occupied by another family for twenty long years. The outgoing family did not clean up the premises before it left; the premises were very dirty indeed. Into these dirty premises the junior senator from Wisconsin charged with all the energy and enthusiasm of a natural-born housekeeper. He found dirt under the rug. He found dirt behind the chiffonier.

He found dirt in all the corners. He found cobwebs and spiders in the cellarway. All this dirt he found and displayed, and the clean-up he personally supervised. Of course it was not done quietly." But then, "natural-born housewives" seldom worked quietly.

Nevertheless, in all his life he had never "seen or heard anything to match the dust and racket of this particular job of housecleaning. Perhaps these extremes are necessary if a one-man party is to be kept in the headlines and in the limelight." But the question now before the nation was whether the necessary housecleaning was the main task before the United States, or "do we face far more dangerous problems, from the serious consideration of which we are being diverted by the dust and the racket?"

It was Flanders' belief that "we are being diverted to a dangerous extent. In very truth, the world seems to be mobilizing for the great battle of Armageddon," and in that struggle, "what is the part being played by the junior senator from Wisconsin? He dons his war paint. He goes into his war dance. He emits his war whoops. He goes forth to battle, and proudly returns with the scalp of a pink Army dentist. We may assume that this represents the depth and seriousness of Communist penetration in this country at this time. . . . Let him not so work as to conceal the mortal danger in which our country finds itself from the external enemies of mankind."

There was no flamboyant rhetoric here, and the whimsicality of the picture provoked (Joe in apron and mop cap making great to-do with a feather duster) drew chuckles on both sides of the chamber; but Senator Cooper of Kentucky was the only one to praise the speech. That evening President Eisenhower conveyed his congratulations to Flanders in an unpublicized personal note. But this same day the Democratic senators caucused on the election issues and decided to stick to economic questions and dodge the issue of McCarthy.

In New York, Joe laughed at Flanders' whimsy. "One of the nicest old gentlemen I have ever met," he said, "but I'm too busy to answer Republican heroes."

That evening the linotypers at *The New York Times* were busy setting an editorial that spoke of the "moral cowardice" shown in the Democratic caucus and warned the Democrats that they were "playing with fire" when they treated McCarthy as a strictly Republican problem. "There have been potential McCarthys in Democratic ranks, too, as the Democrats well know," the senators were reminded. And so passed Tuesday.

[II]

On Wednesday, the dam began to show first signs of cracking. At his press conference Eisenhower appeared in a mood vastly different from the relaxed affability of one week before. Today he was blunt and plainly angry. First he commended Flanders' stand, although withholding detailed comment on the speech until he had read it. Departing from his rule against dealing in personalities, he said curtly that he didn't know whether McCarthy would be speaking for the party in the fall campaign; "no one in the world could say that." On this point he allowed himself to be quoted directly, a permission rarely given. Confronted with Stevenson's taunt that the Republican party was hopelessly divided ("half McCarthy and half Eisenhower") the President blurted, "Nonsense!" While stopping just short of an open break with McCarthy, the President's whole attitude was one of bitterness, and he emphasized in the strongest terms that Vice-President Nixon, in his forthcoming reply to Stevenson, would be speaking for the party. The correspondents were impressed by the sudden change in Eisenhower's tone and speculated on a possible White House decision to muzzle Joe.

At noon, that Wednesday, Senator McCarthy lunched with Defense Secretary Wilson at the Pentagon. Their talk lasted two hours, and when reporters were called in, the two men were laughing jovially, apparently on the best of terms. Both said that they had "no argument" on how to deal with Communists drafted into the Army, and when a newsman brought up Wilson's "damned tommyrot" remark, Joe promptly countered that he had never said the Army "as such" was guilty of "coddling Reds," and Wilson joined in that he "hadn't come to Washington to quarrel with anybody." McCarthy added that he was sure that 99 percent of the officers in the Army were loyal, and his committee was simply helping to clean out "the few rotten apples." The senator dominated the press conference, and incidentally announced that he would reply to Stevenson in a Fulton Lewis, Jr., broadcast over the Mutual network the following evening. And he renewed his threat to compel CBS and NBC to grant him thirty minutes of free time.

Upon returning to the Capitol, McCarthy ran into a rumor that Senator Potter was going to join the Democrats on the investigations subcommittee in demanding the removal of Roy Cohn as subcommittee counsel. Joe called Potter to his office and the two had a long session together, without revealing what was discussed; but reporters sensed that something critical was impending, and there were hints of grave dissension in the subcommittee.

That afternoon McCarthy held a brief public hearing of the subcommittee. Two former Communists, who confessed that they had perjured themselves in previous testimony, recanted and accused former associates at a communications laboratory in New Jersey of being Reds. Noting that Senator Jackson was not present, the chairman tartly remarked that members of the committee who stayed away had "no right to complain about one-man hearings," as Jackson had done recently.

The real surge of news that afternoon, however, was the public reaction to an unprecedented attack on Senator McCarthy made by Edward R. Murrow in his "See It Now" telecast the previous evening. Murrow and his staff had spent two months putting together what was announced as "a report on Senator Joseph R. McCarthy told mainly in his own words and pictures." The entire telecast was given over to this "report" (Murrow would not concede that it was an "attack"), during which carefully edited films showed McCarthy in such vulgarian lapses as belching, picking his nose, ignoring witnesses before his committee, laughing at his own unsubtle humor ("Alger—I mean Adlai"), contradicting himself, and otherwise displaying crudities of manner and glaring inconsistencies. It was an exhibition to repel the fastidious, and the main host of McCarthy's outspoken enemies were well bred, educated, mannerly, genteel. Murrow's graveyard-voice commentary drew on Shakespeare with the question, "Upon what meat does Senator McCarthy feed?" And the ready answer: "Two of the staples of his diet are the investigations (protected by immunity) and the half-truth. . . . It is necessary to investigate before legislating, but the line between investigation and persecution is a very fine one, and the junior senator has stepped over it repeatedly. His primary achievement has been in confusing the public mind as between the internal and the external threat of communism. . . . [His actions] have caused alarm and dismay amongst our allies abroad and given considerable comfort to our enemies, and whose fault is it? Not really his: he didn't create this situation of fear, he merely exploited it, and rather successfully. Cassius was right: 'The fault, dear Brutus, is not in our stars, but in ourselves.' "

Toward the close of the program, which was seen in prime time in thirty-six cities, the audience was admonished that "this is no time for men who oppose Senator McCarthy's methods to keep silent, or for those who approve." And McCarthy was offered equal time, equal position, to reply, "if he believes we have done violence to his words or pictures."

The public response was instantaneous and prolonged. In New York, twenty extra telephone operators at CBS could not keep up with the calls. Final tabulation showed 12,924 calls received praising Murrow, and 1,368 defending Joe. Among the 7,000 letters reaching the New York offices, the ratio was 15 to 1 in favor of Murrow. In Washington, 13 people called to protest, 559 to applaud Murrow. In Macon, Georgia, the letters were running 100 to 1 for Murrow; in Los Angeles, 1,937 to 30; in Chicago, 2 to 1 against Joe. The network reported the response was the heaviest ever recorded.

McCarthy did not see the show; his wife said he had slept through it. When queried about it, the senator said he was inclined to take up Murrow's offer; meanwhile, he had accepted Fulton Lewis' offer of his own broadcast period.

[III]

Amid all the acclaim, a few voices of disagreement were raised, some in surprising quarters. Fulton Lewis explained that he had acted because he was "sickened by the pretense that Mr. Murrow is objective, that he sticks to strictly unbiased fact," when really he "is, and always has been, heavily slanted on the left side." But this attitude was expected from Fulton Lewis. More significantly, Murrow came under fire from sources not at all partial to McCarthy, the charge being made that the CBS commentator had resorted to the very use of "half-truths" for which McCarthy was so heartily denounced, and also that the offer of free rebuttal time was a dubious gesture, heavily weighted in Murrow's favor. The argument over the ethical questions involved was bitter since McCarthy's alleged low ethical standards (or no standards at all) had been cried aloud by his critics, and were in fact a keystone of the opposition to the man and his methods.

Two unexpected critics of the Murrow attack were John Cogley, in *Commonweal,* and Gilbert Seldes, in *Saturday Review.* Both these writers, as well as their magazines, had been strongly anti-McCarthy, basing their opposition on both political and ethical grounds. Now both pointed out that Murrow's telecast, billed as a "report," had in fact been an "attack" because of its one-sidedness. It was indeed a report, but exclusively an adverse report, using only material that had been carefully selected to convey a partisan point of view. As far as it went, it was accurate; but it did not go far enough. It was true, but not the whole truth. Cogley found that Murrow had set out to illustrate a thesis, and had done so brilliantly. Seldes reported, as proof of the selectivity of the material used, that Murrow had viewed 15,000 feet of film in search of exactly the clips suited to his purpose. Other commentators, Cogley observed, might make "a totally different selection of film which would turn Senator McCarthy into a man on a shining white steed—infinitely reasonable, burdened with the onus of single-handedly cleaning out subversives in the face of violent criticism, wholly without self-interest and sincerely devoted to the success of the Eisenhower administration." Cogley believed that film footage could be found to suggest all these noble attributes. "Instead of McCarthy with the chilling giggle, we could be shown shots of the shy bridegroom surrounded by admiring friends, the friendly political opponent who debated with Congressman Eugene McCarthy on television and consistently called him 'Gene' as if they were bosom buddies disagreeing over some abstruse point. We could have had the playful McCarthy who threw his arm around Senator Flanders after the Vermont Republican had lambasted him, and the courteous McCarthy who once found himself in an elevator with Dean Acheson."

Thus, Cogley concluded, the "report" Murrow offered was true in detail, but false in overall effect because only one side of a complex personality and extraordinarily complicated issue had been presented. The effect had been to suggest that there was only one side. And beyond this, Cogley saw a dangerous precedent in Murrow's presentation, because "television is dynamite; combined with selectivity it could explode in any person's or any group's face." Telecasts openly sponsored by political groups might indulge in one-sidedness without harmful effects, because allowance for bias would be made. But a commercially sponsored show, like Murrow's, using selected pictures and not the spoken word, which can be clearly answered, and the fact that "persons who disagreed with Murrow's evaluation of McCarthy had no hand in the selection of the clips to be shown" placed the "See It Now" program in a dif-ferent category—one not only patently unfair to its subject (an "attack" and not a "report"), but fraught with grave potentialities for the future use of the television medium.

All this was seconded by Gilbert Seldes in *Saturday Review.* While he could not personally vouch for the typicality or untypi-cality of clips showing McCarthy as "a giggling psychopath," Seldes was sure they "needed to be balanced by some clips showing him at his best. I have just returned from Milwaukee," Seldes reported, "where his dearest enemies assured me that McCarthy is per-suasive, dangerously agreeable, and—as they put it—'a *great* dem-agogue.' " He recalled that recently in *The New Yorker* magazine Richard Rovere had called McCarthy (who actually gave Rovere the creeps) "a political figure of the first rank . . . quite possibly an authentic genius." Seldes felt that the use of denigratory shots alone smacked of "the partial truth and the innuendo"—long pro-claimed by McCarthy's enemies to be the essence of "McCarthyism."

Seldes also dissented from the view that Murrow's offer of equal time on television constituted fair play. He called it an empty formula that stacked the odds outrageously against the senator. Murrow and his staff were professionals, admitted to be without peers in assembling and projecting an effective television docu-mentary. They had been helped by this professional skill, acquired by long experience in the medium, and they were backed by the vast prestige enjoyed by the "See It Now" program. To millions of viewers, Murrow's program had become "identified with in-tegrity, with fairness, with a sense of responsibility and justice"; and this accumulated prestige formed the background against which each week's broadcast appeared, each half-hour taking on solidity and power from the mere fact of its being one in a con-tinuing series. The half-hour handed over for rebuttal, on the other hand, would come as "merely an interruption" of the series, and a discordant interruption at that.

Increasing the disparity was the matter of cost. Murrow's pro-gram was estimated to have cost some $15,000 to prepare, count-ing salaries and incidentals. What if the subject of a similar "report" could not raise the considerable sum that would be needed to as-semble an effective rebuttal—even supposing, which was unlikely, that he could command the requisite professional talent?

The wave of public enthusiasm, however, swept over such demurrals, and Murrow was acclaimed a hero—tardy but triumphant —in the anti-McCarthy camp. Murrow himself modestly disclaimed any special merit.

The hasty offer by Fulton Lewis of a radio spot for McCarthy to answer Murrow was answered by a station in Cambridge, Massachusetts, which announced that it would not carry the rebuttal, terming it "not meriting a public airing."

On the same day in Montreal, Brother Thomas Austin, assistant general of the worldwide order of Marist Brothers, was interviewed on his arrival from France for a tour of Canada and went out of his way to comment on Senator McCarthy. The senator, he said, was being assailed as a Catholic "because he dared to place his finger on a sore spot—the underhanded domination of communism in spheres where its influence is unsuspected." In London, meanwhile, the *Catholic Herald* was blaming Senator McCarthy for carrying on a "reign of terror" in the United States, while the *Manchester Guardian* was taxing President Eisenhower with being "altogether too kind" to "patrioteers."

Obviously there still was more than one side to this question, even if all were not equally "equal," although the millions who had shrieked with laughter at Joe's belching on "See It Now" had not exactly been encouraged to consider that possibility.

[IV]

On Thursday the dam burst. It started in the forenoon, when Mrs. Annie Lee Moss, a timorous, pathetic widow, suspended from her job with the Signal Corps, appeared in a televised hearing before McCarthy's committee and softly but firmly denied any Communist connection or activities. The hearing was in the Senate caucus room and every seat was taken. Wearing a black coat and frayed white gloves, the witness leaned forward anxiously as she denied that she had belonged to the party and paid dues from 1943 to 1945. She was asked about her knowledge of "Robert Hall," identified by committee counsel Roy Cohn as a Washington correspondent for the *Daily Worker* and a Communist party functionary. Mrs. Moss replied that she knew a Robert Hall, a colored man, in connection with the cafeteria workers union to which she belonged, and that many years ago he had tried to get her son to sell the *Daily Worker,* but her husband had refused to let the boy do it.

At this point a reporter passed a note to Robert Kennedy, attending as counsel to the Democratic minority. Kennedy handed it to Senator McClellan. The note said that the Robert Hall who was the *Daily Worker* correspondent was a white man, and McClellan asked Cohn whether he knew that the man he was referring to was white. Cohn did not and became confused, and McClellan read the note into the record and ordered Cohn to check.

The questioning obviously was going poorly. McCarthy, presiding, excused himself quietly, saying he had to work on his broadcast that evening, and left. Senator Mundt took over as chairman.

The questioning became more and more absurd. Mrs. Moss's job, it developed, had nothing to do with coding machines; she was an operator of teletypes, her work consisting of feeding perforated tapes into the machines.

Asked whether she read the *Daily Worker,* she said it had come to her house for a while, but when a white man called to collect for it, she refused, because she never read it. "He kicked up quite a fuss," she recalled.

Asked if she knew the *Daily Worker* was a Communist newspaper, she said she had never heard of communism until 1948, when the Hiss scandal broke.

"Do you know who Karl Marx is?" asked Senator Symington.

"Who's that?" she asked blankly, and laughter swept the room.

Again and again the crowd broke into applause as the web of accusation fell steadily apart, and Mundt made little attempt to suppress the demonstrations of sympathy for the witness. Cohn insisted that the staff had secret evidence that Mrs. Moss was a Communist, but when challenged to produce it protested that it was impossible at the moment because the accuser was in the hands of the FBI and their permission must be obtained. Thereupon the Democrats exploded in condemnation of "this business of convicting people by rumor and hearsay and innuendo." Mundt ordered Cohn's statement to be stricken from the record, and McClellan wrathfully objected that the remark could be expunged, but it could not be stricken out of the minds of the press and the public. He ripped into Cohn for talking about "secret evidence" that he was unwilling to make public; besides the question of unfairness to the witness, he said, the testimony was going out over television to untold thousands of viewers who had a right to hear and weigh the evidence—all of it. Again and again the room rang with unchecked applause, and the animus against Cohn was plain. From McCarthy's side, the hearing was a disaster, climaxed by Senator Symington's leaning into the microphone and exclaiming to the fragile, bewildered witness with non-lawyer bluntness:

"I may be sticking my neck out, but I think you're telling the truth! If you are not taken back in your Army job, come around and see me. I'm going to see that you get a job!"

The film of the uproar furnished grist for Murrow in his next week's program, and it told eloquently against the senator. To the dimmest intelligence it seemed clear that the case hinged on a bungle over identity—there were several "Annie Lee Moss" listings in the Washington telephone directory—and it focused attention on the slipshod work of McCarthy's staff. As for Cohn, the day's debacle placed the bouncy young counsel squarely on the spot.

This setback, however, was secondary compared to the sensation of that afternoon, when the Army handed to each member of the McCarthy subcommittee, and to the press, a thirty-four-page "chronology" charging that Senator McCarthy and Roy Cohn had persistently exerted undue pressure on the Army to give G. David Schine a direct commission or, failing that, an assignment in the New York area studying evidences of "pro-Communist leanings in West Point textbooks."

This extraordinary indictment charged that Cohn had once threatened to Army counsel John Adams that he would "expose" the Army and put it in the "worst possible light" in connection with the Fort Monmouth investigation unless the commission was forthcoming. It said that in a rage Cohn had vowed he would "wreck the Army" and promised that Stevens was "through" as secretary.

The period covered by the chronology ran from mid-July 1953 to February 1954, and forty-four separate counts of improper pressure were listed. It set forth concrete incidents, such as Schine's telephoning to the Pentagon on the eve of being drafted to inquire whether he might come over that afternoon and "hold up his hand" and be sworn in as a officer. It set forth Cohn's numerous appeals to Stevens to give Schine a New York assignment. McCarthy was represented as having told Adams at one point that he hoped "nothing would occur to stop the ordinary processes of the draft" in Schine's case because "Mr. Schine was of no help to the committee, but was interested in photographers and getting his picture in the papers, and that things had reached a point where Mr. Schine was a pest," and he hoped that Adams would let Stevens know how he felt.

There had followed telephone calls from Cohn "almost every day," with Adams insisting that "the national interest" required that Schine be treated no differently from the 300,000 other young men who were drafted each year; to this Cohn had replied that "if national interest was what they wanted, he'd give them a little" and "show the country how shabbily" the Army was run.

The "almost nightly" disappearances of Private Schine from Fort Dix during his training period, allegedly to wind up committee business, together with regular weekend passes not issued to other trainees, had led General Ryan, commanding at Fort Dix, to protest to the Pentagon, the report went on, although Senator McCarthy had written to Stevens, at Adams' request, urging that Schine be treated just like other draftees; whereupon, it was charged, Cohn had telephoned to Adams saying he would "teach Mr. Adams what it means to go over his head." Later, "using extremely vituperative language," Cohn assertedly had told Adams that the Army had "double-crossed" Cohn, Schine, and McCarthy.

The story ran on and on—pressure, pressure, pressure—demands by Cohn—long-distant telephone calls—"vituperative language"—McCarthy sitting mute while Cohn ranted—appeals to get Schine off KP duty—Senator McCarthy's arguing with Adams that it was senseless to get into "a long-range fight" with Cohn, for even if he should quit as committee counsel or be fired, he would carry on a vendetta in the newspapers accusing the Army of "favoritism" in other cases. Although Cohn was represented as the chief instigator of the attempted intimidation, McCarthy and Frank Carr, the subcommittee's chief investigator, were directly involved, and Cohn was in deep, deep trouble.

[V]

Reacting typically, McCarthy interpreted the Army's accusations as a challenge to a fight, and he accepted the challenge without a second thought. Before he had even read the full text of the chronology, he told reporters that he would be forced to do battle with "one or two" members of the Army high command on the issue. He didn't like to do this, he added, because "the deeper I get into it, I'm convinced that the Army as a whole is damn clean. What some people in the Army do doesn't mean the entire Army." He said he had already instructed his staff to pull out of the files everything bearing on the case and give it to him so it could be "made available to the American public," and it wouldn't be "just Mr. Adams' version."

The subcommittee, it was reported, was up in arms, demanding that Cohn be dismissed; but the chairman would not hear of it. And that evening, in his radio appearance, Joe struck back at Stevenson, Murrow, and Flanders, but he ignored the new imbroglio. He called Stevenson's statement that only one Communist had been found in the government during the previous year "absolutely false"; he accused Murrow of uttering "half-truths"; and he informed Flanders that the "barncleaning" would go on. He made no mention of the President's criticism at the last press conference, but read from a 1935 newspaper article that listed Murrow (one of the "extreme left wing bleeding-heart elements of television and radio") as a member of the advisory council for a summer session of Moscow University, "which taught the overthrow of the entire traditional social order."

Three and one-half hours after the broadcast, Murrow explained publicly that in 1935, as assistant director of the Institute of International Education, whose trustees and directors included John Foster Dulles, Virginia Gildersleeve, Thomas M. Lamont, John Dewey, and Robert M. Hutchens, he had advised on the indicated summer session of Moscow University, but the session had never been held because the Russians had called the whole thing off. In a phrase not original, but quoted by his admirers with as much fervor as if it were, Murrow added:

"If the senator means that I am somewhat to the left of his position and of Louis XIV, he is correct."

The next day the newspapers carried photographs of McCarthy and Cohn taken after the broadcast, showing Joe laughing, but Cohn looking haggard. There was to be no sleep for either of them that night, and the lights blazed in the senator's office until dawn as the full staff toiled at preparing a rebuttal. On Friday McCarthy gave it to the press. He did this without consulting his subcommittee or even providing them with advance copies; Mundt had to borrow a copy from a reporter.

Briefly, McCarthy's countercharges centered on what he contended had been a planned attempt by Adams and Stevens to "blackmail" him into abandoning the Fort Monmouth investigation and "go after the Navy, Air Force, and Defense Department instead." When McCarthy protested he had no evidence to warrant such a change of targets, Adams, he charged, had promised to dig up "plenty of dirt" in the other services.

All these countercharges were contained in a file of office memoranda dated from October 2, 1953, to the very day of the Army's blast. One memo, from Frank Carr to McCarthy, spoke of the way "the Army is going to use Schine as a hostage to pressure us to stop our hearings on the Army." On the same date, a memo from Cohn to McCarthy reported that Adams had got "specific information for use on an Air Force base where there are a large number of homosexuals" and had offered to trade the information for a tip-off on the subcommittee's next Army investigation. Still another memo from Cohn to McCarthy said that Adams had dropped by to say "this was the last chance for me to arrange that law partnership in New York which he wanted. . . . He is serious. He said he had turned down a job in industry at $17,500 and needed a guarantee of $25,000 from a law firm." A note from Carr called McCarthy's attention to the way Adams was "baiting Roy pretty much lately on the 'hostage' situation. They get pretty heated before Roy buys the lunch, but it's going to lead to trouble." The final memo set forth that on the day before, McCarthy had offered to make available to Fred Seaton, Assistant Secretary of Defense, all the memoranda so that the Army might consider them before releasing their own charges.

The first reaction from Stevens was to gasp that McCarthy's accusations were "utterly untrue . . . fantastic." Adams called them "fantastic and false" and pointed out that Joe had never complained to the Army about any action of his. McCarthy, displaying intense anger, retorted that "no investigation by me will ever be ended by threats of blackmail," and Cohn, denying any improper activity on behalf of Schine, said he would not resign.

Both the Republicans and the Democrats on the subcommittee demanded an immediate inquiry to get to the bottom of the affair and, if the Army's charges should stand up, that Cohn be removed.

Outraged by the high-handed manner in which the chairman had issued his rebuttal without consulting anybody, they called for a meeting of the full subcommittee; and when their request was turned down by Joe, they turned on him angrily, pointing out their own responsibility for the actions of the subcommittee. The Republican majority (and that included McCarthy) had agreed, it was complained, to make no comment on the Army's broadside until they had studied it carefully; and in view of the chairman's violating that agreement, even Senator Dirksen declared that the subcommittee would take matters out of McCarthy's hands. "I do mean it!" Dirksen exclaimed. "There will be no fooling about it. This matter has gone far enough!"

To this Joe's reply was to take off on a weekend speaking tour in Wisconsin. He'd be back on Monday, he left word, and he might call the subcommittee together on Tuesday, but he wasn't promising. And away he flew, leaving his committee in a stew, the Pentagon seething, Roy Cohn in a dither, Washington agog, and Senator Potter grimly declaring that if both parties to the dispute should repeat their denials under oath, then "obviously someone is lying," and perjury indictments were a possibility. On all sides it was understood that this was the showdown, with a battle royal in sight. The Capitol, the press, and the public tensely waited the next move —so tensely, and amid so much turmoil, that Senator Murray of Montana, a member of the Senate Labor Committee, deemed it salutary that although in no way involved in the McCarthy affair, they henceforth open their own sessions with the heartfelt invocation:

"Bless us, O Lord, and this committee, which has worked so long in harmony, that we, too, may not fall apart in dissension."

PART SIX

Buccaneer at Bay

"There is nothing from without a man, that entering into him can defile him: but the things which come out of him, those are they that defile the man."

—*Gospel According to St. Mark VII: 15*

"Rougher and Rougher and Rougher"

A feature of Senator McCarthy's kinetic career had been the ver-
tiginous rapidity with which episodes, and episodes-within-episodes,
had developed, riveted public attention for a time, then unaccountably sunk out of sight. The senator was famous for his nimbleness
in uttering a charge, creating a furor, and then, while his opponents
were scurrying to repel that attack, simply vanishing from the field
only to pop up with a fresh attack at an entirely different location.
The result had been that his accusations, like the bow-wave of a
blunt-nosed craft, tended to throw a veritable cascade, while the
rebuttals became lost in the churn of his rapidly receding wake.

To these swift changes some of Joe's critics never became inured.
There had been McCarthy's casual confirmation, during the preceding week of sensations, that he had dropped his $2,000,000
libel suit against former Senator Benton for alleging that Joe was
unfit to sit in the Senate. The suit had been filed, with attendant
hosannas in the press that Joe at last had been smoked out of his
immunity sanctuary, nearly two years before, and McCarthy deliberately made the grounds for dismissal wildly preposterous: his
attorney, Edward Bennett Williams, he said, had ransacked the
United States but had been unable to find one single person who
believed anything Benton said, and consequently he had no basis
for claiming that he had been damaged. The announcement was
greeted with laughter that buried the affair so far as public interest
went, although Benton would not give up. He dared McCarthy to
revive the suit, offering to repeat his allegations at any time, in any
place that McCarthy might designate. "I told the truth about him
and he knows it," Benton insisted obstinately. "McCarthy was guilty
of fraud and deceit in 1951 and he hasn't improved with age."

What Benton, and others like him, would not realize was that the issues of 1951 were dead. An immensity of sound had poured forth since then, heralding crisis after crisis, each one more intense, and after that long crescendo the tunes of 1951 sounded thin and tinkling amid the thunders of the present. People generally were no longer interested in Joe's peccadillos as a soybean gambler: those activities bore the same relation to the present conflict as John Brown's raid to the Battle of Gettysburg. Even in the course of a single month, the scope of his clash with the Pentagon had been enlarged mightily, mainly by his own maneuvering. At the start of February the question had been, "Who promoted Peress?" By the start of March Peress had been shouldered aside and the issue being cried aloud was, "Who is lying—Stevens, McCarthy, Cohn, Adams—who?" And the greater issue was looming: Who should set the tone of the Republican party—Ike, the titular leader, or Joe, the rampaging senator?

Because of the explosions during the week, Vice-President Nixon's official reply to Adlai Stevenson's attack on Saturday proved to be an anticlimax. Nixon plainly hoped to still the tempest, and his low-key broadcast dwelt chiefly on the Eisenhower program for containing communism abroad and for tax reforms at home. Regarding subversion, Nixon struck hard at Stevenson's quip that Washington's Red-hunters were "chasing phantoms"; the danger was real, Nixon repeated, but the job of meeting it must be carried out fairly and properly. He did not censure McCarthy, but, sticking safely to the plural, condemned "those" who "by their reckless talk and questionable methods" had divided the nation on the communism issue and diverted attention from the administration's legislative proposals. Scattershot investigations, he said, had enabled the guilty to "pull the cloak of innocence around themselves," while some "men who have in the past done effective work exposing Communists . . . made themselves the issue rather than the cause they believe in so deeply." The rebuke was obvious, although McCarthy was not named.

If the Vice-President's speech produced any soothing effects, they were not noticeable. During Saturday Joe and Stevens exchanged telegrams, in effect calling each other liars. The Secretary said he was "astounded" by McCarthy's denial of ever trying to get special treatment for Schine, while the senator asked Stevens to "make clear to the press that the only time you and I ever discussed the question of a commission for David Schine was in his presence, at which time I urged and you fully agreed that his case would have to be treated the same as any other draftee's." And he instructed his Washington office to release a letter which he had written to Stevens on the previous December 22, saying that his staff had a right as individuals to intervene with the Army on behalf of Schine, but "as I have told you a number of times, I have an unbreakable rule that neither I, nor anyone in my behalf, shall ever attempt to interfere with or influence the Army in its assignments, promotions, etc., . . . While I am inclined to agree that Mr. Schine would never have been drafted, except because of the fact he worked for my committee, I want to make it clear at this time that no one has any authority to request any consideration for Mr. Schine other than what other draftees get."

"Smokescreen!" scoffed Stevens.

Speaking at a Junior Chamber of Commerce dinner in Manitowoc that Saturday evening, Joe was defiant, telling the crowd of three hundred:

"As long as I am in the United States Senate, and I hope it is a long time, I don't intend to treat traitors like gentlemen. I don't care how high or how low those are who scream at what we are doing. Some people have told me I shouldn't get rough; a Senate friend—a kindly old gentleman—had something to say about it the other day. It's a difficult job to pick out these slimy creatures without getting rough, but if someone can tell me the gentleman's way to dig out Communists, I'll invite them to come on in, the water's fine. All this furor," he concluded, "has been brought about because we dared to expose some people in the military. We've got to get rough; the Communists don't treat our boys like gentlemen!"

Plainly Joe was fighting back in the only style he knew—to jab, and jab again, and again, and again; a Fabian defense utilizing artful reconnoiter was beyond his capacity.

[II]

With the Sunday newspapers, the public began to get a clearer view of the frantic backstage activities that had culminated in the events of that hectic week. The story of Roy Cohn's supposed improper intercession on behalf of Schine had been aired by Drew Pearson as long ago as the previous December, and both the *Baltimore Sun* and the *New York Post* had followed with their own "exposés." But these were notorious baiters of McCarthy, and could be expected to seize any stick to beat the obnoxious senator, so their revelations had been taken with a grain of salt. The publicity had, however, stirred up concern at the Pentagon, and on January 21, 1954 (a date that would assume much importance in the subsequent developments), a group of high-level administration officials had conferred on the matter at the Justice Department. Present were Deputy Attorney General William P. Rogers; Sherman Adams and Gerald Morgan, of the White House staff; Henry Cabot Lodge, who was both United Nations ambassador and a special White House assistant; and John Adams. Sherman Adams had suggested that the Army prepare a chronological record of the appeals said to have been made by Cohn or others to get preferential treatment for Schine.

At this direct urging by the White House (for so John Adams construed the "suggestion") the chronology had been compiled. The Army had no clear-cut plan for using it yet, but rumors of its preparation leaked to some Democratic senators, including Senator McClellan, ranking Democrat on McCarthy's subcommittee. He and Senator Russell of Georgia asked the Army for copies, if the document existed. Its political value to the Democrats was self-evident, and the requests were stalled.

Meanwhile, on January 22, John Adams had called on McCarthy at the senator's home and in a three-hour conversation had intimated (according to later and conflicting versions of the meeting) that real trouble was in store for Joe and his committee unless Roy Cohn were gotten rid of and the Peress and Fort Monmouth investigations were dropped, together with McCarthy's demand that he be given the names of the Army officials responsible for the Peress mix-up. From the way Adams talked, McCarthy suspected that he had White House backing, and this aroused his instinctive resistance. He had talked over Adams' veiled threat with Cohn and had decided to stand firm. ("No one can push me out of anything.") In a subsequent executive meeting of the subcommittee, Cohn was severely reprimanded, but he declined to resign, and McCarthy refused to fire him.

On Monday of the week just past, late in the afternoon, Defense Secretary Wilson had telephoned to Senator Potter. Wilson was worried. He told Potter about the existence of the report and said the Democrats were trying to get copies. Since disclosure by the Democrats would be damaging to the administration, Wilson suggested that perhaps Potter could cushion the effect by arranging to let the subcommittee's Republicans make the disclosure and then taking swift remedial action; that would dampen the Democratic attack that was sure to follow. He proposed that Potter immediately write a formal request for a copy. Potter did, and within thirty minutes a copy of the chronology was in his hands. He read it, and his feeling was one of consternation.

The next day (it was the day Senator Flanders made his "war paint" speech) Potter confronted McCarthy with the report and begged him to fire Cohn instantly; otherwise the entire subcommittee would come under the gun. McCarthy refused, denied that Cohn had done anything wrong, and even hinted at "making things rough" for Potter himself if he persisted. Potter was startled, and so were Dirksen and Mundt when they were apprised of the situation.

On Thursday afternoon the Democrats got copies of the chronology, and as word spread to the press gallery, correspondents raced to check on the news. That evening the eastern newspapers held their front pages open until midnight and later while their Washington bureaus filed furiously.

McCarthy, meanwhile, had agreed to meet with his Republican committee members on Friday morning. Instead, he called in reporters and released his counterattack on the Army, charging an attempt to "blackmail" the committee. Cohn, white-faced and tight-lipped, stood beside the senator as he handed out his statement. Then McCarthy dashed to the airport to fly to Wisconsin. At the last minute he had telephoned to Potter, saying they could get together on his return. "The Army can't get away with this, Charlie," he had snapped. "It's blackmail!" And in the midst of Potter's plea that every minute counted, that already the Democrats were gloating, he had hung up. Racing to board the plane, he paused at a newsstand to buy a paperback, which he was clutching as he came aboard—a Western titled *Fight or Run*.

The violation of his promise to meet with his committeemates infuriated Dirksen and Mundt, and they prepared for a showdown on McCarthy's return to Washington late Sunday night. That evening Roy Cohn, in a "Meet the Press" television interview, flatly denied the Army's charges and also denied that the subcommittee staff was being pressured to subscribe to a "pledge of loyalty" to himself. He specifically denied, in this regard, having threatened two women holdouts, assuring them that "it would be the worse" for those who refused to sign. "Absolutely untrue," he asserted. "I never made any such statement." Eventually all but two of the staff did sign this private loyalty pledge.

[III]

Amid the rising demands for a speedy inquiry into the entire affair, McCarthy met with his subcommittee on Tuesday morning. An investigation, with sworn testimony, looking toward possible perjury action, was unanimously approved, and pending the completion of this "full and free" inquiry, all investigative action by the subcommittee was to be held in abeyance. To insure a fair hearing, McCarthy agreed to step down as chairman, with Senator Mundt replacing him temporarily. Mundt accepted the assignment with great reluctance, for he was facing a reelection campaign and foresaw embarrassments. McCarthy pledged that he would testify as a witness, and that Cohn, Stevens, and Adams would be called. While Cohn would not be suspended pending the outcome, it was agreed that special counsel should be hired for this inquiry—some man of national stature and reputation. McCarthy was urged to call off his speaking dates and stay in Washington to help "bring out all the facts," but he declined, objecting that he was already committed to speak in Chicago, Milwaukee, and Oklahoma City. Mundt and McClellan, acting jointly, at once impounded all the subcommittee files relating to the dispute and ordered that nobody but the new staff, to be hired, should have access to them.

Much dissatisfaction with the decision of the McCarthy committee to investigate the conduct of its own chairman and chief counsel arose in Congress and elsewhere. Senator Estes Kefauver, the Tennessee Democrat who had rocketed to national prominence by his televised inquiry into racketeering, fought to have the Armed Services Committee, of which he was a member, take jurisdiction; but the chairman of that committee, Senator Saltonstall of Massachusetts, would be up for reelection in the fall, and he successfully sidestepped the proposal, although Senator Mundt was heartily in favor of handing the assignment to some neutral group.

At the President's weekly press conference, the charges and countercharges were the subject of questioning, and Eisenhower said that he believed Stevens had told the truth, although it was possible that he might have been misinformed; but Ike refused directly to attack McCarthy. He said that certainly he was not taking the dispute lightly, and to suggest that he was would be ridiculous.

At the Pentagon it was reported that Stevens was overjoyed at the chance to do battle with Joe, now that he had the Defense Department and the White House behind him.

Meanwhile, before a cheering crowd at the St. Patrick's Day dinner of the Irish Fellowship of Chicago, McCarthy exclaimed that he didn't give "a tinker's dam" about criticism of his methods, no matter "how high or how low" the critics were in either party. He repeated "how high or how low" for emphasis and was cheered repeatedly. He pledged that the fight would go on "as long as I am in the United States Senate" and charged that Republicans as well as Democrats, along with "eggheads" and "deluded liberals," were playing into the hands of the Communists by demanding curbs on his authority. The crowd greeted him with shouts of "Give 'em hell, Joe!" "Pour it on!" and "You're in your own ball park!" Most of the city's leading Republicans as well as numerous leading Democrats were on hand, and the toastmaster drew thunderous applause when he introduced the senator as "driving the snakes out of America." McCarthy showed plainly that he was in no mood to compromise, but would fight it out no matter what. He read from a booklet laying down the Communist party line as of September, 1953, a passage urging all members to egg on the dispute between Joe and Ike in order to discredit "Red hunters."

In Milwaukee, two days later, McCarthy rose from a sickbed to address the centennial dinner of the Milwaukee County Young Republican organization. At noon his temperature was 102°, and his doctor reported him suffering from acute virus laryngitis brought on by overwork, excessive fatigue, and exposure. The doctor forbade him to attend the dinner, but Joe overruled him and in a blistering, twenty-count indictment accused the Democratic party of either "treason or gross stupidity." Replying to Stevenson's attack on "McCarthyism," he called him "the attorney for the defense" and challenged him to plead guilty or not guilty to each separate count on behalf of the party.

And the next day, in Oklahoma City, he addressed 1,000 Republicans at a $100-a-plate delayed Lincoln Day dinner, his voice still husky but full of fight. He had intended to speak on Communist infiltration of the press, but dropped that plan when local party leaders told him the crowd wanted to hear about the Army-Cohn-Schine row. In a meeting with reporters, however, he threatened to expose the extent of what he termed the Communist influence in the American press, radio, and television, particularly in Washington. The reporters accepted this as his answer to the heaviest editorial criticism of his stormy career.

Before the wildly enthusiastic crowd, he said that the Army's Cohn-Schine charges had been brought only after he had demanded "the names of those in the Pentagon who knew the records of alleged Communists, but nevertheless promoted them and gave them plush jobs." He got applause when he said he could not and would not accept the advice of "some of my chameleon Republican friends —luckily there are not too many of them—" who urged him to avoid criticism of the administration. Never, he said, would he be a party to "whitewashing or covering up mistakes" just because they were made by his own party. He blamed the press for creating the impression that he was in any contest with the President. "I like him personally," he said, "and as a matter of fact, if he was running for office today I would feel compelled to campaign for him. I think he is doing the best job he can." His dispute with the Army was another matter, and "while I did not start this fight, I guarantee to you that I will finish it!"

The senator spoke for sixty-five minutes to almost continuous applause. Republican National Committeeman Baille Vinson, introducing the speaker, said that he had heard that McCarthy was accused of "playing a little rough with Communists. We down in Oklahoma think that playing rough with Communists is a privilege, and we are proud of him, and hope he will get rougher and rougher and rougher and rougher, until we can't find any Communists either in government or thinking they are going to get back into government."

The next morning the senator attended Sunday Mass in the residence of Bishop Eugene McGuiness, then flew back to Washington, his health fully recovered. During the flight he gave reporters aboard the plane a statement (just in time to catch the morning papers) suggesting that everybody concerned in the Army dispute—himself, Cohn, Stevens, and Adams, at least—should submit to a lie detector test if the committee sanctioned it. He said he had used the polygraph when a judge in Wisconsin and had confidence in it, when it was properly operated.

That Sunday in New York, the Very Reverend Francis B. Sayre, Jr., dean of Washington Cathedral and grandson of Woodrow Wilson, preaching at the Cathedral of St. John the Divine, denounced McCarthy for using methods "diametrically opposed" to divine compassion and called the senator as "another of the devil's disguises."

Meanwhile, in Washington, the Very Reverend James A. Pike, preaching in Dr. Sayre's pulpit, declared that there was "a devilish indecision about any society that will permit an imposter like McCarthy to caper out front while the main army stands idly by."

The theme of "McCarthyism" seemed to be threatening to attain Miltonian grandeur, but whether it would culminate in a "Paradise Lost" or a "Paradise Regained" for its author was inscrutable. One thing was clear: if McCarthy went down, he would go down fighting. Senator Potter had been struck by the spirit of the man at the time he was pleading with Joe to look before he leaped into headlong combat with the Army. On the wall of McCarthy's office hung a motto:

> "Oh God, don't let me weaken. Help me to continue on. When I go down, let me go down like an oak tree felled by a woodsman's ax."

In that attitude Joe was sincere. He would not retreat, his nature would not allow it. By now he had become the prisoner of his cause.

[IV]

The subcommittee was running into difficulties in its search for a counsel to direct the inquiry. The man must have a reputation for ability and impartiality; he must never have expressed any opinion that might indicate bias; he must be willing to drop a lucrative practice for a job paying $1,000 a month, with the certainty of being under heavy attack for as long as the inquiry lasted, and perhaps afterward. The head of the American Bar Association, William J. Jameson, was approached, but after consulting other officials of the organization he declined. United States Judge Harold Medina of New York was sounded out, but the Supreme Court demurred against his selection.

The principals in the dispute, meanwhile, kept up their war of nerves. McCarthy insisted on his right to cross-examine witnesses, and was willing to concede the same privilege to Stevens and Adams or their counsel. On this point Joe was resisting bipartisan pressure, but he would not budge. Senator Symington was agitating to get McCarthy off the subcommittee entirely. Asked his opinion, President Eisenhower thought Joe should have the right to cross-examine, but not the right to sit as a judge of his own case. But already McCarthy had consented to forgo his vote during the proceedings, although remaining a member of the subcommittee.

Because word had been given out that Eisenhower would comment on the dispute, his next press conference was jammed, 212 correspondents being on hand, and again the letdown among those hoping for a more belligerent stand was severe. *The New York Times,* as it had done often and ineffectually before, sounded the tocsin, warning flatly that if the senator were allowed to get away with his demands, "there can be no doubt that he is master of the McCarthy subcommittee that is investigating McCarthy."

Days of press speculation ensued. Three television networks announced they would cover the hearings. Senator Mundt talked about a ten-day inquiry. Washington hummed with reports that the Republican "pros" were more convinced than ever that McCarthy or "McCarthyism" would be the main issue in the autumn elections. The Republican National Committee gave no indication of disavowing the senator as a party speaker, even though Leonard Hall, national chairman, was quoted as saying that McCarthy had done "more harm than good." Rumors of "a settlement by resignations" (Cohn, Adams, Stevens, perhaps others) swept the capital and were denied. The American Civil Liberties Union backed McCarthy's right to cross-examine—but not as a member of the subcommittee. Averell Harriman, speaking for the Democrats, detected in McCarthy's speeches "the hard ring of Hitlerism," while Harry Truman offered Eisenhower unsought advice on what to do with his "great investigator"—send him to Siberia and let him do a little Red-hunting there.

Momentous headlines these days were interspersed with trivial ones, all bearing, directly or remotely, on The Subject—McCarthy. The Army announced that Annie Lee Moss had been reinstated in her job while a loyalty board studied her case. Ben Gold, head of the furriers union in New York, was convicted of perjury in denying Communist party membership. Long, detailed biographies of Wisconsin's junior senator appeared in newspapers and periodicals, recounting his meteoric rise "from farm to fame." Mrs. Peress was forced out of the editorship of a parent-teacher magazine after a near riot over her in a parents-teachers meeting. Announcing the view of Admiral Lewis Strauss, chairman of the Atomic Energy Commission, bold headlines read, "H-Bomb Can Wipe Out Any City, Tests Show"; and on the same day: "Reds (Vietminh) in Mass Attack on Dienbienphu." The Army announced that Private Schine had failed to qualify for the Criminal Investigation Division training course at Camp Gordon, Georgia. Defense Secretary Wilson promulgated a new set of rules governing the drafting of avowed Communists. In Maine, the Republican state convention, at the urging of Senator Margaret Chase Smith, rejected a resolution condemning the investigative methods employed by Senator McCarthy. Responding to press inquiries, the Marine Corps stated that Senator McCarthy had been promoted, with 183 other reserve majors, to the rank of lieutenant colonel a year previously. In his dispute with Edward R. Murrow, McCarthy tried to enlist William F. Buckley, Jr., to reply for him on the offered free time, but CBS ruled out any substitute; so the senator, during a weekend in New York, patched together a filmed answer, as a result of which intensive effort he was put to bed at the St. Regis with another attack of virus laryngitis, accompanied by high fever. Recovering, he flew to Boston to make an off-the-record speech before the Beacon Club Society, Boston's oldest dining club. He was greeted with loud cheers and a few mild boos when he entered the room, and a guest said later that he had ripped into Murrow, vowing to "get him off the air for life."

Then the subcommittee announced it had found a counsel at last, Samuel P. Sears, a Boston attorney—only to have controversy break out within a few hours over Sears' fitness for the job. Newspaper clippings were produced quoting Sears as endorsing McCarthy and saying "the senator has done a great job . . . as he drives the pinks and Commies out of the government," and otherwise approving Joe, even having offered to raise a campaign fund for him in 1952. Although insisting that he could be impartial, Sears bowed out of the picture, leaving the embarrassed subcommittee in what the *Times* called "confusion if not consternation." It was feared that the entire investigation might go on the rocks. In any event, in the opinion of the *Times* and numerous other critics, the Sears bungle

—committed unanimously except for Joe, who was ill in New York—simply emphasized "the unfitness of this committee to conduct the inquiry at all."

So the hunt went on, while the Army succeeded in engaging as their counsel another Bostonian, Joseph Nye Welch, who insisted on serving without pay. With him he brought to Washington two assistants, James D. St. Clair, a partner in Welch's law firm of Hale & Dorr, and Frederick G. Fisher, Jr. Both these also were to serve without compensation. When questioned about his stand on "McCarthyism," Welch said, "I am a registered Republican and a trial lawyer. I am just for facts."

At length, after more hesitations and rebuffs, the subcommittee found an acceptable choice for counsel—Ray Jenkins, of Knoxville, described as "the best trial lawyer in East Tennessee." He also was to serve without pay. Jenkins had flown to Washington at the suggestion of Senator Dirksen for a searching examination before the full subcommittee. After discussion of his qualifications by the members, the final decision was delayed for an hour and a half so that Senator Symington could register his vote. He was playing golf in a foursome that included President Eisenhower; reached by telephone, he voted favorably, and Jenkins' appointment was released to the press.

Joe made his thirty-minute reply to Murrow over forty-two stations of the CBS network. It was rambling and amateurish, totally inadequate to compete with Murrow's finished showmanship and professionalism. Charging that there had been a "deliberate delay" of eighteen months in developing the hydrogen bomb, McCarthy demanded: "If there were no Communists in government, why did we delay . . . even though our intelligence agencies were reporting, day after day, that the Russians were feverishly pushing their own development of the bomb?" Murrow, he said, "as far back as twenty years ago," had been engaged in "propaganda for Communist causes," and he mentioned that the *Daily Worker* had praised Murrow while attacking McCarthy. Even Joe's admirers voted the show dull.

Then, although ground rules for the hearings remained to be worked out, Senator Mundt set April 21 for the start of the public sessions and stated that the hearings would be televised on all networks.

On the Slippery Slope

Of course the show did not get under way on the scheduled date; in this production few happenings would conform to the predetermined pattern. McCarthy, who had flown with his wife to Arizona to shake off that persistent virus infection, objected that on April 21 he was booked to make an Independence Day speech in Houston, Texas. To this Mundt had snorted, "Out in South Dakota, chum, Independence Day is July 4." Joe elucidated: he meant Texas Independence Day, commemorating the Battle of San Jacinto. Mundt grumbled, but put the question to the committee, and a delay of one day was granted reluctantly. But during the waiting period much, much more would occur that would raise public expectancy to fever heat. *The New York Times* had remarked that for six months McCarthy had overshadowed all other domestic issues, and foresaw that from now on all topics foreign and domestic would be not only overshadowed; to a large extent they would be ignored completely.

On all sides pollsters were estimating McCarthy's strength and weakness, and the estimates bore each other out with rare consistency. The Gallup Poll, which had been canvassing public reaction to McCarthy since 1950, found that Joe's popularity had climbed steadily during the last four years. In August, 1951, when Benton was moving to have McCarthy expelled from the Senate, only 15% of those polled looked favorably on Joe. Two years later, 34% favored him, and in January of the current year—after Joe's clash with the State Department over trade with Red China, after Brownell's charges in the Harry Dexter White affair, and after McCarthy's uncovering of a Communist in the Government Printing Office—the senator's popularity had hit a peak of 50% of all those questioned. Now, on the eve of hearings into what Mc-

Carthy had taken to calling "this Cohn-Adams dispute," the popularity rating had dipped slightly to 46%. More significant was the steady shrinkage shown in the percentage of people who said they held no special opinion regarding Joe, either for or against, and the concurrently steady increase of those who were actively hostile to him. In 1951, 63% of those polled had held no decided views about the senator; now, in 1954, only 18% were undecided. Meanwhile, the percentage of those definitely opposed to him had risen from 22% in 1951 to 36% in 1954. Thus the gap between those cheering McCarthy on and those damning him and his works had widened, although nearly half the population still remained definitely in his corner.

The dejected liberals winced under the impact of these figures, but there was no dodging them. With wringing of hands, the avowed left gloomed that the Communist propaganda machine in Europe was exploiting the McCarthy-Army squabble as proof of rising Fascism in the United States, under a neo-Hitler, namely, Senator Joe, who capered at the beck of "Texas oil millionaires" and other sinister elements of the "criminal ruling classes."

At home the press seemed not far behind these propagandists abroad; never had the senator been under such widespread, sustained, and organized attack. In Wisconsin, a movement begun by a country editor—Leroy Gore, publisher of the *Sauk City Star*—to obtain 400,000 signatures to a petition that would force a state recall election on McCarthy, had snowballed into dizzy dimensions and appeared on the verge of success. Although the legality of such a recall election, provided for in Wisconsin law but not in the United States Constitution, was debatable, the "Joe Must Go" organization, improvised almost overnight, underfinanced, and wildly amateurish in its enthusiasm, was confident that they could at least force the issue into the courts, an action which by itself might sufficiently discredit McCarthy to bring about his expulsion by the Senate. The movement had spread beyond Wisconsin and was receiving national attention. In any event it revealed a tide of anti-McCarthyism in the senator's own state.

In the East, a group calling themselves the "I Believe Committee," composed of persons who believed that a court of law should decide on the truth or falsity of Benton's fraud charges against McCarthy, ran full-page advertisements in two New York newspapers and harvested 10,000 signatures and $16,000 in contributions to pay for similar advertisements throughout the nation.

This was the first major operation directed by the so-called clearinghouse of the National Committee for an Effective Congress, aimed at attacking McCarthy by the techniques of a high-powered professional lobby, and the blow was effective.

There was no denying that Joe's enemies were massing. Indicative of this trend was an Associated Press feature article released to Sunday newspapers of April 4, when anticipation over the Army hearings was acute. The article recapitulated the senator's four-year rise, then summarized the current situation in these words:

"Nobody knows the size of his following or of his opposition. He is the object of intense admiration and bitter hostility. But it is plain he has reached a crossroads, with a barrier of restraint reaching from the White House through the leadership of both parties. The word is spreading in Washington that he has 'gone too far.' For the first time influential Republicans are saying privately that Joe has become a party liability. And now it is not 'pinkos.' It is a solid, conservative opposition."

In four years, this Associated Press report said without qualification, Senator McCarthy's accusations had "stirred great passion, cast a shadow over the reputations of many men, encouraged the informer, and brought such terms as 'guilt by association' into the consciousness of a startled and frequently bewildered citizenry."

[II]

Yet on the very Sunday when this unfavorable summarization appeared, the senator received the most vociferous demonstration of support of his career. Appearing as honor guest at the annual communion breakfast of the Holy Name Society of the New York Police Department, he was given a roaring ovation by 6,000 policemen and their friends. The cheering started at the first mention of his name by the toastmaster, Monsignor Joseph A. McCafferty, police department chaplain since 1924. Father McCafferty introduced McCarthy as "one who has devoted his time and talent and his life to the exposure and uprooting of Communists—" Here the speaker was interrupted by fifty seconds of handclapping and cheers before he could proceed. "—out of every phase of our national life, education, business, industry, the government." Somebody yelled, "The Army, too!" Father McCafferty went on to say that McCarthy had been criticized by left-wing politicians and Americans "misled by slanted and biased segments of the press, radio, and screen" and asserted that the senator's mistakes, "which have been few" (cries of "No! No!"), had been magnified a thousandfold, and his accomplishments minimized.

In his own speech, Joe challenged the "civilian Pentagon politicians," if they really wanted to raise the morale of the Army, to spend more time trying to free the thirty-two fliers and nine hundred other American prisoners of the Korean war still unaccounted for. Instead, he exclaimed scornfully, "the bleeding hearts talk about destruction of our morale because the chairman of a committee wants to find out from a general why he has given an honorable discharge and special favors to a Communist."

The audience rose and gave cheer after cheer, until the walls of the Hotel Astor's grand ballroom rang. Reporters noted that among the ranking past and present police and city dignitaries on the dais, a few failed to join in the ovation, or seemed to be applauding perfunctorily, but about the fervor of the ovation there was no possible question: it was a spontaneous tribute to a hero. During the breakfast Cardinal Spellman entered, shook hands with McCarthy and chatted briefly, then left. And the newspapers carried photographs of Joe, flanked by police executives, leading "New York's Finest" in the march down Fifth Avenue from St. Patrick's Cathedral to the Astor Hotel. McCarthy himself described the tumultuous welcome as the greatest tribute he ever received; his enemies were shocked into speechlessness.

And in the Senate the next day, Senator McCarran arose to ask for fair play for McCarthy. The Nevada Democrat's voice was the first to be raised in Joe's support there. To set the record straight, McCarran restated what he saw as the basic question involved. The real issue in the present dispute, he said, was not whether McCarthy or Stevens or anybody else was telling the truth. "All of the principals on both sides of this so-called Army versus McCarthy controversy could be liars in one degree or another and it would not change by one iota the fact that there *is* a conspiracy in the world; that this conspiracy seeks the overthrow of the government of the United States by force and violence; that this conspiracy is active in our country today; that one of the things this conspiracy fears most is exposure; and that the greatest proportion of exposure of portions of the Communist conspiracy in recent years has been done by the investigations of Congressional committees.

"Let us get to the bottom of this controversy by all means," he appealed. "The people of America will not stand for a whitewash of any parties to the controversy on either side. If there have been lies, let the liars be exposed. If their lies have been serious, let them be punished. If their lies have amounted to perjury, let them be prosecuted. Let the truth be exposed to the public gaze. But through it all let us not lose sight of the things that are so much, much more important than who is a liar."

The nation, he warned, was poised "on the edge of war," and the real issue was rapidly coming to be "whether, at long last, the Communists, with the aid of front groups, fellow travelers, Communist sympathizers and dupes, are going to succeed in their efforts to silence the committees of the United States Congress who have been starting to tear away the mask from the sinister operations in this country of the world Communist conspiracy. Rightly or wrongly," he concluded, McCarthy had become "a symbol of anti-communism," and more and more McCarran was concerned with the "growing tendency to identify the anti-McCarthy forces as the forces of truth and decency, and tolerance and civil rights."

Senator McCarran spoke seldom on the floor, and no reply was offered to his appeal. An answer did come the next day from the press, *The New York Times* accusing McCarran of obfuscation. The real issue, the *Times* contended, was "whether McCarthy or Eisenhower is going to run the executive department."

The President would not recognize any such conflict. In an unusual display of temper, he served notice at his press conference that he was through answering questions about McCarthy and he hoped the senator's name would not be brought up again.

Prominent display was given across the country, at this moment, to an attack on Senator McCarthy made by Bishop Bernard J. Sheil of Chicago, founder of the Catholic Youth Organization and widely respected liberal churchman. Addressing the convention of the United Auto Workers, Bishop Sheil ripped into the senator as a "noisy anti-Communist playing for the grandstand. We have been the victims in the past few years of a kind of shell game," he said. "We have been treated like country rubes, taken in by a city slicker from Appleton, Wisconsin. . . . Are we any safer because General George C. Marshall was branded as a traitor? No, we are not, but we are a little less honorable." Emphasizing that he spoke for himself and not for his church, which correctly, he said, took no position on such a political matter, Bishop Sheil did remind his audience that the church "does take a position on lies, calumny, the absence of charity, and calculated deceit. These things are wrong . . . and to call them good . . . is itself a monstrous perversion of morality."

The attack, one of the sharpest McCarthy had yet sustained, drew mixed responses. In New York, Senator Lehman and Rabbi William F. Rosenblum of Temple Israel praised Sheil's statement, but in Brooklyn the Reverend Edward Lodge Curran, pastor of St. Joseph's Church, denounced it as "unsubstantiated and uncharitable" and noted that no member of the American hierarchy had emulated Bishop Sheil. In Chicago, Cardinal Stritch, Sheil's superior, withheld comment except to say that Bishop Sheil had not consulted him in advance. At Sheil's residence, telephone calls ran about 65% against him, but at CYO headquarters they were reported to be 4 to 1 in his favor. Three hundred members of Chicago's Naval Post 372, American Legion, adopted a resolution condemning Sheil; the resolution had been introduced by Philip W. Collins, a prominent Catholic layman. Edward R. Murrow ran a film of Bishop Sheil's speech on his "See It Now" program.

The bishop's attack was welcomed with relief by such outspoken opponents of McCarthy as *Commonweal* because it made clear the division existing among Catholics on the issue of "McCarthyism." Citing a recent poll indicating that 58% of American Catholics supported the senator, contrasted with 49% of Protestants favoring him, *Commonweal* said the difference of only nine points showed— if it showed anything significant—that both groups were deeply split on the issue, and that there was no monolithic "Catholic bloc" rooting for Joe, as frequently was asserted. McCarthy, sunning himself in Tucson, ignored the incident. "If I spent my time reading all the attacks made on me," said he, "I'd do nothing else."

[III]

In the midst of these verbal exchanges, several rapidly breaking events kept bright the public's consciousness of the existence of a Communist menace. First came the sensational suspension by the Atomic Energy Commission of Dr. Robert Oppenheimer, leading atomic scientist, and the scheduling of hearings on him as a security risk. Oppenheimer was denied access to secret data pending an investigation of his associations with Communists over the years. This action launched an episode almost as extensive and as fiercely controversial as that raging around McCarthy, and the senator of course was linked to it.

A few days later the newspapers carried accounts of the forcible rescue by Australian police of a Soviet diplomat's wife, who had been kidnaped by Soviet secret police after she had begged for asylum; the police took the woman off the plane at Darwin, and an infuriated mob severely manhandled the burly armed "couriers" who were attempting to spirit her back to Moscow.

In the news on the same day was an interview with a veteran of the Spanish Civil War, a Spaniard, who had been captured and had spent twenty years in Soviet slave labor camps. Finally released, upon reaching Western Europe he recounted his experience, telling how he and his fellow captives were auctioned off to work on collective farms under conditions differing in no respect from slavery. He told of other slave camps, scattered over the Soviet Union, and the account drove home afresh to Americans the reality of the ever-present threat of communism to freedom everywhere. So the climate of tension was built up in anticipation of the imminent Army-McCarthy hearings.

[IV]

Special counsel Jenkins had been making his case, interviewing prospective witnesses and prodding the principals to submit bills of particulars detailing what they hoped to prove. The Army complied first. It had been agreed that neither side would release its document to the press in advance of the other; but someone, not publicly identified, leaked copies of the Army's countercharges to a few reporters, whereupon Senator Symington released the complete brief. Going beyond the original charges, the Army linked McCarthy directly to the alleged instances of improper pressure on behalf of Schine.

Angered by this breach of the agreement, Roy Cohn telephoned to McCarthy, who was headed for a few days of fishing off the Texas Gulf coast, and for a while it appeared that McCarthy's side might boycott the investigation. Joe demanded that the leak be looked into before anything further was done. The other senators accused him of stalling, and six days later he, Cohn, and Frank Carr filed their joint bill of particulars.

This contained a fresh sensation, for not only were Stevens and

John Adams accused, but also H. Struve Hensel, newly appointed
as an Assistant Secretary of Defense. The only connection Hensel
had had with the affair thus far had been his act of signing—in his
previous capacity as Defense Department counsel—the covering
letter transmitting the Army's original chronology to the Capitol.
Now McCarthy accused him of having profited during the war
through the sale of naval supplies to the government while occupying a "top procurement post." The senator said that Hensel had
learned that the subcommittee, under McCarthy himself, had slated
these wartime deals for a full investigation and had thereupon
joined the attempt to smother Joe's investigation of the Army,
hoping thereby to discredit the senator.

While not repeating the "blackmail" charge, McCarthy's bill of
indictment also averred that Stevens and Adams had followed a
clear pattern of cooperation with the subcommittee's investigation
of conditions at Fort Monmouth as long as individual Communists
were the targets; but "as soon as the probe turned to the infinitely
more important question of who was responsible for protecting
Communist infiltration and protecting Communists who had infiltrated, every conceivable obstacle was placed in the path of the
subcommittee's search for truth." When the Army's charges were
placed "in the proper perspective," it was stated, they would be
found "to have given greater aid and comfort to Communists and
security risks than any other single obstacle ever designed."

The Army's special counsel (referred to as "a Joseph N. Welch")
received a passing swipe for having signed the Army's bill of particulars, in place of Stevens and Adams, despite the fact that he
had come into "the situation long after all of the alleged incidents
were supposed to take place and could, therefore, have no personal knowledge of the matter." Another paragraph read that
"it should be noted also that a law partner of Mr. Welch has, in
recent years, belonged to an organization found by the House
Un-American Activities Committee to be the 'legal bulwark' of
the Communist party, and referred to by the Attorney General as
the 'legal mouthpiece' of the Communists. This same law partner
was selected by Mr. Welch to act as his aide in this matter, and
was discharged only when his Communist-front connection became
publicly known."

This oblique allusion drew no special attention from the press,
although five days previously the newspapers had published in-

conspicuously the information that Frederick Fisher, one of the two assistants whom Welch had brought along from his law firm, had been sent back to Boston in consequence of its being learned that Fisher had once belonged to the National Lawyers Guild, which was then resisting an attempt by the Attorney General to cite it as a Communist front. Fisher's dismissal, with his photograph, had appeared in *The New York Times* and elsewhere without exciting comment; it was taken for granted that Welch had acted to avoid possible embarrassment. McCarthy's allusion placed the Army counsel on notice that the incident had not been overlooked.*

In another direction, the McCarthy rebuttal toned down sharply the strong language that was said to have passed between Cohn and Adams, terming the Army's version grossly exaggerated. The two men had long been personal and social friends, it was pointed out; they had had conversations almost daily ("some jocular, some animated"), which now were being puffed up to the dimensions of "violent, abusive, and threatening" outbursts.

Within five minutes of the charges against himself becoming known, Hensel, fighting mad, struck back. Calling the accusations "barefaced lies," known by McCarthy to be baseless, he taunted the senator with running true to form: when cornered, resorting to "diversionary smears." He dared McCarthy to repeat his charges without immunity. Joe replied from Houston that he would do nothing to hold up the hearings, but "if at some future time Hensel still wants the material repeated—and I don't think he will—away from the committee, I see no harm in that."

In a recorded interview with the Associated Press, McCarthy denied again categorically that he was aiming at either the Presidency or control of the Republican party. His language was forceful. Asked whether the charge was true that he was deliberately provoking a fight with President Eisenhower, he answered:

"I think if you just examine who does the shouting, you might get the answer to that. Whenever I dig out a Communist who was brought in by the old administration, I find someone like the Allslops, Edward R. Murrow, or Drew Pearson shouting that McCarthy is starting a fight with the President. It's so ridiculous

* The slight prominence given to the Fisher development in the press contrasted strikingly with the extensive and even sensational coverage given to the disclosure of the past associations and utterances of the Boston attorney Sears.

that you can't hardly answer it. I'm doing the job that the President promised our administration would do—dig out Communists. I may say that the President has never indicated to me that he was unhappy about digging Communists out."

Conceding that Eisenhower might have said things in press conferences that could be construed as indicating that he was unhappy about McCarthy's methods, the senator insisted that "to me, directly or through anybody on his staff, or anyone else, he has never indicated unhappiness."

Queried about the outcry against his "methods," he expostulated: "You have to name some method that is objectionable. The record is available for anyone to see. We call a man in. We give him every right to counsel. Give him every right to rebut the testimony against him. I can't think of anything we can do in addition to that. You find people screaming about methods, but they never tell what methods they have in mind."

On April 21, McCarthy spoke before a crowd of 5,000 at the San Jacinto battlefield monument, twenty miles south of Houston. He said there was a plot afoot to hamstring his committee by changing the rules so it could not operate. The plot was being cooked up, he contended, by "some devilish clever men," aided by "some good men being used with the assurance that they will be paid off by receiving the praise of the left-wing elements of the press, radio, and television." Referring to the imminent hearings as "this television show of Adams versus Cohn," he departed from his prepared text to advise: "Well, while this show of 'The Private in the Army' would normally be a great waste of time, I suggest you watch on television so you get some picture of what is being done." And he urged that the people write to their senators about what they saw. Then he flew back to Washington.

That same day in New York, at a meeting of the Communist-dominated American Labor Party, the 300 delegates present tendered Dr. Irving Peress a standing tribute of respect. And *The New York Times* earnestly admonished its readers, as they prepared to tune in television's greatest show, to beware of smokescreens, for really it was not Roy Cohn, not the Army, but Senator McCarthy who was, "or who should be, on trial today."

So, at last, the momentous hearings got under way.

A Front of Brass

When the Senate's Permanent Subcommittee on Investigations met on Thursday, April 22, 1954, to open its public investigation of charges of grave misconduct raised against representatives of the Army and against its own chairman and chief counsel, nobody knew what would happen. Nothing exactly like this had ever occurred; no precedent existed either in legislative history or in the brief history of television. The spectacle had been given an enormous advance buildup, and a potential audience of millions of viewers was keyed to expect revelations—although no one knew exactly what. The subcommittee members themselves were as much in the dark as the public. Comparisons with the Kefauver hearings into organized crime were unsatisfactory. The Kefauver hearings had drawn the greatest viewing audience on record; but in that investigation there had been a cast of plainly recognizable "good guys" and "bad guys." In the present instance the identification of the "goodies" and the "baddies" would depend upon each individual viewer's bias, and recent polls had shown the nation sharply divided on the issue of McCarthy and "McCarthyism." Furthermore, this investigation would pit not only the Army against the senator and his aides, but Democrats against Republicans, the executive department against the Congress, and the subcommittee against its own chairman. The conflicts were intricate and overlapping, and the audience was going to need scorecards to follow the action. These the newspapers and radio television commentators and analysts were prepared to supply, in such abundance and variety, however, that they might tend more to confuse and bewilder than to simplify and enlighten. What was sensed clearly was that here was a great, untidy drama about to be played for high stakes, and its very lack of precedent would make it all the more engrossing

499

to the onlooking nation. How engrossing was revealed instantaneously when, at 10:30 A.M., Senator Mundt, presiding as temporary chairman, rapped with a glass ash tray and announced, "The committee will come to order." At that moment the national consumption of electricity took a sharp jump upward as several million television sets were switched on.

The show was being telecast directly from the Senate caucus room by all networks and broadcast by every radio station of any consequence coast to coast. In Wall Street, where the stock exchanges had just begun the day's trading, business came to a virtual halt as clerks and executives in brokerage houses crowded together around sets, looking and listening. And what they were watching and waiting for mainly became clear within a few minutes—it was the performance of the admitted star of the production, Senator Joe McCarthy.

The jam-packed caucus room was cluttered with television and newsreel cameras, lights, and cables. There were some 500 spectators, 130 reporters, and 60 still photographers pushing and elbowing through the crush for angle shots. The crowd was select, made up almost wholly of members of Congress and their friends. Admission was by card only, and many were turned away; latecomers were forced to stand around the walls. All spectators had been searched at the doors, the women required to turn out their handbags (a cause of embarrassment and some sly joking among the onlookers) and the men being frisked for concealed weapons; the precaution had been ordered because of telephoned threats. Uniformed guards were posted around the room.

The seven members of the subcommittee were ranged behind a thirty-six-foot-long mahogany table. Mundt was in the center, with Ray Jenkins, the special counsel, seated at his right. Strung farther along on that side were the Republican members—Senators Dirksen, Potter, and Dworshak of Idaho, whom McCarthy at the last moment had appointed to sit in for him to prevent a tie vote. At Mundt's left sat the Democrats, Senators McClellan, Symington, and Jackson. In front of each senator, for the benefit of the television watchers, was a placard bearing his name. Each senator had his own microphone.

At the far end of the table, beyond the Democratic members, sat McCarthy, flanked by Roy Cohn and Frank Carr. Opposite Mundt stood the witness chair, with Joseph Welch, the Army's counsel, beside it. Immediately in back of the witness chair, so placed that they formed a brilliant background whenever the cameras panned to the witness, sat a galaxy of high-ranking Army brass—more generals than the public was ever likely to see together again. Their chests ablaze with row on row of military ribbons, they sat erect, motionless, silent, registering their unwavering support of their embattled representatives.*

The hearing got under way with an introductory statement by Senator Mundt. It was designed, the temporary chairman said, to give the entire nation a chance to see how a congressional investigation was conducted. Mundt did not mention that the Republicans had fought hard to keep the hearings closed, letting the public see nothing; but McClellan and McCarthy both had stuck to their demand that the testimony be given the widest possible publicity. The chair cautioned the spectators against any manifestation "of approval or disapproval" and said that the guards would "politely escort" to the door any offenders against this rule. It was with difficulty that the audience refrained from applauding this preliminary speech.

There had been much joking among the senators about their roles, with consultation on the use of makeup, the right sort of attire, and how to catch the eye of the camera when one wished to make a point. It was plain that all the participants felt like actors for the nonce, but when the curtain rose there was no sign of constraint apparent among the figures strung along the interminable table; all seemed at ease and on jolly terms with one another.

Senator McCarthy was wearing a dark blue suit and blue-and-white tie; his makeup failed to mask entirely the black shadows on his jowls. Confident and alert, he betrayed no doubt of his ability to breeze through the performance. Beside him sat Roy Cohn, chubbily cherubic with his air of respectful innocence, while on the senator's other side Frank Carr's full-moon beamed im-

---

* Unfortunately color television was not yet in general use. The nation's first color receivers had gone on public sale only one month previously, and the few color telecasts were still experimental. Westinghouse offered 250 sets of their eleven and one-half-inch model, priced at $1,295 each, although they had cost $3,000 each to manufacture. Emerson Radio had sets for rent, but not for sale. They charged $200 for installation and "personal instruction" in how to operate the controls, and a monthly rental fee of $75. This worked out at an annual rental cost of $1,025.

passively, betraying no emotion. In Carr's custody were five briefcases as bulging as himself, stuffed with reference documents.

In an immaculately pressed, single-breasted gray suit, Stevens
was neutral in tone and manner. John Adams looked supercilious
and irascible. Hensel personified pent-up wrath.

The chairman explained the rules: Jenkins would call the witnesses in any order he chose and would first examine them directly,
to allow them to get their stories on the record; then, switching
roles, he would cross-examine them, to develop any discrepancies.
No time limit was set on this. Thereafter, each senator in turn would
have ten minutes to cross-examine, first a Republican and then a
Democrat, alternately, until all had had a turn. If any senator had
further questions to ask, the circle would be gone around again
in the same order, and this process would be repeated as long as
any senator deemed necessary. McCarthy was included in these ten-
minute question periods, but Welch, as Jenkins' opposite, might
cross-examine witnesses without limitation of time.

It was noted that none of the three accused principals on
McCarthy's side was represented by counsel, as were the Army
trio. Jenkins was counsel for the investigating committee, not for
the accused. McCarthy had proposed to retain Edward Bennett
Williams, who had represented him in the Benton libel case, but
Williams had declined when McCarthy insisted on doing his own
cross-examining; Williams felt that he could not accept responsibility for conduct of the case unless he were allowed full control.
Cohn, too, had considered engaging counsel, and had been urged
to do so by McCarthy, but finally had decided to conduct his own
defense. Later he would regret having taken this course.

[II]

Shortly after the camera lights were turned on for the first time,
it became clear who would dominate the proceedings. It was
Senator McCarthy, and this in spite of his having to meet rugged
competition for the star role. No Broadway play or motion picture
was ever so ideally cast: in looks, in manner, in tone of voice, and
in personality, each actor was perfectly suited to the part he was
to play. Jenkins, with his rumpled hair and undershot bulldog jaw,
was the tough courtroom prosecutor, cajoling or menacing as needful. The wily Welch, watching with a self-effacing air, gentle and
old-fashioned in his speech, seemed timidly bemused by the goings-

on, but missed no opportunity deftly to score. Senator Mundt, in the chair, puffing a pipe, was placidly genial and ineffective. Dirksen's lubricating tones rippled and rolled to soothe moments of tension. McClellan, the homespun Arkansas lawyer who never finished high school, was literal, unsmiling, and tenacious—the "honest man" of facts and blunt action. Handsome Senator Symington, aware of his emerging image as a leading contender for the Democratic Presidential nomination, seemed the well-groomed business executive he was, stern but fair, determined not to let the wool be pulled over his eyes. Senator Jackson, youthful-looking but endowed with a vigorous legal mind enriched by both congressional experience and the training received as a prosecutor in his home state, would be resigned to playing a relatively minor role. But even the bit players in this real-life drama were superbly and uncannily "right" for their parts.

Barely had the proceedings got under way when Senator McCarthy moved in.

"Mr. Chairman. Mr. Chairman." His metallic voice sounded from the foot of the table as he leaned over his microphone. "A point of order."

"Let the senator state his point," the chair replied.

Now a parliamentary point of order is one raised to direct the chair's attention to a violation of the rules, or in objection to irrelevant or immaterial digressions, and in most instances it takes precedence over other matters. It is obvious that a presiding officer cannot decide whether a point of order is properly taken until it has been stated, and this was the weapon McCarthy seized upon. What he objected to, it developed, was the right of Stevens and Adams to maintain, or represent to the subcommittee, that their charges had been brought "on behalf of the Department of the Army." The charges had been filed, McCarthy insisted, on behalf of two or three civilians in the Army, and he emphasized *civilians*.

"I may say, Mr. Chairman," came the rasping, insistent voice as Mundt attempted to reply, "that I have heard—may I have the attention of the chair—may I say, Mr. Chairman, that I have heard from people in the military, all the way down from generals with the most outstanding combat records, down to privates recently inducted, and they have indicated they are very resentful of the fact that a few Pentagon politicians, attempting to disrupt our investigations, are naming themselves the Department of the Army."

The way the senator said "Pentagon politicians" made the words

sound like an obscenity. Curtly Mundt overruled the point of order
and cautioned McCarthy against making speeches. Thereupon the
latter interrupted again to assail Stevens and Adams further for their
"attempt to make this a fight between me and the Army." The interruption ended with nothing changed in the record, but McCarthy
had brought home to several million television viewers a technical
contention buried in his formal rebuttal of the charges. This, of
course, had been his purpose all along; and from that moment
Senator McCarthy dominated the cameras almost at will with questions, interruptions, and "points of order" that were essentially
points of disorder, but beyond the ability of the chairman to head
off. Joe in fact kept the show running. While the cameras were
trained on him, interest was high; all the other senators were forced
temporarily into playing supporting roles. When his turn for questioning came he took the full ten minutes, and when his time ran
out he raised a point of order and kept on talking. Nobody seemed
eager to do battle with him; the mild objections interposed by
Jenkins and Welch he rode down brutally. The weakness of the
two lawyers lay in their failure thus far to grasp that the hearing
was not a trial, the caucus room not a courtroom, and that courtroom rules did not apply. The investigation was a loosely governed
proceeding in which audacity could pay off, and of audacity Mc-
Carthy had a limitless supply, backed by a lifetime of skill in using it.

In order to set the ground for the Army's case, Jenkins called
Major General Miles Reber, who had been chief of legislative liaison
for the Army when the Schine affair began. Currently stationed in
Germany, Reber had been flown back to testify. Under Jenkins'
tactful leading, he stated crisply that starting on July 8 of the previous year, Senator McCarthy and Roy Cohn had talked with him
about getting Schine a commission. Repeatedly emphasizing his
sense of "the importance of this case," Reber said he had communi-
cated the request to General John E. Hull, then Vice-Chief of Staff,
inasmuch as General Lawton Collins, Chief of Staff, was absent
from Washington. General Hull had instructed that Schine's application should be handled in exact accordance with standard procedure.

Schine himself had telephoned, saying he would like to come over
to the Pentagon and "hold up his hand," and a date had been set.
Since he might be out of his office when Schine arrived, Reber had
instructed three members of his staff—two colonels and a lieutenant

colonel—regarding the case, and these officers had received the applicant, put him through a physical examination, and given him an application form to fill out. This Schine had done, seeming to show "an attitude of haste and impatience." After he had left, it was found that the form had been only partially completed, and it was sent to the Capitol by courier for completion. The next day it was returned, completed.

General Reber then told of his approaching the Army Transportation Corps and the Office of Psychological Warfare, neither of which found Schine qualified for a commission, mainly because of lack of previous military experience. Meanwhile, Reber was receiving telephone calls from Cohn, and a few from the senator, urging him to make haste, or Schine would be drafted. When finally the Army seemed canceled out as a prospect, at Cohn's request General Reber sounded out the Navy and the Air Force, in the process consulting an admiral, a commander, and a major general, but again he was turned down.

Reber explained that the job of legislative liaison was to receive and act upon calls from congressmen regarding men about to be drafted, and he would not term the calls he had received from Senator McCarthy improper or excessive, but those from Cohn were a different matter; they were "not normal," judging by his ten years of experience in dealing with Congress. "I felt that Mr. Cohn was persistently after me . . . that I was being put under definite pressure," the General described the situation.

McCarthy moved in with a rapid-fire cross-examination that involved other members of the subcommittee and their calls to Reber's office, and the General conceded that the senator himself had not asked for any preferential treatment for Schine, but simply that he be given a chance to apply for a commission and show, if he could, that he was qualified for one. Then, after drawing from the witness the admission that he had been "acutely aware" of Roy Cohn's position as chief counsel for the subcommittee at the time of Schine's application, McCarthy wondered why Reber had been so "acutely aware." Abruptly he asked, "Is Sam Reber your brother?" The reference was to Samuel Reber, formerly acting high commissioner for Germany and at present retired from the State Department. The General replied that Sam Reber was his brother, and McCarthy shot out:

"Now, did anything about Sam Reber's activities make you

'acutely aware' of the fact that Mr. Cohn was chief counsel? . . .
That Mr. Sam Reber, when Mr. Cohn and Mr. Schine were sent to
Europe by me to inspect the libraries, that your brother, Mr. Sam
Reber, repeatedly made attacks upon them? . . . At the time you
were processing the application of this young man, Schine, for a
commission, were you aware of the fact that he had had a very
unpleasant experience with your brother?"

General Reber denied any such knowledge, and in reply to a
question by Senator Symington he stated positively that the first
time he had ever heard his brother mentioned by either McCarthy
or Cohn was "in this hearing today." But McCarthy was not through.
When his question period came around again he began circuitously:

"May I say, general, to begin with, I feel that I should apologize,
and I think we all should apologize to the General of the Army to
keep you here questioning you about the private in the Army who is
still a private despite the special consideration he got. Number
two"—and here came a dagger thrust—"let me say that this committee has nothing in its record that reflected adversely on you, as
far as I am concerned, as far as I know. However, I would like to
ask you this question, and I think it should be on the record, for
the benefit of the committee: were you aware of the fact that your
brother was allowed to resign when charges that he was a bad security risk were made against him as a result of the investigations of
this committee?"

The statement, made with biting underemphasis, by innuendo im-
peaching Reber's testimony as biased, shocked the room, and a
heated wrangle broke out over whether it was relevant. Pounding
the palm of his left hand with his right fist, General Reber excitedly
demanded, through Welch, the right to reply, and he was finally
accorded permission. Looking McCarthy in the eye, he said defiantly:

"I do not know and have never heard that my brother *retired* as
a result of any action of this committee. The answer is '*positively
no.*'"

McCarthy paid no attention to Reber's glare. He had achieved
a dramatic climax and had dominated the scene, mainly for the
benefit of the enormous television audience, and he gave no sign of
retreating. Already he had held the microphone longer than any
other senator, and he had been the only one to interrupt a witness
while speaking. He had clashed with Jenkins several times and more

than once had lectured the chairman for failing to give him un-
divided attention. Yet through it all he had remained at ease, giving
the impression of a tough pugilist, battling every inch of the way,
bullying the referee and bending the rules to suit his purposes, but
not really at odds personally with anybody. It was like a roughhouse
poker session on an extended scale—with 20,000,000 kibitzers
looking on.

Late in the day Secretary Stevens took the stand as the Army's
chief witness, but immediately stepped down to allow General Walter Bedell Smith, Undersecretary of State, whose name had been
brought up in the testimony, to testify before he left for a high-level
diplomatic conference in Geneva.

Smith recounted with military brevity Cohn's having consulted
him about a commission for Schine. Smith had tried the Army, to
no avail, and Cohn had then suggested that the CIA "might arrange
to have Mr. Schine commissioned," since he had investigative experience. Smith had offered to telephone Allen Dulles about it, but
at the last moment Cohn had changed his mind, remarking that the
CIA was "too juicy a subject for future investigation, and it would
not be right to ask them to get Mr. Schine commissioned, and then
investigate the organization later."

Jenkins asked whether General Smith felt that Cohn had tried to
"high-pressure anyone," and got the laconic response, "Not me,
sir!" The crowd laughed heartily.

Then Stevens resumed the stand and read his preliminary statement, which summarized the Army's indictment. He said that from
mid-July of 1953 to the month just past, "David Schine was discussed between one branch or other of the Department of the Army
and Senator McCarthy or members of his staff in more than sixty-
two telephone calls . . . [and] at approximately nineteen meetings
between Army personnel and Senator McCarthy or members of his
staff." Requests made on Schine's behalf, Stevens continued, ranged
from several for a direct commission before he was inducted to
"many for special assignments, relief from routine duty such as KP,
extra time off, and special visitor privileges." And in conclusion, to
make his indignation and the Army's resentment clear (sitting, as
he did, between Lieutenant General Lyman Lemnitzer, Deputy
Chief of Staff for Plans, and Major General Robert N. Young,
Assistant Chief of Staff for Personnel), the Secretary said that
"during my tenure as Secretary of the Army, there is no record that

matches this persistent, tireless effort to obtain special consideration
and privileges for this man." The Schine case, Stevens declared, was
"only one example of the wrongful seeking of privilege, of the perversion of power—it has been a distraction that has kept many men
from the performance of tasks far more important to the welfare
of this country than the convenience of a mere Army private."

In other words, the United States Army was being disrupted and
demoralized by the to-do being made over Private G. David Schine.

[III]

These were the opening bursts of fire. The next day, Friday, the
figurative rattle of small arms sounded again in the crowded caucus
room as Ray Jenkins took the Secretary over the twisting course of
his relations with Senator McCarthy and the subcommittee staff.
Robert Ten Broeck Stevens had been the civilian head of the Army
only one year, and a harrowing year it had proved. Passing by the
preliminary phases of the Schine affair, Jenkins came to various
encounters with Cohn, Schine, and the senator. On one occasion,
for example, Stevens had taken breakfast coffee with Senator Mc-
Carthy in the home of Schine's parents in New York. On October 12
of the previous year he had been a guest of the Schines, with Roy
and Judge Cohn and McCarthy, at dinner in the Waldorf-Astoria;
and the next morning, since he was attending a hearing by Mc-
Carthy's subcommittee in the federal courthouse downtown, he had
been picked up by David Schine in the latter's car and driven to
Foley Square.

During that ride a somewhat unusual conversation had taken
place. Jenkins asked what had been said, and Stevens recalled:
"Well, the conversation was along the line that I was doing a good
job in ferreting out Communists."

"Was that your statement, or his?" inquired Jenkins, amid a ripple
of laughter.

Stevens: "That was Mr. Schine's statement." A gust of merriment
filled the room, and Stevens went on: "He thought I could go a long
way in this field." This time the laughter was louder, and Mundt
fidgeted. "And that he would like to help me." The laughter became
a guffaw, and although Mundt rapped warningly, he himself was
smiling. "He thought it would be a much more logical plan for him

to become a special assistant of mine . . . than being inducted in the Army." McCarthy chuckled with the others.

Then Jenkins took the witness over the events of October 20, when Stevens had flown from Washington with Senator McCarthy, Roy Cohn, and John Adams to inspect the layout of laboratories at Fort Monmouth. Stevens said he had gathered the impression that McCarthy was about ready to turn over to the Army the leads he had uncovered, for prosecution and dismissals. On landing, they had been met by General Lawton, Senator Alexander Smith, and Congressman James C. Auchincloss, the latter two from New Jersey. The group set out on a tour of the installation. When they came to one laboratory which required a special security clearance to enter, there was some hesitation, because Stevens did not know who had clearance and who hadn't. He and Adams were cleared, and making an "on-the-spot decision," he ruled that members of Congress should be considered as cleared. That left out Roy Cohn, and when the group emerged, they found him fuming.

Jenkins asked what had been said. "Well," replied Stevens, "Colonel BeLieu, my military aide, told me that Mr. Cohn . . . had been very provoked, and [had said]: 'This is war! I am cleared for the highest classified information! I have access to FBI files when I want them! They did this just to embarrass me! We will now really investigate the Army!' " Stevens added that later he learned that within earshot of two Fort Monmouth aides Cohn had exclaimed, "This is a declaration of war!"

Laughter mingled with gasps of astonishment in the audience drew a firm rebuke from the chairman, while the cameras swept the long table, scanning the facial expressions of the senators sitting as judges. Roy Cohn sat frozen-faced, nervously flicking glances up to the ceiling.

Then the questioning passed to Stevens' growing resentment, during November of 1953, of "the hammering over the head of the Army persistently, creating the impression that there was espionage in a big way at Fort Monmouth, which I say was not so. I told Senator McCarthy and his associates that . . . if they kept on with these headlines, which in my opinion were entirely unfair, that they could drive me out of office if they wanted to."

"Mr. Chairman," came the voice from the foot of the table, "a point of order. I think the record should show that the chairman of the committee has no control whatsoever over headlines, or over what the press says. If the chair is to be criticized——"

"That is not a point of order," Mundt interrupted. "You will have an opportunity during cross-examination to bring out those points."

But Stevens broke in: "I would like to state right now with reference to that, after an executive committee meeting of this committee, Senator McCarthy goes out and addresses the press, and he tells them exactly what he pleases, and that is where the stories are generated."

McCarthy: "Mr. Chairman, a point of order. If the secretary is going to discuss what I say after an executive meeting, I think that the record should show that his man Adams was present at every executive meeting, and that his man Adams was invited to correct any statement that I made if he felt I was in error. A point of order."

Mundt, wearily: "What is the point?"

McCarthy: "If Mr. Stevens would intimate that some improper statement was made to the press after any meeting, then he should give us the date and the time and the place and tell what the improper statement was."

"That is a question of cross-examination," counsel Jenkins interposed hastily, "and Senator McCarthy will have that opportunity shortly." Then he corrected himself dubiously: "I hope it is shortly."

The slugging had started in earnest. But the mood lightened when Stevens related a telephone conversation he had had with McCarthy regarding Schine, after the latter finally had been drafted and Cohn was trying to have him reassigned to the subcommittee. Speaking from memory, Stevens recollected that the senator had said that such a reassignment would be misinterpreted, and had volunteered that "one of the few things he had trouble with Mr. Cohn about was David Schine. He said that 'Roy thinks Dave ought to be a general, and operate from a penthouse in the Waldorf-Astoria,' or words to that effect. Senator McCarthy then said that he thought a few weekends off might be arranged . . . perhaps for the purpose of 'taking care of Dave's girl friends.' "

"Did you say that that conversation was monitored?" Jenkins inquired, and set off a three-hour wrangle over the admissibility of monitored calls.

Stevens explained that it was standard practice at the Pentagon to have an assistant in the outer office listen in on all calls coming to the Secretary and make notes on them. This was with a view to efficiency, since the monitor could automatically initiate any action required, such as obtaining information, arranging transportation, or checking files, freeing the Secretary from the burden of issuing detailed instructions. The Army possessed transcripts of monitored calls from McCarthy, Cohn, and others (rumor said as many as a hundred), some of which it proposed to offer as evidence.

McCarthy, who had chuckled with the crowd at the account of his "mercy suggestions" for Dave, suddenly grew bitter and lashed out fiercely at the practice of listening in without the caller's knowledge. "One of the most indecent and dishonest things I have ever heard of!" he termed it.

Welch cited a legal danger inherent in revealing the contents of a monitored call without the consent of both parties, and challenged McCarthy to consent, since the Army was willing. But the senator retorted that it would be unfair to release his calls alone, or only selected ones; he demanded that if any were presented, all must be, together with transcripts of all calls made by the other principals and by the members of the subcommittee—in their entirety and chronologically, not edited or arranged in some order chosen by counsel. The argument grew heated, but McCarthy stubbornly held his ground. Finally, on a motion by Senator McClellan, who agreed with McCarthy, it was decided to subpoena all records on monitored calls held by the Army, but to hold up action pending a careful study of the legal aspects. Jenkins was instructed to prepare an opinion for the guidance of the committee, and Mundt stressed that "every conceivable precaution" would be taken to avoid making "a shambles of the whole hearing by introducing evidence and later having some lawyer destroy its validity." The significance of his statement lay in the likelihood, admitted on all sides, of perjury action against somebody, perhaps based on a monitored telephone call.

This issue being disposed of, at least for the time being, the hearing was recessed over the weekend.

"I Show You a Photograph"

The weekend hiatus gave the public an opportunity to collect its impressions of the thus far highly confused goings-on in the Senate caucus room, and those impressions proved to be quite as tangled and conflicting as the testimony so far offered and the issues raised. Even the extent of the public's interest in the fracas was in dispute. *The New York Times* reported that the Hooper ratings on viewers' response showed the spectacle trailing well behind the mark attained by the Kefauver hearings and that department stores and movie houses reported no loss of business, at least in New York City. But elsewhere a sudden spurt in sales of television sets was registered, and shops did notice a decided slacking off of trade during the telecast hours. In Los Angeles, where because of the time differential the program came on at 7:30 A.M., employers reported much tardiness, due to workers' reluctance to break away from their sets, and vehicular traffic was much curtailed.

Newsweek collected representative comments but they seemed to fall into no regular pattern. In Massachusetts, the state's attorney general said, shrugging, that up to the present all the hearing had proved was that "Schine is still a private, while Peress was promoted to major." A Dallas night watchman was worried about "who's paying for this." In St. Louis, two men argued on the street, one saying, "They've got him in a corner," and the other answering, "He'll come out of it bigger than ever." A Texas businesswoman felt that "both sides are getting hurt," while a newspaper editor in Milwaukee was confident that "this is getting nowhere; they won't frame Joe." An ex-GI thought McCarthy was making an ass of himself, but another veteran said the Army was making "more of an ass of itself than usual." In Atlanta the joke was, "They got McCarthy in jail yet?" A stenographer gushed over the senator,

512

"Isn't he handsome!" But a cab driver grumbled, "The way they're going, they'll be at it for another month and a half."

One element with which the telecasts were by no means popular was the broadcasting networks. A trade magazine estimated that in ten days the hearings would cost the networks $10,500,000 in sponsored shows canceled and in expenses, not to mention real fear of a loss of advertising goodwill. NBC took the plunge over the weekend and announced it was discontinuing the live telecasts, and would show filmed highlights only—the practice CBS was following already. ABC said it would keep on with live coverage as long as the committee permitted, both morning and afternoon sessions.

NBC's announcement provided an immediate test of the hearings' appeal to viewers, and irate protests poured in so swiftly and in such volume that the network backtracked and restored the live telecasts.

Editorial comment was mixed. *The New York Times* welcomed the spectacle being acted before the cameras because it showed McCarthy for the first time "very much on the defensive." The *Times* conceded that "he fights with great dexterity. 'Point of order!' has become his trademark. He uses it with great skill to interrupt witnesses and avail himself of the privilege of making long or short speeches. . . . He uses every dodge in his extensive book. . . . It is enlightening to watch him operate [and] the longer the proceedings drag on, the longer the public will have to watch him; and the longer it has to watch him, the more accurately, we believe, will the full picture emerge of what kind of senator he is."

Washington correspondents said that that city was fascinated by the show, although it was too early to predict the outcome. Joe's ardent partisans were for him stronger than ever, while his dedicated enemies were strengthened in their belief that he had been trapped in what would prove his Waterloo. The hatred obsessing both sides plainly was preventing any balanced judgment. Recognizing that the public would have to make up its mind slowly, *The New York Times* provided food for reflection by printing eleven full pages of the verbatim testimony given in the first two days.

McCarthy had flown to Wisconsin for the weekend, and in Wausau he told a luncheon meeting of the Women's Press Club that the most regrettable aspect of the hearings was the way they were wasting the time of half a dozen top-ranking generals for the sole purpose of impressing impressionable television watchers; even General Ridgway, the Chief of Staff, had appeared in the solemn phalanx of brass supporting the Army Secretary. That evening, addressing Roundtable International, a civic organization, the senator praised Secretary Stevens as an innocent used by others. "Bob Stevens is a fine, honest American," said Joe, "but he doesn't know how to handle these hard politicians who are running the Pentagon." He thought Ray Jenkins was running the hearings very fairly, although the whole affair was nothing more than a "red-minnow burlesque." The senator announced that he would be making numerous speeches in Wisconsin during the next few weeks.

[II]

McCarthy showed up for the Monday sessions radiating confidence. He was following his regular daily routine—up between 7 and 7:30, bathe and shave, a couple of cups of tea with his wife, then off to his office, a short distance away. Usually his wife accompanied him, although she was still on crutches from her New York accident. Arriving at about 9 o'clock, he would spend an hour catching up on general business and discussing the day's strategy with Cohn and Carr. Then all three would proceed to the caucus room, Jean McCarthy still in the party. During the testimony she would usually sit close behind her husband, observing attentively. At noon the group would lunch in the Carroll Arms Hotel, next door to the Senate Office Building, usually without other company; then back for the two-hour afternoon session, after which came a stroll back to the office, pursued by well-wishers and autograph hunters, Joe obliging good-naturedly as he strode along. More paperwork, then home around 6:30 for a cocktail and a quiet dinner, after which he might work or watch a Western on television.

McCarthy by now had become a seasoned infighter—far different from the inept amateur who had been a setup for the polished lacing administered by Senator Tydings four years ago; now he could take care of himself in the clinches.

The week opened with Secretary Stevens undergoing vigorous cross-examination by Jenkins. The big, rangy Tennesseean, with his unruly hair and underslung jaw, changed his manner as he bore down on the well-meaning but ineffective Army head. His voice booming in contempt, the counsel sought to establish that Stevens had gone to suspiciously extreme lengths to get the Fort Monmouth investigation called off, because of the bad publicity it was causing. Stevens denied this, saying he only wanted to speed up the hearings so that the Army could finish the job of weeding out security risks, a job which he contended he had been carrying out to everybody's satisfaction until McCarthy interfered. The suggestion that he was "trying to minimize" McCarthy's activity Stevens flatly, if somewhat lamely, denied; he just thought the senator had "greatly overexaggerated" the situation. Tracing Stevens' actions in "courting" McCarthy's goodwill, during the early phases of the Fort Monmouth inquiry—arranging visitors' privileges for the senator and his staff in the exclusive Merchants Club in downtown New York, all at Stevens' personal expense; flying the senator and his staff here and there in the Secretary's personal plane; accepting social favors from Schine's parents; allowing Schine to chauffeur him around New York chummily—why, asked Jenkins with heavy innuendo, had Stevens gone so far out of his way to "make peace with Cohn and Schine," to "humble" himself, to "go traipsing off to New York, hunting this man," if it wasn't because he was afraid of the senator and hoped to get the investigation called off?

His eyes blinking behind heavy, horn-rimmed glasses, Stevens rejected the imputation. And he denied, as "an unequivocal lie," the suggestion that he had proposed a deal to switch the inquiry to another service branch.

Turning to the reasons for the Army's having included Frank Carr in the charges, Jenkins drew from Stevens an account of how Cohn and Carr had called on him at the Pentagon before Schine was drafted, and how Cohn had pressed for a special assignment for Schine, if not a commission, while Carr kept silent. The Secretary could not recall Carr's having spoken a single word, but he insisted that "the very fact that he [Carr] . . . did not object . . . left me with the definite impression that he fully concurred in Mr. Cohn's position."

McCarthy moved in: "Mr. Chairman!"

Senator Mundt: "Point of order?"

McCarthy: "Is this a new theory of 'guilt by silence,' I wonder?"

Mundt was annoyed. "That is a proper question for the senator to ask in his own time," he retorted huffily. "I would appreciate it if no spurious points of order will be made to interrupt the interrogatory."

McCarthy: "Mr. Chairman!"

Mundt, sharply: "Point of order overruled."

McCarthy, hanging on: "I can assure you there'll be no interruptions, unless I think it's of importance. I do think it's important now to make a point of order that the secretary is trying to impute 'guilt by silence' to Mr. Carr."

Only then, amid the laughter, did he subside, having succeeded, in spite of the rebuke from the chair, in getting his point across to the television audience while the incident was still fresh in their minds. During the repartee the cameras had shown Stevens sitting unhappily; under Jenkins' searching attack he was visibly wilting.

Toward the end of the afternoon, while Senator McClellan was taking his turn at questioning the witness, he brought out with some bluntness that as head of the Army Stevens did have the legal power to confer commissions at his discretion, outside of regular channels. Stevens protested that this right was purely academic, because he would never, under any circumstances, exercise it. But McClellan pointed grimly to the "imputation—you might as well face it, sir—that you were trying to buy off this committee from investigating the Army" by withholding a commission from Schine which the Secretary could have granted.

McCarthy let Stevens squirm for a while, then moved in with a "point of order" and a show of righteous indignation, saying: "I think that question is completely improper and unfair and the implication is that this chairman could have been bought off. . . . There is no evidence that this chairman [himself] could have been bought off in any hearing, and never will be bought off in any hearing." Turning to Stevens, he continued, in spite of impatient mutterings from the chair: "Look, Bob, you are accusing Frank Carr of something very serious." Stevens agreed, and McCarthy went on: "You say he tried improperly to influence you. Now, if he said something that was improper, then you should tell us. And if you can't remember anything improper, you should tell us." Stevens became more and more distressed, although he stuck to his "impression," and McCarthy concluded that he was "trying to give us an honest account, although some of my friends don't agree with that, I may say."

Roy Cohn chimed in that he was one of those who did not agree. Finally the chairman's gavel, recessing the hearing until tomorrow, rescued the graying witness from the crossfire poured in by antagonists far more able and ruthless than he would ever be.

[III]

So far the Army side had not shown up well at all, and the longer Stevens remained on the stand, the less convincing his testimony became. Even those who believed the worst of McCarthy could not dodge the all too obvious fact that an extraordinary interest had been taken in G. David Schine at the Pentagon level both before and after he had been inducted. The inevitable question was: what was the motive for this utterly abnormal interest in just another draftee? The way the caucus room echoed with allusions to "Private Schine," "Private Schine," "Private Schine," and the constant linking of his name with those of Army officers of the most exalted rank, drummed that question home, and Stevens' palpable honesty of intent could not efface it.

Then on Tuesday the Army's case received a jolt that threatened a complete disaster. Stevens was under cross-examination again, as Jenkins reverted to the Secretary's alleged eagerness to have the Fort Monmouth investigation stopped. Jenkins brought out that altogether eighty-four separate "contacts"—telephone calls or personal appeals—had been made in reference to either a commission or preferential treatment for Schine, and that in Stevens' opinion Cohn had "used his office in an attempt at perversion of the rules of the Army."

When McCarthy's turn at questioning came, he wanted to know what special consideration Schine in fact had received. "Don't you think, actually, Mr. Secretary," he asked, "that this is all ridiculous in the extreme for this committee and all of these competent Army officers to be sitting here trying to find out why a private in the Army is successively promoted until he is finally up to the very top position of private? What do you think?" He ended with a tight smile and his odd titter of amusement, but Stevens replied gravely, "Well, I think you would have liked to have had him something other than a private."

This brought laughter from the audience, in which McCarthy joined. As the chair rapped for order and the tumult was subsiding, the senator injected, still chuckling: "Oh, don't mind me! Let—for the time being—for the time being—for the time being, let's assume that what you say is right. If I wanted him as something other than a private, I was awfully unsuccessful, wasn't I? Isn't that right?"

"But that wasn't your fault, senator," came the dogged response.

Jenkins then brought out that Stevens had known Schine personally ever since the previous September, had been the guest of Schine's parents, had mingled with Schine socially, and therefore knew him more or less well long before he was drafted. Then came the question: "Mr. Stevens, did you ever have your photograph taken with G. David Schine?" Stevens admitted that might be, because at the Fort Monmouth hearings "there were a lot of photographers around." But Jenkins wanted to know whether the Secretary had "ever, at your suggestion, at a meeting anywhere, any time, said, 'I want my picture taken with David,' and have it done."

Again Stevens demurred; he had never made a statement "just like you made it there," he said, but "if there was a picture being taken, and there were people around, I might be very apt to say, 'Well, let us all step up in here and have a picture.' " But he didn't think he had "ever made any demand to have my picture taken with David Schine."

But Jenkins was pertinacious: "I did not say 'demand,' but was his picture, after David Schine was drafted, ever taken with you alone, at your suggestion, anywhere?"

Stevens: "After he was drafted?"

Jenkins: "Yes. Let me show you a picture, Mr. Stevens, for the purpose of refreshing your recollection."

And the counsel suddenly held up, so that both the witness and the television audience could see it clearly, a three-foot-high blown-up photograph of Schine, in private's uniform, and the Secretary of the Army, standing beside a military airplane facing each other and apparently chatting. The Tennesseean's voice rumbled on remorselessly: "I ask you whether or not this is a photograph of you, the Secretary of the Army, and David Schine, a private in the Army?"

Obviously taken aback, Stevens hedged. He identified himself, and he assumed . . . his voice trailed off.

Jenkins: "What do you say about the soldier boy?"

Stevens: "I do not know whether that is Schine or not."

"Well, Mr. Stevens, you know Schine, do you not?"

"Yes."

"You know him well?"

"That picture does not look very much like him."

"You have had meetings with him and have been in his home and in automobiles with him. What is your best impression about whether or not that was David Schine?"

"I think it probably is," the Secretary sighed.

It developed that the photograph had been taken by a military photographer at Maguire Air Force Base, adjoining Fort Dix, New Jersey, on the previous November 17, when Schine was undergoing basic training at Fort Dix. The day before, according to Stevens' own testimony, the Secretary had lunched with Senator McCarthy and the latter's staff at the Merchants Club in New York, having come up from Washington in response to a report that McCarthy was highly displeased by the statement Stevens had given to the press asserting that there was no current espionage problem at Fort Monmouth. At the luncheon McCarthy had said frankly that the statement didn't give a correct picture of conditions at Monmouth, and Stevens had offered to make a "clarifying statement," stressing that he was not speaking for the McCarthy subcommittee but for the Army alone. Such a statement was given out.

"Designed for the purpose of, shall we say, pacifying or mollifying the senator?" Jenkins queried.

"I had been cooperating right along with the senator," Stevens protested.

McCarthy, Cohn, and Carr were scheduled to hold a hearing in Boston the next day, and Cohn mentioned that he hoped to meet Schine at Fort Dix (on one of those weekend passes that were upsetting General Cornelius Ryan, commander at Dix). As a courtesy, Stevens had flown the whole group in his official plane to Maguire Air Base, where Private Schine was waiting for them. Colonel Kenneth Bradley, commanding at Maguire, was on hand to welcome the Secretary, and from there Stevens offered the use of his plane to take them all to Boston, while he continued on to Washington in another plane. According to Cohn, during the flight to Boston McCarthy commented on the extraordinary helpfulness being displayed by Stevens, adding grimly, "He's turning handsprings to make us stop [the hearings at Monmouth], isn't he?"

During this dramatic passage, the television cameras had caught shots of Stevens stirring uneasily in his chair, of Welch whispering to him secretively, of senators bearing down with questions, and again and again of McCarthy and Cohn with heads together, whispering, their hands cupped over the microphones to guard against being overhead. It was a day of bad omen for the Army, climaxed by what to millions of viewers seemed the Alice-in-Wonderland absurdity of Stevens' guileless response to Jenkins' summarizing question: "The treatment you accorded Schine, then, was just what you accorded every other private in the Army?" With owl-like, deadpan gravity the Secretary replied: "I certainly would treat privates in the Army, one and all of them, the same."

At that point, figuratively, the Army's case collapsed, its main prop knocked out completely.

[IV]

The next morning Jenkins' dramatic surprise of the photograph figuratively exploded in the committee's face and set off a nation-wide sensation.

As the session opened, the Army's counsel, Joseph Welch, ejaculated, "Mr. Chairman!"

The television cameras swung toward the speaker, revealing the heretofore self-effacing Bostonian in a totally different light. Up to now he had personified unobtrusive mildness, had been retiring, almost apologetic in tone and mien as he ventured objections. Now and then his eyes had twinkled, but his air of courtly gravity and punctilious courtesy had been unruffled by anything that had happened. Now he was to burst onto television screens across the nation as a consummate courtroom actor, armed with drollery, biting wit, razor-sharp perceptions, and ruthless reflexes, a master of tactics and timing, and above all exuding a pawky humor that was best described as "Pickwickian"; indeed, he seemed a character straight out of a Dickens novel. Now his high tenor voice broke in angrily, peremptorily: "Mr. Chairman!"

"Mr. Welch, a point of order?" asked Mundt.

"I don't know what it is, but it's a point of something," came the response in a tone that expressed pain and indignation. "I have——"

Mundt insisted on hewing to the line: "A point of order will get stated."

Welch: "My point is that Mr. Jenkins yesterday was imposed upon, and so was the Secretary of the Army, by having a doctored or altered photograph produced in this courtroom as if it were honest!"

The slip of the tongue indicated his agitation. Senator Mundt primly corrected him, saying, "This is a committee room, Mr. Welch."

"A committee room—and produced as if it were honest. I have the photograph which was offered yesterday in evidence, and in respect to which Mr. Stevens was not only examined but cross-examined, and I show you now a photograph in respect to which I charge that what was offered in evidence yesterday was an altered, shamefully cut down picture, so that somebody could say to Stevens, were you not photographed alone with David Schine, when the truth is he was photographed in a group!"

The room—audience and committee members alike—was shocked into immobility for an instant, and Welch seized that minute to address his counterpart, Ray Jenkins, and exonerate him as a fellow attorney from any suspicion of complicity. Behind Welch's words was discernible—especially to all lawyers present—the mutual recognition that the opposing counsel after all were attorneys, not politicians, and merely temporary visitants to a world where apparently the ethical standards binding upon the legal profession did not apply.

"Mr. Jenkins," said Mr. Welch with heartfelt sympathy and compassion "I would like to say with all of my power, sir, I know you would never participate in a trick like this, but I suggest to you that you were imposed upon. I would now like to offer the picture that I have in my right hand"—he held up in plain view, on and off the television screen, a three-foot-high blowup of a photograph showing three figures—"as the original, undoctored, unaltered piece of evidence."

And thereupon erupted a debate that would rage continuously for days.

The third figure in the photograph that Welch produced turned out to be Colonel Bradley, the commander at Maguire Air Force Base. Bradley was standing at the left, with Private Schine between him and Stevens. Except for the inclusion of this third figure, the photograph was identical with the one introduced by Jenkins.*

Swiftly the committee counsel got in a disclaimer of any intention to deceive. The print he had produced, Jenkins said, had been given to him "by one of the parties in interest in this case . . . as being the genuine, authentic photograph, with no intimation or insinuation that it had been cut down," and he had presented it in good faith.

Jenkins' statement was barely uttered before McCarthy moved in with, "Point of order! Mr. Welch, under the guise of making a point of order, has testified that a picture is doctored. I now have before me, and I may say this: yesterday is the first time that I saw either of these pictures, the picture that was introduced yesterday and the one Mr. Welch puts in today; and he makes the completely false statement that this is a group picture, and it is not."

Jenkins whispered to Mundt, and the latter broke in: "Counsel advises the chair, may I say——"

McCarthy cut him off with an impatient, "May I finish my point of order?"

Mundt: "Counsel advises the chair that the senator is engaging in a statement or cross-examination rather than a point of order."

McCarthy's upper lip tightened, in a sign of rising temper, and his eyes narrowed to slits as he struck back through almost clenched lips: "I am getting rather sick of being interrupted in the middle of a sentence!"

Senator Stuart Symington had had a surfeit of Joe's tactics. He burst out: "If this is not a point of order, it is out of order! The counsel says it is not a point of order, and it is not a point of order if the counsel says it is not a point of order!"

McCarthy turned to Symington as if rebuking a naughty boy, and snapped, "Oh, be quiet!"

Symington bristled. "I haven't the slightest intention of being quiet! Counsel is running this committee, and you are not running it!"

McCarthy: "Mr. Chairman, do I have the floor?"

Mundt: "The chair has the floor, and nobody is endeavoring to determine whether Senator McCarthy is speaking to a point of

---

* Actually there was a fourth figure in the print, that of a man standing in the background at the far left with his back to the camera, and so obscured as to be unrecognizable. Later he would be identified as Frank Carr.

order. Will you state your point of order and then speak to it?"

McCarthy: "Mr. Chairman, may I suggest that when I start to say something, I not be interrupted in the middle of a sentence, and that Mr. Symington or no one else has the right to interrupt unless they address the chair, and unless the chair recognizes them. I am getting awfully sick of sitting down here at the end of the table and have whoever wants to interrupt in the middle of a sentence. Now, Mr. Welch . . . said this picture was doctored. . . . I can see no doctoring, except that a Colonel Bradley . . . his picture was not included. When Mr. Welch, under the guise of a point of order, said this was a group picture, I suggest that the chair make the record clear that Mr. Welch was not speaking the truth, and that the only change——"

Here Jenkins bulled his way into the harangue to repeat that neither McCarthy nor Welch had made a point of order, but statements of fact. "Mr. Chairman," came McCarthy's insistent demand, whereupon Senator Mundt made a speech about points of order and how everybody concerned would be given a chance to testify under oath about the picture and whether it was doctored or not; so there was no point of order involved, although the situation was "a bit unusual."

But McCarthy had no intention of being hushed. "Mr. Chairman"—he leaned into the microphone with one eye on Mundt and the other on the scrutinizing cameras—"call it a point of order or call it what you may, when counsel for Mr. Stevens and Mr. Hensel and Mr. Adams makes a statement and he is allowed to do it without interruption, and if that statement is false, do I have the right to correct it, or do we find halfway through my statement that Mr. Welch should not have made his statement and therefore I cannot point out that he was lying? I think that is an important question."

Repeating that both sides would have an opportunity to testify under oath about the photograph, Mundt got the interrogation going again; and on and on it would go.

[V]

Who had procured the photo? It had come from the office of David Schine—a small framed print hung on the wall—obviously a trophy that the young man was proud of. Cohn testified, James

Juliana, the subcommittee aide who had made the blowups, and others testified concerning its procurement, with the advantage shifting from side to side. Juliana explained that he had been instructed to obtain a photograph from Schine showing Stevens and Schine together and to make some blowups, without being told anything more, and he had carried out his instructions to the letter. Cohn testified at length, sparring quite successfully with Welch, saying he had ordered no cutdown in the photo and arguing that whether two men or three appeared in the print, the significance of the picture remained unchanged, which indeed was the case. Here was a photograph of an Army private enjoying the unique privilege of a weekend pass while still in basic training—a privilege extended to no other trainee—chatting amiably, to all appearances, with the head of the Army, on a military reservation; the photograph taken by military personnel, with no immediate or subsequent protest or order forbidding such a registering of a highly peculiar familiarity —and the incident taking place weeks after the Secretary had complained that he was being improperly pressured, or hectored, to grant trainee Schine preferential treatment. What was the reason for this exception to all principles of discipline? There was the important question. Was it to "appease" Senator McCarthy and get the Fort Monmouth hearings suspended, as McCarthy's side contended? Was it simple good nature? Was it merely a lamentable and unsoldierly sloppiness of conduct? Or was it a cat-and-mouse game by which Cohn could be jollied along by the granting of small favors to Schine, while the major one (a commission or special assignments) was withheld? These were the questions the answers to which the public tried to puzzle out as witnesses jousted with counsel and senators, and as political overtones kept obtruding to add complexity to the situation. The drama was electric, and the fact that both sides seemed to have been caught in misdemeanors spiced the suspense.

McCarthy was constantly active, full of audacity and surprises, zealously backing up his staff when they came under fire. His tactic was obvious: to contradict unfavorable testimony immediately, lest it remain unchallenged in the minds of television watchers. A viewer who heard the hostile testimony today might not be watching to hear the rebuttal tomorrow; so adverse testimony must be challenged instantly. For this reason, and in the face of the candid resentment of the lawyers involved, he resorted to interruptions and points of order, genuine or spurious, continually. In the first five days of the hearings he raised forty-six points of order, although all the other senators combined raised only twenty-seven. On other interruptions his score was thirty-six, against twenty-nine by all the others. On television and in the hearing room he dominated the action. His movements were watched minutely. He might rise and stalk out of the room, and a tremor of expectancy would race through the crowd. He would return, and the excitement would subside. He was never unaware of the camera's searching eye, and the public was insatiable for details about him. *Newsweek* even printed a photo of a memo that Joe had passed to the TV crews. Scribbled on a memo blank carrying the printed heading, "Senate of the United States—Memorandum," it read: "Could I have time off from camera for 10 seconds to use handkerchief?" The writing was firm and legible.

Joe was tireless in his questioning of Stevens, who for his part grew more and more evasive and contradictory, and was showing signs of exhaustion. Reverting from the disputed photograph to Stevens' objection to the Fort Monmouth hearings, the senator observed that Stevens had "succeeded in getting the hearings on Communist infiltration of the military suspended. Your success is complete as of today, is it not?" Stevens replied that he didn't know whether the hearings had been suspended, but McCarthy pointed out that "there have been no hearings since your office issued the attacks upon Mr. Cohn, Mr. Carr, and myself. In other words, you have been successful, have you not?"

Refusing to admit that there had been any such "success" on his part, Stevens became entangled in a quibble over just what he had said in testimony the day before. McCarthy grew impatient. "Bob," he insisted, "I am asking you a very simple question. Did you yesterday say that you wanted to have the hearings suspended?" Stevens wanted to "look up the record" before replying, so McCarthy held off the question until the afternoon session. But again Stevens hedged, explaining that he had not yet looked up the record. Under pressure he repeated that he would "look it up"; but of one thing he was sure—whatever he had said was the truth.

"How did you finally get the hearings suspended?" McCarthy pounded away. "They are suspended as of today. We both agree as to that, I believe. How did you finally succeed?"

Stevens, stubbornly: "They aren't suspended, as far as I know."

McCarthy: "Are the hearings still going on?"

Stevens: "Are they still going on? You know about that."

McCarthy: "Bob, don't give me that. You know the hearings were suspended the day you or someone filed your charges. . . . You know that, don't you? Let's not be coy."

Stevens: "I'm not being coy at all."

Cohn was called to the witness chair, and under questioning by McCarthy he swore that at Maguire Air Force Base, in the presence of Cohn, McCarthy, and Schine, Stevens had called over a military photographer and said, "I want my picture taken with Dave." Cohn made his answer to the question emphatic: "Yes, sir . . . Mr. Stevens stated that he wanted to have a picture taken of himself and Dave. And you [McCarthy] heard it, and I heard, and Frank Carr I know particularly heard it."

Under oath, Stevens professed inability to recollect making any such request.

At one point Senator Symington deplored that the hearings would tend to discourage reputable businessmen from entering government service if they must face "the type of smear and the type of lies" to which Stevens was being subjected; but Cohn disclaimed any culpability, reminding the senator tartly that "we did not make these charges, these 'smear' charges, against Mr. Stevens. He made them against us. I assume no responsibility in that regard."

Symington, whose dander was raised by Cohn's brashness and McCarthy's disdain, retorted that he could not recall "Mr. Stevens accusing any of the principals on the other side of blackmail or falsehood"; but after a whisper from Bobby Kennedy, the minority members' attentive counsel, he corrected himself. "I beg your pardon. He did accuse them of falsehood, but to the best of my knowledge he did not accuse them of blackmail. I think it is a two-way stretch." Tempers were fraying on both sides.

Senator Jackson put the direct question to Stevens on each separate charge made against him in McCarthy's bill of particulars, and drew categorical responses, repeated over and over: "False," "Equally false," "Completely false," "False," "False," "False."

Senator Dworshak, who hated being involved in the business and usually waived his question periods, pinned Stevens down on the latter's claim that a definite feeler had been put out toward the Pentagon, through George Sokolsky, the columnist friendly to McCarthy, to the effect that further investigation of the Army by McCarthy's committee would "either be terminated or be conducted along reasonable lines" if a commission were forthcoming for Schine. Stressing that this was a serious accusation, amounting to a claim that the subcommittee's "entire pattern of investigation could be influenced so easily," Dworshak asked whether the Secretary would stand back of the charge, and Stevens replied firmly, "That is right; yes, sir."

Jenkins took up the Inspector General's report on Schine's alleged irregularities at Fort Dix and asked whether the Secretary of the Army had been aware at the time that this trainee was being granted special privileges. Stevens said he had learned about that later—that Schine had been excused from KP duty, failed to appear in his uniform, hired others to clean his rifle and tidy up his quarters, and received an inordinate number of leaves and passes. These infractions of the rules Stevens said he had found out about later; but when Jenkins asked whether he had known that Schine took "unusual liberties with the officers . . . put his arm around a commissioned officer and fraternized with him and talked to him as though he were his equal in rank or superior," the Secretary admitted, amid a gust of laughter, that he had "never heard that one." Nor had he heard about Schine's putting his arm around his company commander and confiding that he "was there on a special assignment, to wit . . . to modernize the American Army and streamline it along modern lines."

To the accompaniment of more laughter, Jenkins asked whether the Secretary had known that when the trainees at Fort Dix were transported elsewhere, "Private Schine almost invariably rode in the cab of the truck, whereas the other soldiers, sometimes numbering forty or fifty, were packed like cattle or sheep in the bed of the truck and exposed to the weather." Stevens said this was the first time he had heard that charge, and McCarthy joined in instantly to repel such a slur upon the Army; he wished to assure the mothers of America, he said, that their sons in the military were not treated "like cattle" but with decency and respect.

Had Stevens known, Jenkins resumed, that Private Schine had been allowed to use the telephone at Fort Dix to call "a girl friend in New York City . . . and did so sometimes as many as four times a day"? Stevens conceded that he had been told about that, and the counsel drew blood when he asked whether General Ryan, commanding at Fort Dix, had telephoned to the Secretary regarding special treatment for Private Schine. No, Ryan had not called him directly, Stevens answered, but he had talked with John Adams. Thereupon Jenkins asked whether Stevens knew "whether or not Mr. Adams, by way of appeasement of this committee," had "directed General Ryan to permit this special treatment for Private Schine." Stevens did not know that, and he insisted that there had been "absolutely and completely" no appeasement.

The openings for McCarthy, when his question period came around, were too inviting to overlook, and the senator began with Schine's calls to girl friends, about which so much fuss was being made. Wasn't there a regular telephone center at Fort Dix, he asked, where "almost any night you can go in there and find hundreds of privates calling people, I assume many of them calling their girl friends?" And was it "special consideration to allow a private to call his girl friend?" No, Stevens would not say it was, and Mc-Carthy drove home the point with, "In other words, you don't think that we intervened as a committee to allow Private Schine . . . to call up his girl friend?" Well, not if he did it at the proper time, Stevens allowed, and McCarthy went on to quote the praise of Private Schine voluntarily given by his commanding general at Camp Gordon, in Georgia, describing him as "a good soldier with excellent character and superior efficiency." How did that square with his reported misconduct at Fort Dix, the senator wanted to know. Stevens thought the answer was that Schine's record at Camp Gordon was "an entirely different thing from his record at Fort Dix, sir." Which was an answer but hardly clarifying.

Then a surprise witness was summoned—Private G. David Schine. Innumerable times his name had fallen from the lips of generals and other high-ranking military and civilian figures, but until now he had been invisible, an all-pervading presence, felt but not seen. A flutter of excitement passed through the room as the handsome, twenty-seven-year-old private entered, trim in his uniform, respectful in his manner, and was sworn. He was unaccompanied by counsel, and reporters were at a loss to decide whether his cordovan shoes were GI issue, although they certainly had a brilliant gloss.

The most renowned private in the United States Army proved to be a cooperative and collected witness, well-spoken, courteous, and correctly deferential to his superiors in rank and age. He was plainly intelligent, responsive to questions, and as plausible as he was likable. He testified that after the disputed photograph had been snapped, he had asked the cameraman not to release it for publication, because "I had had to pose for it upon request," but had said that he would appreciate having a print for himself. Later the print came in the mail. To a question from Welch, he replied that he had told the cameraman, "I had to pose for it, because I was asked to by Secretary Stevens."

"Are you suggesting, sir," insinuated Welch, "that it was repulsive to pose for that picture?" Private Schine said that he was suggesting nothing. Welch tried again: "Are you suggesting, sir, that you were ordered by the Secretary of the Army to pose for that picture?" The answer came in a tone that was restrained and candid: "I am saying, sir, that I was asked by the Secretary of the Army to stand next to him and be photographed."

With the outlook for possible perjury action thus growing stormier, Jenkins insisted on getting his own story into the record under oath. Taking the witness stand, he recited in detail exactly how the disputed photograph came to him, ending with an avowal that seemed to be offered on the behalf of the other "outsider" in the affair, Counsel Welch, also: "Gentlemen, I would not, under any circumstances, present to this committee a spurious document. No intimation has ever been given to me by Mr. Welch or Mr. Stevens or Mr. Adams that I would be handed a document that was not genuine and authentic. No intimation has ever been made to me by Mr. Cohn or any member of his staff that any document might be handed to me for use on direct or cross-examination that was not genuine and authentic." Then Jenkins had himself unsworn and resumed his role as committee counsel. To some viewers his words had sounded curiously like an expression of pained astonishment that nobody had warned him or his high-principled opponent from Boston that in Washington they might be venturing among liars.*

---

* The constant assumption in the press of the lofty ethical standards governing the tactics of both special counselors, at this stage of the hearings, caused quiet amusement among the cynical. Their avoidance of the tricks of courtroom pleading was widely commented upon, yet the careers of both were replete with instances of the use of devices that while permissible were at least open to question if judged by the strictest ethical standards. Both men, like all conspicuously successful trial lawyers, were skilled actors, Welch a consummate one. Jenkins had defended scores of capital cases in Tennessee and boasted that he had never lost a client to the electric chair. He once appeared on behalf of a bail bondsman accused of shooting a photographer, and the actual photograph of the man firing a pistol squarely at the camera was introduced as evidence of murderous assault. Jenkins brought the defendant into court on a stretcher and represented the accuser as having deliberately and callously provoked a cripple into justifiable self-defense by unbearable taunts and insults. He won an acquittal. Welch's resort to subtler devices, based not at all on principle, would become apparent during the current hearings.

A Calm View of Bedlam

At the end of the second week, the net effect which the hearings were producing upon the nation was in doubt. The public's interest remained intense, whatever the public's judgment might be. The Hooper ratings on the television response fluctuated, dropping as low as 9 and jumping up to 30 when some crisis occurred. The sense of latent drama never left the caucus room; long stretches of monotonous questioning as each senator went over the same ground repetitiously (with an eye on the home folks watching) would suddenly be broken by a chance statement and the scene would come alive, tingling with suspense, as the verbal fencers clashed.

The statistics of the inquiry themselves were dramatic. What had started with some minor questions about an $83-a-month Army private had mushroomed into an investigation that was costing the taxpayers $3,500 a day in salaries and expenses, and the television networks millions of dollars in lost revenue. The hearings consumed some 500 man-hours of government work daily, occupying almost the full time of eight United States senators, the Secretary of the Army, the Army's chief counsel, an Assistant Secretary of Defense, two major generals, a colonel, two lieutenant colonels, at least fifteen other Army officers, enlisted men, and civilian employes, eight lawyers, fifteen members of the subcommittee's staff, and a dozen other government employes. It was keeping millions of Americans glued to their television sets, to the detriment of their own concerns, and was commanding more attention nationally than matters as grave as the current Geneva conference seeking to work out a permanent settlement of the future of Indo-China. It was certain to figure largely in the coming national elections. And no end was in sight.

Seasoned political observers were constantly struck by the atmosphere of crude, overwhelming drama. Writing in *The New*

530

York Times, the veteran Arthur Krock commented on how inevitably and surely Senator McCarthy seized and held the spotlight, hour after hour, day after day, in spite of his attitude that the whole dispute really had nothing to do with himself at all, but lay between Stevens and Adams, on the one side, and the subcommittee staff on the other. But in spite of "all the confusion, the repetition, the ineptness or worse of some members of the cast," Krock emphasized, "the hearings abound with high drama. Suspense, active excitement, and other elements which invest human conduct with interest are all present. Sometimes they are like the whodunit thrillers that rely on the testimony of a guilty witness, under the prodding of a cross-examiner, to bring the tale to its denouement. Sometimes they have the flavor of one of those courtroom melodramas when an innocent suspect is browbeaten with the tactics of a bucko mate and the gallery dissolves in tears. And sometimes, though more rarely, they provide the relief of comedy.

"The millions who saw and heard the proceedings when Private Schine was suddenly summoned to the stand and was closely interrogated by two most experienced trial lawyers would have a long search to find a book, a play, or a movie with comparable dramatic quality. And like many other melodramas, but few as good, the quest was for proof or disproof of the witness's involvement in a suspected conspiracy concerning a photograph that had been altered. The four chief figures couldn't have been improved upon by the best casting expert on Broadway—the handsome young private in his uniform, testifying without counsel; the suave attorney for the Army in which the youth serves; the criminal lawyer with the menacing mien and craggy eyebrows who holds the brief for the Senate of the United States; and McCarthy in the role of the private's protector."

That the tension was telling was underlined by a remark made by the eminent medical authority Dr. Charles Mayo, who urged that the inquiry be called off because it was raising the nation's blood pressure dangerously. "I look at it," he confessed, "but I don't agree that it should be happening." And how McCarthy's name permeated all discussion, dominating the confusion, was underscored by an anecdote passed around at this time concerning Edgar Eisenhower, the President's banker brother from Tacoma. In the East for a visit, he telephoned to friends in Vermont, and the family's six-year-old daughter answered. "Do you know who this is?" asked the caller. "Oh, yes," replied the child, "you are President McCarthy's brother."

The President himself made no secret of his disgust with the business. Asked at a press conference whether Defense Secretary Wilson had discussed the "Schine matter" with him, Ike glared and blurted incredulously, "You mean talking about this private?" The reporters laughed, but not the President; and when the correspondent persisted with his question, saying, "Yes, and about the pressure being put on for him," Eisenhower flushed and snapped angrily, "Never heard of it." Adding grimly that he hoped the whole business would be concluded very quickly, he strode out of the room.

[II]

Next to McCarthy, the actor in the drama who was conceded to come closest to stealing the show was Army counsel Welch. During the animated passages he would sit watching quietly, studying the participants (McCarthy seemed to fascinate him). To one observer he suggested "a gentleman viewing Bedlam with calm." Then when his chance came, he would launch "Welchisms" that often scored heavily as well as wittily for his side.

One such moment occurred during the argument over the cropped photograph. Jim Juliana was disclaiming any knowledge of the source of the original print. With a raffish leer Welch pried, "Did you think this came from a pixie?" The spectators laughed, priming Welch to continue. "Where did you think this picture I hold in my hand came from?" Quick to run interference for his staff, McCarthy moved in with, "Will that question be reread?" It was so ordered by the chair, and in an expressionless tone the reporter read, "Did you think this came from a pixie?"

Facing Welch, McCarthy asked: "Would counsel, for my benefit, define—I think he might be an expert on this—the word 'pixie'?"

Welch twinkled and replied roguishly: "I should say, Mr. Senator, that a pixie is a close relative of a fairy." The room rocked with mocking laughter, and when it died down Welch went on, with deadly innuendo: "Shall I proceed, sir? Have I enlightened you?"

The intent was unmistakable, and this time McCarthy joined in the laugh, although his smile was strained. Attempting a light retort, he hit back: "As I said, as I said, I think you might be an authority on what a pixie is." *

But though Welch's flick of the cat's paw that drew blood was beyond him, the senator came off effectively in other scrimmages before the cameras. Better than any of his associates, he understood the television audience's desire for action, and one form of action that he could provide, with maddening results upon his colleagues, was the sort of temporary chaos that would tie up the proceedings for maybe half an hour. A typical scene followed his interposition during the questioning of Secretary Stevens about Frank Carr's role in the Schine affair.

"Mr. Chairman!" came the familiar rasping note.

"Have you a point of order?" asked Mundt.

"Is this a new species of guilt by silence, I wonder?" The senator chuckled, and the chair sternly ruled that McCarthy could ask that question on his own time. To this the senator responded with a speech conveying that that was just what he intended to do. Senator McClellan, thoroughly annoyed, exclaimed that if everybody was

---

* The listening audience, and millions were listening, thoroughly understood the unscrupulousness of Welch's thrust. One of the stories that had been diligently circulated to "explain" the influence that Roy Cohn was supposed to exercise on McCarthy attributed it to a homosexual attachment, although no scrap of solid evidence was ever offered to sustain the inference. The frequent camera shots of Cohn and McCarthy in the hearing room, whispering, almost cheek to cheek to avoid being overheard, had been seized upon as substantiation. They were, of course, nothing of the sort: Welch was shown in similar poses whispering to Stevens, Jenkins to Mundt, and others, without any sinister significance being drawn. The climate of moral tolerance in 1954, and that of conversational permissibility, were far stricter than either would be two decades later. An imputation of homosexuality in 1954 carried a social and moral stigma that was ineffaceable, and to attribute to an individual what was then classified as a criminal aberration without sustaining proof was no less than malicious defamation. Thus Welch's sly (and *sly* is the proper adjective in this instance) resort to so unjustifiable and damning a tactic against his opponent must regretfully be placed in the category of those methods that were so angrily denounced as elements of "McCarthyism," namely, guilt by innuendo—character assassination. That this same innuendo would subsequently be repeated on the floor of the United States Senate would render Welch's unscrupulousness the more reprehensible, because it paved the way. The enemies of McCarthy were prone to present themselves as the party of honor, of decency, of truth, and of honesty, and to attribute only the meanest of motives to either the senator or to all who supported either him or his techniques. "McCarthyism," however, by the very definition coined by McCarthy's foes, is still "McCarthyism," whether practiced by men or by angels.

going to make speeches, he would reserve the right to make one, and the exasperated chair agreed, threatening to discontinue recognizing senators or counsel on points of order. McCarthy retorted that he would keep on raising points of order "whenever I find flagrant dishonesty on the part of a witness," whereupon the chairman repeated that he *would not be interrupted* "on points of order that are not in fact points of order." McCarthy stuck to his right to ask questions of the chair, and Mundt reviewed the rules. Senator Symington proposed that the rules be changed, since they weren't working, causing McCarthy to protest that it would be "dishonest" to change the rules "halfway through the game"—until the badgered Mundt banged for order and declared that the rules were not going to be changed, and could they get back to the question, which was— he had forgotten what it was. "I am completely at sea—I'll have to ask the witness—were you in the process of making a statement?" But the witness, Stevens, had his own protest to make against McCarthy's implying that he was committing "flagrant dishonesty." He said that he resented the slur—and the fracas started all over again. The Marx Brothers could not have done better by the television customers.

Another point on which McCarthy raised hackles more than once was the array of solemn-faced, tight-lipped Army brass that daily adorned the hearings, lending color and stony stoicism although apparently little else to the sometimes zany proceedings. The senator had asked repeatedly who was taking care of the national defense with the brains of the Army stationed in the caucus room. Who, during their absence, was running the Pentagon? To this theme he returned one day as soon as Mundt opened the session.

"Mr. Chairman!" came the dreaded hail.

"Do you have a point of order?" Mundt began wearily, but Joe set him straight. "Not a point of order, Mr. Chairman, but I should like to suggest that until we have identified all the generals and other officers here and know why they are here—because I think the committee takes more and more criticism for holding up the work of the Army by this investigation, and I think we should know——"

"That is not a point of order," Mundt broke in, "and the chair does not propose to go around the audience identifying our guests, and they have a right to be here as long as they refrain from manifestations of approval or disapproval."

McCarthy: "I do think that regardless of whether it is a point of order or not—I don't think it is a point of order—but I do think we should know just how many generals and colonels are ordered over here by the civilians in the Pentagon; why they are here and not doing their work in the Pentagon?"

Mundt: "If you have a question to ask of the secretary along that line . . . you may ask it on your own time."

McCarthy: "I will ask that." And when his turn for cross-examination came around he plunged in—after heartily endorsing a proposal by Senator Potter that they hold night sessions "so that we can get through with this circus as quickly as possible." Then addressing Stevens, who was on the stand, he noted that "there are three Army officers, a general, two full colonels, one sitting beside Mr. Hensel—I beg your pardon—two lieutenant colonels and one two-star general sitting here, one behind Mr. Hensel, two to his left. Are they here to aid and assist Mr. Hensel?"

Stevens: "They are here to represent the Department of the Army with me."

McCarthy: "Are they here for the purpose of helping Mr. Hensel?"

Stevens: "They are here for the purpose of helping me if I need to call upon them."

McCarthy was not to be put off. "Are they here also for the purpose of helping Mr. Hensel?"

Stevens gave up. "No. Mr. Hensel has already testified that he has his own counsel."

"Then," said McCarthy, "could I suggest—may I have the names of these two colonels? May I have the names of the colonels?"

Stevens: "Lieutenant Colonel Wood is the lieutenant colonel seated next to Mr. Hensel, General Caffrey is to his left, and Colonel Murray is sitting in the second row."

McCarthy looked toward the chair earnestly: "Mr. Chairman, I want to make a point that may seem relatively unimportant, but we have been shifting seating arrangements around here so often. The understanding is that Mr. Hensel, as a party in dispute, may sit here with his counsel at the table. If these young men are not here—I beg your pardon—if the officers are not here to aid Mr. Hensel and they are here to aid Mr. Stevens, I think they should move back of Mr. Stevens. I don't like to have men with combat records—and I can see that they have outstanding combat records, apparently, from the ribbons they wear—I don't like to have them sitting here and lending dignity to Mr. Hensel by sitting at his left."

The thrust was outrageous—so outrageous as to be breathtaking.

Hensel, whose fund of patience was minimal, appeared to be on the verge of apoplexy.

"Mr. Chairman!" he cried, but McCarthy kept on speaking through barely opened lips: "His lawyers can sit here with him."

"Mr. Chairman!" Hensel pleaded, and back came Mundt's threadbare, "Do you have a point of order?"

"I think that remark was uncalled for," Hensel barked, "and Senator McCarthy ought to be asked to apologize for that! I am serious, sir!"

The audience erupted in applause and Mundt banged the gavel in a fluster. "May the chair remind the audience," he called out sternly—"just a minute, Mr. Hensel—may the chair remind the audience for the final time that you are here as the guests of the committee. There are to be no manifestations of approval or disapproval." Then to Hensel: "You have raised a point of order?"

Hensel had indeed. "I am quite serious about the request for an apology, Mr. Chairman," he said with flushed face. "I do not think that remark of Senator McCarthy about my dignity was called for! I think I have plenty of dignity and deserve all that I have!"

Mundt granted that "your statement will be incorporated in the record," but said the chair had "no power to enforce an apology on the part of any of the participants to this dispute."

Through all the turbulence McCarthy sat unmoved, in his element. The scene went over big on television. It showed battling Joe, unafraid to take on single-handed the Army brass, the Defense Department, anyone, no matter how powerful or awesome—the fighter who could not be daunted. And one result was clearly registered on the screen: as the days went by, the array of beribboned military chests dwindled and faded away, as old soldiers are supposed to do, and by the end of the inquiry the dignity of the uniform was being upheld by a sergeant and a corporal.

Meanwhile, millions of bewildered Americans were saying to themselves in wonderment: "Is this the way United States senators carry on the serious business of the government?"

[III]

So far the evidence adduced by the hearings had been inconclusive. Both sides had scored, but neither had scored definitively. The prevailing impression was that Stevens' testimony had done the

Army little good and some harm, while the reaction to McCarthy's antics depended entirely upon one's bias for or against the senator. There had been manifested no pronounced trend of public sentiment, nor was there any appreciable falling off of interest in the proceedings. Even the one subject that had brought on the most heated clashes—the cropped photograph—was still moot. The picture undoubtedly showed the Secretary of the Army posing with the controversial Private Schine, and the question still had not been satisfactorily answered—why?

Newsweek felt that the bedrock issue—"Who is lying, the Army or McCarthy?"—would never be settled finally. "Regardless of what answer the subcommittee eventually may give, there will be millions of Americans who will violently disagree with it." The motives underlying the actions of Cohn, Stevens, McCarthy, Adams and the others were just as important as the actions themselves, and while the testimony could bring out what was done, why it was done could never be pinned down absolutely and would always remain in dispute.

McCarthy, it was observed, appeared to be as indifferent to the sensibilities of his colleagues as he was to those of his avowed antagonists. Over the weekend he succeeded in roiling his committee associates further by ignoring an executive meeting of the subcommittee which he himself had called and taking off for Milwaukee to make a speech ridiculing the whole investigation.

Critical comment on the hearings over the weekend was generally unfavorable. *The New York Times* stigmatized the Senate for ever letting McCarthy get started on his four-year course of raising Cain. In the same issue, William S. White, the *Times* correspondent assigned to the Senate, reported that the real professionals in Congress felt that the affair had become a mess which was hurting everybody, although opinions differed as to how much and in what way. A reaction against McCarthy seemed to be taking shape in the Senate, White reported; on one of the senator's necessarily rare appearances there, to vote on a bill, it was noticed that several Republican senators had carefully avoided him, and a couple even "looked straight through him." But White cautioned that the same thing had happened before, without producing any lasting effect. Stevens' performance most senators considered disastrous, one growling sourly that "if he hadn't played footsie with the private we wouldn't be in this hole." The mail reaching the Capitol indicated that many voters felt the same.

Arthur Krock, looking over the field of inquiry, listed his own five "strongly invited" conclusions so far as follows:

1. "The only way to 'appease' McCarthy is to surrender—permanently."

2. Stevens and his advisers were undergoing the "usual painful experience of those who engage in battle with McCarthy if they take the field with chinks in their armor."

3. Those in the Pentagon who first leaked the report of efforts by McCarthy's aides to get preferential treatment for Schine "would have been wiser if they had not attempted this type of counter-warfare against a senator skilled in ruthless guerrilla tactics."

4. Senator Potter "perhaps wishes he had never asked Secretary Wilson" for the Army's "chronology."

5. President Eisenhower was feeling that his Administration and his party had been let down "in what can be called 'the distasteful case of Private Schine.'"

To which White added the glum footnote: "It may be stated with complete confidence that some members of the subcommittee are unhappily aware of all this and profoundly, if vainly, wish they had never had to sit at all."

Regardless of party, the senators were dismayed by the way the hearings dragged along. Secretary Stevens was still on the stand, and nobody ventured to hazard a guess as to when McCarthy would testify; indeed, his critics were predicting that he would never be sworn, but at the crucial moment would stage a walkout. Welch saw no way to speed the investigation except to call the principals in rapid succession and eliminate all but the most indispensable secondary testimony, but he could get no general agreement on this plan. McCarthy jauntily guessed that the committee "might be able to finish the hearings about 1970, at the rate we're going now"; he professed to see no feasible way to hurry things along.

He appeared to be impervious to the sense of outrage and disgust that was spreading on Capitol Hill at the spectacle being offered to the nation. Representative Emanuel Celler of Brooklyn expressed this feeling and illustrated his attitude toward the Wisconsin senator by an anecdote about Gladstone and Disraeli, the rival British statesmen. Disraeli had used the words "misfortune" and "calamity" in a speech, and he was asked how he distinguished between them. He replied: "If somebody were to throw Mr. Gladstone into the

Thames, that would be a misfortune. But if somebody fished him out, that would be a calamity."

In the Senate, meanwhile, Senator Maybank of South Carolina deplored the "hamming" and "playing to the gallery." He agreed that the reciprocal accusations should be thoroughly investigated, but "I am against doing it in a televised vaudeville show." Senator Smith of New Jersey called the hearings "perfectly terrible," while Senator Aiken of Vermont perhaps came closest to the home truth when he said that millions were watching "to see who gets skinned, without caring much who is."

[IV]

As the "vaudeville show" entered its third week, the stridency of the performers became more pronounced. Secretary Stevens had admitted that at one point he had sought McCarthy's views on relieving General Lawton of the command at Fort Monmouth—although the Secretary's memory was blurred as to why he had considered transferring the General, all that he was sure of being that it was *not* because Lawton had "over-cooperated" with the senator's investigation. At any rate, McCarthy had taken a dim view of the proposal and it had been shelved for the time being.

Nerves were obviously taut at the week's start. McCarthy and Cohn questioned Stevens in turns, although the Secretary had already been eight days on the stand; and although Joe remarked that in view of the weak case the Army had presented he really felt there was no need to call witnesses to disprove it; still he expected to cross-examine the wilting Secretary two days longer. The ten-minute rule for each senator's questioning was rigorously applied by the chairman, but interruptions and "points of order" strung out the periods indefinitely. Once, in a slip of the tongue, Mundt warned McCarthy that he had only "thirty minutes" left, and hastily corrected himself to say "thirty seconds"; it turned out that he was right the first time.

Repeatedly a senator would begin, "Now, to expedite the hearings," but no expedition developed. Political partisanship was open, Senator McClellan seldom missing a chance to observe that "this, after all, is a Republican family quarrel." The personal bitterness that existed between Adams, on one side, and Cohn and McCarthy, on the other, was plainly evident: At one point the senator began

a question with, "John, do you——" but was tartly cut off, "It's Mr.
Adams to you, senator." But although in the House of Representatives Henderson Latham, a Democrat from Georgia, bemoaned the
hearings as "the sorriest spectacle of our generation," coming just at
the moment when "Indo-China and all of Southeast Asia are being
lost to the free world," the public's interest in the proceedings remained unabated. The galleries of the House and Senate were deserted, while the caucus room remained crowded daily, with standees
along the walls.

The tensions of Monday, that week, were eclipsed by Tuesday's
injection of what was discerned at once as "a new and absorbing
mystery," when Senator McCarthy produced what purported to be
a carbon copy of a letter written by J. Edgar Hoover, director of
the FBI, to a high Army official in 1951, containing classified information regarding suspected security risks employed in the Fort
Monmouth radar laboratories. This surprise development, which
was speedily whipped up to a national sensation by the adroitness
of counsel Welch, focused on the basic issue of the constitutional
balance between the executive and the legislative branches of the
government. Private Schine was left far behind.*

Roy Cohn had been questioning Secretary Stevens regarding a
civilian worker at Fort Monmouth named Coleman, who had been
suspended from his job and then rehired although his personnel file
contained an FBI warning that he should be regarded as a security
risk. The point at issue was this: at the outset of the Monmouth investigation, Cohn had been given access to the personnel files of
employes, and he had made notes on their contents. Coleman's case
was one of those involved. Then the subcommittee requested copies
of the files. These were sent to the Pentagon, photocopies were
made, and the copies were delivered to the subcommittee. But the
papers delivered from the Pentagon proved to be incomplete; Cohn
swore that he had seen and had taken notes on certain documents

---

* The striking parallels between this controversy and the national furor resulting
from the unauthorized publication in 1971 of classified material gleaned from the
so-called Pentagon Papers will become obvious as the story unfolds. Curiously,
the roles of the contending parties in the two instances were exactly reversed:
The elements, principally the press, which savagely denounced McCarthy's infringement of the executive authority in 1954, in 1971 ardently defended such
infringement, even going to law to defend their right and duty to publish government secrets, stolen or otherwise obtained, which they deemed of national concern and not in violation of national security.

that were no longer in the files. When he queried John Adams about this, the latter sent a written explanation to the effect that the missing documents had been found to contain information relating to loyalty, and therefore had been withheld in compliance with Presidential directives forbidding the disclosure of such data. Under the Army's interpretation of these directives, executive agencies were enjoined from turning over to congressional committees any information on employes' "loyalty," although "personnel" data could be supplied.

The distinction sounded like hairsplitting, and McCarthy and Cohn charged that the Army had deliberately "stripped" the files of information vital to the subcommittee's investigation, and that this had been done without any notification or acknowledgment until the subcommittee itself discovered the deletions. Or as McCarthy put it to Adams, "until we caught you redhanded."

Irked by Stevens' repetition, under Cohn's tactful but persistent questioning, of "I have no such recollection," the senator interrupted:

"Mr. Stevens, could I have your attention? Mr. Stevens, would you consider it a rather serious matter if during this period of [your] 'great cooperation' with the committee, a personnel file had been stripped in the Pentagon and given to us and represented as a complete file?"

Stevens spoke vaguely of "presidential directives," and McCarthy retorted, "There is no presidential directive prohibiting the committee's getting a personnel file, is there?" Stevens agreed that was correct, "according to my understanding." McCarthy then asked the chair "to order the secretary to produce the letter which they wrote to us, after we caught them stripping the file, in which they gave their explanation for the stripping."

Welch chimed in that such a letter, if it existed, must be in the subcommittee's files, so "why not fish it out?" Because, replied McCarthy, it could not be located, although it had been received. The Army then produced the letter, and Adams read it aloud, Welch protesting all the while against such "foolishness." That aroused McCarthy, and he addressed the witness: "Mr. Adams, you have just heard Mr. Welch speak of 'foolishness.' Would you consider it foolishness to have a file stripped and not tell the committee it was stripped, presented to the committee as a complete file?"

"We told the committee by this letter that it had been stripped, senator," Adams said testily.

McCarthy: "After we caught you redhanded, then you gave us the material!"

Then Stevens resumed the stand and was questioned by McCarthy about the alleged "stripping"; but the Secretary sidestepped, professing to be unable to recall certain critical conversations, until McCarthy pinned him down with: "Mr. Secretary, a number of senators have raised the point that you are being kept on the stand too long. Now if you would try to answer the questions——"

"I am trying very hard to," the Secretary interjected, and McCarthy went on, emphasizing each phrase with a dip of the head: "The question is this, and it is very simple . . . Do you recall discussing with Mr. Adams the removal of material from the Coleman file, keeping in mind that Coleman was the man, the friend of Julius Rosenberg [here McCarthy, of course, was reminding the television public], identified as a member of the Young Communist League, that he had stolen secrets from the radar laboratory? I assume that you would consider him a rather important person, perhaps even more important than a private . . . I now ask you the simple question, and if you will just answer it we can go on to another subject . . . Let me repeat, do you now remember whether or not you ever discussed with Mr. Adams the removal of material from Coleman's personnel file before it was given to the committee?"

Again came the disclaimer: "I do not recall any such conversation."

Picking up a paper lying on the table in front of him, McCarthy went on: "Mr. Secretary, I would like to give you a letter, one which was written, incidentally, before you took office but which was in the file, I understand, all the time you are in office—I understand it is in the file as of today—from the FBI, pointing out the urgency in connection with certain cases, listing the fact, for example, that Coleman had been in direct connection with espionage agents——"

Committee counsel Jenkins interrupted to suggest that it would first be proper to establish that the letter was in the Secretary's file at the time he came into office and had been there since then. McCarthy thought the point well taken, and addressing the chair ostensibly (but the millions of television viewers actually) he explained:

"May I say, Mr. Chairman, that the reason for questioning Mr. Stevens on this letter and submitting it to him is not because it was written to him—it was written before he came into office—but because it is part of a series of letters from the FBI warning of the tremendous danger of Aaron Coleman and associates handling top-secret radar or other material; that those repeated warnings were disregarded and ignored until this committee opened its investigation; that while the letter was not written to Mr. Stevens, it was ignored by him and his subordinates, no attention being paid to this letter until the hearings were over."

This was a bombshell. It went to the heart of the contention on which McCarthy had been hammering for four years, namely, that repeated warnings by the FBI of dangerous infiltration of government agencies by Communists or their allies had been ignored and flouted until disclosures produced by congressional investigations had forced action. Now, however, instead of accusing a previous, Democratic administration of such acts of delinquency, the senator included officials of his own party's government—Eisenhower appointees—of the same defiant betrayal or at least culpable disregard of the nation's interest and security. The charge was laid squarely on the White House doorstep, and McCarthy was informing the chair and the nation that he held in his hand one of those flouted, top-secret FBI warnings that would prove the truth of all he had said, over and over again.

The excitement was almost unbearable as McCarthy handed the letter to the wary Jenkins for identification. The Army's counsel, Welch, was watching keenly, the moment having arrived for the deployment of all his skill to blunt, turn aside, or smother this direct attack on the good faith of the men whom he represented.

Cautiously Jenkins stated that the document "purports to be a letter written January 26, 1951, from the Federal Bureau of Investigation and signed by J. Edgar Hoover, the director. It is addressed to Major General [A. R.] Bolling, assistant chief of staff, G-2, Department of the Army, Washington, D. C. The . . . letter contains pertinent information with respect to Coleman, perhaps others, who should be investigated." The question now, Jenkins went on, was whether this letter (it was only a carbon copy, not the original) was in the Army's file when Stevens became Secretary, and whether he had known, or "by the exercise of diligence" should have known, of it, and taken action on its contents.

This provided Welch with his opening and he moved in, assuring the chair that "this purported copy did not come from the Army files, nor does the senator for a moment suggest that"—a statement

that said nothing, since the paper in Jenkins' hand obviously had
come from McCarthy's own files, being only a copy of an original.

McCarthy was ready for Welch and objected immediately that
"if Mr. Welch is going to say that there is not a copy of this in the
Army files, he should be sworn, because that statement is untrue."

"I did not say that," Welch retorted. "I said that this purported
copy did not come from the Army files, and you know I am quite
right, sir. And," he added, fixing McCarthy with a searching eye,
"I have an absorbing curiosity to know how in the dickens you got
hold of it."

By this byplay Welch shifted attention from the pertinence of the
document and its contents to the question of what right the senator
had to have it in his possession. Chairman Mundt broke in to remind
Welch again that "all investigative agencies in this town operate on
the rule that they do not have to disclose the sources of their information. Your absorbing curiosity will have to be satisfied some
other way."

"By J. Edgar Hoover!" Welch shot back instantly.

McCarthy suggested that Stevens read the letter before being
questioned about it; but Welch took the paper from the hand of
Jenkins and in a whisper advised the Secretary, with the consequence that the latter expressed doubt of his having the right to
read "any letter written by Mr. J. Edgar Hoover unless I have specific approval."

In Washington, FBI reports were considered sacrosanct—out of
bounds for any congressional inquiry—and Welch bore down on
this point by announcing that the letter was headed "Personal and
Confidential, via Liaison," which seemed to him to be "rather severe words of a confidential nature." He therefore supported Stevens
in the Secretary's refusal to read the document, or to have it discussed "in this room" unless it was released by Hoover. It was agreed
that the FBI director should be consulted immediately, and on that
expectant note the session was adjourned.

[V]

Wednesday's session opened tensely. Robert A. Collier, one of
Jenkins' assistants, had been assigned to contact Hoover. Taking
the stand, Collier testified that he had consulted the FBI chief and
that Hoover had stated that the document in question was not a
copy of any letter in the FBI files. There was in the file, under the

date of the letter, January 26, 1951, a fifteen-page interdepartmental memorandum that had been sent to General Bolling. In Collier's presence, Hoover had compared this fifteen-page memorandum and the two-and-one-quarter-page carbon copy of a letter, and had stated that the subject matter in both was the same, and in some instances the language was "exact or identical." As for releasing the material, Hoover referred the committee to the Attorney General, his superior, who alone could give permission.

From this it appeared clear that the McCarthy document, cast in the form of a letter—starting "Dear Sir," and concluding "Sincerely yours," with "J. Edgar Hoover" typed underneath—actually was a digest, and in some places a verbatim extract, of the fifteen-page memorandum. Collier was firm in quoting the FBI director as saying that there was no copy of the McCarthy letter, "or anything like it," in the FBI files. So that, as Counsel Welch immediately averred, "this document . . . is a carbon copy of precisely nothing, is that right?" Collier would only say that Hoover had stated it was not a carbon copy of anything in the FBI files. But Welch was scornful: "Let's have it straight from the shoulder. So far as you know, this document in this courtroom sprung yesterday by Senator McCarthy is a perfect phony, is that right?"

Collier held firm: "No, sir. That is your conclusion. I will not draw such a conclusion."

Welch: "You just told us it is a carbon copy of precisely nothing, haven't you?"

Collier: "I have said it is not a copy of a document in the FBI file. I will not say it is a copy of nothing, because if it was typed as a carbon, there must have been an original."

Welch: "You would think so, but we can find no trace of an original, can we?"

"Not yet," was the laconic reply; and Welch went on to promise that if the original was in the Army's files, it would be tracked down, "even if we have to keep fourteen colonels up fourteen nights."

Then Jenkins called a surprise witness—Senator McCarthy. And to the chagrin of all those who had predicted that he would never submit to examination under oath, Joe raised his right hand and was sworn.

Let the witness tell, in his own words, Jenkins began, how he got possession of the letter, and when, and give "any other knowledge" regarding it that he might have. McCarthy was happy to oblige, and he waded in swinging. The first clout was a haymaker.

"First let me make it very clear, Mr. Jenkins and Mr. Chairman," he said, "that I will not under any circumstances reveal the source of any information which I get as chairman of the committee. One of the reasons why I have been successful, I believe, to some extent, in exposing communism, is because the people who give me information from within the government know that their confidence will not be violated. It will not be violated today. There was an attempt to get me to violate that confidence some two or three years ago, before the Tydings committee. I want to make it very clear that I want to notify the people who give me information that there is no way on earth that any committee, any force, can get me to violate the confidence of those people. . . . That is the rule which every investigative agency follows . . .

"This [letter] came to me from someone within the Army. As I recall the time—I do not recall the date—he stated very clearly [that] the reason why he was giving me this information was because he was deeply disturbed, because even though there were repeated reports from the FBI to the effect that there was Communist infiltration—indications of espionage in the top-secret radar laboratories—that nothing was being done. He felt that his duty to his country was above any duty to any Truman directive to the effect that he could not disclose this information.* And may I say, Mr. Chairman and Mr. Counsel, now that I am on the stand, it has been now established that this is a completely accurate résumé of all of the information in that FBI report, but that our informant, whoever he was, was very careful not to include any security information. . . . I call the chair's attention to the fact that there is no security information in this, and I urge, Mr. Chairman, that this be made available to the public."

Might they understand, Jenkins queried, that the senator had got the document from the FBI?

"I did not," replied McCarthy. Then from whom? "From a young officer in the intelligence department."

Counsel Welch took up the questioning. "Senator McCarthy, when you took the stand you knew, of course, that you were going to be asked about this letter, did you not?"

Yes, said McCarthy, he assumed that would be the subject.

---

* Compare the identical defense of his actions made by Daniel Ellsberg, the man who in 1971 passed the purloined top-secret Pentagon Papers to newspapers which published the material, pleading in justification a paramount duty to the nation.

Welch repeated: "And you, of course, understood that you were going to be asked the source from which you got it?"

McCarthy: "I never tried to——"

Welch, sharply: "Did you understand you would be asked the source?"

McCarthy: "I never try to read the minds of senators to know what they will ask."

Welch, gently: "Could I have the oath which you took read to us slowly by the reporter?"

This request seemed fatuous to the chair. "Mr. Welch," Mundt remonstrated, "you were present. You took the oath yourself. He took the same oath you took."

Calmly Welch addressed the witness: "The oath included a promise, a solemn promise, by you to tell the truth, comma, the whole truth, comma, and nothing but the truth. Is that correct, sir?"

McCarthy: "Mr. Welch, you are not the first individual that tried to get me to betray the confidence and give out the names of my informants. You will be no more successful than those who have tried in the past, period."

Welch: "I am only asking you, sir, did you realize when you took that oath that you were making a solemn promise to tell the whole truth to this committee?"

"I understand the oath, Mr. Welch."

"And when you took it, did you have some mental reservation, some Fifth or Sixth Amendment notion that you could measure what you would tell?"

The reply was scornful: "I don't take the Fifth or Sixth Amendment!"

Welch: "Had you some private reservation when you took the oath that lets you be the judge of what you will testify about?"

McCarthy: "The answer is, there is no reservation about telling the whole truth."

Welch let the next question fall softly: "Thank you, sir. Then tell us who delivered the document to you."

McCarthy's reply was equally direct: "The answer is 'no.' You will not get that information."

Welch: "You wish, then, to put your own interpretation on your oath and tell us less than the whole truth?"

McCarthy: "Mr. Welch . . . I repeat, you will not get their names, you will not get any information which will allow you to identify them so that you or anyone else can get their jobs. You go right ahead and try until doomsday and you will not get the names of any informants who rely upon me to protect them!"

Here Senator Dirksen raised a point of inquiry as to whether the subcommittee would be justified in compelling a witness to "reveal the source of a document when he has pledged himself to respect the confidence and not reveal the source." He requested a ruling by the chair, and also the opinion of counsel.

Jenkins at once observed that the right to conceal a source of information is "one of the most elementary principles engrafted in the law. Otherwise, law-enforcing officers would be so ham-strung and hampered that they would never be able to ferret out crime." He unhesitatingly held that McCarthy need not divulge the name of his informant. Mundt heartily concurred.

Welch then passed to another line of questioning, trying to get McCarthy to admit that he knew that no original of the carbon copy was to be found in the Army files. McCarthy shrugged and said that he had no idea what would be found. "You have access to them; I do not," he said. "So let's not waste our time by asking these questions."

Senator Symington got into the record that he believed McCarthy's letter was "fraudulent," and that he thought the 1948 ban on releasing loyalty data to congressional committees should be lifted. McCarthy agreed thoroughly with this view, saying, "I am just as unhappy with that directive since we have the new administration as when we had the old. I frankly can see no reason, senator, why a committee of senators representing the people should not have information about communism, sabotage, espionage, the same way that we get information about robbery, crooks, graft, corruption."

These digressions impelled Senator Jackson to suggest that it was "high time that this hearing get on the track; we have been sidetracked too long." And Senator McClellan, stressing the gravity of the issues involved, moved that the transcript of each day's testimony be dispatched to the Attorney General, for him to take whatever action might be indicated. The charges, said McClellan, were far too serious to be skimmed over lightly, dealing as they did with highly reprehensible conduct. "They strike at the integrity of the Army and also at the integrity of the Senate. Gentlemen, in my opinion we durst not wipe these charges off and at the same time do our duty." And since the hearings were being televised, he felt that it would not be difficult for the public to decide "who is guilty of dilatory tactics and who is trying to obstruct."

Senator Jackson rejoined the argument, observing that Senator McCarthy had used the word "blackmail," which the law made a felony punishable with a prison sentence. Senator Potter (who had been deluged with mail blaming him for having brought on the spectacle) finally complained that he was being "brain-washed," protesting pitiably that "I never dreamed that we would have a parade of special attorneys! I assumed that this matter could be handled quietly!"

Others felt more and more at sea as the merry-go-round turned dizzily, and to assist its readers *The New York Times* took to printing a daily capsule summary of what the original charges had been. Already they seemed faint and far away.

[VI]

Thursday's session was the most explosive yet. Overnight Chairman Mundt had written to Attorney General Brownell requesting a ruling on whether it would be injurious to the nation's security to divulge the contents of McCarthy's "FBI letter," and Brownell had replied that such disclosure would in fact be harmful, and that Senator McCarthy had no right to possess the document. This brought into play the paramount issue—the people's right to know—and McCarthy seized the opportunity to address an impassioned appeal to the subcommittee not to bow submissively to the executive's demands, but to decide, "once and for all," whether "we are lackeys to obey and afraid to overrule a decision made by someone in the executive department." For his part, he was of a mind to publish the letter himself, after striking out all that pertained to security.*

---

* Again it is pertinent to note the similarity with the Pentagon Papers dispute, in which the roles of the principals were almost exactly reversed. *The New York Times* in 1954 belabored McCarthy, as it had done before, for his readiness to "flout the law" by accepting and utilizing information abstracted from classified sources. Other newspapers also condemned him harshly for his audacity in this respect. Should the course be persisted in, it was contended in editorial after editorial, it could lead only to anarchy. That was in 1954. In 1971 some of the same newspapers, notably *The New York Times,* would come under executive fire for doing precisely what McCarthy had done seventeen years before, on the same grounds. His reasoning in 1954 was denounced as base and fallacious; in 1971 that reasoning was defended to the point of appeal to the courts; and the United States Supreme Court—by a split decision, it is true—in 1971 upheld the newspapers' defiance of executive orders and their right to publish matter which in their judgment the public should know, even though the information had been passed to them by an unauthorized source.

McCarthy presented his case well. After Brownell's letter had been read, he obtained the floor and began:

"I note that Mr. Brownell's letter reveals that the material cannot be submitted in any form. As the chair will recall, I suggested that we delete any security information, anything that would indicate the source of the information, informants, et cetera. That has all been done . . . as far as I can tell. As the chair knows, this has been authenticated as to paragraphs 1, 2, 3, 4, 5, 6, 7, and 8, which is the entire body of the letter, or document, call it what you may . . . as an accurate résumé of the memorandum from J. Edgar Hoover."

He then entered a formal demand that the Attorney General be called before an executive session of the subcommittee and questioned as to why he refused to sanction the release of information not security-related. There was precedent for releasing certain FBI data, he said, and cited Brownell's recent revelations about Harry Dexter White, taken from highly confidential files. In his Chicago speech, Brownell had named, on the basis of FBI reports, McCarthy said, "not the live spies that we are discussing here, who are still poised with a razor over the jugular vein of this nation. . . . He named a very important dead spy. I don't criticize him for that. I think that was information that the public should have had—and should have had long ago. His veracity was questioned . . . he then made public FBI reports . . . which had never been discussed before. . . . He didn't make available the names of any informants, and I think it was a job well done. But he has established a precedent. . . . As the chair well knows, I have never . . . disclosed the name of a single informant, and . . . the chair knows also that I never obtained any information from the FBI. But when I receive FBI material which is disseminated and is in the hands of loyalty board members with Communist records, I can no longer respect any classification of that. In other words, once it is in the conduit, available to Communists, I think maybe that I have no duty to keep this material secret, and I don't intend to.

"As far as I personally am concerned," he went on, with great determination, "there is no Truman directive or any other directive which is designed not for the security of this nation, but to prevent embarrassment of those responsible for covering up Communists—no such directive will keep me from making available to the public the type of information which we have here, showing gross neglect . . .

"Mr. Chairman, I think the time has come when we should decide as a committee . . . whether or not we are forever to continue operating under that Truman blackout order of 1948. . . . I don't think that a congressional committee is bound—if I may have the chair's attention—I don't think that any congressional committee is bound by the opinion of anyone in the executive as to whether or not they are entitled to certain information. . . . I am getting very, very weary sitting here and acting as though we are playing some little game, when the committee's activities may well determine whether this nation will live or die. We have to clean out those responsible . . . not dead ones, but live ones."

At last permitted to inject a word, Senator Mundt stated that he would rule against calling the Attorney General, unless overruled by the other members. No one challenged him, although McCarthy, at his most insistent, repeated that "this is a most serious matter . . . We are not playing any games here. You would think we were, the way we have been bandying things back and forth. We are getting right down, Mr. Chairman, to the point where the blue chips are down, and if we neglect, Mr. Chairman, if we neglect to get to the bottom of the facts because of some Truman order of 1948, then every one of us sitting at this table should not be in the Senate."

Again Mundt declined to agree to call Brownell; but McCarthy pounded on:

"There is no reason on God's earth, Mr. Chairman, why the Attorney General should not be called in executive session and made to answer why parts of these letters—not having to do with security, but which might be awfully embarrassing, I agree, to some people—should not be made available, number one, to the members of the committee, and then, the next question, whether they should be made available to the public. I think both. . . . We can get information about dishonesty, about corruption, about graft, but it seems we cannot get information about something a thousand times worse, namely, treason."

Mundt stood on his ruling unless a majority of the subcommittee demanded a reversal, which it did not.

Later in the session, as McCarthy was questioning Stevens (who was nearing the limit of his endurance; this was his eleventh day on the stand), Ray Jenkins attempted to spare the witness; but McCarthy plowed ahead, saying, "This is no trial of Mr. Stevens. . . . The contention which I have made over the past number of months is that somebody is trying to cover up his improper conduct over in the Pentagon, that they are using a fine, not overly experienced secretary as their tool. These individuals, who they are I don't know, but they are somebody deathly afraid of being exposed."

McCarthy's throwing down the gauntlet to the administration on the issue of using classified documents made pallid all previous sensations, and all signs now pointed to a showdown. Surely it must come soon, and interest in the drama quickened. The battle, however disorderly, was growing grimmer.

The Purloined Letter

[I]

Behind the scenes a feverish search was being carried on to find some way of ending the hearings agreeably to both sides, and without either losing face before the public. But the Army was stubbornly resisting a quick solution, and the Democrats backed up the Pentagon; the Democrats believed the Republicans were being hurt worse by the disclosures than was their own party. President Eisenhower wanted the hearings ended because in his opinion they were costing the United States its self-respect at home and its prestige abroad. A survey of European press reaction seemed to bear him out.

In England the press had been rather slighting the rowdy spectacle, only the *Manchester Guardian* devoting much space to it. The *Guardian* hoped the committee would finally muzzle McCarthy but had little expectation that that would come to pass. The senator had been investigated before, it was pointed out, and look at the results!

The *London Daily Mirror,* a tabloid, carried dispatches from a correspondent who, signing himself "Cassandra," pictured the proceedings as "a steamy miasma of muddy incompetence," which he expected to get worse, because "the stink, the stench, and the stain can only be counteracted by a bigger stink and stench and stain." The testimony he dismissed for the most part as "verbal garbage."

On the continent the reaction was totally unfavorable. *Die Tat* of Zurich termed the "nauseating spectacle" no longer a political fight: "Here a fanatic runs amuck in his own party." In Vienna, the *Arbeiter-Zeitung* said the hearings were stripping the world of its "faith that America is really fighting for freedom." The *Rotterdam Afternooner Nieuw Courant* foresaw the contest ending in a draw, because it was "already very clear that the Army accusations are based on the truth," but on the other hand it was just as clear that Stevens had gone "very far in his efforts to gratify McCarthy."

At home the reaction was increasingly vehement. Most newspapers were urging that the hearings be terminated, in the name of national sanity; a few of McCarthy's bitterest enemies demanded that they go on. The committee members were being deluged with letters and telegrams, a torrent, ranging in content from public indignation through obscene denunciation to itching powder. (Mundt got the itching powder in a letter from New York.) McCarthy's office reported receiving 5,000 to 6,000 letters a day, running 4 to 1 in his favor. Mundt was getting about 1,500 daily, and 75 telephone calls, strongly in favor of McCarthy. The senator's heaviest support seemed concentrated in the New York area, eastern Massachusetts, and Southern California. The three Democratic committee members were getting fewer letters, but the ones they received were, if possible, more bitter. All agreed that they could recall no such outpouring.

Behind the scenes, McCarthy was sympathetic to Dirksen's attempts to transfer the interrogation to executive sessions after Joe and Stevens had completed their testimony. Although confident that his side was ahead on points so far, McCarthy appreciated that the trend might be reversed at any moment by some surprise the Army might spring. In a strategy huddle, Frank Carr put his finger on the ever-present danger: this inquiry, he pointed out, was being conducted before an audience of millions, who would render the final verdict; and on television it was not so necessary to *be* right as to *look* right.

In another weekend foray into Wisconsin, McCarthy told cheering audiences that the hearings were a deplorable waste of time, devoted mainly to "trying to find out who shined Schine's shoes." Why, he demanded, should the time of eight senators, the Secretary of the Army ("with a rather bad memory"), and seven to ten generals be taken up with a "red minnow burlesque," when they ought to be working on matters concerning the national defense?

"We took a tremendous beating in Indo-China in the last few days," he reminded the crowds, referring to the fall of Dienbienphu. "What happens in Southeast Asia not only can but will affect the lives of everyone here today."

[II]

So the hearings were resumed, with one change visible: wherever McCarthy went, and seated just behind him during the sessions, were two plainclothesmen, one from the Capitol police, the other from the city force. The guards had been assigned as a result of mailed threats, although nothing suspicious had occurred in the caucus room; in fact, the audience there had earned good marks for its orderliness and restraint, only three or four disrupters having been ejected, one of these a man who had thumbed his nose at McCarthy.

At the outset, Mundt announced that he would not vote to end the public hearings if the Democrats opposed that action. That the latter promptly did. McCarthy made his position on this issue clear: "I believe that many of the senators—at least I hope so—are smarting under the public pressure to get this circus about Schine's shoes called off. As long as we are going to have hearings, Mr. Chairman, I should prefer they be in public. If we are in executive session public opinion cannot operate so well." Welch said the Army would make known its feeling on the next day.

The only acerbic moments came while McCarthy was questioning Stevens about the latter's insistence that there were "doggone few Reds" in the Army.

"Will you agree with me," asked the senator, "that one Communist, in a key spot, could result in the death of the nation?"

"You mean in a key spot like Major Peress?" shot back Stevens.

McCarthy, nettled, read from testimony given by Earl Browder in another investigation, paying no heed to objections by Jenkins and Mundt that it was not relevant, and Stevens, catching the implication, asked, "Does this mean I am a Communist?" The room rocked with laughter. But McCarthy's temper was up.

"That's awfully funny, isn't it, Mr. Secretary. That's terribly funny," he said, sneering. "There has been no claim by anyone, and you know it, that you were a Communist, or that you were a Communist sympathizer. I have made that clear to you at all times, that I felt you were anti-Communist. I have also made it very clear to you that I thought you were very naively and unintelligently anti-Communist, and you know that, Mr. Secretary."

When the senator took to addressing his associates by their full titles, or as "Mister," it was a sign of anger; ordinarily he used their first names, or even a nickname—"Stu" and "John" and "Bob" and "Roy."

That day was Stevens' thirteenth as witness, and the next morning he failed to appear; Welch explained that he was fighting a virus infection and had been told to stay home.* A decision had to be reached on a modified curtailment plan that Dirksen had drawn up. Welch doubted that the Army would accept it. Nor, in Welch's opinion, would the Army accede to any other "magic formula for shortening the hearings. I think the American people will demand and should have the long, hard furrow plowed." When requested by the chairman to ascertain the views of the Secretary by telephone, Welch withdrew, dropped a dime into a pay telephone, and returned to announce cheerily: "Mr. Chairman, due to the wonderful invention of television, the secretary was able to follow what had happened. He was therefore ready to talk."

"And what was Mr. Stevens ready to say?" inquired Mundt.

"He said, 'No.' "

So the plan was rejected, with Mundt casting the deciding vote. Thereupon Senator Dirksen, all his peace overtures having failed, made ready to divulge certain facts that contradicted some of the Army's contentions. And two days later he did.

In the interim General Cornelius E. Ryan, commander at Fort Dix while Schine trained there, was thoroughly grilled on his unhappy encounter with that "man apart." To illustrate the special treatment that Schine had received at Fort Dix, General Ryan produced two large charts. On one chart the dates of Schine's absences from the base were blacked out; the second chart indicated in a shade of light gray the leaves granted to the average trainee.

McCarthy immediately interrupted to denounce the charts as "phony and dishonest." Pointing to the square marked "November 3," he called attention to the fact that on Schine's chart it was blacked out, whereas on the other chart it was left white. November 3 was the date of Schine's induction. "There is certainly no reason why a man should get a black mark for being inducted?" he challenged Ryan, and the General hastily agreed. "November 23" also was blacked out on Schine's chart, but left blank on the other. That

---

* An aide revealed later that the Secretary had spent the day watching the proceedings on television, the show having developed a "horrified fascination" for him.

was the day Schine started basic training, and he didn't merit a black mark for that, did he? Not at all, assented Ryan. Then about the telephone calls; other trainees made telephone calls, didn't they? Then why shouldn't they show on the second chart, when they were marked down on Schine's record? McCarthy's answer to that question was that an attempt was being made to mislead people by giving Schine's chart a host of black marks.

Then Captain Joseph J. M. Miller, who had commanded Private Schine's company during his training at Fort Dix, was called. He told of Schine's riding to the rifle range in the cab of a truck, and being found there arguing with the sergeant in charge, whereupon the captain had "admonished" him—only to be interrupted by Schine's wondering whether he might possibly lower his voice, because there were "others present" (the whole gawk-eyed squad) and it was embarrassing to him.

This was too much for McCarthy. This questioning into "the private life of Private Schine" was totally irrelevant to the issue, he stormed, and he refused to waste time on it. He was going back to his office to catch up on neglected work, he said, and "will the chair or someone call me when we get through with this drivel?" And out he stalked—straight to the men's room.

John Adams, in turn, came under a pounding cross-examination by Jenkins, after volunteering the first public statement about the January 21 meeting of administration leaders at the Justice Department to discuss McCarthy's threat to subpoena the members of the Army's loyalty board in order to find out why they had been "shielding and promoting Communists," such as Irving Peress. McCarthy had maintained for a long time that the Army's charges had been brought as a result of this subpoena threat, and the Army had denied this. Adams listed the administration bigwigs who had attended the meeting, among them Sherman Adams, Attorney General Brownell, and Deputy Attorney General William P. Rogers. The case of Private Schine had been discussed and Sherman Adams had suggested that a record be compiled of the day-by-day attempts made by Cohn and others to get special treatment for Schine, the witness said.* But he denied that he had attempted to put pressure on McCarthy on January 22, the night after this meeting with high-level White House spokesmen, or had hinted at a

* This was the first official admission linking the Army's subsequent actions directly with the White House.

possible disclosure of damaging information if any subpoenas were served. Using his by now familiar tone of contempt, Jenkins forced Adams to admit that all or portions of the original Army "chronology" had been shown to five newsmen, known to be hostile to McCarthy, more than a month before it was given to members of Congress; but Adams again denied that this had been intended to serve as a "sword" over the committee. Adams frequently was caught in contradictions, and his venomous dislike of Roy Cohn came through plainly.

[III]

The next day John Adams was recalled to the stand, and he at once created a sensation by refusing to discuss further the critical January 21 meeting, at which administration plans were laid for dealing with McCarthy. He said that he had been ordered to keep silence on that topic by the acting Secretary of Defense, Robert B. Anderson, who had said that he was "transmitting instructions," although Adams did not know from whom. This was an unconcealed defiance of congressional authority by the execuitve branch, and Senator Symington demanded a showdown on the issue. He moved that Adams be required to answer, since he had introduced the topic voluntarily. Senator McClellan felt that the committee should find out whether there was "somebody higher than Stevens directing the Army's action," and Symington repeated that this January 21 conference was "perhaps the most important conference of all, because it was where most, if not all, of this business started."

After considerable heated debate, Symington consented to withhold his motion until after the weekend, and Adams was ordered to have ready a written report, by the time the hearings should resume, explaining why the administration was imposing the blackout. But before the session ended, three members of the subcommittee—Dirksen, Mundt, and Potter—in another sensational move temporarily resigned their positions as judges, and after being sworn as witnesses took the stand to contradict John Adams and get into the record the parts they had played at that turning point.

Senator Dirksen recounted that on the afternoon of January 22 Gerald Morgan, a White House assistant, and John Adams had come to him and had urged him to use all his influence to have the subpoenas for the loyalty board members stopped, insinuating that unless they were stopped, grave charges against Cohn and perhaps others would be preferred and the entire subcommittee might be placed in a bad light. The next morning, Dirksen said, he had called in Frank Carr and requested him to withhold the subpoenas if they had not already been issued. Then that afternoon, the Republican members of the subcommittee had met in McCarthy's office, and Dirksen had told them what had occurred. He pointed out that charges against Cohn and others undoubtedly had been prepared, and the Army was ready to use them to discredit the entire subcommittee, if they could. He had also said that this was the first time he had heard about the Cohn-Schine controversy, but if what John Adams had told him was true, then Cohn should be fired out of hand, and probably John Adams, too. Although he had pressed for immediate action, Dirksen concluded, nothing had been done at that time.

Mundt followed Dirksen on the stand and said that he, too, had been approached by John Adams on January 22 and had been urged to exert his influence to stop the subpoenas. At the same time he had been told about the Schine affair, in a way, he said, that had struck him as "a strange juxtaposition of topics."

Next Senator Potter testified that on January 22 he had been approached by a close friend, Deputy Army Counsel Louis Berry, with a request to use his influence to kill the subpoenas, and coincidentally had been told about the Schine difficulty.

Each of the three senators, after they had testified, gravely had themselves "unsworn" and resumed their roles as judges.

McCarthy's attitude during this startling testimony puzzled everybody. While John Adams was testifying, Joe read a newspaper, and as the questioning went on, he listened intently but entered not a single point of order. What surprise had he to spring, the capital wondered.

[IV]

During the weekend recess, excitement continued high, for now a key to the responsibility for the hearings that were turning out so unrewardingly for everybody seemed to lie in those two dates—January 21 and 22. On the first date the administration had moved finally toward a showdown—a decisive test of strength. On January 22 McCarthy and the other Republican members of the subcommittee had been approached with a veiled "deal" proposal—drop the subpoenas and the Cohn-Schine matter would be dropped—but McCarthy had defiantly told the Army to "go to hell." One week later he had opened up on the Peress case.

When the hearings resumed on Monday, a letter was presented to the chairman, written by the Attorney General and dealing with the "FBI document" held by Senator McCarthy. Without preamble, the committee was informed that criminal prosecution might be started against all involved in the "preparation and dissemination" of the altered, condensed, but still confidential FBI report.

At the same time, President Eisenhower allowed it to become known that the order forbidding testimony regarding the January 21 conference had been issued by himself. This made the issue crystal-clear—congressional authority against the authority of the White House.

Faced with this obstacle, the subcommittee, after an agitated debate, voted to recess the hearings for one week. All the senators were angry and resentful. McCarthy denounced the President's action as an "iron curtain." McClellan called the order a mistake and said that so far as he was concerned, "these hearings are termi-nated," for he agreed with Senator Dirksen that it would now be impossible to get the facts.

An outcry arose in the press against what some critics suspected was a step toward preparing a "whitewash." In an emotional edi-torial *The New York Times* demanded that "the hearings must go on," that McCarthy must not be permitted to go scot-free. The decision to recess the *Times* called "incredible," "stupid," and "harmful" to the public weal. McCarthy was depicted as shedding crocodile tears; had the January 21 conference occurred at cabinet level, it was argued, even he "would not have the effrontery to demand a transcript," and the conference certainly had taken place at "near cabinet level."

In his press conference that week, the President for the first time displayed willingness to discuss the affair. He said he thought the hearings should go on because all the facts had not been brought out yet, and the subject was of intense interest to Americans every-where. He defended his "gag" order, saying that far from trying to derail the investigation, he was merely trying to get it back on the rails. He had no intention of changing his order, he made clear.

nt's press secretary, gave out the statement orally in Brownell's
me, and McCarthy retorted with a renewed invitation to all
deral employes to give him any information regarding commu-
sm or other misconduct. And his colleagues were jolted by his
etching a phrase he had used continually—"twenty years of
eason"—to "the past twenty-one years of treason."

This audacious bracketing of the current Administration with
ose of the Democratic years left all who heard him momentarily
eechless. What was McCarthy trying to do? Commit political
ra-kiri? Unabashed, he repeated that if a State Department em-
oye had not rapped on Mundt's door at 2:30 A.M., "Alger Hiss
ight now be an assistant secretary of state, instead of a federal
nvict."

Exclaimed Symington, torn between wrath and dismay: "If the
nator is right, we don't have a good government, we don't have a
d government, we just don't have any government at all!" Re-
arking on the silence of the Republicans when their President was
cluded in McCarthy's charge of "treason," Symington admitted
being "a little astonished at the amount of defense this adminis-
ation is getting from Democratic members of the committee and
e abysmal silence on the right!"

Privately, Mundt pointed out that most congressional investiga-
ons started from classified information leaked by government
orkers.

"I don't mind if President Eisenhower calls it reprehensible," he
id comfortably. "If I were President Eisenhower or Brownell I'd
o everything I could to stop it. But I'm down here, and I do all
can to get it. That is the way you play the game."

[VI]

It was still anybody's ball game, although the number of specta-
rs still uncommitted was growing smaller. Opinion polls showed
steady drift of fence-straddlers into the ranks of those frankly
ostile to the senator, while the number of his adherents remained
ationary at around 35 percent of those polled; this Macedonian
halanx showed no sign of cracking.

McCarthy's defiant notification to all "loyal" government work-
rs that he expected them to turn over to him any information they

McCarthy's reply was to accuse the White House of asking him
to play with a stacked deck. "I'm willing to play with any kind of a
deck they use, but I don't think anyone on my staff should," he
said. "For the first time since I got into a fight to expose Communists, I am sort of at a loss to know what course to take. I think
the White House made a great mistake." Thinking the matter over,
he amplified his remarks to include the insinuation that the administration was in effect hiding behind the Fifth Amendment
against possible self-incrimination. "They must have something to
hide," he insisted, and he assured reporters that he would be on
hand when the hearings resumed.

The senator spent most of that week of May 17 speaking in
Wisconsin. At Fort Atkinson he was cheered when he warned the
President that the blackout order might lead the Republican party
to "commit suicide before the television cameras. . . . If nothing
happened at that conference, there is no reason why the participants
shouldn't testify."

During that week the nation at large had another topic of absorbing interest to ponder—the Supreme Court's decision banning
school segregation. Nevertheless, interest in the Army-McCarthy
imbroglio showed signs of mounting, instead of falling off. And
Mundt severely rebuked those who predicted that the investigation
would be dropped.

On schedule, the hearings reconvened, and that day the Army
wound up its case with Stevens and John Adams accepting responsibility for preferring the Army's charges. McCarthy again assailed
the Presidential order of secrecy as "a type of Fifth Amendment
privilege" and told his colleagues that they were not required to
conform to Presidential directives. He said he was "deeply concerned" by the attitude taken by Senators McClellan and Symington
that the passing of unauthorized information to him, and his retaining it in his possession, was a criminal offense. If anybody wished
to indict him for that, let him go right ahead, said Joe. Furthermore, he was startled to find two of his Democratic colleagues "in
effect notifying the two million people who work for this government that it is a crime for those employes to give the chairman of
an investigating committee evidence of Communist infiltration,
treason. I think it will discourage them. As far as I am concerned,
I would like to notify those two million federal employes that I feel

it is their duty to give us any information which they have about graft, corruption, communism, treason; and that there is no loyalty to a superior officer which can tower above and beyond their loyalty to their country."

Senator McClellan protested earnestly: "If this theory is followed . . . you can have no security system in America. It will destroy it totally and irrevocably, if all who have information give it out indiscriminately." And he called for a legal ruling to establish beyond cavil whether Congress was entitled to get classified information and make it public; and "if we are not entitled to get it by subpoena, are we entitled to get it by theft?"

To this McCarthy responded cogently by summing up his own position:

"The Attorney General issued a statement the other day to the effect that the executive has the sole duty and right to enforce the law. That is correct. From that he apparently jumped the huge gap and said that therefore the Congress could not investigate whether or not they are badly enforcing the law. . . . As chairman of the investigating committee, I have no choice—I have the duty—but to examine and expose any wrongdoing in the executive branch. . . . I want to make it very clear that while I am chairman of the committee I will receive every evidence of wrongdoing, graft, corruption, treason from every government employe who will give it to me. I feel that the government employes have a high duty to do that. . . . I am not setting myself above any law. I feel that I have an oath as senator, an oath as the chairman of an investigating committee. That oath binds me to get information of wrongdoing in government. I feel there is no valid directive of any kind which can say that, as chairman of the committee, I must not do that. If the Congress passes a law and the President signs it . . . then there is nothing I can do except abide by it. But I just will not abide by any secrecy directive of anyone. I think you and I have seen Presidents come and go. . . . We have a duty to do our job even though we may differ with a perfectly honest version of what the President thinks his job is."

Chairman Mundt tried to halt the argument, but McCarthy got in the last word, and it was in praise of Mundt: "If a State Department employe had not knocked on the door of the present chairman of this subcommittee, and gave him information about treason, Alger Hiss would not be in jail today."

[V]

On Wednesday, Senator Dworshak introduc[ed] miss Frank Carr and Struve Hensel as parties also as witnesses. The Democrats immediatel[y] McCarthy interjected that because of the Pr[e] the inquiry would "never get at the facts of t[he] can get the truth," and so he was in favor of or of anything that would "get this show off Clellan wanted to know why the individuals wh[o] serious, damnable charges . . . against Mr. were right in the room, didn't "step up here an[d] them?" Counsel Welch, rising to the drama, [joined] fully with Dworshak to split his motion into t[wo] the cases of Carr and Hensel separately. Dw[orshak] Welch, tremulous with emotion, begged again voice" might be heeded. But Dworshak remi[nded] are practical enough to know that you must h[ave] compensating feature," and by a straight part[y] the motion was adopted. Welch sang its requie[m] in the heart," he mournfully reproached the [Democrats] "May I say, sadly, gentlemen"—his voice quav[ered] strange to me that these Republican lips of m[ine] sixty-four years, with the single exception of admired—that these lips can convince only De[mocratic] enemies, and that the Republicans, whom I l[ove] my words are dust and ashes."

The scene was played to the hilt, and at the tators drew a long, audible breath. The feelin[g] that McCarthy's side had scored. Some pers[ons] timated that Welch was really relieved to get of going through with the Army's nebulous ca[se] knowing in advance that the vote would go seized the opportunity to feign brokenhearted inevitability.

The next day the White House released a approved by the President, saying that the executive branch "cannot be usurped by any seek to set himself above the laws of our land.

came upon regarding wrongdoing—especially Communist infiltration—received the strongest condemnation in the press generally. Protested the usually even-tempered *Commonweal:* "If every clerk in Washington is to set himself up as an authority on what should or should not be released from confidential files, the anarchic principle has carried the day. . . . The atom spies have claimed that they passed information to the Soviet because they felt they were thereby serving the interests of peace and humanity."

The constitutional threat imposed by McCarthy's flouting of the Presidential authority was emphasized as basic and of the utmost gravity; for McCarthy, as *Commonweal* observed, had become that dangerous thing, the man of one idea, one fixed motive for action, one fixed principle, and one standard of conduct, endlessly repeating his hallucinatory chant: "Communists in government." To him "all the operations boil down to one: eliminating people whom *he* judges subversive." To allow this beater of one drum to dominate the orchestra of reciprocal powers would be folly incredible, *Commonweal* cautioned; in effect, "the peaceful overthrow of the United States Presidency."

The end of this week of thickening confusion found McCarthy heading for a quiet Wisconsin resort, where he told reporters that "no power on earth" could force him to identify his sources of information. Behind him, in the capital, he left his party divided, and both Democrats and Republicans in a stew of embarrassment. In weekend interviews, Senators Mundt, Dworshak, McClellan, and Jackson deplored the injection of partisan politics into the hearings, and Senator Symington predicted that "fur is going to fly" in the coming week's sessions. The anomaly was that the Democrats, still smarting under McCarthy's attacks on Democratic Presidents, felt compelled to defend Eisenhower on the general issue of constitutional power, while many Republicans, alarmed by the schism engendered by McCarthy's truculence and the tougher attitude adopted by the White House, elected to remain "determinedly neutral," waiting to see where the ball would land. Some observers foresaw the likelihood of both Eisenhower and McCarthy figuring actively in the fall elections, working both sides of the political street, as it were, and this prospect sent a shudder of dread through aspiring Democratic candidates in more than a hundred districts where the margin of victory or defeat was likely to be narrow.

[VII]

The week of fresh conflict was started by the President. Speaking at the Waldorf-Astoria in New York at the opening of the bicentennial celebration of Columbia University, he told 2,200 alumni that he was confident that knowledge and understanding would "drive from the temple of freedom all who seek to establish over us thought control—whether they be agents of a foreign state or demagogues thirsty for personal power." Although McCarthy was not named, the President's entourage, when sounded out, said, "Who else?" And it was noticeable that although the applause when the President rose was tepid, his allusion to "demagogues" brought shouts of "Hooray!" and half a minute of stormy handclapping.

McCarthy captured the spotlight at the very start of the week's first session by proposing that all the principals in the dispute take a lie detector test, beginning with himself. If they would do that, he said, "we might be able to end this thing in twenty-four hours instead of twenty-four days."

The suggestion was summarily rejected, and the Democratic members pressed for a clear ruling on the legality of government employes turning over secret information to the senator. Ruling or no ruling, Joe insisted that "I just will not abide by any secrecy directive by anyone."

Roy Cohn was the day's principal witness, and he proved to be as sweet-tempered as his features were ingenuous. Welch expressed grave doubts about the genuineness of the subcommittee memoranda which had been entered in reply to the Army's charges: had they really been dictated on the dates shown? Or had they been concocted—thrown together hastily after the Army's charges were known? McCarthy bristled at this insinuation and demanded that Welch be put under oath; and Welch admitted that he had no proof. But it seemed odd that McCarthy's secretary, Mary Driscoll, who had typed the memos, had no "clear recollection" about them, and had destroyed her shorthand notes.

Consistently Cohn rebuffed the accusation that he had ever threatened to "wreck the Army," or had "declared war," as asserted by Adams. While he could not recall saying that Stevens was "through" as Secretary of the Army, he could tell Welch "under oath here, that I never, never threatened to wreck the Army, that

I am sure he knows I could not wreck the Army, and the whole thing is just a little bit ridiculous."

The sensation of the day, however, was a second direct attack on McCarthy made by Senator Flanders in the Senate. The attack was listened to in silence except for a few chuckles from the Democratic side when Flanders referred to the Wisconsin senator as a "Dennis the Menace . . . spreading division and confusion wherever he goes." Senator Knowland, the majority leader, sat red-faced while the Vermonter charged that the hearings were not going to the "real heart" of the matter, which was the "mystery concerning the personal relationships of the Army private, the staff assistant, and the senator. There is the relationship of the staff assistant to the senator. There is the relationship of the staff assistant to the Army private. It is natural that he should wish to retain the services of an able collaborator, but he seems to have an almost passionate anxiety to retain him. Why? And then there is the senator himself. Does the staff assistant have some hold on the senator? . . . Does the committee plan to investigate the real issues as stake?"

Having thus brought to the floor of the Senate the rumors of some homosexual relationship, Flanders assailed McCarthy as a religious menace, too. Despite the fact that his "closest associates," Cohn and Schine, were Jews, Flanders said that McCarthy had inspired "foreboding in our fellow citizens of Jewish faith and blood." Also, the senator had uttered "no word of rebuke" when Matthews had "charged the Protestant ministry with being in effect the center of Communist influence in this country." And the senator had "driven his blundering ax deep into the heart of his own church," too. Recalling the police breakfast at which Monsignor Caffery had "gone into a public eulogy" of McCarthy that had evoked both "cheers and silences," Flanders made a point of the fact that Cardinal Spellman had entered "and shook hands with our senator. He arrived late and left early, but he did shake hands. Does this mean that the imprimatur of 'nihil obstat' has been set by the church on these debonair campaigns to divide Americans from each other on religious lines? It looked like a pretty serious business. But soon, thank God, from Chicago another voice was heard . . . that of Bishop Sheil." McCarthy, Flanders concluded, could not have done a better job for the Communists, in dividing his country and his party, had he been in the pay of Moscow. And to crown all, he had "achieved the incredible success of trapping Republican senators into a detailed and relentless search for some significant evidence of subversion in the Republican administration—and this is an election year!"

Upon receiving word of this attack, McCarthy demanded that Flanders make good his accusations before the subcommittee. The latter replied that he would be glad to appear, "but I would have to begin by making a statement that I have nothing to testify, and that I read it all in the newspapers." A reply which brought from McCarthy that he couldn't decide whether the attack was the product of "senility or viciousness."

Flanders' gratuitous insinuation of sexual depravity, admittedly based on nothing but gossip circulated by McCarthy's least scrupulous enemies, did not pass unrebuked by either partial or impartial critics in the press. Professed anti-McCarthyites publicly condemned it, and sterner judgments scored it roundly as a perfect example of "McCarthyism" at work. *Commonweal,* a magazine that had opposed Senator McCarthy consistently for years as a menace to free institutions, remarked that Joe had not invented "McCarthyism"; he had simply given the concept "its richest illustration to date."

" 'McCarthyism' can strike anywhere," the comment continued; "it is even quite possible to find it on the anti-McCarthy front. When, for instance, anti-McCarthy partisans blast whole religious or national segments of society and tar them with the brush meant for the senator and his lackeys, they are, we submit, engaging in 'McCarthyism.' When they spread unfounded rumors about the senator and his staff, they are playing the McCarthy game. When they systematically use innuendo to say what they cannot repeat under oath or even repeat forthrightly without oath; when they make hazy general charges that cannot be substantiated; when they attempt to score for their side in the present Washington hearings by arbitrarily associating McCarthy with unsavory (but never established) connections; when they make sly appeals to racial or religious feelings; when these tactics are used—even against the senator—there is a word to describe them—perhaps the senator's most lasting contribution—the one he has made to the dictionary."

Because this rebuke echoed the revulsion of many fair-minded Americans, who were both for and against McCarthy himself, it carried weight. Flanders' speech, *Commonweal* submitted, "was a timid exploration into the McCarthyist wilderness. The Vermont

senator hinted darkly that there was some personal bondage between McCarthy and the Messrs. Cohn and Schine. The junior
senator, then, quite properly, invited Flanders to specify under
oath whatever it was he was hinting about. Flanders had no answer
except to say that all he knew was what he read in the newspapers.

"Again, the Vermonter tried to turn McCarthy into a special
foe of the nation's Jews and Protestants, on the flimsiest evidence.
The Jews: McCarthy's anticommunism parallels Adolf Hitler's,
ergo, McCarthy must share Hitler's racist attitudes (despite his relationship with Cohn and Schine). The Protestants: McCarthy had
no word of rebuke for (Protestant) J. B. Matthews' charges against
a small minority of the Protestant clergy, ergo, he must be anti-
Protestant. The Winconsin senator, Flanders said, after contrasting
the treatment McCarthy received at the hands of Cardinal Spellman of New York and Bishop Sheil of Chicago, had even 'driven
his blundering ax deep in the heart of his own church.' What Flanders apparently meant was that Catholics, like Jews and Protestants,
are divided on the McCarthy issue. . . . Americans, as Americans, are divided on the McCarthy question. Some honestly believe
that he is a great national asset; others, like the editors of this
magazine, are convinced he is a dangerous demagogue. But except
among the most fanatical, a sense of unity and abiding loyalty to
each other as fellow-Americans transcends any such disagreement. . . .

"Flanders has struck again. We think this attempt was inept, to
say the least, and bound to fail. Anyone who tries to out-McCarthy
McCarthy is up against the master himself, and needs considerably
more cunning than Mr. Flanders with his own blundering ax has so
far revealed."

The Monitored Calls

[I]

And on the hearings drifted. For millions of television viewers they had become a habit; even when dull they fascinated because of the feeling that at any instant pandemonium might break loose— generally as a result of McCarthy's wading into a scrimmage, swinging right and left. There was a certain hypnotic appeal in the senator's single-handed defiance of the arrayed forces of the administration. Clearly there could be no backing down by either side, and Joe was confident that he would not be the one to suffer defeat. His tactics did not match his audacity in brilliance; he blundered again and again, disingenuously, but always hewed to his grim cardinal precept—"Attack! Attack!"

The caucus room continued to be crowded day after day, with a waiting line. Among Washington's hostesses competition was spirited to secure the best seats for being caught by the television camera's roving lens. The prize position was directly behind Senator Mundt, because in his capacity as chairman he drew the cameras' stare most frequently. It became a game to speculate on who would occupy that coveted seat each day, and the pageant of spring hats that passed across the television screens, nodding victoriously behind "Papa Mundt," was formidable. One day Mrs. Jenkins held sway there, on another Mrs. Mundt or Mrs. John F. Kennedy, wife of the senator, who was a close friend of McCarthy. Perle Mesta, the noted party-giver of Truman days, showed up there in a bonnet obviously created for the occasion. When reporters asked whether she was back in town to resume her role of "the hostess with the mostest," she swept her hand over the room and conceded gallantly: "Later, perhaps. I can't compete with this."

The consensus seemed to be that the McCarthy side had suffered a loss on points in the recent clashes; certainly the odium being heaped upon the senator here and abroad had in no way slackened. From Edinburgh the elders of the Church of Scotland thundered against "McCarthyism," while in this country Dr. John Alexander Mackay, president of Princeton University and retiring moderator, told the General Assembly of the Presbyterian Church in the U.S.A. that the "invisible informer" had begun to "haunt the halls of learning and the chambers of government," and sternly he denounced "patriotic lying."

A swift response came from another ecclesiastical spokesman, Dr. Daniel A. Poling, editor of *Christian Herald,* who assured the All-American Conference to Combat Communism that "on the current scene the principal 'informers' are not 'invisible' and not liars, 'patriotic' or otherwise." Some had even risked their lives to unmask treason, he pointed out.

The Rabbinical Assembly of America, meanwhile, was deploring the "climate of fear" which they felt overhung the nation and lectured government leaders for lending themselves to controversies that "drag their good names, and the names of all of us, into disrepute." A New York rabbi specifically blamed Senator McCarthy for the current rash of "panty raids" that were enlivening college campuses.*

Canadian radio listeners were convulsed by a burlesque skit titled "The Investigator," in which McCarthy's voice and inflections were imitated so exactly that most of the audience thought they were hearing the senator himself.† And *Look* magazine conducted a poll that showed McCarthy's vote-getting potential at an all-time low. Nevertheless, in Sauk City, Wisconsin, Leroy Gore admitted that his "Joe Must Go" recall drive was likely to fail, unless "the sleeping giant of anti-McCarthyism can be aroused" in urban centers. On all sides a feeling was apparent that the coming week would provide the long-awaited showdown on the engrossing issues involved.

---

* The good rabbi was quite serious. His line of reasoning ran: springtime is a difficult season for the young male; it makes him restless, aggressive, a prey to primal urges. McCarthy's activities exacerbated these urges; and the ebullition was worked off by boisterously invading girls' dormitories and snatching filmy specimens of feminine underwear.
† The author of the lampoon, it developed, was a Canadian who had been deported from the United States after being identified before the House Un-American Activities Committee as a Communist party member.

[II]

The week opened with a curiously incongruous scene of joviality when Senator Mundt, on his fifty-fourth birthday, was presented with a birthday cake and two boxes of cigars—a special gift from McCarthy, who had complained of the quality of the chair's cigars. Mundt said laughingly that this was a new experience for him—celebrating his birthday on television—and the atmosphere throughout that day remained relatively peaceful. A start was made on reading into the record the monitored telephone calls between the Pentagon and the members of the subcommittee. After a long legal argument, all the parties concerned had given their written consent to have their calls introduced, without exception; Senator Symington especially had stipulated that everything must be disclosed—a "goldfish-bowl policy—all or nothing."

The millions of Americans watching and listening (the accepted estimate of the daily television audience had been pegged at around 20,000,000) received a fascinating glimpse of how the political machine operates behind the scenes, where the real decisions are made. The first calls read were those between Stevens and Senator Dirksen, including the Secretary's outraged protest against the interpretation placed by the press on his "surrender luncheon" with McCarthy, Mundt, and Dirksen. He might have to do something—and "it might get drastic," Stevens had exclaimed—to dispel the impression that he was a "yellowbelly." The most intriguing factor to the listeners was the cozy way top leaders in the government called each other by first names or nicknames—"Dick" (Vice-President Nixon), "Karl" (Mundt), "Charlie" (Potter), "Stu" (Symington), "Bob" (Stevens), and "Jerry" (Major General Wilton B. Persons, Presidential assistant). The telephone calls really were "inside stuff," never so baldly exposed to the public before.

With the public appetite thus whetted for the disclosure of confidences, the reading of Senator Symington's monitored calls the next day supplied the ammunition for a blazing-hot clash between the Missouri Democrat and Senator Joe. Symington's repugnance to McCarthy had been obvious from the beginning, but the dislike had been held for the most part within the bounds of courtesy. This day's revelations were to blow all ideas of restraint to smithereens.

The first call had been made by Stevens to Symington, on February 20. McCarthy had just issued his blast at General Zwicker and had called the General to testify publicly. The Pentagon was in an uproar, and Stevens was excitedly conferring with members of the subcommittee, determined not to allow Zwicker to be further "browbeaten" and "humiliated" by Joe. Symington advised the Secretary not to worry; but Stevens exclaimed that when he had told McCarthy that Zwicker would be forbidden to appear, "he really started to beat my brains out. I'm a coddler of Reds, you see!"

"Did you have anybody on the phone?" Symington asked; and responded, when Stevens said he had, "That's good. Keep the recording."

Then Symington urged that nothing be done until "I get into touch with Clifford [Clark Clifford, onetime political adviser to President Truman] . . . Let me talk with Clifford about it and I'll call you."

A short while later Symington reported back: "I talked to our legal friend. He thinks it was a mistake for you to call Mac [McCarthy]." Then, after saying he was writing a request to McCarthy to delay the proposed hearing until Symington returned from a two-week trip to Europe, the senator went on: "I would suggest two things to you, old fellow. One, let's counterpunch this stuff and not lead; two, I think your people over there are pretty harassed and I don't blame them, but maybe some of them can't see the forest for the trees. This boy gets awfully rough. . . ."

"Well, Stu," came Stevens' response, "probably it was poor politics and poor judgment to call him——"

"It isn't a question of politics at all. It's a question of the integrity and fighting morale of the Army, and therefore everybody in my opinion who has a concept of what is decent will break their back to help you in any way they can."

Later that afternoon Symington had called again, saying: "I'll give you a little piece of gratuitous advice. My friend said yesterday, 'This guy got any steel in him?' I said, 'Sure . . . right.' He said, 'If he has steel he can do a great service.' He said also, 'He has got to be careful of every move he makes, carefully thought out.' I think you may have this fellow on the run a little bit. But he is terrifically agile in getting around something. . . . I think you are in shape to protect your Army . . . provided you stay tough. . . . One other fellow that is on your side, and I know he is absolutely tops, and that is Bill Rogers [Deputy Attorney General]. I mean, you can't go wrong with Bill."

"We have been in touch with him, of course," Stevenson rejoined, and Symington speculated, "This fellow may be sick, you know."

Then the next morning Symington had called Stevens again; he was upset by a report in the newspapers that Stevens had agreed to appear before McCarthy at any time. "If you and I are going to work together," Symington remonstrated, "we have got to be on the table with each other . . . we can throw the blocks in this thing. . . . If you are going to play with McCarthy, you have got to forget about any of those Marquis of Queensbury rules. . . ."

As these words were read, Symington sat rigid, his jaw set grimly, his face blood-red in color; apoplexy seemed imminent. Here was the Republican Secretary of the Army conniving with a Democratic senator and that senator's Democratic advisers on how to "throw the blocks" into Senator McCarthy and the operations of the Republican-controlled investigations subcommittee.

But there was more to come; and in the reading of these further monitored calls, the dates became all-important.

Symington had gone abroad, and on his return he had telephoned Stevens on March 8 to inquire about a rumor going the rounds of the Capitol to the effect that the Army had compiled a report on the improper pressure that had been exerted by Roy Cohn to get preferential treatment for Private Schine. Stevens replied vaguely, belittling the rumor. Symington said he would like to see the report, adding that "naturally it is of great interest to us."

Stevens had hedged, saying, "Personally, I very much doubt whether it would be available, Stuart"; and when Symington had tried to pin him down as to whether such a report existed, the Secretary ducked and dodged, admitting nothing, and finally expressed his personal feeling that "anything in that line would prove to be very much exaggerated." He had no personal complaint regarding his treatment by McCarthy or the subcommittee, Stevens insisted, although "when he got after Zwicker, of course, then I hollered, but so far as I personally am concerned, I don't have a lot of stuff so far as my contact with Joe or the committee is concerned." Concluding with his belief that "I don't think there is too much there," Stevens said he would "talk with Adams and find out what I can see." Symington responded that he would "appreciate this being private between you and me."

This conversation, in which the Army Secretary brushed aside the Schine matter as unimportant, had taken place on March 8.

Two days later a copy of the report Stevens was so vague about
(the famous Army "chronology") had been given to Senator Potter,
and the day after that it was transmitted to the full subcommittee
and made public.

[III]

Definitely a plot seemed to be unfolding, and McCarthy took full
advantage of the opening thus afforded to his side. He requested
that two witnesses be subpoenaed—Clark Clifford and Senator
Symington, whom he now addressed sarcastically as "Sanctimonious
Stu."

The monitored telephone calls clearly proved, said Joe indignantly, that Stevens had been ready to cooperate with the committee, telling Symington that he didn't think there was anything
serious in the charges rumored to have been drawn up, and that
Symington, with Clifford, "the chief political adviser of President
Truman—and I assume the chief political adviser of the man who
would be President on the Democratic ticket in 1956 [an allusion
to Symington's Presidential aspirations]—is doing the advising. I
believe the next day—anyway, a matter of a day or two—these
charges were issued, issued under the Secretary's name, charging
Mr. Cohn, Mr. Carr, and myself with almost everything except
murdering our great-great-grandmother.

"Number two," McCarthy went on, while Symington appeared
to be choking, "Mr. Symington should be subpoenaed. If he refuses
to honor that subpoena . . . I would suggest that we take this to
the Senate floor . . . and see whether or not the Senate will order
him to give us the truth. At that time, I will quote in detail all the
statements made by Sanctimonious Stu when he told how everything had to be laid on the table.

"And number three, Mr. Symington should do exactly what I
did. He should disqualify himself, because never before in the history of this Senate as far as I know have we had the man who
instigated the charges insist on sitting as judge."

Red with rage, Symington assured both the chair and "all people within the sound of my voice" that he would be glad to discuss
the matter on the Senate floor with the "distinguished junior senator
from Wisconsin—especially as I always tell the truth."

"How about under oath?" challenged McCarthy, and Symington

retorted that there had been a time when Joe was invited to testify before a Senate committee investigating him, and had refused; but "you take it to the floor any time you want, and I will meet you there with pleasure. . . . Millions of Americans have been told by Senator McCarthy that the Eisenhower administration, this Republican administration, has added another year of treason to our proud history. . . . I am a Democrat, but first and foremost I am an American. It is little comfort to me that these terrible charges are directed against a Republican administration, Republican officials, and our Republican commander-in-chief. It would appear that some of us want to end up in this country with just plain anarchy."

McCarthy's retort was laced with sarcasm: "Mr. Chairman, I may say I was rather amused to hear Senator Symington worrying about the Republicans, when he had been conniving secretly to get the top political adviser of the Democrats to try to get the Republicans to commit suicide. It may seem very clever to Senator Symington at this time that he got Clark Clifford to mislead a fine, naive, not too brilliant Republican Secretary of the Army. But in the end this is going to be bad for his party and for the country, because the two-party system cannot survive if you have the chief political adviser of one calling the shots for the other. If our two-party system does not survive, our republic cannot survive."

At this point the exchange was temporarily halted by the chairman, and Roy Cohn was recalled to the stand. Under teasing insinuations from Counsel Welch, the witness was brought to concur in Welch's soothing belief that "in spite of all the dismay that others may have felt in this room, or the dismay that the country may have felt at all the language that has taken place here, the country, and particularly the mothers and fathers of the boys in the service, may rest easy." The astute Army attorney was bent on syruping over the blisters that the hearing was suddenly raising. "It is a beautiful Army, Navy, and Air Force, is it not?" he asked, beaming.

Feeling on safe ground, Cohn assented entirely: "It certainly is, sir."

But McCarthy was not one to be soft-soaped or to drop an advantage gained, and he continued to rub salt into Symington's wounds, demanding that the latter testify under oath as to how he and Clifford had managed to get Stevens to issue the charges which only a couple of days before Stevens had belittled as "very much exaggerated" and of slight consequence. Let the committee find out what part Symington had taken "in calling on these hearings, what part he took in trying to induce Secretary Stevens not to testify and to call off the investigations of communism." This expression of willingness to discuss the matter on the Senate floor, in order to avoid testifying under oath, why, "that's such an obvious dodge that I don't think a single one of our jury of millions of people will be deceived." Let "our friend, Sanctimonious Stu——"

Barked Symington: "Senator McCarthy, I object to that reference to my first name! You better go to a psychiatrist!"

"Why, Mr. Chairman, when he was advising us that he wanted all of the facts laid on the table . . ." McCarthy forged ahead, saying a few simple questions were all he wanted Symington to answer. Again and again, each time more grimly, the latter repeated that he would do so if McCarthy would answer a few simple questions that had been asked in 1952 about his financial dealings and other matters. Finally the chair succeeded in ending the colloquy, but the bitterness remained and would flare up again.

One net result of the incident was clear: Symington's Presidential boom had been sunk without a trace by buccaneer Joe, with piratical efficiency and by the use of only two words—"Sanctimonious Stu." The Democratic command would never entrust their highest hopes to a standard-bearer to whom, between blushes, that scarifying epithet had been applied—unjustly or not—before 20,000,000 television viewers.

"No Sense of Decency?"

McCarthy's side received an undoubted boost from the revelations contained in the monitored calls. For some time the tide had been running rather against the senator and his associates; now the Army's side seemed definitely on a spot. The calls showed that not only had Stevens turned to influential Democrats for political counsel, but that Deputy Attorney General Rogers had been quarterbacking the Pentagon's moves, obviously on orders from higher up; a clear refutation of Stevens' and Adams' testimony that they alone were responsible for the steps taken. Not they, but the White House, it now seemed transparently clear, had instigated the attempt to stop Joe.

Not all the monitored calls had been introduced yet, and as he took off that weekend for more speechmaking in Wisconsin, McCarthy, with his consistent disregard for protocol and orderly procedure but his acute sense of timing to insure maximum publicity, gave to the wire services transcripts of three telephone conversations between himself and Stevens. He marked these for release after 7 P.M. Saturday—just in time for inclusion in the Sunday papers, where they would receive the widest display.

The substance of these calls had been related in part by Stevens weeks before. One call, dated November 7, just after G. David Schine had been inducted, showed the senator requesting "one personal favor" of the Secretary, namely, "for God's sake don't put Dave in service and assign him back to my committee. From three standpoints: one, I couldn't get away with it more than a week; the newspapers would be back on us and you would have to send him back into uniform anyway. Two, this thing [the Monmouth investigation] has been running along so cleanly so far they haven't been able to beat your brains out. There is nothing the leftwingers

578

would like better; they don't like the cooperation between the committee and the Army. And the third thing, they would say I asked for him. He is a good boy, but there is nothing indispensable about him. From my desk today I can pick up perhaps a half-dozen letters from mothers whose boys are in worse shape than Dave, and it would be embarrassing if held to me. . . ."

Then had come the famous suggestion that "maybe a few weekends off" might be arranged: "Roy—it's one of the few things I've seen him completely unreasonable about. He thinks Dave should be a general and work from the penthouse of the Waldorf."

The transcript showed Stevens replying: "From the start you never have done or said anything that spurred me on this situation at all, other than to take a friendly interest."

McCarthy then had underscored the political realities of the situation for this "honest, naive, not too brilliant" Army Secretary, telling him, with explicit clarity: "If you put him into service to work with the committee, all the devil would break loose, and the President would be calling you not to play favorites. . . . I think, for Roy's sake, if you can let him come back for weekends or something so his girl friends won't get lonesome—maybe if you shave his hair off he won't want to come back."

The transcript containing political dynamite was that of a call made by Stevens to McCarthy on February 20—the call that led to Stevens' appeal to Symington for help. Stevens already had told the other members of the subcommittee that he was ordering General Zwicker not to obey McCarthy's subpoena to appear in a public hearing. He told how upset he was over the treatment accorded Zwicker in executive session, and McCarthy had advised him not to follow the "coverup" policy adopted by the previous administration, but to undertake a genuine housecleaning. "You have got a wonderful opportunity here, Robert," the senator had said, "to take the position that the Congress knows about traitors no matter where they are. . . . To try to cover up, as has gone on before, that will be impossible, I will guarantee you! I have had a most insulting session with the general . . . to tell me that the commissioning of Communists was an order against discrimination because of political beliefs, that is jargon! You don't recognize that."

Stevens: "That is exactly what has been used in reference to this type of thing, Joe."

McCarthy: "Let me ask you this: is it your position that you are going to try to keep from us the names of the officers who protected these men?"

Stevens: "I am going to prevent my officers from going before your committee until you and I have an understanding as to the abuse they are going to get."

This lit the fuse and McCarthy exploded: "You are going to order them not to appear before my committee? Just go ahead and try it, Robert! I am going to kick the brains out of anyone who protects Communists! If that is the policy of you—you just go ahead and do it! I will guarantee that you will live to regret it!"

"Joe, you know——" Stevens tried to break in, but the torrent of words kept on: "Let me finish! This is your time, I didn't call you. If this new administration of the Army is going to try to protect the hangovers from the old, that in turn protected Communists, the people will know about it, and I guarantee you, Bob, that you will learn before you are through that instead of protecting Communists you should be helping us uncover them. I don't care whether an officer is a general or what he is, when he comes before me with the ignorant, stupid, insulting aspect of those who appeared, I will guarantee you that the American people will know about it. . . . If you have nothing to hide——"

Stevens: "I have absolutely nothing to hide, one hundred percent."

McCarthy: "Let me get this straight, then . . . You are calling me this morning to tell me you are going to order officers of the Army not to come before our committee, and I understand yesterday you went to see each member of the committee. Did you tell them that?"

Stevens: "Yes, I told them I was not going to let Zwicker appear on Tuesday."

McCarthy: "Would you consider yourself subpoenaed for ten o'clock Tuesday morning?"

Stevens: "I will take that under advisement."

But the senator was through with palaver. "If you don't want to appear, all right," he snapped. "I am telling the press that you have been told to appear. If you decide not to we will take steps from there on. I am through with this covering-up of Communists. I am sorry that Bob Stevens is one that is doing it, too!"

And here McCarthy cut the connection with a slam.

[II]

The release of these transcripts before they had been introduced as evidence threw counsel for both sides into dismay: how could there be any orderly procedure if the principals were allowed to disclose unsworn testimony outside the hearing room? McCarthy was debonair about their concern, explaining lightly that he would place the texts in the record on Monday. For the moment he was congenially taken up with being the chief attraction at the celebration in Ripon, Wisconsin, of the Republicans' centennial as a party. He told a laughing, cheering crowd of 5,000 that Senator Symington had helped to bring on the hearings in Washington as part of a plot to destroy President Eisenhower and the Republican party. In a slashing personal attack he ridiculed "Sanctimonious Stu's Presidential pretensions, saying the Missourian was "running about as fast as anyone can" for his party's nomination—"and now we have the would-be candidate for the Democratic nomination as President saying to the Republican Secretary of the Army, 'We can throw the blocks into this thing!' What is the thing? It is the sellout of the American people! It is advice to the Republican party how best to commit suicide!"

The applause was hearty when the senator expressed his repugnance to "eavesdropping on the telephone." And he indicated that his long experience in bluffing at the poker table had stood him in good stead, because Symington, he said, had consented to the introduction of his damaging telephone conversations only because "he thought I already had copies of them. He was wrong. I didn't have copies!"

In the best of humors, Joe also disclosed the secret of his style of fighting. A northwoods guide named Indian Charlie, he chuckled, long ago had told him: "If you see somebody approaching with unfriendly intent, kick him as quick and as hard as you can under the belt, and keep on kicking until you have him helpless." (The version finding its way into print was considerably toned down from Joe's language; in those days of newspaper prudery, expressions as earthy as his were not considered "fit to print.")

A second sensation was provided that weekend by the *Chicago Tribune*'s publication of the leaked transcript of a telephone call made by Secretary Stevens to G. David Schine just before the latter was drafted, explaining in a fatherly way that there was "no appropriate way" by which Schine could avoid basic training. The subject had been canvassed three times with Defense Secretary Wilson, Stevens said, and "we feel that it is almost a must, in the situation as it now stands; and after going over the situation three times now, insofar as you are concerned, it is Mr. Wilson's and my conviction that this is the wise thing to do, Dave." But hope was held out for the future. "Having done that," Schine was promised, "then I think there is an excellent chance that we can pick you up and use you in a way that would be useful to the country and to yourself." What that way would be Stevens could not say, but he was profuse in assurances that "I personally would like to arrange it in such a way that you could come into the Army . . . [and] that you could use the knowledge and ability you have in certain fields. But I won't discuss it over the phone."

Schine replied graciously that "I am certainly happy to know you have talked it over with Mr. Wilson and that you are both thinking about it."

What the average draftee thought of all this it is needless to ask. Inevitably the question sprang to mind: "Why this extraordinary consideration, on the highest level, for a prospective private—why?" It is hardly an overstatement to say that the Army's case was not strengthened.

[III]

Upon resumption of the hearings after these weekend diversions, this conversation, together with the transcripts of McCarthy's calls, was entered in the record. Then the Pentagon's talks with McClellan, Mundt, Cohn, and Carr were introduced; and although the Army had fought to have these entered, none of them seemed to bear out the Army's contention of undue pressure having been exerted on behalf of Schine. There were no texts of calls between Cohn and John Adams, because Adams had not monitored any until February, and by then he and Cohn were not speaking to each other. One conversation between Adams and Frank Carr related some cheerful information about Private Schine: at Camp Gordon, Adams said, "something had happened to him"; he had become "circumspect . . . a damn fine soldier." He had even gotten rid of his Cadillac and bought "a secondhand Chevy" for off-duty use.

On Monday McCarthy had entered formal demands that Senator Symington step down as a judge and testify under oath, both which demands again were rejected. He also formally requested that Clark Clifford be subpoenaed; but the next day, when the Democrats supported this request, to everyone's bewilderment Joe opposed it. Counsel Welch was baffled. Studying McCarthy intently, he said slowly, in a tone as if of dawning comprehension:

"Looking at you, Senator McCarthy, you have, I think, something of a genius for creating confusion, throwing in new issues, new accusations, and creating turmoil in the hearts and minds of the country that I find troublesome. And because of your genius, sir, we keep on, just keep on, as I view it, creating these confusions. Maybe I am overimpressed by them, but I don't think they do the country any good."

McCarthy retorted that perhaps Welch meant that he had a genius for "bringing out facts which may disturb people." Then he suggested that a two-week recess might be necessary because Cohn was scheduled to report for National Guard duty at Camp Kilmer—where General Zwicker was in command. Cohn held a lieutenant's commission in the New York National Guard. "He's going down to get that preferential treatment from General Zwicker," the senator explained. "I can't ask for his deferment because that would be asking for special favors, and we don't want any investigation of this committee for granting special favors to Mr. Cohn."

Thus alerted, Counsel Jenkins at once requested and received a postponement of Cohn's guard duty.

The feeling of exacerbation in the caucus room had become more and more noticeable as the days dragged by. The explosions of temper grew more bitter, and noisy demonstrations by the spectators —although frowned upon by the chair—became more frequent. Both Symington and McCarthy received scattered applause, for instance, when they entered the room at the start of each session.

On Wednesday morning Cohn again took the stand, under cross-examination by Welch. The Army counsel had given up hoping for a clear-cut verdict in his clients' favor; he was now trying to score points, even if on trivial matters, and in this endeavor he used all the wiles of a veteran trial lawyer who had every trick of forensic feigning, every cadence of courtroom histrionics, at his command. This day he bore down on Cohn's disclaimer of having threatened to "wreck the Army," or having given way to a fit of rage. Cohn represented himself as too balanced, too reasonable, even-tempered, and restrained to have yielded to blind anger, although several witnesses had testified that they had heard him utter violent threats when shut out of the radar laboratory at Fort Monmouth. By persistent needling, Welch tried to provoke the witness into losing his temper, without success. He brought out that Cohn had been aware of a "disturbing" security situation at Fort Monmouth as early as March or April of the previous year; yet Cohn admitted that when he met Secretary Stevens for the first time, in September, he had made no mention of this alarming situation.

"Don't you know," Welch prodded, "that if you had really told him what your fears were, and substantiated them to any extent, he would have jumped in the next day with suspensions?"

Cohn replied that he did not know any such thing, and Welch switched to the number of alleged subversives or Communists who were known by Cohn to be in defense plants. "I'm in a hurry," he insisted. "I don't want the sun to go down while they're still in there if we can get them out." *

The witness was doubtful. "I'm afraid we won't be able to work that fast."

Welch was persistent. "How many are there?"

"I believe the figure is approximately one hundred and thirty."

"Approximately one three oh."

"Those are people, Mr. Welch—"

"I don't care. You've told us who they are. And how many plants are there?"

"I see sixteen offhand."

"Sixteen plants. Are you alarmed at that situation, Mr. Cohn?"

"Yes, sir, I am."

"Nothing could be more alarming, could it? . . . Will you not, before the sun goes down, give those names to the FBI and at least have those men put under surveillance?"

"If there is need for surveillance," responded Cohn, "I can well assume that Mr. John Edgar Hoover and his men know a lot better

* Exactly four years before, the first official reaction to McCarthy's charges of Communist infiltration of the government had been a demand by John E. Peurifoy, Undersecretary of State, that the senator furnish the names of any such subversives in the State Department, promising that "if I can find a single one, he will be fired by sundown"; a rhetorical statement, like Welch's, that in the light of the practical difficulties was meaningless, and in both instances, of course, known to be so.

than I . . . I do not propose to tell the FBI how to run its job."

"Then they've got the whole one hundred and thirty, have they, Mr. Cohn?"

"I'm sure of it, sir, and a lot more."

"Then what's all the excitement about, if J. Edgar Hoover is on the job, chasing those one hundred and thirty Communists?"

"Mr. Welch, all the excitement——"

The Army counsel cut in. "Well, then, as a second line of defense, let's send the one hundred and thirty names to the Department of Defense tonight. Would you mind doing that?" he pleaded.

"Whatever the committee directs on that, sir, I will——"

Again Welch cut in. "I wish the committee would direct that all the names be sent to both the FBI and to the Department of Defense with extreme suddenness."

Chimed in Senator Symington: "Mr. Chairman, I so move."

McCarthy had been watching this ragging of his counsel with increasing impatience. Basically, the senator's character was primitive in its intolerance of complexities. To him all issues appeared in primary colors—stark red or sheer white, without shadings, blendings, or gradations. His idea of loyalty was feudal: total and unquestioning allegiance. He demanded absolute fealty and he gave it. He would have made a superb chieftain of a Highland clan, or feudal border raider, baron or knight, upon whose protection any vassal or kern of his fief might call at any time with assurance of being heard. To attack any person on McCarthy's side was to attack McCarthy; there could be no hesitation about it, and the response would be automatic, heedless of possible risk or collateral consequences. In the shifting world of politics such a character was archaic and dangerous to its possessor.

Now he saw a henchman hard-pressed, and without a moment's reflection he plunged impetuously to the rescue—figuratively rushing in with claymore flashing. His eyes narrowed to slits (imparting to his features a look that to the *New Republic* seemed "almost satanic"), the upper lip drew taut with anger, and he interrupted:

"Mr. Chairman, in view of Mr. Welch's request that information be given if we know of anyone who might be performing any work for the Communist party, I think we should tell him that he has in his law firm a young man named Fisher, whom he recommended incidentally to do work on this committee, who has been, for a number of years, a member of an organization which is named, oh, years and years ago, as the legal bulwark of the Communist party, an organization that always swings to the defense of anyone who dares to expose Communists." * The caucus room sat in hypnotized silence, and McCarthy went on, speaking clearly, incisively, though his lips scarcely moved:

"I assume that Mr. Welch did not know of this young man at the time he recommended him as the assistant counsel for this committee, but he has such terror and such a great desire to know where anyone is located. You may be serving the Communist party, Mr. Welch, and I thought we should just call to your attention the fact that your Mr. Fisher, who is still in your lawn firm today, whom you asked to have down here looking over the secret and classified material, is a member of an organization, not named by me but named by various committees, named by the Attorney General, as I recall. He belonged to it after it had been exposed as the legal arm of the Communist party. Knowing that, Mr. Welch, I just felt that I had a duty to respond here to your urgent request that *before sundown* [the words were emphasized with withering sarcasm] that if we know of anyone serving the Communist cause we let the agency know. We're now letting you know your man did belong to this organization for either three or four years. Belonged to it long after he was out of law school. And I have hesitated bringing that up, but I have been rather bored with your phony requests to Mr. Cohn here, that he personally get every Communist out of government *before sundown*. . . . Now, I'm not asking you at this time to explain why you tried to foist him on this committee. That you did, the committee knows. Whether you knew that he was a member of that Communist organization or not, I don't know. I assume you did not, Mr. Welch, because I get the impression that while you are quite an actor, you play for a laugh, I don't think you have any conception of the danger of the Communist party. I don't think you yourself would ever knowingly aid the Communist cause. I think you're unknowingly siding with it when you try to burlesque this hearing in which we're attempting to bring out the facts."

He stopped, and after a moment of stunned silence, Welch spoke to a point of personal privilege. Leaning over the microphone, deliberately and gravely he began:

"Senator McCarthy, I did not know—may I have your attention?"

---

* Sic. McCarthy's grammar frequently became fouled when he was angered.

The senator was riffling through a mass of papers, apparently looking for something, and he responded lightly, "I can listen with one ear."

"Now, this time, sir, I want you to listen with both," said Welch sternly, and continued: "Senator McCarthy, I think until this moment—you won't need anything in the record when I finish telling you this—until this moment, senator, I think I never really gauged your cruelty or your recklessness. Fred Fisher is a young man who went to Harvard law school and came into my firm and is starting what looks to be a brilliant career with us. When I decided to work for this committee, I asked Jim St. Clair, who sits on my right, to be my first assistant. I said to Jim, 'Pick somebody in the firm to work under you that you would like.' He chose Fred Fisher and they came down on the afternoon plane. That night, when we had taken a little stab at what this case was about, Fred Fisher and Jim St. Clair and I went to dinner together. I then said to these two men, 'Boys, I don't know anything about you, except that I've always liked you, but if there is anything funny in the life of either of you that would hurt anybody in this case, then speak up quick.' And Fred Fisher said, 'Mr. Welch, when I was in law school, and for a period of months after that, I belonged to the Lawyers Guild,' as you have suggested, senator. . . . And I said, 'Fred, I just don't think I'm going to ask you to work on this case. If I do, one of these days that will come out, and go over national television, and it will just hurt like the dickens.' And so, senator, I asked him to go back to Boston. Little did I dream that you could be so cruel and reckless as to do an injury to that lad. It is true, he is still with Hale & Dorr. It is true that he will continue to be with Hale & Dorr. It is, I regret to say, equally true that I fear he shall always bear a scar needlessly inflicted by you. If it were in my power to forgive you for your reckless cruelty, I would do so. I like to think I'm a gentle man, but your forgiveness will have to come from someone other than me."

The tremulous voice broke—but McCarthy would not let the rebuke pass. "Mr. Chairman, Mr. Chairman," he responded, undeterred, "may I say that Mr. Welch talks about this being cruel and reckless. He was just baiting, he has been *baiting,* Mr. Cohn here for hours, requesting that Mr. Cohn *before sundown* get out of any department of the government anyone who is serving the Communist cause. Now, I just give this man's record, and I want to say, Mr. Welch, that it had been labeled long before he became a member, as early as 1944——"

"Senator, may we not drop this?" cut in the counsel. "We know he belonged to the Lawyers Guild. . . . Let us not assassinate this lad further, senator. You have done enough. Have you no sense of decency, sir, at long last? Have you no sense of decency?"

"I know this hurts you, Mr. Welch——"

"Senator, I think it hurts you, too!" came the interjection.

"Mr. Chairman," McCarthy persisted, "I'd like to finish this. . . . Mr. Welch talks about any sense of decency. It seems that Mr. Welch is pained so deeply he thinks it improper for me to give the record, the Communist-front record, of a man whom he wanted to foist upon this committee. But it doesn't pain him at all, there's no pain in his chest, about the attempt to destroy the reputation and take the jobs away from the young men who are working here on my committee. And, Mr. Welch, if I have said anything that is untrue, then tell me. I have heard you and everyone else talk so much about laying the truth upon the table. But when I heard the completely phony Mr. Welch . . . saying, now, *before sundown,* you must get these people out of government . . . So I just want you to have it very clear, very clear, that you were not so serious about that when you tried to recommend this man for this committee."

"Mr. McCarthy, I will not discuss this further with you," came Welch's emotion-packed response. "You have sat within six feet of me and could ask, could have asked me about Fred Fisher." The voice rose and the old man seemed to struggle against tears. "You have seen fit to bring it out, and if there is a God in heaven, it will do neither you nor your cause any good! I will not discuss it further. I will not ask Mr. Cohn any more questions. You, Mr. Chairman, may, if you will, call the next witness."

Thunderous applause shook the caucus room. The men around the committee table sat immovable, and the chair made no attempt to curb the tumult. McCarthy, isolated at his end of the long, long table, sat with head bowed as the handclapping kept up, staring down at the litter of papers before him. Finally Mundt gaveled a recess.

As the glaring television lights faded and principals, counsel, and witnesses filed out, McCarthy glanced toward the watching reporters and in a quizzical gesture held out both hands, palms upward. It seemed as though he were asking, in bewilderment, "What did I do wrong?" Such, at least, was the construction placed upon that mute appeal by some of those to whom it was directed. Yet it might just as readily have been interpreted as the fatalistic gesture of the gambler who sees himself wiped out by an unlucky cast of the dice and accepts the fact with a shrug of resignation— "There goes the game!"

There indeed the game had gone, whether McCarthy sensed it or not. That dramatic outburst by Joseph Welch, provoked by McCarthy's own demonic obsessions, marked the turn of the tide that, rising swiftly, would incontinently overtake and then engulf the still defiant but impotent King Canute McCarthy.

"Fretful Lightning"

[I]

At this point in the (some people thought) pointless proceedings in Washington, the *St. Louis Post-Dispatch* cartoonist Fitzpatrick caricatured the cast of characters—Welch, Jenkins, McCarthy, Mundt—in a page-wide strip under the flabbergasted caption: "If this were played upon a stage, now, I should condemn it as improbable fiction."

Another observer compared Secretary Stevens' brushes with Senator McCarthy to "Little Lord Fauntleroy trying to reform a Dead End Kid."

The United Press contributed to the feeling of national zaniness by distributing a "Key to the Language of the Hearings," a lexicon giving the "true meanings" of the phrases that had been used constantly in the hearing. These included:

"Point of order" (It's my turn to contribute to the disorder here)

"Mr. Chairman" (Turn those cameras this way, boys)

"The gentleman" (Courtesy title)

"My friend" (My opponent)

"My learned friend" (That dope)

"My distinguished friend" (A worse stinker I never met)

"I shall be happy to enlighten the gentleman" (Hold still for this one, you rat)

"Would you please repeat the question?" (How will I ever get out of this?)

"I shall have to refresh my recollection" (I need time, dad)

"I do not question your integrity" (You bet your sweet life I do)

"Hearing room" (Archaic expression meaning room in which you can hear. Also archaic, room in which one receives a hearing)

"Let's keep politics out of this" (Your politics, that is)

590

"I hope this discussion won't be taken out of my time" (I'm entitled to my full ten minutes on television)

"An unnamed person" (I'll slip the press a note in just a minute)

"May I have your attention" (Ah, that's better—two cameras)

But beneath the implausibility and extravagance lay profound significances: The stakes for which the participants were playing were enormous, bound to have worldwide repercussions, and the final score could not be chalked up yet. In recent days the tide had been swinging in McCarthy's favor as the weaknesses in the Army's case became apparent, and it seemed that all McCarthy would need to do would be to maintain the advantage gained, avoid missteps, and he might emerge not only the winner hands down, but even strengthened by the ordeal. At precisely this juncture McCarthy had blundered, tripped up by his own temper, and had given Welch an opening for a diversionary stroke, an opening which the veteran counsel had exploited with devastating effect.

Thrilling as the actual scene had been, there had been a drama within the drama of which the viewing public was unaware. The fact of Fred Fisher's brief association with Welch at the outset of the inquiry, and of his elimination and the reason for it, was no secret; it had been published in the newspapers at the time it happened. McCarthy's raking it up had shocked Welch and other attorneys in the know because it violated the ethics lawyers work by—it flouted a private, quid-pro-quo, backstage agreement between counsel not to raise the incident.

Early in the proceedings, an understanding had been reached between Welch and McCarthy's side that the Fisher incident would not be introduced, in return for Welch's "laying off" Roy Cohn's military record. There was nothing suspicious or irregular about this record, but it might have been used unscrupulously in testimony, to no relevant purpose. McCarthy had been informed of this agreement and had endorsed it; but his anger had overcome him in the heat of Cohn's cross-examination and he had cast aside all restraint. This betrayal of their agreement had angered and alienated Welch personally, besides arousing his resentment of the injustice done to Fisher; professional indignation was mingled with his humanitarian revulsion.

Cohn had tried to head off McCarthy at the very start, showing great agitation as the irate senator plowed ahead, passing him a note reminding him of the understanding and shaking his head in protest. McCarthy read the note, remarked that "Mr. Cohn would rather not have me go into this," and went right on.

There had been another hidden factor contributing to the violence of the encounter. The pressure on the committee to end the hearings was building up. Although the Democrats said they wanted the interrogation to continue, in the belief that the Republicans were being hurt, actually both sides would have been glad to call a halt if a way could be devised that would save face all around. Welch himself, according to those close to him, was on the watch for a means to wind up the hearings, and when McCarthy gratuitously provided a chance to make a continuation less attractive to any of the parties involved, Welch had seized upon it with maximum effectiveness—at one stroke ridding himself of Cohn, from whom it was obvious nothing more of consequence could be drawn, and turning the tide of public sentiment against the senator. Both ends had been achieved not by testimony, but by courtroom histrionics.

The degree of Welch's sincerity when professing the pangs of heartbreak over McCarthy's scurvy treatment of a defenseless lad became an immediate subject of debate, and the argument would continue for years. Fred Fisher, of course, in that hearing room was never "defenseless"; he was being accorded a most astute and telling defense by a master pleader. As Welch moved out of the room for the recess, his face was etched in grief. Spectators pressed close to murmur sympathy and press his hand. Passing into the corridor, he paced along slowly, and as cameramen preceding him ground away, he appeared to brush back tears. The United Press confined itself to reporting that the old man "appeared to be wiping his face" with his handkerchief. "I am close to tears," he was quoted as saying. "Here is a young kid with one mistake—just one mistake—and he is trying to crucify him. I don't see how in the name of God you can fight anybody like that! I never saw such cruelty . . . such arrogance!" The reporters, having got their statement, melted away, and Welch moved deeper into the maze of the building.

(Years afterward, a lawyer who paced that corridor with Welch gave an ampler version. Said this witness: "We walked out of the hearing together, down the hall, around the corner, around another corner, through the corridors of the Senate Office Building, until finally reporters had quit trailing us and the flash bulbs had quit exploding. Then Welch looked at me, and without changing his expression, the tears still streaming down his face, asked, 'Well, how did it go?' " To that there could be but one possible answer: It *went,* to perfection.) *

McCarthy's comment during the recess was curt: "Too many people can dish it out, but can't take it."

[II]

And that afternoon, breezy, relaxed, and confident, he opened his defense with a lecture on the progress achieved by communism during recent years. Producing a large map to illustrate his theme, he propped it up in view of the cameras and assured the committee that "I've got a good hog-calling voice, Mr. Chairman, and I think I can speak loudly enough so that the mike will pick it up. You see here, Mr. Jenkins . . . " The counsel let him ramble at will, assisting with an occasional question. To the audience, most of the information seemed old hat; they had heard it over and over during the last four years, from Joe and others; and also, so exhaustively had the subject been what Senator Dirksen called "ventilated" during that time that the gaps in McCarthy's reasoning—his some-times farfetched assumptions and tendentious conclusions, the sweeping generalizations, often based on questionable or exag-gerated statistics—were apparent to all but the willfully obtuse of the senator's diehard believers. The novelty had worn off: time had moved on although Joe had not, and to this fact he was im-pervious.

All the following day he spent on the stand, questioned sharply by Jenkins. He denied that he had ever asked anybody in the Army to give Schine a direct commission. He denied that he or his staff had used "one iota of improper influence" to get favors for Schine. Since this was in flat contradiction of both Stevens and General Reber, it posed the issue of perjury squarely. Asked about Cohn's "declaration of war" against the Army, the senator pointed out that Cohn had not denied uttering such a threat, but had said he could not remember making it. Testimony regarding this had been given by, among others, Colonel Kenneth BeLieu, Secretary Stevens' aide, and McCarthy commended Cohn for "not calling the young man who made that statement a perjurer, and I was very happy to see him do that. I don't think he made that statement, number one.

* Source: Robert Griffith, *The Politics of Fear,* University of Kentucky Press, 1970, p. 259.

Number two, there is no war between the committee and anyone except Communists and those guilty of graft and corruption."

He said he had not taken seriously the Army's efforts to call off the Monmouth investigation until January, considering some actions that Cohn had resented mere "ribbing" or "needling." And he agreed with Jenkins that the Army Secretary was "fundamentally honest" and as much opposed to communism as any man he knew; he bore him no ill will, he said.

Senator McClellan remarked that McCarthy had named Stevens as part of a blackmail plot, and raised the question: "What is an honest blackmailer?"

Over the objections of the Democrats, the Republican majority of the committee that day voted to end the hearings with McCarthy's testimony and that of Frank Carr, which he had volunteered to offer, although he had been formally dropped as a witness. Counsel Jenkins welcomed their approach to "the very twilight of the drama, when the curtain is falling rapidly"; but the descent was to be achieved only with many a jerk, jar, and rattle.

[III]

The excitements of the next day came unheralded. The first was sprung by Senator Flanders. Entering the caucus room while McCarthy was recounting his memory of how the famous "cropped photograph" had been taken, the Vermonter shambled up to the witness chair and stood there patiently, blinking placidly, while Joe continued. As he remembered it, McCarthy was saying, Stevens had been in a hurry and had called out something like, "Dave, come over here," or "Dave, I want a picture"—Joe guessed because the Secretary, being "a good-natured individual," wanted to "make Dave feel good." Schine had two coats, and he had handed one to an officer to hold while he posed—McCarthy didn't know the officer but was told he was the "commanding officer," and the situation had amused him because there stood "a colonel holding a private's coat. That wasn't the way we did things in the Marine Corps!"

Here noticing Flanders, McCarthy paused and turned toward him. Flanders silently handed him an envelope. McCarthy ripped it open and read the contents aloud: an announcement that Flan-

ders was going to make a speech against Joe in the Senate that afternoon and inviting McCarthy to be present.

Having delivered his message, in full view of the television audience, Flanders turned to leave, but was halted by Joe's voice.
Swiveling in his chair, McCarthy addressed the old man sharply:
"Number one, I will be unable to be present because I will be
testifying. Number two, I don't have enough interest in any Flanders
speech to listen to it. Number three— Senator, may I have your
attention? Number three, you have indicated . . . you have information of value to this committee. You suggested that this committee was not getting at the heart of this matter—let me finish,
Mr. Flanders. At that time you did not have the courtesy that you
have today of letting me know that you were speaking. . . . If you
have any information of value, what you should do is take the oath,
let us cross-examine you."

Mundt cut the exchange short with a grumbled, "We seem to be
good for one surprise a day," and Flanders shambled out. Later
McCarthy told reporters, "I think they should get a man with a net
and take him to a good, quiet place."

Shortly after this, during a recess, Welch encountered McCarthy
in a corridor; the senator was talking with Joe Foss, Marine ace
of World War II now running for governor of South Dakota. Mc-
Carthy started to introduce his companion, but Welch brushed him
aside with an icy, "You have broken the bonds between us," and
turned away. "Okay," said Joe with a smile, and kept on talking to
Foss.

With Cohn temporarily back on the stand, Senator Jackson
undertook to poke fun at a proposed program for combating communism on a global scale drawn up by Schine when he was a committee aide, and rejected by the State Department. Robert Kennedy,
acting as counsel for the minority members, fed the questions to
Jackson, who read them with satirical humor. For instance, Schine
had suggested the ideological struggle be carried on through fra-
ternal orders—the Elks, for example—and Jackson, himself an
Elk, laughingly questioned whether there was an Elks lodge in
Pakistan. This seemed very funny to Jackson and drew a laugh from
the crowd. Jibe after jibe followed, plainly angering Cohn, who
defended Schine's ideas, and the minute the session was adjourned
he rushed at Kennedy, excited and gesticulating. In the heated ex-

change some reporters nearby said they heard Cohn threaten to "get Jackson for this," and obviously Roy was infuriated. For a moment it appeared that the pair would come to blows, but they were separated, and Senator Mundt ordered them to keep their private quarrel, whatever it was about, out of the hearings. "I don't know what it is about and I don't care, but it is of long standing and it has no business mixing in committee business. They are just popping off and they can stop it!"

Meanwhile, Flanders delivered his promised speech, the third he had made against McCarthy in a few weeks. And he gave this attack a more serious aspect by putting it in the form of a motion that the Senate strip McCarthy of his committee assignments unless he purged himself of the personal charges leveled against him by Benton in 1952 and never answered. For two years, Flanders told a scattering of his colleagues on the Senate floor, but with the galleries well filled, the Wisconsin senator had been in contempt of the Senate and he should be called to account. McCarthy had called the Benton charges a smear, and Flanders conceded that "a smear is a most annoying thing—one which is perhaps—I will not say definitely—not unknown to the junior senator from Wisconsin. But there is this about a smear: it can be removed by a dry cleaning process which involves a vigorous application of the truth. That process the senator from Wisconsin was unwilling to apply. The smear remains." Since it would be unfair not to give McCarthy a reasonable time to "change his general accusation of smear to detailed answers concerning his personal affairs," Flanders stated that he would allow his motion to lie on the desk for a while, during which interval it could be brought to a vote at any time at the request of any senator.

Flanders' action caused a flurry among the Senate's leaders since a bitter floor fight would surely result if the motion should be called up. Senator Knowland, the majority leader, warned of a further split in Republican ranks, foresaw damage to the administration's legislative program, and termed Flanders' action unjustified; but the Vermonter replied that while it might be embarrassing to the leadership, "it's past time for them to be talking like that now." Scolded by Knowland for having acted without prior consultation, "contrary to established procedure," Flanders said he had purposely consulted no one "because if I did consult them they might talk me out of it."

McCarthy seemed not at all perturbed. Back in Milwaukee for

the weekend, he was given an uproarious welcome by the state Republican convention, the cheers, whistling, and siren-blowing of the 3,000 delegates obliterating a feeble attempt at dissent. When he said defiantly that he would be bound by his own ideas of duty rather than by party regularity, the throng went wild.

"I personally don't give a tinker's dam what any newspaper, radio station, or news columnist says about me," he shouted. "I intend to do the best I can, even if I leave a few scars on my own party, because I believe the test of loyalty is not whether you play the game or follow the leader."

His twenty-minute speech was interrupted repeatedly by shouts of approval, and when an occasional voice cried out in protest, it was hooted down. The convention voted a resolution commending the senator and his accomplishments. As an afterthought, another resolution was passed commending President Eisenhower.

The next day, in Sioux Falls, South Dakota, McCarthy forecast to an American Legion convention that the hearings in Washington would result in no clear-cut decision; that the Democrats would file their report and the Republicans would file theirs, unable to agree. His voice was hoarse and he was obviously weary; and directly afterward he and his wife, who was constantly at his side, flew back to Washington for a final week of rancor and surprises.

[IV]

As the week began, reporters sensed a stirring in the caucus room: although every seat was taken, there was a feeling that the crowd was glancing toward the exits. The outbursts of temper rang like the many that had been heard before. McCarthy was patient with "the completely phony" Mr. Welch; Welch grieved over McCarthy; Symington and McCarthy exchanged barbs; Chairman Mundt vainly tried to quell what he called "mid-morning madness." Frank Carr took the stand and gave his associates unqualified support, although Welch attacked the basis of his actions in the squabble. Particularly, Welch as much as said that one key memorandum entered by the McCarthy side to back up their accusations had been falsified if not forged. The memo, apparently dictated by Carr and attributed to him, Welch insinuated had been concocted after the Army had entered its bill of particulars, and dated back several weeks. Carr denied this. McCarthy's secretary, Mary Driscoll, again proved vague as a witness, even professing to have no

preference as to which typewriter she used—a paragon among secretaries, Welch complimented her, as he admitted suavely that
he had no proof of his suspicion. The FBI document also figured
again, leading McCarthy to repeat his defiance of any security classification and his pledge to accept information about "wrongdoing
in government despite orders of anyone in the executive branch,
from the President on down. . . . I will not protect people in
crime against my government."

The most heated clashes occurred between Symington and Mc-
Carthy toward the close. In questioning Carr about the subcommittee's files, Symington brought out that numerous committee
employes who lacked clearance had access to the file room. Mc-
Carthy broke in to register his resentment of "these personal innuendoes against these young men who have been working so hard at
very low salaries to dig out Communists, without the help, I may
say, of men like Symington." As the bell rang summoning the senators to a roll-call vote in the Senate, Symington shouted that "the
files of what you call *my* staff, *my* director, *my* chief of staff, have
been the sloppiest and most dangerously handled files that I have
ever heard of since I have been in the government!"

Although Mundt hastily declared the recess, McCarthy kept
shouting into the microphone, ordering the official reporter to put
his words into the record. He called Symington's remark "the most
dishonest, the most unfounded smear" upon his entire staff; and,
when Symington turned to leave, exclaimed tauntingly: "You can
run away if you like, Stu . . . You jump up and run away without
answering the question . . . leaving a smear upon the name of
each and every one. . . . That is the same thing that the Communist party has been doing too long!"

Clutching his own microphone, his face a mask of fury, Symington retorted that any time anyone said anything critical of anybody
on McCarthy's staff, he was called a Communist—which was the
only answer he would give to the senator. And out he marched, to
considerable applause, evoked not so much by his words as by the
vehemence with which he had spoken. Joe continued to bark: "He
runs away. He won't answer the question. . . . Before this is over,
the American people will have a better picture of it!" Then, seeing
that everyone was leaving, he desisted, shrugging, "I guess we
must go vote now," and followed the others amid a smattering of
applause. At the door a woman counseled him comfortably, "Smooth
down your feathers, Joe."

On the next-to-last day, another major clash occurred between Welch and McCarthy. The Army counsel had brought the senator, at tedious length, to concur that he was a witness, and not a judge, in the controversy at issue. Using his "humility" approach, Welch pressed the point:

"Senator McCarthy, I want to say something to you, sir, with some gravity, if I may. I have, on more than one occassion, heard you say casually, quote, 'Now that the Army charges have proved entirely false,' unquote, and you have said such things, have you not? Just 'yes' or 'no.' "

"I think I have said the 'Stevens-Adams charges.' This is not an Army charge."

"May I remind you, senator," Welch continued, in his gently modulated, still-small-voice-of-conscience tone, "with all humility on my part, that you are a witness in this case and not a judge. You will agree to that, sir?"

"I'm a witness."

"And not a judge?"

"You are certainly right."

"And that your testimony today and what you may hereafter give must be weighed on the one hand by this committee, is that right, sir?"

"Obviously."

"And the country must also—or will, at least, make up its mind?"

"Yes, I think the jury that's watching on television will make up its mind, watching all the witnesses."

"And may I suggest to you, sir, that whatever the outcome, it would be more graceful, at least, for you to await the verdict rather than to announce it, so you think, from the witness chair?"

"Mr. Welch," Joe said, bristling, as Welch and everyone watching him by this time expected he would do, "may I tell you, sir, that when you or anyone else makes charges against my staff which . . . are completely unfounded—and you and I will agree now that the charges against Mr. Carr were completely without foundation— that I will not be graceful when it comes to that sort of situation. I have a duty. Let's make this clear, Mr. Welch. This is no game. This is no game. . . . And I just want to tell you, Mr. Welch, as long as it is proven now that these charges are completely fraudulent, completely unfounded, I don't think there would be anything graceful about my trying to intimate that there is something truthful about them." And on the speech rolled. The audience, those present and those thousands of miles away, had heard it many times before.

And yet, in spite of every hindrance, the end did come at last. In farewell speeches as judges the senators one by one bowed themselves out of the spotlight. Then McCarthy appealed for unanimity in getting back to the proper business of the subcommittee, outlining several investigations which he said had been marking time.

Senator McClellan put his determination bluntly, saying: "I do not believe that the testimony that has been given here . . . can be, in any process of reasoning, reconciled." He called the "lengthy and unpleasant" hearings "one of the most disgraceful episodes in the history of our government."

Senator Potter furnished the by now almost mandatory "one surprise a day" by filing a formal statement (which he later read on television) saying that he believed the principal accusations made by both sides had been borne out, even though the testimony was "saturated with statements which were not truthful and which might constitute perjury." He also believed there had been subornation of perjury, and he called for criminal prosecutions.

When Potter's statement was shown to Senator McCarthy, he appeared shocked. Senator Dirksen pleaded with Potter to withhold it from the record, but Potter would not.

It was, however, appropriate that the most gifted thespian of this all-star cast, Welch, should ring down the curtain. As he spoke the epilogue, the eagerly attentive audience could almost hear violoncellos sighing softly in the wings.

"I, alone," came the richly whimsical voice, infinitely sophisticated for all its homespun surface tone, "I, alone, came into this room from deep obscurity. I, alone, will retire to obscurity. As it folds about me softly, as I hope it does quickly, the lady who listened and is called Judith Lynden Welch will hear from me a long sigh of relief. I am sorry that this play had to take place in the fretful lightning and the ominous roll of noises from Indo-China and around the world. It saddens me to think that my life has been lived either in wars or turmoil. I can say, as I have already indicated, that I could do with a little serenity. I will allow myself to hope that soon there will come a day when there will, in this lovely land of ours, be more simple laughter."

No less yearning for serenity, Chairman Mundt thereupon adjourned the hearings *sine die*.

PART SEVEN

A Daniel Come
to Judgment

"QUONDAM: Having been formerly.
A ludicrous word."
        —Johnson's *Dictionary*

"A Challenge to Civilization?"

A general casting-up of balance sheets ensued, with the conclusion that, so far as the public was concerned, little had been changed: Those who had hated McCarthy before hated him still, and the hard core of his determined supporters had not been diminished. By general consensus, no clear verdict could possibly be rendered, the evidence on both sides being best described as "a mixed bag." It appeared beyond doubt that there had been an effort to get preferential treatment for Schine, although nothing like the unrelenting campaign which the Army charged. On the other side, the testimony showed beyond doubt that Secretary Stevens and John Adams had courted the goodwill of McCarthy and his staff egregiously in their attempt to halt or at least blunt the bad publicity the Army was getting as a result of the senator's investigations.

The only apparent change of much significance in the public view of McCarthy seemed to be a slight "edging away" from the senator. A Gallup survey showed an increase among those who believed McCarthy and Cohn had used improper means on behalf of Schine, the percentage rise being from 40 to 46. This trend was most pronounced among those who had watched the hearings ten times or more, suggesting that the longer people watched the senator in action, the less they inclined toward him. *Commonweal* long since had envisioned the ironic possibility that McCarthy might go down to defeat ultimately because people grew bored with him, rather than on a matter of principle. Boredom can be as destructive as moral indignation, and during the dreary repetitions of the television show the audience had often been bored. Joe's pitch had become stale. The crowd was seeing too much of him; the old rallying cries sounded dated. And gradually, among an important segment of the populace which heretofore had tolerated McCarthy rather

than positively endorsed him (often loving him mainly for the enemies he attracted), a feeling was discernible that perhaps Joe had
served his purpose, and that fresh leadership now was required.

Even Joe's friends agreed that McCarthy's personal performance
on television had been harmful to his cause. His heavy jowls, his
scowl, his crudity, his ruthlessness, his defiance, his bull-in-a-china-
shop lunges, his impudent interruptions, his tendentious speeches,
had built up the stereotype of a villain which no stage "heavy" could
improve upon. And while from first to last he had dominated the
action, his fascination for the audience was not altogether popularity; at times it had been the fascination of utter incredulity. At
first his courageous grappling with the Army, fellow senators, and
the administration had given him an underdog appeal; but his
reckless laying about with a bloody cleaver had alienated much of
this sympathy.

The grand-total statistics of the hearing were stupefying: thirty-
six days of testimony; thirty-two witnesses; 2,000,000 words in
7,424 pages of transcript; the cost to the government $100,000,
and to radio and television interests upward of $10,000,000;
115,000 spectators in and out of the caucus room, with standees
every day; 20,000,000 more or less enthralled citizens looking on
daily. And what had it all proved? Well, one answer ran, by Stevens'
own testimony it had firmly established that there was no rank in
the Army lower than private.

[II]

The press reaction was not restrained. The *Louisville Courier-
Journal* said bluntly: "In this long, degrading travesty of the democratic process there have been no heroes. Senator McCarthy has
shown himself to be evil and unmatched in malice. Secretary
Stevens stands naked as a man of weak principle and little pride."

The *Kansas City Star* felt that "everyone involved in the hassle
got hurt—most of all the country."

To the *Buffalo Evening News* "the bitter battle ended with no
clearcut winners—only losers . . . with all wounds open, with
daggers flying, with hate triumphant."

The *New York Daily News* put it in everyday speech: "As to who
was lying, it seemed to us that both sides pulled some fast ones."

And the *Pittsburgh Post-Gazette* felt that the conflict had now progressed to a different phase: "The Senate has yet to deal with a colleague whose obsessive hunt for subversives at times borders on lunacy."

Still Senator Flanders' motion lay undisposed of. Senator Knowland wished to refer it to the Rules Committee, where it could be trusted to stay buried, inasmuch as the chairman of that committee was Senator Jenner, McCarthy's ardent ally. Flanders was resisting this attempted maneuver and at last was receiving organized help.

McCarthy had produced his usual extreme effect upon Flanders, and from simple tolerance the latter had progressed to viewing his Wisconsin colleague as the incarnation of absolute evil. In a television interview, Flanders insisted that what was at stake, in his opinion, was the survival of Western civilization. "This difficulty goes back over the last 1,500 years," he said. "That is the stage upon which this little incident is being played. Anyone who cannot see this as the crisis of this civilization is blind."

While the television audience might not be either prepared or equipped to wrestle with a proposition of such magnitude, the haters of McCarthy were. Convinced that Flanders would stand fast, a number of knowledgeable volunteers came to his aid, providing advice, money, and strategy-planning by Capitol Hill experts. This group supplemented his meager clerical staff, lobbied at the Capitol, wrote speeches, raised funds, organized demonstrations, brought pressure to bear on senators from influential men and women in their home states, and gave Flanders' motion the systematic backing it had previously lacked.

The brunt of this activity fell on the so-called clearinghouse of information about McCarthy established under cover of the National Committee for an Effective Congress. This counter-intelligence group had been functioning sporadically; now it swung into full action, assembling a corps of both paid and voluntary workers, with the object of preventing the demise of Flanders' motion by parliamentary sleight-of-hand. Under coaching, Flanders dropped his demand that Senator McCarthy be deprived of his committee assignments and substituted Senate Resolution 301, calling for a vote of general censure. As introduced, this resolution read:

"*Resolved,* that the conduct of the junior senator from Wisconsin is unbecoming a member of the United States Senate, is contrary to senatorial traditions, and tends to bring the Senate into disrepute, and such conduct is hereby condemned."

The twelve-man Republican policy committee voted to support Senator Knowland in a motion to table the resolution without debate. The Democratic policy committee voted to leave the issue open for each senator to vote as his conscience bade him. Seeking a middle road, Senator Smith of New Jersey proposed the appointment of a bipartisan committee to examine the conduct of Senator McCarthy and report to the Senate. The practical reality of the situation was that few senators relished the prospect of taking a stand on McCarthy on election eve. So the chips were down when Flanders' resolution was called up for action in the Senate on July 30. McCarthy was on hand, just back from a seventeen-day vacation with his wife south of the border. Picking up the reins of his subcommittee immediately, he had blocked a Democratic demand for a housecleaning of the staff. This he had done by refusing to accept the proxy of Senator McClellan, who was absent in Arkansas, engaged in a hot primary fight. Although Senator Potter had voted with the Democrats, the minority had been unable to carry the day. But facing a certain vote for his dismissal as soon as McClellan returned to Washington, Roy Cohn resigned as chief counsel. McCarthy accepted the resignation with expressed regret; his feeling was that Roy had been "mantrapped in the rough game of politics we play down here."

The Flanders resolution promised a test of strength, and on the day of the debate the Senate galleries were crowded. In the front row of the section reserved for the wives of senators Jean McCarthy was seated.

Ninety senators were on the floor, an unusually high number. McCarthy bounced in, greeting friends, clapping them on the back, waving gaily to Jean. He seemed in the best of spirits as the business got under way.

Flanders led off, speaking for twenty minutes. He contended that McCarthy had "spread contempt over the entire Senate" by his behavior. The attack was fumbling, but the speech was merely the kickoff in a debate of extraordinary bitterness.

Immediate objection to Flanders' loosely worded resolution came from an unexpected quarter. Senator Wayne Morse, who was by no means an ally of McCarthy, termed the motion an invitation to "procedural tyranny" and "lynch law." If the senator were to be condemned, Morse insisted, people had a right to know for what acts he merited censure. "I think there are plenty of such acts," he said, "but I think they ought to be stated in a bill of particulars" and then taken up in a judicial way, with presentation of proof, before a verdict was reached.

Senator Fulbright thereupon offered an amendment to the resolution, listing six specific charges, ranging from acceptance of the $10,000 Lustron fee, through the Annie Lee Moss, General Zwicker, and General Marshall incidents, to McCarthy's urging government employes to violate their oaths of office by feeding him secret information. McCarthy read a newspaper during most of Fulbright's speech.

New Jersey's Smith, anxious to effect a peaceful compromise, invited McCarthy to "join with us . . . play ball with us," and work out some way to get rid of "some of the things that have occurred" for which the senator might have merited censure. This overture brought McCarthy to his feet with a statement that if "playing ball" meant "I would quit digging out Communists, then I will never play that brand of ball!"

Senator Dirksen, speaking in McCarthy's favor, ticked off the strange agglomeration of forces that were egging on the Senate to "do something about McCarthy." The list included the *Daily Worker,* the CIO, the ADA, the Committee for an Effective Congress (which had set up a lobbying center in the Carroll Arms Hotel, next door to the Senate Office Building)—these, said Dirksen, were the sort of partisans who had "jumped into bed" with Flanders.

For three days the debate went on, and toward the end McCarthy treated the Senate to another of his virtuoso performances. In a speech that flouted every canon of the Senate, he cited his critics by name, dealt in personal insults, and taunted his accusers with unveracity, but he did not yield an inch. He denied nothing. He asked for no hearing, for no vindication. For days, he said, he had sat "listening to scurrilous, defamatory, false statements," and he compelled Flanders to read into the *Record,* one by one, thirty-three specific accusations, which Flanders admitted had been prepared at his request by the Committee for an Effective Congress,

and in support of which not one scrap of documentation or proof
was offered.* The indictment took exception to practically everything about McCarthy and his entire career. His staff assistants
were ridiculed, a description of Roy Cohn's asserted arrogance
drawing laughter when Flanders interpolated (but withheld from
the official *Record*) that "Mr. Cohn habitually rang three bells for
the Senate elevator [the signal reserved for senators], and when the
elevator boy asked him, 'Where is the senator?" he said, 'I am
here.' " Flanders said he enjoyed reading the long list.

The violence of McCarthy's headlong counterattack almost
succeeded in placing his accusers on the defensive. He demanded
that they pledge themselves to honor subpoenas in any investigation of his actions and "either indict themselves for perjury or
prove what consummate liars they are." And at the close he stalked
out, disdaining to remain for Fulbright's rebuttal, in which the
latter accorded Joe "the most extraordinary talent for disruption
and causing confusion . . . that I have ever seen." The scene
was not televised, and the public caught only a pale reflection of
the ferocity of the drama. On the strength of that performance,
the *New Republic* was tempted to credit McCarthy with more than
talent—with positive genius, of a malevolent sort.

The sense of the Senate had gravitated toward adopting a procedure that conformed to its traditions, as an immediate vote of
censure would not. The action decided upon was to authorize
the appointment by the Vice-President of a select committee, composed of three Republicans and three Democrats, to examine the
charges against the Wisconsin senator and report their recommendations to the Senate. Senator Knowland offered the motion
and it was accepted gratefully on both sides of the aisle. The vote
authorizing the committee was 75 to 12, with eight senators not
voting and McCarthy voting "present."

[III]

The committee chosen by Vice-President Nixon to conduct the
investigation was carefully selected to assure the public a dignified,
impartial inquiry. All six members were conservatives, representa-

---

* Even the *New Republic* confessed that this scattershot blast included "many
acts of a boorish man which still do not constitute grounds for punishment by
the Senate."

ting states in the South and West where McCarthy had never been a major issue. Only one was up for reelection, and he faced no opposition to speak of.

The Republicans were Arthur V. Watkins of Utah, Frank Carlson of Kansas, and Francis Case of South Dakota; the Democrats were John C. Stennis of Mississippi, Edwin C. Johnson of Colorado, and Sam J. Ervin of North Carolina. Ervin, Stennis, and Watkins were former judges. All were jealous of the dignity of the Senate, and all accepted the assignment reluctantly and from a sense of duty only.

This was especially true of Senator Watkins, who was named chairman. In him there was no trace of levity. Sixty-seven years old, a devout Mormon, president of his church, of unblemished integrity, possessing granite determination, he had been elected to the Senate at the same time as McCarthy, and their desks adjoined each other.

Watkins made clear at once that this investigation would be marked by none of the antics that had characterized the Army hearings. Radio and television were to be excluded, and for a while Watkins even meditated excluding the press and issuing a transcript after each day's session. In the end he relented and let reporters in, but under stern control.

In the opinion of most observers, McCarthy was in serious trouble. The most celebrated of Senate investigators had become its most investigated member. Four committees had undertaken the task, and this one, the fifth, would have available an accumulation of data extending back for years.

This time McCarthy did entrust his defense to counsel, choosing Edward Bennett Williams. The attorney accepted only after Joe had promised to refrain from interfering and to leave the conduct of the case in counsel's hands. And except for one or two outbursts, he kept this promise; but what Williams did not realize until too late was that McCarthy had made no promise about remaining silent outside the hearing room. This oversight was to cost the attorney sleepless nights.

Watkins made his objective plain at the start. "Let's get off the front pages and back among the obituaries," he said. "That would suit us just fine." The wish sounded as grim to the reporters as it did to Joe. And on August 30, the hearings got under way.

A Study in Severity

Almost overlooked in the hubbub about the censure hearings were the findings of the investigations subcommittee on the Army-McCarthy hearings. As most people had expected, there were two main reports, both strictly party-line affairs. The Republicans—Mundt, Dirksen, and Dworshak—mildly criticized everybody, reprehended Roy Cohn severely for his actions in behalf of Schine, did the same toward Adams and Stevens, but found that the charges on neither side had been proved. The Democrats—McClellan, Symington, and Jackson—denounced Cohn's conduct, held McCarthy equally blamable, and castigated Stevens for lack of integrity when confronted with blatant misbehavior. Senator Potter filed his individual judgment, calling for perjury indictments all around. And Senator Dirksen put on record his "supplementary views" to the effect that the testimony had certainly reflected an "extraordinary readiness on the part of the Secretary of the Army to please Mr. Schine," but failed to exhibit "pressure, improper or otherwise, in any significant degree."

The *New York Daily News* remarked that the "four soft, wet reports fell with four soft, wet thuds." *The Nation* dismissed the entire fracas as a hoax and a farce—conducted by "the wrong methods, by the wrong committee, assigned to investigate the wrong set of charges, filed by the wrong accusers." Thus ended the mighty "Army-McCarthy Affair." The public glanced at the contradictory conclusions and forgot them, though what had crossed their television screens the public would never forget. The Watkins Committee's inquiry was the new focus of national interest.

These hearings offered a striking contrast to the ballyhooed spectacle of a few weeks before. The setting was the familiar Senate caucus room; but there were no hot lights, no air of expectancy, no hubbub, rather the coolly deliberate, subdued atmosphere of a courtroom. Significantly, this time McCarthy was not seated with his peers at the long table; he and his counsel were assigned seats at a small table facing the six men who would judge his conduct. The arrangement underlined, none too subtly, that he was a defendant.

The first task of the committee had been to reduce the mass of accusations and evidence to manageable dimensions; discard the rumors, hearsay, and extraneous matter, and then organize the substantive accusations into clearly defined categories. One category covered McCarthy's personal finances. A second took in his attitude toward senators and Senate committees. A third covered his acceptance of classified information without authorization. The fourth concerned his encouraging government employes to break the law. And the fifth related to his asserted abuse of witnesses before his committee, especially General Zwicker.

McCarthy made his bid to dominate the hearings at the outset. He had prepared a preliminary statement, which had been handed to the committee and the press before the session started; and he requested permission to read it. Chairman Watkins stated coldly that although the statement was not relevant, "we are not going to prevent Senator McCarthy from making that statement, and we will now permit him to proceed."

"Thank you, Mr. Chairman," responded McCarthy. But Watkins was not through.

"And we want it understood," the dry voice went on, "that this is not a precedent to the reception of any matter in the way of testimony or evidence that is irrelevant, incompetent, and immaterial."

Under the handicap of that damper, McCarthy read his statement without much zest. It proved to be a tedious rehash of all his alarms regarding the danger of Communist infiltration and his own part in carrying on the struggle, "as best I know how," against an "unholy alliance" of three inimical forces, differently motivated but rallying to a common standard—"the Communists and their sympathizers . . . those who do not sympathize with communism but deny that it presents a serious threat . . . those who profess to appreciate the strength of the Communist fifth column but balk at taking vigorous measures to stamp it out." Should these interlocking forces prevail, he warned, their victory would be celebrated over "the grave of American civilization."

The statement read, Senator Watkins announced that the committee "will now proceed to consideration of matters . . . deemed of first importance. . . . Number one, 'Incidents of contempt of the Senate or a senatorial committee.' " And that was the end of Joe's opening gambit.

McCarthy's counsel moved to dismiss the first group of charges on legalistic grounds, contending that the 83rd Congress had no power to review decisions or actions taken by the 80th, 81st, or 82nd Congresses. Williams was allowed to make an oral statement, although Watkins explained that the committee had already weighed that point and had decided against him; nevertheless he might file a brief. As Williams attempted to elaborate his oral argument, he was told curtly but politely: "You can submit your brief. You are not being denied a hearing; submit your brief."

Distressed by this tactic, but bound by his pledge not to interfere, McCarthy retreated to the corridor and vented his shock over the microphones there.

Returning to the committee room, he tried a maneuver that had served repeatedly to plunge the Senate and previous committee hearings into inextricable confusion: He attacked the makeup of the committee on the ground of bias.

The evening before, he and Williams had called to the attention of the press and the committee an item that had appeared in the *Denver Post* the previous March 12, in which Senator Johnson had been quoted as saying: "In my opinion there is not a man among the Democratic leaders of Congress who does not loathe McCarthy. . . . I do not think there are more than half a dozen Republicans who think McCarthy is all right."

When the committee convened on the morning after this disclosure, Senator Johnson asked permission to make a statement.

"Mr. Chairman," the big Coloradan said deliberately, "I did not say, on March 12 or at any other time, that I personally loathed Senator Joseph McCarthy. I did agree that some of my Democratic colleagues did not like Senator McCarthy, [but] I have full faith in my ability to weigh the charges . . . against Senator McCarthy . . . without prejudice."

Williams was not satisfied; he wished to discuss Johnson's fitness to sit as a judge. But Watkins cut him short: "I do not think it is necessary to this hearing. . . . Senator Johnson was appointed by the Senate and this committee has no authority to remove him or even accept a resignation of his from the committee. Since that is the record, why is it necessary to clutter it up with a lot of extraneous matter . . . immaterial to this hearing? We are not trying Senator Johnson."

This was more than McCarthy could bear, and unmindful of his promise to abstain from interfering, he broke in:

"Mr. Chairman, I have desisted from making any comments so far, and I would like to ask a question, if I may——"

Bang went Watkins' gavel. "Just a moment, senator," he said. "Let us get this clear: when your counsel speaks on a matter, that precludes you from addressing the chair on the same matter. If you want to take it over yourself, why, then, state it, and we will let you finish it. But we are not going to let both of you argue this matter."

Surely they had a right to ask Senator Johnson whether the newspaper had quoted him correctly, Williams urged, and Watkins agreed that they certainly did have that right; but on their own time, outside the hearing room.

"Mr. Chairman," McCarthy exploded, "are we entitled to know whether or not the quotations of March 12th are correct or incorrect? I would like to know whether the *Denver Post*——"

Bang went the gavel. "You may get it, senator, and I am going to rule on this, and I have already ruled, you may get that some other place. But this committee has no jurisdiction over such matters whatsoever. This committee was appointed by the Senate; the only condition laid down was that there should be three Democrats and three Republicans, and here there are three Democrats and three Republicans, and this committee is not going to take on the job of the Senate and is not going to decide whether this committee is a proper committee or not. This committee is——"

"Mr. Chairman"—McCarthy's voice rose in the familiar insistent whine—"I should be entitled to know whether or not——"

Watkins: "The senator is out of order."

"Can't I get Senator Johnson to tell me——"

"The senator is out of order."

"——whether it is true or false?"

"The senator is out of order. You can go to the senator and question him and find out. That is not for this committee to consider. We are not going to be interrupted by these diversions and sidelines. We are going straight down the line." And the merciless gavel banged for a recess.

McCarthy was out of control. Vainly his counsel tried to calm him. Rushing into the corridor, Joe shouted into the radio and television microphones, "This is the most unheard of thing I ever heard of!"

But Watkins' ruling stuck, and day by day evidence was read into the record by the drab voice of the committee counsel, while McCarthy slumped in smouldering anger or in sullen indifference. Denied the right to disrupt, he was helpless. Physically he had deteriorated; he had acquired a paunch, and his jowls hung slack. Now and then he would start to life, but every attempt to inject himself into the humorless proceedings was instantly squelched by the implacable chairman. The record was all that Watkins deemed admissible, and it unrolled in ruthless candor.

Privately Joe told reporters that all he wanted was to "get this thing over with"; and when the time came for him to enter his defense, he did so with a rush. He denied nothing, but justified his whole conduct, year by year, item by item. He would not concede that he had abused witnesses. He called General Zwicker "arrogant, evasive, and irritating, well meriting castigation." Regarding his statement that Zwicker was not fit to wear the uniform, he was unrepentant, insisting: "I said that then, and I say it now, and I'll say it again." Yes, he admitted, he had called Senator Flanders "senile" and suggested that "a man with a net" ought to take him away, but Flanders had vilified him with "obscenities." As for the famous two-and-one-quarter-page document drawn from an FBI report which McCarthy had brandished in the Army hearings, he scoffed that it was not "so very confidential," and urged the committee to read it. Williams handed the paper to Watkins, who mumbled something about "a serious matter . . . no place to argue it," and slipped it into his pocket, and that was that.

Williams called General Lawton as a witness and drew from him that in conversation with General Zwicker three months before the latter's clash with McCarthy, he had formed the definite opinion that Zwicker was antagonistic to the senator. Another witness, who had been seated in front of Zwicker during a subcommittee hearing, testified that he had overheard Zwicker mutter "you s.o.b." in reference to McCarthy.*

* Senator Malone's biting comment was: "And I don't think he meant Senate Office Building."

Joe's judges afforded him every opportunity to bolster his case. Several times the chairman indicated a possible loophole, suggesting that this or that action "might have been an honest mistake, might it not?" McCarthy scorned to take advantage of such weaseling; in fact, the *New Republic* thought that the mere idea of hiding behind "an honest mistake" was "enough to make Joe McCarthy vomit."

[II]

Hewing steadily to the line, the committee was able to begin assembling its recommendations in late September, just as the political forecasters were studying the outcome of the September primary elections for clues to any shift in the wind of McCarthy's popularity with voters. But no positive trends were discernible— except in Wisconsin. On Joe's home grounds the results in four primary contests, two of them of major significance, appeared to show that the senator's stock in his home state was at its rock-bottom low. In all four contests the senator had been an issue; and the four winners all had openly repudiated him.

Then the Watkins Committee filed its report with the Senate. It was exhaustive, voluminous, and unanimous, and its recommendations were clear-cut.* On two counts the committee recommended censure; thirty-three counts were thrown out for reasons fully stated; and on three groups of charges the senator was given the benefit of the more charitable construction and no censure was suggested, although his conduct under these headings was reprobated in terms so harsh they fell just short of censure.

The first charge on which censure was recommended was contempt of the Gillette subcommittee in 1951, including McCarthy's characterization of Senator Hendrickson of New Jersey as "a living miracle . . . without brains or guts." His attitude toward the subcommittee was termed "contemptuous, contumacious, and denunciatory, without reason or justification, and obstructive to legislative processes."

The second count on which censure was urged was McCarthy's treatment of General Zwicker; this was held to be "reprehensible" and without justification.

---

* As published in *The New York Times,* it filled forty-six columns of fine type.

The committee had winnowed the original forty-odd accusations against McCarthy until only nineteen remained for consideration, and on most of these the verdict was just short of total condemnation.

Presentation of this report on the eve of the November elections threw the Senate leadership into a tailspin, and agreement was quickly reached between Knowland and Lyndon Johnson to postpone consideration until after the voting. Most senators breathed easier on learning that they would not be compelled to take a stand on the controversial recommendations immediately.

McCarthy had taken no part in the election campaign, turning down all invitations to speak on behalf of Republican candidates. When the returns were in, it was found that the Democrats had regained control of Congress—control which they would assume when the new Congress met in January. The question, of course, was hotly debated as to what influence McCarthy's absence had played in determining the outcome. It was anybody's (and just about everybody's) guess; nobody really knew, or was able to convince anyone else that he knew.

On November 8 the Senate—the lame-duck Senate—was to convene in extraordinary session to debate the censure of its most rambunctious member. Those adverse to McCarthy were not sanguine. One of his less courtly critics. *The Nation,* sourly reflected:

"Joe is about to be branded 'uncouth' and 'no gentleman.' But on that we thought everybody agreed, Joe included."

"Once More unto the Breach"

[I]

The occasion was unparalleled. Although three other senators (and only three) had been censured by their fellows since the start of the republic, never before had the Senate been called together for the sole purpose of disciplining one of their select number.*

Joe showed up looking trimmer, healthier, and more cheerful than he had for weeks, his waistline slimmed down, his color good, and the sluggishness that had weighed him down during the recent hearings replaced by energy and his customary aggressiveness. He bragged to reporters, "I can go fifteen rounds!" and he almost looked it.

The Watkins report had been filed almost on the anniversary of the McCarthys' marriage, and Jean McCarthy joked that it had been an appropriate first-year present—paper, of course. But the brilliant gathering of Washington's political elite who had toasted the couple twelve months before was conspicuously missing now. In politics-ruled Washington, the McCarthys had passed under a social cloud; recently Mrs. Eisenhower had observed a studied coolness toward the senator's wife, to whom for a while she had been most cordial.

McCarthy harbored no illusion that he would escape censure. In most respects politically he was clear-sighted and realistic, and he knew the temper of the Senate as well as any man living. He predicted an easy victory for his foes, censure requiring only a majority vote and not one of two-thirds, as expulsion would; but

---

* In 1902, Senators Tillman and McLaurin, South Carolina Democrats, were censured for resorting to "abusive and provocative" language—and fisticuffs—on the floor. In 1919, Senator Bingham, Connecticut Republican, was censured for bringing a lobbyist into an executive meeting.

he seemed to feel that he could absorb the blow and emerge later stronger than ever.

That he still commanded political muscle was obvious. In the Senate he could count on a small but intensely loyal group of supporters who would not falter, and their votes might provide enough countervailing influence to affect some votes in either party. The overriding issue—anticommunism—was still his: a pre-election canvass conducted by the Republicans in ten critical states had shown that, next to foreign policy, the threat of domestic communism topped all other subjects of concern to the electorate. Meanwhile, a movement was under way nationally to collect ten million signatures on a petition protesting against the censure of McCarthy. Called "Ten Million Americans Mobilizing for Justice," the drive was under the direction of retired Air Force General George E. Stratemeyer, an ardent supporter of Joe. Daily the senator's office was crowded with well-wishers.

On November 10, Senator Watkins led off the debate with a restrained, dispassionate presentation of his committee's findings. Both sides were prepared for a no-holds-barred struggle, and a few of McCarthy's extreme partisans were talking about a chance to stave off defeat; he did not share their optimism. His opponents were wary, knowing him to be resourceful, audacious, and fast-acting—more so than most of his colleagues. More than once, when apparently on the ropes, he had rallied and routed an over-confident opponent by a surprise attack. This time his antagonists were determined to win by nothing less than a knockout. And the Watkins indictment was so lethally comprehensive, calm, and judicial in tone that it was felt the Senate could not do otherwise than adopt its recommendations.

One maneuver that McCarthy's enemies dreaded was a possible attempt to filibuster the report to death. The 83rd Congress would expire on December 24, and should no vote be taken by then, the report, also, would die, the incoming Senate having no authority to act on a report to its predecessor. McCarthy's defenders, under the leadership of Senator Dirksen, denied any intention of filibustering, but the other side remained suspicious.

Joe could hardly have exuded greater confidence. On November 14, sixteen hundred of his admirers tendered him a birthday banquet (it was his forty-sixth birthday) in Milwaukee, and he assured them, amid cheers, that "regardless of what is done at this circus in Washington . . . I intend to continue . . . until our civilization wins this war against foreign ideologies." The crowd sang, "Nobody loves McCarthy but the people," and one well-wisher pumped Joe's hand so enthusiastically that he banged the senator's right elbow on the furniture and inflicted a painful injury.

Meanwhile, with guns firing in the Senate chamber, conciliators were busy backstage seeking a formula that would provide an "out" mutually acceptable to all parties, circumventing censure. These peacemakers were actuated by different motives: some wished to spare McCarthy the odium of being censured, while others wished to spare his colleagues the odium certain to flow from taking an unpopular stand in the controversy.

Joe was scornful of compromises. He would not head off censure by apologizing for his remarks or actions; he would not apologize to anyone; he had taken his stand and would not retreat one inch. And he had not only a case to present, but the actions of some of his accusers were questionable enough; yet perversely he seemed bent on harming his own cause. The only style of fighting he comprehended was attack, and he attacked wildly, furiously, without logic or precision. His attacks were not only ill-considered, they were ill-tempered and ill-timed, and their effect was self-destructive. He was the despair of his defenders, for he stopped at nothing. He seemed like a battle-maddened corsair, who, foreseeing inevitable defeat, chooses to blow his ship and himself to kingdom come rather than strike his colors. The match was applied when he inserted in the *Record* a speech full of fury denouncing the debate as a "lynch party" and a "lynch bee," and maintaining that in trying to discredit him, Senator Watkins and his associates had made themselves the "unwitting handmaidens" and the "attorneys-in-fact" of the Communist party.

This outrageous affront struck at each senator, insulting the dignity and self-respect of each too flagrantly to be passed over. Too long had they consented to be bullied, by their silence acquiescing; too long had they been browbeaten and abused. Now the Senate, even the Senate of the United States, rebelled.

Senator Ervin, a member of the Watkins Committee, demanded McCarthy's expulsion from the Senate, holding censure too lenient a penalty for so gross an offense. Senator Stennis, another committee member, protested that the good work McCarthy had done iu fighting communism gave him no license to bespatter the entire

Senate with "slush and slime." Half a dozen Republicans crossed the aisle to pump Stennis' hand, and the shocked Watkins thanked his colleague "from the bottom of my heart."

Driven to desperation, Senator Jenner, Joe's staunch supporter, finally warned him to his face that he alienated friends every time he opened his mouth. One of McCarthy's most trusted advisers, Clarence E. Manion, the former dean of Notre Dame law school, was brought in to add his caution, but it had little effect.

Meanwhile, cracks had been appearing in the anti-McCarthy front, starting with a declaration by Senator Case, a Watkins Committee member, that further study of the Peress case had convinced him that censure for asserted abuse of General Zwicker would not be warranted, and that he would not vote for censure on that count. Case's objection was concurred in by several influential Democrats, including McClellan of Arkansas and Russell of Georgia. In the new Congress McClellan would head the committee now under McCarthy, and Russell would become chairman of the powerful Armed Services Committee, and both announced that they would not condemn McCarthy for the Zwicker incident.

Dramatically, at the height of the bitterness, Senator Capehart pleaded with his associates not to contribute to the deep division already existing among Americans on the subject of McCarthy. Anywhere in the United States, he said, "if there are six people gathered together and the subject of McCarthy or 'McCarthyism' is brought up . . . those pople will take sides, and before it is over the division will become very, very bitter." And McCarthy's "devoted few" defenders continued to denounce the efforts to "wash out . . . the one man in the United States who has been trying to fight communism at home, on the grounds that he has been a little too rough."

Then precisely at this climax, Senator McCarthy was taken to the hospital. The elbow injured by the overzealous admirer's handshake had brought on a serious infection and intensive treatment was required. With the defendant in the case unable to appear, the Senate voted a two-week recess.

[II]

McCarthy's enemies were infuriated. They declared that this was another trick, that the senator was shamming, that he had "run out" in order to give the "fixers" time to patch up some crawling compromise. But McCarthy did return to the Senate, his right arm in a sling, and the debate was resumed on November 29.

By now the Senate was sick of the McCarthy question and was only desirous of winding up the business. As for the public, most people had given up trying to unravel the tangled skein of charge and countercharge, and the division in opinion, for or against the embattled senator, was permanently settled. Senator Flanders, the meek cause of the storm on the Senate floor, sat through the hurricane patiently and placidly, seldom speaking and occasionally encountering difficulty in staying awake.

On the next-to-last day of the debate, Senator Watkins spoke again, this time in a spirit of indignation. He had thought, he said, that he had been ordered to conduct an investigation, but "at times I have felt that I am on trial." Without equivocation, he called for censure. Then Senator Knowland at last joined the Eisenhower-led lineup against Joe and announced that he would vote for censure. Immediately Lyndon Johnson, minority leader, broke his silence and said he, too, would vote for censure. McCarthy's language toward fellow senators, said Johnson, would be "more fittingly inscribed on the wall of a men's room. . . . In my mind there is only one issue here—morality and conduct. Each of us must decide whether we approve or disapprove of certain actions as standards of senatorial integrity."

Senator Dirksen worked for a compromise to the last minute, several times hitting upon a formula that was acceptable to the other side, but each time McCarthy refused to budge. The night before the vote was to be taken, Dirksen and Senator Goldwater pleaded for hours with McCarthy to accept a substitute resolution that would express disapproval of his conduct, but without formal censure, if it were accompanied by a semi-apology on his part. He listened to their plea and said no. To surrender, he explained doggedly, would be disloyal to all those who had fought for his cause; it would be unfair to the millions who believed in him— "they would think I crawled."

On December 2 the vote was taken. In a parliamentary shuffle the Zwicker indictment had been quietly eliminated, Lyndon Johnson having warned Watkins privately that at least fifteen Democrats would vote against it. Substituted was a resolution of general censure for contempt of the Senate as a whole, based on McCarthy's slurring of the debate as a "lynch bee." The resolution regarding contempt of the Gillette subcommittee in 1951 was retained. But in the final wording neither resolution contained the word "censure"; instead, McCarthy's conduct on both counts was found to have been contrary to the ethics and traditions of the Senate, and tending to bring the Senate into disrepute, and was "hereby condemned."

On roll call, the two-count "condemnation" was approved by 67 to 22. Every Democrat present (44) voted to condemn, and so did 22 Republicans. Senator Morse of Oregon, who since leaving the Republicans had listed himself as an Independent, voted with the majority. Senator Wiley, McCarthy's Republican Wisconsin colleague, did not vote, and the only Democratic senator neither voting nor announcing his stand was John F. Kennedy of Massachusetts, who was in a hospital in New York. Senator McCarthy voted "present." *

A curious scene followed the announcement of the vote. Senator Styles Bridges of New Hampshire arose to inquire whether the Senate had actually voted on a resolution of censure. Vice-President Nixon read the texts, in which the word used was "condemned."

"Then," said Bridges, "it is not a resolution of censure," whereupon Senators Jenner, Malone, and Welker broke into hysterical laughter. Calling for a dictionary, Senator Fulbright read aloud the definitions of "censure" and "condemn" to prove that they were interchangeable.

Exercising his prerogative, the Vice-President struck the word "censure" out of the title, making it read: "Resolution Relating to the Conduct of the Senator from Wisconsin, Mr. McCarthy."

As the session broke up, Joe, his arm in a sling, was asked by a reporter what he thought of the vote.

"Well," he replied wryly, "it wasn't exactly a vote of confidence."

Asked what he proposed to do next, he said he would go right on "digging out communism, crime, and corruption."

But as he said it, his face was gray and his shoulders stooped.

---

* Kennedy would be haunted for years by questions concerning the possible political expediency of that hospital visit, and its possible strategic timing.

And Addenda...

"Whether to see life as it is, will give us much consolation, I know not; but the consolation which is drawn from truth, if any there be, is solid and durable; that which may be derived from errour, must be, like its original, fallacious and fugitive."

—Samuel Johnson, in a letter
to Bennet Langton, Esq.

[I]

Since this is not a biography, the rest of the story may be told more briefly. December 2, 1954, marked the effective end of the McCarthy Affair, although its backwash would churn on long afterward.

Four years of unremitting turbulence, of strain and drawing upon all his reserves of energy, had affected McCarthy physically as well as mentally, and his health had been undermined at the same time that his tactical judgment had been warped. Once his sense of timing had been acute; now it seemed to have abandoned him. During the censure debate his friends had been alarmed by his occasional lapses into brooding and petulant moodiness. He became convinced that he was being pursued with deliberate malice by Eisenhower, and after the vote he muttered privately that the resolutions would never have been voted except for the President's interference. The fact that nearly half the Republican representation in the Senate had voted against censure indicated to him that only pressure from the White House had dragooned the others into joining the Democrats in the campaign to destroy him. The Democrats had voted as a party, without a single defection, he pointed out, while twenty-two Republicans had helped to chastise one of their own party. Unless White House pressure had been exerted on these "suicidal" twenty-two, Joe reasoned, so unnatural an alliance could not be accounted for. He knew that Flanders had been covertly encouraged by the White House. He knew that at the close of the Army hearings Joseph Welch had been invited to a private meeting with the President to receive the latter's congratulations. And Senator Knowland's last-minute lining up with the enemy could only have been in obedience to a White House command.

Had not Eisenhower publicly felicitated the Senate upon "a job
well done"?

The spark that set off the final explosion came when Joe learned
that Senator Watkins had been summoned to the White House to
receive the Presidential praise personally. Five days after the censure vote, McCarthy burst into a hearing of his own subcommittee,
at which Senator Mundt was presiding, and said he wished to make
a statement. Mundt, seeing his agitation, advised against it, but
Joe insisted. "They're shooting at me from the other end of the
Avenue!" he exclaimed. "I've got to say something!" And over
Mundt's protest he then read into the record his "swan song" as
committee chairman:

"During the Eisenhower campaign I spoke from coast to coast
promising the American people that if they would elect the Eisenhower administration that they could be assured of a vigorous,
forceful drive against Communists in government. Unfortunately,
in that I was mistaken. I find that the President, on one hand, con-
gratulates senators who hold up the work of our committee, and
on the other hand urges that we be patient with the Communist
hoodlums who as of this very moment are torturing and brain-
washing American uniformed men in Communist dungeons. . . .
There has been considerable talk about an apology to the Senate
for my fight against communism. I feel rather that I should apologize to the American people for what was an unintentional deception upon them."

This was the last straw: political madness could go no further.
Even those sympathizers who had stuck with him through all his
previous battles dropped away. Most of the senators who had voted
against censure quickly dissociated themselves from the outburst.
McCarthy's most fervent advocate in the military, General James A.
Van Fleet, former commander of the Eighth Army in Korea, fired
off a telegram: "Withdrawing all support. Shocked by your personal bitter attack on our great President."

A rumor flared that McCarthy was planning to head a third
party, and it gained such currency that Eisenhower was asked about
it at his press conference. He replied that if there were people who
wished to break away from his party and administration, they
were at liberty to do so. He believed that he had put together a
progressive program, and he hoped that all who thought the way

he did would help to implement it; that was all he could say. It was sufficient: for all practical purposes, McCarthy thereby became a pariah in his party, politically as good as dead.

[II]

In the Senate, Joe became the man who wasn't there. The censure carried no stated penalties: he was still a senator, deprived of none of his privileges; but except in cold formalities his existence was ignored. When he arose to speak, the chamber emptied. If he presented a motion, it was booted to death by a contemptuously crushing vote. He continued to utter the same phrases and belabor the familiar themes, but his words were as hollow as those of a baby babbling in a barrel. He wrote speeches; they might have been written in smoke.

Even this might not have been final, had McCarthy retained his forum—the nation's front pages. Often the press had been accused of "creating" McCarthy by inflating him and his pronouncements in the early stages, and to some extent the criticism was justified. It was argued that had the press, in the days after the Wheeling speech, buried it "back among the obituaries," Joe's anticommunism crusade might never have got off the ground; that it was the persistence of reporters that had forced Senator Lucas to take cognizance of McCarthy's random shot; and that under the eagerness of the press for sensational headlines the issue had snowballed and made the senator a celebrity overnight.

But if the newspapers had erred by overplaying the senator when he was obscure, they atoned now by consigning him to obscurity again—the obscurity of occasional mention in the back pages. And in imposing this virtual blackout on the man who had so long been the source of some of the press's biggest and most exploitable sensations, the press was aided by the spirit of the times. The temper of public feeling at the moment McCarthy first appeared nationally had carried him, with the avid collaboration of the press, to instantaneous celebrity and spreading influence; and that public mood had been built up by the actions of others over a long stretch of time. At the critical instant McCarthy had precipitated the crisis, and the press reaction had been a part of that precipitation. Now the temper of the times had changed, and the vote of censure had caused a different precipitation of sentiment regarding Joe. Senator Monroney, once a newspaperman, had predicted the effect the Senator's condemnation would have.

"The difference between McCarthy before censure and McCarthy after censure is the difference between getting headlines on page one and being buried back with the classified ads," he said. "From here on out, McCarthy will wear a scarlet 'C' on his chest—a 'C' for censure. From here on out, when newsmen write about him, they will describe him in the lead of their stories as the man who was condemned by his colleagues for his conduct."

And so it was. Censured on December 2, before the end of the year McCarthy had virtually vanished from the news columns. Within two weeks of the censure, the Gridiron Club's annual skit, in which the Washington press corps traditionally lampooned current headline figures, gave the chief roles to President Eisenhower and Senator Watkins and alluded to McCarthy only once, as a "loud-mouthed kid" who had "elbowed his way to obscurity."

And when the new Congress met, "McCarthyism" was no longer an issue. "I don't even think about that any more," said Senator Jackson when queried. Senator Dworshak was equally debonair. "Haven't heard a thing about that lately," he confessed.

Privately, the totality of Joe's downfall did evoke some compassion among a few of his colleagues, although they were careful not to betray it publicly. Looking at the despondent figure across the chamber, one senior senator (not identified by name) remarked to a reporter: "They're hitting him from every angle. He feels caged. In my book he has it coming, but believe me, I don't take pleasure in the sight."

[III]

All his life Joseph Raymond McCarthy had squandered his physical resources as recklessly as his material means, and both were near an end. His visits to Bethesda Naval Hospital became more frequent, and at home the few friends who still called saw the deterioration. He had spurts of energy, but these alternated with periods of lassitude and depression. Mostly he was perplexed by what had happened to him. He preached the same doctrine, but the words that had inflamed throngs and awakened resounding echoes in the press now fell flat—ignored. Why? Millions of Americans still rejected the harsh verdict of his colleagues. (At least a million, maybe more, had signed that last-minute petition against censure.) Why were their voices not heeded? From time to time he inclined toward this or that explanation of the mystery, but he never solved it. Joe was never good at introspection, and he could not grasp that in the judgment of those who controlled the channels of public information he had been ticketed "quondam—having been formerly, a ludicrous word."

Occasionally some event would bring him momentarily to public notice. In April, 1955, he called in reporters and with great satisfaction exhibited a United States Treasury check for $1,056.75— a refund on excess income taxes he had paid during the 1947–1952 period. An exhaustive investigation of his returns had been started under the Truman administration, in connection with the inquiry into Benton's charges of financial skullduggery—including the allegation that money contributed to "fight communism" was being diverted to his personal use. For three years Treasury auditors had "looked into every dollar," Joe told the reporters, and not only had been unable to find anything improper, but had discovered a substantial overpayment of taxes through failure to take advantage of all the provisions of the law.

Well, in Joe's opinion apologies now were due by the Watkins Committee to the American people for having included unsubstantiated charges of financial chicanery in its report to the Senate.

Senator Watkins was unimpressed. "No apology is called for," he said icily, "as he is not purged of contempt." Newspapers that had printed reports that McCarthy was in tax trouble (the *Washington Star* had published that he owed the government $25,000) retracted nothing.

Nor was McCarthy to get satisfaction in the Peress-Zwicker affair. Upon assuming the chairmanship of the investigations subcommittee in the new Congress, Senator McClellan had picked up that inquiry (left unresolved during the Army hearings) and drawn from Secretary Stevens and others damaging admissions. The final report issued by the committee (written by Robert F. Kennedy as chief counsel, succeeding Roy Cohn) severely castigated the Army spokesmen for "deception" and "gross imposition" and listed "some forty-eight errors of more than minor importance" of which the Army had been guilty in its mishandling of the case. And as a result of further testimony by General Zwicker, on April

12, 1955, Senator McClellan forwarded the record to the Justice
Department to determine whether or not Zwicker should be prosecuted for perjury. There the matter rested for a year and a half,
although with an old soldier at 1600 Pennsylvania Avenue there
was little doubt what the decision would be. It came on December
11, 1956, in a letter to McClellan informing him that "the complex
legal and factual problems involved . . . have been carefully considered and all the evidence developed has been examined in the
light of the technical requirements necessary to establish an offense
under the existing law," and as a result "a criminal prosecution
will not be undertaken."

To McCarthy this was intolerable. "As I read it," he exclaimed,
"the clear implication of this letter is that even the Justice Department felt that General Zwicker lied, and that only technical difficulties stood in the way of a successful perjury action." Nobody
was listening, and a month later Zwicker was nominated for promotion to major general.

At McCarthy's urging, the Senate Armed Services Committee
examined Zwicker and adduced further apparent conflicts of testimony which he could not explain satisfactorily; nevertheless, over
McCarthy's protest, the promotion was recommended to the Senate.
On April 1, 1957, McCarthy carried his opposition to the Senate
floor. The chamber was all but empty as he read the conflicting
testimony into the *Record* and commented bitterly: "I had hoped,
after the Peress incident, that General Zwicker would be quietly
retired. When he subsequently committed perjury I was sure we
had seen the last of him as an Army officer—that his next appearance would probably be in a criminal court. Little did I dream
that he would, in effect, be honored for the crime by being promoted to major general."

When the bell rang for a roll call, absent senators flocked in,
and Zwicker's promotion was approved by 70 to 2. The two dissenting votes were cast by McCarthy and Malone.

[IV]

In every way, it seemed, the tide of history was running against
the Wisconsin senator. The spirit of coexistence was making headway, although President Eisenhower continued to discourse on
Russian "duplicity." But soothing words of peace issued regularly

from Moscow, and the necessity to resist the inroads of communism at home lost its urgency. The Soviets assiduously soft-pedaled that issue. In August, 1955, Premier Nikolai A. Bulganin departed from custom in addressing the Supreme Soviet by refraining from denouncing by name the leading free-world figures; the only Westerner singled out for attack by name was Wisconsin's Joe McCarthy, and even him Bulganin ridiculed rather than reviled.

All that year Joe kept working fitfully, although to little effect. His mail still ran to thousands of letters every week. But although his assistants said they found his mind as keen as ever, he spent much time and energy in futile backward glancing. Particularly he regretted having entrusted his defense against censure to counsel. That had been a mistake, he felt. "I was fighting for my life, and they wouldn't let me fight!" he moaned to Cohn. "I had to sit there and take it. I felt like a coward. They back you into a corner, and you have to do one of two things: you jump off a roof, or you stand up like a man and fight your way out! I lost without fighting!" The thought was searing.

His cause did appear to score a point when John Paton Davies, Jr.—one of the postwar advisers on China policy in regard to whom McCarthy had accused the Eisenhower administration of "batting zero"—was finally dropped from the State Department. McCarthy had linked Davies and John Stewart Service to the famous phrase "agrarian reformers," which had been used so misleadingly in reference to the followers of Mao Tse-tung.

But the pendulum swung in the opposite direction when the government dismissed the indictment against Owen Lattimore, after failing to bring the case to trial. The appeals court had reinstated two of the counts that the lower court had thrown out of the indictment; but in spite of this, political reasons were found to justify allowing the indictment to die. Lattimore and his apologists, of course, were jubilant and crowed loudly over the crestfallen senator.

Not that McCarthy totally lacked recognition and support. He kept up his speaking activities, and was well received by handpicked audiences. But ill-health was increasingly plaguing him. During the Army hearings he had dropped in at Bethesda Naval Hospital almost daily for relief from excruciating headaches. In the autumn of 1955, after a speech in Wisconsin, he had stumbled on the steps leading to the platform and wrenched his right knee so badly a brace was required for support. This, in turn, induced an infection that put him in the hospital again.

During an epidemic of hepatitis which occurred in the 1950's, McCarthy had contracted the disease, but apparently had shaken it off. The regimen prescribed for victims of this malady—a disease of the liver—is rest, a strict diet, and no alcohol whatever. Joe refused to submit to such rules. During 1956 he began to drink heavily, sometimes in secret, and he received medical warnings: his recovery from the hepatitis attack had not been complete. He lost weight, and his face took on a puffy appearance and the yellow tint indicative of jaundice. Several times, when appearing as a public speaker, he was so weak he had to be helped on and off the platform. Less and less was he seen at the Capitol, and during his rare attendance at committee hearings he would sit staring vacantly, now and then starting to life and interjecting questions, as if determined to arouse his faculties. Since often the questions were wide of the mark, his colleagues made little effort to conceal their annoyance.

Early in 1957 he was well enough to appear on a television program, and during the telecast he disclosed that his wife and he had adopted a five-week-old baby girl from the New York Foundling Hospital, an institution in which Cardinal Spellman took particular interest. The child had been named Tierney Elizabeth, and Joe, to the amusement of his friends, instantly became a doting father.

At the beginning of March, the thoroughness of McCarthy's isolation in the capital was made clear by a social note: of the 529 members of Congress, Senator McCarthy, according to Presidential press secretary Hagerty, was the only one who had not been invited to at least one social function at the White House. Hagerty added that the omission had not been unintentional.

A month after that, Mrs. Eisenhower entertained the wives of the senators at luncheon, and it was observed that Jean McCarthy was not among the guests. Inquiry elicited that an invitation had been extended, and McCarthy said one had come orally—too late. Jean treated the matter lightly: she had seen no invitation, she said, but in any event, "when they woudn't invite my husband to the White House because of his fight against communism, I would hardly go anyway."

McCarthy's speech against the promotion of General Zwicker

on April 1 marked his last appearance in the Senate. His looks on that occasion shocked those of his colleagues who regarded him at all; he seemed old, his face was a ghastly hue, and he limped.

During the rest of that month his health grew progressively worse, and on Sunday, April 28, he again was admitted to Bethesda Naval Hospital. On Wednesday, May 1, the news services carried a brief announcement of his illness but reported him somewhat improved; he had been taken out of the oxygen tent, it was stated. His illness had been diagnosed as acute hepatitis. This was the first public disclosure of his condition, and *The New York Times* printed the half-dozen lines on page 32.

The next day the *Times* reported the senator's condition unchanged, still grave. That was good for page 63.

Twenty-four hours later Joe McCarthy was back on the front page of *The New York Times* and virtually every other newspaper in the world, a feat he accomplished by the simple act of dying.

Millions of words were poured out in brightest eulogy and blackest hatred. In Europe the press called him "the grand master of witch-hunting" and ridiculed and flayed him as "the snooper senator" and "destroyer of the innocent." The *London Daily Sketch* termed him "the world's most hated man." The Moscow radio took satisfaction in the removal of "this double-dyed reactionary . . . hunting down and subjecting to terrorist persecution all who opposed him."

In America the press for the most part marked time. A few editorializers spoke of the passing of "a great patriot," though the adjective most frequently applied to the senator and his career was the question-begging "controversial." The *Syracuse Post-Standard* (the paper against which Joe had won a libel suit) stressed that the senator had "made himself the biggest figure in the nation from 1950 to 1952." But again and again the caution was given that history alone would define his true stature, and time assign him his true niche.

[V]

Death came to McCarthy at forty-eight, the cause being stated as "acute hepatitic failure," a breakdown in the functioning of the liver. Burial, it was decided, should be in Appleton, beside his parents. Funeral services were held in Washington first. At St.

Matthew's Cathedral, where the senator had been married, a solemn pontifical requiem mass was offered by Archbishop Patrick A. O'Boyle, with eulogy by Monsignor John K. Cartwright.

Then the flag-draped casket was borne to the Capitol, escorted by an honor guard of United States Marines. Carried into the Senate chamber, past McCarthy's flower-banked desk, it was placed in the well, just below the rostrum. Vice-President Nixon and Speaker Sam Rayburn, with dignitaries of the Congress, special guests, and seventy senators, were on hand, although neither the President nor Mrs. Eisenhower attended; they had telegraphed condolences to Mrs. McCarthy.

Only twenty-three senators had previously been accorded a funeral service in the Senate chamber, the last having been William E. Borah in 1940. There were prayers, but no speeches; these would come later, at a Senate memorial session. Then came the final "insertion in the *Record*":

"Thereupon, at 11 o'clock and 22 minutes A.M., the casket was borne from the Senate chamber, and the service was concluded."

Notes on Sources, Method,
and Some Conclusions

The main sources from which this account has been drawn are those by which the event was recorded originally, namely, newspapers, periodicals, radio, television. Such sources as private letters, secret diaries, or subsequent constructions and revelations have been used sparingly, since their contents were not accessible to the public at the time.

This approach was chosen by design, the aim being to convey something of the episode's immediacy by recounting it in its own contemporaneous terms. The McCarthy affair was a spectacular conflict fought between the partisans of two irreconcilable sets of assumptions. It was a drama played on the world stage before an audience of millions, and to appreciate the impact it produced on that audience it must be viewed through the eyes of its time, not through the distorting lenses of hindsight.

The published record is enormous; probably the biblical span of threescore years and ten would afford insufficient time to sift through every scrap of the printed word that has survived. Selection being necessary, the following general plan was adopted:

For the day-by-day ("serialized," as it were) narrative, the file of *The New York Times,* in itself enormous, was chosen as the main source. This was for two reasons: first, because no other newspaper covered the subject as consistently and exhaustively, year after year; second, because despite its editorial detestation of Senator McCarthy, in its news reports the *Times* did make a conscientious effort to record what was said and what happened as objectively and as accurately as possible. If this effort failed occasionally, that was only to be expected of human fallibility; but on the whole the record comes as close to impartiality as was perhaps possible in those days of flaming commitment one way or the other.

But the McCarthy affair took in more than Senator McCarthy; it embraced the times, and it took in his opposition; therefore representative expressions of his opponents' point of view were necessary, too. For this purpose three magazines of liberal opinion were selected—*The Nation, New Republic,* and *Commonweal.* These three shared the same dogged hostility to the senator and his activities; they were able to articulate the reasons for their hostility; and *Commonweal,* in addition, reflected an important but often neglected factor in the equation—the liberal Catholic reaction to McCarthy and his work.

The official record relating to the senator is almost inexhaustible. Besides the hundreds, if not thousands, of pages in the *Congressional Record,* there are the reports of five Senate investigations of McCarthy, with their transcripts of testimony covering tens of thousands of pages. To give these their ordinary designations in place of their cumbersome official titles, they include the Tydings Committee hearings and report; the Gillette subcommittee report on the Maryland election campaign; the Hennings Report on Senator Benton's charges against McCarthy; the Army-McCarthy hearings and reports; and the Watkins Committee hearings and report. There are also the reports of other Senate and House committees, and the debates on the floor of the Senate. To list them *in extenso* would be a labor of supererogation; they await anyone who has the hardihood to delve into them, in any major library.

As for the books on the McCarthy phenomenon that have accumulated, most of them since his death, these, with a very few exceptions, have lain outside the scope of this narrative. One exception is Anderson and May's *McCarthy: the Man, the Senator, the "Ism."* This 1952 study, although strongly biased and tendentiously written, nevertheless is still the fullest account of McCarthy's background—his family, schooling, and early Wisconsin career. There is no definitive biography of the senator, and none can be written until McCarthy's papers, now under seal at Marquette University, are released for purposes of research. Of such release there appears to be no likelihood for a long time to come.

No final and definitive history of the McCarthy Affair, either, can be compiled until his papers are available for study; gaps in our knowledge will remain, and this present account is not offered as being definitive at all. But it is authentic. By design it contains practically nothing that is new. Everything here set down, barring a handful of minor details, has been published somewhere, in some form, at some time. That may be a merit of the book—a safeguard against unwarranted or fanciful inventions.

In keeping with the informal, contemporaneous method, source references, bibliography, and similar paraphernalia of scholarship have been dispensed with as extraneous to the design of the book. An irreducible minimum of footnotes has been retained, and most sources are plainly indicated in the text.

Just as this is not a biography of Joseph Raymond McCarthy, neither is it a special plea for any or several of the protagonists; as was cautioned on the title page, this is a story without a hero. That there will ever be any unanimity of judgment regarding McCarthy seems improbable; certainly there is no more agreement today than there was during his heyday. Attempted analysis of the cause or causes which underlay the traumatic upheaval associated with his name will go on. Numerous theories have been advanced, but as these are more or less mutually contradictory, it is unlikely that the truth has been hit upon yet. It may never be, for Pilate's question remains unanswered and unanswerable.

The subtleties of dialectic are for others to unwind; but one thing about McCarthy is clear: he rose on the crest of a wave of national excitement, and he became the symbol of a collective movement. But that eminence was attained at a price: as the tide receded, leaving bare the bleached bones of innumerable errors committed both for and against McCarthy, and others committed long before he appeared, the guilt for those errors, in addition to his own, became attached to the symbol, and McCarthy the symbol became McCarthy the scapegoat for his era—for its excesses, for its derangements, for its effects, which went far, far beyond him. So the balance is maintained, of truth and untruth, favor and disfavor.

McCarthy's peculiar achievement was that he seized upon and dramatized in overwhelmingly effective terms a dilemma which lay latent in the national consciousness. He did not create the crisis of his time, he came to it as a stranger; but he projected the drama of the crisis more vividly and arrestingly than anyone else. He was a player, not the playwright. Historically his case may be unique: surely no politician ever reached power by a more curious route, or did less with it when gained.

Three incidents epitomize the depth to which the senator's prestige sank and his achievements seemed to be washed out during his final, "quondam" phase.

Incident number one: When John Stewart Service—whose removal from the State Department McCarthy had demanded in his first anti-Communist speech, at Wheeling, West Virginia, on February 9, 1950—was dismissed in 1951, he did not contest the action. But in 1955, after McCarthy had ceased to be a threat to anyone, John Stewart Service instituted legal action to have Dean Acheson's order of dismissal set aside on technical grounds. Service contended that under the department's own rules, once a suspected employe had been cleared by the departmental loyalty board, the Secretary of State had no power to intervene and reverse the decision. The court accepted the contention, ruled that in effect Service had never been legally separated from government employment, and ordered his reinstatement with accrued back pay.* In September, 1957, four months after Senator McCarthy's death, John Stewart Service returned to the State Department and remained there until his retirement. And in 1971, during the thawing of relations between the United States and Peking, John Stewart Service revisited China at the invitation of the Communist regime.

Incident number two: Corliss Lamont, an avowed apologist for Soviet policies who refused to answer questions before McCarthy but declined to invoke the protection of the Fifth Amendment, was indicted for contempt of the Senate. Lamont fought the indictment on constitutional grounds and on the basis that McCarthy had not only exceeded his authority by investigating subversion in the government, but had flouted the Senate's positive command to stay out of that field of inquiry.

The Senate Committee on Government Operations (originally called the Committee on Expenditures in the Executive Department) was the parent committee from which McCarthy's subcommittee on investigations derived its authority. Obviously the parent committee could not confer upon its subsidiary powers which exceeded its own. Created by the Reorganization Act of 1946, the Government Operations Committee was instructed to look into matters pertaining to the "economy and efficiency" of the govern-

---

* This turned out to be a relatively modest sum, because all he was entitled to was the difference between what he would have been paid and what he had earned in private employment in the interim.

ment—budgeting, accounting, expenditures, reorganizations, the relations between federal and state governments, and those between the United States and foreign organizations of which it was a member. Nowhere was subversion included.

At the start of the Eighty-third Congress, in 1953, Senator McCarthy, taking over as the new chairman of the Committee on Government Operations, filed his request with the Senate for funds to operate during the coming year. This request (Senate Resolution 40) was routinely referred to the Rules Committee, of which Senator Jenner was chairman, and was reported favorably to the Senate by that committee, with this appended limitation:

". . . It is also intended that certain aspects of improper influence in government shall be investigated, but any inquiries undertaken will in no way interfere or transgress those investigations which other Senate and House of Representatives committees may be engaged in making in comparable areas of government operation, such as subversion."

This was plain and explicit: the Rules Committee, or rather its chairman, Senator Jenner, was warning McCarthy off, so far as investigation of subversion was concerned; in the Senate, that activity had already been assumed by Jenner's own internal security subcommittee. Accompanied by this blunt prohibition, McCarthy's budget request was granted, and in due course McCarthy spent the funds mainly in investigating subversion.

On July 27, 1955 (McCarthy having been censured seven months before), United States Judge Edward Weinfeld ruled that the senator's questioning of Lamont had been unwarranted and without authority in law, and therefore no offense had been committed by Lamont's refusal to answer. The indictment was dismissed. The government appealed, but was not only overruled again, but reprimanded for its persistence in trying to press to trial indictments "for offenses that cannot be supported by law." This higher ruling came on August 14, 1956, and ended the matter. It also exposed the McCarthy Episode as a monstrous fantasy, resting on nothing whatever except Joe McCarthy's limitless audacity.

Incident number three: When Frank Costello, the racketeer, was resisting deportation proceedings, he was advised to retain as counsel Edward Bennett Williams. Costello spurned the suggestion. "Not that guy," he said indignantly. "Wasn't he the lawyer for McCarthy?"

Implacably the tide ran on against the late senator, until in 1972, in another February, President Richard M. Nixon, onetime friend of Joe McCarthy, made the long flight to Peking to dance a diplomatic gavotte with "those murderers" of twenty years before, Mao Tse-tung and Chou En-lai. In Appleton, Wisconsin, the snow whorls on McCarthy's grave danced eerily. His ghost was not still.

Index